*The Jossey-Bass Handbook
of Nonprofit Leadership
and Management*

Second Edition

The Jossey-Bass Handbook of Nonprofit Leadership and Management

Second Edition

Robert D. Herman and Associates

JOSSEY-BASS
A Wiley Imprint
www.josseybass.com

Published by Jossey-Bass
A Wiley Imprint
989 Market Street, San Francisco, CA 94103-1741   www.josseybass.com

Jossey-Bass books and products are available through most bookstores. To contact Jossey-Bass directly call our Customer Care Department within the U.S. at 800-956-7739, outside the U.S. at 317-572-3986, or fax 317-572-4002.

Jossey-Bass also publishes its books in a variety of electronic formats. Some content that appears in print may not be available in electronic books.

Library of Congress Cataloging-in-Publication Data

The Jossey-Bass handbook of nonprofit leadership and management/
Robert D. Herman and associates.—2nd ed.
p. cm.
Includes bibliographical references and index.
ISBN 0-7879-6995-8 (hardcover)
1. Nonprofit organizations—Management.   I. Herman, Robert D., 1946–
HD62.6.J67   2004
658'.048—dc22
2004015799

Printed in the United States of America
SECOND EDITION
HB Printing   10 9 8 7 6 5

CONTENTS

vii

TABLES, FIGURES, AND EXHIBITS

TABLES

FIGURES

EXHIBITS

PREFACE

All of us associated with *The Jossey-Bass Handbook of Nonprofit Leadership and Management* are pleased to have the opportunity to present this second edition. Of course, all the chapters have been revised and updated to reflect current research, theory, and practice. Most chapters are again written by the same authorities who wrote the first-edition chapters, though second authors have changed in a couple of instances.

Also, one chapter has been added in place of a chapter prepared for the first edition; Chapter Eleven, "Strategic Alliances," considers one of the areas of rapid development since the publication of the first edition. Chapter Twenty-Three, on finding and keeping the right employees, has two new authors, Mary Watson and Rikki Abzug, both of whom have substantial expertise in researching and experience in working with nonprofit organizations. Their chapter deals with a perennial issue in nonprofit organizations, attracting and retaining excellent employees, usually without the ability to pay as much as private sector or often government employers.

Nonprofit organizations continue to be different, even as they change and evolve due to the changing funding and institutional environments they face. They are unlike both business and government in certain fundamental ways while similar in other ways. Nonprofit organizations, like businesses, rely on voluntary exchanges to obtain revenues and other resources. In business, customers supply the resources for the service they receive. Unlike business, nonprofit organizations (especially publicly supported charities, the sort of nonprofit organization on which this volume focuses) typically depend, at least to some extent, on one group, donors or government, for the resources necessary to provide a different group, the clients or beneficiaries, with services. Indeed, one reason nonprofit organizations exist is that the services they offer would not be provided otherwise. This is the justification for the tax and other public policy preferences nonprofit organizations receive—they provide public goods that would otherwise not be provided, either by business or by government.

A public good, in the economic sense, is one that has two special features: first, it costs no more to provide it to many than it does to a few, and second, there is no easy way to prevent those who have not contributed to its provision from consuming it once it has been produced (economists call this the "free rider" problem). The production of public goods—clean water, for example—is typically the responsibility of government. In *The Nonprofit Economy* (Harvard University Press, 1988), Burton Weisbrod argues that democratic governments are constrained to provide public goods at the level that satisfies the median voter, as preferences for and willingness to pay taxes in support of public goods varies. Thus there is unsatisfied demand for some public goods, and nonprofit organizations are often created to meet such demands.

Nonprofit organizations, like governments, generally supply services with public goods characteristics, but unlike governments, they cannot compel users to pay for those services. Moreover, nonprofit organizations, unlike governments, need not provide their services to all who meet eligibility requirements. Nonprofit organizations may serve particular interests and groups. The particularism of nonprofit organizations enhances the articulation and advocacy of a wide range of values and causes. In this way, nonprofit organizations contribute to pluralism and the strengthening of civil society.

To summarize, nonprofit organizations are in some ways similar to and are yet different from both businesses and governments. Some, of course, are more similar to businesses; those that depend almost entirely on government funding are more similar to government; and others, including all volunteer nonprofit organizations, are substantially different from both business and government.

This volume is based on the premise that the distinctive (and varied) character of nonprofit organizations affects the leadership and management of such organizations. Those at the helms of organizations working in the nonprofit sector have become increasingly aware of the significance of their work in North American societies. The following indicators all testify to the growing importance of nonprofit organizations in Canada and the United States over the past twenty to twenty-five years: the number and strength of sector-serving associations have increased; publications by and about nonprofit organizations continue to expand; and the number of university programs devoted to research and teaching about nonprofit management, philanthropy, and volunteerism has substantially grown.

As those working in North American nonprofit sectors have become more aware of being part of a sector, interest in the distinctive leadership and management challenges that nonprofit organizations face has also increased. While the swelling volume of publications relating to voluntarism, philanthropy, and nonprofit management has served the sector well in many ways, all too often advice on financial management, human resource management problems and solutions (for both employees and volunteers), and organizational strategies and leadership has only been available in fragmentary pieces published in far-flung periodicals and sometimes not easily available sources. The need for a single volume that offers a comprehensive and thorough treatment of the functions, processes, and strategies of nonprofit organizational leadership and management remains. This second edition will continue to meet that need.

INTENDED AUDIENCE

In that this handbook is designed to provide comprehensive and in-depth descriptions of effective leadership and management practices that apply throughout a nonprofit organization, we believe and intend the volume to be of utmost value to a wide range of practitioners. It will be especially useful to anyone who has come to a management or leadership position from a program service background, to anyone who has moved from a relatively specialized management niche into a position with extensive responsibilities, and to everyone who seeks a solid core of support for the wide range of knowledge and skills that nonprofit leadership requires. In addition to those in paid staff positions, this volume will benefit board members and other volunteer leaders who are interested in enlarging their understanding of the nature of nonprofit organizations. This handbook will also be useful to those, both in formal education programs and in self-directed learning, who want to prepare for careers in nonprofit management. Finally, we believe this book will continue to be an important resource to those who work with nonprofit organizations as consultants, technical assistance providers, regulators, and funders.

OVERVIEW OF THE CONTENTS

The volume is organized into five parts. Part One is devoted to describing the context and institutions within which nonprofit organizations currently operate and the context in which they are likely to work in the near future. Nonprofit organizations have been shaped and will be continue to be shaped by the historical times and forces, by social institutions, laws and regulations, political and economic trends and events, and increasing globalization. The chapters in Part One consider how these large-scale phenomena have affected and are affecting nonprofit organizations and their leadership and management. In Chapter One, Peter Dobkin Hall deftly describes the complex history of philanthropy and nonprofit organizations in the United States, showing how and why the nonprofit sector has been invented. Jon Van Til, in Chapter Two, describes how both social institutions and sector institutions affect nonprofit organizations. In Chapter Three, Thomas Silk uses an extended illustrative case to clarify the crucial legal and regulatory environment in which U.S. nonprofit organizations operate. The number, types, activities, and operations of nonprofit organizations are greatly influenced by political and economic events. In Chapter Four, Lester M. Salamon analyzes the impact of large-scale economic, political, and demographic forces on various segments of the nonprofit sector. Helmut K. Anheier and Nuno Themudo, in Chapter Five, describe the increasing internationalization of nonprofit and nongovernmental organizations and consider questions of the role of such organizations in creating a global civil society.

Part Two covers key leadership issues in nonprofit organizations. Boards of directors of nonprofit organizations hold the prime leadership position and are expected to provide, in large part, leadership in defining their organization's mission and values. In Chapter Six, Nancy R. Axelrod analyzes the continuing challenge of developing board leadership and describes some promising approaches for helping boards meet their leadership obligations. In Chapter Seven, Dick Heimovics and I examine the crucial role of chief executives in nonprofit organizations and describe the board-centered, external, and political leadership skills of especially effective chief executives. One of the key leadership tasks facing boards and executives is that of strategically designing programs to most effectively achieve an organization's mission. John M. Bryson provides guidelines for the effective use of strategic planning and management by nonprofit organizations in Chapter Eight. In an era in which many businesses, as well as government and nonprofit organizations, have been revealed as lacking all ethical sense, nonprofit leaders must meet the challenge of creating and sustaining organizational cultures that uphold the highest ethical standards. Thomas H. Jeavons offers important advice about how this can be achieved in Chapter Nine. Nonprofit leaders continually face questions of whether, when, and how to affect legislation relevant to their organizations' missions. Bob Smucker answers those questions in Chapter Ten. Nearly all nonprofit organizations now face questions about whether and with whom to form strategic alliances of various types so as better to accomplish their missions. John A. Yankey and Carol K. Willen, in a welcome addition to this second edition, address these issues in Chapter Eleven.

The contributions in Part Three get at the heart of nonprofit organizational operations. Increasing numbers of nonprofit organizations have recognized the need to explicitly manage their exchanges with a wide range of constituents. Brenda Gainer and Mel S. Moyer, in Chapter Twelve, provide nonprofit leaders with a thorough analysis of the uses of marketing, highlighting the important ways that marketing efforts can help improve mission accomplishment. Most nonprofit organizations rely on volunteers, many to a substantial extent. In Chapter Thirteen, Jeffrey L. Brudney describes the issues and choices to be considered in designing and running effective volunteer programs. In Chapter Fourteen, Vic Murray considers the difficulties of evaluating nonprofit organizational effectiveness and suggests some useful ways of practically dealing with the considerable challenges. As Steven Rathgeb Smith observes in Chapter Fifteen, contracting with government is a fact of life for many nonprofit organizations, though contracting brings predictable (as well as unpredictable) problems. Smith provides concrete advice about effectively dealing with problems. Governments and other funders have become more demanding about evidence of program effectiveness. John Clayton Thomas, in Chapter Sixteen, reviews how nonprofit organizations can successfully undertake both outcome assessment and more thorough program evaluations.

Part Four takes up topics crucial to developing and managing financial resources. While an ever-increasing number of publications offer advice on specific fundraising techniques, few of those publications deal with issues of how fundraising should be integrated with the mission and culture of a nonprofit organization. In Chapter Seventeen, Robert E. Fogal not only tells how to design and manage the fundraising program but also provides perspective on integrating mission and fundraising. The past decade has seen increasing interest on the part of some traditional funders for nonprofit organizations to become more self-supporting, and many nonprofit organizations have made efforts to become more commercial (also sometimes described as social entrepreneurship). Cynthia W. Massarsky, in Chapter Eighteen, describes the full range of commercial income options nonprofit organizations might consider, giving special attention to issues of thorough planning and analysis before deciding on an earned income strategy. Robert N. Anthony and David W. Young, in Chapter Nineteen, cover the principles and management uses of financial accounting, while Young, in Chapter Twenty, explains how nonprofit managers can use management accounting information to manage operations more efficiently. One important way that nonprofit organizations can control both costs and exposure to losses is through better risk management. Melanie L. Herman, in Chapter Twenty-One, provides thorough and readable guidelines for making decisions about a comprehensive risk management program.

Part Five contains four chapters on any nonprofit's most important assets—the people who, whether as employees or volunteers, make the organization what it is. In Chapter Twenty-Two, Stephen McCurley specifies how an organization can find, engage, and keep volunteers who are suited to it and its work. Mary R. Watson and Rikki Abzug, in Chapter Twenty-Three, describe not only the steps and appropriate practices for selecting employees but also the many (nonfinancial) ways in which nonprofit organizations can retain the committed and excellent employees that often make nonprofit organizations great places to work. In Chapter Twenty-Four, Nancy E. Day focuses specifically on establishing and operating compensation and benefit programs that suit a nonprofit organization and the needs and expectations of its employees. Nancy Macduff, in Chapter Twenty-Five, considers how nonprofit organizations can assess their training needs and then design and carry out appropriate programs for both paid and volunteer staff.

In the Conclusion, I offer a personal assessment of the current environment and the forces pushing many nonprofit organizations to become "more businesslike," arguing that there are risks to doing so and suggesting some steps that nonprofit organizations and associations serving the sector can take to maintain the distinctiveness and legitimacy of the sector.

Like the first edition, this second edition of the handbook presents the best and most applicable practical leadership and management information currently available on a wide range of topics. That the information is the best and most applicable is a result, I believe, of deriving practical implications not solely from current practice but even more from the latest research and the most current theory. I believe and hope that this second edition, like the first, will be a widely used reference, serving to inform leaders, leaders-to-be, managers, and managers-to-be for many years to come.

ACKNOWLEDGMENTS

I especially want to acknowledge and thank all of the chapter authors. I was pleased that nearly all of the authors of chapters in the first edition were willing take part by revising and updating their chapters for this second edition. Most authors, over the intervening decade, had become even busier, and I know that meeting the deadlines and doing a thorough job was often difficult. I also greatly appreciate the efforts of the new authors who have prepared wholly new chapters. They too faced short deadlines, but without a foundation to start with. I also want to thank the readers Jossey-Bass asked to review the first edition and make suggestions for the second edition. Though we did not always follow your suggestions, the contributors and I appreciate the value of those suggestions and the serious thinking that went into them. Thanks are also due to many people who responded to my solicitation to provide suggestions about revisions; those suggestions were often very helpful.

I thank Allison M. Brunner, editorial assistant at Jossey-Bass, who has responded to my frequent questions and importunings with helpful good humor. I also appreciate the support and guidance of Dorothy Hearst, senior editor at Jossey-Bass, who has calmly dealt with the problems and concerns I presented to her.

Finally, my thanks to my wife, Charlotte, for all her support over the years and during the months when I was using much of our time on this volume.

Kansas City, Missouri   Robert D. Herman
August 2004   Editor

THE EDITOR

Robert D. Herman is a professor in the Cookingham Institute of Public Affairs, H. W. Bloch School of Business and Public Administration, University of Missouri, Kansas City. He teaches in the institute's M.P.A. specialization in nonprofit management, which he helped create. He is also a senior fellow with the university's Midwest Center for Nonprofit Leadership. He received his B.A. degree (1968) in economics from Kansas State University and his M.S. (1971) and Ph.D. (1976) degrees, both in organizational behavior, from Cornell University.

Herman's previous research has concentrated on the effective leadership of nonprofit charitable organizations, including chief executive–board relations. His current research focuses on investigating nonprofit organizational effectiveness.

He is past president of the Association of Voluntary Action Scholars (now known as the Association for Research on Nonprofit Organizations and Voluntary Action). He has also served on several boards of nonprofit organizations and works with nonprofit organizations, in the United States and internationally, in consulting and advisory capacities.

He is coauthor of *Executive Leadership in Nonprofit Organizations* (with Dick Heimovics, 1991), coeditor of *Nonprofit Boards of Directors* (with Jon Van Til, 1989), and author of many articles on nonprofit leadership and governance.

THE CONTRIBUTORS

Rikki Abzug is on the faculty of the Nonprofit Management Program at the Robert J. Milano Graduate School of Management and Urban Policy, New School University. Previously, she was the associate director of Yale University's Program on Nonprofit Organizations. She has been a public, nonprofit, and for-profit management and market research consultant for over fifteen years, providing consulting services to management groups in the United States, Poland, and Ukraine. Abzug sat on the board of the Association for Research on Nonprofit Organizations and Voluntary Action (ARNOVA) and was a founding board member of the Alliance for Nonprofit Governance. She has published dozens of articles on governance and sectoral and institutional theory and serves on the editorial board of *Nonprofit and Voluntary Sector Quarterly.* She holds a Ph.D. degree in organizational sociology from Yale University and lives in New Jersey with her husband, the surrealist painter Patrick Brady, and two daughters.

Helmut K. Anheier is a professor and director of the Center for Civil Society at UCLA's School of Public Policy and Social Research and Centennial Professor of Social Policy at the London School of Economics, where he founded in 1998 and directed the Centre for Civil Society. Prior to this he was a senior research associate and project codirector at the Johns Hopkins University Institute for Policy Studies and associate professor of sociology at Rutgers University. Before embarking on an academic career, Anheier served as social affairs officer to the United Nations. He obtained his Ph.D. degree from Yale University in 1986.

Robert N. Anthony is Ross Graham Walker Professor of Management Control, Emeritus, at the Harvard Business School. He received his D.B.A. degree (1952) from Harvard University. He is the author or coauthor of numerous books and journal articles on management control generally and management control specifically in nonprofit organizations. He is coauthor, with David W. Young, of *Management Control in Nonprofit Organizations,* currently in its seventh edition. His books have been translated into fifteen languages.

Nancy R. Axelrod is an independent consultant in Washington, D.C. She is the founding president of the National Center for Nonprofit Boards (now Board-Source), where she served as the chief executive officer from 1987 to 1996. She previously served as vice president of the Association of Governing Boards of Universities and Colleges, where she designed and conducted educational programs for college and university trustees and their presidents. Axelrod is the author of *Chief Executive Succession Planning: The Board's Role in Securing Your Organization's Future* (2002), *Advisory Councils* (2004), and numerous articles and op-ed pieces.

Jeffrey L. Brudney is professor of public administration and policy, adjunct professor of social work, and a member of the Nonprofit and Community Service faculty in the College of Business at the University of Georgia. He is cofounder and codirector of the Institute for Nonprofit Organizations and the Master of Arts in Nonprofit Organizations degree program at Georgia. His areas of research and teaching interest include volunteer involvement in the public sector, nonprofit management education, and research methods and statistics. Brudney has received several national and international awards, including the Herbert Kaufman Award for excellence in research, the William E. Mosher and Frederick C. Mosher Award for the best article written by an academician published in *Public Administration Review,* the Mentor's Award from the American Political Science Association, and the John Grenzebach Award for outstanding research in philanthropy for education for his book *Fostering Volunteer Programs in the Public Sector: Planning, Initiating, and Managing Voluntary Activities* (1990).

John M. Bryson is a professor of planning and public affairs in the Hubert H. Humphrey Institute of Public Affairs at the University of Minnesota. He is the author of *Strategic Planning for Public and Nonprofit Organizations* (3rd ed., 2004) and coauthor (with Farnum Alston) of *Creating and Implementing Your Strategic Plan* (2nd ed., 2004). He consults widely with public and nonprofit organizations in the United States and the United Kingdom.

Nancy E. Day is associate professor of human resources and organizational behavior at the Bloch School of Business and Public Administration at the University of Missouri–Kansas City. Prior to entering academics, she worked as a
consultant specializing in compensation program and performance management
as well as a human resource practitioner for a municipality. She received her
B.S. degree in psychology and education (1976) from Southwest Missouri State
University, her M.A. degree in counseling psychology (1979) from the University of Missouri–Kansas City, and her Ph.D. degree in social psychology (1987)
from the University of Kansas. She researches in rewards and diversity issues
and has published in *Personnel Psychology, Personnel Review,* the *Journal of
Management Education,* and elsewhere.

Robert E. Fogal has been a fundraising professional since 1979. Currently executive director of the Saint Mary's Duluth Clinic Foundations in Duluth, Minnesota, he has held senior development positions in higher education and
human services. Previous experience also includes serving as director of The
Fund Raising School of the Indiana University Center on Philanthropy, extensive involvement in international education, and performing as a professional
musician. He holds a Ph.D. degree in folklore and ethnomusicology from Indiana University.

Brenda Gainer is director of the Nonprofit Management and Leadership Program
and currently holds the Royal Bank Professorship in Nonprofit Management at
the Schulich School of Business at York University in Toronto, Canada. Her main
fields of research are consumer behavior and marketing management for nonprofit organizations, with a particular emphasis on the cultural sector and gender issues. She has been teaching graduate courses in management at York since
1987 and also teaches a variety of executive and professional development
courses in marketing, consumer behavior, and management for nonprofit, arts,
and public sector clients. She also acts as a consultant on marketing research,
audience development, and strategic management, and her articles have appeared in numerous business journals.

Peter Dobkin Hall is Hauser Lecturer on Nonprofit Organizations at the John F.
Kennedy School of Government, Harvard University. Associated with Yale's Program on Non-Profit Organizations from 1978 to 1999, he also held teaching ap-
pointments in Yale's Department of History; Divinity School; Ethics, Politics,
and Economics Program; and School of Management. Hall's publications include *Sacred Companies: Organizational Aspects of Religion and Religious Aspects of Organizations* (1998), *Inventing the Nonprofit Sector and Other Essays
on Philanthropy, Voluntarism, and Nonprofit Organizations* (1992), *Lives in
Trust: The Fortunes of Dynastic Families in Late Twentieth Century America*

(1992), and *The Organization of American Culture, 1700–1900: Organizations, Elites, and the Origins of American Nationality* (1982).

Dick Heimovics is Levitt Professor of Human Relations at the Bloch School of Business and Public Administration, University of Missouri–Kansas City where he is also Senior Fellow at the Midwest Center for Nonprofit Leadership. He received his Ph.D. degree (1975) from the University of Kansas. He is coauthor, with Robert D. Herman, of *Executive Leadership in Nonprofit Organizations: New Strategies for Shaping Executive-Board Dynamics* (1991) as well as author of other books and numerous articles on issues in organizations and nonprofit leadership. He has served on the boards of many nonprofit organizations and has consulted with a wide range of nonprofit, public, and for-profit organizations.

Melanie L. Herman serves as executive director of the Nonprofit Risk Management Center, a Washington, D.C.–based resource center serving the nonprofit community (http://www.nonprofitrisk.org). The center provides training, technical assistance, and informational resources on a wide range of topics, including risk management, liability, employment practices, accountability, insurance, and child abuse prevention. Herman has spent her entire career in the nonprofit sector and has authored and coauthored more than fifteen books covering a wide spectrum of risk management issues. Each year she delivers numerous workshops, seminars, and keynote presentations on risk management, liability, and insurance topics. Her most recent books are *Playing to Win: A Risk Management Guide for Nonprofit Sports and Recreation Programs* (2004) and *Risk Management: A Comprehensive Guide* (2003). She holds a B.A. degree in urban affairs from the American University and a J.D. degree from George Mason University. She is a member of the District of Columbia Bar.

Thomas H. Jeavons is the general secretary (chief executive) of Philadelphia Yearly Meeting of the Religious Society of Friends, the largest Quaker judicatory in the United States. He is also a consulting scholar for the Rockefeller Institute of Government's Roundtable on Religion and Social Welfare Policy at the State University of New York in Albany and was the founding director of the Center on Philanthropy and Nonprofit Leadership at Grand Valley State University (1992–1996). He holds a B.A. degree in philosophy from the University of Colorado (1975), an M.A. degree in theology from the Earlham School of Religion (1978), and a Ph.D. degree in management and cultural studies from the Union Institute (1992). He is the author of several books and numerous chapters and articles on nonprofit management, ethics, and fundraising.

Nancy Macduff is a practitioner and academic. For fourteen years she served as executive director of a community-based youth organization and for nine years as manager of volunteers for a government-based program. Currently she is on the faculty at Washington State University, teaching an online certificate course in the management of volunteer programs. She is the author of six books on the management of volunteer programs, numerous journal articles, and chapters in several books on volunteer management. Her company, Macduff/Bunt Associates, provides consultation and training services for volunteer programs and nonprofits around the world.

Cynthia W. Massarsky is president of CWM Marketing Group, a consulting firm specializing in marketing and business development for the nonprofit sector. CWM's services include developing new business ventures, conducting strategic planning, and analyzing financial and organizational risk. The firm also provides various services to grantmakers. Prior to founding CWM in 1990, Massarsky was product and marketing manager for Scholastic; director of marketing and licensing for Marlo Thomas's Free to Be Foundation; vice president of New Ventures, a business development firm that guided nonprofit organizations in developing nonprofit enterprise; and director of development for the national office of the Foundation Center. Her writing has been widely published. She holds a B.A. degree from Simmons College and an M.B.A. degree from Cornell University.

Stephen McCurley is an internationally known trainer and consultant in the field of effective volunteer involvement. He is currently a partner in VM Systems, a management consulting firm specializing in helping organizations improve their utilization of volunteers. He has served as a consultant on volunteer program development to the AARP, the National Association of Partners in Education, the U.S. Tennis Association, Special Olympics International, the National Park Service, the Points of Light Foundation, and many other groups. He is the co-editor (with Susan Ellis) of the *e-Volunteerism* online journal. He is one of the founding faculty of the Institute on Advanced Volunteer Management, held in the United Kingdom annually. He is the author of fourteen books and more than 120 articles on volunteer involvement, including the best-selling basic text, *Volunteer Management*.

Mel S. Moyer is professor emeritus of marketing and senior scholar in the Schulich School of Business at York University, Toronto. He is the founding director of the Schulich School's Voluntary Sector Management Program. His research interests include organizational politics and marketing. His chapter in the first edition of this book was based on a research project on the nature of patterns for judging organizational effectiveness in nonprofit organizations, funded by the Social Science and Humanities Council of Canada.

Vic Murray is adjunct professor in the School of Public Administration at the University of Victoria in British Columbia, Canada. Until July 1995, he was director of the Voluntary Sector Management Program in the Schulich School of Business at York University, Toronto. In the nonprofit sector, his interests focus on the areas of board governance, strategic planning, interorganizational collaboration, and the assessment of organizational effectiveness. He is also an active consultant in these areas. He is the author of over one hundred books, articles, and papers in the fields of organizational behavior and nonprofit management. He is also the director of the Voluntary Sector Knowledge Network (http://www.vskn.ca), a Web-based service providing information on a wide range of issues related to the management of nonprofit organizations.

Lester M. Salamon is a professor at the Johns Hopkins University and director of the Johns Hopkins Center for Civil Society Studies and of its Comparative Nonprofit Sector and Listening Post projects. Prior to this, he served as director of the Center for Governance and Management Research at the Urban Institute and as deputy associate director of the U.S. Office of Management and Budget. He received his Ph.D. degree in government from Harvard University and is the author, most recently, of *The State of Nonprofit America* (2002), *The Resilient Sector* (2003), and *Global Civil Society* (2004). Salamon received the 2003 ARNOVA Distinguished Leadership Award for his work on the nonprofit sector in the United States and abroad.

Thomas Silk practices at the San Francisco law firm he founded in 1972, known today as Silk, Adler & Colvin, which specializes in nonprofit and exempt organization law. He received his A.B. degree from the University of California, Berkeley, in 1959 and his J.D. degree from the university's school of law (Boalt Hall) in 1963; after graduation, he worked for the U.S. Department of Justice in Washington, D.C. He has taught nonprofit law at Boalt Hall and at other law schools and universities and has consulted and lectured on nonprofit law development in Asia and Europe. He is the coauthor and editor of *Philanthropy and Law in Asia* (1998). Recent publications include chapters in *The Exempt Organization Tax Review* (2004), *Serving Many Masters: The Challenges to Corporate Philanthropy* (2003), and *California Tax Lawyer* (2003).

Steven Rathgeb Smith is professor of public affairs in the Daniel J. Evans School of Public Affairs at the University of Washington. He also is the director of the Nancy Bell Evans Center on Nonprofit Leadership at the Evans School. Smith is coauthor of *Nonprofits for Hire: The Welfare State in the Age of Contracting* and *Adjusting the Balance: Federal Policy and Victim Services* (1995) and co-editor of *Public Policy for Democracy.* He is the editor of *Nonprofit and Voluntary Sector Quarterly,* the journal of the Association for Research on Nonprofit Organizations and Voluntary Action (ARNOVA). His recent publications examine the government-nonprofit relationship, the development of social services in the United States and abroad, the role of faith-related agencies in the provision of social welfare services, and the implications for citizenship of the growing importance of nonprofit organizations in providing public services.

Bob Smucker is executive director of Charity Lobbying in the Public Interest (CLPI), a national organization whose mission is to promote, support, and protect advocacy and lobbying rights of charities. He was formerly vice president for government relations at INDEPENDENT SECTOR from its founding in 1980 until 1997 and has been a lobbyist for charities for more than thirty years at the local, state, and national levels. During that time, he wrote *The Nonprofit Lobbying Guide,* one of the most widely read and used books on lobbying. Prior to working at INDEPENDENT SECTOR, Smucker was the vice president for government relations at the National Mental Health Association. He has written numerous articles on lobbying by nonprofits in the United States.

Nuno Themudo is an assistant professor in nongovernmental organizational management and international development at the Graduate School of Public and International Affairs, University of Pittsburgh. Between 2001 and 2003, he taught at the Centre for Civil Society at the London School of Economics. He obtained his Ph.D. degree at the London School of Economics in 2004.

John Clayton Thomas is a professor and former chair in the Department of Public Administration and Urban Studies in the Andrew Young School of Policy Studies at Georgia State University in Atlanta. He previously taught at and directed the L. P. Cookingham Institute of Public Affairs at the University of Missouri–Kansas City. He has written three books and more than forty articles in the areas of program evaluation, public management, and urban government and politics. He has more than twenty years' experience in teaching master's-level courses on program evaluation to practitioners from the nonprofit and public sectors. Thomas has also consulted and conducted training for governments and nonprofit agencies in a variety of states. He earned a Ph. D. degree in political science at Northwestern University and B.A. (magna cum laude) and M.A. degrees in journalism and mass communications at the University of Minnesota.

Jon Van Til is professor of urban studies and community planning at Rutgers University, Camden, N.J. He directs the urban studies program and is former director of the Rutgers-Camden program in Citizenship and Service Education (Camden CASE). His books include *Critical Issues in American Philanthropy* (1990), *Mapping the Third Sector: Voluntarism in a Changing Social Economy* (1988), *Nonprofit Boards of Directors* (coedited with Robert D. Herman, 1988), and *Shifting the Debate: Public/Private Sector Relations in the Modern Welfare State* (coedited with Susan Ostrander and Stuart Langton, 1987). Van Til served as editor in chief of *Nonprofit and Voluntary Sector Quarterly* (formerly the *Journal of Voluntary Action Research*) from 1978 through 1992. He was twice elected president of the Association of Voluntary Action Scholars and is the founding board chair of the Center for Nonprofit Corporations (Trenton, N.J.). He writes a regular column in *Nonprofit Times* and has published in a variety of scholarly journals. In 1994, he received the Distinguished Research and Service Award from ARNOVA.

Mary R. Watson is assistant professor at the Milano Graduate School of Management and Urban Policy, New School University, in New York City. She earned her Ph.D. degree (1997) in organization studies at the Owen Graduate School of Management at Vanderbilt University. Her research and teaching address contemporary human capital issues in organizations, with emphasis on social impact implications. Watson has done research in the for-profit and nonprofit sectors, including work on career paths, the constitution of interorganization fields, and ethics in multinational operations. She has been published in the *Academy of Management Journal, Communication Yearbook,* and the *IRRA Research Annals.* Watson has consulted to the nonprofit, for-profit, and government sectors. She was recently a plenary speaker at the first annual national conference on nonprofit human resources, sponsored by Action Without Borders (http://idealist.com). She has developed and taught international management courses in Germany, Argentina, and Uruguay.

Carol K. Willen, as director of education and manager of Center-Wide Initiatives at the Mandel Center for Nonprofit Organizations at Case Western Reserve University, administers the center's multidisciplinary graduate programs in nonprofit leadership and management. Prior to joining the Mandel Center, she spent fifteen years in the field of philanthropy, including a decade as senior program officer for education at the Cleveland Foundation. She also served as executive director of a private family foundation and worked in a corporate philanthropic program. She has done independent consulting for higher education institutions and philanthropic foundations and taught at several universities. A graduate of the University of Michigan, she earned her master's and Ph.D. degrees at Harvard University.

John A. Yankey is the Leonard W. Mayo Professor at the Mandel School of Applied Social Sciences and the Mandel Center for Nonprofit Organizations at Case Western Reserve University. A former public administrator and a part-time lobbyist, he teaches in the areas of strategic planning, legislative and political processes, and strategic partnerships among nonprofit organizations. His research over the past decade has focused on the development of nonprofit strategic alliances. Yankey has a very active consultation practice with nonprofit organizations in facilitating strategic planning processes and conducting strategic alliance feasibility studies.

David W. Young is professor of accounting and control in Boston University's School of Management, a lecturer in physician management education programs at Harvard University, and a principal in the Crimson Group, a firm specializing in customized in-house management education programs for physicians and other health care professionals. From 1992 to 1995, he served as commissioner and chair of the Massachusetts Hospital Payment System Advisory Commission (HospPAC), charged with monitoring access, quality, and fair-market standards as the state shifted to a more market-oriented health care system. He has been nominated four times for BU's prestigious Metcalf Award for teaching excellence. Young is the author of several books and coauthor (with Robert N. Anthony) of *Management Control in Nonprofit Organizations,* currently in its seventh edition. He holds a B.A. degree from Occidental College, an M.A. degree from the University of California at Los Angeles, and a doctorate from the Harvard Business School.

*The Jossey-Bass Handbook
of Nonprofit Leadership
and Management*
Second Edition

PART ONE

CONTEXT
AND INSTITUTIONS

While people have probably always engaged in informal voluntary efforts, the establishment and character of formal nonprofit organizations are greatly affected by social, political, legal, and economic institutions. The United States and Canada have, by international standards, large nonprofit sectors of long standing. To fully understand current (and evolving) nonprofit management and leadership practices and issues, we need to understand how institutions have shaped and influenced nonprofit organizations.

This part of the book contains five chapters that describe and analyze the historical evolution of the U.S. nonprofit sector; how nonprofit organizations are affected and affect our society's major institutions; the legal and regulatory environment within which U.S. nonprofit organizations, particularly charities, must operate; how nonprofit organizations have responded to changes in the recent relationship of governments to nonprofit organizations and in the political economy more generally; and how the increasingly international and global character of philanthropy affects the leadership and management of nonprofit organizations that operate internationally.

CHAPTER ONE

Historical Perspectives on Nonprofit Organizations in the United States

Peter Dobkin Hall

Although charitable, educational, and religious organizations (such as the Roman Catholic Church) are thousands of years old and some in the United States (such as Harvard College) were founded in colonial times, the concept of "nonprofit organizations" as a unified and coherent "sector" dates back only to the 1970s.

In fact, over 90 percent of nonprofit organizations currently in existence were created since 1950. Worldwide, most nongovernmental organizations (NGOs) have come into being in the past thirty years. Nonprofits and NGOs are the most rapidly growing types of organizations in the world.

It is difficult to generalize about what nonprofit organizations are, what they do, and how they do it. They vary enormously in scope and scale, ranging from informal grassroots organizations with no assets and no employees through multibillion-dollar foundations, universities, religious bodies, and health care complexes with thousands of employees or members. While some provide traditional charitable, educational, and religious services, the law in many countries, including the United States, permits them to provide almost any kind of good or service on a not-for-profit basis. Sources of revenue vary: some nonprofits are supported by donations, others depend on income from sales of goods and services, and many receive most or all of their revenues from government. Modes of governance range from the autocracy of sole trustees selected from among the descendants of charitable donors through broadly representative boards composed of ex officio elected officials or directors elected by members of the organization.

Because of the complexity and diversity of nonprofit organizations, the term *nonprofit* itself has a variety of meanings. It can refer to entities classified by the Internal Revenue Code as 501(c)(3) charitable tax-exempts or to a more inclusive universe of 501(c)(4) civic organizations, which are themselves exempt from taxation but do not allow deductibility of donations. Good arguments can be made for including other noncharitable nonprofits such as cemeteries; veterans' and fraternal and sororal organizations (such as the Masons and the Elks); political parties; and other organizations covered by section 501(c). However inclusive, restricting the term to organizations accorded nonprofit status by the tax code remains problematic, since it does not include churches and other religious organizations that enjoy the privileges of 501(c)(3)s but are not legally required to incorporate or seek exempt status. There is also a vast realm of unincorporated associations (such as Alcoholics Anonymous and other self-help groups) that perform many of the functions of incorporated nonprofits as providers of charitable, educational, and religious services but whose assets do not merit—or that ideology does not permit—formal institutionalization.

Because their numbers have grown so rapidly, because they are so diverse, and because their impact is so far-reaching—touching on every aspect of our lives and every level of institutions—nonprofits have been the focus of intense controversy as legislators, the courts, and the public have struggled to come to terms with this organizational revolution. At the same time, because the non-profit universe has been in a process of emergence, everyone within it had to struggle to define and legitimate it.

For all these reasons—diversity, complexity, and disagreement about how to define them—nonprofits pose particular difficulties for scholars trying to explain their history. While elements of the "nonprofit sector" date back to biblical and classical times (religious bodies, for example), other important aspects of it are entirely new (hospitals and universities, for instance). At best, in trying to understand the history of nonprofits, we can identify the various ideas and institutions that make up today's nonprofit domain and show how they have evolved over time.

ASSOCIATIONS IN EARLY AMERICA

The basic legal vehicles of today's nonprofits—the corporation and the trust— were known to colonial Americans. Philanthropy and volunteer service—giving money and time—were also features of early American life. But because the colonists understood the role of government and the rights and responsibilities of citizenship so differently, these vehicles and practices little resembled the forms they take in modern America.

To begin with, there was no clear demarcation between the public and the private realm. All corporations, to the extent that they were permitted to exist, were considered public agencies (Davis, 1918; Dodd, 1960; Hurst, 1970; Seavoy, 1982). Most common were municipal corporations: townships (Hartog, 1983). In most colonies, religious congregations were public corporations supported by taxation and enjoying monopoly powers. The early colleges, Harvard (founded in 1638), William and Mary (1689), and Yale (1701), were sustained by government grants and governed by clergymen who, as officials of the government-supported ("established") churches, were public actors (Whitehead 1976). No private corporation as we understand the term today existed in America before the 1780s. Many of these institutions—churches, townships, and colleges—accepted gifts and bequests from donors and held them in trust as endowments, though it would be decades before American courts would have the power to enforce or adjudicate trusts.

Citizens often pitched in to maintain roads, to build meetinghouses, to fight with militias, and to assist with other public tasks (McKinney, 1995). While superficially resembling modern volunteers, these citizens were usually compelled by law to labor on behalf of the public. Service of this kind was a common way of paying taxes in a primitive colonial economy in which barter usually took the place of money. Militia duty and service in public office were often required by law—and those who failed to "volunteer" to serve were often punished by fines.

Despite obvious differences, these colonial institutions resembled modern nonprofits in important ways (Zollmann, 1924). They were self-governing, with decisions made by members who often delegated power to governing boards. More important, they had no owners or stockholders. As public bodies, they were exempt from taxation. And like modern nonprofits, they could accept donations and bequests for charitable purposes, such as supporting education and poor relief.

During the eighteenth century, population growth, economic development, and closer contact with England and other European countries changed American institutions. More people and the founding of new towns made it harder to maintain social and political unity. Artisans, merchants, and laborers living in seaports, dependent on trade and exposed to new ideas from Europe, developed different ways of thinking and living from subsistence farmers living in isolated landlocked villages. Even in the backcountry, conflict developed between farmers who began to grow crops for sale to urban merchants—tying themselves to the emerging market economy—and those who continued to produce largely to satisfy their own needs. To complicate matters, England's efforts to integrate the colonies into its growing commercial empire brought political changes. In many colonies, elected officials were replaced by royal appointees, and the Congregationalist religious monopoly was broken by the establishment of Anglican churches.

New ideas accompanied these social, economic, and political changes. Out of a century of religious warfare and political strife in Europe came philosophies that asserted the "natural rights" of citizens, including freedom of speech, assembly, and worship, and questioned the authority of arbitrary and oppressive government (Bailyn, 1992). New ideas also included more sophisticated understandings of law, particularly as it affected economic rights (Katz, 1971; Katz, Sullivan, and Beach, 1985; Nelson, 1975; Horowitz, 1977).

Closer ties to Europe brought not only new ideas but also new institutions. After an apprenticeship as a printer in London, young Benjamin Franklin returned with firsthand knowledge of the various kinds of voluntary associations being formed by English tradesmen (Morgan, 2003). Freemasonry, a fraternal order whose members were committed to a variety of radical political and religious ideas, spread rapidly through the colonies in the mid-1700s. Masonry provided a model for other forms of private voluntary associations, most notably Franklin's Junto, a club of young Philadelphia tradesmen who pooled their books, trained one another in debating and writing, and supported one another's political and economic ambitions.

Closer ties with Europe also transformed American religious life as evangelists associated with dissenting sects crossed the ocean to spread their doctrines (Ahlstrom, 1972; Finke and Stark, 1992; Hatch, 1989; Butler, 1990). Soon American cities and towns were filled with competing churches, with Methodists, Baptists, and other religious enthusiasts crowding out the older Congregationalists and Methodists. Although Pennsylvanians and Rhode Islanders had long enjoyed religious toleration, the notion that people could freely choose how to worship and were free to form and support their own congregations, free of government interference, was a novel idea to most Americans. In many places, religious dissenters demanded and succeeded in obtaining many of the same rights as members of established churches, including exemption of their congregations from taxation. This set an important precedent for the secular associations that would proliferate in the nineteenth century.

The American Revolution drew on all these intellectual and organizational developments: religious revivals and political theories that affirmed the importance of individual rights, experience in organizing voluntary associations, and the use of associations in politics. Groups like the Sons of Liberty and the Committees of Correspondence helped mobilize citizens to fight for American independence.

VOLUNTARY ASSOCIATIONS
IN THE NEW REPUBLIC, 1780–1860

Despite their importance during the Revolution, many Americans distrusted voluntary associations and feared the power of wealthy private institutions. These feelings were fueled by popular uprisings like Shays's Rebellion, in which Revolutionary War veterans led armed resistance to tax collectors, and the establishment of the Society of the Cincinnati, an association of army officers that critics believed sought the creation of a titled aristocracy. This fueled resistance to efforts to charter corporations and to enact legal reforms that would make it easier to set up and enforce charitable trusts.

Led by Virginia, many states actively discouraged private charity (Wyllie, 1959; Miller, 1961). In 1792, the Commonwealth of Virginia annulled the British laws that authorized the establishment of charitable trusts and confiscated endowments administered by the Anglican Church. Favoring public over private institutions, Virginia established the first state university in 1818 (Dabney, 1981). This would become a common pattern in many southern and western states.

The South was not alone in its suspicion of private charitable enterprise. In 1784, New York established the Regents of the University of the State of New York, a regulatory body that oversaw all charitable, education, religious, and professional organizations. In the 1820s, the state enacted laws limiting the size of institutional endowments and the size of bequests that testators could leave to charity.

In contrast, the New England states actively encouraged private initiatives of all sorts. By 1800, Massachusetts and Connecticut had chartered more corporations than all the other states combined. Voluntary associations—formal and informal; religious and secular—flourished. By the 1820s, legal reforms gave further encouragement to private charities by protecting trustees from liability and liberalizing the kinds of investments they could make. As a result, the New England states became national centers for education, culture, and science as the wealth from the region's industrializing economy poured into the coffers of its colleges, hospitals, libraries, and museums (Hall, 1982).

These growing differences in the treatment of private associations, charity, and philanthropy inevitably had political consequences. With the rise of popular politics and the intensification of efforts to disestablish churches in states where some religious groups still enjoyed monopoly privileges and tax support, conservative elites went on the defensive, using colleges and other private institutions to protect their power. These struggles came to a head in the Dartmouth College Case (*Trustees of Dartmouth College* v. *Woodward*, 17 U.S. 518, 1819; Tobias, 1982). In 1819, the U.S. Supreme Court was asked to decide whether the state of New Hampshire had exceeded its powers in taking over a privately endowed educational institution and turning it into a public institution. The court, in ruling that a corporation was a private contract and hence protected by the contracts clause of the United States Constitution, gave assurance to donors that the institutions they founded and supported would be safe from government interference. Later, in the Girard Will Case (*Vidal* v. *Executors of Girard*, 43 U.S. 127, 1844), the Court would affirm the legal basis for private philanthropy, even in states like Pennsylvania, which had annulled British charity statutes.

Because the Constitution granted significant power to the states, these federal court decisions had limited impact. Every state had its own laws governing corporations, associations, and charities. Some, like the states of New England, encouraged private philanthropy and protected charitable corporations. Most, however, restricted private initiatives and, as a matter of public policy, favored public ones. This preference did not, it should be noted, preclude private giving to public institutions. State colleges and universities, public libraries, and other government-run agencies benefited from this growing practice of public philanthropy.

During the first half of the nineteenth century, voluntary associations played increasingly important roles in the nation's public life. Political parties, embryonic in 1800, had become powerful national institutions. As Americans became concerned about slavery, drunkenness, violations of the Sabbath, treatment of the insane, and other causes, voluntary associations, organized on a national basis with state and local chapters, became the preferred vehicles for social movements promoting reform. Churches began organizing themselves into national denominations that supported a wide variety of educational and charitable initiatives, domestic and foreign missions, and substantial publishing enterprises (Foster, 1965; Mathews 1969). Fraternal organizations, such as the Masons and the Odd Fellows, commanded the loyalties of hundreds of thousands of Americans (Skocpol and others, 1998) .

Beginning in the 1830s, European emigrants, displaced by war, revolution, and economic distress, began to flock to our shores. Some, like the Germans, brought with them their own rich traditions of voluntary action. Others, like the Irish, brought forms of charitable engagement. The Roman Catholic Church, to which many Germans and Irish belonged, began creating a benevolent empire of schools, orphanages, temperance societies, and social welfare organizations to serve its members. Although its hierarchical structure excluded laity from involvement in church governance, the church became an increasingly important factor in the nation's associational life (Dolan, 1992; Oates, 1995).

In addition to these national associations, there were thousands of free-standing local charitable corporations and voluntary associations devoted to practically every imaginable purpose (Ryan, 1981). As the French visitor Alexis de Tocqueville noted while visiting America in the 1830s:

> Americans of all ages, all conditions, and all dispositions constantly form associations. They have not only commercial and manufacturing companies, in which all take part, but associations of a thousand other kinds, religious, moral, serious, futile, general or restricted, enormous or diminutive. The Americans make associations to give entertainments, to found seminaries, to build inns, to construct churches, to diffuse books, to send missionaries to the antipodes; in this manner they found hospitals, prisons, and schools. If it is proposed to inculcate some truth or foster some feeling by the encouragement of a great example, they form a society. Wherever at the head of some new undertaking you see the government in France, or a man of rank in England, in the United States you will be sure to find an association. [1840/1945, p. 106]

In his enthusiasm, de Tocqueville somewhat exaggerated the universality of voluntary associations. While they were used for many purposes and by people at all levels of society, including women and African Americans who were excluded from the political process, there remained significant geographical variations in citizens' willingness to use them, depending on whether state laws restricted their activities and authorities were willing to subsidize them directly, through government grants and contracts, or indirectly through tax exemption.

In states where private initiative was discouraged, tasks of education, healing, and care for the dependent and disabled were often carried out by public agencies. Public provision did not preclude private support, however. State universities accepted private donations. Firefighting in most towns and cities was provided by volunteer companies. Along with newer forms of voluntary action, older traditions of public philanthropy and volunteerism continued to flourish.

NATION BUILDING, 1860–1890

Associations, private charities, and giving and volunteering all played prominent roles in the Civil War (1861–1865), which provided opportunities for further advancing the claims of private eleemosynary enterprise. Among the first units to rally to the defense of the Union were private military companies, groups of civilians for whom soldierly training was a form of recreational and social activity. Once the fighting began in earnest, private groups rushed to care for the injured and provide comfort for soldiers still in the field. The United States Sanitary Commission, the United States Christian Commission, and other groups organized fundraising events, made clothing and bandages, and mobilized volunteers in towns and cities throughout the country to meet the medical, public health, and other needs of armed forces (Brockett, 1864; Cross, 1865; Moss, 1868; Frederickson, 1965).

At the war's end, the victorious Union faced the immense task of "reconstructing" states devastated by fierce fighting and preparing millions of slaves for freedom (Fleming, 1906; McFeely, 1968; Butchart, 1980; Richardson, 1986). To do this, the government turned to voluntary organizations to build and staff schools, to teach civic and vocational skills to newly freed men and women, and to reform southern industry and agriculture (Swint, 1967). Reconstruction also showed some of the darker possibilities of voluntary associations as embittered southerners organized groups like the Ku Klux Klan to terrorize blacks and the northern volunteers who were helping them.

The Civil War transformed America, not only establishing the preeminent authority of the federal government in important areas such as civil rights but also unifying the country economically and culturally. Military needs had forced standardization of railroad equipment, consolidation of the telegraph industry, and the creation of a national financial market, centered in New York. Government spending and growing demand from an increasingly urbanized population fueled increases in the scope and scale of manufacturing and commercial enterprises that sought national and international markets. The government-funded transcontinental railroad, completed in 1869, opened vast areas of the West for agricultural and industrial development. Growing industries and advancing technology required managers and experts for efficient and profitable operation.

Educational institutions found opportunities in this prospect of unbounded growth. "The American people are fighting the wilderness, physical and moral, on the one hand, and on the other are struggling to work out the awful problem of self-government," declared Harvard's new president, Charles W. Eliot, in 1869. "For this fight they must be trained and armed." Having spent the war years in Europe studying the relationships between higher education and economic development, Eliot himself was well prepared to lead the transformation of Harvard, a sleepy local college before the war, into a modern research university.

Eliot's clarion call was met with enthusiasm. Gifts and bequests to the university increased from $1.6 million for the period 1841–1865 to $5.9 million for the years 1866–1890 (Sears, 1922). Business leaders largely replaced clergymen and lawyers on its governing boards (Veblen, 1918). Curricular reforms encouraged specialization, while new graduate departments and professional schools provided facilities for advanced training and research (Veysey, 1965; Rudolph, 1968; Hawkins, 1972). Harvard's transformation into a research university set the pace for American higher education—and the generosity and imagination of its donors set a standard for philanthropists throughout the country (Curti and Nash, 1965).

Universities became hubs for a universe of new associational and philanthropic institutions and activities (Bledstein, 1976; Hawkins, 1992; Geiger, 1986, 1993). Hospitals, museums, and other arts organizations became research centers, closely tied to university medical schools, scientific disciplines, and new programs in the fine arts and music (Fox, 1963; Starr, 1982; Di Maggio, 1986). New academic disciplines and professions gave rise to professional and scholarly societies (Buck, 1965; Haskell, 1977). University-trained managers and experts became increasingly important not only to industry but also to governments, which were beginning to grapple with the social welfare, public health, transportation, and policing problems of growing cities (Wiebe, 1967; Brint, 1994).

Beginning in the 1870s, the American economy was shaken by a series of crises. The collapse of the stock market in 1873 was the beginning of a depression that lasted for years and impoverished hundreds of thousands of workers. Economic distress encouraged the growth of labor unions and radical political organizations whose conflicts with employers and government authorities became increasingly violent. In 1877, a national railroad strike provoked large-scale rioting and looting in major cities. In 1886, labor's campaign for a ten-hour workday culminated in the Haymarket bombing in Chicago, which killed a dozen policemen and led to the roundup and execution of radical politicians and journalists.

Among the few calm voices in the period was that of a Pittsburgh steel executive, Andrew Carnegie (Wall, 1970). An immigrant from Scotland, Carnegie had worked his way up from being a child laborer in a textile mill to serving as the right-hand man of the president of the Pennsylvania Railroad. From there, he became a pioneering and fabulously successful steel manufacturer. By the 1880s, he was well on his way to becoming one of America's wealthiest men.

In 1886, Carnegie began writing a series of articles on the labor crisis that argued that shorter hours, better working conditions, and employer recognition of workers' right to organize were in the interests of both capital and labor. At the same time, he suggested that the enlarged scope and scale of modern industry had fundamentally changed not only economic relationships but also the nature of political life (Carnegie, 1886a, 1886b). He summed up his thinking in an 1889 essay, "Wealth," which urged the "men of affairs" who had most profited from advanced industrial development to use their "genius for affairs" to reinvest their fortunes in society. Inherited wealth, he believed, was bad both for heirs and for society—and he went so far as to recommend confiscatory estate taxation to prevent the passing on of large fortunes (Carnegie, 1889). More important, he argued that intelligent philanthropy could not only eliminate the root causes of social problems but also sustain the competitive processes essential to continuing progress.

Carnegie was harshly critical of traditional charity, which, he believed, only responded to suffering rather than addressing the causes of poverty. "It were better for mankind that the millions of the rich were thrown into the sea," he wrote, "than so spent as to encourage the slothful, the drunken, the unworthy. Of every thousand dollars spent in so-called charity today, it is probable that nine hundred and fifty dollars is unwisely spent—so spent, indeed, as to produce the very evils which it hopes to mitigate or cure" (Carnegie, 1889).

"The best means of benefiting the community," Carnegie urged his fellow millionaires, "is to place within its reach the ladders upon which the aspiring can rise"—"institutions of various kinds, which will improve the general condition of the people; in this manner returning their surplus wealth to the mass of their fellows in the forms best calculated to do them lasting good" (Carnegie, 1889). This included libraries, parks, museums, public meeting halls (like New York's famous Carnegie Hall), and educational institutions.

In popularizing the idea that businessmen could use the same "genius for affairs" that had made them rich to reform society, Carnegie set an example for his fellow tycoons. Before Carnegie, most philanthropy had been small-scale and conventional. After Carnegie, philanthropy, organized and focused through foundations, would assume an unprecedented scale and scope, becoming an important source of innovation in addressing problems of education, health, and social welfare.

The consolidation of American political, economic, and social institutions between the Civil War and the First World War was as much the result of the actions of elite institutions like universities and powerful leaders like Andrew Carnegie as it was the outcome of associational activity at all levels in society (Sklar, 1988). In the second half of the nineteenth century, America became, in Arthur Schlesinger Sr.'s phrase, "a nation of joiners" (1944, p. 24). Immigrants, who flooded the nation in ever-growing numbers, organized mutual benefit associations that gave them solidarity and provided help in times of sickness and distress (Soyer, 1997; Li, 1999). Physicians, lawyers, engineers, and other professionals organized associations to set standards, exchange information, and pressure government (Calhoun, 1965; Calvert, 1967; Auerbach, 1976; Abbott, 1988; Kimball, 1995). Businesses organized trade associations to advocate for legislation favoring their interests (Naylor, 1921). Wage earners organized trade unions to press employers to improve pay and working conditions. War veterans organized the Grand Army of the Republic to promote sociability and to advocate for pensions and other benefits. Advocacy groups, which drew members from across the social spectrum, agitated for prohibition, women's suffrage, civil service and charities reform, and other causes (Clemens, 1997). Most important of all were the fraternal and sororal organizations—the Freemasons, Odd Fellows, Knights of Columbus, Rebekahs, and dozens of others—whose chapters became centers of sociability and civic activity, as well as sources of social insurance, for men and women throughout the country (Dumenil, 1984; Beito, 2000; Kaufman, 2002; Skocpol, 2003).

Widespread participation in these broad-based associations was probably the most powerful and effective school of democracy. By participating in associations, citizens learned how to be self-governing, to argue and persuade, to raise funds and manage finances, to form alliances and coalitions. The fact that most of these associations were national entities whose architecture mirrored that of government itself—with national, state, and local organizations—helped bind the nation together by accustoming Americans to engaging with one another beyond the locality. If, as de Tocqueville suggested, Americans in the first half of the nineteenth century had learned the principle of association in their schoolyards, in the second half of the century associations became the great school of democracy, teaching adults and children alike the values and skills needed for a vibrant and inclusive public culture.

NEW CHARITABLE VEHICLES, 1890–1930

The kind of large-scale targeted giving Carnegie recommended faced a number of obstacles. The most important of them were legal barriers to private charity in states like New York. At the time that Carnegie wrote, New York state courts had already invalidated a million-dollar bequest to Cornell on the grounds that the donation, if accepted, would render the university's endowment larger than the amount that the legislature had authorized it to hold. The courts had also invalidated former presidential candidate and corporation lawyer Samuel Tilden's multimillion-dollar charitable bequest to establish the New York Public Library (Ames, 1913). Without major legal reform, the wealthy, who were increasingly gravitating to New York, the nation's financial center, could not be philanthropically generous even if they wanted to be.

Another obstacle was the lack of organizational vehicles for large-scale philanthropy. Wealthy men like the devoutly religious John D. Rockefeller, who controlled America's petroleum industry by the 1890s, tried to be conscientious givers, personally considering and carefully weighing the thousands of begging letters that poured into their offices (Harr and Johnson, 1988; Chernow, 1998). Rockefeller's situation was summed up by his chief assistant, John W. Gates, who exclaimed to his employer, "Your fortune is rolling up, rolling up like an avalanche!" he told him. "You must keep up with it! You must distribute it faster than it grows! If you do not, it will crush you and your children and your children's children" (Harr and Johnson, 1988, p.82). The solution was the creation of corporate entities, staffed by experts, to scientifically distribute this surplus wealth. The problem was that American law had traditionally required that charitable trusts be specific in designating classes of beneficiaries.

The failure of the Tilden Trust, combined with anxieties about the increasing anger of average Americans toward the rich and big business, fueled a coordinated effort to reform charity laws in the leading industrial states ("American Millionaires," 1893). By 1893, New York, Pennsylvania, Ohio, and Illinois had altered their charity statutes, permitting the kind of wholesale philanthropy that Carnegie had advocated. Philanthropists proceeded cautiously onto this new legal ground. The first recognizably modern foundations included Rockefeller's General Education Board, established in 1901 to benefit black schools in the South) but later broadened to include higher educational nationally, Andrew Carnegie's Carnegie Endowment for the Advancement of Teaching, established in 1905, and Margaret Olivia Slocum Sage's Russell Sage Foundation, established in 1907 to systematically address social welfare issues on a national basis (Fosdick, 1962; Lagemann, 1999; Glenn, Brandt, and Andrews, 1947; Hammack and Wheeler, 1994). In 1911, Carnegie took the bold step of establishing the largest foundation of all, the Carnegie Corporation of New York, for the general purpose of "the advancement and diffusion of knowledge and understanding" (Lagemann, 1992).

John D. Rockefeller, not to be outdone and smarting from the court-ordered breakup of the Standard Oil monopoly, applied to Congress for a charter for a $100 million foundation dedicated to "the betterment of mankind" (Fosdick, 1952). The request set off a furor among politicians and journalists, who worried about the influence foundations of this size could have on public policy and about their economic power. Rockefeller eventually obtained a charter from the New York state legislature in 1913.

Concerns about the power of foundations and the continuing concentration of wealth continued to grow. In 1915, Congress empanelled the special Commission on Industrial Relations, which held well-publicized hearings over a period of two years (U.S. Congress, 1916). The charges aired during these hearing led foundations to be cautious and secretive about their involvement in public affairs—a stance that would fuel public suspicions of philanthropy's motives and methods that would erupt periodically for the rest of the century (Katz, 1981).

Grantmaking foundations were not the only new charitable vehicles created in the decades before the First World War. In 1910, Cleveland's chamber of commerce convened a committee to consider problems of charitable fraud, abuse, and inefficiency. Appeals for charity were multiplying, but donors had no way of knowing whether they came from reputable organizations. The number of charitable organizations seek aid was increasing, producing duplicated efforts and wasted resources. The donor base was shrinking, with an increasing proportion of donations coming from a smaller number of donors. The committee eventually brought forth a new kind of charity—the Community Chest (Seeley and others, 1957; Cutlip, 1965). Led by businessmen, the Community Chest proposed to conduct a single annual fund drive for all of Cleveland's charities. The organization's distribution committee would assess the city's charities and allocate funds to the most worthy. The Community Chest proposed to broaden the donor base by soliciting employees of the city's business firms. Aggressively publicized, the Community Chest idea spread rapidly. By 1930, hundreds of towns and cities had adopted this form of federated fundraising. The Community Chest is the ancestor of today's United Way.

Cleveland also fostered cooperation among the city's social agencies through its Charities Federation. Establishing lines of communication between agencies allowed them to coordinate their activities, improve their management, and use their resources more efficiently. It also enabled private agencies to work more closely with government to address social problems.

The Community Chest and the Charities Federation addressed problems of current giving and spending. In 1925, Cleveland banker Frederick Goff sought to make the establishment and management of charitable endowments more efficient. He proposed the idea of the community foundation, an institution empowered to receive charitable trusts of various sizes and for various purposes (Hall, 1989b; Hammack, 1989; Magat, 1989). These would be placed under common management under the authority of a board made up of leading bankers. A distribution committee, often made up of public officials and others serving ex officio, would allocate undesignated or discretionary funds to worthy organizations. Like the Community Chest, the community foundation was intended to democratize charitable giving while at the same time giving civic leaders control of a community's charitable resources.

None of these innovations would have been possible without the enthusiastic backing of business leaders. Not only did their ideas and money sustain charitable, educational, and religious institutions, but their companies also became important to the effort to improve society (Heald, 1970; Hall 1989a). Under the banner of "welfare capitalism," corporations not only contributed generously to community institutions but also established pension plans, initiated educational programs, and supported social and athletic activities for their employees and their families (Brandes, 1976; Brody, 1980). Many firms sold products intended to improve Americans' health and quality of life.

These charitable innovations were only a small part of a far broader associational revolution in the first three decades of the twentieth century. Membership in fraternal and sororal organizations peaked in numbers of organizations and members in the mid-1920s (Skocpol, 2003). Businessmen's service organizations—Rotary, Kiwanis, Lions, and others—appeared in every town and city (Charles, 1993). Businesses organized trade associations to advocate, lobby, and educate the public and government about their interests. Herbert Hoover, writing in 1922, envisioned these trade associations working closely with other kinds of "voluntary organizations for altruistic purposes" (p. 42) to advance public welfare, morals, and charity; to elevate public opinion; to improve public health; and to solve social problems combining the pursuit of self-interest with higher values of cooperation and public service (Hoover, 1922; Galambos, 1966; Hawley, 1974, 1977; Karl, 1969, 1976). A nation based on public interest volunteerism, he believed, would not need the radical remedies of socialism and communism to address problems of inequality and injustice.

Accompanying this associational revolution was a related transformation of fundraising (Cutlip, 1965). As the needs of hospitals, universities, and other organized charities grew, fundraising became professionalized. Firms like John Price Jones & Company combined sophisticated business methods with aggressive marketing techniques in raising funds for the World War I loan drives and later for Harvard and other universities.

Reform-oriented social movements and other kinds of organized advocacy continued to grow during this period (Sealander, 1997). Efforts to eliminate child labor, enfranchise women, restrict immigration, and protect the rights of minorities influenced public policy through demonstrations, advertising campaigns, lobbying, and litigation. Particularly notable were the efforts of the National Association for the Advancement of Colored People (NAACP) and other groups in the vanguard of the effort to halt the epidemic of lynchings and race riots in which thousands of black citizens perished between 1890 and 1930. Sadly, perhaps the most influential social movement of the period was the revived Ku Klux Klan, which during the 1920s commanded the loyalty of hundreds of thousands of followers throughout the country, directing its energies against African Americans, Jews, Catholics, labor organizers, and others.

BIG GOVERNMENT, THE NONPROFIT SECTOR, AND THE TRANSFORMATION OF PUBLIC LIFE, 1930–1980

Between 1930 and 1980, American public life was transformed by huge growth in the scope and scale of government, which in turn stimulated commensurate expansion of private institutions. The two were closely connected since government, as it took on increasing responsibilities for managing economic, political, and social matters, was able to use its awesome power to stimulate growth and activity in the private sector. Just as the public sector activities like construction of the interstate highway system and petroleum industry subsidies stimulated the growth of the privately owned automobile industry, so public sector subsidies of charitable giving (tax breaks for donors, exemptions for charities, voucher programs like the G.I. Bill, and increasingly generous grants and contracts) stimulated the growth of nonprofit enterprises of every kind.

This was an incremental process. In the 1930s, no one envisioned that the emergency powers assumed by the federal government to deal with the Great Depression would become permanent and central features of public life. Nor could anyone imagine the extent to which the increasing activism of government would stimulate the growth of the private sector.

The nation was ill-prepared to deal with the catastrophic economic collapse that began with the stock market crash of October 1929. Even if the discipline of economics had been better developed, its retrospective insights could not have offered much understanding of this unprecedented event. In any event, government lacked the necessary tools of economic management to engage problems of mass unemployment and business failure on this scale.

President Herbert Hoover, a millionaire mining engineer who had entered politics with an international reputation as a humanitarian, was philosophically opposed to the idea of big government. His attempts to deal with the Depression through the system of voluntary associations whose growth he had fostered as secretary of commerce and later as president, proved ineffective. His successor, Franklin D. Roosevelt, entered office with similarly conservative views. The centerpiece of his recovery program, the National Recovery Administration (NRA)—with its motto "We do our part"—was similarly based on voluntaristic principles, promoting economic revival through cooperation between business and government (Himmelberg, 1976).

When the NRA was declared unconstitutional in 1935, Roosevelt turned to more activist remedies, with attempts to restore consumer buying power through massive public works projects like the Works Projects Administration (WPA) and the Civilian Conservation Corps (CCC), agricultural subsidies, and a national system of social insurance (Social Security). He also proposed major tax reforms, which introduced steeply progressive income and estate taxes with the intent of using the tax system to redistribute the wealth owned by the richest Americans. These tax reforms had little impact on average Americans, few of whom earned enough money to owe income tax. But they proved to be a powerful incentive for the wealthy to avoid taxation through large-scale charitable giving.

Roosevelt's New Deal established the paradigm for the later growth of government. While the federal government increased the scope of its responsibilities and assumed leadership for making policy in important areas, most federal programs were carried out by state and municipal agencies and by nongovernmental organizations funded by government contracts, user fees, and private contributions indirectly subsidized through tax exemptions and deductions.

During the Second World War and afterward, as the United States assumed leadership of the free world, federal government policies played a key role in stimulating growth in the number and importance of nonprofit organizations.

The most important of these involved taxation (Witte, 1985; Webber and Wildavsky, 1986). The income tax, which few Americans had had to pay before the 1940s, was universalized: not only were most wage and salary earners subject to it, but the government began withholding estimated tax liabilities from employees' paychecks. At the same time, tax rates were sharply increased on estates and business corporations. The intent of the new tax policies went beyond gathering revenue for government: "loopholes"—exemptions, deductions, and tax credits—were provided to encourage charitable giving to private institutions classified as tax-exempt by the Internal Revenue Service (IRS) (Howard, 1997). The growth of nonprofit organizations was also stimulated by increased spending in the form of government grants, contracts, and vouchers (like the G.I. Bill, which subsidized higher education for returning soldiers).

These policies had dramatic effects (Weisbrod, 1988). By 1940, there were only 12,500 charitable tax-exempt organizations registered by the IRS—along with 179,742 religious congregations (which did not have to apply for exemption) and 60,000 noncharitable nonprofits (such as labor unions and fraternal associations) that enjoyed various tax privileges.[1] By 1980, there were 320,000 charitable tax-exempt nonprofits, 336,000 religious bodies, and 526,000 noncharitable nonprofits. Today, there are more than 600,000 charitables, 400,000 religious congregations, and 600,000 noncharitables—a total of more than a million and a half nonprofits of various types (Hall and Burke, 2004). Government policies played a crucial role in fueling the growing scope and number of nonprofit organizations, not only indirectly by creating incentives for individuals and firms to contribute to private organizations serving governmental ends but also directly through grants and contracts. By the 1970s, between 12 and 55 percent of total nonprofit revenues were direct payments from the federal government (Salamon, 1987).

Although the scope and scale of its responsibilities vastly increased in the second half of the twentieth century, the size of the federal government—at least as measured by the size of its civilian workforce—did not. The number of federal civilian employees remained unchanged between 1950 and 2000, while the number of state and local employees doubled and tripled, respectively, and the number of nonprofit organizations grew from the thousands to more than a million. Quite clearly, "big government" as it developed after the Second World War took a very different form than conventionally supposed. Doing its work through states and localities and through policies that encouraged flows of resources to private actors, the American welfare state was a remarkable example of what Lester Salamon has called "third-party government." (See Chapter Four for more about the relationship between governments and nonprofit organizations.)

Of the proliferating organizations in the nonprofit sector, none attracted more attention in the years following the war than foundations (Andrews, 1950). As taxes on incomes and estates increased, the founders of the huge fortunes built in the boom years of the twentieth century were increasingly likely to use foundations as mechanisms for avoiding taxation. When Henry Ford died in 1947, stock in his closely held company was divided into two classes (MacDonald, 1956; Greenleaf, 1964; Nielsen, 1971; Sutton, 1987). The voting stock was retained by the family, and the nonvoting securities were given to the Ford Foundation, which sold them at an immense profit. The Ford Motor Company passed to the next generation without paying a penny in taxes—and the largest foundation in the world was created in the process.

Stratagems like this helped fuel an enormous increase in the number and importance of foundations. From a mere 203 in 1929, the number of foundations with assets exceeding $1 million grew to 2,058 by 1959, the vast majority of them established in the 1950s (*Foundation Directory*, 1960; Andrews, 1956). In 1929, their assets represented only 10.7 percent of the total property controlled by charitable tax-exempt organizations; by 1973, their share was 21.7 percent. Thanks to liberalized laws regarding corporate philanthropy, the growing universe of private and community foundations was further enlarged by corporate foundations and organized corporate contributions programs (Andrews, 1952; Useem, 1987; Hall, 1989a; Himmelstein, 1997).

While Ford and other foundations established by wealthy families at this time undoubtedly performed valuable services, some politicians and journalists wondered whether average citizens, who were becoming increasingly sensitive to their own tax burdens, either approved of the loopholes that permitted multimillionaires to evade taxes or sympathized with the sometimes controversial uses of foundation grants (Lundberg, 1968; Nielsen, 1971; Andrews, 1969). Between 1952 and 1969, congressional committees investigating foundations and "other tax-exempt entities" cast an increasingly skeptical eye on their activities. With the federal government assuming primary responsibility for education, health, and social welfare, many Americans wondered whether private philanthropy, subsidized by tax breaks, had outlived its usefulness.

Despite these periodic outbursts of regulatory enthusiasm, funds from foundations, corporations, and new government programs (the National Institutes of Health, National Science Foundation, National Endowment for the Arts, and National Endowment for the Humanities, among others) continued to fuel the growth and transformation of nonprofit enterprises. Industries like the performing arts and health care, which had been almost entirely for-profit in ownership before 1950, became dominated by nonprofit firms in the course of the next half-century. On the other hand, industries like elder care, which had been largely nonprofit, became for-profit in ownership as government social and medical insurance programs made nursing homes an increasingly profitable enterprise.

The increasing centrality of government also encouraged the growth of special-interest advocacy organizations as stakeholders affected by or benefiting from government programs sought to influence legislators in their favor (Berry,

1977, 1997; Jenkins, 1987; Jenkins and Craig, 1986; Jenkins and Halcli, 1999). Policy research ("think tanks") and policy advocacy groups like the Business Advisory Council, the Conference Board, the Committee for Economic Development, and the Business Roundtable, formed a privatized policy establishment (Critchlow, 1985; Smith, 1991a, 1991b; Rich, 2004).

Increasing government activism and foundation funding also stimulated grassroots social movement activity intended to influence public policy. The civil rights movement of the 1950s and 1960s gave rise to a host of movements promoting the rights of women, children, the unborn, the disabled, the health of the environment, and a variety of international causes (Minkoff, 1995; Proietto, 1999; Berkeley Art Center Association, 2001; Fleischer and Zames, 2001; Minton, 2002; Stroman, 2003). On the whole, these social change organizations differed in significant ways from their nineteenth-century predecessors. Earlier organizations had been broadly based membership organizations in which volunteers and local chapters played central roles. Late-twentieth-century social change organizations were increasingly likely to be based in the national capital and to be run by professional managers, policy experts, communications specialists, and lobbyists (Skocpol, 2003).

Changing political culture, combined with a more educated, affluent, and mobile citizenry, helped kill off traditional kinds of voluntary associations. Membership in fraternal and sororal organizations began to drop sharply after the Second World War as Americans moved to the suburbs and substituted television and other privatized forms of entertainment and recreation for more collective forms of social engagement (Skocpol, 1999). Even such venerable organizations as the Parent-Teacher Association (PTA) began to decline as suburban parents preferred to devote their energies to parent-teacher organizations focusing more narrowly on the schools their own children attended rather than broader educational issues (Crawford and Levitt, 1999). According to political scientist Robert Putnam (2000), all forms of civic engagement—voting, attending public meetings, church attendance, and participation in athletic associations like bowling leagues—declined sharply after the 1960s.

Taking the place of traditional voluntary and membership-based engagement was a growing domain of narrowly focused, professionally managed nonprofit organizations that obtained their funding from a mix of earned revenues, government and foundation grants and contracts, and corporate contributions (Hall, 2003). These organizations were more likely to provide specific kinds of services (child day care, elder care, education, health services) and to engage in advocacy, lobbying, and public education than to promote generalized sociability and civic engagement. Writing on public culture in the late twentieth century, management guru Peter Drucker (1989, p. 204) noted that "the nonprofit organizations of the so-called third sector . . . create a sphere of effective citizenship," a "sphere of personal achievement," in which the individual "exercises influence, discharges responsibility, and makes decisions. . . . In the political culture of mainstream society," Drucker concludes, "individuals, no matter how well-educated, how successful, how achieving, or how wealthy, can only vote and pay taxes. They can only react, can only be passive. In the counterculture of the third sector, they are active citizens. This may be the most important contribution of the third sector.

In his enthusiasm for the possibilities of the sector, Drucker overlooked the fact that organizations that did not depend on volunteers or donations, did not seek to recruit members, and were narrowly focused on service provision and advocacy were likely primarily to engage the energies and interest of "knowledge workers" empowered by the high-tech economy rather than the mass of citizens.[2] It appeared that the "nation of joiners" celebrated by Schlesinger in the 1940s were left without opportunities for joining.

The major exception to this trend was religion. Although rising more slowly than the general population, membership in religious bodies and attendance at worship services increased steadily through the second half of the twentieth century (Finke and Stark, 1992; Fogel, 2000). More impressive were increases in the numbers of congregations and new religious organizations (Roof, 1999). While the mainstream denominations (Catholic, Protestant, Jewish) declined, their place was being taken by freestanding congregations, often of an evangelical bent, and by groups that stood outside the Western religious traditions (Wuthnow, 1998; Eck, 2001). In addition, ecumenical and parachurch organizations like Habitat for Humanity, which drew on members' religious commitment but were nonsectarian, grew steadily (Wuthnow, 1994; Baggett, 2001; Bender, 2003). New religious organizations were more likely to be politically active: the conservative revolution of the 1980s and 1990s owed much to its ability to mobilize voters and bring pressure to bear on legislators (Reed, 1996). Even more important, the new religious organizations were likely to be broadly based in ways that cross lines of class, occupation, education, and ethnicity, making them especially potent in imparting civic values and skills (Verba, Schlozman, and Brady, 1995).

As religious organizations have assumed a new visibility in public life generally, they have also gained recognition as centrally important parts of the nonprofit sector (Wuthnow, 1988; Wuthnow, Hodgkinson, and Associates, 1990; Cherry and Sherrill, 1992; Demerath, Hall, Williams, and Schmitt, 1998). This is the case not only because they constitute a large part of the nonprofit universe but also because they serve as paths of recruitment into secular activities and as platforms for secular or faith-based service provision in a variety of areas. The debate over charitable choice stemming from the welfare reforms of the mid-1990s was not so much an argument about church-state separation as it was an effort to codify government support for faith-based social services that had been a feature of America's human services regime for decades (Carlson-Thies and Skillen, 1996; Cnaan, 1999, 2002; Chaves, 2001; Hall, 2001).

THE CONSERVATIVE REVOLUTION
AND THE NONPROFIT SECTOR, 1980–2000

For much of the twentieth century, foundations and secular nonprofit organizations had been generally associated with liberal political causes. Conservatives, regarding nonprofits as liberal—if not subversive—organizations, had not only sought to curtail their privileges but also generally avoided using nonprofits to advance their own purposes. This began to change after the defeat of Barry Goldwater in 1964, when conservative leaders realized that criticizing liberalism was insufficient as a basis for political success: victory required alternative policies and relentless efforts to sway the public in their favor (Hodgson, 1996). To achieve their ends, conservatives would have to overcome their aversion to nonprofits in order to create their own "establishment" of think tanks, advocacy organizations, and foundations (Blumenthal, 1986; Berry, 1997; Rich, 2004).

A number of factors fueled this resolve. One was the emergence of a new cadre of moneyed conservatives, mostly from fast-developing areas of the South and West, whose wealth was based on defense production and extractive industries (Sale, 1975). They had a vital economic interest in being able to sway government policies in their favor. Another factor was the political mobilization of conservative Christians, particularly in the South, due to civil rights legislation and court decisions on school prayer, abortion, and tax exemptions for segregated private schools that they believed threatened their way of life. The convergence of big new money and a broad-based religious movement with a social agenda created new opportunities for conservative Republicans to begin organizing around "wedge issues" like reproductive rights that broke up long-standing liberal political coalitions. The mobilization of conservative voters, in turn, created the conditions for articulating a positive set of conservative policies that could credibly challenge liberal orthodoxies.

Although moderate Republicans regained control of the party after the Goldwater defeat, the conservatives worked doggedly to seize control of the local and state party organizations—helped along by the 1970s Watergate scandal, which discredited the moderate leadership of Richard Nixon. By the eve of the 1980 election, conservatives were ready to take power with Ronald Reagan as their standard-bearer.

Reagan assumed office with strong opinions on the role of nonprofit organizations in public life. He believed that big government had stifled private initiative, and he intended to undo the damage through a combination of "jaw-boning" higher levels of corporate giving (through the President's Task Force on Private Initiatives) and cutting government spending. What he, like most Americans, failed to understand was the extent to which the nonprofit sector had become dependent on government spending. By the time he took office, nearly a third of the annual revenues of private research universities came from government grants and contracts, and direct federal support for nonprofits in industries like human services ranged as high as 90 percent (Salamon, 1987). All in all, as an influential Urban Institute report pointed out in 1982, the federal government had become the largest single source of revenue for secular nonprofit organizations, and for this reason, massive cuts in government social spending would devastate the nonprofit sector (Salamon and Abramson, 1982).

Through the 1980s and into the 1990s, the emphasis in conservative social policy was on devolution (shifting responsibilities to states and localities) and privatization (shifting responsibilities for service provision to private sector actors). The rationales for these policies included the belief that not only would more local and private service provision be more flexible and responsive to the needs of beneficiaries but also that competition for contracts among private providers would also produce greater efficiency and effectiveness in service provision (Olasky, 1992).

Although it remains to be seen whether privatized social services have fulfilled any of these promises, it is clear that among the most important effects of these policies was to increase the need for professionally trained nonprofit managers and entrepreneurs—people who could master an increasingly complex and turbulent policy and funding environment. Although Republican leaders like George H. W. Bush might enthuse about the "thousand points of light" in America's community-serving nonprofit organizations, the reality was that these organizations were being driven by circumstances into being less and less responsive to client and community needs while becoming more businesslike in their attitudes and operations. At the same time, as traditional manufacturing and commercial businesses either disappeared or were driven from urban centers to the suburbs, for-profit enterprises were being rapidly replaced by nonprofit service providers, making the nonprofit sector an increasingly important part of the national economy.

Despite the election of centrist Democrat Bill Clinton in 1992, the conservative revolution entered a new and more radical phase in 1994 when Republicans took control of the House of Representatives and increased their plurality in the Senate. Under the banner of the so-called Contract with America, conservative leaders set out to dismantle the government social programs created during the previous century (Gillespie and Schellhas, 1994). This agenda went well beyond the desire to devolve and privatize without altering the basic tasks of social programs. Rather, it was based on fundamental challenges to a variety of liberal articles of faith: that the tax system should be used to redistribute wealth, that alleviating poverty required changing social conditions, and that church and state should be strictly separated. Asserting that liberal social programs had succeeded in creating a "permanent underclass" by rewarding welfare recipients for deviant behavior, the conservatives proposed to eliminate most entitlement programs and to strictly limit eligibility. The key to dealing with poverty and dependency, conservatives believed, was changing the values and behavior of the poor. The dependent, the disabled, and the unemployed would have to rejoin the workforce and in doing so would regain their self-respect and self-sufficiency. Not surprisingly, given their heavily sectarian constituency, conservatives looked to religious bodies and faith-based organizations to play central roles in transforming the values and behavior of the poor. Section 104 of the Personal Responsibility and Work Opportunity Reconciliation Act of 1996 set forth the terms of government's new relationship to religious nonprofits.

Although the conservative revolution in many ways favored nonprofit enterprises, especially with the huge expansion of contracted programs, it also intensified competition for contracts by allowing for-profit businesses to be eligible for grants and contracts. While conservative education reforms encouraged nonprofits through voucher programs and charter schools, they also put nonprofit schools in competition with for-profit enterprises like the Edison Schools, which, with their access to equity financing, had the capacity to operate entire urban school systems. In such an environment, skilled management, entrepreneurial attitudes, and political acumen became crucial to the survival of nonprofits.

Health care, which until the 1970s had been dominated by nonprofits, underwent major changes as legislators sought to control the rising cost of entitlement programs like Medicare and Medicaid (Gray, 1983, 1986, 1991). As government became more vigilant about health care costs, hospitals were forced to become more businesslike in their operations. Many converted to for-profit ownership. Others, while remaining nonprofit, turned their operations over to for-profit firms. Seeking economies of scale, hospitals consolidated into national and regional chains, as did formerly nonprofit health insurance plans like Blue Cross Blue Shield.

By putting nonprofits in competition with for-profits offering similar services and by demanding higher levels of accountability for decreasing government funding, conservative policies helped erode many of the boundaries between nonprofit and for-profit enterprises (Weisbrod, 1997; Hall, 2003). Nonprofits had to become more commercial and more entrepreneurial to survive. Whether nonprofits' commitments to missions of public service could survive such relentless attention to the bottom line remained in doubt as the twenty-first century dawned (Weisbrod, 1998).

THE NONPROFIT SECTOR
AND THE GLOBAL CHALLENGE

Nonstate actors—nonprofit organizations, NGOs, network organizations—are assuming extraordinary importance as the world's economy becomes more globalized (Salamon and Anheier, 1996, 1997; Anheier and Salamon, 1998).[3] Despite growing global flows of goods, information, and labor, the nation-state remains the primary unit of governmental organization, and international governmental bodies remain weak. For this reason, NGOs operating transnationally have become the major mechanisms of world governance (Lindenberg, 1999).

These organizations take a variety of forms (Khagram, Riker, and Sikkink, 2002). Some mediate relationships between states (Brown and Fox, 1998, 1999; Brown, Khagram, Moore, and Frumkin, 2000; Brown and Moore, 2001). Some, like the U.S. Agency for International Development, are governmental bodies operated to serve the interests of the United States by promoting economic development. Others, like the World Bank, the International Monetary Fund, the World Health Organization, and UNESCO, are international quasi-governmental bodies connected to the United Nations and governed by boards representing the UN's member states.

Many NGOs, like CARE, the International Red Cross, and a variety of religious charities, are based in the United States or Europe but conduct their operations elsewhere (Lindenberg and Dobel, 1999). Others are genuinely transnational, based on coalitions of indigenous and transnational NGOs. Often operating in opposition to nation states, these promote human rights, sustainable development, and environmental objectives (Fisher, 1993, 1998; Edwards, 1999). Unlike the quasi-governmental bodies, which deal primarily with governments, these transnational NGOs work directly with indigenous peoples, communities, and organizations. Among the most important of these are groups like CIVICUS, which promotes the development of nonprofit sectors throughout the world. Some of the largest grantmaking foundations, notably Ford, Rockefeller, and the Bill and Melinda Gates foundations, have global programs that fund health, education, research, and economic development activities in developing countries.

The tragic events of September 11, 2001, called attention to the significance of NGOs and network organizations connected to religious movements. Along with terrorist networks like Al-Qaeda, there are Islamic charities and foundations that operate worldwide to support religious education, provide relief, and foster economic and political development in Muslim communities.

In some respects, transnational organizations are nothing new. The scientific community has long been transnational and anchored in nongovernmental professional and disciplinary bodies. Transnational human rights advocacy dates back at least as early as the anti–slave trade movement of the late eighteenth century. Most major religious bodies are transnational organizations. International relief organizations have been operating since the nineteenth century. Grantmaking foundations have had international programs since the 1920s (Curti, 1965).

Contemporary global and transnational NGOs differ from their predecessors in important respects. Many are genuinely transnational, located either in many countries or, as in the case of Al-Qaeda, not anchored in any nation-state. Beyond the reach of national authorities, these entities are difficult to police and control (Brown and Moore, 2001; Goodin, 2003). Of equal importance is the extent to which transnational NGOs are linked to indigenous organizations outside the advanced nations of Europe and North America. Their capacity to give voice to victims of authoritarian regimes, to protest economic exploitation, and to resist the power of Western corporations and governments has dramatically transformed global public policymaking. Advances in information technology have vastly increased the influence of transnational NGOs, making available information that corporations and governments may attempt to suppress and making it possible for transnational and indigenous groups to form coalitions and alliances. Recent worldwide protests against economic globalization and the U.S. invasion of Iraq may signal the emergence of new kinds of political forces.

The nature of globalization and the role of transnational nonstate actors is far from clear. To some observers, they represent a kind of neocolonialism, the means by which an integrated global economy, anchored in the advanced nations of the West, is being created. To others, they represent a new empowering force for democracy and social and economic justice. One thing is clear, however: nonprofit organizations, so highly developed in the United States in the course of the twentieth century, offer important possibilities to nations engaged in creating their own civil societies.

CONCLUSION

In this chapter, I have followed a long and complex strand of institutional development. Beginning in the seventeenth century, when the nation-state was still emergent, legal systems were primitive, and boundaries between government and private initiative were ill-defined, I have traced the ways in which voluntary associations, eleemosynary corporations, and philanthropy became indispensable components of the national state and the industrializing economy in the United States in the nineteenth century. I have suggested that neither business nor government could stand alone: both required broadly based participation by citizens, producers, and consumers in organizations and activities that created the shared values and skills that enabled formal institutions of government and business to function effectively.

In the years between 1830 and 1950, the private, donative, and voluntary character of much of nonprofit enterprise seemed self-evident, as did the boundaries between public and private initiative. In the second half of the twentieth century, these defining characteristics became less well-defined as nonprofits on the one hand became more dependent on government subsidies and were increasingly entrusted with responsibilities formerly borne by government agencies and on the other hand became more commercial and entrepreneurial.

Globalization, which has enabled nonprofits to operate beyond national borders, has further eroded traditional boundaries between public and private domains and commercial and charitable activities. Because privatization is a global movement, NGOs outside the United States are increasingly taking the place of nation-states in service provision, relief, and development assistance. Many development activities, such as microloan programs, more resemble commercial activities than charitable ones. And overall, important aspects of the emergent global institutional order depend on the governance functions of NGOs rather than on governmental entities.

In significant ways, today's centrally important but poorly demarcated roles and responsibilities of nonprofits and NGOs are more like those of three centuries ago, when the nation-state was aborning, than like the associations and eleemosynary corporations of a century ago, whose character and functions were relatively well defined and clearly bounded.

History shows, if nothing else, that ownerless collectivities of the nonprofit type are remarkably flexible instruments that can be put to a multitude of uses, empowering the masses in democracies, shaping public opinion for the benefit of elites, carrying out the tasks of government in authoritarian regimes, promoting peace and prosperity, and spreading terror. What the future holds for nonprofits is anybody's guess.

Notes

1. Few tasks are more difficult than accurately counting the number of nonprofit organizations in the United States. The fundamental difficulty involves the definition of the nonprofit universe. In corporation law, a nonprofit is any non-stock-issuing corporation that does not distribute its surplus, if any, in the form of dividends. Under the federal tax code, a nonprofit is any organization or association classified in section 501(c) of the IRS Code—a universe that includes not only charitable entities—501(c)(3)s—but also many other kinds of organizations, including political parties, labor unions, cooperatives, cemetery companies, and black lung trusts. Because some of these noncharitable nonprofits, like those classified as 501(c)(4)s (social welfare organizations, civic organizations, and

associations of employees), engage in many of the same educational and service provision activities as charitables without offering donor deductibility of donations, excluding them from a definition of the nonprofit sector unreasonably narrows the scope of the definition. To complicate matters, religious bodies, which enjoy tax exemption and deductibility of donations by right (and hence are not required to apply for these privileges) are not included in IRS statistics of registered nonprofits—despite the fact that they are the largest single category of nonprofit organization in the United States and receive more than half the funds donated to American nonprofits.

To further complicate matters, many groups engaged in charitable, educational, religious, and other activities associated with nonprofits are unincorporated and do not seek exempt status (Smith, 2000).

2. It is impossible to provide exact figures on the number of donative and voluntary nonprofits versus those supported by dues, fees, commercial income, and grants and contracts from government, corporations, and foundations. Studies of local organizational populations (Hall, 1999) and national membership associations (Skocpol, 1999, 2003) suggest a vast die-off of traditional donative, voluntary, and membership associations and their replacement by professionally managed nonprofit organizations. Despite these trends, such organizations as religious congregations—one of the most vigorously expansive nonprofit domains—remain heavily dependent on volunteers and almost entirely dependent on donations. Counterbalancing this, however, is the huge growth of nonprofit service providers incident to the court-ordered deinstitutionalization of the mentally disabled. These use no volunteers and depend entirely on government subsidies.

3. Walter W. Powell (1990) defines network organizations as " patterns of communication and exchange characterized by "interdependent flows of resources" and "reciprocal lines of communication" (pp. 295–296). An example of a network organization is the open source network of computer programmers cooperating to develop the LINUX operating system. These entities lack the hierarchical structures and financial incentives that are typical of conventional firms.

References

Abbott, A. D. *The System of Professions: An Essay on the Division of Expert Labor.* Chicago: University of Chicago Press, 1988.

Ahlstrom, S. E. *A Religious History of the American People.* New Haven, Conn.: Yale University Press, 1972.

"American Millionaires and the Public Gifts." *Review of Reviews,* 1893, *37*(7), 48–60.

Ames, J. B. "The Failure of the Tilden Trust." In *Essays in Legal History and Miscellaneous Legal Essays.* Cambridge, Mass.: Harvard University Press, 1913.

Andrews, F. E. *Philanthropic Giving.* New York: Russell Sage Foundation, 1950.

Andrews, F. E. *Corporation Giving.* New York: Russell Sage Foundation, 1952.

Andrews, F. E. *Philanthropic Foundations.* New York: Russell Sage Foundation, 1956.

Andrews, F. E. *Patman and the Foundations: Review and Assessment.* New York: Foundation Center, 1969.

Anheier, H. K., and Salamon, L. M. *The Nonprofit Sector in the Developing World: A Comparative Analysis.* New York: St. Martin's Press, 1998.

Auerbach, J. S. *Unequal Justice: Lawyers and Social Change in Modern America.* New York: Oxford University Press, 1976.

Baggett, J. P. *Habitat for Humanity: Building Private Homes, Building Public Religion.* Philadelphia: Temple University Press, 2001.

Bailyn, B. *The Ideological Origins of the American Revolution.* Cambridge, Mass.: Belknap Press, 1992.

Beito, D. T. *From Mutual Aid to the Welfare State: Fraternal Societies and Social Services, 1890–1967.* Chapel Hill: University of North Carolina Press, 2000.

Bender, C. *Heaven's Kitchen: Living Religion at God's Love We Deliver.* Chicago: University of Chicago Press, 2003.

Berkeley Art Center Association. *The Whole World's Watching: Peace and Social Justice Movements of the 1960s and 1970s.* Berkeley, Calif.: Berkeley Art Center Association, 2001.

Berry, J. M. *Lobbying for the People: The Political Behavior of Public Interest Groups.* Princeton, N.J.: Princeton University Press, 1977.

Berry, J. M. *The Interest Group Society.* (3rd ed.) New York: Longman, 1997.

Bledstein, B. *The Culture of Professionalism: The Middle Class and the Development of Higher Education in America.* New York: Norton, 1976.

Blumenthal, S. *The Rise of the Counter-Establishment: From Conservative Ideology to Political Power.* New York: HarperCollins, 1986.

Brandes, S. *American Welfare Capitalism.* Chicago: University of Chicago Press, 1976.

Brint, S. *In an Age of Reform: The Changing Role of Professionals in Politics and Public Life.* Princeton, N.J.: Princeton University Press, 1994.

Brockett, L. P. *The Philanthropic Results of the War in America. Collected from Official and Other Authentic Sources, by an American Citizen. Dedicated by Permission to the United States Sanitary Commission.* New York: Sheldon & Co., 1864.

Brody, D. "The Rise and Decline of American Welfare Capitalism." In D. Brody (ed.), *Workers in Industrial America.* New York: Oxford University Press, 1980.

Brown, L. D., and Fox, J. (eds.). *The Struggle for Accountability: The World Bank, NGOs, and Grassroots Movements.* Cambridge, Mass.: MIT Press, 1998.

Brown, L. D., and Fox, J. *Transnational Civil Society Coalitions and the World Bank: Lessons from Project and Policy Influence Campaigns.* Working Paper no. 3. Cambridge, Mass.: Hauser Center for Nonprofit Organizations, Harvard University, 1999.

Brown, L. D., Khagram, S., Moore, M. H., and Frumkin, P. *Globalization, NGOs, and Multi-Sectoral Relations.* Working Paper no. 1. Cambridge, Mass.: Hauser Center for Nonprofit Organizations, Harvard University, 2000.

Brown, L. D., and Moore, M. H. *Accountability, Strategy and International Non-Governmental Organizations.* Working Paper no. 7. Cambridge, Mass.: Hauser Center for Nonprofit Organizations, Harvard University, 2001.

Buck, P. H (ed.). *Social Sciences at Harvard, 1860–1920: From Inculcation to the Open Mind.* Cambridge, Mass.: Harvard University Press, 1965.

Butchart, R. E. *Northern Schools, Southern Blacks, and Reconstruction, 1862–1875.* Westport, Conn.: Greenwood Press, 1980.

Butler, J. *Awash in a Sea of Faith: Christianizing the American People.* Cambridge, Mass.: Harvard University Press, 1990.

Calhoun, D. H. *Professional Lives in America: Structure and Aspiration, 1750–1850.* Cambridge, Mass.: Harvard University Press, 1965.

Calvert, M. A. *The Mechanical Engineer in America: Professional Cultures in Conflict.* Baltimore: Johns Hopkins University Press, 1967.

Carlson-Thies, S. W., and Skillen, J. W. (eds.). *Welfare in America: Christian Perspectives on a Policy in Crisis.* Grand Rapids, Mich.: Eerdmans, 1996.

Carnegie, A. "An Employer's View of the Labor Question." *Forum,* 1886a, *1,* 114–125.

Carnegie, A. "Results of the Labor Struggle." *Forum,* 1886b, *1,* 538–551.

Carnegie, A. "Wealth." *North American Review,* 1889, *148,* 653–664, and *149,* 682–698.

Charles, J. A. *Service Clubs in American Society: Rotary, Kiwanis, and Lions.* Urbana: University of Illinois Press, 1993.

Chaves, M. "Religious Congregations and Welfare Reform: Assessing the Potential." In M. Silk and A. Walsh (eds.), *Can Charitable Choice Work? Covering Religion's Impact on Urban Affairs and Social Services.* Hartford, Conn.: Pew Program on Religion and the News Media, Leonard E. Greenberg Center for the Study of Religion in Public Life, Trinity College, 2001.

Chernow, R. *Titan: The Life of John D. Rockefeller Sr.* New York: Random House, 1998.

Cherry, C., and Sherrill, R. (eds.). *Religion, the Independent Sector, and American Culture.* Atlanta: Scholars Press, 1992.

Clemens, E. S. *The People's Lobby: Organizational Innovation and the Rise of Interest Group Politics in the United States, 1890–1925.* Chicago: University of Chicago Press, 1997.

Cnaan, R. A. *The Newer Deal: Social Work and Religion in Partnership.* New York: Columbia University Press, 1999.

Cnaan, R. A. *The Invisible Caring Hand: American Congregations and the Provision of Welfare.* New York: New York University Press, 2002.

Crawford, S., and Levitt, P. "Social Change and Civic Engagement: The Case of the P.T.A." In T. Skocpol and M. Fiorina (eds.), *Civic Engagement in American Democracy.* Washington, D.C.: Brookings Institution Press, 1999.

Critchlow, D. T. *The Brookings Institution, 1916–1952: Expertise and the Public Interest in a Democratic Society.* De Kalb: Northern Illinois University Press, 1985.

Cross, A. B. *The War and the Christian Commission.* Baltimore, 1865.

Curti, M. *American Philanthropy Abroad.* New Brunswick, N.J.: Rutgers University Press, 1965.

Curti, M., and Nash, R. *Philanthropy and the Shaping of American Higher Education.* New Brunswick, N.J.: Rutgers University Press, 1965.

Cutlip, S. M. *Fund Raising in the United States: Its Role in America's Philanthropy.* New Brunswick, N.J.: Rutgers University Press, 1965.

Dabney, V. *Mr. Jefferson's University: A History.* Charlottesville: University Press of Virginia, 1981.

Davis, J. S. *Essays on the Earlier History of American Corporations.* Cambridge, Mass.: Harvard University Press, 1918.

Demerath, N. J., III, Hall, P. D., Williams, R. H., and Schmitt, T. (eds.). *Sacred Companies: Organizational Aspects of Religion and Religious Aspects of Organizations.* New York: Oxford University Press, 1998.

Di Maggio, P. J. "Cultural Entrepreneurship in Nineteenth-Century Boston." In P. J. Di Maggio (ed.), *Nonprofit Enterprise in the Arts.* New York: Oxford University Press, 1986.

Dodd, E. M. *American Business Corporations Until 1860, with Special References to Massachusetts.* Cambridge, Mass.: Harvard University Press, 1960.

Dolan, J. P. *The American Catholic Experience: A History from Colonial Times to the Present.* South Bend, Ind.: University of Notre Dame Press, 1992.

Drucker, P. F. *The New Realities: In Government and Politics, in Economics and Business, in Society and World View.* New York: HarperCollins, 1989.

Dumenil, L. *Freemasonry and American Culture, 1880–1939.* Princeton, N.J.: Princeton University Press, 1984.

Eck, D. L. *A New Religious America: How a "Christian Country" Has Become the World's Most Religiously Diverse Nation.* New York: HarperCollins, 2001.

Edwards, M. "International Development NGOs: Agents of Foreign Aid or Vehicles for International Cooperation." *Nonprofit and Voluntary Sector Quarterly,* 1999, *28*(4 suppl.), 25–37.

Eliot, C. W. "The New Education." *Atlantic,* 1869, *23,* 203–220, 358–367. Reprinted as "Inaugural Address as President of Harvard." In C. W. Eliot, *Educational Reform: Essays and Addresses.* New York: Century, 1898.

Finke, R., and Stark, R. *The Churching of America, 1776–1990: Winners and Losers in Our Religious Economy.* New Brunswick, N.J.: Rutgers University Press, 1992.

Fisher, J. *The Road from Rio: Sustainable Development and the Nongovernmental Movement in the Third World.* Westport, Conn.: Praeger, 1993.

Fisher, J. *Nongovernments: NGOs and the Political Development of the Third World.* West Hartford, Conn.: Kumarian Press, 1998.

Fleischer, D. Z., and Zames, F. *The Disability Rights Movement: From Charity to Confrontation.* Philadelphia: Temple University Press, 2001.

Fleming, W. L. (ed.). *Documentary History of Reconstruction: Political, Military, Social, Religious, Educational and Industrial: 1865 to the Present Time.* Cleveland, Ohio: Arthur H. Clark Co., 1906.

Fogel, R. W. *The Fourth Great Awakening and the Future of Egalitarianism.* Chicago: University of Chicago Press, 2000.

Fosdick, R. B. *The Story of the Rockefeller Foundation.* New York: Harper, 1952.

Fosdick, R. B. *Adventure in Giving: The Story of the General Education Board, a Foundation Established by John D. Rockefeller.* New York: Harper, 1962.

Foster, C. I. *"An Errand of Mercy": The Evangelical United Front, 1790–1837.* Chapel Hill: University of North Carolina Press, 1965.

Foundation Directory: Edition 1. New York: Russell Sage Foundation, 1960.

Fox, D. M. *Engines of Culture: Philanthropy and Art Museums.* Madison: State Historical Society of Wisconsin, 1963.

Frederickson, G. M. *The Inner Civil War: Northern Intellectuals and the Crisis of the Union.* New York: Harper, 1965.

Galambos, L. *Competition and Cooperation: The Rise of a National Trade Association.* Baltimore: Johns Hopkins University Press, 1966.

Geiger, R. L. *To Advance Knowledge: The Growth of American Research Universities, 1900–1940.* New York: Oxford University Press, 1986.

Geiger, R. L. *Research and Relevant Knowledge: American Research Universities Since World War II.* New York: Oxford University Press, 1993.

Gillespie, E., and Schellhas, B. (eds.). *Contract with America: The Bold Plan by Rep. Newt Gingrich, Rep. Dick Armey and the House Republicans to Change the Nation.* New York: Times Books, 1994.

Glenn, J. M., Brandt, L., and Andrews, F. E. *The Russell Sage Foundation, 1907–1947.* New York: Russell Sage Foundation, 1947.

Goodin, R. E. *Democratic Accountability: The Third Sector and All.* Working Paper no. 19. Cambridge, Mass.: Hauser Center for Nonprofit Organizations, Harvard University, 2003.

Gray, B. H. (ed.). *The New Health Care for Profit: Doctors and Hospitals in a Competitive Environment.* Washington, D.C.: National Academy Press, 1983.

Gray, B. H. (ed.). *For-Profit Enterprise in Health Care.* Washington, D.C.: National Academy Press, 1986.

Gray, B. H. *The Profit Motive and Patient Care: The Changing Accountability of Doctors and Hospitals.* Cambridge, Mass.: Harvard University Press, 1991.

Greenleaf, W. *From These Beginnings: The Early Philanthropies of Henry and Edsel Ford, 1911–1936.* Detroit: Wayne State University Press, 1964.

Hall, P. D. *The Organization of American Culture, 1700–1900: Institutions, Elites, and the Origins of American Nationality.* New York: New York University Press, 1982.

Hall, P. D. "Business Giving and Social Investment in the United States." In R. Magat (ed.), *Philanthropic Giving: Studies in Varieties and Goals.* New York: Oxford University Press, 1989a.

Hall, P. D. "The Community Foundation in America." In R. Magat (ed.), *Philan-thropic Giving: Studies in Varieties and Goals.* New York: Oxford University Press, 1989b.

Hall, P. D. "Vital Signs: Organizational Population Trends and Civic Engagement in New Haven, Connecticut, 1850–1998." In T. Skocpol and M. P. Fiorina (eds.), *Civic Engagement in American Democracy.* Washington, D.C.: Brookings Institution Press, 1999.

Hall, P. D. "Historical Perspectives on Religion, Government, and Social Welfare in America." In M. Silk and A. Walsh (eds.), *Can Charitable Choice Work? Covering Religion's Impact on Urban Affairs and Social Services.* Hartford, Conn.: Pew Program on Religion and the News Media, Leonard E. Greenberg Center for the Study of Religion in Public Life, Trinity College, 2001.

Hall, P. D. "The Welfare State and the Careers of Public and Private Institutions Since 1945." In L. J. Friedman and M. D. McGarvie (eds.), *Charity, Philanthropy, and Civility in American History.* New York: Cambridge University Press, 2003.

Hall, P. D., and Burke, C. B. "Voluntary, Nonprofit, and Religious Entities and Activities." In S. Carter and others (eds.), *Historical Statistics of the United States: Millennial Edition.* New York: Cambridge University Press, 2004.

Hammack, D. C. "Community Foundations: The Delicate Question of Purpose." In R. Magat (ed.), *"An Agile Servant": Community Leadership by Community Foundations.* New York: Foundation Center, 1989.

Hammack, D. C., and Wheeler, S. *Social Science in the Making: Essays on the Russell Sage Foundation, 1907–1972.* New York: Russell Sage Foundation, 1994.

Harr, J. E., and Johnson, P. J. *The Rockefeller Century.* New York: Scribner, 1988.

Hartog, H. *Public Property and Private Power: The Corporation of the City of New York in American Law, 1730–1870.* Ithaca, N.Y.: Cornell University Press, 1983.

Haskell, T. L. *The Emergence of Professional Social Science: The American Social Science Association and the Nineteenth-Century Crisis of Authority.* Urbana: University of Illinois Press, 1977.

Hatch, N. O. *The Democratization of American Christianity.* New Haven, Conn.: Yale University Press, 1989.

Hawkins, H. *Between Harvard and America: The Educational Leadership of Charles W. Eliot.* New York: Oxford University Press, 1972.

Hawkins, H. *Banding Together: The Rise of National Associations in American Higher Education, 1887–1950.* Baltimore: Johns Hopkins University Press, 1992.

Hawley, E. W. (ed.). *Herbert Hoover as Secretary of Commerce: Studies in New Era Thought and Practice.* Iowa City: University of Iowa Press, 1974.

Hawley, E. W. "Herbert Hoover, the Commerce Secretariat, and the Vision of an 'Associative State.'" In E. J. Perkins (ed.), *Men and Organizations.* New York: Putnam, 1977.

Heald, M. *The Social Responsibilities of Business: Corporation and Community, 1900–1960.* Cleveland: Case Western University Press, 1970.

Himmelberg, R. F. *The Origins of the National Recovery Administration: Business, Government, and the Trade Association Issue.* New York: Fordham University Press, 1976.

Himmelstein, J. L. *Looking Good and Doing Good: Corporate Philanthropy and Corporate Power.* Bloomington: Indiana University Press, 1997.

Hodgson, G. *The World Turned Right Side Up: A History of the Conservative Ascendancy in America.* Boston: Houghton Mifflin, 1996.

Hoover, H. *American Individualism.* New York: Doubleday, 1922.

Horowitz, M. J. *The Transformation of American Law, 1780–1860.* Cambridge, Mass.: Harvard University Press, 1977.

Howard, C. *The Hidden Welfare State: Tax Expenditures and Social Policy in the United States.* Princeton, N.J.: Princeton University Press, 1997.

Hurst, J. W. *The Legitimacy of the Business Corporation in the Law of the United States, 1780–1970.* Charlottesville: University Press of Virginia, 1970.

Jenkins, J. C. "Nonprofit Organizations and Policy Advocacy." In W. W. Powell (ed.), *The Nonprofit Sector: A Research Handbook.* New Haven, Conn.: Yale University Press, 1987.

Jenkins, J. C., and Craig, E. "Channeling Black Insurgency: Elite Patronage and the Development of the Civil Rights Movement." *American Sociological Review,* 1986, *51,* 812–830.

Jenkins, J. C., and Halcli, A. L. "Grassrooting the System? The Development and Impact of Social Movement Philanthropy, 1953–1990." In E. C. Lagemann (ed.), *Philanthropic Foundations: New Scholarship, New Possibilities.* Bloomington: Indiana University Press, 1999.

Karl, B. D. "Presidential Planning and Social Science Research: Mr. Hoover's Experts." *Perspectives in American History,* 1969, *3,* 347–409.

Karl, B. D. "Philanthropy, Policy Planning, and the Bureaucratization of the Democratic Ideal." *Daedalus,* 1976, *105,* 129–149.

Katz, S. N. "The Politics of Law in Colonial America: Controversies over Chancery Courts and Equity Law in the Eighteenth Century." In D. Fleming and B. Bailyn (eds.), *Law in American History.* New York: Little, Brown, 1971.

Katz, S. N. "The American Private Foundation and the Public Sphere, 1890–1930." *Minerva,* 1981, *19,* 236–270.

Katz, S. N., Sullivan, B., and Beach, C. P. "Legal Change and Legal Autonomy: Charitable Trusts in New York, 1777–1893." *Law and History Review,* 1985, *3,* 51–89.

Kaufman, J. *For the Common Good? American Civic Life and the Golden Age of Fraternity.* New York: Oxford University Press, 2002.

Khagram, S., Riker, J. V., and Sikkink, K. (eds.). *Restructuring World Politics: Transnational Social Movements, Networks, and Norms.* Minneapolis: University of Minnesota Press, 2002.

Kimball, B. A. *The "True Professional Ideal" in America: A History.* Lanham, Md.: Rowman & Littlefield, 1995.

Lagemann, E. C. 1992. *The Politics of Knowledge: The Carnegie Corporation, Philanthropy, and Public Policy.* Chicago: University of Chicago Press, 1992.

Lagemann, E. C. *Private Power for the Public Good: A History of the Carnegie Foundation for the Advancement of Teaching.* New York: College Entrance Examination Board, 1999.

Li, M. *We Need Two Worlds: Chinese Immigrant Associations in a Western Society.* Amsterdam, Netherlands: Amsterdam University Press, 1999.

Lindenberg, M. "Declining State Capacity, Voluntarism, and the Globalization of the Not-for-Profit Sector." *Nonprofit and Voluntary Sector Quarterly,* 1999, *28* (4 suppl.), 147–167.

Lindenberg, M., and Dobel, J. P. (eds.). "Globalization and Northern NGOs: The Challenge of Relief and Development in a Changing Context." *Nonprofit and Voluntary Sector Quarterly,* 1999, *28*(4 suppl.).

Lundberg, F. *The Rich and the Super-Rich: A Study in the Power of Money Today.* New York: Lyle Stuart, 1968.

MacDonald, D. *The Ford Foundation: The Men and the Millions.* New York: Reynal & Co., 1956.

Magat, R. (ed.). *"An Agile Servant": Community Leadership by Community Foundations.* New York: Foundation Center, 1989.

Mathews, D. "The Second Great Awakening as an Organizing Process." *American Quarterly,* 1969, *21,* 23–43.

McFeely, W. S. *Yankee Stepfather: General O. O. Howard and the Freedmen.* New Haven, Conn.: Yale University Press, 1968.

McKinney, H. J. *The Development of Local Public Services, 1650–1860: Lessons from Middletown, Connecticut.* Westport, Conn.: Greenwood Press, 1995.

Miller, H. S. *The Legal Foundations of American Philanthropy.* Madison: Wisconsin State Historical Society, 1961.

Minkoff, D. C. *Organizing for Equality: The Evolution of Women's and Racial-Ethnic Organizations in America, 1955–1985.* New Brunswick, N.J.: Rutgers University Press, 1995.

Minton, H. L. *Departing from Deviance: A History of Homosexual Rights and Emancipatory Science in America.* Chicago: University of Chicago Press, 2002.

Morgan, E. S. *Benjamin Franklin.* New Haven, Conn.: Yale University Press, 2003.

Moss, L. *Annals of the United States Christian Commission.* Philadelphia: Lippincott, 1868.

Naylor, E. H. *Trade Associations: Their Organization and Management.* New York: Ronald Press, 1921.

Nelson, W. E. *Americanization of the Common Law: The Impact of Legal Change on Massachusetts Society, 1760–1830.* Cambridge, Mass.: Harvard University Press, 1975.

Nielsen, W. *The Big Foundations.* New York: Columbia University Press, 1971.

Oates, M. J. *The Catholic Philanthropic Tradition in America.* Bloomington: Indiana University Press, 1995.

Olasky, M. N. *The Tragedy of American Compassion.* Washington, D.C.: Regnery, 1992.

Powell, W. W. "Neither Network nor Hierarchy: Network Forms of Organization." In *Research in Organizational Behavior* (Vol. 12). Greenwich, Conn.: JAI Press, 1990.

Proietto, R. "The Ford Foundation and Women's Studies in American Higher Education: Seeds of Change?" In E. C. Lagemann (ed.)., *Philanthropic Foundations: New Scholarship, New Possibilities.* Bloomington: Indiana University Press, 1999.

Putnam, R. D. *Bowling Alone: The Collapse and Renewal of American Community.* New York: Simon & Schuster, 2000.

Reed, R. *Active Faith: How Christians Are Changing the Soul of American Politics.* New York: Free Press, 1996.

Rich, A. *Think Tanks, Public Policy, and the Politics of Expertise.* New York: Cambridge University Press, 2004.

Richardson, J. M. *Christian Reconstruction: The American Missionary Society and Southern Blacks, 1861–1890.* Athens: University of Georgia Press, 1986.

Roof, W. C. *Spiritual Marketplace: Baby Boomers and the Remaking of American Religion.* Princeton, N.J.: Princeton University Press, 1999.

Rudolph, F. *The American College and University: A History.* New York: Knopf, 1968.

Ryan, M. P. *Cradle of the Middle Class: The Family in Oneida County, New York, 1790–1865.* New York: Cambridge University Press, 1981.

Salamon, L. M. "Partners in Public Service: The Scope and Theory of Government-Nonprofit Relations." In W. W. Powell (ed.), *The Nonprofit Sector: A Research Handbook.* New Haven, Conn.: Yale University Press, 1987.

Salamon, L. M., and Abramson, A. J. *The Federal Budget and the Nonprofit Sector.* Washington, D.C.: Urban Institute, 1982.

Salamon, L. M., and Anheier, H. K. *The Emerging Nonprofit Sector: An Overview.* New York: St. Martin's Press, 1996.

Salamon, L. M., and Anheier, H. K. *Defining the Nonprofit Sector: A Cross-National Analysis.* New York: St. Martin's Press, 1997.

Sale, K. *Power Shift: The Rise of the Southern Rim and Its Challenge to the Eastern Establishment.* New York: Random House, 1975.

Schlesinger, A. M. "Biography of a Nation of Joiners." *American Historical Review,* 1944, *50*(1), 1–25.

Sealander, J. *Private Wealth and Public Life: Foundation Philanthropy and the Reshaping of American Social Policy from the Progressive Era to the New Deal.* Baltimore: Johns Hopkins University Press, 1997.

Sears, J. B. *Philanthropy in the Shaping of American Higher Education.* Washington, D.C.: Bureau of Education, Department of the Interior, 1922.

Seavoy, R. E. *The Origins of the American Business Corporation, 1784–1855.* Westport, Conn.: Greenwood Press, 1982.

Seeley, J. R., and others. *Community Chest: A Case Study in Philanthropy.* Toronto, Ontario, Canada: University of Toronto Press, 1957.

Sklar, M. J. *The Corporate Reconstruction of American Capitalism, 1890–1916: The Market, the Law, and Politics.* New York: Cambridge University Press, 1988.

Skocpol, T. "Advocates Without Members: The Recent Transformation of American Civic Life." In T. Skocpol and M. P. Fiorina (eds.), *Civic Engagement in American Democracy.* Washington, D.C.: Brookings Institution Press, 1999.

Skocpol, T. *Diminished Democracy: From Membership to Management in American Civic Life.* Norman: University of Oklahoma Press, 2003.

Skocpol, T., and others. "How Americans Became Civic." In T. Skocpol and M. P. Fiorina (eds.), *Civic Engagement in American Democracy.* Washington, D.C.: Brookings Institution Press, 1999.

Smith, D. H. *Grassroots Associations.* Thousand Oaks, Calif.: Sage, 2000.

Smith, J. A. *Brookings at Seventy-Five.* Washington, D.C.: Brookings Institution Press, 1991a.

Smith, J. A. *The Idea Brokers: Think Tanks and the Rise of the New Policy Elite.* New York: Free Press, 1991b.

Soyer, D. *Jewish Immigrant Associations and American Identity in New York, 1880–1939.* Cambridge, Mass.: Harvard University Press, 1997.

Starr, P. *The Social Transformation of American Medicine.* New York: Basic Books, 1982.

Stroman, D. F. *The Disability Rights Movement: From Deinstitutionalization to Self-Determination.* Lanham, Md.: University Press of America, 2003.

Sutton, F. X. "The Ford Foundation: The Early Years." *Daedalus,* 1987, *116,* 41–91.

Swint, H. L. *The Northern Teacher in the South, 1862–1870.* New York: Octagon Books, 1967.

Tobias, M. *Old Dartmouth on Trial.* New York: New York University Press, 1982.

Tocqueville, A. de. *Democracy in America,* vol. 2 (Henry Reeve, trans.). New York: Random House, 1945. (Originally published 1840)

U.S. Congress. *Industrial Relations: Final Report and Testimony Submitted to Congress by the Commission on Industrial Relations.* 64th Congress, 1st Session, S. Doc. 154. Washington, D.C. U.S. Government Printing Office, 1916.

Useem, M. "Corporate Philanthropy." In W. W. Powell (ed.), *The Nonprofit Sector: A Research Handbook.* New Haven, Conn.: Yale University Press, 1987.

Veblen, T. *The Higher Learning in America; A Memorandum on the Conduct of Universities by Business Men.* New York: Huebsch, 1918.

Verba, S., Schlozman, K. L., and Brady, H. *Voice and Equality: Civic Voluntarism in American Politics.* Cambridge, Mass.: Harvard University Press, 1995.

Veysey, L. R. *The Emergence of the American University.* Chicago: University of Chicago Press, 1965.

Wall, J. F. *Andrew Carnegie.* New York: Oxford University Press, 1970.

Webber, C., and Wildavsky, A. *A History of Taxation and Expenditure in the Western World.* New York: Simon & Schuster, 1986.

Weisbrod, B. A. *The Nonprofit Economy.* Cambridge, Mass.: Harvard University Press, 1988.

Weisbrod, B. A. "The Future of the Nonprofit Sector." *Journal of Policy Analysis and Management,* 1997, *16,* 541–555.

Weisbrod, B. A. (ed.). *To Profit or Not to Profit: The Commercial Transformation of the Nonprofit Sector.* New York: Cambridge University Press, 1998.

Whitehead, J. S. *The Separation of College and State: Columbia, Dartmouth, Harvard, and Yale, 1776–1876.* New Haven, Conn.: Yale University Press, 1976.

Wiebe, R. M. *The Search for Order.* New York: Hill & Wang, 1967.

Witte, J. F. *The Politics and Development of the Federal Income Tax.* Madison: University of Wisconsin Press, 1985.

Wuthnow, R. *The Restructuring of American Religion: Society and Faith Since World War II.* Princeton, N.J.: Princeton University Press, 1988.

Wuthnow, R. (ed.). *"I Come Away Stronger": How Small Groups Are Shaping American Religion.* Grand Rapids, Mich.: Eerdmans, 1994.

Wuthnow, R. *After Heaven: Spirituality in America Since the 1950s.* Berkeley: University of California Press, 1998.

Wuthnow, R., Hodgkinson, V. A., and Associates. *Faith and Philanthropy in America: Exploring the Role of Religion in America's Voluntary Sector.* San Francisco: Jossey-Bass, 1990.

Wyllie, I. G. "The Search for an American Law of Charity." *Mississippi Valley Historical Review,* 1959, *46,* 203–221.

Zollmann, C. *American Law of Charities.* Milwaukee, Wisc.: Bruce, 1924.

CHAPTER TWO

Nonprofit Organizations and Social Institutions

Jon Van Til

T he work of nonprofit managers takes place in organizations identified by society as voluntary, charitable, or nonprofit, as Peter Dobkin Hall explains in Chapter One. The task of this chapter is to look at the ways in which the work of nonprofit managers forms an important part of the institutional life of society.

A clear understanding of the concept of an institution is indispensable. An institution is any aspect of society that relates to meaning in a special way. An institution organizes meaning, manifests meaning. It makes clear to the people living in a society just what it is that their society values most highly. Among the basic institutions of Victorian England, as Gilbert and Sullivan put it, were "the army, the navy, the church and the stage." In our own time and place, a list might include the family, the church, the workplace, and the mall. And maybe the nonprofit organization as well, although this latter is a relative newcomer to the primary ranks of institutional life.[1]

In this chapter, I will treat the nonprofit organization as an institution, one surrounded by and subject to the influence of other institutions. I will examine the institutional environment within which the nonprofit organization exists, I will seek to enumerate the principal institutional actors who perform within nonprofit organizations, and I will endeavor to clarify the mission of the nonprofit organization manager in fulfilling the institutional role of the nonprofit organization.

THE HUMAN SIDE OF
NONPROFIT INSTITUTIONS

It all begins, Susan Ostrander and Paul Schervish (1990) remind us, with the simplest of human choices: How do we spend our time and money? If some of our time is spent advancing the work of nonprofit organizations and some of our money is spent making sure those organizations can survive, then we may have chosen to do less fishing than we might have otherwise done or bought a less fancy fishing pole (or traveled to a more remote river).

But then it all depends, doesn't it? If volunteers spend their time showing a group of youngsters how to fish, they might be doing all the fishing they really wanted to. And if the donor's money is spent to support a nonprofit organization that allows youth to fish, then the donor's money may still have gone for the purchase of poles or the transport to fish-laden waters. Such is the transformational power of the individual act of giving: it allows us to do things we would have done only for ourselves and makes the same action into something that benefits others as well.

And that is what makes an institution: the pulling together by people in a way that makes collective meaning out of actions that are important to them. This is not to say that everything that gets done in the name of nonprofit organizations is institutional or even of value. The work of nonprofit organizations can be subverted by people as weak, devious, and malevolent as those who scheme, from time to time, in the halls of governments and corporations.[2]

How things look depends a lot on where we're looking from. Nonprofit administrators see the world, quite naturally, from the perspective of their own organizations. And from that perspective, they, like other executives, see most immediately the structure of their own organizations. Demanding as the tasks of managing any organization are, executives can hardly focus all their attention on it. Students of organizational life observe that the best administrators practice, by a combination of preference and necessity, a "mixed scanning" approach (see Etzioni, 1968, pp. 284–285) that keeps, in soft focus, distant specks on the organization's environment as well as the more immediate troubles directly on the executive's desk. Organizational scholar Henry Mintzberg (1980) identifies the variety of roles played by the successful executive, which include directing, motivating, coordinating, innovating, serving as an external spokesperson and gladiator, and managing crises. If nonprofit administrators are truly to be effective, they need to recognize that their organization is linked in myriad ways to the world outside it. Theirs, like any other organization, exists in a complex net of relations with other organizations and institutions, each of which affects each other in some way.

Sociologist Talcott Parsons (1951) provided a way of seeing this nesting of all organizational life in the context of broader social forces when he noted that any organization must meet four challenges if it is to survive. These challenges, in everyday language rather than the jargon used by Parsons, may be expressed as follows:

1. The need to meet basic life challenges
2. The need to meet goals shared with others
3. The need to secure resources adequate to sustain the organization
4. The need to relate to other organizations as each organization pursues its particular tasks

These challenges are so important that all societies create institutions to provide for them. Thus (paralleling the list just given):

1. *Family and community structures* develop to meet basic needs for meaning and support.
2. *Political institutions* emerge to define and articulate public goals.
3. *Economic institutions* arise to develop resources.
4. *Social institutions* are established to harmonize the various actions of organizations.

These categories of institutions are often thought of as "sectors" in society. Think of it this way: we divide our institutions into four major sectors to accomplish our social tasks. Corporations and businesses (the first sector) make most of our products and hire most of our labor: this sector provides jobs that amount to 80 percent of our payrolls. Government (the second sector) provides a military capacity and a number of ancillary regulatory and welfare services: it meets about 13 percent of our national payrolls. Voluntary and nonprofit organizations (the "third sector") address a number of educational, charitable, and membership purposes: its payroll amounts to more than 7 percent of the national total and is supplemented by much valuable voluntary effort as well. Finally, households and other informal community organizations (neighbors, kin, and so on) perform the lion's share of home management and child raising, though usually without the transfer of cash (Van Til, 2000).

To the nonprofit organization administrator, these sectors and the various cultural, political, economic, and social forces that form them should be seen as part of the organization's environmental field, the arena within which it seeks to operate effectively. The first portion of this chapter will focus on the environment of nonprofits.

The ability to scan the environment, however, is just one part of the administrator's task. To be effective, nonprofit managers will also need to understand the workings of the nonprofit sector—the immediate organizational world inhabited by their organizations. This sector (the third sector) includes the many givers, intermediaries, and regulators that impinge on the nonprofit organization. And as Ostrander and Schervish (1990) remind us, it also includes that all-important member of the sector, the beneficiary who receives the services provided by the organization.

THE ENVIRONMENT OF NONPROFIT MANAGEMENT

Nonprofits, like other institutions, are subject to various forces in the environment in which they operate—cultural, social, and demographic.

Cultural Forces

Perhaps the most powerful influence on nonprofit organizations is the culture that surrounds them. Thus it has been contended that the role of nonprofits is unique to the American experience, where a frontier mentality gave rise to a distrust of both government and business as institutions capable of solving human problems. Recent research, however, has blasted this view as itself a cultural myth, finding that voluntarism and nonprofit organizations have been part of many cultures throughout the sweep of human history (Lohmann, 1992; Ilchman, Katz, and Queen, 1998).

The fact that voluntarism characterizes other societies, however, does not detract from the fact that it has been, and continues to be, an important aspect of life in America. It reflects forces of local activism that are important drives in American history and represents a considerable strength in the American way of life.

The basic cultural carriers in any society are the family, the church, and the school. This is as true in a contemporary democratic society as it is in a totalitarian one, as the Nazi exaltation of "Kinder, Küche, und Kirche" (children, kitchen, and church) reminds us. Each of these cultural institutions shapes and influences the scope and scale of the nonprofit organization in many important ways.

The Family. Recurrently in American history, "culture wars" that divide our population erupt over questions of family structure and policy. Early in the summer of 2003, for example, Supreme Court Justice Antonin Scalia spoke for many Americans, and offended at least as many others, when he noted that the Supreme Court's majority had "taken sides in the culture war" by finding that privacy rights protect homosexual relations in *Lawrence* v. *Texas* (41 S.W. 3d 349). Later that summer, an openly gay bishop was approved for consecration by the Episcopal Church, following a bitter debate within the governing circles of that church. And at about the same time, President Bush joined Senate majority leader Bill Frist in vigorously opposing the idea of marriage between homosexuals. Pennsylvania's junior senator, Rick Santorum, raised a bit of a ruckus that same summer when he proclaimed his belief that sexual activity should be limited to what Alfred Kinsey once quaintly called "heterosexual outlets," leading Pennsylvania Governor Ed Rendell to quip that while Pennsylvanian Tom Ridge was guarding our nation from frontal attack (as secretary of homeland security), Santorum focused his efforts on "guarding our rear" ("Rendell Steals Show," 2003).

Debates over "family values" present nonprofit managers with a minefield of issues confronting their own work. Some of these issues deal with the family directly: Should community organizations take a stand in favor of the normative superiority of the married heterosexual two-parent family in preference to "alternate" forms of family life? Can teenagers be advised about, or provided with, abortion services without their parents' knowledge or consent? Should schools offer instruction on the use of condoms as well as outfit their students with this particular form of disease and birth control? Other issues affect the nonprofit organization more indirectly, though they often require at least as much delicacy to resolve: Should the needs of parents be given special consideration at the workplace when children's emergencies arise? Should the ire of the Roman Catholic Church be tempted when partnerships with pro-choice organizations such as Planned Parenthood are proposed? Should welfare reform plans requiring recipients to work be supported? Will efforts to strengthen "fragile families" lead feminist critics to oppose efforts to reward fathers who stand by their children?

Lurking behind these issues is a fundamental social fact: the family as an institutional force in society is in the process of being fundamentally reshaped. For some, this reshaping means the emergence of a "postmodern family," as Judith Stacey (1990) calls it. A single model of family no longer holds. Families now come in many configurations, due to changing cultural and personal circumstances.

For others, this reshaping means the disappearance of the father as a presence. A clear majority of children born to low-income parents do not issue into families headed by a married couple, and the proportion is rising among middle-income parents as well. Mincy and Pouncy (1977) have observed that what had previously been seen as a "crisis" of the black family may well involve an instance of "cultural lead"—with even the white middle-class joining in the advance of unmarried childbearing. In U.S. society as a whole, nearly 44 percent of all children born in 2002 would at one time have been identified by society as "illegitimate" (U.S. Department of Health and Human Services, 2003).

The implications of these cultural changes in the family are clear for nonprofit organizations: these organizations are increasingly expected to perform functions formerly reserved to the family. The social service agency provides day care; the school instills values and breakfast as well as instruction; the university offers its students as tutors and hallway monitors; the counselor valiantly seeks to substitute for father and, increasingly in the drug-infested areas of the metropolis, mother as well. And the bill for these services mounts, no matter how cost-effective the nonprofit organization. The fourth sector (family, church, and school) is simply not performing its functions in our modern society, and it is to volunteerism and nonprofit organizations (the third sector) that society increasingly turns to raise, and control, its youth.

Religion. A second institutional keeper of the cultural flame is religious institutions. Themselves prominent members of the nonprofit community, such institutions manifest by their doctrine and practice basic values of a society: conceptions of behavior, thought, and attitude that are transmitted from generation to generation as the elements of life as properly lived.

Nonprofit administrators must recognize the role that religious values and institutions play in their communities. Religious leaders articulate underlying values and concerns of their communities with a particular sensitivity, though certainly not with a unanimity of view. The interplay of the different theological conceptions, social values, and organizational structures in the religious sphere ensures a lively and compelling social process.

The rise in expectations regarding the ability of faith-based organizations to deliver social services, a central domestic policy initiative of the current Bush administration, has introduced new levels of controversy into contemporary discussions. Though the charitable choice provision dates from the 1996 welfare reform act and governments have long contracted with religiously affiliated organizations, Bush's creation of the Office of Faith-Based and Community Initiatives set off bitter disputes between and among religious leaders. I described this conflict in a column in the *NonProfit Times* (Van Til, 2001, p. 33):

> Not only did Bush's apparent allies on the right, the "fundamentalist reverends" Falwell and Robertson, begin to damn the new initiative with very faint praise, but Bush's own surprise point man in the office, John Di Iulio, made it clear that his heart did not belong with the right-wing on this issue, but rather with the set of African-American crime-fighting ministers of the night like Boston's Eugene Rivers. Di Iulio, an academic who achieved notoriety for warning about the dangers of youthful "super-predators" in the 1990s, had chosen the ghetto faith basers as his cause by the millennium's turn, and was recently introduced to a conference as "a man of God, appointed and anointed to lead this faith-based initiative."
>
> Rivers rushed to the defense of the new office, and was quoted in *The Atlanta Constitution* to the effect that it would not be "an illogical inference" to conclude that racism is why conservative religious leaders have been so lukewarm about Bush's initiative. "There is a racial dimension that must be looked at," said Rivers. The conservative religious right does not "accept the viability of

the black ministry to support the poor." And, he added, "We reject the assumption that we can't manage the money."

Not to be left out of a good fight, fundamental Protestant leaders began to mix things up with those of Catholic persuasion. The *Los Angeles Times* reported dissatisfaction within the Protestant community over the amount of time Bush was spending with Catholic leaders. Richard Cizik, vice president for government affairs for the National Association of Evangelicals, has been quoted as saying: "It's probably hurt him with the religious right because they've felt ignored. . . . This could come back to bite him."

As this article makes clear, no nonprofit manager should be without an appreciation of the complexities involved in the interplay of church, state, and service in contemporary society. Nor should anyone lose track of the various ways in which the persistently religious culture of the contemporary United States can affect perceptions of the work of nonprofit agencies. As Andrew Greeley (2001) has persuasively argued, religion in America is not in decline, churches will not lose their adherents, and religious belief is not in the process of withering away.

Education. The third major cultural force at play in society involves education, both formal and informal. Education is more than formal schooling and the massive institutional structure that aims to provide it. Education also includes the many ways by which individuals learn to think about the world and to participate in what has been called the "learning society." Such institutions as the mass media, as well as informal learning environments, such as community associations, should be included in this expanded view of education.

Many schools and colleges are moving in this direction as they develop new programs to assist students in learning the values of civic and voluntary participation. As Peter Hall (1992) has noted, schools convey important orientations toward service by their curricula. If they put a value on service that even approaches the weight they give football and other collective sports endeavors, schools might be able to assist students in learning that we live in the kind of society in which we all rise or fall together. As a collection of programs begins to emerge under the rubric of "national service," nonprofit managers will have many opportunities to assist young Americans in finding appropriate placements in their agencies and communities.

Meanwhile, comparative testing shows an increasing advantage being secured by students in many countries overseas. Assisting schools in achieving their daunting goal of educating youngsters is becoming a more widely shared community responsibility and one that nonprofit managers will increasingly be called on to assist.

As the challenge of enhancing education is recognized as a societywide need, many nonprofit managers will choose to monitor the state of education as a cultural element in their communities. Are they perceived as well-educated individuals? Do their organizations have a "learning style" congruent with those prevalent in their communities? Are their organizations perceived as "willing to learn"? Will they take advantage of the change to assist in the improvement of education as a community process, say, by playing an active role in encouraging service learning? All of these factors will affect the success of individual nonprofit organizations in the communities they serve.

Social and Demographic Conditions

We live in an age of troubling paradox. The triumph of democracy and capitalism is celebrated in some portions of the globe and imposed militarily on others, but U.S. electoral participation declines and living standards stagnate. The morning paper cites the weekly poll on presidential preference, but "none of the above" or "anybody but Bush" rises as the candidate of choice. On the state level, wrestlers and entertainers emerge as governors in Minnesota and California. The blessings of "being an American" are ritually cited, but the connectedness of individuals, especially youth, seems to recede before the lures of mass consumption and private indulgence. What David Reisman (1950) called "the lonely crowd" perpetuates itself as a nation of individualist onlookers—of television, in malls, and even in recreation. Political scientist Robert Putnam (2000) summed up our age in a challenging phrase: we have even learned to do our bowling alone.

Social scientists have constructed a list of characteristics of effective persons in society—people who can function productively in a modern society. Such individuals possess, to some degree:

- Enough *human capital* to be able to work gainfully and productively in the workplace

- Enough *personal capital* to sustain a loving relationship within the confines of family, kin, neighborhood, and community

- Enough *cultural capital* to understand the role of human creativity and to partake in a shared cultural life in modern society

- Enough *economic capital* to ensure participation in decisions regarding the creation of new economic products, as both owner and consumer, as well as the resources enabling a modicum of personal and family wealth

- Enough *social capital* to permit a full and warm joining with others to address issues of public and community concern by means of voluntary associations and a variety of bureaucratic organizations as well.

To a very real extent, what most nonprofit organizations do in their work is try to build many of these forms of capital, especially social, personal, and cultural capital. It is imperative that nonprofit organization managers understand the ways in which their work is affected by the powerful social forces abroad in our world. This is a time of great turbulence, of great change. Indeed, the time has come, as a young political scientist named Woodrow Wilson foresaw a century ago, when our country has awakened, "surprised to find herself grown old—a country crowded, strained, perplexed." In such a situation, Wilson observed, it will be necessary for America "to pull herself together, adopt a new regimen of life, husband her resources, concentrate her strength, steady her methods, sober her views, restrict her vagaries, trust her best, not her average, members. That will be the time of change" (Schlesinger, 1992, pp. 14–15).

Among the pressing challenges presented in this time of change are those of poverty, racism, alienation, and incapacity. Let us review each of these forces briefly and tie them to the work of nonprofit organizations.

Poverty and Economic Malaise. Living standards for the large majority of Americans have stopped growing. Both in our cities and in many small towns and rural areas, poverty is actually increasing. Even within the seemingly placid suburban areas inhabited by the new majority of Americans, structural unemployment annually removes hundreds of thousands of heads of households from positions formerly viewed as secure. In many urban areas, living standards mimic those of the Third World, with few human needs assured in a chaos of crime, housing decay, and hunger. Federal poverty statistics show the poverty rate holding steady at 12 percent, and a staggering total of one of every six American children grows up in poverty (U.S. Census Bureau, 2003).

Even for Americans not living below the poverty line, economic insecurity has become a fact of life in an era troubled by recurring recessions and jobless recoveries. Consumer confidence remains unsteady, and employee confidence has been riddled by the daily announcements of major corporate layoffs and reductions in force. "Jobless recoveries" from recessions may become the norm, and economic insecurity emerges as a fact of life for older workers and aspiring entrants to the labor force alike.

Racism. For many of the nearly one in three Americans who belongs to a minority group (13 percent are Hispanic, 12.7 percent African American, 4 percent Asian, and 2.7 percent "other" (Infoplease, 2003), and especially the one in eight who identify as black Americans, life continues to unfold in an atmosphere of white racism and racial discrimination, subtle though it may be. A significant proportion (perhaps as many as one-half) of the black population has been relegated to a condition of multigenerational undereducation, unemployment, and social alienation. For those who have escaped poverty, the specter of personal and social slight remains an ever-present threat.

Many black Americans find their lives confined to urban areas that provide few opportunities for education, employment, or health care. Such cities as

Gary, Indiana; East Saint Louis, Illinois; and vast stretches of North Philadelphia—"Type 2" cities, as Robert Catlin (1993) calls them—provide a nearly impossible environment for social stability or mobility.

Alienation. The alienation of the ghetto dweller is not unique in American society. With the loss of the employer's commitment to the provision of job security has come the loss of the worker's commitment to the provision of quality performance. With growing uncertainty in the authority and trustworthiness of religious leaders (in particular, Catholic priests) has come a loss in the individual's ability to find meaning and connection in everyday life. With the transformation of politics into late-night television entertainment has come the loss of individual participation in community problem solving. With the decline of the urban, and even suburban, community has come the privatization inherent in what Robert Reich (1991) has characterized as our "ZIP-code society."

Alienation, as Hegelian philosophy reminds us, is multiple: from society, from others, from self, and ultimately from meaning itself. Americans tend to be cynical about their standing in public life, and this cynicism has increased in the aftermath of the events of September 11, 2001. The Harris Poll found in a survey conducted in December 2003:

- 69 percent believe that "the rich get richer and the poor get poorer."
- 60 percent believe that "most people with power try to take advantage of people like you."
- 56 percent feel that "what you think doesn't count very much anymore."
- 46 percent believe that "the people running the country don't really care what happens to you."
- 67 percent feel that "the people in Washington are out of touch with the rest of the country."

Incapacity. A fourth collection of social problems clusters around questions of personal incapacity. As society becomes more complex and the literacy and numeracy required to perform even its most minimal functions increases, a growing number of individuals find themselves facing one or another set of personal incapacities. These incapacities may be physical (such as the disability following an automobile accident or an assault with a deadly weapon), socioenvironmental (such as the disability that results from being "computer illiterate"), or mental (such as the disability resulting from maternal drug use or growing up in a polluted environment).

The enhancement of social and economic opportunities for disabled individuals has become the goal of ambitious legislation and a growing social change agenda. Spurring all this movement is a sense that many individuals are being left behind through no fault of their own and that something must be done to ensure their living lives that are as normal as possible nevertheless.

GOVERNMENT, POLITICS, AND LAW

A player that looms larger than it perhaps deserves in American life is our system of government—permeated with the historic love of freedom born of colonial domination by the Old World and the wildly successful experiment of democracy. From another perspective, government in the United States may be regarded as a narrowly confined and limited tool for action and change. Supported by tax rates that are increasingly stingy in comparison with other developed nations and heavily focused on the delivery of military capacity abroad and public safety at home, government in America more resembles Hobbes's watchman than it does the cradle-to-grave service provider of the Scandinavian welfare state. This tendency toward global military domination and domestic security means that public funds for the support of domestic programs (education, social services, income support) are ever and continuously limited.

Despite these limits, however, governmental institutions (which include political parties and the framework of laws created by government) affect the daily work of the nonprofit manager, directly and indirectly. Government affects the nonprofit world directly in that it decides which nonprofit organizations it will recognize as eligible for tax deductions and which nonprofit organizations it will select as a contracting partner in the delivery of publicly mandated services. Indirectly, government affects the nonprofit world in its choices of which services to provide itself, which reduce the opportunities for services nonprofits might provide.

Welfare Mix

The choices a nation's government makes regarding the degree to which it will provide social service programs vitally affects the size and scale of its nonprofit sector. If that government chooses to fund and provide the full range of services of the modern welfare state—services that may include free health care, access to subsidized education at all levels, and guaranteed employment—the range of services provided by voluntary organizations will be limited. If, on the other hand, that government chooses to provide only a limited range of services—for example, health care only to the poor and aged, free education only through the secondary level, and little or no guaranteed employment—the nonprofit sector will have a more open field for the development of its programs.

The British have come to identify this problem as the "welfare mix": Which services does government provide? Which are offered by nonprofits? Which are left to the economic marketplace? The American response may best be identified as that of a reluctant and limited welfare state. Our history shows that we adopt welfare programs a generation or more after they are pioneered in western Europe, and usually only under the pressure of a looming economic catastrophe, such as the Great Depression of the 1930s, the social turmoil of the 1960s, or the long economic decline of the late 1980s and early 1990s.

The preferred American response has been to provide two levels of services directly: (1) to those in poverty, a set of services designed to provide a minimum level of food, shelter, and educational opportunity; (2) to those no longer able to work owing to advanced age, a more lavish set of programs designed to ensure adequacy of income and health care. This "dual welfare system" (on the one hand, Temporary Assistance for Needy Families, food stamps, and Medicaid, and on the other, Social Security and Medicare) is provided with quite different dispositions. Assistance aimed at the poor is given grudgingly, with frequent checks for eligibility and cheating. Assistance provided to those who have been employed throughout their lifetimes is typically provided as a right and not a privilege and carries none of the stigma typically associated with the receipt of welfare, food stamps, or Medicaid.

Within the boundaries of the welfare mix, nonprofit entrepreneurs conduct a constant search for niches in which to place nonprofit organizations. Few nonprofits choose to provide income directly (a government monopoly), but many provide the services government provides only sporadically, such as health care, housing, and higher education. Large numbers of nonprofit organizations also present themselves as potential providers of services government chooses to fund but not directly provide itself—services like sheltering the homeless, feeding the hungry, and counseling those without family support. Other organizations take advocacy as their focus and seek to influence policy and public opinion toward priorities that seem most basic to them.

The welfare mix is always under pressure to change. Democrats and Republicans differ sharply as to its proper form. With the election of Ronald Reagan to the presidency in 1980, for instance, the die was cast for a considerable reduction in welfare state funding, almost entirely taken from the housing budget. A direct result of this policy choice was the drastic increase in homelessness that accompanied a reduction in federal spending on housing from $29 billion to $15 billion during the Reagan years (Piven and Cloward, 1982). The narrow electoral victory of George W. Bush over Al Gore in 2000 led to another set of tax cuts for the wealthy and program cuts for lower-income Americans.

As the party domination of national and state governments shifts and as new problems come to rule the national agenda, one can anticipate a never-ending shift in the content of the welfare mix. From a strategic point of view, nonprofit managers cannot afford to ignore these processes and must seek to anticipate and plan for the implications they will have for the organizations they serve. These forces become for many such organizations the basic context of their work, whether their organizations focus primarily on the delivery of service or on the mounting of advocacy.

Certification

Government not only affects the reach of nonprofit organizations by preempting certain service areas but also sets the stage for nonprofit action by certifying those organizations it will recognize as tax-exempt. By controlling this identification, government determines which nonprofits can inform their supporters that donations are tax-deductible. The deductibility of such contributions effectively socializes the individual charitable contribution, ensuring that each donor's gift is "matched" by the taxpaying citizenry as a whole. (At a 33 percent tax rate, the donation of $1,000 to a charitable organization, for instance, costs the donor $667 in after-tax dollars, while the remaining $333 that is deducted from the giver's tax liability is effectively paid by every other taxpayer in the country.) By ceding government the power to certify organizations as exempt, nonprofit organizations also cede a good deal of their sometimes claimed independence. Having the ability to certify these organizations amounts to a considerable restriction of their independence. Efforts led by Congressman Ernest Istook (R-Okla.) in the 1990s similarly sought to prevent nonprofits engaged in advocacy or lobbying from the receipt of any federal contracts, even if the lobbying, as is required by law, was clearly supported only by voluntary nongovernmental time and contributions (see Van Til, 2000, ch. 3).

Of course, allowing the deduction of charitable donations further advances the ability of government to support the organizations it approves. And when an individual's gift is effectively matched by all taxpayers, as I have explained, the power of the wealthy giver is magnified at the expense of the preferences of those of lesser wealth.

Regulation

In addition to certifying nonprofit organizations, various governments at every level, from federal to local, regulate the work of nonprofits in a variety of ways. In some cases, this regulation accompanies the provisions of contracts between government and nonprofits. In others, regulations are part of the public responsibility to ensure the general health and welfare.

Behind many regulations stand important community values. Thus what may seem to one person to be a reasonable regulation may seem to another to be undue harassment. The members of the suburban church congregations who offered meals to the homeless in a suburban Pennsylvania county, for example, found their work declared illegal by a township regulation requiring that food served outdoors be cooked in regulated and inspected kitchens. Project organizers pointed out that other mass feeding occurred routinely in the suburban town in such events as backyard picnics. They questioned the application of the regulation to their activity, noting that it was not being applied to more reputable and influential township residents. As a result of their advocacy, the homeless feeding project continued.

NONPROFITS AND THE ECONOMY

A final set of institutional actors and outcomes that must centrally concern the nonprofit administrator are those of the economic order—regional, national, and global. Nonprofit managers will need to be alert to matters of productivity, distribution, and globalization in their work.

Productivity

Productivity issues are those most commonly thought of in terms of "growth." When the economy grows, people tend to feel hopeful and optimistic. When it stagnates, people tend to feel as though they are being left behind.

Nonprofit organizations are directly related by these sentiments, for they affect levels of charitable giving, and they also affect the range and magnitude of problems that are brought to nonprofits for succor and resolution. In times of growth, nonprofits may find a bit of a surplus in their operating budgets. In times of stagnation or decline, however, they face double trouble: a greater range of needs waiting at their doors but also shrinking resources, from both public and charitable sources, with which to fund the staff and services required. Thus in recent years, many nonprofit organizations, especially those supporting arts and culture, have been subject to funding declines as total donations grew only slowly (if at all) in a recessionary era and were deflected, to some extent, toward disaster relief in the wake of the attacks on New York and Washington of September 11, 2001.

Distribution

How society distributes its wealth and income also critically affects the work of nonprofit organizations. The long sweep of human history has shown a reduction of patterns of inequality in the distribution of income since the inception of the Industrial Revolution. This pattern continued in the United States through out most of the twentieth century but has been reversed since 1980. Since that date, the rich have increased their wealth and income while the middle and working classes have stagnated and the poor have lost. This "reverse Robin Hood" pattern, in full gallop in the early years of the twenty-first century, has made the work of nonprofit organizations particularly perilous.

When a society begins to blame its poor not only for inducing their own poverty but also for costing its wealthier members more in the way of crime, services, and education, a nasty downward cycle confronts nonprofit organizations. The issues of distribution are certainly important to monitor and confront if a vital nonprofit sector is to be sustained.

Globalization, Including Mass Media

A third economic force that needs monitoring by the nonprofit manager is the onrushing global economy. We have never before lived as fully in one world as we do today. The transnationalization of economic life has many implications: (1) It reduces the prospect of world war (but not regional wars), since corporations are powerful in many countries and do their work globally—and therefore do not want to fight themselves or see their profits reduced by war. (2) It has created a single financial market, which makes all national economies interdependent. (3) It creates the possibility for international problem solving in a world whose problems (like AIDS or SARS or abortion, in an age of RU-486, for example) know no borders. (4) It opens the possibility for the creation of a transnational philanthropic system, in which, for example, Japanese-owned corporations that do business in the United States participate in the support of American nonprofit organizations.

Among the forces that have been globalized are the mass media. With their hunger to report sensational news, events of fleeting interest in a local community may flash for a few moments on the TV screens of the world, where world leaders are known to monitor CNN on a constant basis, even directly from their own offices.

For the nonprofit organization leader, the transnationalization of the media means that a particularly dramatic case may lead to transitory international attention and perhaps some checks in tomorrow's mail. But it also means that a transgression will be noted and possibly punished with as swift a sword. Thus many Catholic priests, accused of sexual misconduct with youthful parishioners, have quickly been relieved from parish work and subjected to removal from office. Still most dramatic among the cases of executive malfeasance in the nonprofit world is that of William Aramony of United Way of America, who abused the perquisites of his office so baldly that he earned himself a long prison sentence. One world, one economy, one information system: it is a new world, and one a nonprofit manager will need to understand and exploit, at least in terms of the interests and values of his or her particular organization.

MAJOR PLAYERS ON THE NONPROFIT STAGE

I have so far reviewed the environmental field in which nonprofit organizations are sited. The next part of the chapter deals with the sector itself, its principal players, and their roles.

The third sector, as I prefer to call it, is a world of thoughts and dreams, individuals and groups, needs and solutions. Its principal actors are givers, intermediaries, regulators, nonprofit and charitable organizations, and beneficiaries and customers.

Givers

Givers are people who join with others in meeting their own and others' perceived needs by means of a voluntary organization. For the giver, it is not enough to rely on the benefits provided by the other sectors of society. An additional level of involvement is perceived, and that involves joining with others of like mind in supporting the work of a voluntary or nonprofit organization.

Givers rely, like the rest of us, on the other three sectors. They are citizens who vote, complain about government inaction, and enjoy the blessings of governmental services. They are also persons who live in families and experience the joys and frustrations inherent in that venerable human institution. And they make their livings, or seek to, within the confines of the world of economic organizations.

But there is something that the three other sectors are not able to provide that these individuals seek through involvement in the third sector. Perhaps they volunteer, as more than half of the American population does on a regular basis, in assisting persons who may require their assistance, whether it be a group of youngsters on a local swim team or a group of homeless persons thankful to receive a hot meal on a regular basis.

Givers also make financial contributions to nonprofit organizations. Sometimes these gifts are large, such as the $100 million gift made by a New Jersey industrialist to a regional public college in 1992; sometimes these gifts are small, such as the quarter you may have placed in a UNICEF tin carried by a trick-or-treater last Halloween. The varieties of giving, and the attitudes underlying them, are increasingly the subject of an emerging subfield of fundraising (see, for example, Burlingame, 1992).

The question of the attitude underlying giving has long concerned social scientists. After many studies of the subject, it appears clear that giving is performed out of a variety of motives. Some are largely altruistic: some people find it rewarding to assist others without receiving any evident reward themselves. But of course, they do receive a psychic reward in the form of their feeling of having done "the right thing." So have they acted entirely without concern for their own well-being?

Other gifts come with strings attached, such as the aforementioned gift of $100 million by industrialist Henry Rowan to Glassboro State College. A substantial piece of the gift was earmarked to provide tuition and educational programs for the employees of the company Rowan owns. In return, and apparently unsolicited by Rowan, officials of the college and the state of New Jersey rushed to enact a name change: from Glassboro State to Rowan College of New Jersey.

During the Nixon presidency, Americans learned about the laundering of money. Had they been more attuned to the history of philanthropy, they might have been more prepared for these revelations. Giving to nonprofit organizations involves a transformative process: money made in the first sector (business) is not spent in the fourth sector (the household) for personal use but is rather donated to the third sector (a certified nonprofit organization), where it receives an immediate reward from the second sector (government) in the form of a forgiveness of taxation.

Thus is raised the question of "tainted money." The argument goes as follows. A fair amount of money that individuals make in the world of corporate business comes to them as a result of ethically dubious activity. What is to ensure that this money is somehow purified when it is offered to a nonprofit organization, especially when a third of it returns to the donor in the form of a tax deduction? Often cited as a case in point is Andrew Carnegie or John D. Rockefeller, neither of whom was known for particularly humane treatment of his employees or his competitors.

In opposition comes the standard response of the successful nonprofit administrator: "Tainted money? 'Taint enough of it around for my organization!" A variety of ethical dilemmas are thus suggested: Should nonprofit organizations participate with corporations in "cause-related marketing" schemes? Should nonprofit organizations accept donations from donors who make their profits from legal but addictive drugs such as tobacco or alcoholic beverages? Should fundraising advisers work on contracts that provide them a fixed share of the monies that are raised by campaigns they counsel? Should educational institutions accept funding when it is accompanied by specific requests for board control or program revision?

Since we live in a world in which the alchemic transformation of dross to gold has been shown to be a problematic process at best, I ordinarily advise that nonprofit managers examine these questions fully and deeply before they accept a donation. They should be at least as sophisticated as the young lady from Kent:

> There was a young lady from Kent
> Who said that she knew what it meant
> When men asked her to dine,
> Gave her cocktails and wine—
> She knew what it meant, but she went.

Intermediaries

Very little is accomplished without the use of intermediaries in the modern world. In the nonprofit organizational world, intermediaries link the money and time of donors with the needs the organizations themselves seek to meet. These intermediaries are variously known as consultants, trainers, counselors, and program officers. They work for their own firms, support centers, fundraising firms, "sector-serving organizations," and foundations. They apply a good deal of the grease to the rails of American philanthropy and volunteerism.

Of all these intermediary institutions, the foundation is the most visible. Typically established by an individual of considerable wealth, the foundation provides support through its program for a wide range of nonprofit organizations.

Nonprofit organization managers, as a matter of professional course, get to know the lay of the foundation land. They learn that foundations come in three major varieties: national, regional, and community. National foundations support programs that are seen to have a particular impact on a pressing problem of broad concern to the foundation, the solution of which might be applicable in other parts of the country or the world. Regional foundations support programs that are perceived to have a particular impact on problems of the region, typically problems identified by the donors themselves. Community foundations draw support from many local donors and seek to enhance the social capacity of organizations in a particular city or metropolitan area.

Foundations operate in the context of an etiquette of "giving and getting" that differs quite considerably from the rough-and-tumble of daily organizational contact. Historically, foundations sought to create an aura of refined dignity in their offices and processes, with the "grant seeker" typically left to play the role of humble supplicant. In more recent times, foundation officers have come to recognize that the grant seeker is its very lifeblood, in that a foundation is only as good as the programs it is able to attract to it. Considerable effort has been devoted, in many foundations, to reducing the perceived distance between seeker and grantor. And in many cases, the sheer volume of queries and prospectuses that reach a foundation officer conjures up the image of a paper-glutted office rather than a bastion of corporate gentility.

Sector-serving organizations, such as INDEPENDENT SECTOR, the Council on Foundations, the Association of Fundraising Professionals, and literally hundreds of associations of like-minded nonprofit organizations, serve as the "trade associations" of the sector. They share information on legislation, grant opportunities, social trends, and research as these pertain to the interests of their members. They assert the interests of their members in the legislative process, and they engage in public relations campaigns aimed at convincing Americans that the work of nonprofit organizations is of considerable value and merit.

University-based centers on voluntarism, philanthropy, and nonprofit organizations, of which there are now more than forty, provide educational, training, and research services to individuals aspiring to enter the field of nonprofit management and to those already established in positions in the field. Typically funded by a major regional foundation in their area, these centers are beginning to develop degree programs (usually at the master's level) and to otherwise secure their rather perilous niches in the tottering structure of American higher education.

Closer to the firing line of everyday organizational give-and-take is the office of the support or technical assistance provider. Typically, this is an individual, "mom and pop," or small group venture that lives and dies on the basis of accumulating and discharging the responsibilities of many short-term contracts. Consultants strive to project the image of "taking charge" and providing important services to organizations that reach out to them for assistance. The aristocrats of the consultant trade are the "fundraising counsel," a fascinating group of individuals who adopt both the élan of the old-line foundation and a kind of locker-room camaraderie based on having located and secured for their clients a considerable amount of philanthropic wealth.

Regulators

Regulators are few and far between in the nonprofit sector (Gaul and Borowski, 1993). But when they enter the scene, the sector trembles. Principal among this group are state agencies of taxation and attorneys general; the IRS, generally overwhelmed in its policing of nonprofit fraud; nonprofit organizations that serve as sector monitors; program evaluators; and congressional subcommittees. The work of these various bodies, taken as a whole, yields only a sporadic product.

The process by which an organization receives tax exemption tends to be a onetime review conducted in full rigor only before the organization moves into a fully operational mode. Once the exemption is granted, the major requirement of tax agencies involves the completion of an annual form, the 990, which is at best a perfunctory reporting device. Few are the nonprofit organizations whose exempt status is questioned after initial certification, assuming annual filing of the 990.

Sector-monitoring organizations, like the Better Business Bureau and the Charities Information Bureau (now merged as the BBB Wise Giving Alliance), and the more recently established Charity Navigator and American Institute on Philanthropy, are similarly noteworthy for the limits of the services they provide. Some, like the BBB Wise Giving Alliance, respond to individual complaints and queries regarding the legitimacy of the practices of nonprofit organizations. Others compute data on the proportion of agency funding that actually reaches the intended beneficiaries of the nonprofit's service. Typically, however, a bogus charity does not begin to suffer before its malevolence reaches the press and courtroom. The *Chronicle of Philanthropy,* a basic source of news in the field, reported that "fraudulent activity—including check forgery, money laundering, and other forms of stealing—has long troubled nonprofit organizations, but people who study it say it has intensified in recent years" (Wolverton, 2003).

Program evaluators are required by most federal grants and some foundations. Their work is intended to reassure the funder that the recipient organization has indeed delivered the service promised in the initial proposal. The work of a professional evaluation consultant is often of great value to the delivery of the program, providing an ongoing "formative" contribution to the program as well as a formal "summative" report. However, the evaluation component is typically cast as a part of the program, rather than as an external review, and is therefore not seen as a purely regulatory device.

The form of regulation that strikes the deepest fear in the nonprofit organization's heart is that of the congressional subcommittee. As detailed by several historians (see especially Hall, 1992), this process raises, from time to time, the threat of removing the charitable deduction for nonprofit organizations. As far back as the 1950s, Congressman Wright Patman (D-Tex.) led a series of hearings that resulted in the recasting of foundation practice, requiring all foundations to provide at least a fixed proportion of their assets in annual contributions. And in the 1980s, Congressman J. J. Pickle (D-Tex.) raised the specter of removing tax exemption as a means of coping with the increasingly intractable federal budget deficit. When the specter of changes in federal tax codes presents itself, the national and regional structure of sector-serving organizations mobilizes for action. While some people argue that such change would be beneficial, the typical response of the sector servers is one of impending disaster. The net effect of this process, however, is never thoroughgoing regulation but rather sporadic intervention. Most of the time, the nonprofit sector pursues its various ends in American life in a self-regulated or even unregulated fashion.

Nonprofit and Charitable Organizations

Some 1.6 million nonprofit organizations exist in the United States, employing approximately 10 percent of the total workforce (Van Til, 2000). These denizens of the third sector comprise an army over half the size of government. They constitute a formidable array of institutional forces providing religious, educational, social, health, and cultural services.

The work of nonprofit organizations involves three major forms of activity: service, advocacy, and member benefit. These are elaborated in the work of David Horton Smith (1992), among others. Service helps individuals in need resolve immediate and pressing problems. Advocacy defines a set of policies that other institutions, including governmental and corporate structures, might follow to more fully achieve a just and humane society. Member benefit provides association members with the collective structure within which to enjoy both colleagueship and the articulation of common interests.

The work of nonprofit organizations as an institutional force is the subject of a number of useful volumes, including the works of Lohmann (1992), Hall (1992), Wolch (1990), O'Neill (1989), Van Til (1988, 2000), O'Connell (1983, 1999), Douglas (1983), Salamon (1999), and Frumkin (2002). These volumes, as well as the one before you, belong in a prominent place on the reading shelf of all nonprofit managers. They document, in considerable detail, the rapid expansion of the nonprofit sector in American life over the past half-century; they also show the ways in which nonprofit organizations have come to stand as institutions unto themselves in American life: Boy Scouts and Girl Scouts, the

Catholic Church and the Salvation Army, the Brookings Institution and the Heritage Foundation, Blue Cross and the Mayo Clinic, Yale and Amherst, the Ford Foundation and the Getty Trust, the National Football League and the Motion Picture Academy of America.

Beneficiaries and Customers

Who benefits from the activity of a nonprofit organization? An initial list might go as follows:

- Those who directly receive services from the nonprofit organization
- Those in whose name the nonprofit organization advocates
- Members of the nonprofit organization who receive direct membership benefits
- Staff members employed by the nonprofit organization
- Those who enjoy the benefits of the nonprofit organization as consumers or customers
- Members of the general public who find a higher quality of life available to them as a result of the work of the nonprofit organization

In an intriguing presentation, historian Rudolph Bauer (1993) suggested that volunteers tend to treat nonprofit organizations as though they were providers of charitable service, while board members tend to see them as political organizations. Meanwhile, staff behave as though the organization is a business. In this way, Bauer observed, a third-sector organization tends to take on the coloration of business (first sector), politics (second sector), and community (fourth sector). It all depends on one's point of view, which itself is determined by one's role within the organization.

CONCLUSION: A COUPLE OF BIG QUESTIONS

The nonprofit sector arises as an institutional response to social disquiet and need. Its leaders give the obligatory nod to de Tocqueville (1835–1840) in their encomiums and routinely observe the importance of the third sector to American pluralism. But do nonprofit organizations serve as tools of a democratic process, or are they too often simply tax-free businesses in disguise, another form of organization out to preserve advantage in an age of grab and greed? And what of the role of individual voluntary action in the modern mass society? How does it contribute to the values of participation in a strong democracy?

The role of the nonprofit sector as an institutional contributor to the building of a viable democratic society is a matter that requires continuing attention.

Though it has been probed in the literature in the field on an intermittent basis, it is clear that the relationship with democratic theory and institutions is considered as at best a question of secondary importance by many in the field. Such issues as management capacity, fundraising stratagems, and public relations predominate in professional conferences and literature, including this handbook. The ways in which voluntary action and nonprofit organization may serve to expand the democratic horizon raise questions that typically do not find their way onto the nonprofit agenda.

Nonprofit organization leaders will be well advised to take the work they do in a manner both serious and clear-minded. At stake is not only the success of their organizations and the welfare of their clients and members but also the precarious health of the nonprofit sector as an institutional actor in contemporary society. Nonprofit managers will do well to understand this institutional field and the importance of their own role in it.

Notes

1. My use of the concept of an institution in this chapter is essentially descriptive (Kramer, 1998). For a more involved theoretical construction, see Powell and Di Maggio (1991), Van Til (1988), or Lohmann (1992).

2. Perhaps the most dramatic example of the perversion of nonprofit organizations involves their use by the Hitler government. For a full review of this experience, see Bauer (1990).

References

Bauer, R. "Voluntarism, Nongovernmental Organizations, and Public Policy in the Third Reich." *Nonprofit and Voluntary Sector Quarterly,* 1990, *19*, 199–214.

Bauer, R. Plenary presentation to Conference on Well-Being in Europe and the Third Sector, Barcelona, Spain, May 1993.

Burlingame, D. (ed.). *The Responsibilities of Wealth.* Bloomington: Indiana University Press, 1992.

Catlin, R. *Racial Politics in Urban Planning: Gary, Indiana, 1980–1990.* Lexington: University of Kentucky Press, 1993.

Douglas, J. *Why Charity?* Thousand Oaks, Calif.: Sage, 1983.

Etzioni, A. *The Active Society.* New York: Free Press, 1968.

Frumkin, P. *On Being Nonprofit.* Cambridge, Mass.: Harvard University Press, 2002.

Gaul, G. W., and Borowski, N. A. *Free Ride: The Tax-Exempt Economy.* Kansas City, Mo.: Andrews & McMeel, 1993.

Greeley, A. "The Future of Religion in America." *Society,* 2001, *38*(3), 32–37.

Hall, P. D. *Inventing the Nonprofit Sector and Other Essays on Philanthropy, Voluntarism, and Nonprofit Organizations.* Baltimore: Johns Hopkins University Press, 1992.

Harris Poll. "Modest Increase in Nation's Alienation Index, According to Harris Poll." PRNewswire [http://www.forrelease.com/D20031231/nyw036.P2.12312003154505 .24915.html]. Dec. 31, 2003.

Ilchman, W. F., Katz, S. N., and Queen, E. L., II (eds.). *Philanthropy in the World's Traditions.* Bloomington: Indiana University Press, 1998.

Infoplease. "Population of the United States by Race and Hispanic/Latino Origin, Census 2000 and July 1, 2002" [http://www.infoplease.com/ipa/0/7/6/2/1/5/ A0762156.html]. 2003.

Kramer, R. M. *Nonprofit Organizations in the 21st Century: Will Sector Matter?* Washington, D.C.: Aspen Institute Nonprofit Sector Research Fund, 1998.

Lohmann, R. A. *The Commons: New Perspectives on Nonprofit Organizations and Voluntary Action.* San Francisco: Jossey-Bass, 1992.

Mincy, R. B., and Pouncy, H. "Paternalism, Child Support Enforcement, and Fragile Families." In L. M. Mead (ed.), *The New Paternalism: Supervisory Approaches to Poverty.* Washington, D.C.: Brookings Institution, 1977.

Mintzberg, H. *The Nature of Managerial Work.* Upper Saddle River, N.J.: Prentice Hall, 1980.

O'Connell, B. (ed.). *America's Voluntary Spirit.* New York: Foundation Center, 1983.

O'Connell, B. *Civil Society: The Underpinnings of American Democracy.* Lebanon, N.H.: University Press of New England, 1999.

O'Neill, M. *The Third America: The Emergence of the Nonprofit Sector in the United States.* San Francisco: Jossey-Bass, 1989.

Ostrander, S., and Schervish, P. G. "Giving and Getting: Philanthropy as a Social Relation." In J. Van Til and Associates, *Critical Issues in American Philanthropy: Strengthening Theory and Practice.* San Francisco: Jossey-Bass, 1990.

Parsons, T. *The Social System.* New York: Free Press, 1951.

Piven, F. F., and Cloward, R. *The New Class War: Reagan's Attack on the Welfare State and Its Consequences.* New York: Pantheon, 1982.

Powell, W. W., and Di Maggio, P. (eds.). *The New Institutionalism in Organizational Analysis.* Chicago: University of Chicago Press, 1991.

Putnam, R. *Bowling Alone: The Collapse and Revival of American Community.* New York: Simon & Schuster, 2000.

Reich, R. B. *The Work of Nations: Preparing Ourselves for 21st-Century Capitalism.* New York: Knopf, 1991.

Reisman, D. *The Lonely Crowd.* New Haven, Conn.: Yale University Press, 1950.

"Rendell Steals Show at DLC Event." *Philadelphia Inquirer,* Aug. 3, 2003, p. B02.

Salamon, L. M. *America's Nonprofit Sector.* (2nd ed.) New York: Foundation Center, 1999.

Schlesinger, A. M., Jr. "Faded Glory." *New York Times Magazine,* July 12, 1992.

Smith, D. H. "A Neglected Type of Voluntary Nonprofit Organization: Exploration of the Semiformal, Fluid-Membership Organization." *Nonprofit and Voluntary Sector Quarterly,* 1992, *21,* 251–270.

Stacey, J. *Brave New Families: Stories of Domestic Upheaval in Late Twentieth Century America.* New York: Basic Books. 1990.

Tocqueville, A. de. *Democracy in America.* New York, 1835–1840.

U.S. Census Bureau. "Poverty, Income See Slight Changes; Child Poverty Rate Unchanged, Census Bureau Reports." *Department of Commerce News,* press release [http://www.census.gov/Press-Release/www/2003/cb03-153.html]. Sept. 26, 2003.

U.S. Department of Health and Human Services. "U.S. Birth Rate Reaches Record Low." *HHS News,* press release [http://www.cdc.gov/nchs/releases/03news/lowbirth.htm]. June 25, 2003.

Van Til, J. *Mapping the Third Sector: Voluntarism in a Changing Social Economy.* New York: Foundation Center, 1988.

Van Til, J. *Growing Civil Society: From Nonprofit Organization to Third Space.* Bloomington: Indiana University Press, 2000.

Van Til, J. "Faith-Based Initiative." *NonProfit Times,* June, 2001, pp. 33–34.

Wolch, J. *The Shadow State.* New York: Foundation Center, 1990.

Wolverton, B. "Fighting Charity Fraud." *Chronicle of Philanthropy,* Aug. 7, 2003.

CHAPTER THREE

The Legal Framework of the Nonprofit Sector in the United States

Thomas Silk

Non-profit, non-business, non-governmental are all negatives.
One cannot, however, define anything by what it is not. What, then,
is it that all these institutions do? They all have in common—and this
is a recent realization—that their purpose is to change human lives.
—Peter Drucker, *The New Realities*

A t a legal conference in Moscow, I was approached by a Russian lawyer who was trying to make sense of the interplay of laws that govern the charitable sector in the United States. What was needed, he suggested, was not more detailed treatments of state corporation and trust laws or federal and state tax laws pertaining to the charitable sector. What was missing, he said, was an overview with practical detail, a "bird's-eye and worm's-eye view" of U.S. charitable law. This chapter is based on the paper I wrote in response to that request. It takes the form of a case study and commentary featuring a hypothetical charitable advocacy organization that, although fictional, is a composite of many existing organizations. The case study provides the basis for the commentary on legal and regulatory issues that are frequently encountered during the life cycle of a charitable organization in the United States. To allow consideration of a broad range of legal issues, the case study considers the growth and development of a large and successful charitable organization.

PREFORMATION

Jim and Beth Rankin received their doctorates in oceanography in 1995. After graduation, they taught marine science at neighboring universities and conducted academic research. They formed a discussion group with their colleagues, which met weekly. In the first year, the group included about twenty people who discussed

63

their research findings about the ocean environment. It soon became apparent to the members of the group that the oceans were threatened and that citizens as well as social institutions, including the federal and state governments, were blissfully unaware of the threat and its significance. Existing environmental organizations were concerned with other issues pertaining to land and air and had not yet begun to consider marine issues.

In 1997, the Rankins decided to do something about the problem. They expanded their discussion group to fifty members, and they enlisted the aid of their colleagues in giving speeches about the environmental threat to the oceans to any local organizations that would listen. Their goal was clear and entirely lacking in modesty: to change the attitude and behavior of people toward the oceans. Changes in the policies of government and business, they believed, would follow in time.

The Rankins began to encounter a pleasant but persistent problem. After they gave a speech, members of the audience would ask where they could contribute money to support the Rankins' work. By this time, the Rankins had come to think of themselves as organizers as well as academics. They decided to form a new nonprofit environmental organization to protect the oceans.

For several years, the Rankins met regularly with colleagues and gave speeches about environmental threats to the oceans. In many countries, such meetings and public speeches would be regulated by government. In America, however, the Bill of Rights to the U.S. Constitution limits government regulation of speech and the related right of association. Private meetings and speech may not be regulated. Public speech and meetings may not be regulated as to content, but reasonable restrictions as to time, place, and manner may be imposed. The early environmental activities of the Rankins and their colleagues therefore proceeded lawfully, despite the absence of government knowledge or authorization. Government involvement did not occur until the Rankins decided to conduct their activities within a formal legal entity.

FORMATION

The Rankins were not required to form a charitable organization, or any organization at all, in order to advocate for environmental preservation. It was, rather, the benefits of charitable status and the corporate form that led them to choose this approach. Had they wished to operate without governmental oversight and without legal formalities, they would have been entirely free to do so, but they would have had to forgo the accompanying benefits. The benefits are both symbolic and practical. A formal organization would have its own separate identity, which would symbolize their mission and could survive their retirement or death. Moreover, the corporation, rather than the Rankins as individuals, would be legally responsible for the project's acts and omissions.

The tax benefits of forming a separate charitable organization are even more significant. A tax-exempt charity, as the name implies, generally pays no tax on its income. Of equal importance, charities may offer potential donors not only the satisfaction of contributing to a good cause but also the ability to lower their income tax bills. This is because individuals and corporate taxpayers who contribute to charitable organizations may, under the federal tax system and those of many states, reduce, by the amount of their allowable contributions, the income base on which their tax is calculated.

The formation of legal entities is regulated, in almost all instances, by state law rather than by federal law. In California, the Rankins would have three legal entities to choose from: a nonprofit public benefit corporation, a charitable trust, or an unincorporated nonprofit association. The association form is seldom used because its few rules contain little protection against liability and leave many operational questions unanswered. The nonprofit corporation has largely replaced the more ancient legal form, the charitable trust, as the entity of choice for new nonprofit organizations. This has come about because charitable trusts are largely creatures of case law, while nonprofit corporations are creatures of statutory law. Modern statutory rules governing organizational formation, operation, and termination contain protections against liability and provide comprehensive legal guidance to the directors and members of nonprofit corporations but not to trustees of charitable trusts.

Name

The Rankins wanted a name that was dramatic. They considered many possibilities and settled on the international distress signal, SOS, as an acronym for Save Our Seas, only to learn that another organization in a distant state was already using that name. But they kept returning to the notion that the problem was global in scope and that water comprises more than two-thirds of our planet. Late one night, the name came to them: Planet Water.

The Rankins were not able to use their initial choice of name, SOS, because another charitable organization was already using it. Had they attempted to use that name, both the government and the other charity could have taken steps to prevent it.

No state will allow the formation of a new corporation whose name is deceptively similar to that of another organization. Moreover, the civil law of unfair competition allows an existing organization to prevent a new organization from using a name that exploits the value that the prior organization has built into the name. To avoid name-related problems, new organizations commonly search the state corporation registry and, with increasing frequency, the federal trademark registry as well before a name is finally chosen. After the name has been chosen and the organization has been formed, the name will be registered under the federal and state trademark laws, a practice that is becoming standard.

Incorporation

With the help of an attorney, Planet Water was incorporated in California in 1999 as a nonprofit corporation. Its purpose, as stated in its articles of incorporation, is to encourage and promote the environmental protection of the oceans. The articles were signed by the Rankins and were mailed to California's secretary of state for filing. Within a week, the Rankins were notified that the document had been accepted and filed. They opened a bank account for Planet Water with $1,000 that they had managed to save from their salaries. At the same time, Planet Water applied to the Internal Revenue Service over the Internet for an employer identification number, which it received immediately.

The bylaws of Planet Water provide for a voting membership of all individuals who pay dues. They also make provision for a fifteen-person board of directors elected by the members for three-year terms.

A common name for the enabling document of a nonprofit corporation in the United States is *articles of incorporation.* State practice varies, however, and synonyms (such as *constitution, certificate, charter,* and *organic document*) are also encountered.

In California, the content of articles of incorporation is largely standardized by statute. Articles generally contain the name of the organization, the law under which it is being incorporated (for example, the Nonprofit Public Benefit Corporation Law), its purposes, the manner in which the net assets are to be distributed in the event of dissolution, and the names of the incorporators. California law requires only one incorporator. However many incorporators there are, they need not be U.S. citizens or even residents.

The incorporator submits the articles to the secretary of state, together with the minimum state income tax prepayment (which is refunded, with interest, if the corporation later receives tax-exempt status). The secretary of state reviews the articles of incorporation for form but not for content. If the articles are correct in form, they will be accepted for filing and given a corporate number. The corporation's legal existence begins on the date that the articles are accepted for filing by the secretary of state.

Once the articles have been filed and returned, the individuals who have incorporated the organization then meet to adopt its bylaws. The bylaws prescribe the organizational rules that, so long as they are not inconsistent with state law, govern the corporation. They usually contain sections describing the board of directors (its powers, the term of office and manner of election of the directors, and the rules for conducting meetings); the members, if any (their rights and duties and rules for members' meetings); the duties of officers; and other similar matters relating to the formal governance of the corporation. At the same meeting, the incorporators will usually elect the first board of directors and the officers and authorize the opening of a bank account, specifying which individuals have authority to withdraw funds.

The next step is commonly to visit the local office of a bank and to open the new charity's bank account. Banks generally require evidence of the organization's legal existence (here, the file-stamped articles) and of the connection between the organization and those who will manage the bank account (usually, a resolution adopted by the board of directors appointing signatories on the bank account).

State law requires that minutes—a written record of a meeting—be made of all meetings of the organization's board of directors and committees. There is no requirement that the minutes be filed with any governmental agency. They must be produced, however, if they are requested in connection with any audit of the organization by a governmental agency.

The bylaws are effective as soon as they are adopted by the incorporators. It is not necessary to obtain the approval of any governmental agency.

Tax Exemption

Planet Water applied simultaneously to the Internal Revenue Service and to the California Franchise Tax Board for federal and state tax exemption as a charitable organization.

In those applications, the Rankins described the purpose and intended activities of Planet Water and included a proposed budget listing the anticipated receipts and expenditures of Planet Water for the next three years. The California Franchise Tax Board exemption was issued in two months. Three months later, the IRS exemption letter was in hand.

The revenues of nonprofit organizations are generally exempt from federal income tax. Business revenues are a major exception. If the nonprofit organization is actively engaged in a business whose conduct is unrelated to its exempt purpose, then it is taxable on the net receipts from that activity at the same rates that apply to a business corporation. There are many exceptions and exclusions, however, to the scope and coverage of that complex tax. It does not apply, for example, to passive investment income, such as most types of dividends, interest, rents, and royalties.

California law is substantially the same: a nonprofit organization is exempt from state income tax except on its unrelated business income. In both jurisdictions, the exemption process entails the filing of an application for exemption and a review by the tax agency of the proposed purposes and activities of the nonprofit organization. It is in this review that the content of the charitable organization is scrutinized for the first time by any governmental agency.

The exercise of discretion by the IRS is reviewable internally and in court. Federal law gives an organization extensive opportunities to challenge a proposed determination by the IRS that it fails to qualify as charitable. The initial deter-mination is usually made at a regional office of the IRS. The organization may appeal the adverse proposed determination administratively, within the IRS, at the regional and national levels. If those appeals do not succeed, the organiza-tion may file an action in federal court, where a neutral judge will review the administrative proceedings and make an independent determination as to whether the organization qualifies as charitable.

When Planet Water applied for tax-exempt status, it represented to the IRS and the Franchise Tax Board that it fit the statutory definition of a charitable or-ganization. The statutory definition—contained in a federal statute, section 501(c)(3) of the Internal Revenue Code, and also in corresponding provisions of the laws of many states—requires that a tax-exempt charitable organization be formed only for certain permitted purposes: religious, charitable, scientific, testing for public safety, literary, educational, fostering national or international amateur sports competition, or the prevention of cruelty to children or animals. It must be organized exclusively for one or more of those purposes; that is, its governing document must limit its activities to proper goals. And it must be op-erated exclusively for one or more of those purposes. Hence it may not engage in activities that serve other purposes, except to an insubstantial degree.

The federal statute explicitly prohibits certain activities by tax-exempt char-itable organizations. No part of a charity's net earnings may be regularly di-verted to the benefit of any private person or entity. This means that the charitable organization's funds must be used to carry out its charitable program and may not be paid to individuals except as reasonable compensation for nec-essary services performed for the charity or as fair and reasonable payment for the use or acquisition of property required by the organization.

The federal statute bars a charity from engaging in electioneering—activity in support of or in opposition to a candidate for public office—and it also pro-vides that no substantial part of a tax-exempt charity's activities may involve attempts to influence legislation. Except for churches, charities that are broadly supported (as opposed to charities that are supported chiefly by a single family or business entity) may make expenditures to influence legislation amounting to 20 percent of their total expenditures in any taxable year, subject to a maxi-mum of $1 million per year for the largest organizations. Since Planet Water in-tended to work for the passage of pro-environment legislation, it notified the Internal Revenue Service, in its application for tax exemption, that it would en-gage in lobbying activity to the extent permitted by law.

Although American tax-exempt charitable organizations are subject to these limits on their political activity, they are nonetheless free to engage in activities that in many other countries would be considered political. For example, Planet Water has sponsored rallies, parades, and other law-abiding demonstrations op-posing the pollution of the oceans. It regularly buys full-page advertisements in major newspapers to advocate its views. It has led international consumer boycotts of products that endanger marine life. The activities of Planet Water in attempting to change the attitudes and behavior of all sectors of society—business, government, nonprofit, and citizens—are intended to target power relationships between and within those sectors. Its activities are political in the most fundamental sense. So long as it refrains from involvement in campaigns for public office and complies with the limits on its lobbying expenditures, however, the political activities of Planet Water, like those of other American charities, are limited only by the willingness of its supporters to finance them.

OPERATION

The operation of a nonprofit charitable organization typically means that the organization provides a service or set of services (often called programs), attracts members (though some nonprofit organizations do not have legally recognized members except for the board of directors), has a governing body, employs staff, and manages its finances. All of these operations are affected by laws and regulations.

Program

Since its formation, Planet Water's activities have become extensive. All are reviewed each year by its board of directors. Old programs are continued or dropped, and new ones added, and all are tested by whether they advance the goals of oceanic environmental education and constituency building.

Research has become an important component of its program. Planet Water has designed and is conducting a five-year study of San Francisco Bay and of Chesapeake Bay for the purpose of developing a scientific baseline against which to measure the environmental health of those bodies of water. Both studies are funded by the federal government.

Planet Water conducts an extensive public education program. It offers a training course in marine environmental policy issues for volunteers. There are about 425 volunteers, each of whom makes a commitment to give ten speeches a year. Planet Water publishes, in seven languages, a quarterly magazine and widely popular books that are filled with handsome photographs and informative articles on ocean themes. It has produced numerous related television programs.

Children are not overlooked. Planet Water publishes an ocean science curriculum for elementary school teachers. It commissions and publishes books for children designed to acquaint them with the world's oceans, and each summer it operates a sea camp for children at eight coastal locations. After a flurry of publicity in the national press about the killing of dolphins, Planet Water launched an "adopt-a-dolphin" campaign, which has resulted in the formation of Dolphin Clubs for schoolchildren across America.

Active in lobbying nationally and internationally, Planet Water has been credited with contributing significantly to the International Whaling Commission's global ban on whaling and the enactment of the Clean Water Act and the Ocean Dumping Ban Act.

Planet Water also makes modest grants in support of water-related environmental activities of other groups, both foreign and domestic.

Planet Water receives donations from the public and grants from other charities, but most of its income is generated by its own activities, including publications and government contracts. It is entirely legal and proper in the United States for a charitable organization to charge a reasonable fee for goods or services it provides. However, its activities must be conducted in a noncommercial manner, and the conduct of those activities (not just the use to which the proceeds are put) must be substantially related to the accomplishment of the charity's exempt purpose. If not, the organization may be taxed on the proceeds of the activity at corporate rates. Furthermore, an organization's tax exemption may be revoked if its unrelated business activities are so extensive in comparison with its charitable activities that the organization fails to carry out a charitable program reasonably commensurate with its financial resources.

During its annual review of Planet Water's programs, the board of directors examines each program to determine whether it satisfies these standards. In considering Planet Water's magazine, for example, the board determined that the magazine helps Planet Water advance its educational purposes by informing a wide audience about marine issues. But is it improperly commercial? Like many commercial publications, the magazine is well designed and filled with color photographs. But these graphic techniques help the magazine convey its educational message more effectively. The magazine is distributed through conventional commercial channels, including subscriptions and newsstand sales. But it is also made available at reduced rates to schools, libraries, and other public facilities. Moreover, the board has decided to continue to distribute foreign-language editions of the magazine, even though their costs far exceed the revenues derived from them, in order to reach a global audience with information about the global problem of marine pollution. The board concluded that publishing and distributing the magazine contributes substantially to the accomplishment of Planet Water's exempt purposes and that the magazine is not operated in a commercial manner.

In a market economy, the success of a business enterprise depends not only on the decisions made by its directors, officers, and staff but also on whether investors are willing to risk their money on the enterprise and on whether consumers are willing to buy the goods or services it produces. The economic dynamics of much of the charitable sector are similar. Planet Water will survive only if the public supports it, whether with volunteer time, donations of money, or purchases of the educational materials and services that Planet Water provides. Planet Water's staff and board, therefore, are constantly concerned with improving Planet Water's performance and level of response of the public to the organization itself, as well as in the marine issues it advocates.

In recent years, Planet Water has received, with increasing frequency, requests for grants from individuals and other smaller and sometimes informal environmental groups. After extensive consideration, the board of directors decided that an important part of Planet Water's mission was to support informal citizen-based environmental activity related to the oceans. The board agreed to set aside 5 percent of Planet Water's annual revenues to fund this effort. Each year, the board grants a total of $1 million, usually in amounts of $5,000 or less.

Planet Water has adopted a written grant procedure that provides that it will consider proposals for support of emerging charitable organizations and informal groups engaged in activities to preserve oceans, lakes, and rivers. The written proposal must describe the problem to which the organization or group is responding, and it must also contain a description of the activities the grantee intends to conduct, including a budget that shows, in detail, how the money requested will be spent to carry out those activities. The staff of Planet Water reviews all proposals received and recommends to the board of directors those that it believes should be funded. The board considers them at its quarterly meetings. Planet Water receives far more proposals than it is able to fund, even with $250,000 available each quarter. Last year, the staff recommended to the board only one out of every ten proposals it received. The board, in turn, funded about 80 percent of the proposals recommended to it by the staff.

Once a grant is approved, the staff sends a letter to the grantee, advising it of the grant award and enclosing a check. The grantee is required to submit periodic written reports to Planet Water, explaining how the grant is being spent and how those expenditures are consistent with the representations made by the grantee in its proposal.

When Planet Water received its federal tax exemption as a charitable organization, it was also classified by the IRS as a public charity, based on its representation that it would have a broad base of financial support. As a public charity, Planet Water is not limited in making grants to organizations that have achieved formal recognition of their charitable and tax-exempt status. It may make grants to support any activity that furthers its own charitable purposes, whether that activity is conducted by a formal charitable organization, an informal group, a business, or an individual. If the grantee is not a formal charity, however, Planet Water must restrict the grant to charitable purposes and must require written reports so that it can be assured that the grant was used for a proper charitable purpose and not for a personal or business purpose. So long as it adheres to these standards, Planet Water may make grants abroad as well as in the United States.

Membership

Planet Water now has three hundred thousand members worldwide, who pay annual dues of $25 each. They receive a quarterly magazine and are invited to attend the annual meeting at which the Rankins, who serve as joint executive directors, report on the current status and future prospects of Planet Water. It has chapters in major coastal cities in the United States and affiliates in twelve other countries. Members vote by mail for directors to fill terms that have expired.

Planet Water's bylaws provide that a member is anyone whose current dues are paid. Over three hundred thousand people around the world have paid their annual dues for the current year and have the right, under the bylaws, to vote for members of the board of directors. They also receive Planet Water's magazine.

Planet Water is not required by law to have voting members. California law permits a public benefit corporation like Planet Water to operate with a self-perpetuating board of directors, and most of them do so, often giving donors the honorary title of "member." Vacancies on the boards of such corporations are filled by the vote of the remaining directors rather than by members.

But Planet Water's members are more than honorary because they have the right to vote for directors. California law gives such members the right not only to vote for directors but also to nominate them. The consent of the membership is required if the board wants to remove a director. Planet Water's members also have the rights to receive annual reports on its finances; to inspect and copy its tax returns, minutes, and other records; to vote on the manner in which its assets will be distributed upon dissolution, termination, or merger with another corporation; to receive written notice a reasonable time in advance of any membership meeting; to sue to protect the charity against wrongful acts by its directors; to vote on amendments to the charity's articles of incorporation; and to vote on bylaw amendments that would affect their rights as members.

Despite the presence of these rights, however, voting members of a public benefit corporation are not personally responsible for the charity's debts, liabilities, or other obligations. And members are not personally liable for improper actions of directors, unless the member personally benefits from such an act.

Unlike stockholders of a business, voting members of a public benefit corporation do not own the corporation, nor do they have any right to its assets. Their rights pertain to governance and access to information about the organization. The corporation's assets are held in charitable trust, for the benefit of the public.

Governing Body

The governing body of Planet Water is its board of directors. Except for the Rankins, who are paid as staff members and who have been elected to the board on a continuing basis over the years, the fifteen board members serve without compensation.

They are, however, reimbursed for their travel, meal, and lodging expenses in connection with attending board meetings. The board meets quarterly, in January, April, July, and October. At the July meeting, the board reviews the goals and objectives of the organization and makes, usually on recommendation of the Rankins, the modifications it believes to be suitable. At the October meeting, the board reviews and approves the program and financial budget for each quarter of the next year. At the following year's meetings, the primary task of the board, apart from developing the budget for the new year, is to review the program and financial performance of the organization in comparison with the budget, to consider policy issues put before them by the two executive directors, and to approve grants.

Between board meetings, policy decisions are made by an executive committee consisting of the four officers who are also board members. The day-to-day management decisions are made by the Rankins in accordance with the program and financial budget approved by the board of directors.

Asked to say whether the board or the staff ran Planet Water, an impartial observer would probably say that the staff did. After all, the board meets only four times a year, and then only to set policy, to adopt a budget, and to make grants. But under the law, it is the board who is responsible for the operations of the organization. The organizational role of the staff is to carry out the policies set by the board.

State law defines the responsibilities of Planet Water's directors in broad terms. Like directors of other public benefit corporations in California, they must act in good faith and in the best interest of the charity, with the same degree of thoughtfulness that a reasonable person would apply to the decision-making process. In traditional legal terms, directors owe the corporation a duty of loyalty and a duty of care. If directors adhere to this standard in performing their duties as directors, they will not be penalized personally for acts or omissions that turn out later to have been mistaken.

The distinction between board responsibility and staff management can produce unexpected results. Suppose, for example, that the staff member in charge of payroll fails to pay the employment taxes on time, and the government assesses fines and penalties against Planet Water. The attorney general of California will automatically demand that the individual members of the board of directors, not the employee, personally reimburse Planet Water for the charitable dollars lost to the organization due to the payment of those fines. This is because, under the law, it is the directors, rather than the staff, who are responsible for the acts of the organization. So long as the directors can demonstrate that they acted responsibly (by, for example, requiring the staff to keep and monitor a calendar of all filing dates), they will probably not be penalized.

The day-to-day decisions about Planet Water's operations are made by its joint executive directors and other senior staff members. They consult with the executive committee on major decisions between board meetings, but the board is generally not involved in these decisions except to ratify actions previously au-thorized by the executive committee. The board, with fifteen members who are geographically dispersed, is simply too cumbersome a body to respond quickly. State law generally leaves the organization free to decide how many directors it will have (California law requires a minimum of one director). As an organiza-tion becomes larger, however, the size of its board of directors tends to follow suit, since the practice is to bring people onto the board who are resourceful and who are in a position to contribute expertise or other resources, including money.

Directors, as we have seen, owe a duty of loyalty to the charity: they must put the best interests of the charitable organization before any personal benefit to themselves. But a charity is not prohibited from dealing with a board mem-ber in his or her professional capacity. Planet Water's board, for example, in-cludes its attorney, Susan Cohen; Larry Yee, who owns the public relations agency that produces Planet Water's advocacy advertisements and direct mail appeals; and Jim and Beth Rankin, its founders and codirectors—all of whom are compensated for the professional services they render. Rather than bar a charity from benefiting from the expertise of its board members, California law allows such transactions, so long as the interested director—that is, the direc-tor with a financial stake in the transaction—discloses all the material facts to the other directors and they alone decide that the benefit to the corporation out-weighs the benefit to the individual director.

At least four of Planet Water's fifteen directors are interested directors. Cali-fornia law permits such interested directors to serve on the board, but only if they make up no more than 49 percent. In practice, the founders of a new or-ganization may have difficulty attracting a sufficient number of outside direc-tors. The hope of the founders is that their cause will have sufficient public appeal that the increase in activities will lead to greater outside recognition and an expansion of the number of resourceful supporters who will be willing to volunteer time to serve as board members and in other capacities.

Some foundations follow a policy of refusing to make grants to organizations that have employees on their boards. The laudable purpose of that policy is to strengthen the independence of the board. The unfortunate consequence, how-ever, is that deserving charities may be disqualified simply because they are at an early stage in their development.

Staff

The paid staff of Planet Water now consists of 312 people, ranging from accountants to zoologists. When employees are hired, they are given three documents: a letter containing a description of their duties and their salary, a personnel policy describing the health plan and retirement and other benefits, and an evaluation form. Each year, the board of directors reviews and sets the salary and benefits for the Rankins.

The compensation for all other employees is decided as the result of an annual evaluation by the two executive directors, subject to review and approval by the board. In determining the appropriate amount of salary and benefits, the Rankins rely on an annual compensation survey published by a national nonprofit management organization. From that survey, they determine the range within which other non-profit organizations of comparable size pay their employees for performing compa-rable tasks. The amount paid to the employee within that range by Planet Water will depend on how well the employee has fared in the evaluation.

A charitable organization is not exempt from the extensive body of federal, state, and local labor law regulating employment. Planet Water must comply with laws requiring that the amount of wages paid to employees meet a certain min-imum standard. It must pay the employees additional compensation if they work more than an eight-hour day or a forty-hour week. California and San Francisco have stronger antidiscrimination laws than the federal government. Those laws, taken together, prohibit Planet Water from discriminating on the basis of race, religion, national origin, sex, sexual orientation, physical or men-tal disability, and age in the hiring, promotion, or termination of employees.

One type of law applies only to employees of a charitable organization: laws limiting the amount of compensation that an employee may receive. Federal and state laws prohibit the payment of excessive compensation to employees of charitable organizations. The compensation they receive must be reasonable in relation to the services they perform. There is, by comparison, no such restric-tion on the amount of compensation that may be received by employees of busi-ness organizations.

An individual who wants to engage in a particular activity must take this lim-itation into account when deciding whether to conduct that activity as a charity or as a business. For example, suppose that a teacher wants to form a school to teach foreign languages, and suppose further that the salary range for language teach-ers in nonprofit schools in her area is $20,000 to $40,000. If the teacher wants her school to be a charity, she must be content with receiving a salary within that range. On the other hand, she is free to form her school as a business, instead, and to receive as much compensation as her business can generate.

Finances

The finances of Planet Water, which were precarious indeed at the beginning, have now stabilized. Its annual revenues are about $20 million, made up of dues and fees (40 percent), book sales (16 percent), individual contributions (13 percent), government contracts (8 percent), royalty income (7 percent), investment income (6 percent), joint-venture income (5 percent), foundation grants (4 percent), and corporate contributions (1 percent).

Dues and fees are paid by members and participants. At $25 each, three hundred thousand members generate dues of $7.5 million. Parents of the two thousand children who attend the summer sea camp pay a fee of $250 per child.

The source of the income from book sales is Planet Water's extensive program of publishing educational books on the ocean environment.

Individual contributions are derived mainly from direct mail campaigns. Each year, Planet Water conducts four campaigns, reaching twenty million households. The core of the solicitation for funds is often a copy of a recent Planet Water advertisement in the *New York Times* dramatizing the consequences of an oil spill or other environmental catastrophe at sea. Over the years, as the public has learned more about the effective work of Planet Water, the amount of bequests has also increased.

The government contracts include, in addition to the bay studies, the service of Planet Water as portkeeper of four coastal ports to monitor compliance with restrictions on the discharge of pollutants into the waters of those ports by shipping, industry, and local governments.

Planet Water receives extensive royalty income. It licenses the use of its name and logo to approved manufacturers of over one hundred products, ranging from T-shirts to windsurfers, in return for a 3 percent fee or royalty based on the gross receipts from sales.

Planet Water's fund balance is now $5 million. Investment decisions are made by the board of directors on recommendation of the finance committee. The funds of Planet Water available for investment are allocated equally among four outside investment managers. Once a year, the committee meets with its advisers to review their investment performance. The board of directors has instituted a policy of replacing, every third year, the investment adviser with the poorest performance record.

Planet Water is also engaged in a joint venture with a commercial organization. They are partners in the design, manufacturing, and marketing of submersible vehicles that are used to gather data on pollution beneath the ocean surface. The vehicles are also sold to the public for recreational use.

Grants from foundations have increased each year, although they remain a small percentage of overall receipts. The amount of corporate contributions has not improved in recent years.

Except for joint-venture income, the sources of financing for Planet Water are fairly representative of a large nonprofit environmental organization. The amount and types of funds received will differ, of course, from organization to organization. A large performing arts organization, such as a symphony orchestra or an opera, would typically receive much of its support from ticket sales, but significant amounts would also come from government and foundation grants, individual and corporate contributions, and investment income. A charitable organization providing a social service, such as housing advice to the poor, would in the past have been supported primarily by government grants. Due to reduced government funding, however, that organization would now be supported, at a reduced level, by foundation and corporate grants and individual contributions.

Most of Planet Water's income is exempt from federal and California income taxes. Even the income that may appear to be commercial in nature—from book sales, government contracts, royalties, and investments—will probably qualify as tax-free to Planet Water. Commercial income requiring no significant activity on the part of the charity to produce it, such as income from investment and royalties, is not subject to the unrelated-business tax. The commercial income that does involve sustained activity, such as the sale of books or the performance of government contracts, qualifies for that reason as business income. Since the activities of publishing environmental books and conducting environmental research further the purpose of Planet Water, they generate related business income, which is not subject to the tax imposed on unrelated business income.

The joint-venture income, from the sale for recreational use of the submersible vehicles, would be taxed as unrelated business income. Income from the sale or rental of such vehicles for environmental research purposes would probably be treated as related income because of its connection to Planet Water's purposes and would therefore not be subject to tax.

The direct mail campaign is a form of solicitation for charitable contributions. There is, as yet, no federal regulation of such solicitation. There is an enormous diversity of laws at the state and local level, however. In California alone, more than two hundred cities and counties have enacted laws regulating charitable solicitations. Before Planet Water solicits funds either by mail or door-to-door, it must review the laws of the particular localities and states where it will be soliciting. Those rules often require a charity to register with a governmental agency and to disclose its program and its finances. Charities, like businesses and individuals, may not obtain money by fraud or misrepresentation. The government may not regulate charitable solicitation without restriction. Charitable fundraising is an exercise of constitutionally protected free speech, and in recent decisions, the U.S. Supreme Court has struck down state and local laws regulating charitable solicitation on the grounds that they were unduly restrictive of free speech.

The investment of charitable funds is regulated primarily at the state level. Most states require the governing body of the charity to make its assets productive. This means that the surplus funds of the charity must be invested prudently and may not be allowed to lie idle. For example, members of the board of directors of a California charitable foundation were fined by a court because they allowed foundation funds to remain in a non-interest-bearing checking account in excess of the amount needed to meet current expenditures. The court required them to pay to the foundation the amount of interest that the foundation would have received had its excess funds been deposited in a savings account.

State laws do not ordinarily specify which types of investments a charitable organization must choose. California does, however, regulate the process by which the choice is made: it requires the directors to exercise reasonable and prudent judgment. In addition, many states have laws that, like California's, protect the members of boards of directors from liability that might otherwise arise as a consequence of unwise investment decisions, so long as the decisions are made on the basis of advice from a competent professional investment manager.

COMPLIANCE

Each year, Planet Water must submit reports to tax and regulatory agencies. Annually, at the federal level, Planet Water must file a report with the Internal Revenue Service, setting forth its receipts and expenditures, explaining the general nature of its activities, and disclosing the name of each large contributor and each director, officer, top official, highly compensated employee, and consultant. The report discloses the salaries and benefits provided to highly compensated employees.

Each year, at the state level, Planet Water must file similar reports with the California Franchise Tax Board and the Registry of Charitable Trusts. It must also disclose the names of its current officers to the secretary of state.

At the local level, Planet Water must file an annual form with the City and County of San Francisco to qualify for an exemption from property tax on any land, buildings, and office equipment that it owns in San Francisco. Planet Water must describe the nature of its property and explain how it is used in carrying out its charitable purpose.

Each quarter during the year, Planet Water must file with federal and state tax authorities a form that describes the amount of income and other taxes it has withheld from the salaries of its employees and paid to the tax authorities.

Planet Water must comply with separate charitable solicitation laws imposed by most states and by some cities, which require that all charitable organizations that raise funds in their area must register and report on a periodic basis with the appropriate authority.

Recently, antiterrorist laws adopted in response to the tragedy of September 11, 2001, impose new due diligence procedures for charitable organizations in the conduct of its domestic and international activities.

Government review of a charitable organization occurs most commonly in connection with the annual reports filed by a charity. Random audits are made of those reports. In recent years, sophisticated computer programs have been designed by tax and charitable regulatory agencies. Those programs are applied to the reports to identify legal compliance issues from the information contained in them. An organization may also be selected for audit because of a complaint made by an individual or because a newspaper article describing improper charitable activity comes to the attention of the government agency.

If a charitable organization's report is selected for audit, a government auditor may schedule a visit to the office of the organization. The auditor is empowered to examine any document and to interview any person connected with the charitable organization. Despite this extensive audit power, most charitable organizations have never been audited by any government organization. When they do occur, most audits take no more than a few days, assuming that no serious violation of law is uncovered. In most cases, the result of an audit is a "no change" letter, indicating that the organization is in compliance with the laws and regulations of the governmental agency conducting the audit.

On September 23, 2001, the President issued Executive Order 13224, declaring a national emergency and prohibiting the donation of money, food, clothing, or medicine to specified donees. Within a month thereafter, Congress enacted the USA PATRIOT Act. Those measures list specially designated nationals, blocked persons, and allegedly terrorist organizations and criminalize the knowing provision of material support and resources to them.

TERMINATION

The board of directors does not plan to terminate Planet Water. The directors believe there is a continuing need for its work. Its goals, they have concluded, are not likely to be realized in the foreseeable future.

In a recent interview, Beth Rankin was asked how she would know when Planet Water had accomplished its mission. "No one is more aware than I am," she said, "that the changes in public attitudes toward the environment have not been due solely to our modest efforts. We happened on an idea whose time had come. On the other hand, I am convinced that we have made some difference. But there is still a long way to go. I will know that we have reached our goal," she concluded, "when the act of polluting water that belongs to everyone is every bit as socially unacceptable as fouling the water you serve in your own home."

The determination of when a charitable organization should end its existence is ordinarily a private matter, made not by the state but by the governing body of the organization.

The government has extensive powers in the event of abuse, but the exercise of those powers is surrounded with important protections.

On the federal level, for example, the Internal Revenue Service has the power to in effect terminate the existence of a nonprofit organization by proposing to revoke its tax exemption. Revocation is proper only if specific violations of law have occurred, such as failing to conduct legitimate charitable activities, conducting activities in a manner that confers an improper economic benefit on an individual, or engaging in excessive lobbying or electioneering. In the event of a proposed revocation, the organization has extensive rights to present evidence and to oppose that action within the IRS. If the IRS is unpersuaded, the organization can challenge the proposed IRS action in court.

At the state level, the powers of the tax agency and the protections of the organization are similar. In addition, the state attorney general has extensive powers to investigate the activities of a charitable organization to ensure that it complies with the law. The attorney general, however, has no power to act against the organization independently. If that office discovers violations of law and decides to impose penalties over the charity's objections, the attorney general must take the charity to court. The court, not the attorney general, will decide, after a full trial, whether the organization has violated the law, whether a penalty or other remedy should be imposed under the law, and if so, what the appropriate remedy or penalty should be. Nevertheless, due to the cost of litigation and the potential of harmful adverse publicity, most disputes between charities and state attorneys general are resolved by settlement rather than by litigation.

If the organization voluntarily dissolves or terminates and has money or property, those assets must, in California and in most other states, be distributed by the organization to another charitable organization with similar purposes. The attorney general reviews all proposed terminations to ensure that charities comply with this rule. For example, if Planet Water's directors voted to end the organization's existence, they could distribute its assets only to other charitable tax-exempt organizations whose purpose was to protect and preserve marine life and the oceans in general. If they wanted to distribute a portion of Planet Water's assets to organizations working on other important social problems, such as homelessness, the attorney general would step in to prevent it. This is because under the law of charitable trusts, a charity's assets must be used for the purpose stated in its governing document, unless that purpose becomes illegal, impossible, or, in some states, impracticable. Environmental protection, Planet Water's purpose, will no doubt remain viable for the foreseeable future.

CHAPTER FOUR

The Changing Context of
American Nonprofit Management

Lester M. Salamon

The nonprofit sector has long been the hidden subcontinent on the social landscape of American life, regularly revered but seldom seriously scrutinized or understood. In part, this has been due to the role that these organizations play in our national mythologies and in the political ideologies that have been constructed on them. Indeed, a lively ideological contest has long raged over the extent to which we can rely on nonprofit institutions to handle critical public needs, with conservatives focusing laserlike on the sector's strengths to fend off calls for greater reliance on government and liberals often restricting their attention to its weaknesses instead to justify calls for greater government action. Through it all, though largely unheralded and perhaps unrecognized by either side, a classically American compromise has taken shape. This compromise was forged early in the nation's history, but it was broadened and solidified in the 1960s. Under it, nonprofit organizations in an ever-widening range of fields were made the beneficiaries of government support to provide a growing array of services—from health care to scientific research—that Americans wanted but were reluctant to have government provide directly (Salamon and Abramson, 1982; Salamon, 1987; Smith and Lipsky, 1993). More

This chapter draws heavily on Lester M. Salamon, *The Resilient Sector: The State of Nonprofit America* (Washington, D.C.: Brookings Institution Press, 2002).

than any other single factor, this government-nonprofit partnership is responsible for the emergence of the U.S. nonprofit sector in the shape we see it in today.

During the past twenty years, however, that compromise has come under considerable assault. At the same time, the country's nonprofit institutions have faced an extraordinary range of other challenges as well—significant demographic shifts, fundamental changes in public policy and public attitudes, new commercial impulses, growing competition from for-profit providers, shifts in the basic structure of key industries in which nonprofits are involved, massive technological developments, and changes in lifestyle, to cite just a few. Although nonprofit America has responded creatively to many of these challenges, the responses have pulled it in directions that are at best not well understood and at worst corrosive of the sector's special character and role.

This changing context has fundamentally shaped the nature of contemporary nonprofit operations. No serious understanding of nonprofit leadership and management can proceed very far, therefore, without taking this changing context into account.

The purpose of this chapter is to examine some of the salient features of this changing context of nonprofit action. To do so, the discussion falls into three parts. The first part examines some of the major challenges that American nonprofit organizations have confronted over the recent past and some of the opportunities they have also had available to them. The second part then assesses the implications these challenges and opportunities have had for nonprofit managers and how the sector's leaders and organizations have responded. The final part identifies the risks that these responses have brought with them and the steps that may be needed to reduce them.

The basic impression that emerges from this analysis is a message of *resilience,* of a set of institutions and traditions that has been facing enormous challenges and also important opportunities but has been finding ways to respond to both, often with considerable creativity and resolve. Indeed, nonprofit America appears to be well along in a fundamental process of "reengineering" that calls to mind the similar process that large segments of America's business sector has undergone since the late 1980s (Hammer and Champy, 1993; Carr and Johnson, 1995). Facing an increasingly competitive and changing environment, nonprofit organizations and the institutions and traditions that support them have been called on to make fundamental changes in the way they operate. And that is just what they have been doing.

Like all processes of change, this one has been far from even. Some organizations have been swept up in the winds of change while others have hardly felt a breeze or, having felt it, have not been in a position to respond. What is more, it is far from clear which group has made the right decision or left the sector as a whole better off because the consequences of some of the changes are far from certain and at any rate are mixed.

CHALLENGES AND OPPORTUNITIES: THE CHANGING CONTEXT OF NONPROFIT ACTION

Nonprofit America has endured an extraordinary time of testing in the recent past. To be sure, it is not alone in this. For-profit corporations and governments have also experienced enormous challenges over the past twenty years. But the challenges that nonprofit organizations face are especially daunting since they go to the heart of this sector's operations and raise questions about its very existence. Fortunately, however, the sector has also enjoyed a variety of important opportunities. Let us examine this mixture of challenges and opportunities, which has been shaping the context of nonprofit action and seems likely to continue to do so.

Challenges

The recent challenges faced by nonprofit organizations in the United States can be grouped for convenience under four main headings: the fiscal challenge, the competitive challenge, the effectiveness challenge, and the technology challenge.

The Fiscal Challenge. First of all, nonprofits have had to cope with a significant fiscal squeeze. To be sure, fiscal distress has been a way of life for this sector throughout its history. But this eased significantly during World War II, and even more so in the 1960s, when the federal government expanded its funding, first, of scientific research and then of a wide range of health and social services. What is not widely recognized is that the government efforts to stimulate science and overcome poverty and ill health during this period relied heavily on nonprofit organizations for their operation, following a pattern that had been established early in our nation's history (Whitehead, 1973; Warner, 1894). Consequently, by the late 1970s, federal support to American nonprofit organizations outdistanced private charitable support by a factor of 2 to 1, and state and local governments provided additional aid. What is more, this support percolated through a wide swath of the sector, providing needed financial nourishment to colleges, universities, hospitals, health clinics, day care centers, nursing homes, residential treatment facilities, employment and training centers, family service agencies, drug abuse prevention programs, and many more. Indeed, much of the modern nonprofit sector took shape during this period as a direct outgrowth of expanded government support (Salamon and Abramson, 1982; Salamon, 1995).

Federal Retrenchment. This widespread pattern of government support to nonprofit organizations suffered a severe shock, however, in the early 1980s. Committed to a policy of fiscal restraint and seemingly unaware of the extent to which public resources were underwriting private nonprofit action, the Reagan administration launched a significant assault on federal spending in precisely the areas where federal support to nonprofit organizations was most extensive—social and human services, education and training, community development, and nonhospital health. Although the budget cuts that occurred during this period were nowhere near as severe as originally proposed, federal support to nonprofit organizations, outside of Medicare and Medicaid, the large federal health finance programs, declined by approximately 25 percent in real-dollar terms in the early 1980s and did not return to its 1980 level until the late 1990s (Abramson, Salamon, and Steurle, 1999). Although some state governments boosted their own spending in many of these areas, the increases were not sufficient to offset the federal reductions. Indeed, outside of pensions, public education, and health, overall government social welfare spending declined by more than $30 billion between 1981 and 1989. Nonprofit organizations in the fields of community development, employment and training, social services, and community health were particularly hard-hit by these reductions.

Although, as we will see, these fiscal pressures eased significantly during the 1990s, the experience of the 1980s and early 1990s left a lingering financial scar. That scar has been reopened in the early years of the new century by a combination of tax reductions, economic recession, and increased military and antiterrorism spending that is causing new cutbacks in health, education, and social welfare funding and hence new pressures on nonprofit finances (Wilgoren, 2003; Rosenbaum, 2003).

From Producer to Consumer Subsidies: The Changing Forms of Public Support.
Not just the amount but also the form of government support to the nonprofit sector changed during this period. For one thing, during the 1980s and 1990s, government program managers were encouraged to promote for-profit involvement in government contract work, including that for human services (Kettl, 1993). More significant, instead of relying on producer-side subsidies like grants and contracts to finance services, the federal government shifted to forms of assistance such as vouchers and tax expenditures that channel aid to the consumers of services instead, thus requiring nonprofits to compete for clients in the market, where for-profits have traditionally had the edge (Salamon, 2002c). Already by 1980, the majority (53 percent) of federal assistance to nonprofit organizations took the form of such consumer subsidies, much of it through the Medicare and Medicaid programs. By 1986, this stood at 70 percent, and it continued to rise into the 1990s (Salamon, 1995, p. 208).

In part, this shift toward consumer subsidies resulted from the concentration of the budget cuts of the 1980s on the so-called discretionary spending programs, which tended to be producer-side grant and contract programs, while Medicare and Medicaid—both of them consumer-side subsidies—continued to grow. In part also, however, the shift toward consumer-side subsidies reflected the ascendance of conservative political forces that favored forms of assistance that maximized consumer choice in the marketplace. The price of securing conservative support for new or expanded programs of relevance to nonprofit organizations in the late 1980s and early 1990s, therefore, was to make them vouchers or tax expenditures. The new Child Care and Development block grant enacted in 1990 and then reauthorized and expanded as part of the welfare reform legislation in 1996, for example, specifically gave states the option to use the $5 billion in federal funds provided for day care to finance voucher payments to eligible families rather than grants or contracts to day care providers, and most states exercised this option. By 1998, well over 80 percent of the children receiving day care assistance under this program were receiving it through such voucher certificates, and an additional $2 billion in federal day care subsidies was delivered through a special child care tax credit (U.S. House of Representatives, 2000, pp. 912, 923). Nearly $7 billion was thus provided in new consumer-side day care subsidies, much more than the $2.8 billion allocated for producer-side subsidies to social service providers for day care and all other forms of social services under the federal government's Social Services block grant. Nonprofit day care providers, like their counterparts in other fields, were thus thrown increasingly into the private market to secure even public funding for their activities. In the process, they were obliged to master complex billing and reimbursement systems and to learn how to "market" their services to potential "customers." Worse yet, the reimbursement rates in many of these programs have often failed to keep pace with rising costs, putting a further squeeze on nonprofit budgets and making it harder to sustain mission-critical functions such as advocacy and charity care (Gray and Schlesinger, 2002).

Not only did government support to nonprofit organizations change its form during this period, but so did important elements of private support. The most notable development here was the emergence of "managed care" in the health field, displacing the traditional pattern of fee-for-service medicine. By 1997, close to 75 percent of the employees in medium and large establishments and 62 percent of the employees in small establishments were covered by some type of managed care plan (U.S. Census Bureau, 2000, p. 119). More recently, managed care has expanded into the social services field, subjecting nonprofit drug treatment, rehabilitation service, and mental health treatment facilities to the same competitive pressures and reimbursement limits that hospitals have been confronting.

Tepid Growth of Private Giving. Adding to the fiscal pressure nonprofits have been facing has been the continued inability of private philanthropy to offset cutbacks in government support and to finance expanded nonprofit responses to community needs. To be sure, private giving has grown considerably over the recent past. But giving for human service, arts, education, health, and advocacy activities lagged behind the overall growth of the economy (62 percent versus 81 percent after adjusting for inflation). Indeed, as a share of personal income, private giving has been declining steadily in the United States, from an average of 1.89 percent in the early 1970s down to 1.75 percent in the early 1980s and 1.64 percent in the early to mid-1990s (Salamon, 2002b, p. 14). Although this trend was reversed in the boom times of the late 1990s, it has resumed its downward course (AAFRC Trust for Philanthropy, 2001, p. 170). As a consequence, private philanthropy has actually lost ground as a share of total nonprofit income, falling from 18 percent of the total outside of religion in 1977 to 12 percent in 1997 (Salamon, 2002b, p. 14).

The Competitive Challenge. In addition to a fiscal challenge, nonprofit America has also faced a serious competitive challenge. This, too, is not a wholly new development. But the changing forms of public sector support coupled with the difficulties nonprofit organizations have confronted in securing capital for new technologies seem to have enticed for-profit competitors into an ever-widening range of fields and to have given them a competitive edge. Thus, as shown in Table 4.1, the nonprofit share of day care jobs dropped from 52 percent to 38 percent between 1982 and 1997, a decline of some 27 percent. Similarly sharp declines in the relative nonprofit share occurred among rehabilitation hospitals, home health agencies, health maintenance organizations, kidney dialysis centers, mental health clinics, and hospices. In many of these fields, the absolute number of nonprofit facilities continued to grow, but the for-profit growth outpaced it. And in at least one crucial field—acute care hospitals—while the nonprofit *share* increased slightly, a significant reduction occurred in the *absolute number* of nonprofit (as well as public) facilities, so that the for-profit share of the total increased even more.

The range of for-profit firms competing with nonprofits has grown increasingly broad, moreover. For example, the recent welfare reform legislation, which seeks to move large numbers of welfare recipients from welfare dependence to employment, attracted defense contractors like Lockheed-Martin into the social welfare field. What these firms offer is less knowledge of human services than information-processing technology and contract management skills gained from serving as master contractors on huge military system projects, precisely the skills now needed to manage the subcontracting systems required to prepare welfare recipients for work. Even the sacrosanct field of charitable fundraising has recently experienced a significant for-profit incursion in the form of financial service firms such as Fidelity and Merrill Lynch. By 2000, the Fidelity Charitable Gift Fund had attracted more assets than the nation's largest community foundation and had distributed three times as much in grants (AAFRC Trust for Philanthropy, 2001, p. 53).

Table 4.1. Growing For-Profit Competition in Selected Fields, 1982–1997.

Dimension and Field	Percentage Nonprofit		Percentage Change in Relative Nonprofit Share
	1982	*1997*	
Employment			
Child day care	52	38	−27
Job training	93	89	−4
Individual and family services	94	91	−3
Home health	60	28	−53
Kidney dialysis centers	22	15	−32
Facilities, participation			
Dialysis centers	58[a]	32	−45
Rehabilitation hospitals	70[a]	36	−50
Home health agencies	64[a]	33	−48
Health maintenance organizations	65[a]	26	−60
Residential treatment facilities for children	87[b]	68	−22
Psychiatric hospitals	19[a]	16	−16
Hospices	89[c]	76	−15
Mental health clinics	64[b]	57	−11
Higher education enrollments	96	89	−7
Nursing homes	20[b]	28	+40
Acute care hospitals	58[a]	59	+2

[a]Initial year for data is 1985, not 1982.

[b]Initial year for data is 1986, not 1982.

[c]Initial year for data is 1992.

Sources: U.S. Census Bureau, 1999; Gray and Schlesinger, 2002; National Center for Education Statistics, 2000.

The Effectiveness Challenge. One consequence of the increased competition nonprofits are facing has been to intensify the pressure on them to perform and to demonstrate that performance. This runs counter to long-standing theories in the nonprofit field that have emphasized this sector's distinctive advantage precisely in fields where "information asymmetry" makes it difficult to demonstrate performance and where "trust" is consequently needed instead (Hansmann, 1981).

In the current climate, however, such theories have few remaining adherents, at least among those who control the sector's purse strings. Government managers, themselves under pressure to demonstrate results because of the recent Government Performance and Results Act, are increasingly pressing their nonprofit contractors to deliver measurable results too. Not to be outdone, prominent philanthropic institutions have jumped onto the performance bandwagon. United Way of America, for example, launched a bold performance measurement system in the mid-1990s complete with Web site, performance measurement manual, and video in order to induce member agencies to require performance measurement as a condition of local funding. Numerous foundations have moved in a similar direction, increasing the emphasis on evaluation both of their grantees and of their own programming (Porter and Kramer, 1999). In addition, a new "venture philanthropy" model stressing focused attention on performance measures has been gaining notoriety and adherents (Letts, Ryan, and Grossman, 1997). Chapters Fourteen and Sixteen of this book provide detailed reviews of various approaches to conceiving and measuring the effectiveness of programs and overall nonprofit organizational effectiveness.

The Technology Challenge. Pressures from for-profit competitors have also accelerated the demands on nonprofits to incorporate new technology into their operations. Indeed, technology has become one of the great wild cards in the evolution of the contemporary nonprofit sector, as it has of the contemporary for-profit and government sectors. Like the other challenges identified here, technology's impact is by no means wholly negative. For example, new information technology is increasing the capacity of nonprofits to advocate, reducing the costs of mobilizing constituents and connecting to policymakers and allies. Technology is also opening new ways to tap charitable contributions. The September 11 tragedy may well have marked a turning point in this regard: 10 percent of the funds raised came via the Internet (Wallace, 2001, p. 22). However, the extent to which nonprofits raise money online is highly variable.

But enticing as the opportunities opened by technological change may be to the nation's nonprofit institutions, they pose equally enormous challenges. This is due in important measure to the capital requirements that technology poses, requirements that are especially difficult for nonprofits to meet because of their inability to enter the equity markets and raise funds. But new technologies are also raising a variety of philosophical issues involving such matters as creative control and intellectual property rights in the arts (Wyszomirski, 2002).

Opportunities

But challenges are not the whole story. Nonprofits in America have been presented with a number of opportunities as well, owing to changes in demographics, philanthropy, visibility, and government spending.

Social and Demographic Shifts. In the first place, nonprofit America has been the beneficiary of a significant range of social and demographic shifts that have increased not only the need but also the demand for its services. Included here are the following:

- The doubling of the country's elderly population between 1960 and 2000 and the prospect that there will be four times as many elderly Americans in 2025 as there were in 1960, which will increase the need for nursing home and other elderly services

- The jump in the labor force participation rate for women, particularly married women, from less than 20 percent in 1960 to 64 percent in 1998, which translates into increased demand for child care services (U.S. Census Bureau, 2000, pp. 408–409)

- The doubling of the country's divorce rate, from one in every four marriages in the 1960s to one in every two marriages in the 1980s and thereafter, and the resulting sharp jump in the number of children involved in divorces, from less than 500,000 in 1960 to over one million per year in the 1980s and 1990s (U.S. Census Bureau, 2000, p. 101)

- A fivefold increase in the number of out-of-wedlock births, from roughly 225,000 in 1960 to more than 1,250,000 million per year by the mid-1990s, which has increased the need for a variety of work readiness, health, and child care services (U.S. Census Bureau, 2000, p. 71)

- The doubling that occurred in the number of refugees admitted to the United States, from 718,000 between 1966 and 1980 to 1.6 million during the next fifteen years (U.S. House of Representatives, 2000, p. 1363)

Taken together, these and other sociodemographic changes have expanded the demand for many of the services that nonprofit organizations have traditionally provided, such as child day care, home health and nursing home care for the elderly, family counseling, foster care, relocation assistance, and substance abuse treatment and prevention. The pressure on the foster care system alone, for example, has ballooned as the number of children in foster care doubled between the early 1980s and the early 1990s. At the same time, the welfare reform legislation enacted in 1996, with its stress on job readiness, created additional demand for the services that nonprofits typically offer. But the demand for these services has spread well beyond the poor and now encompasses middle-class households with resources to pay for them, a phenomenon that one analyst has called "the transformation of social services" (Gilbert, 1977).

The New Philanthropy. Also working to the benefit of the nonprofit sector are a series of developments potentially affecting private philanthropy. These include the intergenerational transfer of wealth between the Depression-era generation and the postwar baby boomers that is anticipated over the next forty years (Avery and Rendell, 1990; Havens and Schervish, 1999); the greater corporate willingness to engage in partnerships and collaborations with nonprofit organizations that has resulted from globalization (Smith, 1994; Nelson, 1996); the dot-com phenomenon, which accumulated substantial fortunes in the hands of a small group of high-tech entrepreneurs; and the new "venture philanthropy" mind-set that many of these new entrepreneurs have adopted. Together, these developments are injecting a substantial amount of new blood and new energy into the philanthropic field.

Greater Visibility and Policy Salience. Another factor working to the advantage of nonprofit organizations has been a spate of political and policy developments that has substantially increased their visibility. This has included the neoliberal ideology popularized by the Thatcher and Reagan regimes on both sides of the Atlantic, with their antigovernment rhetoric and emphasis on the private sector; the significant role that "civil society" organizations played in the collapse of communism in central Europe in the late 1980s; and the recent emphasis on the importance of "social capital" to the development of democracy and the market system.

Resumption of Government Social Welfare Spending Growth. Finally, and perhaps most important of all, government social welfare spending, which had stalled and in some cases reversed course in the early 1980s, resumed its growth in the late 1980s and into the 1990s. The principal reason for this was a steady broadening of eligibility and coverage under the basic federal entitlement programs—Medicare, Medicaid, and the Supplemental Security Income program (SSI). For example, the number of children covered by SSI, a program originally created to provide income support to the elderly poor, increased from seventy-one thousand in 1974 to over one million in 1996 largely as a result of aggressive efforts to enroll disabled children following a 1990 Supreme Court decision that liberalized SSI eligibility requirements. Medicaid coverage was extended to fifty distinct subgroups during the late 1980s and early 1990s, including various groups of women and children, the homeless, newly legalized aliens, people with AIDS, recipients of adoption assistance and foster care, and broader categories of the disabled and the elderly. Consequently, between 1980 and 1998, Medicaid coverage doubled, and the program was transformed from a relatively narrow health and nursing home program into a veritable social service entitlement program (U.S. House of Representatives, 2000, pp. 892–893).

Thanks to these and other changes, spending on the major federal entitlement programs jumped nearly 200 percent in real terms between 1980 and 1999, more than twice the 81 percent real growth in the U.S. gross domestic product (see Table 4.2). Although reimbursement rates under these programs were still often not sufficient to cover the full costs of the services, the expansion in the pool of resources available was substantial.

What is more, federal policymakers also created a variety of new programs during this period to improve the life chances of children and to provide assistance for homeless people, people with AIDS, children and youth, people with disabilities, volunteerism promotion, drug and alcohol treatment, and home health care (Smith, 2002). Renewed federal activism was mirrored, and in some cases anticipated, moreover, by activism at the state and local level. In some cases, state and local governments replaced cuts in federal spending with their own new or expanded programs. In other cases, states found new veins of federal funding to tap as old ones ran dry. The most striking example here is what became known as the "Medicaid maximization strategy," under which programs formerly funded entirely by the states or by federal discretionary programs subjected to Reagan-era budget cuts were reconfigured to make them eligible for funding under the more lucrative and still growing Medicaid or SSI program (Coughlin, Ku, and Holahan, 1994; U.S. House of Representatives, 2000).

Table 4.2. Growth in Federal Entitlement Program Spending, 1980–1999.

Program	Spending (billions of constant 1999 U.S. dollars)[a]		Percentage Change, 1980–1999
	1980	1999	
Medicare	79.9	212.0	+ 165
Medicaid[b]	56.8	189.5	+ 222
Supplemental Security Income[b]	9.5	30.9	+ 225
Total	146.2	432.4	+ 196
U.S. gross domestic product	4,900.9	8,856.5	+ 81

[a]Based on chain-type price deflators for the service component of personal consumption expenditures.

[b]Includes both federal and state spending.

Sources: U.S. House of Representatives, 2000, pp. 100, 912, 214; Council of Economic Advisers, 2002, tab. B-2.

Finally, the federal welfare reform legislation enacted in 1996 produced a fiscal windfall for the states when welfare rolls surprisingly began to fall while federal payments to the states remained fixed at their 1996 level. Under the welfare reform legislation, states were permitted to use these funds to finance a variety of work readiness, child care, and related human service programs considered necessary to help welfare recipients find work, and many of these are run by nonprofit organizations.

THE NONPROFIT RESPONSE: A STORY OF RESILIENCE

How has nonprofit America responded to this combination of challenges and opportunities? Conventional wisdom would lead us not to expect much. Nonprofits are not to be trusted, Professor Regina Herzlinger explained to readers of the *Harvard Business Review* in 1996, because they lack the three basic accountability measures that ensure effective and efficient operations in the business world: the self-interest of owners, competition, and the ultimate bottom-line measure of profitability.

In fact, however, nonprofit America has responded with amazing resilience. To be sure, the resulting changes are hardly universal. What is more, there are serious questions about whether they are in a wholly desirable direction. Yet there is no denying the dominant picture of resilience, adaptation, and change. More specifically, three broad threads of change are apparent: growth, commercialization, and professionalization.

Overall Growth

Perhaps the most vivid evidence of the nonprofit sector's resilience is the striking record of recent sector growth. Between 1977 and 1997, the revenues of America's nonprofit organizations increased 144 percent after adjusting for inflation, nearly twice the 81 percent growth rate of the nation's economy. Nonprofit revenue growth was particularly robust among arts and culture organizations, social service organizations, and health organizations, in each of which the rate of growth was at least twice that of the U.S. economy. However, even the most laggard components of the nonprofit sector (education and civic organizations) grew at a rate that equaled or exceeded overall U.S. economic growth (Salamon, 2002b, p. 51).

Growth occurred, moreover, not only in the revenues of the sector, which can be affected by the performance of just the larger organizations, but also in the number of organizations. Between 1977 and 1997, the number of 501(c)(3) and 501(c)(4) organizations registered with the Internal Revenue Service increased by 115 percent, or about twenty-three thousand organizations a year, and growth was faster in the more recent part of the period than in the earlier part (Weitzman, Jalandoni, Lampkin, and Pollack, 2002, pp. 4–5).

Commercialization

What accounts for this record of robust growth? While many factors are responsible, the dominant one appears to be the vigor with which nonprofit America embraced the spirit and the techniques of the market. The clearest reflection of this is the substantial rise in nonprofit income from fees and charges, indicative of the success with which nonprofit organizations succeeded in marketing their services to a clientele increasingly able to afford them. In fact, even with religious congregations included, fees and charges accounted for nearly half (47 percent) of the growth in nonprofit revenue between 1977 and 1997—more than any other source (see Table 4.3).

Fee income not only grew in scale but also spread to ever-broader components of the sector. Thus after adjusting for inflation, the fee income of arts and culture organizations jumped 272 percent, of civic organizations 220 percent, and of social service organizations over 500 percent between 1977 and 1997. Even religious organizations boosted their commercial income during this period, largely from the sale or rental of church property (Chaves, 2002, p. 284).

Another reflection of the commercialization of the nonprofit sector has been its success in adapting to the new terrain of public funding, which has also grown more commercial as a consequence of the shift to "consumer-side" subsidies. Despite this shift, nonprofits managed to boost their government support 195 percent in real terms between 1977 and 1997, proportionally more than any other

Table 4.3. Changing Structure of Nonprofit Revenue, 1977–1997.

| | | Share of Total | | | | Share of Revenue Growth, 1977–1999 | |
| | | All | | Excluding Religion | | | |
Revenue Source	Percentage Change, 1977–1997	1977	1997	1977	1997	All	Excluding Religion
Fees, charges	145	46	47	51	51	47	51
Government	195	27	33	31	37	37	42
Philanthropy	90	27	20	18	12	16	8
Total	144	100	100	100	100	100	100

Sources: Weitzman, Jalandoni, Lampkin, and Pollack, 2002; Council of Economic Advisers, 2002.

source, and these figures do not include the windfall from welfare reform. Government accounted for 37 percent of the sector's substantial growth during this period, increasing its share of the total from 27 percent in 1977 to 33 percent in 1997. And with religious congregations excluded (since they do not receive much government support), government's share of the sector's revenue increased from 31 percent to 37 percent (Salamon, 2002b, p. 54).

Also indicative of the commercialization of the nonprofit sector has been the significant growth of commercial ventures within the sector and the expanding pattern of partnerships with business (see Chapter Eighteen for further detail on commercial ventures). Commercial ventures such as museum gift shops and online stores, the rental of social halls by churches, and licensing agreements between research universities and commercial firms have long been a feature of nonprofit operations, but they have recently experienced substantial growth (Lipman and Schwinn, 2001). Especially interesting has been the emergence of "social ventures," business ventures that serve not primarily to generate income but rather to carry out the basic charitable missions of nonprofit organizations (for example, training ex-convicts for productive jobs by establishing a catering business in which they work and are trained) (Young and Salamon, 2002).

These developments point, in turn, to a broader and deeper penetration of the market culture into the fabric of nonprofit operations. Nonprofit organizations are increasingly "marketing" their "products," viewing their clients as "customers," segmenting their markets, differentiating their output, identifying their "market niche," formulating "business plans," and generally incorporating the language and the style of business management into the operation of their agencies. Indeed, management expert Kevin Kearns (2000) argues that nonprofit executives are now "among the most entrepreneurial managers to be found anywhere, including the private for-profit sector" (p. 25).

As the culture of the market has spread into the fabric of nonprofit operations, old suspicions between the nonprofit and business sectors have significantly softened, opening the way for nonprofit acceptance of the business community not simply as a source of charitable support but as a legitimate partner for a wide range of nonprofit endeavors. This perspective has been championed by charismatic sector leaders such as Bill Shore (1995), who urge nonprofits to stop thinking about how to get donations and start thinking about how to "market" the considerable "assets" they control, including particularly the asset represented by their reputations. This has meshed nicely with the growing willingness of businesses to forge strategic alliances with nonprofits in order to generate "reputational capital." The result has been a notable upsurge in strategic partnerships between nonprofit organizations and businesses manifested, for example, in a variety of "cause-related marketing" arrangements and increasingly in broader partnerships that mobilize corporate personnel, finances, and know-how in support of nonprofit activities.

Professionalization

If commercialization has been the chief vehicle for the nonprofit sector's response to the challenges and opportunities it has recently faced, professionalization has been a close second. Nonprofit America has become astonishingly more professional over the past two decades. The process began in the fundraising sphere, where a veritable revolution has occurred, as reflected in the emergence and growth of specialized fundraising organizations, such as the National Society of Fund-Raising Executives (1960), now known as the Association of Fundraising Professionals (AFP); the Council for the Advancement and Support of Education (1974); the Association for Healthcare Philanthropy (1967); and the National Committee for Planned Giving (1988). Equally impressive has been the transformation in the technology of charitable giving through the development of such devices as workplace solicitation, telethons, direct mail campaigns, telephone solicitation, e-philanthropy, and a host of complex "planned giving" vehicles such as "charitable remainder trusts." Entire organizations have surfaced to manage this process of extracting funds, and for-profit businesses, such as Fidelity, have also gotten into the act.

Other evidence of the growing professionalization of the nonprofit field has included the construction of a set of sectorwide infrastructure institutions, such as INDEPENDENT SECTOR, the Council on Foundations, the Association of Small Foundations, the Forum of Regional Associations of Grantmakers, and state nonprofit organizations (Abramson and McCarthy, 2002); the development of a sizable research and educational apparatus focused on this sector, including nonprofit degree or certificate programs in close to one hundred colleges and universities; and the creation of a nonprofit press (*Chronicle of Philanthropy, NonProfit Times, Nonprofit Quarterly*). What was once a scatteration of largely overlooked institutions has thus become a booming cottage industry attracting organizations, personnel, publications, services, conferences, Web sites, headhunting firms, consultants, rituals, and fads—all premised on the proposition that nonprofit organizations are distinctive institutions with enough commonalities despite their many differences to be studied, represented, serviced, and trained as a group.

IMPLICATIONS FOR NONPROFIT MANAGERS

Nonprofit America has thus responded with extraordinary creativity and resilience to the challenges and opportunities it has confronted over the past twenty years. The sector has grown enormously as a consequence—in numbers, in revenues, and in the range of purposes it serves. In addition, it seems to have expanded its competencies and improved its management, though these are more difficult to gauge with precision. To be sure, not all components of the sector have experienced these changes to the same degree or even in the same direction. Yet what is striking is how widespread the adaptations seem to have been.

On balance, these changes seem to have worked to the advantage of the nonprofit sector, strengthening its financial base, upgrading its operations, enlisting new partners and new resources in its activities, and generally improving its reputation for effectiveness. But they have also brought significant risks, and the risks may well overwhelm the gains.

Risks

The nonprofit sector's response to the challenges of the past twenty years, creative as it has been, has exposed the sector to a number of important risks.

Growing Identity Crisis. First off, nonprofit America is increasingly suffering under an identity crisis as a result of a growing tension between the market character of the services it is providing and the continued nonprofit character of the institutions providing them. This tension has become especially stark in the health field, where third-party payers, such as Medicare and private HMOs, increasingly downplay values other than actual service cost in setting reimbursement rates; where bond-rating agencies discount community service in determining the economic worth of bond issues and hence the price that nonprofit hospitals have to pay for capital; and where fierce for-profit competition leaves little room for conscious pursuit of social goals (Gray and Schlesinger, 2002). Left to their own devices, nonprofit institutions have had little choice but to adjust to these pressures, but at some cost to the features that make them distinctive. Under these circumstances, it is no wonder that scholars have been finding it so difficult to detect real differences between the performance of for-profit and nonprofit hospitals and why many nonprofit HMOs and hospitals have willingly surrendered the nonprofit form or sold out to for-profit firms (Rosner, 1982; Herzlinger and Krasker, 1987; Salkever and Frank, 1992; James, 1998).

Increased Demands on Nonprofit Managers. These tensions have naturally complicated the job of the nonprofit executive, requiring these officials to master not only the substantive dimensions of their fields but also the broader private markets in which they operate, the numerous public policies that increasingly affect them, and the massive new developments in technology and management with which they must contend. They must do all this, moreover, while balancing an increasingly complex array of stakeholders that includes not only clients, staff, board members, and private donors but also regulators, government program officials, for-profit competitors, and business partners and while also demonstrating performance and competing with other nonprofits and with for-profit firms for fees, board members, customers, contracts, grants, donations, gifts, bequests, visibility, prestige, political influence, and volunteers. No wonder that burnout has become such a serious problem in the field despite the excitement and fulfillment the role entails.

Increased Threat to Nonprofit Missions. Inevitably, these pressures pose threats to the continued pursuit of nonprofit missions. Nonprofit organizations forced to rely on fees and charges naturally begin to skew their service offerings to clients who are able to pay. What start out as sliding fee scales designed to cross-subsidize services for the needy become core revenue sources essential for agency survival. Organizations needing to raise capital to expand are naturally tempted to locate new facilities in places with a client base able to finance the borrowing costs. When charity care, advocacy, and research are not covered in government or private reimbursement rates, institutions have little choice but to curtail these activities.

How far these pressures have proceeded is difficult to say with any precision. As William Diaz (2002) has observed, support for the poor has never been the exclusive, or the primary, focus of nonprofit action. Nor need it be. What is more, many of the developments identified in this chapter have usefully mobilized market resources to support genuinely charitable purposes. Yet the nonprofit sector's movement toward the market is creating significant pressures to move away from those in greatest need, to focus on amenities that appeal to those who can pay, and to apply the market test to all facets of their operations (James, 1998).

Disadvantaging of Small Agencies. A fourth risk resulting from the nonprofit sector's recent move to the market is that smaller agencies will be at an increasing disadvantage. Successful adaptation to the prevailing market pressures increasingly requires access to advanced technology, professional marketing, corporate partners, sophisticated fundraising, and complex government reimbursement systems, all of which are problematic for smaller agencies. Market pressures are therefore creating not just a digital divide but a much broader "sustainability chasm" that smaller organizations are finding increasingly difficult to bridge. Although such agencies can cope with these pressures in part through collaborations and partnerships, these devices themselves often require sophisticated management and absorb precious managerial energies. As the barriers to entry and especially to sustainability rise, the nonprofit sector is thus at risk of losing one of its most precious qualities—its ease of entry and its availability as a testing ground for new ideas.

Potential Loss of Public Trust. All of this, finally, poses a further threat to the public trust on which the nonprofit sector ultimately depends. Thanks to the pressures they are under and the agility they have shown in response to them,

American nonprofit organizations have moved well beyond the quaint Norman Rockwell stereotype of selfless volunteers ministering to the needy and supported largely by charitable gifts. Yet popular and press images remain wedded to this older image, and far too little attention has been given to bringing popular perceptions into better alignment with the current realities and to justifying these realities to a skeptical citizenry and press. As a consequence, nonprofits find themselves vulnerable when highly visible events, such as the September 11 tragedy, let alone instances of mismanagement or scandal, reveal them to be far more complex and commercially engaged institutions than the public suspects. Reflecting this, the proportion of respondents in recent polls registering "a great deal of confidence" in nonprofit organizations stood at only 18 percent as of May 2002 (Light, 2003). The more successfully nonprofit organizations respond to the dominant market pressures they are facing, therefore, the greater the risk they face of sacrificing the public trust on which they ultimately depend.

Resetting the Balance: The Task Ahead

What all of this suggests is that a better balance may need to be struck between what Bradford Gray and Mark Schlesinger (2002) term the nonprofit sector's "distinctiveness imperative," the things that make nonprofits special, and the sector's "survival imperative," the things nonprofits need to do in order to survive. To be sure, these two imperatives are not wholly in conflict. Nevertheless, the tensions between them are real, and there is increasing reason to worry that the survival imperative may be gaining the upper hand. To correct this, steps will be needed in both domains, and the steps will require support from many different quarters.

Steps to address the nonprofit sector's distinctiveness imperative could include revisiting the sector's fundamental rationale through organizational strategic retreats and broader sectorwide positioning exercises, more sustained public information campaigns designed to clarify the actual operations of contemporary nonprofit institutions, and possible shifts in public policy to increase the salience of the sector's public benefit activities. Actions on the survival side of the equation could include passage of tax incentives to help even the playing field for nonprofit generation of capital, reconfiguring government and private reimbursement systems to make provision for mission-critical nonprofit functions, and shifting from a tax deduction to a tax credit system for charitable contributions in order to provide additional stimulus to private charitable giving.

CONCLUSION

The context of nonprofit management has changed massively in recent years. Until now, nonprofit managers have had to fend for themselves in deciding what risks it was acceptable to take in order to respond to this changing context.

Given the stake that American society has in the preservation of these institutions and in the protection of their ability to perform their distinctive roles, this may now need to change. Americans need to rethink in a more explicit way whether the balance between survival and distinctiveness that nonprofit institutions have had to strike in recent years is the right one for the future and, if not, what steps might now be needed to allow nonprofit managers to shift this balance for the years ahead.

References

AAFRC Trust for Philanthropy. *Giving USA 2000.* Indianapolis, Ind.: AAFRC Trust for Philanthropy, 2001.

Abramson, A. J., and McCarthy, R. "Infrastructure Organizations." In L. M. Salamon (ed.), *The State of Nonprofit America.* Washington, D.C.: Brookings Institution Press, 2002.

Abramson, A. J., Salamon, L. M., and Steurle, C. E. "The Nonprofit Sector and the Federal Budget: Recent History and Future Directions." In E. T. Boris and C. E. Steurle (eds.), *Nonprofits and Government: Collaboration and Conflict.* Washington, D.C.: Urban Institute Press, 1999.

Avery, R., and Rendell, M. *Estimating the Size and Distribution of the Baby Boomers' Prospective Inheritances.* Ithaca, N.Y.: Department of Consumer Economics, Cornell University, 1990.

Carr, D. K., and Johnson, H. J. *Best Practices in Reengineering: What Works and What Doesn't in the Reengineering Process.* New York: McGraw-Hill, 1995.

Chaves, M. "Religious Congregations." In L. M. Salamon (ed.), *The State of Nonprofit America.* Washington, D.C.: Brookings Institution Press, 2002.

Coughlin, T. A., Ku, L., and Holahan, J. *Medicaid Since 1980: Costs, Coverage, and the Shifting Alliance Between the Federal Government and the States.* Washington, D.C.: Urban Institute Press, 1994.

Council of Economic Advisers. *Economic Report of the President, 2002.* Washington, D.C.: Executive Office of the President, 2002.

Diaz, W. "For Whom and For What: The Contributions of the Nonprofit Sector." In L. M. Salamon (ed.), *The State of Nonprofit America.* Washington, D.C.: Brookings Institution Press, 2002.

Gilbert, N. "The Transformation of Social Services." *Social Services Review,* 1977, *51,* 624–641.

Gray, B., and Schlesinger, M. "Health." In L. M. Salamon (ed.), *The State of Nonprofit America.* Washington, D.C.: Brookings Institution Press, 2002.

Hammer, M., and Champy, J. *Reengineering the Corporation: A Manifesto for Business Revolution.* New York: HarperBusiness, 1993.

Hansmann, H. "The Role of Nonprofit Enterprise." *Yale Law Journal,* 1981, *89,* 835–901.

Havens, J. J., and Schervish, P. G. *Millionaires and the Millennium: New Estimates of the Forthcoming Wealth Transfer and the Prospects for a Golden Age of Philanthropy.* Boston: Social Welfare Research Institute, Boston College, 1999.

Herzlinger, R. "Can Public Trust in Nonprofits and Governments Be Restored?" *Harvard Business Review,* Mar.-Apr. 1996, pp. 97–107.

Herzlinger, R., and Krasker, W. S. "Who Profits from Nonprofits?" *Harvard Business Review,* Jan.-Feb. 1987, pp. 93–106.

James, E. "Commercialism Among Nonprofits: Objectives, Opportunities, and Constraints." In B. Weisbrod (ed.), *To Profit or Not to Profit: The Commercial Transformation of the Nonprofit Sector.* New York: Cambridge University Press, 1998.

Kearns, K. P. *Private Sector Strategies for Social Sector Success: The Guide to Strategy and Planning for Pubic and Nonprofit Organizations.* San Francisco: Jossey-Bass, 2000.

Kettl, D. *Shared Power: Public Governance and Private Markets.* Washington, D.C.: Brookings Institution Press, 1993.

Letts, C. W., Ryan, W., and Grossman, A. "Virtuous Capital: What Foundations Can Learn from Venture Capitalists." *Harvard Business Review,* Mar.-Apr. 1997, pp. 2–7.

Light, P. C. "To Give or Not to Give: The Crisis of Confidence in Charities." Brookings Institution, Reform Watch Brief no. 7 [http://www.brook.edu/comm/reformwatch/rw07.htm]. Dec. 2003.

Lipman, H., and Schwinn, E. "The Business of Charity: Nonprofit Groups Reap Billions in Tax-Free Income Annually." *Chronicle of Philanthropy,* Oct. 18, 2001, p. 25.

National Center for Education Statistics, *Digest of Education Statistics, 2000.* Washington, D.C.: National Center for Education Statistics, U.S. Department of Education, 2000.

Nelson, J. *Business as Partners in Development: Creating Wealth for Countries, Companies, and Communities.* London: Prince of Wales Business Leaders Forum, 1996.

Porter, M., and Kramer, M. R. "Philanthropy's New Agenda: Creating Value." *Harvard Business Review,* Nov.-Dec. 1999, pp. 121–130.

Rosenbaum, D. "Bush Plans Little More Money for Bulk of Federal Programs." *New York Times,* Jan. 22, 2003, p. A19.

Rosner, D. *A Once Charitable Enterprise: Hospitals and Health Care in Brooklyn and New York, 1885–1915.* Princeton, N.J.: Princeton University Press, 1982.

Salamon, L. M. "Partners in Public Service." In W. W. Powell (ed.), *The Nonprofit Sector: A Research Handbook.* New Haven, Conn.: Yale University Press, 1987.

Salamon, L. M. *Partners in Public Service: Government-Nonprofit Relations in the Modern Welfare State.* Baltimore: Johns Hopkins University Press, 1995.

Salamon, L. M. "The New Governance and the Tools of Public Action: An Introduction." In L. M. Salamon (ed.), *The Tools of Government: A Guide to the New Governance.* New York: Oxford University Press, 2002a.

Salamon, L. M. (ed.). "The Resilient Sector: The State of Nonprofit America." In L. M. Salamon (ed.), *The State of Nonprofit America.* Washington, D.C.: Brookings Institution Press, 2002b.

Salamon, L. M. (ed.). *The Tools of Government: A Guide to the New Governance.* New York: Oxford University Press, 2002c.

Salamon, L. M., and Abramson, A. J. *The Federal Budget and the Nonprofit Sector.* (Washington, D.C.: Urban Institute Press, 1982).

Salamon, L. M., and Abramson, A. J. "The Federal Budget and the Nonprofit Sector: Implications of the Contract with America." In D. F. Burlingame, W. A. Diaz, W. F. Ilchman, and Associates, *Capacity for Change? The Nonprofit World in the Age of Devolution.* Indianapolis: Indiana University Center on Philanthropy, 1996.

Salkever, D. S., and Frank, R. G. "Health Services." In C. T. Clotfelter (ed.), *Who Benefits from the Nonprofit Sector?* Chicago: University of Chicago Press, 1992.

Shore, B. *Revolution of the Heart: A New Strategy for Creating Wealth and Meaningful Change.* New York: Riverhead Books, 1995.

Smith, C. "The New Corporate Philanthropy." *Harvard Business Review,* May-June 1994, pp. 105–116.

Smith, S. R. "Social Services." In L. M. Salamon (ed.), *The State of Nonprofit America.* Washington, D.C.: Brookings Institution Press, 2002.

Smith, S. R., and Lipsky, M. *Nonprofits for Hire: The Welfare State in the Age of Contracting.* Cambridge, Mass.: Harvard University Press, 1993.

U.S. Census Bureau. *U.S. Economic Census.* Washington, D.C.: U.S. Government Printing Office, 1999.

U.S. Census Bureau. *Statistical Abstract of the United States, 2000.* (120th ed.) Washington, D.C.: U.S. Government Printing Office, 2000.

U.S. House of Representatives, Committee on Ways and Means. *2000 Green Book: Background Material and Data on Programs Within the Jurisdiction of the Committee on Ways and Means, 106th Congress, 2d Session.* Washington, D.C.: U.S. Government Printing Office, 2000.

Wallace, N. "Online Giving Soars as Donors Turn to the Internet Following Attacks." *Chronicle of Philanthropy,* Oct. 4, 2001, p. 22.

Warner, A. *American Charities: A Study in Philanthropy and Economics.* New York: Crowell, 1894.

Weitzman, M. S., Jalandoni, N. T., Lampkin, L. M., and Pollack, T. H. *The New Nonprofit Almanac and Desk Reference.* San Francisco: Jossey Bass, 2002.

Whitehead. J. S. *The Separation of College and State: Columbia, Dartmouth, Harvard, and Yale.* New Haven, Conn.: Yale University Press, 1973.

Wilgoren, J. "New Governors Discover the Ink Is Turning Redder." *New York Times,* Jan. 14, 2003, p. A20.

Wyszomirski, M. J. "Arts and Culture." In L. M. Salamon (ed.), *The State of Nonprofit America.* Washington, D.C.: Brookings Institution Press, 2002.

Young, D., and Salamon, L. M. "Commercialization and Social Ventures." In L. M. Salamon (ed.), *The State of Nonprofit America.* Washington, D.C.: Brookings Institution Press, 2002.

CHAPTER FIVE

The Internationalization of the Nonprofit Sector

Helmut K. Anheier
Nuno Themudo

The past few decades have witnessed the expansion of nonprofit sectors to levels unknown in the past, accounting for about 6 percent of total employment in member nations of the Organization for Economic Cooperation and Development (OECD) (Salamon and others, 1999). While most remain domestic organizations, the scope of the nonprofit sector is increasingly international in scope, and some larger nonprofits have grown into veritable global actors (Anheier, Glasius, and Kaldor, 2001; Clark and Themudo, 2003; Lewis, 2001; Lindenberg and Bryant, 2001). Oxfam, Save the Children, Amnesty International, Friends of the Earth, the Red Cross, and Greenpeace have become the "brand names" among international nongovernmental or nonprofit organizations (INGOs), with significant budgets, political influence, and responsibility. Indeed, by the late 1990s, the ten largest development and relief INGOs alone had combined expenditures of over $3 billion, equivalent to about half of the official U.S. aid budget at the time (Lindenberg and Dobel, 1999).

The internationalization of the nonprofit sector is not a recent phenomenon (Anheier and Cunningham, 1994). Of course, the Roman Catholic Church and Islam have long had transnational aspirations and maintained far-reaching operations for centuries. The modern, internationally active nonprofit organization emerged from antislavery societies, most notably the British and Foreign Anti-Slavery Society in 1839 and the International Committee of the Red Cross (ICRC), founded by Henri Dunant in 1864 after his experiences in the Battle of Solferino. By 1874, there were 32 INGOs, which increased to 1,083 by 1914 (Smith, Chatfield, Pagnucco, and Chatfield, 1997), including political organizations like the Socialist International, peace movements, learned societies, and business and professional associations.

What seems new, however, is the sheer scale and scope that international and supranational institutions and organizations of many kinds have achieved in recent years. In this chapter, we describe the growing internationalization of the nonprofit sector and explore some of its causes. What are the key drivers behind this internationalization process and its growing momentum? What are the management and policy implications of internationalization, and what are likely future developments?

BECOMING INTERNATIONAL, GOING GLOBAL

Before presenting the contours of internationalization, a word on terminology is in order, as certain concepts and terms are used cross-nationally in rather inconsistent and sometimes confusing ways (Najam, 1996; Lewis, 2001). For *nonprofit organization,* we adopt the definition developed by Salamon and Anheier (1997) for cross-national research, which refers to organizations that are organized, private, self-governing, non-profit-distributing, and voluntary. *Nongovernmental organization* (NGO) is a somewhat imprecise term that originated in the League of Nations in the 1920s, came to prominence in the UN system, and is today used largely to refer to nonprofit and non-government-related organizations working in the field of international relations, environment, human rights, humanitarian assistance, and development cooperation (Glasius and Kaldor, 2002). Our use of the term is broader. Here we will use *international nongovernmental organizations* (INGOs) to refer to nonprofit organizations that make significant operating expenditures across national borders and do not identify themselves as domestic actors. *International philanthropy* refers primarily to the activities of foundations and other nonprofit institutions in the United States and other countries that support causes and meet needs abroad.

Internationalization takes place when a national organization decides to expand into another country, either by setting up an affiliate or branch office or by collaborating financially or otherwise with an existing organization abroad. Examples might be Save the Children setting up offices in Asian countries, Greenpeace opening an office in Spain, or the Ford Foundation making grants to recipient organizations in Nigeria. Another possibility is that various national organizations decide to get together and create a federation (International Federation of Red Cross and Red Crescent Societies, Friends of the Earth), an alliance (Oxfam International), or a campaign coalition (International Campaign to Ban Landmines).

INTERNATIONALIZATION
AND THE NONPROFIT SECTOR

Since no comprehensive data are available on the internationalization of the nonprofit sector, we begin our analysis by presenting three related facets of globalization and philanthropy: (1) the scale and revenue of international activities of the nonprofit sector in the United States and selected countries, (2) the rise of international nongovernmental organizations and the emergence of what has been called global civil society (Anheier, Glasius, and Kaldor, 2001; Kaldor, 2003), and (3) the growth of international philanthropy.

International Activities of the Nonprofit Sector

The Johns Hopkins Comparative Nonprofit Project (Anheier and Salamon, 2005; Salamon, Sokolowski, and List, 2003; Salamon and Anheier, 1996) attempted to measure basic economic indicators on the size of international nonprofits in a broad cross section of countries. These data allow us to fathom at least some aspects of the scale of international nonprofit activities, albeit from a country-based perspective. For the twenty-eight countries for which such data are available, INGOs amount to 1 to 2 percent of total nonprofit sector employment, or 134,0000 full-time-equivalent jobs. They also attracted a larger number of volunteers, who represent another 154,000 jobs on a full-time basis. In the United States, estimates suggest that more than four million people volunteer for international causes, which would equal about 45,000 full-time jobs, or close to a third the number of paid employment in the field. In Germany, the more than 100,000 volunteers would represent an equivalent of 28,500 full-time jobs, substantially more than the actual amount of paid employment in the international field (see Table 5.1).

For some countries, it is possible to examine the growth for the 1990s. Between 1990 and 1995, employment in INGOs grew by 8 percent in France (Archambault, Gariazzo, Anheier, and Salamon, 1999, p. 89), over 10 percent in Germany (Priller and others, 1999, p. 115), and by more than 30 percent in the United Kingdom (Kendal and Almond, 1999, p. 188). Even though the data are limited, the resulting pattern is in line with some of the other evidence we will present in this chapter: since the early 1990s, international nonprofit activities have expanded significantly, and even though they continue to represent a small portion of national nonprofit economies, their share has increased nonetheless.

In terms of revenue structure, the international nonprofits, as measured by the Johns Hopkins team, receive 29 percent of their income through fees and charges, including membership dues; 35 percent from both national and internal governmental organizations in the form of grants and reimbursements; and 36 percent through individual, foundation, or corporate donations. With vol-

Table 5.1. Size of International Nonprofit Sector Activities in Five Countries, 1995.

| International Activities | Employment and Volunteers | | |
	Full-Time-Equivalent Employment	Percentage of Total Nonprofit Sector Employment	Volunteers in Full-Time-Equivalent Jobs
United Kingdom	53,726	3.6	7,298
United States	123,253	1.7	45,026
Germany	9,950	0.7	28,510
France	17,403	1.8	30,986
Japan	7,693	0.3	37,785

Sources: Salamon and others, 1999; Anheier and List, 2000.

unteer input factored in as a monetary equivalent, the donation component increases to 58 percent of total "revenue," which makes the international nonprofit field the most "voluntaristic and donative" part of the nonprofit sector after religious nonprofit (73 percent), civic and advocacy (56 percent), and environmental groups (56 percent), and far more than is the case for domestic service-providing nonprofits in these countries.

As Table 5.2 suggests, the revenue structure of international activities differs significantly from that for the nonprofit sector as a whole. Most of the difference is due to a more pronounced share of private giving combined with a reduced portion of income from private fees and payments: whereas the voluntary sector in the United Kingdom receives, as a whole, 44 percent of its revenue in the form of private fees and payments, the corresponding share is only 27 percent for international activities. At the same time, private giving makes up about one-third. We find even more dramatic reversals in the importance of commercial income and giving in the case of the United States, France, and Germany. Even in Japan, where private donations make up 3 percent of the sector's revenue as a whole, giving amounts to 27 percent for international activities. By contrast, the share of government payments changes much less.

These findings suggest that the revenue structure of international nonprofit sector activities is characterized to a significant extent by private giving. The international component of the nonprofit sector benefits more from volunteer commitment and general mobilization of the population behind particular causes (for example, human rights, humanitarian assistance, peace and international understanding) than more conventional nonprofit activities in social services, culture and the arts, or housing, which are increasingly financed by the public sector and commercial revenue sources.

Table 5.2. Revenue Structure of International Nonprofit Sector
Activities Versus Total Nonprofit Sector in Five Countries, by Revenue Source, 1995.

Country	Field	Public Sector (%)	Private Giving (%)	Private Fees and Payments (%)
		Revenue Source		
United Kingdom	International	40	33	27
	Total nonprofit sector	47	9	44
United States	International	31	50	19
	Total nonprofit sector	30	13	57
Germany	International	51	41	8
	Total nonprofit sector	64	4	32
France	International	43	40	17
	Total nonprofit sector	58	8	35
Japan	International	19	27	54
	Total nonprofit sector	45	3	52

Sources: Salamon and others, 1999; Anheier and List, 2000.

The pronounced donative and volunteer element applies also to INGOs of significant size and with complex organizational structures that increasingly span many countries and continents (Anheier and Themudo, 2002; Anheier and Katz, 2003). Examples include Amnesty International with more than one million members, subscribers, and regular donors in over 140 countries and territories. The Friends of the Earth Federation combines about five thousand local groups and one million members (see Anheier and Katz, 2003). The International Union for the Conservation of Nature brings together 735 INGOs, 35 affiliates, 78 states, 112 government agencies, and some ten thousand scientists and experts from 181 countries in a unique worldwide partnership. Much of the international coordinating work involved is done on a volunteer basis.

The Rise of International Nongovernmental Organizations

Figure 5.1 shows the exponential growth in INGO numbers in the twentieth century. As readily indicated by the upward trend in the figure, the number of known INGOs increased from under five thousand in the 1970s to about thirty thousand by 2001. The number of INGOs reported in the early 1980s would make up under one-third of the stock of INGOs twenty years later. Even though analysts are divided on the question as to whether, and by what measure, aid flows to developing countries have increased, decreased, or remained stable

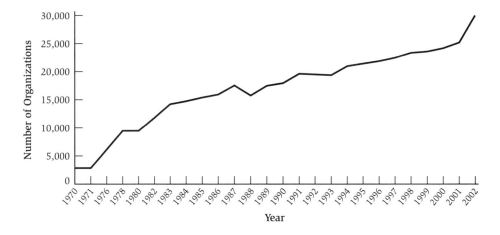

Figure 5.1. Growth in the Number of International Nongovernmental Organizations, 1970–2002.

Note: Includes only INGOs present in at least three countries.

Source: Union of International Associations, 2002.

over recent decades, one consistent finding is that the INGO share has increased significantly. In the 1970s, INGO aid as a share of all aid flows from OECD countries to developing countries was 11 percent. The INGO share has since doubled, with most of the gain in the 1990s, a period that coincides with the significant expansion of INGO operations more generally (see Figure 5.2). What is more, INGO contributions increased in both relative and absolute terms as official aid flows decreased, as Figure 5.3 illustrates for the period 1970–1999.

The change in the economic weight and political importance of INGOs is highlighted even further when we look at the composition of INGO aid flows. Although some analysts diagnosed a decrease of total official aid in real terms over the course of the 1990s (Smillie and Hailey, 2001), official aid channeled through INGOs increased during that period. Using data on INGOs registered with the United States Agency for International Development (USAID), the world's largest donor, we found that in just twenty years, total income of INGOs more than doubled from $2.3 billion in 1982 to $5 billion in 1992 and then more than tripled to $16.8 billion in 2001 (see Table 5.3). These figures are consistent with Fowler (2000), who estimated that total income for INGOs rose from around $6 billion in the early 1990s to about $13 billion by the end of the decade.

Private giving and official funding alike fueled this growth. According to some sources, shown in Table 5.3, private giving increased from $3.4 billion in 1992 to $12.8 billion in 2001. A separate estimate by Clark (2003) found that private donations, including individual, foundation, and corporate contributions, more than doubled from $4.5 billion in 1988 to $10.7 billion in 1999. These figures

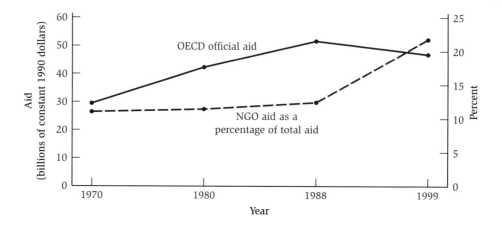

Figure 5.2. Aid from the OECD to Developing Countries and Share of NGOs as a Percentage of the Total, 1970–1999.

Note: U.S. dollar GDP deflators from the World Bank. Percentage of NGO aid calculated as a percentage of total OECD and total NGO aid.

Sources: OECD Development Assistance Committee; Clark, 1991, 2003; Lindenberg and Bryant, 2001; Development Initiatives, 2000; United Nations Development Programme, 2001.

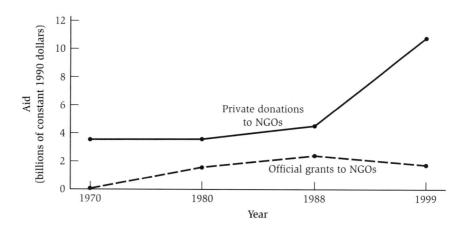

Figure 5.3. Composition of NGO Aid to Developing Countries, 1970–1999.

Note: U.S. dollar GDP deflators from the World Bank.

Sources: OECD Development Assistance Committee; Clark, 1991, 2003; Lindenberg and Bryant, 2001; Development Initiatives, 2000; United Nations Development Programme, 2001.

Table 5.3. Income of INGOs Registered with USAID, 1982–2001 (in billions of U.S. dollars).

Income Source	1982	1992	1996	1997	1998	1999	2000	2001
Private	1.30	3.40	6.30	7.10	8.33	9.40	10.33	12.80
Public	1.07	1.60	2.40	2.40	2.54	2.90	3.91	4.05
Total	2.37	5.00	8.70	9.50	10.87	12.30	14.24	16.85

Notes: Data on private resources from INGOs' own reports. Data on public resources include U.S. foreign aid and international donors (bilateral and multilateral aid). Public income for 1982 and 1992 includes U.S. foreign aid only. Data for 1992–1999 are for U.S. private voluntary organizations (PVOs) only. Data for 2000–2001 include around $1 billion from non-U.S. PVOs registered with USAID. All figures include funds for central and eastern Europe.

Sources: United States Agency for International Development, 1995, 1998–2003.

underscore the significant expansion of INGOs in the changing development field of the 1990s and the major private mobilization effort they represent.

Official funding by governments and multilateral agencies to INGOs is generally divided into humanitarian assistance and development aid. INGOs have benefited from a rise in funding dedicated to humanitarian assistance in the 1990s (Lindenberg and Bryant, 2001; Wallace, 2000). Moreover, many donors have increased the proportion of humanitarian aid they channel through INGOs. In the 1990s, the European Commission's Humanitarian Office increased the share of its humanitarian assistance funds channeled through INGOs from just over 25 percent in 1990 to around 45 percent in 1995 and 62 percent in 1999. Similarly, Wallace (2000) shows that in less than ten years, between 1988 and 1995, NGOs more than quadrupled their income for development and humanitarian assistance from the Department for International Development, the donor agency in the United Kingdom, from £33.6 to £161 million. One consequence of this growth was that the World Bank, the European Union, and bilateral aid agencies have institutionalized their relationship with INGOs, creating dedicated divisions within their organizations to deal with INGOs (Lindenberg and Bryant 2001).

Dispersal. The significant growth of INGOs since the 1970s, shown in Figure 5.1, is, of course, not equally spread across the world. Europe and North America have the greatest number of INGOs and higher membership densities than other regions of the world (see Anheier and Katz, 2003). And even though, as we will show, cities in Europe and the United States still serve as the INGO centers of the world, a long-term diffusion process has decreased the concentration of INGOs to the effect that they are now more evenly distributed around the world than ever before.

Figure 5.4 shows the growth in membership for different world regions. As is to be expected, INGO memberships increased in all regions, but more in some

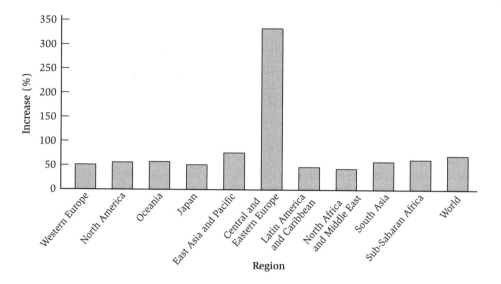

Figure 5.4. Growth in INGO Membership, 1990–2000, by Region.

Source: Union of International Associations, 1990, 2000.

than in others. The highest expansion rates are in central and eastern Europe, including central Asia, followed by East Asia and the Pacific. The growth in central and eastern Europe is clearly linked to the fall of state socialism and the introduction of freedom of association, whereas the growth in Asia is explained by economic expansion and democratic reform in many countries of the region.

Figure 5.5 adds a different dimension and shows the INGO membership growth in relation to economic development. Growth rates throughout the 1990s were higher in middle-income countries (East Asia, central and eastern Europe, parts of Latin America) than in the high-income countries of western Europe, the Pacific, and North America. What is more, the expansion rate of INGOs in low-income countries is higher than that for richer parts of the world.

Together, these data indicate that the growth of INGOs involves not concentration but dispersion. In organizational terms, as a group, INGOs today are less a Western-based phenomenon than in the past, and the significant growth rates of recent years have benefited their reach and expansion outside North America and the European Union. In the terms of Held and colleagues' dimensions of globalization (Held, McGrew, Goldblatt, and Perraton, 1999), the INGO phenomenon has attained wider reach and higher density, a finding also supported by Anheier and Katz (2003).

To illustrate the process of dispersion, it is useful to review some basic patterns of INGO locations over time and to go back briefly to the beginnings of modern INGO development. In 1906, only 2 of the 169 INGOs had their headquarters out-

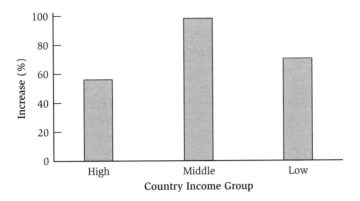

Figure 5.5. Growth in INGO Membership, 1990–2000, by Country Income Group.

Sources: Union of International Associations, 1990, 2000.

side Europe; in 1938, only 36 of the total of 705 INGOs existing at that time were located outside Europe. By 1950, reflecting a significant increase of U.S.-based INGOs and the establishment of the United Nations, 124 of the 804 existing INGOs were not based in Europe. Following the independence movement and the generally favorable economic climate of the 1950s and early 1960s, the number of INGOs increased to 1,768, of which 83 percent were located in Europe, 10 percent in the United States, and 1 to 2 percent in each of the other regions, Asia, South America, Central America, Africa, the Middle East, and Australia (Tew, 1963).

By 2001, much of this concentration has given way to a more decentralized pattern around an emerging bipolar structure of INGOs, with two centers: western Europe and North America. Europe still accounts for the majority of INGO headquarters, followed by the United States, but other regions like Asia and Africa have gained ground, as we have seen in Figures 5.4 and 5.5. Nonetheless, among the ten countries hosting the greatest number of intercontinental organization headquarters in 2001, we find eight European countries (United Kingdom, France, Switzerland, Belgium, the Netherlands, Germany, Italy, and Austria), next to the United States and Canada (Union of International Associations, 2002, vol. 5, p. 81). In terms of cities, we find that by 2001, the traditional role of Paris (729), London (807), Brussels (1,392), Geneva (272), and New York (390) has not been diminished in absolute terms. They dominate less, however, in relative terms: nearly a dozen other cities on four continents have more than one hundred INGO headquarters, and another thirty-five on five continents more than fifty.

Organizational Links. The infrastructure of global civil society in terms of INGOs has not only become broader in geographical coverage but also became much more interconnected throughout the 1990s. In 2001, the Union of International

Associations reported over ninety thousand such links among INGOs, and thirty-eight thousand between INGOs and international governmental organizations. The average number of links per organization jumped from 6.7 in 1990 to 14.1 in 2000—an increase of 110 percent.

Composition. Next to scale and connectedness, field of activity or purpose is another important dimension in describing the scope of INGOs. When looking at the purpose or field in which INGOs operate (see Figure 5.6), we find that among the INGOs listed in 2001, two fields dominate in terms of numbers: economic development and economic interest associations (26.1 percent) and knowledge-based INGOs in the area of research and science (20.5 percent). At first, the pronounced presence of these activities and purposes among INGOs seems a surprise, yet it is in these fields that needs for some form of international cooperation, exchange of information, recognition, standard setting, and other discourse have long been felt. There are thousands of scholarly associations and learned societies that span the entire range of academic disciplines and field of human learning. Likewise, there is a rich tradition of business and professional organizations reaching across national borders, forming international chambers of commerce, consumer associations, and professional groups in the fields of law, accounting, trade, engineering, transportation, civil service, and health care.

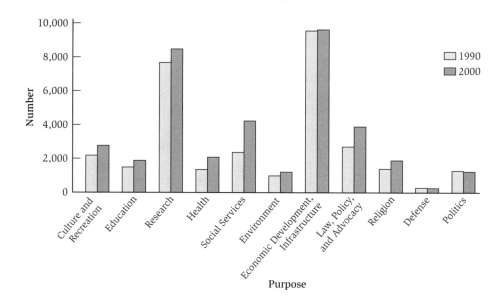

Figure 5.6. INGOs, 1990–2000, by Purpose.

Source: Union of International Associations, 2000.

Indeed, the earliest available tabulation of INGOs by purpose lists 639 organizations in 1924, with nearly half in either economic interest associations (172) or learned societies and research organizations (238) (Otlet, 1924). Only 55 organizations fell into the category "political," 28 in sports, 25 in religion, and 14 in arts and culture. In other words, the political, humanitarian, moral, and religious values components of INGOs are more recent phenomena. Although some of the oldest humanitarian organizations date back to the nineteenth century (for example, the Red Cross or the Anti-Slavery Society), their prominence at the transnational level is a product of the latter part of the twentieth century.

Indeed, as Figure 5.6 shows, by 2000, values-based INGOs in the areas of law, policy, and advocacy (12.6 percent), politics (5.2 percent), and religion (5.2 percent) make up the second largest activity component, accounting for a total of 23 percent of all INGOs. This is followed by a service provisions cluster, in which social services, health, and education together account for 21 percent of INGO purposes. Smaller fields like culture and the arts (6.6 percent), the environment (2.9 percent), and defense and security (0.07 percent) make up the balance. Yet next to a greater emphasis on values, the changes in the composition of purposes that took place in the 1990s brought a long-standing yet often overlooked function of INGOs to the forefront: service delivery has become a visible and important part of INGOs. Indeed, the social services as a purpose grew by 79 percent between 1990 and 2000, health services by 50 percent, and education by 24 percent.

Thus INGO activity has expanded significantly since 1990, in terms of both scale and connectedness. We also saw that the relative focus on these organizations, taken together, shifted more toward values-based activities and service provision. Overall, the expansion of INGOs and the values-activity shift reflect both quantitative and qualitative changes. Throwing some light on these developments will be the task in the next section, once we have taken a brief look at international philanthropy.

International Philanthropy

Philanthropy is perhaps the least international component of the nonprofit sector; at the same time, foundations are among its most visible international components. Large foundations such as the Ford Foundation and the Rockefeller Foundation, the network of Soros Foundations in central and eastern Europe and now central Asia, the Robert Bosch or Bertelsmann Stiftung in Germany, or the Rowntree Foundation in the United Kingdom enjoy high cross-national recognition. Prominent examples of international philanthropy are the Bill and Melinda Gates Foundation's program to develop vaccines for malaria and the AIDS virus, the John D. and Catherine T. MacArthur Foundation's grantmaking program in environmental protection and natural resource management, and the Ford Foundation's support of human rights.

At the same time, the relative share of U.S. foundation grants to international affairs, development, and peace remained steady for much of the 1990s, between 3 and 4 percent of total grant dollars awarded. But in 2000, that share slipped to 2.8 percent, although the number of grants grew by 12 percent and the amounts awarded by 20 percent, from $350 million to $414 million. In other words, while funding of international affairs grew in the 1990s in absolute terms, it declined in relative terms somewhat, being overshadowed by the growth in other funding arenas (Foundation Center, 2002).

The picture for cross-border giving by foundations is different, however. According to the Foundation Center (2002), U.S. private foundations, including corporate foundations, made about $2.5 billion in grants in other countries in 2001, up from $1.5 billion in the early 1990s. Whereas in 1982, around 5 percent of all grant dollars went abroad, that share increased to 16 percent twenty years later.

The United Kingdom receives about 12 percent of all U.S. grant dollars, and western Europe 13 percent. Like Europe, Latin America received about a quarter (22 percent); Asia and Pacific, 19 percent; sub-Saharan Africa, 19 percent; eastern Europe, Russia, and central Asia, 6 percent; North Africa and the Middle East, 6 percent; and North America and the Caribbean, 7 percent (Foundation Center, 2002, pp. 52–54). In terms of program fields and areas of activities, U.S. grant dollars were distributed as follows (p. 62):

18 percent to international development

15 percent to health

13 percent to international affairs

11 percent to education

10 percent to social science and policy analysis

9 percent to the arts

10 percent to environmental protection, natural resource management, and science

8 percent to human rights

3 percent for religious purposes

3 percent for other purposes

Information on transnational philanthropy in other countries is much more limited. In Europe, five countries—Sweden, the United Kingdom, Germany, the Netherlands, and Italy—have large foundations that engage in grantmaking abroad, yet as in the United States, most foundations remain domestic actors, constrained by their founders' original purposes, embodied in their deeds, and held back by the higher transaction costs of operating across borders.

International philanthropy also includes individual giving. In *Giving USA 2002,* the American Association of Fundraising Counsel Trust for Philanthropy shows that philanthropic giving in the United States, including both individual and foundation giving, to the "international sector" nearly doubled from $2.2 billion to $4.2 billion between 1991 and 2001. As a percentage of total giving, however, it has remained constant, at 2.1 percent of the total in 1991 and 2.0 percent of the total in 2001.

FACTORS FAVORING INTERNATIONALIZATIONS

The complex internationalization picture depicted so far in this chapter tells one simple story: that of an overall increase in the international activities of the nonprofit sector in absolute terms and in many of its facets also in relative terms. How can we account for this? The internationalization of nonprofit activities is aided by both demand- and supply-side factors. Key demand-side drivers include changes in the international aid system and rising needs for humanitarian and developmental services abroad.

Changes in the International Aid System

The rise of INGOs' profile is a consequence of both successful local and voluntary action and of the increasing popularity that they enjoy with governments and donors (Edwards and Hulme, 1995). Ideological changes such as "new public management" in the public sector and the rise of the "new policy agenda" in the international aid system, which combines neoliberal market privatization with democratic governance, have put INGOs at the forefront of policy implementation (Edwards and Hulme, 1995; Lewis, 2001).

Clarke (1998) argues that since the 1980s, the political environment favored INGOs as agents of development. Conservatives, neoliberals, and radicals all saw INGOs as a solution to problems with the state. Conservatives saw INGOs as private agents that are more efficient, more flexible, and more innovative than state agencies. Delivering development aid through INGOs was therefore a way to reduce the state apparatus and achieve greater efficiency. Neoliberals, on the other hand, saw INGOs as providing a necessary balance to state power. INGOs bring about greater pluralism and democratization of the development process. Finally, radicals saw INGOs as bottom-up initiatives capable of promoting social change and addressing inequalities of power. INGOs therefore became the favorite instrument—some even suggested the "magic bullet" (Edwards and Hulme, 1995)—of development policy.

NGO involvement came to be seen as a precondition for good governance and reducing corruption in the use of development aid funds. Lewis (2001) suggests the search for alternative development models as a key reason for the growth of INGOs since the 1970s. The failure of large-scale state-led development models to deliver the promised results encouraged a search for alternative, more bottom-up development models. Development thinking moved toward more participatory approaches to development and to "putting the last first" (Chambers, 1986). INGOs therefore seemed an important vehicle for citizen mobilization. More recently, INGOs have taken center stage in official donor efforts to strengthen civil society in non-Western contexts (Lindenberg and Bryant, 2001).

Growing Needs

The last two decades have witnessed various high-profile humanitarian emergencies that received worldwide media attention and public support. Prominent examples are the famine in Ethiopia in the mid-1980s, which led to the Live Aid fundraising efforts; the complex emergencies in the Balkans; floods in Poland; genocide in Rwanda; hurricane Mitch in Central America; and reconstruction efforts in the Middle East. The growing recognition of humanitarian needs in distant areas has generated a demand for INGOs to address them. Indeed, as we have shown, there has been a rise in private giving for humanitarian emergencies and development work, partly due to the development of international media that now provide nearly instant information about international disasters and emergencies around the world (Lindenberg and Bryant, 2001). The growth in "global sympathy" and the expansion of INGOs are in part reflections of this trend.

The rise in demand from private and government sources is not, however, sufficient to explain the strong rise of INGOs. There are important supply-side stimuli to the internationalization of the nonprofit sector, which have reduced the cost of INGO action and therefore encouraged its expansion. Such supply-side factors include new political opportunities and important technological and social changes that have enabled INGOs to operate more freely and more cheaply across borders.

Political Opportunities. The end of the Cold War has reduced the barriers to INGO action, facilitating their internationalization. INGOs could now move into countries previously under Soviet influence, and the end of many regional conflicts formerly fueled by the Cold War allowed INGOs broader access across the globe. Similarly, the spread of democracy increased the legal and political space for INGO and local nonprofits alike (Clark, 2003; Lindenberg and Bryant, 2001).

Political space increased even under nondemocratic regimes. Nonprofit organizations working in antagonistic environments are often able to mobilize a supportive international network to put pressure on a repressive government—the so-called boomerang effect (Keck and Sikkink, 1998). These international support networks have given greater visibility and therefore security to small nonprofits working in nondemocratic nations and created a new international arena in which they can fight national and local causes. Successful examples of such networks include the Narmada Dam campaign in India, which mobilized local, national, and international environmental and grassroots groups to stop the project. They were successful despite the initially favorable stance of the Indian government and of the World Bank. The ability to unite interests in an effort to put greater pressure on political targets provides another incentive for the internationalization of the nonprofit sector.

New spaces have also opened in the global governance system (Clark, 2003; Boli and Thomas, 1999). Ever since the 1972 Stockholm Conference, INGOs have been gaining access and influence in UN-organized global summits on various social issues such as the environment, women, and housing. This participation was institutionalized in the 1992 Earth Summit, which took place in Rio de Janeiro, Brazil, when INGOs were invited to several sessions. At the same time, the Rio summit inaugurated the tradition of creating parallel summits for nonprofits and other civil society organizations, with results of the discussion fed into the official governmental discussions taking place (Fisher, 1993). What is more, the development of more favorable national legal systems has been another important driver of NGO expansion. Countries that lacked adequate legal and fiscal treatment of nonprofit organizations introduced better regulatory frameworks (Stuart, 2003).

Technology Change. Technological progress, especially in information and communications (e-mail, Internet), has dramatically facilitated cooperation across borders (Clark and Themudo, 2003; Lindenberg and Bryant, 2001), leading to a major drop in communication costs for transnational organizations. Technology has also facilitated the emergence of newer organizational forms in the nonprofit sector: "dot causes" (Clark and Themudo, 2003). Dot causes such as Attac are social networks that mobilize support for particular policy campaigns, primarily (but not necessarily exclusively) through a Web site. They fit Keck and Sikkink's definition of transnational advocacy networks as "actors working internationally on an issue, who are bound together by shared values, a common discourse, and dense exchanges of information and services" (1998, p. 2). Some of the earliest examples were the Free Burma campaign network, started in 1995, followed by networks waging campaigns against Shell Oil in Ogoniland (Nigeria) and against McDonald's in various places around the world (O'Neill, 1999).

World Political Culture

The development of a world culture or world society is a generally less discussed but we believe important supply-side driver contributing to the internationalization of the nonprofit sector (Boli and Thomas, 1999). World society researchers argue that a world culture of institutions such as citizenship, human rights, science and technology, socioeconomic development, education, religion, and management has emerged that penetrates virtually all human endeavor (Meyer, Boli, Thomas, and Ramirez, 1997). This increasingly global social organization of rationalized modernity has its logic and purposes built into almost all nation-states, which, bound by international treaties to remain domestic actors, "spin off" INGOs as agents of international contact next to the transnational corporation. INGOs are one way in which countries open up to globalization.

Globalization

Berger (1997) suggests that attitudes toward globalization are a reflection of four conflicting cultures that themselves are closely allied to specific institutions. The *Davos Culture* is the global culture, lifestyle, career patterns, and expectations of the international business community. The *Faculty Club* is the intellectual response to globalization, focused largely on reform and trying to "tame" and "humanize" the process and the realm of many INGOs. *MacWorld* is the name applied to the spread of consumerism and the Americanization of popular culture. And *Religious Revival* refers to the efforts of largely Protestant and Islamic groups at proselytizing and gaining greater influence. The values systems around these cultures are on a collision course, as they make very different claims on the nature of globalization, with INGOs as one institutional vehicle to advance one's cause, especially for the *Faculty Club* and *Religious Revival* camps.

Kaldor, Anheier, and Glasius (2003) develop a different though complementary approach to identifying political and values positions on globalization held by INGO leaders, political parties, governments, business executives, and individuals. Kaldor and colleagues argue that there are very few out-and-out supporters of globalization—groups or individuals who favor all forms of global connectedness, including trade, money, people, law, and politics; at the same time, there are very few total rejectionists. Rather, the dominant responses to globalization are mixed. Specifically, "regressive globalizers" are individuals, groups, and governments who favor globalization on their own terms and when it is in their particular interest. Reformers or "redistributive globalizers" are groups, individuals, governments, and multilateral institutions who, like Berger's Faculty Club, favor "civilizing" or "humanizing" globalization.

As summarized in Table 5.4, the development of INGOs over the past three decades has shown a remarkably consistent trajectory (Kaldor, Anheier, and Glasius, 2003). Three observations seem particularly noteworthy:

- The growth and expansion of INGOs seems closely associated with a major shift in cultural and social values that took hold in most developed market economies in the 1970s. This shift saw a change in emphasis from material security to concerns about democracy, participation, and meaning and involved, among other things, a move toward cosmopolitan values such as tolerance and

Table 5.4. Phases of INGO Development.

Decade	Infrastructure Growth	Fields	Form Innovation	Changes in Political Values	Popular Participation
1970s	Medium growth	Economics, research and science	Humanitarian membership-based INGOs	Rise of post-materialism	Slow increase
1980s	Acceleration of growth	Values-based	INGOs linked to International Social Movement	Cosmopolitan values	Mobilization
1990s	High growth	Values-based, service provision	Corporate NGOs	Consolidation	Slow increase
2000s	Moderation in growth	Service provision (likely)	Social forums, "dot causes"	Resilience	Increase around social forums

Source: Adapted from Kaldor, Anheier, and Glasius, 2003.

respect for human rights (see Inglehart, 1990; Inglehart and Baker, 2000). These values facilitated the cross-national spread of social movement around common issues that escaped conventional party politics, particularly in Europe and Latin America, and led to a broad-based mobilization in social movements, with the women's, peace, democracy, and environmental movements as the best example of an increasingly international "movement industry" (Diani and McAdam, 2003; McAdam, Tarrow, and Tilly, 2001).

• The 1990s brought a political opening and a broad-based mobilization of unknown proportion and scale (Kaldor, 2003) that coincided with the reappraisal of the role of the state in most developed countries and growing disillusionment with state-led multilateralism in the Third World among counterelites (Edwards, 1999). In addition to this broadened political space, favorable economic conditions throughout the 1990s and the vastly reduced costs of communications and greater ease of organizing facilitated the institutional expansion of global civil society in organizational terms (Anheier and Themudo, 2002; Clark, 2003).

• By 2002, the changed geopolitical environment and the economic downturn challenged both the by then relatively large number of INGOs and the broad values base of cosmopolitanism in many countries around the world, particularly among the middle classes and elites. As a result, new organizational forms and ways of organizing and communicating have gained in importance, with social forums and Internet-based mobilization as prominent examples. At the same time, frictions between the American and European visions of the world's future have arisen.

IMPLICATIONS FOR MANAGEMENT

For governance and management, the growth of INGOs into global actors has brought new organizational challenges (Clark, 2003; Lindenberg and Bryant, 2001; Young, 1992; Young, Koenig, Najam, and Fisher, 1999). Some are characteristic of nonprofit organizations generally and have become amplified by increased size, professionalization, and other changes associated with growth. Others, however, seem generic to the transnational character of INGOs and appear closely linked to the complexity of the diverse political, economic, and cultural environments in which they operate. We have discussed the implications of internationalization for INGO organizational forms elsewhere (Anheier and Themudo, 2002). Here we will examine some key implications for INGO management.

Critical challenges develop from the need to remain responsive to a diverse and dispersed constituency base, which poses crucial questions of accountability, effectiveness, and legitimacy (Edwards and Hulme, 1995). Moreover, INGOs are facing problems associated with increased organizational size and resource and information flows (Lindenberg and Dobel, 1999; Salm, 1999). We will briefly discuss each in turn. An essential aspect of the complexity of managing across borders is dealing with varying national regulatory frameworks for nonprofit activity with different fiscal regimes and definitions of acceptable advocacy and campaign work. To be effective, INGOs need to understand these national limitations when working in different countries. Moreover, many national regulatory frameworks require every INGO to establish a full national organization with its own board. In such cases, disputes may arise about who the "real" owners of the national branch are: its board or the international headquarters that created it.

A critical question INGOs have to face is the potential conflict between constituents' involvement and efficiency. Specifically, it is the conflict between the values of inclusion and participation in decision making, on the one hand, and organizational needs for efficiency, on the other. Public choice economics and the sociology of collective action (see Michels, 1962; Olson, 1965) have long suggested that democratic decision making and participation may take too much time and scarce resources and may in the end lead to untenable compromises.

By contrast, centralized decision making may not be sensitive to local conditions and may miss out on important information that can be essential for both legitimacy and efficiency. Edwards, Hulme, and Wallace. (1999, p. 134) suggest that most INGOs "try to defend the values-based approach of a global social movement inside an operational framework that drives the organization further into the marketplace. The result is unsurprising muddle and a great deal of internal tension." In campaigning INGOs, this problem is aggravated by what Clark (2003) called the "democracy paradox." INGOs campaign for more democracy of global governance structures but are far from democratic themselves. While these challenges will also be played out in domestic nonprofits, the dispersion of INGOs' constituency base increases the complexity of the problem. The high cost of bringing all constituencies together in one place precludes easy solutions. How can INGOs ensure that constituents in remote geographical areas remain as visible to headquarters and decision makers as constituents closer to the core?

On a different level, traditional government oversight of nonprofit organizations tends to break down at the international level. Perhaps with the exception of extreme cases of fraud, national authorities do not have jurisdiction to supervise INGO activities across borders. Similarly, individual givers in the North have little opportunity to verify the quality of the services being provided by INGOs in the South. Operating internationally therefore creates an opportunity to escape national regulations and supporter accountability. This is particularly true in humanitarian emergency situations when beneficiaries are highly vulnerable and lacking the power to demand ethical behavior from INGO staff. In such environments, special arrangements need to be in place to check opportunistic behavior by INGO staff and organizational partners. Although all nonprofits need to pay careful attention to accountability, because of the distances involved, INGOs have less direct accountability options available to them, and ensuring adequate accountability systems is a particularly challenging task. Scandals could easily destroy hard-earned public trust in these organizations (Gibelman and Gelman, 2001). As a result, INGOs have responded by formulating various self-regulating codes of practice, such as the International Code of Conduct in Humanitarian Relief, drawn up by the International Federation of Red Cross and Red Crescent Societies, to which many other INGOs working in relief have adhered.

INGO progress on dealing with these accountability and legitimacy challenges has been patchy. In an evaluation of accountability of international organizations commissioned by the One World Trust, Kovach, Neligan, and Burall (2003) measured two dimensions of global accountability (member control and access to information) in INGOs, transnational corporations, and other intergovernmental agencies such as the World Trade Organization (WTO). Their evaluation pointed to a mixed assessment of INGO accountability. On the one hand, INGOs such as the Red Cross and Amnesty International topped their evaluation table as the most accountable organizations they surveyed, ahead of organizations such as the OECD and the WTO. On the other hand, INGOs such as the World Wildlife Federation or CARE ranked as less accountable than corporations such as Rio Tinto (a transnational mining corporation) and GlaxoSmithKline (pharmaceutics). Generally, INGOs performed better than other international organizations in "member control of the organization" but performed less well on providing "access to information."

INGOs' higher profile has brought about new demands for accountability (Edwards and Hulme, 1995). NGOs must ensure that their accountability matches their increased power. The recent backlash against the American Red Cross for its handling of the September 11 fund drives home the point that INGOs must treat accountability and transparency very seriously. This is an essential element in their future sustainability because much of INGO legitimacy rests with their claims of accountability to their members, the poor, and the public good.

A related challenge concerns the "dilution of legitimacy" over long chains of partnership arrangements spanning multiple countries. In development, INGOs often do not work directly with beneficiaries but instead work with national and local organizations that work with the beneficiaries. Their claim to represent the interests of the poor thus depends on legitimacy chains of cooperation between various INGOs (Hudson, 2000). Ensuring accountability and legitimacy over networks of organizations working together internationally therefore poses another key challenge so as to avoid the distance between INGOs working internationally and beneficiaries at the local level limiting their organizational legitimacy and effectiveness.

A final challenge concerns the relations between headquarters and national affiliates and the optimum degree of centralization or decentralization of decision making (Lindenberg and Dobel, 1999). In complex task environments, decisions should be made where information is greatest, at the local level. On the other hand, centralization facilitates resource allocation to where needs are greatest. INGOs have been responding to the challenge of the optimal organizational form by adopting compromise forms such as the international federation (Anheier and Themudo, 2002; Young, Koenig, Najam, and Fisher, 1999) and by innovating into new organizational forms such as the "bumble bee federation" (Lindenberg and Dobel, 1999), rotating headquarters, and dual headquarters structures (Anheier and Themudo, 2002).

CONCLUSION

We conclude with a reflection on some of the consequences of the internationalization of the nonprofit sector. The internationalization of the sector both reflects and expands the role of INGOs and their recognition as global players—as testified by the Nobel Peace Prize awards to Doctors Without Borders and the Campaign to Ban Landmines. Boli (1999, p. 298) concluded that "INGOs exercise a surprising degree of authority in the contemporary world. This authority is neither coercive nor commanding; above all, it is cultural. It depends on widely and deeply legitimated theories of the ultimate sources of sovereignty, the proper institution of rational action, the worthwhile ends of human endeavors, and the proper organization of collective structure to solve social problems."

However, the internationalization of the nonprofit sector has not been homogeneous across different regions of the world. Access to cheaper technology and travel, knowledge of English, and the openness of domestic political structure vary dramatically between countries. Similarly, access to wealthy private donors, foundations, and government resources varies within and between countries. In this sense, when it comes to internationalization, "all NGOs are all equal, but some are more equal than others," which has implications for global governance and equity considerations in general.

We also argue that INGOs are likely to enter a new phase of seeking adequate responses to a changed and uncertain geopolitical situation. This process will likely lead to social innovations such as social forums, new kinds of alliances and coalitions, and the increased use of Internet-based forms of communicating and organizing. Indeed, the contrast between the 1990s and the 2000s is striking: The 1990s represented a period of both growth and consolidation, represented by the rapid growth of INGOs and a increasing emphasis on public management and corporate approaches. At the beginning of the twenty-first century, by contrast, we are witnessing a renewed mobilization of people and movements and a renewed emphasis on self-organization and activism. In the 1990s, the predominant political force behind globalization was a coalition between supporters and reformers, in transnational corporations as well as in governments and intergovernmental organization, and in INGOs—symbolized by the World Economic Forum in Davos, Switzerland. Could it be that Web-based platforms and social forums as vehicles for mobilization and activism are replacing this coalition, leading to more open and more participatory debates about the world's future?

References

AAFRC Trust for Philanthropy. *Giving USA 2002.* Indianapolis, Ind.: AAFRC Trust for Philanthropy, 2003.

Anheier, H. K., and Cunningham, K. "Internationalization of the Nonprofit Sector." In R. D. Herman and Associates, *The Jossey-Bass Handbook of Nonprofit Leadership and Management.* San Francisco: Jossey-Bass, 1994.

Anheier, H. K., Glasius, M., and Kaldor, M. "Introducing Global Civil Society." In H. K. Anheier, M. Glasius, and M. Kaldor (eds.), *Global Civil Society 2001.* Oxford, England: Oxford University Press, 2001.

Anheier, H. K., and Katz, H. "Mapping Global Civil Society." In M. Kaldor, H. K. Anheier, and M. Glasius (eds.), *Global Civil Society 2003*. Oxford, England: Oxford University Press, 2003.

Anheier, H. K., and List, R. *Cross-Border Philanthropy: An Exploratory Study of International Giving in the United Kingdom, United States, Germany, and Japan.* West Malling, England: Charities Aid Foundation; London: Centre for Civil Society, London School of Economics, 2000.

Anheier, H. K., and Salamon, L. M. "The Nonprofit Sector in Comparative Perspective." In W. W. Powell and R. Steinberg, R. (eds.), *The Nonprofit Sector: A Research Handbook*. New Haven, Conn.: Yale University Press, 2005.

Anheier, H. K., and Themudo, N. "Organizational Forms of Global Civil Society: Implications of Going Global." In H. K. Anheier, M. Glasius, and M. Kaldor (eds.), *Global Civil Society 2002*. Oxford, England: Oxford University Press, 2002.

Archambault, E., Gariazzo, M., Anheier, H. K., and Salamon, L. M. "From Jacobin Tradition to Decentralization." In L. M. Salamon and Associates, *Global Civil Society: Dimensions of the Nonprofit Sector.* Baltimore: Johns Hopkins Center for Civil Society Studies, 1999.

Berger, P. L. "Four Faces of Global Culture." *National Interest*, 1997, *23*(7), 23–29.

Boli, J. "Conclusion." In J. Boli and G. M. Thomas (eds.), *Constructing World Culture: International Nongovernmental Organizations Since 1875*. Stanford, Calif.: Stanford University Press, 1999.

Boli, J., and Thomas, G. M. (eds.). *Constructing World Culture: International Nongovernmental Organizations Since 1875*. Stanford, Calif.: Stanford University Press, 1999.

Chambers, R. *Rural Development: Putting the Last First*. New York: Longman, 1986.

Clark, J. *Democratizing Development: The Role of Voluntary Agencies*. Bloomfield, Conn.: Kumarian Press, 1991.

Clark, J. *Worlds Apart: Civil Society and the Battle for Ethical Globalization*. Bloomfield, Conn.: Kumarian Press, 2003.

Clark, J., and Themudo, N. "The Age of Protest: Internet-Based 'Dot-Causes' and the 'Anti-Globalization' Movement." In J. Clark (ed.), *Globalizing Civic Engagement: Civil Society and Transnational Action*. London: Earthscan, 2003.

Clarke, G. "Nongovernmental Organisations and Politics in the Developing World." *Political Studies*, 1998, *46*, 36–52.

Development Initiatives. "Global Development Assistance: The Role of NGOs and Other Charity Flows" (mimeo). Somerset, England: Development Initiatives, July 2000.

Diani, M., and McAdam, D. *Social Movements and Networks: Relational Approaches to Collective Action*. Oxford, England: Oxford University Press, 2003.

Edwards, M. "Legitimacy and Values in NGOs and Voluntary Organizations: Some Skeptical Thoughts." In D. J. Lewis (ed.), *International Perspectives on Voluntary Action: Reshaping the Third Sector*. London: Earthscan, 1999.

Edwards, M., and Hulme, D. (eds.). *Beyond the Magic Bullet: NGO Performance and Accountability in the Post–Cold War World.* London: Macmillan, 1995.

Edwards, M., Hulme, D., and Wallace, T. "NGOs in a Global Future: Marrying Local Delivery to Worldwide Leverage." *Public Administration and Development,* 1999, *19,* 117–136.

Fisher, J. *The Road from Rio: Sustainable Development and the Nongovernmental Movement in the Third World.* Westport, Conn.: Praeger, 1993.

Foundation Center. *International Grant-Making.* New York: Foundation Center, 2002.

Fowler, A. *The Virtuous Spiral: A Guide to Sustainability of NGOs in International Development.* London: Earthscan, 2000.

Gibelman, M., and Gelman, S. "Very Public Scandals: Nongovernmental Organizations in Trouble." *Voluntas,* 2001, *12*(1), 49–66.

Glasius, M., and Kaldor, M. "The State of Global Civil Society: Before and After September 11." In H. K. Anheier, M. Glasius, and M. Kaldor (eds.), *Global Civil Society 2002.* Oxford, England: Oxford University Press, 2002.

Held, D., McGrew, A., Goldblatt, D., and Perraton, J. *Global Transformations: Politics, Economics and Culture.* Cambridge, England: Polity Press, 1999.

Hudson, A. "Making the Connection: Legitimacy Claims, Legitimacy Chains, and Northern NGOs' International Advocacy." In D. J. Lewis and T. Wallace (eds.), *New Roles and Relevance: Development NGOs and the Challenge of Change.* Bloomfield, Conn.: Kumarian Press, 2000.

Inglehart, R. *Culture Shift in Advanced Industrial Society.* Princeton, N.J.: Princeton University Press, 1990.

Inglehart, R., and Baker, W. "Modernization, Cultural Change, and the Persistence of Traditional Values." *American Sociological Review,* 2000, *65,* 19–51.

Kaldor, M. *Global Civil Society: An Answer to War.* Cambridge, England: Polity Press, 2003.

Kaldor, M., Anheier, H. K., and Glasius, M. "Global Civil Society in an Era of Regressive Globalization." In M. Kaldor, H. K. Anheier, and M. Glasius (eds.), *Global Civil Society, 2003.* Oxford, England: Oxford University Press, 2003.

Keck, M., and Sikkink, K. *Activists Beyond Borders: Advocacy Networks in International Politics.* Ithaca, N.Y.: Cornell University Press, 1998.

Kendall, J., and Almond, S. "United Kingdom." In L. M. Salamon and Associates, *Global Civil Society: Dimensions of the Nonprofit Sector.* Baltimore: Johns Hopkins Center for Civil Society Studies, 1999.

Kovach, H., Neligan, C., and Burall, S. "The Global Accountability Report: Power Without Accountability?" One World Trust [http://www.oneworldtrust.org]. 2003.

Lewis, D. J. *The Management of Non-Governmental Development Organisations: An Introduction.* London: Routledge, 2001.

Lindenberg, M., and Bryant, C. *Going Global: Transforming Relief and Development NGOs.* Bloomfield, Conn.: Kumarian Press, 2001.

Lindenberg, M., and Dobel, J. P. "The Challenges of Globalization for Northern International Relief and Development NGOs." *Nonprofit and Voluntary Sector Quarterly*, 1999, *28*(4 suppl.), 2–24.

McAdam, D., Tarrow, S., and Tilly, C. *Dynamics of Contention.* New York: Cambridge University Press, 2001.

Meyer, J. W., Boli, J., Thomas, G. M., and Ramirez, F. O. "World Society and the Nation-State." *American Journal of Sociology*, 1997, *103*(1):144–181.

Michels, R. *Political Parties: A Sociological Study of the Oligarchical Tendencies of Modern Democracy.* New York: Free Press, 1962.

Najam, A. "Understanding the Third Sector: Revisiting the Prince, the Merchant, and the Citizen." *Nonprofit Management and Leadership,* 1996, *7*(2), 203–219.

Olson, M. *The Logic of Collective Action.* Cambridge, Mass.: Harvard University Press, 1965.

O'Neill, K. "Internetworking for Social Change: Keeping the Spotlight on Corporate Responsibility." Discussion Paper no. 111. Geneva, Switzerland: United Nations Research Institute for Social Development, 1999.

Otlet, P. *Tableau de l'Organisation Internationale: Rapport Général à la Conférence des Associations Internationales.* Publication no. 114. Geneva, Switzerland: Union of International Associations, 1924.

Priller, E., and others. "Germany." In L. M. Salamon and Associates, *Global Civil Society: Dimensions of the Nonprofit Sector.* Baltimore: Johns Hopkins Center for Civil Society Studies, 1999.

Salamon, L. M., and Anheier, H. K. *The Emerging Nonprofit Sector: An Overview.* Manchester, England: Manchester University Press, 1996.

Salamon, L. M., and Anheier, H. K. *Defining the Nonprofit Sector: A Cross-National Analysis.* Manchester, England: Manchester University Press, 1997.

Salamon, L. M., and Associates. *Global Civil Society: Dimensions of the Nonprofit Sector.* Baltimore: Johns Hopkins Center for Civil Society Studies, 1999.

Salamon, L. M., Sokolowski, S. W., and List, R. *Global Civil Society: An Overview.* Baltimore: Johns Hopkins Center for Civil Society Studies, 2003.

Salm, J. "Coping with Globalization: A Profile of the Northern NGO Sector." *Nonprofit and Voluntary Sector Quarterly*, 1999, *28*(4 suppl.), 87–103.

Smillie, I., and Hailey, J. *Managing for Change: Leadership, Strategy and Management in Asian NGOs.* London: Earthscan, 2001.

Smith, J., Chatfield, C., Pagnucco, R., and Chatfield, C. A. *Transnational Social Movements and Global Politics: Solidarity Beyond the State.* Syracuse, N.Y.: Syracuse University Press, 1997.

Stuart, J. (ed.). *The 2002 NGO Sustainability Index for Central and Eastern Europe and Eurasia.* Washington, D.C.: United States Agency for International Development, 2003.

Tew, E. "Location of International Organizations." *International Organizations,* 1963, *8,* 492–493.

United Nations Development Programme. *Human Development Report 2001.* New York: United Nations Development Programme, 2001.

Union of International Associations. *Yearbook of International Associations: Guide to Global Civil Society Networks.* Munich, Germany: Saur, 1990.

Union of International Associations. *Yearbook of International Associations: Guide to Global Civil Society Networks.* Munich, Germany: Saur, 2000.

Union of International Associations. *Yearbook of International Associations: Guide to Global Civil Society Networks.* Munich, Germany: Saur, 2002.

United States Agency for International Development. *Foreign Assistance: Private Voluntary Organizations' Contributions and Limitations.* Washington, D.C.: United States Agency for International Development, 1995.

United States Agency for International Development. *Report of Voluntary Agencies Engaged in Overseas Relief and Development Registered with the U.S. Agency for International Development.* Washington, D.C.: United States Agency for International Development, 1998, 1999, 2000, 2001, 2002, 2003.

Wallace, T. "Development Management and the Aid Chain: The Case of NGOs." In D. Eade (ed.), *Development and Management.* Oxford, England: Oxfam, 2000.

Young. D. "Organizing Principles for International Advocacy Associations." *Voluntas,* 1992, *3*(1), 1–28.

Young, D., Koenig, B., Najam, A., and Fisher, J. "Strategy and Structure in Managing Global Associations." *Voluntas,* 1999, *10*(4), 323–343.

PART TWO

KEY LEADERSHIP ISSUES

Governance and leadership are important areas in which nonprofit organizations differ significantly from businesses and government agencies. Boards of directors (or trustees) of nonprofit organizations are legally responsible for the conduct of organizational affairs and are expected to provide leadership in defining their organizations' missions, values, and strategies. Experience and systematic research have shown that chief executives of nonprofit organizations often play central leadership roles as well.

The six chapters in this part of the book collectively examine the leadership roles that boards and chief executives are expected to enact in nonprofit organizations, the difficulties that sometimes prevent boards or executives from carrying out their prescribed roles, and the strategies and techniques that have proved useful in enhancing the leadership effectiveness of both boards and executives. The first chapter in this part focuses on the board side of the board–chief executive leadership relation and draws on the increased body of research to present ways for boards to carry out their responsibilities more effectively. The next chapter examines the chief executive role, emphasizing how chief executives can facilitate board effectiveness. Later chapters highlight the leadership roles of boards and executives, as well as other constituencies, in strategic planning, creating and maintaining an ethical organizational culture, advocating for legislation or regulatory actions pertaining to organizational missions, and effectively engaging in strategic alliances with other organizations. Each of these chapters provides important details about the issues and practices that constitute strategic planning, lobbying, and strategic alliances.

CHAPTER SIX

Board Leadership and Development

Nancy R. Axelrod

The governance landscape has changed over the past decade, but some things remain the same. Hopes and frustrations regarding nonprofit boards continue to fuel the demand for tools to help boards fulfill their responsibilities. On the supply side, the number of research studies, educational programs, publications, and consulting services directed to the performance of nonprofit boards has increased to address what board and staff members presumably want and need.

Much of the recent literature revisits governance challenges such as the quest for strategic focus and the areas in which the responsibilities of the board overlap with those of the staff. A great deal of the literature strikes a prescriptive or aspirational tone. Some of it probes more deeply beneath the traditional roles ascribed to boards. The best of it illuminates the different ways that boards are perceived to add value and the multiple ways in which the construct of board effectiveness changes according to the eyes of the beholder.

What has clearly not changed is the subtext that predates the latest wave of governance research and resources: too many boards are performing below par and individual board members are underdeployed. Some analysts suggest that this is the norm given the steady turnover among volunteer board members and chief executives, as well as the institutional life cycle and environmental changes that provide opportunities for boards to either progress or regress. After all, even high-performing boards can be jolted off track by a leadership transition or a critical incident that alters the rules of engagement. Other observers argue that the board development industry has been tackling the wrong issues, ignoring systemic problems, or providing superficial board development interventions.

The climate in which boards operate, however, is changing. After several years of steady financial growth at many nonprofits, the current crop of board and staff members has worked in the wake of a weaker economy to build infrastructure, diversify revenue, and maintain financial stability as their traditional funding sources are scaled back. Increased generational and multicultural diversity has had an impact not only on the services that nonprofits deliver but also on what boards are expected to look like in relation to the communities they serve. The past decade has also brought unprecedented technological advances that provide new opportunities and new vulnerabilities for nonprofit leaders competing in the new networked economy. All of this has triggered an avalanche of advice from just about every quarter that exhorts boards and professional staff to become more effective, more efficient, and more entrepreneurial.

The tough economy, changing demographics, and rapid technological change are not the only issues that have raised the bar for good governance. The corporate scandals that rocked Wall Street in the early 2000s and the questionable practices uncovered at a number of nonprofit organizations over the past several years have heightened public scrutiny of boards. Well-publicized cases of mismanagement have revealed improper accounting, fraudulent practices, ethical lapses, financial irregularities, and lax oversight. What most of these cases have demonstrated at the board level is not so much a pattern of malfeasance as a pattern of "nongovernance."

THE LIMITATIONS OF MODELS AND BEST PRACTICES

Over the past two decades, theorists, consultants, and practitioners have proffered a broad array of models, prescriptions, and tools for building effective boards. These approaches range from crafting an inviolate division of labor between the board and the staff to delegating de facto leadership and development of the board to the chief executive. Differences in mission, stage of the organization's development, strengths and weaknesses of staff and board leaders, and critical issues facing the organization render off-the-shelf governance templates advocated by others inadequate for most boards.

Nevertheless, it is tempting to use a kind of mix-and-match approach from the burgeoning menu of benchmarks. Even this approach, however, yields mixed results because benchmarks and best practices typically presume that there is a single best way, certain preconditions are in place, and consensus exists on what constitutes success. Rather than borrow policies or practices advocated by others, organizations would be better served if their leaders determined which practices were consistent with their mission, visions, and values and how these practices can be continually improved.

Launching a quest for the best model in reaction to dissatisfaction with the status quo is putting the cart before the horse. This search is elusive without an appraisal—long overdue at many organizations—of how the board is perceived to make a difference. One hopes that the following metaphor will not resonate with most nonprofit leaders:

> In many organizations, the board is viewed in a way similar to an appendix, a part of the body without apparent purpose but capable of serious inconvenience. The combination of apparent superfluity with the capacity to inflict real discomfort makes many question the need to have a board. Seeing only their inconvenience and failing to understand their value are strong disincentives to invest in their competence and effectiveness. In this way, a board blessed with a measure of good will but little understanding of anything about its role except that it is "in charge" will fail, and in its failing perpetuate the notion that it's more trouble than it is worth. [Robinson, 2001, p. 12]

Governance models and board development interventions can be helpful once the criteria of board effectiveness have been defined. For some, board effectiveness will look like keeping the board out of operations or the absence of dissent in the boardroom. For others, it will look like narrowing the locus of the board's work to carrying out its fiduciary obligations and reacting to management's recommendations. Others will find superior performance only when board members are meaningfully engaged in shaping institutional character, direction, and strategy.

A large number of organizations have enacted either incremental or radical changes to governance mechanisms. Though some of these changes have resulted in significant improvements, there is little evidence in too many cases of a causal connection between the changes made and improved board performance. In the final analysis, determining how the board can add the greatest value and what constitutes board effectiveness should represent strategic choices, not default practices. It is encouraging to note the growing number of retreats, plenary sessions dedicated to board effectiveness, and board self-assessment exercises dedicated to tackling important questions such as these:

- Why does our board matter beyond its legal and symbolic functions?
- What is working well?
- What areas need attention or improvement?
- What performance measures will demonstrate improved board performance or effectiveness?
- What steps can we take to improve the board's performance and effectiveness?

Once there is consensus on the answers to these questions, the courage to change and the will to act become greater hurdles than figuring out which models are suitable and what needs to be done.

THE BOARD'S RESPONSIBILITIES

An overriding responsibility of a governing board is that of fiduciary, which requires a duty to act for the good of others. The Internal Revenue Service recognizes the tax-exempt status granted to nonprofit organizations based on the broad concept that they operate for the benefit of the general public. Unlike the governing board of a for-profit corporation, which is accountable to either the owners or the shareholders of the corporation, the nonprofit board is ultimately accountable to the public if it is a 501(c)(3) charitable institution (and others, such as members, an industry, or a profession, if it is set up as a professional or trade association).

The principal legal requirements that apply to nonprofit boards can be found in the fiduciary responsibilities developed from well-established principles of nonprofit corporation law and the provisions imposed by state statutes, federal laws, and legal documents such as articles of incorporation and bylaws. What they have in common is the premise that the board is ultimately responsible for ensuring that the organization it governs fulfills its mission. Board members are expected to serve as stewards to protect the assets of the organization and make sure that it operates in accordance with applicable laws.

A central paradox of nonprofit boards is that the board holds ultimate power but does not ordinarily wield it operationally unless the organization does not have any paid staff members. State statutes, the certificate of incorporation, or the bylaws assign the "management" of the business, property, and affairs of the organization to the board. A board with professional staff typically delegates the administration of the organization's day-to-day business to staff unless there is a compelling reason, such as a leadership vacuum, to justify board members' serving as surrogate administrators on a temporary basis.

State requirements vary, but generally, board members are held to three standards of conduct: the duty of obedience, the duty of care, and the duty of loyalty. The duty of obedience requires board members to be faithful to the organization's mission and to act in a way that is consistent with the central goals of the organization and applicable federal, state, and local laws. The duty of care requires board members to exercise reasonable care by staying informed, participating in decisions, and acting in good faith when they make decisions on behalf of the organization. The duty of loyalty requires board members to put the interests of the organization first when making decisions affecting the organization.

Although the fiduciary role is fundamentally the same for all nonprofit boards, legal obligations (or bylaws) do not provide much guidance on *how* boards should carry out their work. In fact, the roles and performance expectations of boards and their members are often as poorly defined at the institutional as at the statutory level. Within individual organizations, one often finds divergent perceptions about the board's primary roles as well as a gap between what the board is expected to do and how it actually spends its time. Ambiguous expectations have created a fertile market for programs and services that delineate board responsibilities, and consumers are often bewildered by the ambivalent assumptions these resources convey about the structure, values, and culture of the organization to be governed. Does it make sense, for example, to advise boards to confine their work to policy formulation when board members may be needed to engage in operational matters of strategic importance?

"Governance has the legitimacy and credibility to continuously attend to issues related to strategic direction," observe the authors of *The Will to Govern Well*. "This does not mean that other groups cannot come together to think about things in different ways, but such groups must serve the board as sources of insight, ideas, and information. If governance is not actively engaged in considering strategic direction, the association may find that board decisions about policy, program, and budget have little reference or relevance to the significant strategic issues confronting the organization, and instead, priorities will be set in the budgeting process—based on politics, perceptions, and past practice" (Tecker, Frankel, and Meyer, 2002, p.7).

Specific board responsibilities naturally vary from organization to organization, but Exhibit 6.1 describes four primary roles ascribed to most governing boards. The precise mix of board responsibilities for each organization can be defined only after the chief executive and board determine how the board can add the greatest value to the organization and the expectations of board and board member performance that these responsibilities convey. Furthermore, the focus of the board's work is likely to shift according to the organization's needs and priorities at different times during its life cycle.

THREE WAYS TO ENHANCE BOARD EFFECTIVENESS

Some experts question whether the traditional roles attributed to boards, along with their legally prescribed fiduciary obligations, are sufficient to enable boards to fulfill their potential. First, certain conventional responsibilities assigned to boards may reflect services that can be rendered as well or better by professional staff, direct service volunteers, paid consultants, or a combination of such individuals. Second, some roles may be necessary but insufficient to benefit from the kind of intellectual capital that some nonprofit leaders want from their

Exhibit 6.1. Primary Governance Roles Ascribed to Boards.

Primary Governance Roles Ascribed to Boards	*Ways in Which Boards Fulfill These Roles*
1. Define and advance the organization's mission.	• Establish the mission at the time that the organization is formed. • Ensure that the mission is clearly articulated and understood and supported by board members. • Regularly review the mission and revise it if necessary. • Engage in strategic thinking to determine the strategic directions and priorities against the organization's mission, vision, values, and changes in the internal and external environment. • Help shape institutional strategy to advance the mission.
2. Ensure, develop, and conserve the organization's resources (including funds, property, and human resources).	• Ensure that adequate financial resources are secured to support the organization. • Ensure that the organization's current revenues are stable, and encourage the cultivation of sources of revenue that are sustainable for the long term. • Ensure that income is managed properly and that financial statements are accurate, intelligible, comprehensive, and timely to reflect the true financial condition of the organization and key financial transactions. • Ensure that accumulated assets (both funds and property) are protected. • Ensure that policies and practices are in place to protect the well-being, safety, and development of staff, volunteers, clients, and members. • Establish risk management policies and practices that adhere to legal standards and ethical norms, protect the organization from legal action, and safeguard the organization's integrity.
3. Provide oversight of management, and ensure assessment of the organization.	• Select, support, and regularly review the performance of the chief executive officer consistent with the expectations articulated by the board. • Hold management accountable for performance. • Monitor the organization's performance and its progress against goals.

Exhibit 6.1. Primary Governance Roles Ascribed to Boards (continued).

Primary Governance Roles Ascribed to Boards	*Ways in Which Boards Fulfill These Roles*
	• Ensure that policies are in place to evaluate the organization's programs and services to determine if they advance the mission and are effective in meeting the needs of beneficiaries. • Select and orient new board members. • Provide continuing education for board members. • Periodically assess the performance of the board.
4. Engage in outreach as a bridge and a buffer between the organization and its stakeholders (clients, members, the communities it serves, regulators, donors, the public).	• Serve as ambassadors to communicate the organization's mission, policies, programs, and services to its various stakeholders. • Interpret and communicate to the organization the needs of the communities served by the organization. • Define the organization's position on public policies and serve as advocates. • Protect the organization from inappropriate intrusions by government and special interests. • Promote the organization to donors and potential donors.

board members. Third, agreement on the responsibilities of the board and expectations of its individual members does not automatically mean that the board will successfully execute its job description.

Board effectiveness continues to be invoked as if it were a monolithic construct. Effectiveness of course means different things to different people, but complaints about board performance reflect recurring themes. Three of the most common complaints are that the board does not spend enough time on the things that matter most; board meetings and other forums are overly scripted and choreographed and offer little opportunity to explore emerging issues, consider viable alternatives, and make thoughtful decisions; and individual board members seem to perform better than the group as a whole. Some analysts speculate that a fundamental design flaw exists in matters of structure and process. Others complain that the current structure is fine; it is the execution that needs improvement.

Most boards are never given opportunities to frame a vigorous defense for their existence or to build their performance in ways that establish that they do in fact matter. Boards have the potential to bring substantial value to the work of an organization, but that value will remain largely untapped if it is not understood, articulated, and cultivated. Assigning value is a necessary first step in any process designed to make boards better. We need to be convinced that boards matter before we can engage in a heartfelt effort to make them effective. Without an honest exploration of the issue of value, reforming things like composition and committee structures, or rethinking the role of board and staff become empty gestures. [Robinson, 2001, p.13]

Dissatisfaction with board performance has spurred more thoughtful research on the actual behaviors of boards and the variables that affect their operation and performance. The following three approaches provide ways to view and ultimately improve board effectiveness. Once nonprofit leaders have defined the board's "value proposition" (beyond its legal and symbolic functions), each of these areas offers a springboard for evaluating current performance, setting goals for improvement, identifying concrete steps to strengthen effectiveness, and documenting changes over time.

Assessing the Board's Competencies

In an attempt to reconceptualize governance as part of the Governance Futures project sponsored by BoardSource and the Hauser Center for Nonprofit Organizations at Harvard University, Ryan, Chait, and Taylor (2003, p. 52) observe that in recent years, "the field of nonprofit governance has approached the challenge of board improvement by continually trying to narrow the scope of the proper work for boards to a set of canonical responsibilities. Given the persistent dissatisfaction with board performance, perhaps this approach should be reconsidered. We can start with three questions. Why have we felt compelled to narrow board work to certain prescribed functions? Have we trimmed board service to the right set of essentials? And does the official job description really advance better governance?"

The research team of Chait, Holland, and Taylor (1996) spent several years of intensive study trying to determine why some nonprofit boards excel while others falter. From their initial research on boards reputed to be either very effective or ineffective, they discovered a pattern of behaviors distinguishing high-performing boards from their less successful counterparts. Although even the most effective boards in their study had not mastered every one of the six competencies described in Exhibit 6.2, they exhibited a greater overall degree of proficiency on each competency than less effective boards.

Chait, Holland, and Taylor have advanced the field by providing a tool to measure board performance and empirically assess the impact of a variety of board development interventions that are linked to specific, observable practices. To make use of the inventory of practical suggestions they offer to enhance board performance, practitioners (and especially chief executives) will need to determine if they can genuinely embrace and invest in building the kind of strong, active board that is characterized by the six competencies described in Exhibit 6.2.

Exhibit 6.2. Board Development Practices Linked to Board Competencies.

Competency	Some Practices That Demonstrate Competency
Contextual: The board understands and takes into account the culture, norms, and values of the organization it governs.	• Orientations that include explicit introduction to the organization's values, norms, and traditions. • Former members, administrators, and "living legends" conveying the organization's history. • Current leaders discussing the concepts of shared governance, collegiality, and consensus. • Leaders reviewing the organization's hallmark characteristics and basic values that set it apart from competitors.
Educational: The board takes the necessary steps to ensure that members are well informed about the organization, the profession, and the board's own roles, responsibilities, and performance.	• Setting aside time at each meeting for a seminar or workshop to learn about an important matter of substance or process or to discuss a common reading. • Conducting extended retreats every year or two for similar purposes and for analyzing the board's operations and mistakes. • Meeting periodically with "role counterparts" from comparable organizations. • Rotating committee assignments so members come to know many aspects of the organization. • Establishing internal feedback mechanisms such as evaluative comments from members at the end of each meeting and conducting annual surveys of board members on individual and collective performance.
Interpersonal: The board nurtures the development of its members as a group, attends to the board's collective welfare, and fosters a sense of cohesiveness.	• Creating a sense of inclusiveness through events that enable members to become better acquainted with one another, building some "slack time" into the schedule for informal interaction, and sharing information widely and communicating regularly. • Communicating group norms and standards by pairing new board members with a mentor or coach. • Ensuring that the board has strong leadership by systematically grooming its future leaders and encouraging individual skills development.
Analytical: The board recognizes complexities and subtleties in the issues it faces and draws	• Analyzing issues and events taking into account multiple potential outcomes and points of view. • Seeking concrete and even contradictory information on ambiguous matters.

Exhibit 6.2. Board Development Practices Linked to Board Competencies (continued).

Competency	Some Practices That Demonstrate Competency
on multiple perspectives to dissect complex problems and to synthesize appropriate responses.	• Asking a few members to be critical evaluators or "devil's advocates," exploring the downside of recommendations. • Developing contingency and crisis plans. • Asking members to assume the perspective of key constituencies by role playing. • Brainstorming alternative views of issues. • Consulting outsiders and seeking different viewpoints.
Political: The board accepts as one of its primary responsibilities the need to develop and maintain healthy relationships among all key constituencies.	• Broadening channels of communication by distributing profiles of board members and annual board reports, inviting staff and consumers to serve on board committees, inviting outside leaders to address the board, visiting with staff, and establishing multiconstituency task forces. • Working closely with the chief executive to develop and maintain processes that enable board members to communicate directly with stakeholders. • Monitoring the health of relationships and morale in the organization. • Keeping options open and avoiding win-lose polarizations. • Being sensitive to the legitimate roles and responsibilities of all stakeholders.
Strategic: The board envisions and shapes institutional direction and helps to ensure a strategic approach to the organization's future.	• Focusing the board's attention on strategic issues by asking the chief executive to present an annual update on organizational priorities and strategy, establishing board priorities and work plans, and developing an annual agenda for the board and its committees. • Structuring the board's meetings to concentrate on strategic priorities. • Reinforcing attention to priorities by providing key questions for discussion in advance of meetings, reserving time at each meeting for the chief executive to discuss future issues, and making use of a "consent agenda." • Monitoring the use of board time and attention.

Source: Adapted from Holland and Blackmon, 2000, pp. 8–9. Text may not be reproduced without written permission from BoardSource.

Building the Board's Capacity
to Work as a High-Performing Group

One of the values assigned to boards is that an effective group can make better decisions than any individual. But moving from a mere working group to a high-functioning team does not happen overnight—in either the nonprofit or the for-profit sector. In his study of what makes teams effective, Patrick Lencioni (2003) notes that although most people believe in teamwork and proclaim its virtues, few organizations actually practice it. "In fact, they often end up creating environments where political infighting and departmental silos are the norm. And yet they continue to tout their belief in teamwork, as if that alone will somehow make it magically appear" (p. 1).

Teamwork demands hard work and often substantial behavioral changes from strong individual board members who may be set in their ways, used to calling the shots, and more skilled at suppressing conflict rather than at voicing differences. Chait, Holland, and Taylor (1996) found that without an intentional effort to develop the capacity of the individuals on a board to work as a team, the natural tendency is for board members to drift away from the long-term view, strategic focus, and collective actions we associate with effective boards.

The correlation between the board's ability to work as a robust group and its performance is also starting to be recognized in the for-profit sector, thanks to the governance breakdowns at major companies that resulted in the Sarbanes-Oxley corporate reform legislation enacted in 2002. When corporate governance expert Jeffrey Sonnenfeld (2002) examined the boards of Enron, WorldCom, and other once great companies that experienced meltdowns, he found no broad patterns of incompetence or corruption among their boards. Quite the contrary, Sonnenfeld found that most were following best governance practices regarding meeting attendance, board size, committee structure, the financial literacy of individual board members, accountability mechanisms in place such as codes of ethics and conflict of interest policies—and even ratio of inside to outside directors.

When Sonnenfeld compared boards of high-profile companies that failed with corporate boards considered the best in the field, he isolated the degree to which the board is performing as a "high-functioning work group" as the most salient difference. Sonnenfeld (2002) concluded that what makes "great boards great" in the corporate sector relates to group traits such as whether there is a climate of trust and candor among board members and between the board and management; whether information is shared openly and on time; whether board members feel free to challenge one another's assumptions and conclusions; whether management encourages lively discussion of strategic issues; and whether boards assess their own performance collectively and individually.

When Salovey and Mayer coined the term "emotional intelligence" in 1990, they introduced the significant role that social and other noncognitive abilities play in predicting success for individuals in daily life and in the workplace. In a similar fashion, the unspoken rules that drive how individual board members behave as a group are likely to have a profound impact on the performance of the board as a whole. Striving for teamwork is important, but it should not trump common sense, healthy skepticism, or the search for meaningful alternatives. Boards that don't come together as a well-performing group can create barriers to their own effectiveness that range from dysfunctional harmony and groupthink to control of the governance process by a few.

Perhaps the miracle is the number of nonprofit boards that do exhibit the tolerance for multiple viewpoints, courage to ask difficult questions, capacity to express dissent, and communication skills to work through tough issues without members' either attacking each other or resorting to "pathological politeness." Boards that demonstrate these competencies have a much greater chance of never hearing the two interrelated questions that invariably follow crises and scandals: Why and how were these questionable practices allowed to happen? Where was the board?

Like many other things, governance is not complex in theory, but behaviorally, it is complex and challenging work. Interpersonal behaviors and group dynamics that form the "culture" of the board have been marginalized as the soft side of governance because they are hard to talk about and even more difficult to measure. Chait, Holland, Taylor, Sonnenfeld, and others have advanced the field by demonstrating that the way in which board members work together is at least as important as the work they do. They have also reminded us that qualitative changes in behaviors, relationships, and group process within every board can and should be subject to performance criteria and measurement.

Recognizing the Chief Executive's Role

Historically, some boards and executives have sought comfort if not cognitive closure by confining policy formulation to boards and assigning implementation to staff. Ryan, Chait, and Taylor (2003) capture the inadequacy of this old bromide restricting boards to the domain of policy:

> Many board members have trouble staying there, and when they cross the boundary into management territory, many executives and consultants are quick to condemn them as either woefully ignorant or downright mischievous. Whatever the reason, when boards so "misbehave," managers proffer the official job description as guidance or wave it like a restraining order. But in reality, it's hard to discern the line that divides policy and strategy from administration and operations. How can we be sure an operational matter is not of sufficient significance to warrant the board's attention? It doesn't help to assert that governors should not manage when the difference between management and governance is not crystal clear. It's also hard to govern at arm's length from the organization and without first-hand knowledge of the "business." How can a board develop strategy without direct contact with the operational realities

of the organization—which is precisely where new strategies and ideas often emerge and are invariably validated or discredited? How can a board evaluate the performance of an organization without some direct knowledge of the enterprise? [p. 52]

A high tolerance for ambiguity can and should be tempered by a conscious effort to clarify the respective roles of board and the chief executive, especially in areas in which more than one stakeholder group has authority. But updated job descriptions for both parties will not eliminate gray areas or the continuous need for good judgment that serve the interests of the organization. The kinds of governance breakdowns that have occurred in the past at nonprofit organizations such as United Way of America circa 1992 suggest that the difference between responsible oversight and meddlesome intrusion sometimes cannot be determined until after the fact, with the clarity and wisdom of hindsight. Boards ultimately have more power than the executive, which they can use to control or support the executive. Executives can either hoard or share information with the board. The way that executives and board members choose to exchange their respective powers (as well as their alignment on shared mission, vision, and values) will do more to affect the quality of governance than any ironclad agreement on proper boundaries.

Research conducted by Herman and Heimovics (1991) found that especially effective chief executives differed most from their counterparts not in their fundraising prowess or their management accomplishments per se but in how they treat their boards. They described six specific board competencies associated with this "board-centered" chief executive: facilitating interaction in board relationships; showing consideration and respect toward board members; envisioning change and innovation with the board; promoting board accomplishments and productivity; initiating and maintaining a structure for board work; and providing helpful information to the board.

It would be hard to understate the key role the chief executive officer plays in determining where and how the board invests its time. Just as individual board members are capable of sleeping on the job or micromanaging, chief executives can be guilty of "undermanaging" their responsibility to help engage board members in meaningful governance. If chief executives are not willing to play an active role in creating the kinds of strategic boards many claim they need, these hopes will not be fulfilled by exhortation. Chait (2003) advises chief executives who want their boards to "govern more and manage less" to take the time to "articulate an institutional strategy for careful, periodic review by the board; structure board materials to direct board members' attention to issues of policy and strategy; structure board meetings to direct board members' attention to issues of policy and strategy; and equip board members with the capacity to monitor organizational performance and progress" (p. 12).

THE DISCIPLINE OF BOARD DEVELOPMENT

Most individuals who serve on boards do not receive any formal preparation for their role. Yet new and more experienced board members approach their positions with a wide array of expectations about what it means to be a good board member. The path to good governance becomes steeper when board members encounter unclear expectations, ambiguous performance indicators, or weak accountability mechanisms once they join the board.

It is hard to find a nonprofit leader who does not proclaim the virtue of a high-performing board. It is even harder to find leaders who adequately invest in the orientation and continuing education of their boards. The gap between the rhetoric and reality of board development is not surprising. In day-to-day operations, many nonprofits are overwhelmed with insufficient financial resources and overworked staff and volunteers. The time and dollars that must be channeled into board development are often put on hold to attend to the immediate and the urgent. And for some, the concept of a strong, active board holds all the charm of a colonoscopy. Nonprofit executives may be reluctant to educate and engage the board for fear that this will breed meddlesome board members who begin to act more like part-time administrators than stalwart policymakers.

Once again, the underlying question of how to strengthen the effectiveness and performance of a board depends a great deal on what kind of board one genuinely wants to have. As noted earlier, Chait, Holland, and Taylor (1996) found that the most effective boards in their study demonstrated and cultivated their competencies in a variety of ways included in Exhibit 6.2. These practices are presented as examples of practical board development strategies linked to specific competencies attributed to effective boards rather than cookie-cutter remedies that serve every organization. Benchmarkers should be careful to analyze best practices of other boards in light of their own culture and circumstances, or they may find that their efforts can be more harmful than constructive.

FOUR VEHICLES FOR BOARD DEVELOPMENT

The most board-savvy executives recognize that a board can provide the organization with the high-quality support to which it is entitled only when it has the tools for good governance. The intentional steps that a chief executive takes (with the help of formal or informal board leaders) to inform, educate, and engage board members can be seamlessly woven into the regular business of the board. To raise the financial literacy of one board, for example, the chief executive, the chief financial officer, and chair of the board finance committee inserted into the finance committee's regular budget report to the board a review of three issues: the organization's financial status, the performance measures used to link the financial plan to the strategic plan, and a review of the greatest risk areas. This served to educate board members with lower financial IQs, inform board members who did not serve on the finance committee, and elevate the financial discussion to issues with governance implications.

The following four vehicles provide opportunities to design and implement meaningful board development interventions.

Creating a Dedicated Board Development Committee

If the board does not have facilitative leadership from its chief executive and board chair, board development efforts are more likely to be episodic and ephemeral. Senior staff, consultants, and other board members can be enlisted to help these "chief board development officers" plan and conduct programs to ensure that board development is a continuous process. A growing number of boards have established what is variously referred to as a board development or governance committee to assist the chief executive and chair in helping the board fulfill its responsibilities (see Exhibit 6.3).

Historically, these committees have morphed out of more traditional nominating committees to work beyond the domain of identification, recruitment, and selection of board members. When these committees are well formed and staffed, they can exert significant influence and impact on the board's performance.

Evaluating the Board's Performance

Behavioral science research provides considerable support for the notion that feedback has an important effect on performance. Whereas Chait, Sonnenfeld, and others highlight the capacity to seek feedback on its own performance as one of the benchmarks of an effective governing board, many boards do not embrace assessment until problems surface. This is changing as a result of the growing pressure on boards to model the behavior they expect of others in the organization and the increasing supply of board evaluation tools available on the market.

There are a number of ways that a board can seek feedback on its performance. They include dialogue on a dimension of the board's work at a special forum, retreat, or regularly scheduled board meeting; constituency surveys; third-party reviews; internal reviews by an ad hoc or standing committee of the board; reflective discussion of critical incidents; feedback solicited at the conclusion of each board meeting; and more comprehensive board self-assessments (see Exhibit 6.4).

The value of a formal board self-assessment process is that it allots a specific time, a priority, and a forum to self-improvement. Board members, like most individuals, are not inclined toward unbiased self-analysis. Nevertheless, a constructive board self-assessment process yields individual perceptions about the

Exhibit 6.3. Sample Governance Committee Job Description.

The governance committee is responsible for ongoing review and recommendations to enhance the quality of the board of directors. The work of the committee revolves around five major areas.

1. Help create board roles and responsibilities
   - Lead the board in regularly reviewing and updating the board's description of its roles and areas of responsibility and what is expected of individual board members.
   - Assist the board in periodically updating and clarifying the primary areas of focus for the board, and help shape the board's agenda for the next year or two, based on the strategic plan.
2. Pay attention to board composition
   - Lead in assessing current and anticipated needs related to board composition, determining the knowledge, attributes, skills, abilities, influence, and access to resources the board will need to consider to accomplish future work of the board.
   - Develop a profile of the board as it should evolve over time.
   - Identify potential board member candidates and explore their interest and availability for board service.
   - Nominate individuals to be elected as members of the board.
   - In cooperation with the board chair, contact each board member eligible for re-election to assess his or her interest in continuing board membership and work with each board member to identify what he or she might be able to contribute to the organization.
3. Encourage board development
   - Provide candidates with information needed prior to election to the board.
   - Design and oversee a process of board orientation, sharing information needed during the early stages of board service.
   - Design and implement an ongoing program of board information, education, and team building.
4. Assess board effectiveness
   - Initiate periodic assessment of the board's performance, and propose, as appropriate, changes in board structure and operations.
   - Provide ongoing counsel to the board chair and other board leaders on steps they might take to enhance board effectiveness.
   - Regularly review the board's practices regarding member participation, conflict of interest, confidentiality, and so on, and suggest needed improvements.
   - Periodically review and update the board policy and practices.
5. Prepare board leadership
   - Take the lead in succession planning, taking steps to recruit and prepare for future board leadership.
   - Nominate board members for election as board officers.

Source: Bobowick, Hughes, and Lakey, 2001, p. 20. Text may not be reproduced without written permission from BoardSource.

Exhibit 6.4. Ingredients of an Effective Formal Board Self-Assessment Process.

- A customized questionnaire for eliciting information from each board member that views the board's performance against predetermined criteria that apply to the organization (such as its mission and the responsibilities of the board)

- A survey form that provides opportunities for multiple-choice rankings, open-ended responses, and "don't know" or "not applicable" options for responses

- A process that allows board members to be candid without fear of awkwardness, compromising themselves, or having their questionnaire responses attributed directly to them

- A forum for exploring the results and their consequences, facilitated by an individual with good group process skills and sufficient detachment from the governance process to help the group reach its own conclusions

- A plan of action with concrete, assignable, and actionable steps and measurable indicators to act on the results

- A genuine commitment from the board officers and the chief executive that the results of the process will inform the work of the board.

board's value, strengths, and weaknesses that will shed light on how the board views itself. This can in turn inform the steps the board can take to improve its performance. Because formal board self-assessments take time, it is unrealistic to expect board members (and the professional staff engaged in the planning and implementation) to participate in this kind of evaluation process annually. The board self-assessment process should be scheduled at a time when the board and the chief executive are most willing to learn from and act on the results. This process can be enhanced by planning in advance to schedule a meeting or retreat dedicated to exploring the results of the self-assessment; deciding on ways to improve the board's performance; and preparing a plan of action to follow through on the results.

Designing Better Meetings

To date, corporate governance research suggests no systematic patterns of association between board effectiveness and structural factors such as board size, committee structure, or the number and duration of board meetings. But the process and substance of meetings can influence how the board performs. Board members who are asked to sit through mind-numbing show-and-tell meetings with predetermined outcomes can't be faulted for wondering how their presence makes any material difference beyond compliance with the fiduciary obligation to show up and the opportunity to perfect the skill of yawning with one's mouth closed. The problem with this approach to board meetings is that it leaves little room to advance the thoughtful discussion and constructive debate associated with a high-performing group. It also increases the danger of resorting to either groupthink or dysfunctional harmony to skirt complex issues.

Board members often complain that they are too seldom invited to examine embryonic issues, consider options before a committee has presented its recommendation, or explore the stakes of a strategic issue with governance implications before action must be taken by the board. Organizations that have created these opportunities for board members provide space for this kind of dialogue in a number of ways, including bundling routine items into a consent agenda for matters that require board approval but not necessarily board discussion; designing plenary sessions within board meetings that encourage dialogue rather than decision making; breaking the board into smaller groups to encourage creativity and give more board members less comfortable with speaking in front of larger groups more air time; and enlisting an outside facilitator to liberate the board chair and chief executive from chairing or steering the board toward one direction. Periodic retreats are also becoming more commonplace as a means of enabling the board to depart from the press of its regular business to address specific objectives such as reviewing the results of a board self-assessment, strategic planning, addressing a strategic issue in greater depth, and providing an opportunity for team building.

Board meetings should not be limited to presenting information or voting on action items. They should provide opportunities for airing multiple viewpoints, new approaches, and even dissensus. But creating the conditions for board members to genuinely think together and directing the board to issues of strategy (rather than "administrivia") are not natural acts. Listening to understand differences of opinion and probing for information constitute skills that are often missing in the home and the office as well as the boardroom. The capacity for dialogue is advanced when the chief executive takes the time to frame the context, the potential strategy, and the questions that the board should address. It is enhanced when suitable governance information, rather than administrative data, is shared with board members in advance so that they come to the meeting prepared to contribute. And it is fostered when the board chair and the chief executive genuinely invite board members to raise concerns, voice criticisms, and express ideas *in the boardroom* that challenge the status quo.

Strengthening Board Structure to Align with Substance

There are no generic templates that apply to board size and structure, but the adage that form should follow function works just as well for governance. Boards that start with the question of "What is the work that the board needs to do?" *before* determining the ideal size, composition, committee structure, or meeting format are in a better position to assess whether the ensuing changes provide benchmarks to emulate or merely interesting trends to note.

According to BoardSource (National Center for Nonprofit Boards, 2000), the median size of a board is seventeen members. Some organizations with large boards (more than twenty members) are downsizing. The impetus to reduce the number of board members varies. Motives include increasing the capacity of the organization to actively engage each board member, reducing the costs generated by boards, and delegating some of the work to other groups such as advisory councils that can fulfill discrete, nonfiduciary board functions. Boards that want to reduce their size should be forewarned that their members face the angst of what one board chair described as "asking the turkeys to vote for Thanksgiving."

Traditional standing board committees are no longer considered sacrosanct. Several boards have reduced the number of standing committees to those deemed essential and increased the number of task forces or ad hoc groups that are formed to carry out specific assignments and then disbanded when the work has been completed. Committees are under greater pressure to ensure that they are fulfilling a legitimate function; working with the right composition, leadership, and staffing; and operating in a cross-disciplinary manner with both members of the board who do not serve on the committee as well as with related committees (rather than functioning like independent silos).

High-performing boards require tools as well as leadership from the board chair, the chief executive, and the informal leaders on the board, the committee officers, and their staff liaisons. Holland and Jackson (1998) remind us that board development efforts are more likely to succeed when they are not offered as a quick fix or detached from the regular work of the board:

> Board members cannot learn to work together as an effective team during a single retreat or from a few readings. Such learning must be integrated into the board's regular business and become a part of members' ongoing work (Taylor, Chait, and Holland, 1996). We found that most members were motivated by a desire to contribute to improving their organization's performance, not the board's own functions, so changes should be framed in terms of enhancing the organization. Pressures to revert to business as usual may become overwhelming if continued attention is not given specifically to strengthening the ways the board adds value to the organization. [p.127]

ACTIVATING ACCOUNTABILITY MECHANISMS

Over the past few years, widely publicized scandals and allegations of unseemly practices or conflicts of interest have lowered public trust and heightened pubic scrutiny of nonprofit as well as for-profit organizations. Although Americans are increasingly concerned about ethical practices in all of their institutions, violations of legal and ethical standards in charitable organizations are particularly troublesome. Board members must now be much more aware of the public repercussions of decisions they make on executive compensation, financial expenditures, and personnel policies.

Even when there are no improprieties, the financial literacy of board members can be problematic. Too many board members cannot interpret the financial statements of the institutions they govern. Though more and more board members are demanding greater transparency in reports, too many remain unaware of key financial transactions or the true financial picture of the organizations they govern. This often remains submerged until better questions are asked, financial formats are changed to help board members interpret financial implications, or disaster erupts.

The increased level of scrutiny and the growing awareness that nonprofits live in financial glass houses have heightened expectations on nonprofit boards to ensure legal and ethical integrity. Most of the provisions of the Sarbanes-Oxley corporate reform legislation enacted in the early 2000s in response to governance breakdowns at major companies such as Enron and WorldCom apply to publicly traded companies. But these events have resonated in nonprofit boardrooms in a number of ways. Some board members have regarded them as a wake-up call to demand better governance information, ask more probing questions, and challenge management when something does not smell right. Other nonprofit leaders view the corporate reform measures as an opportunity to voluntarily comply with regulations perceived to strengthen governance and management practices at their own organizations. New legislative, regulatory, and enforcement initiatives that are not voluntary may be on the horizon if nonprofit boards are not perceived to be up to the task of keeping their own houses in order.

The fundamental lessons learned from this period and the measures put into place to strengthen governance and self-regulation will have a profound impact on the future of the nonprofit sector. Policies, practices, and regulations enacted to strengthen accountability should take into account the systemic problems that can trigger mismanagement, malfeasance, or nongovernance. New rules, regulations, or codes of ethics are of questionable value when they are imposed by board members and chief executives who do not model the values statements so prominently displayed in annual reports and on Web sites. Safeguards designed to prevent abuses will be meaningless if they are activated without attending to the manner in which board members work together, where they decide to spend their time, and how management and board choose to interact.

SUMMARY

During the past decade, the supply of governance research and resources has increased in response to the continuing need for board development and the subtext that too many boards are underperforming. All boards are expected to fulfill fiduciary obligations, and most boards are expected to discharge respon-

sibilities that relate to four primary roles: to define and advance the organization's mission; to ensure, develop, and conserve resources; to provide oversight
of management and ensure assessment of the organization; and to engage in
outreach as a bridge and a buffer between the organization and its stakeholders. Some nonprofit leaders find these conventional roles sufficient, while others want more from their boards.

Determining how the board can add the greatest value and what constitutes
board effectiveness should represent strategic choices for nonprofit leaders
rather than default practices. Efforts to enhance board effectiveness are not
likely to result in significant improvements until key leaders have determined
what they most want and need from their board members beyond their fiduciary obligations. Recent research on the competencies that distinguish effective boards, the impact of the board's capacity to function as a high-performing
group, and the role of the chief executive in developing the board can inform
approaches to defining and strengthening board effectiveness.

The quality and commitment of the individuals selected to serve will not automatically result in an effective board. This is why adequate resources must be
channeled into the recruitment, orientation, continuing education, and engagement of board members. Successful board development efforts can be launched
from a variety of platforms, including a dedicated board development committee, a process for evaluating board performance, interventions to improve the
content and process of board meetings, and efforts designed to strengthen board
structure that meet institutional needs, cultures, and developmental stages.

Over the past few years, widely publicized scandals and allegations of improper practices have lowered public trust and heightened scrutiny of nonprofit
as well as for-profit organizations. The policies and practices that nonprofit leaders put into place to strengthen governance, accountability, and transparency
will have a profound impact on the future of the nonprofit sector. If boards do
not provide the responsible self-regulation and proactive governance the public expects of them, nonprofit organizations may have to comply with new legislative and regulatory requirements from government agencies.

References

Bobowick, M. J., Hughes, S. R., and Lakey, B. M. *Transforming Board Structure:
Strategies for Committees and Task Forces.* Washington D.C.: BoardSource, 2001.

Chait, R. P. *How to Help Your Board Govern More and Manage Less.* Washington, D.C.:
BoardSource, 2003.

Chait, R. P., Holland, T. P., and Taylor, B. E. *Improving the Performance of Governing
Boards.* Phoenix, Ariz.: Oryx Press, 1996.

Herman, R. D., and Heimovics, R. D. *Executive Leadership in Nonprofit Organizations:
New Strategies for Shaping Executive-Board Dynamics.* San Francisco: Jossey-Bass,
1991.

Holland, T. P., and Blackmon, M. *Measuring Board Effectiveness: A Tool for Strengthening Your Board.* Washington, D.C.: BoardSource, 2000.

Holland, T. P., and Jackson, D. K. "Strengthening Board Performance: Findings and Lessons from Demonstration Projects." *Nonprofit Management and Leadership,* 1998, *9*(2), 121–134.

Lencioni, P. M. "The Trouble with Teamwork." *Leader to Leader,* Summer 2003, pp. 1–7.

National Center for Nonprofit Boards. *The Nonprofit Governance Index.* Washington, D.C.: National Center for Nonprofit Boards (now known as BoardSource), 2000.

Robinson, M. K. *Nonprofit Boards That Work.* New York: Wiley, 2001.

Ryan, W. P., Chait, R. P., and Taylor, B. E. "Problem Boards or Board Problem?" *Nonprofit Quarterly,* 2003, *10*(2), pp. 49-53.

Salovey, P., and Mayer, J. D. "Emotional Intelligence." *Imagination, Cognition, and Personality,* 1990, *9,* 185–211.

Sonnenfeld, J. A. "What Makes Great Boards Great." *Harvard Business Review,* September 2002, pp. 106–113.

Taylor, B. E., Chait, R. P., and Holland, T. P. "The New Work of the Nonprofit Board." *Harvard Business Review,* Sept. 1996, pp. 36–46.

Tecker, G. H., Frankel, J. S., and Meyer, P. D. *The Will to Govern Well: Knowledge, Trust, and Nimbleness.* Washington, D.C.: American Society of Association Executives, 2002.

CHAPTER SEVEN

Executive Leadership

Robert D. Herman
Dick Heimovics

Nonprofit organizations are distinctive forms of organization, differing in fundamental ways from business and government. Like businesses, nonprofit organizations engage in voluntary exchanges to obtain revenues and other resources, and like governments, they usually provide services with public goods characteristics. Robert Payton (1988) has suggested that philanthropy is voluntary (private) action for public purposes. Nonprofit organizations—particularly those classed as 501(c)(3) publicly supported charities under the U.S. Internal Revenue Code—are the chief instruments for actualizing philanthropy.

We believe that the distinctive character of nonprofit organizations presents special challenges for the leadership of such organizations. Leaders of nonprofit organizations must integrate the realms of mission, resource acquisition, and strategy. The choice of a mission for an organization depends on the potential for acquisition of sufficient resources to carry out that mission. Conversely, the acquisition of certain kinds of resources can influence the mission an organization chooses to undertake. Any mission, no matter how great the cause, is likely to fail if the organization lacks necessary and sufficient resources to pursue it. Moreover, decisions about strategies for acquiring resources must be consistent with the mission and ethical values of the organization. Actions in one realm affect the other realms. The leadership challenge is to see that decisions and actions in one realm are not only consistent with those in other realms but also mutually reinforcing.

153

Although we recognize that leadership does not and cannot occur only at the top of an organization, we also recognize that organizationwide leadership is fundamentally the responsibility of the individuals at the top. For nonprofit organizations, such system-level leadership is the responsibility of the chief executive and the board. In fact, the chief executive–board relationship is crucial to effective organizational leadership. Whereas Chapter Six focused on board leadership, this chapter will focus on executive leadership—both in relation to the organization and in relation to the board.

The chief executive position in nonprofit organizations is usually demanding and difficult. We believe that the demands and difficulties can be more effectively met if CEOs both understand and develop the skills to focus on the essential relationships and tasks it entails. In these pages, we first describe the psychological centrality of CEOs. In spite of the formal hierarchical structure that makes the CEO subordinate to the board, the day-to-day reality as it is experienced by CEOs, board members, and staff is that CEOs are expected to accept the central leadership role in nonprofit organizations. This often requires that CEOs take responsibility for enabling their boards to carry out the boards' duties.

We go on to describe the specific board-centered leadership skills that characterize especially effective chief executives. Next, we address the importance of executive leadership in the external environment. Here we develop strategies for leadership across the boundaries. We continue by describing our research on the "political" skills of especially effective CEOs and providing guidelines for thinking and acting in politically effective ways. The importance of this criterion of leadership is also examined in light of the hesitancy of chief executives to espouse or advocate political action as an important aspect of their leadership. Our closing summary emphasizes that the essence of effective executive leadership is an external orientation in which the strategies pursued are directed at the tasks of mission accomplishment and resource acquisition.

EXECUTIVE CENTRALITY

Like other formal organizations, a nonprofit organization is typically understood as necessarily hierarchical, with the board of directors in the superior position. The board is expected to define mission, establish policies, oversee programs, and use performance standards to assess financial and program achievements. The chief executive is hired to assist the board and works at the board's pleasure. This conception is the application of what organizational theorists have labeled the "purposive-rational" model (Pfeffer, 1982) or the "managed systems" model (Elmore, 1978) to nonprofit organizations. This model, generally derived from Max Weber's description of bureaucracy (1946), conceives of organizations as goal-directed instruments under the control of rational decision makers where responsibility and authority are hierarchically arranged. This rational, managed systems model is also the commonplace or conventional "theory" of many organizational participants. It is how, many people believe, organizations do and should work.

Much of the substantial normative literature on nonprofit boards accepts this conventional model (for example, Alexander, 1980; Bower, 1980; Conrad and Glenn, 1976; Swanson, 1978), putting the board at the top of the hierarchy and at the center of leadership responsibility. Based on a legal requirement and a moral assumption, the normative literature has advanced a heroic ideal (Herman, 1989) for nonprofit boards. United States law holds that a nonprofit board is ultimately responsible for the affairs and conduct of the organization. The moral assumption is that the board conducts the organization's affairs as a steward of the public interest, in a manner consistent with the wishes and needs of the larger community.

Notwithstanding the wide dissemination of this normative model, the actual performance of boards often falls short of the ideal. Middleton's thorough review of the empirical literature (1987) shows that nonprofit boards seldom completely fulfill their assigned duties and roles (for an updated version of this review, see Ostrower and Stone, 2005). Consequently, the notion that chief executives are simply agents of the board cannot be supported. Recognizing that the relationship between boards and chief executives is more complex than the normative model envisions, many people have invoked a "partnership" or "team" metaphor to describe (and prescribe) the executive-board relationship. Such terms are more appropriate than the conventional model's depiction of the relation as superior-subordinate. However, the partnership and team conceptions remain misleading. Middleton (1987, p. 149) uses the phrase "strange loops and tangled hierarchies" to describe more accurately the complex executive-board relationship. Boards retain their legal and hierarchical superiority (and sometimes must exercise it), while executives typically have greater information, more expertise, and a greater stake in and identification with the organization. Thus both parties are dependent on the other, but they are not exactly equals. This complex, interdependent relation is not fundamentally changed even when nonprofit organizations adopt the corporate model of designating the chief executive "president" and letting the executive vote on board decisions.

The complex executive-board relationship can be better understood, and new and more effective standards and practices relating to the executive-board working relationship can be developed, if other organizational models are used. We have found that a "social constructionist model" of organizations provides very important insights into the chief executive's organizational role and the dynamics of effective executive-board relations. In contrast to the managed systems model, the social constructionist perspective abandons assumptions of hierarchically imposed order and rationality, emphasizing that what an organization is and does emerges from the interaction of participants as they attempt to arrange organizational practices and routines to fit their perceptions, needs, and interests. The social constructionist model recognizes that official or intended goals, structures, and procedures may exist only on paper. Actual goals, structures, and procedures emerge and change as participants interact and socially construct the meaning of ongoing events.

In interviews with nonprofit CEOs, we asked them to fully describe two critical events in their organizations, one of which turned out successfully and one unsuccessfully. We then asked the CEOs, board presidents, and senior staff to assess the extent to which the skills and abilities and the hard work and effort of each party (that is, the CEO, the board, and the staff), as well as good or bad luck, affected the outcome of each critical event.

In the successful critical events, all participants (the chief executives, the board presidents, and the staff) credited the executives with contributing the most, through their skills and their hard work, to that outcome. In successful events, the chief executives assign much more credit to their boards than the board presidents do. In the unsuccessful critical events, the executives assign more blame to themselves than to others or bad luck. This is atypical. Laboratory studies have repeatedly confirmed the "self-serving" hypothesis—that individuals see themselves as causes of successful outcomes and others or luck as responsible for failure. Board presidents and staff, consistent with the self-serving hypothesis, saw the chief executive as most responsible, assigning less responsibility to themselves or to luck. In short, all (including chief executives themselves) see the executive as centrally responsible for what happens in nonprofit organizations (see Heimovics and Herman, 1990, for a thorough report).

We have had several occasions to present and discuss this empirical support for our concept of executive psychological centrality. The nonprofit chief executives to whom we have presented our results have always confirmed that their experience matches our finding. But what does the reality of executive centrality imply for more effective action?

We believe that two implications are indicated. One, since chief executives are going to be held responsible, they should take full control, running things as they think best. The board then becomes either the proverbial rubber stamp or a combination rubber stamp and cash cow. Obviously, there are many instances of this manipulative pattern. Alternatively, since chief executives are going to be held responsible and since they accept responsibility for mission accomplishment and public stewardship, they should work to see that boards fulfill their legal, organizational, and public roles. We believe that this second implication is the much wiser choice. Not only is it consistent with legal and ethical duties, but it is also more likely to enhance organizational effectiveness.

We are not advocating that chief executives dominate or "demote" their boards. Boards, in addition to their legal and moral duties, can contribute a great deal to achieving their organizations' missions. What our results and experience demonstrate is that chief executives can seldom expect boards to do their best unless chief executives, recognizing their centrality, accept the responsibility to develop, promote, and enable their boards' effective functioning.

BOARD-CENTERED LEADERSHIP
SKILLS OF EFFECTIVE EXECUTIVES

We have come to the view that chief executives must often enable and develop their boards' abilities to carry out their duties and responsibilities largely as a result of our research on the leadership skills of effective nonprofit chief executives. We wanted to determine what behaviors or skills distinguished especially effective nonprofit chief executives from others. We selected a sample of especially effective chief executives by asking several knowledgeable participants in a metropolitan nonprofit sector to identify executives they judged to be highly effective. The nominators held positions—such as heads of foundations, federated funding agencies, technical assistance providers, and coalitional organizations—that required them to make and act on judgments of executive effectiveness. Chief executives who received at least two independent nominations as highly effective were included in the effective sample. A comparison sample was selected from among executives who received no nominations and who had held their position for at least eighteen months. Executives from both the effective and comparison samples were interviewed, using the critical event approach, by interviewers unaware of the sample distinction or the research hypotheses. The interviews were tape-recorded and transcribed.

We analyzed the interviews by training raters to note the presence of various leadership behaviors, using an inventory developed by Quinn (1983,) based on Yukl's analysis (1981). Recognizing that a CEO's relationships with the board and staff would probably differ, we had the raters determine executive leadership in relation to each (see Herman and Heimovics, 1990, for a technical report on this research).

The results confirmed the importance of distinguishing between executive leadership in relation to the board and the staff. Analysis showed that executive leadership in relation to staff and in relation to the board are independent and distinct factors. Effective and comparison executives differed little in leadership with their staffs. The most important finding was that the effective executives provided significantly more leadership to their boards. This does not mean that the effective executives ordered their boards around. Rather, as the descriptions of their behavior in the critical events showed, the effective executives took responsibility for supporting and facilitating their board's work. The effective executives value and respect their boards. As a result, they see their boards as at the center of their work. Their leadership is board-centered. We found the following six behaviors specifically characterized the board-centered leadership of the especially effective executives.

- *Facilitating interaction in board relationships.* The effective chief executive is aware of and works to see that board members engage in satisfying and productive interaction, with each other and with the executive. The executive is skilled at listening (that is, at hearing the concerns behind the words) and at helping the board resolve differences.
- *Showing consideration and respect toward board members.* The effective executive knows that board service is an exchange and seeks to be aware of the needs of individual board members. The executive also works with the board president to find assignments that meet those needs.
- *Envisioning change and innovation for the organization with the board.* Given their psychological centrality and their centrality in information flows, chief executives are in the best position to monitor and understand the organization's position in a changing environment. However, appropriate response to this external flux requires that board members be apprised of the trends, forces, and unexpected occurrences that could call for adaptation or innovation. The executive encourages the board to examine new opportunities, to look for better ways of doing things and better things to do. In short, the executive challenges the board consistently to think and rethink the connections among mission, money (and other resources), and strategy.
- *Providing useful and helpful information to the board.* In addition to the usual routine information, such as financial statements, budget reports, and program service data, boards need relevant and timely information that can aid in decision making. Since the executive will have access to a great deal of information, of all kinds and quality, he or she must find ways of separating the important from the trivial and of communicating the important to the board. One key rule followed by effective executives is no surprises. The temptation to hide or delay bad news is understandable, but it must be resisted. Effective executives realize that problems are inevitable and know that by sharing the bad news, solutions are more likely to be found.
- *Initiating and maintaining structure for the board.* Like other work groups, boards require the materials, schedules, and work plans necessary to achieve their tasks. Effective executives take responsibility to work with the board president and other members to develop and maintain consistent procedures. In many effective organizations, the board has annual objectives. It is important that the chief executive support the work of the board in reaching those objectives.
- *Promoting board accomplishments and productivity.* The effective executive helps set and maintain high standards (about attendance, effort, and giving). Through the board president and committee chairpersons, the executive encourages board members to complete tasks and meet deadlines.

Executives who have learned these key board-centered leadership skills have hardworking, effective boards. The board-centered executive is likely to be effective because he or she has grasped that the work of the board is critical in adapting to and affecting the constraints and opportunities in the environment. In short, the effective executive knows that leadership is not solely an internal activity.

LEADERSHIP ACROSS THE BOUNDARIES: IMPACT IN THE EXTERNAL WORLD

As other chapters in this volume demonstrate, the complexity and unpredictability of the world in which nonprofit, charitable organizations operate is great and seemingly continually increasing. Such change and unpredictability make the challenge of integrating mission, resource acquisition, and strategy even greater and require that chief executives effectively engage in leadership across the boundaries. Our research, in conjunction with that of others, suggests four specific strategies for enhancing external impact.

Spend Time on External Relations

Spending time on external relations may seem too obvious to deserve mention. However, both systematic evidence and experience show that routine activities and the inevitable day-to-day office problems can easily absorb nearly all an executive's time. Executives must learn to delegate much of the management of internal affairs and focus on the external. Dollinger (1984) found that small business owners and managers who spent more time on boundary-spanning or external activities were more successful.

Develop an Informal Information Network

Information about what happened in the past (such as is found in financial statements and program evaluations) is important, but information about what might happen in the future (whether that future is next week or next year) is even more important. Information on possible futures is much more likely to be widely scattered, partial, and ambiguous. To acquire, evaluate, and integrate this "soft" information, executives (and others) need to communicate with government agencies, foundations, accrediting bodies, professional associations, similar nonprofit organizations, and so forth. They must attend meetings and lunches, breakfasts and legislative sessions.

Important, useful information is more likely flow when the parties are more than acquaintances. Face-to-face communication helps build reciprocal credibility and trust. A successful network is built and sustained when people are willing and able to understand and accept the interests of others, and it requires exchanging reliable information without violating confidentiality. It means not only investing time but also helping others with their concerns in exchange for help with your own. As Huff (1985) observes, a network is important for more than sharing information. Networks are also deeply involved in making sense of an often rapidly changing field. Different kinds of information are available from different parts of an organization's environment. Information gleaned from a professional associate will be different from that available from a corporate giving officer. Both are likely to be important to a particular policy or program delivery issue. The whole network has an important role in defining emerging issues and in pointing the way to new program practices.

Know Your Agenda

Strategic planning, as John Bryson very helpfully demonstrates in Chapter Eight, provides organizations with a rational process for deriving specific goals and objectives from their missions. Thus the strategic plan structures the executive's work. Both Kotter (1982) and Huff (1985) have found that executives supplement the strategic plan with agendas that are both more immediate and more long-range. The executive's agenda, whether taken directly from the plan or consistently supplemental to it, provides a short list of goals or outcomes that the executive sees as crucial. Knowing and using the agenda to focus work offers a basis for effectively allocating time and effort. A limited, focused agenda also helps bring order and direction in a complex and rapidly changing environment. Concentrating on the agenda also allows the executive to use external interactions to advance those goals. Huff (1985) has described three strategies effective executives often employ in advancing their agenda as dramatizing events, "laying a bread crumb trail," and simplifying.

Dramatizing events entails calling attention to the relationship between networking events and the executive's agenda. For example, an executive who wants to add staff fluent in Spanish to expand services to Spanish-speaking communities might send clippings about growth in the city's Latino population and its service needs to board members. The executive might also feature a digest of such stories in the organization's newsletter and see that the newsletter goes to regular funders. The key is to dramatically or memorably connect public issues to the organization's agenda.

Another good example of how to dramatize events comes from the chief executive of an agency serving the developmentally disabled. She encouraged a friend who taught creative writing at a local university to engage a class in developing a story about a day in the life of her agency. The story was included in the materials made available to those attending an annual banquet and awards dinner for the organization. The story was presented to many stakeholders and others to give them a "real feel for the work of the agency." Clearly, the executive director had additional uses for the story. The description skillfully catalogued the creative work of a staff constrained by limited resources. Copies of the story became part of the publicity program of the agency and were conveniently included in reports to funders and in grant applications.

Just as dramatizing external events is a way of focusing attention, so is the "laying of a bread crumb trail." Over time, through various communications, a chief executive points the way to an important decision. As Huff (1985, p. 175) puts it, organizational action requires that an executive edit his or her concerns "into a smaller number of items that can be comprehended by others. Repetition of these concerns is almost always necessary to gain the attention of others and convince them of serious intent." Such a strategy is probably widely applicable, but we find it especially germane in executive-board relations.

Consider, for instance, the strategy of the chief executive of an organization that operates group homes for the mentally ill. The organization's original facility, called Tracy House, was an old building in great need of repair. Operations at the house did not quite break even. Surpluses from the operation of other facilities covered the shortfall. The executive, based on what he was hearing from the network of licensing, funding, and accrediting bodies, believed that new standards would require modifications that, combined with no growth in state daily rates, would mean operating the facility at an increasing deficit. So he began laying a bread crumb trail for board members, both formally in board meetings and informally in conversations in other settings.

Part of his problem was that a few board members had a strong emotional attachment to Tracy House; they had personally painted it and made repairs to meet licensing standards. Instead of pointing out again that Tracy House was decrepit, he provided an update on the state funding prospects, noting the financial implications for each facility, which made the burden of carrying the home's deficit obvious. Some time later, he mentioned the possibility of federal housing funds' becoming available for group home construction, observing that this would permit the organization to "get out from under" Tracy House. In this way, when the decision was finally made to sell Tracy House, it was a foregone conclusion. The trail of markers not only defined and focused the issue but also brought everyone to the same conclusion, making what could have been a painful decision easy.

The last strategy identified by Huff is to keep things as simple as possible. A complex and interdependent world enhances the tendency for inaction and drift. Before we can make a decision about X, we have to see what happens with Y, and Y depends on what A and B do. To make decisions and take action, individuals must risk simplifying the situation. As Huff (1985) observes, behaving as though the situation is simpler than you know it to be can help bring about more simplicity. Acting in relation to the agenda is an important way of simplifying, or creating order in a disorderly world.

Improvise and Accept Multiple, Partial Solutions

The point of leadership across the boundary is to position the organization in the larger environment and match its capabilities with the demands for its services and the resources available. Of course, the inevitable fact is that neither organizational capabilities nor environmental demands and resources are static. A short, clear agenda and the strategies to carry it out provide a compass pointing the way to where the executive, who has integrated to the greatest extent possible the preferences of the stakeholders, wants to go.

The metaphor of the compass, however, is not complete because the executive (reflecting the stakeholders' varying preferences) wants to go to several places. For example, the agenda might include increasing total revenues, diversifying revenue sources, acquiring a new facility, and expanding a particular program. Not only are these different goals, but there are likely to be different paths to each. Furthermore, the most direct path to one may make paths to the others longer or more difficult to find. Finding the combination of paths that most efficiently leads to goals may often be beyond calculation, particularly when the environment keeps changing. The upshot is that executives must sometimes be willing and able to improvise, to take an unexpected path when it presents itself.

Sometimes chief executives find they cannot, at least within a crucial period, reach a goal in exactly the form imagined. As Huff (1985, p. 167) observes, an "administrator's ability to perceive issues is almost always bigger than the ability to act on issues. As a result, the administrator often must be content to work on a small part of the larger whole." That is, sometimes the organization may have to go someplace a little different from what was at one time imagined because that is where the only available path leads. Huff suggests that a "specific action should rarely be taken unless it is compatible with several different issues" (p. 168). Or in the terms of our metaphor, an action that leads to movement on paths to two or three places at once is particularly useful.

For an especially compelling illustration of this sort of creative leadership, let us look at the case of a nonprofit organization that required a facility with large spaces. For several years, the organization used an old warehouse that a business corporation provided for free. However, the corporation made it clear that it was interested in selling the warehouse and that the organization might have to relocate. As a few years passed and the corporation lacked success in selling the warehouse and had little apparent necessity for doing so, the issue of obtaining a suitable, more permanent facility was increasingly put on the back burner. One day, the chief executive received a call from a corporate officer saying that a tentative agreement to sell the warehouse had been reached and that the organization would have to vacate in six months. The first thing the chief executive did was to call the board. Staff were also quickly informed to avoid the spread of rumors. The chief executive found that many board members and staff assumed that the organization should try to find another old warehouse. However, the executive knew that old warehouses had disadvantages: high energy costs, lack of parking, inaccessibility, and so forth. The executive thought this was an excellent opportunity to rethink what sort of facility would be most appropriate.

After conferring with the board chairman and other key board members, a facility planning committee was formed. The executive was interested in connecting the facility issue to other agenda issues, especially those of enhancing collaboration with other community organizations and adding a demonstration day care program for children. As the facility planning committee identified alternative ways of securing a replacement facility and the costs associated with each, a board member suggested that the executive meet with an official from a local community college. Although the college was not in the same service field as the organization, the college had enough money available through a bond issue to construct a new building but not enough money to finish and equip the building. Following quick negotiations, the organization agreed to provide funds to finish and equip the facility in exchange for a ten-year lease of two floors at a very low rental rate. This solution, though not perfect, moved the organization along on several agenda issues simultaneously. This progress was achieved because the executive worked with and through the board and linked action on one issue with progress on others. (An extensive treatment of both board-centered leadership skills and boundary-spanning leadership can be found in Herman and Heimovics, 1991.)

In emphasizing the importance of externally oriented leadership, we do not wish to suggest that internal operations can be ignored by chief executives. As the chapters in Parts Three, Four, and Five of this volume attest, designing, implementing, and improving the various internal systems and procedures are important and challenging. We believe that nearly all executives and boards are well aware of the importance of these issues. What seems to us to be less well comprehended is the importance of understanding and influencing, when possible, people and systems beyond the organization's boundaries. Effective executive leadership beyond the boundaries is based on a "political" orientation and on political skills. In the next section, we define what we mean by a political orientation, describe recent research that finds effective executives are more politically skillful than others, and suggest how executives can enhance their political acumen.

USING THE POLITICAL FRAME

Our studies have shown that not only do successful executives provide significantly more leadership for their boards than those not deemed especially effective, but they also work with and through their boards to position their organization in its environment. Special effort is extended externally across the boundaries of the organization to manage the organization's dependence on the factors that determine the availability of the resources to carry out the mission and to establish the legitimacy of the organization. In short, effective executives boundary-span to seek and act on opportunities in the environment to help shape the future health and direction of the organization.

Why do some executives engage in more external and board-centered actions than other executives? Our further research helps answer the question (see Heimovics, Herman, and Coughlin, 1993, and Heimovics, Herman, and Jurkie-wicz, 1995, for more details about this study). Effective executives are more likely than other executives to "frame" their orientations toward external events in political ways. This political orientation helps explain how effective executives work "entrepreneurially" to find resources and revitalize missions for their organizations. Effective chief executive officers use a political frame to understand and deal with the challenges of resource dependency their organizations face.

A multiple-frame analysis for understanding organizations and leadership developed by Bolman and Deal (2003) forms the basis for our examination of the political orientation of the effective executive. Bolman and Deal identify four distinct organizational perspectives, or "frames," that leaders may adopt to understand the many realities of organizational life: structural, human resource, political, and symbolic. Knowledge of these frames, their various strengths, and their appropriate use can help leaders understand and intervene in their organizations more effectively. The following brief discussion summarizes these frames.

In the structural frame, clarity in goal setting and role expectations provides order and continuity in organizations. Clear procedures and policies and the view of the organization as a rational and hierarchical system are characteristic of this frame. Adherence to accepted standards, conformity to rules, and the creation of administrative systems confer on the organization its form and logic. Following procedures (for example, personnel systems and board performance standards) to define individual and organizational effectiveness is also characteristic of this frame, as is the emphasis on certainty in mission and clarity of direction. Leaders who rely strongly on the structural frame regard effectiveness as largely determined by clear procedures and clear goals.

According to the human resource frame, people are the most valuable resource of any organization. The effective leader, as defined by this frame, searches for an important balance between the goals of the organization and the hopes and aspirations of its members by attending to individual hopes, feelings, and preferences, valuing relationships and feelings, and advocating effective delegation. Nonprofit leaders who use this frame believe in delegation because it not only "empowers" others to take initiative but also provides opportunities for personal growth and development. This frame defines problems and issues in interpersonal terms and encourages open communication, team building, and collaboration.

The political frame assumes ongoing conflict or tension over the allocation of scarce resources or the resolution of differences—most often triggered by the need to bargain or negotiate to acquire or allocate resources. As viewed by the political frame, conflict resolution skills are necessary to build alliances and networks with prominent actors or stakeholders to influence decisions about the allocation of resources. The informal realities of organizational life include the influence of coalitions and interest groups. Politically oriented leaders not only understand how interest groups and coalitions evolve but can also influence the impact these groups have on the organization. Those who use the political frame exercise their personal and organizational power and are sensitive to external factors that may influence internal decisions and policies.

According to the symbolic frame, realities of organizational life are socially construed. Organizations are cultural and historical systems of shared meaning wherein group membership determines individual interpretations of organizational phenomena. Organizational structure, politics, and human relations are inventions of the cultural and historical system. Leaders evoke ceremonies, rituals, or artifacts to create a unifying system of beliefs. This frame calls for charismatic leaders to arouse "visions of a preferred organizational future" and evoke emotional responses to enhance an organization's identity, transforming it to a higher plane of performance and value (Bass, 1985).

Our research on the use of frames began by revisiting the critical-incident interviews that served as the source of data for our prior research about board-centered behaviors and psychological centrality of the chief executive. Two coders, unaware of differences in the two samples and the hypotheses of this aspect of our research, read and coded the transcribed interviews to determine which frames were used by the chief executives. Analysis revealed that the structural frame was the dominant frame for both the effective and comparison executives. The substantial reliance on the structural frame may be a reflection of the attention of both groups of executives to aspects of events that may be relatively close at hand, immediately demanding, and perhaps amenable to action.

The use of the political frame differed significantly, however, between effective and comparison executives. Not only did comparison executives use the political frame less, but they seemed to differentiate little in their use of the political frame. The comparison executives were almost twice as likely to employ the structural frame and 70 percent more likely to use the human resource frame than the political frame. By contrast, the political frame was the second most dominant frame for the effective executives, who were almost as likely to use it as the structural frame. Most significant, effective executives were twice as likely as the comparison executives to engage in actions defined by the political frame.

We are particularly confident about our findings on the substantial use of the political frame by effective executives. Most of the critical events described by both groups of executives occurred in the environment external to their organizations. Both effective and comparison executives were more likely to choose an external event than an internal event to describe as critical. Examples of environmental events were usually incidents that dealt with the challenges of resource dependency, such as mergers, alliances, fundraising strategies, legislative lobbying, collaboration with other agencies, relations with government officials, new program developments, or program decline. We distinguished these kinds of events from internal critical events, such as a personnel action or problems with implementing an administrative system or procedure.

We then analyzed the data by location of events to determine if this variable explained differences in frame use. Again we found significant differences between our two groups of executives in the political frame. Comparison executives were substantially less likely to rely on the political frame than the effective executives were when dealing with events in the external environment of the organization, where the political frame is assumed to be most important.

We also found that effective executives not only relied more on the political frame but also dealt with events in more cognitively complex ways than those not deemed to be especially effective. In other words, effective executives integrate and employ multiple frames and do not rely on single perspectives, as the comparison executives do. We suspect that the use of multiple frames by effective executives contributes to a deeper understanding of the complexities and volatility of the leadership challenges faced in the fast-changing and complicated environment of nonprofit organizations. Environmentally induced events are characteristically turbulent, fast-changing, and uncertain.

Most service-providing nonprofit organizations are highly dependent on a wide variety of external organizations, ranging from state and local government administrators and politicians, accrediting bodies, and federated funding organizations to foundation and corporate boards. All these groups represent power centers whose actions can directly affect the mission and vitality of the nonprofit organizations that depend on them. The ability of nonprofit executives to understand and act politically, as well as through other frames, in relation to complex sets of interrelated actors helps explain why some executives are more effective than others.

In a final analysis of our interviews (Heimovics, Herman, and Jurkiewicz, 1995), we discovered an interesting extension to our findings about the political orientation of effective chief executives. We conducted a second, independent four-framed analysis of the interviews using Argyris's distinctions between espoused theories and theories-in-use as a coding criterion. For Argyris (1982), espoused theories are values and actions about which individuals are conscious and aware and which they might use to advocate effective leadership as distinct from what they might actually do, their theory-in-use. An espoused theory could be considered a personal philosophy or a statement of a leadership belief, but it is not a description of a particular action taken. Argyris has shown that commonly there are incongruities between what people espouse as their leadership action and how they actually behave. This was the case in our research.

Recall that effective executives were twice as likely as our comparison executives to engage in actions defined in the political frame. However, both sets of executives were much more inclined to present (espouse) their leadership from the structural and human resource frame than the political. Furthermore, both our effective executives and those not deemed especially effective enacted more political behavior than they espoused. In summary, whereas the use of the political frame was the most strongly distinguishing and most important criterion of executive effectiveness, executives without respect to effectiveness acted in political ways and advocated a less politicized philosophy. Why might this be the case?

The espoused structural frame argues for the importance of rationality and the values of structures that best fit organizational purposes and environmental demands. Apparently, nonprofit executives prefer to present themselves as structured and orderly and embracing of the human resource frame. Perhaps it is important to appear as if one is ordered and rational and concerned about others regardless of whether one behaves that way. This finding is especially intriguing in light of the findings about the nature of the political frame, where order and rationality and concern for others are subordinate to a very different and distinguishing set of assumptions and skills.

We know from Pfeffer (1981) that power is most effectively exercised unobtrusively and that overt political pronouncements are divisive and likely to be met with challenges. Wrong (1988) distinguished between political operatives who say and those who do. He concludes that the doers are more effective. Even Machiavelli (1513) recognized that long-term leader effectiveness depends on the eschewal of a highly politicized philosophy. In short, it may be important and effective to act in accordance with the political frame, as our research suggests and as Pfeffer (1982) contends; it may not be acceptable to espouse this frame as part of a leadership philosophy. Our research argues that nonprofit executive leadership effectiveness must encompass the ability to operate within a political framework, regardless of the proclivity to espouse a political agenda.

SUMMARY

Nonprofit leaders continually face the challenge of integrating mission, money (and acquisition of other resources), and strategy. Both boards and chief executives play crucial and interdependent roles in meeting this continuing challenge. Both must ask, "How well are we collectively meeting our responsibilities—to define and refine the organization's mission, to secure the resources necessary to achieve our mission, and to select and implement strategies appropriate to and effective in mission accomplishment and resource acquisition?" Chief executives must ask this question not only of themselves but also in relation to their boards. Are their boards meeting these responsibilities? If the answer is yes, a chief executive will surely want to understand how this happy state of affairs has been achieved and take pains to see that it is maintained. If the answer is no, a chief executive will want to consider the following four fundamental executive leadership strategies. Our research suggests that executives who use these strategies are more likely to lead organizations that effectively meet their responsibilities.

Effective executives accept and act on their psychological centrality. Our research shows that chief executives, board members, and others regard the chief executive as primarily responsible for the conduct of organizational affairs. This is, we think, a fact of life in nonprofit organizations, however strongly we or others might want it to be otherwise. This fact implies that chief executives must often accept the responsibility for enabling their boards to carry out their leadership roles.

Effective executives provide board-centered leadership. Boards can make a difference in how nonprofit organizations meet the challenge of integrating mission, money, and strategy. Boards are much more likely to be active, effective bodies when they are supported by a chief executive who, recognizing his or her psychological centrality, is willing and able to serve the board as enabler and facilitator.

Effective executives emphasize leadership beyond their organizations' boundaries. Given the extensive dependence of nonprofit organizations on their external environments, executives generally recognize the importance of "networking" and other external activities for understanding the changes in that environment. Beyond the information value of external relations, some executives recognize the importance and value of affecting events in the environment. Exercising external leadership is difficult and demanding, since executives often can bring little, if any, financial or political power to bear. The leadership resources they are likely to have in greater abundance are expertise, trustworthiness, the moral stature of their organizations, and skills in coalition building and conflict resolution.

Effective executives think and act in political ways. Effective executives are realists. They recognize and accept that their organizations and the larger world are composed of groups with differing interests. Thus an important part of the leadership role consists of building coalitions, bargaining, and resolving conflicts. Politically astute executives are not immoral or manipulative. However, they are comfortable with the fact that interests differ and sometimes conflict. They are also comfortable with and skilled at negotiating, compromising, and forming alliances, although they are unlikely to proclaim these political skills as an aspect of their leadership strategies.

These four executive leadership strategies are highly interrelated. An executive who enhances his or her board-centered leadership skills will also likely become more attentive to externally oriented leadership. An executive who becomes more active in and skilled at leadership in the external environment will likely develop more politically oriented ways of thinking and behaving. Obviously, these skills are increments to a solid base of other knowledge and skills, such as those of program services, financial management, human resource management, fundraising, planning, evaluation, and the like. These board-centered, external, and political leadership skills are what distinguish especially effective nonprofit chief executives.

References

Alexander, J. G. "Planning and Management in Nonprofit Organizations." In T. D. Connors (ed.), *The Nonprofit Organization Handbook.* New York: McGraw-Hill, 1980.

Argyris, C. *Reasoning, Learning, and Action: Individual and Organizational.* San Francisco: Jossey-Bass, 1982.

Bass, B. M. *Leadership and Performance Beyond Expectations.* New York: Free Press, 1985.

Bolman, L. G., and Deal, T. E. *Reframing Organizations: Artistry, Choice, and Organizations.* (3rd ed.) San Francisco: Jossey-Bass, 2003.

Bower, M. "The Will to Manage the Philanthropic Organization." In T. D. Connors (ed.), *The Nonprofit Organization Handbook.* New York: McGraw-Hill, 1980.

Conrad, W., and Glenn, W. E. *The Effective Voluntary Board of Directors: What It Is and How It Works.* Chicago: Swallow Press, 1976.

Dollinger, M. J. "Environmental Boundary Spanning and Information Processing Effects on Organizational Performance." *Academy of Management Journal,* 1984, *27,* 351–368.

Elmore, R. F. "Organizational Models of Social Program Implementation." *Public Policy,* 1978, *26,* 185–228.

Heimovics, R. D., and Herman, R. D. "Responsibility for Critical Events in Nonprofit Organizations." *Nonprofit and Voluntary Sector Quarterly,* 1990, *19,* 59–72.

Heimovics, R. D., Herman, R. D., and Coughlin, C.L.J. "Executive Leadership and Resource Dependence in Nonprofit Organizations: A Frame Analysis." *Public Administration Review,* 1993, *53,* 419–427.

Heimovics, R. D., Herman, R. D., and Jurkiewicz, C. L. "The Political Dimension of Effective Nonprofit Executive Leadership." *Nonprofit Management and Leadership,* 1995, *5,* 233–248.

Herman, R. D. "Concluding Thoughts on Closing the Board Gap." In R. D. Herman and J. Van Til (eds.), *Nonprofit Boards of Directors: Analyses and Applications.* New Brunswick, N.J.: Transaction, 1989.

Herman, R. D., and Heimovics, R. D. "An Investigation of Leadership Skill Differences in Chief Executives of Nonprofit Organizations." *American Review of Public Administration,* 1990, *20,* 107–124.

Herman, R. D., and Heimovics, R. D. *Executive Leadership in Nonprofit Organizations: New Strategies for Shaping Executive-Board Dynamics.* San Francisco: Jossey-Bass, 1991.

Huff, A. S. "Managerial Implications of the Emerging Paradigm." In Y. S. Lincoln (ed.), *Organizational Theory and Inquiry: The Paradigm Revolution.* Thousand Oaks, Calif.: Sage, 1985.

Kotter, J. P. *The General Managers.* New York: Free Press, 1982.

Machiavelli, N. *The Prince* (W. K. Marriott, trans.). New York: Knopf, 1992. (Originally published 1513)

Middleton, M. "Nonprofit Boards of Directors: Beyond the Governance Function." In W. W. Powell (ed.), *The Nonprofit Sector: A Research Handbook.* New Haven, Conn.: Yale University Press, 1987.

Ostrower, F., and Stone, M. "Boards of Nonprofit Organizations: Research Trends, Findings, and Prospects for the Future." In W. W. Powell and R. Steinberg (eds.), *The Nonprofit Sector: A Research Handbook.* New Haven, Conn.: Yale University Press, 2005.

Payton, R. *Philanthropy: Voluntary Action for the Public Good.* Old Tappan, N.J.: Macmillan, 1988.

Pfeffer, J. *Power in Organizations.* New York: Ballinger, 1981.

Pfeffer, J. *Organizations and Organization Theory.* Boston: Pitman, 1982.

Quinn, R. E. "Applying the Competing Values Approach to Leadership: Toward an Integrative Framework." In J. G. Hunt and others (eds.), *Managerial Work and Leadership: International Perspectives.* New York: Pergamon, 1983.

Swanson, A. *The Determinative Team.* Hicksville, N.Y.: Exposition Press, 1978.

Weber, M. *From Max Weber: Essays in Sociology* (H. H. Gerth and C. W. Mills, trans. and eds.). New York: Oxford University Press, 1946.

Wrong, D. *Power: Its Forms, Bases, and Uses.* Chicago: University of Chicago Press, 1988.

Yukl, G. A. *Leadership in Organizations.* Upper Saddle River, N.J.: Prentice Hall, 1981.

CHAPTER EIGHT

The Strategy Change Cycle

*An Effective Strategic
Planning Approach for
Nonprofit Organizations*

John M. Bryson

This chapter presents an approach to strategic planning for nonprofit organizations and collaboratives. The process, called the Strategy Change Cycle, does what Poister and Streib (1999, pp. 309–310) assert strategic planning should do. Specifically, they believe strategic planning should

- Be concerned with identifying and responding to the most fundamental issues facing an organization
- Address the subjective question of purpose and the often competing values that influence mission and strategies
- Emphasize the importance of external trends and forces as they are likely to affect the organization and its mission
- Attempt to be politically realistic by taking into account the concerns and preferences of internal, and especially external, stakeholders
- Rely heavily on the active involvement of senior-level managers and, in the case of nonprofits, board members, assisted by staff where needed
- Require the candid confrontation of critical issues by key participants in order to build commitment to plans
- Be action-oriented and stress the importance of developing plans for implementing strategies

- Focus on implementing decisions now in order to position the organization favorably for the future

The Strategy Change Cycle becomes a *strategic management* process—and not just a *strategic planning* process—to the extent that it is used to link planning and implementation and to manage an organization in a strategic way on an ongoing basis (Poister and Streib, 1999). The Strategy Change Cycle draws on a considerable body of research and practical experience, applying it specifically to nonprofit organizations (Bryson, 2004a).

Two quotes help make the point that strategic thinking, acting, and learning are more important than any particular approach to strategic planning. Consider first a humorous statement from Daniel Boone, the famous American frontiersman: "No, I can't say as I ever was lost, but once I was bewildered pretty bad for three days" (Faragher, 1992, p. 65). When you are lost in the wilderness—*bewildered*—no fixed plan will do. You must think, act, and learn your way to safety. Boone had a destination of at least a general sort in mind, but not a route. He had to wander around reconnoitering, gathering information, assessing directions, trying out options, and in general thinking, acting, and learning his way to where he wanted to be. In Karl Weick's words (1979), he had to "act thinkingly," which often meant acting first and then thinking about it. Or as Bob Behn (1988) put it, he had to "manage by groping along." Ultimately—but not initially, or even much before he got there—Boone was able to establish a clear destination and a route that worked to get him there. Boone thus had a strategy of purposeful wandering—because although he was not exactly lost, he had to work at finding himself where he wanted to be. Wandering with a purpose is therefore an important aspect of strategic planning, in which thinking, acting, and learning matter most.

Next, consider a quote from poet and essayist Diane Ackerman: "Make-believe is at the heart of play, and also at the heart of so much that passes for work. Let's make-believe we can shoot a rocket to the moon" (1999, p. 7). She makes the point that almost anything is possible with enough imagination, ambition, direction, intelligence, education and training, organization, resources, will, and staying power. We have been to the moon, Mars, the rings of Jupiter, and a host of other places. We as citizens of the world have won world wars and cold wars, ended depressions, virtually eliminated smallpox, unraveled the human genome, watched a reasonably united and integrated Europe emerge, and seen democracy spread where it was not thought possible. Now let's think about having a good job for everyone, adequate food and housing for everyone, universal health care coverage, drastically reduced crime, effective educational systems, secure pensions and retirements, a dramatic reduction in greenhouse gas emissions, the elimination of weapons of mass destruction, the elimination of HIV/AIDS, the realization in practice of the Universal Declaration on Human Rights, more peace and cooperation on a global scale, and so on. And then let us get to work. We can create institutions, policies, projects, products, and services of lasting public value by drawing on our diverse talents—and have done so again and again throughout history (Boyte and Kari, 1996), and clearly, nonprofit organizations have an important role to play (Letts, Ryan, and Grossman, 1999; Light, 2002). We can use strategic planning to help us think, act, and learn strategically—to figure out what we should want, why, and how to get it. Think of strategic planning as the organization of hope, as what makes hope reasonable (Forester, 1989; Baum, 1997).

A TEN-STEP STRATEGIC PLANNING PROCESS

Now, with the caution that strategic thinking, acting, and learning matter most, let us proceed to a more detailed exploration of the ten-step Strategy Change Cycle. The process, presented in Figure 8.1, is more orderly, deliberative, and participative than the process followed by an essayist such as Ackerman or a wanderer like Boone. The process is designed to "create public value" (Moore, 2000) through fashioning an effective mission, meeting applicable mandates, organizing participation, creating ideas for strategic interventions, building a winning coalition, and implementing strategies. The Strategy Change Cycle may be thought of as a *process strategy* (Mintzberg, Ahlstrand, and Lampel, 1998) or *processual model of decision making* (Barzelay, 2001), whereby a leadership group manages the process but leaves much of the content of what the strategies will be to others. The ten steps (or occasions for dialogue and decision) are as follows:

1. Initiate and agree on a strategic planning process.
2. Identify organizational mandates.
3. Clarify organizational mission and values.
4. Assess the external and internal environments to identify strengths, weaknesses, opportunities, and threats.
5. Identify the strategic issue facing the organization.
6. Formulate strategies to manage the issues.
7. Review and adopt the strategic plan or plans.
8. Establish an effective organizational vision.
9. Develop an effective implementation process.
10. Reassess strategies and the strategic planning process.

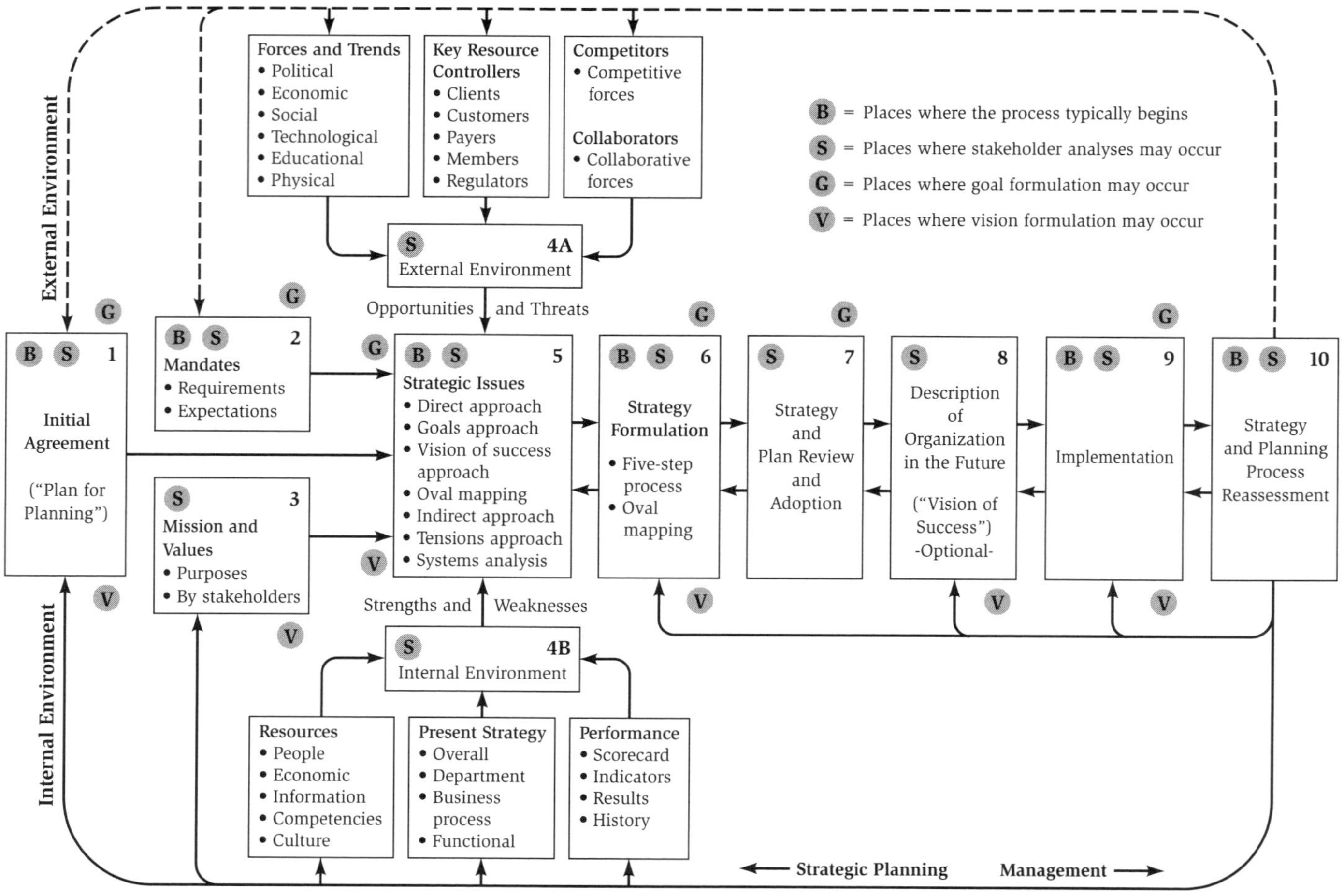
External Environment
Internal Environment
B = Places where the process typically begins
S = Places where stakeholder analyses may occur
G = Places where goal formulation may occur
V = Places where vision formulation may occur
Forces and Trends
• Political
• Economic
• Social
• Technological
• Educational
• Physical
Key Resource Controllers
• Clients
• Customers
• Payers
• Members
• Regulators
Competitors
• Competitive forces
Collaborators
• Collaborative forces
S 4A External Environment
Opportunities and Threats
B S 1 Initial Agreement ("Plan for Planning")
B S 2 Mandates
• Requirements
• Expectations
S 3 Mission and Values
• Purposes
• By stakeholders
B S 5 Strategic Issues
• Direct approach
• Goals approach
• Vision of success approach
• Oval mapping
• Indirect approach
• Tensions approach
• Systems analysis
B S 6 Strategy Formulation
• Five-step process
• Oval mapping
S 7 Strategy and Plan Review and Adoption
S 8 Description of Organization in the Future ("Vision of Success") -Optional-
B S 9 Implementation
B S 10 Strategy and Planning Process Reassessment
Strengths and Weaknesses
S 4B Internal Environment
Resources
• People
• Economic
• Information
• Competencies
• Culture
Present Strategy
• Overall
• Department
• Business process
• Functional
Performance
• Scorecard
• Indicators
• Results
• History
Strategic Planning
Management

Figure 8.1. The Strategy Change Cycle.

Source: Copyright © 1995, 2003 by John M. Bryson.

These ten steps should lead to actions, results, evaluation, and learning. It must be emphasized that actions, results, evaluative judgments, and learning should emerge at each step in the process. In other words, implementation and evaluation should not wait until the "end" of the process but should be an integral and ongoing part of it.

The process is applicable nonprofit organizations and collaboratives. The only general requirements are a "dominant coalition" (Thompson, 1967), or at least a "coalition of the willing" (Cleveland, 2002), able to sponsor and follow the process, and a process champion willing to push it. For small nonprofit organizations, many well-informed strategic planning teams that are familiar with and believe in the process should be able to complete most of the steps in a two- or three-day retreat, with an additional one-day meeting scheduled three to four weeks later to review the resulting strategic plan. Responsibility for preparing the plan can be delegated to a planner assigned to work with the team, or the organization's chief executive may choose to draft the plan personally. Additional reviews and signoffs by key decision makers might take additional time. Extra time might also be necessary to secure information or advice for specific parts of the plan, especially its recommended strategies. For large organizations, however, more time and effort are likely to be needed for the process. And when applied to a collaborative, the effort is likely to be considerably more time-consuming in order to promote the involvement of substantial numbers of leaders, organizations, and perhaps members or citizens (Huxham, 2003).

Note that in practice, the Strategy Change Cycle bears little resemblance to the caricature of strategic planning occasionally found in the literature as a rigid, formal, detached process (see Mintzberg, Ahlstrand, and Lampel, 1998). Instead, the Strategy Change Cycle is intended to enhance strategic thinking, acting, and learning; to engage key actors with what is, as well as with what can be; to engage with the important details while abstracting the strategic message in them; and to link strategy formulation with implementation in wise, technically workable, and politically intelligent ways.

Step 1: Initiating and Agreeing on a Strategic Planning Process

The purpose of the first step is to negotiate agreement among key internal (and perhaps external) decision makers or opinion leaders about the overall strategic planning effort and the key planning steps. The support and commitment of key decision makers are vital if strategic planning in an organization is to succeed. Further, the involvement of key decision makers outside the organization is usually crucial to the success of nonprofit programs if implementation will involve multiple parties and organizations (Nutt and Backoff, 1992; Eden and Ackermann, 1998; Light, 1998; Huxham, 2003).

Obviously, some person or group must initiate the process. One of the initiators' first tasks is to identify exactly who the key decision makers are. The next task is to identify which persons, groups, units, or organizations should be involved in the effort. These two tasks will require some preliminary stakeholder analysis, which we will discuss in more detail shortly. The initial agreement will be negotiated with at least some of these decision makers, groups, units, or organizations. In practice, a *series* of agreements must typically be struck among various parties as support for the process builds and key stakeholders and decision makers sign on. Strategic planning for a nonprofit organization or collaborative is especially likely to work well if an effective policymaking body is in place to oversee the effort.

The agreement itself should cover

- The purpose of the effort
- Preferred steps in the process
- The form and timing of reports
- The role, functions, and membership of any group or committee empowered to oversee the effort, such as a strategic planning coordinating committee (SPCC)
- The role, functions, and membership of the strategic planning team
- The commitment of necessary resources to proceed with the effort
- Any important limitations or boundaries on the effort

As noted, at least some stakeholder analysis work will be needed in order to figure out whom to include in the series of initial agreements. A *stakeholder* is defined as any person, group, or organization that can place a claim on an organization's (or other entity's) attention, resources, or output or is affected by that output. Examples of a nonprofit organization's stakeholders include clients or customers, third-party payers or funders, employees, the board of directors, members, volunteers, other nonprofit organizations providing complementary services or involved as partners in joint ventures or projects, banks holding mortgages or notes, and suppliers.

Attention to stakeholder concerns is crucial: *the key to success in nonprofit organizations and collaboratives is the satisfaction of key stakeholders* (Light, 1998; Moore, 2000). A stakeholder analysis is a way for the organization's decision makers and planning team to immerse themselves in the networks and politics surrounding the organization. An understanding of the relationships—actual or potential—that help define the organization's context can provide valuable clues to identifying strategic issues and developing effective strategies

(Moore, 2000; Bryson, 2004b). In this regard, note that the stakeholder definition is deliberately quite broad for both practical and ethical reasons. Thinking broadly, at least initially, about who the stakeholders are is a way of opening people's eyes to the various webs of relationships within which the organization exists (Feldman and Khademian, 2002) and of ensuring that the organization is alerted to its ethical and democratic accountability responsibilities, since they always involve clarifying *who* and *what* counts (Mitchell, Agle, and Wood, 1997; Behn, 2001).

For many nonprofit organizations, the label "customer" will be given to their key stakeholder, particularly if an organization is trying to "reinvent" itself (Osborne and Plastrik, 1997, 2000), "reengineer" its operations (Hammer and Champy, 1993; Cohen and Eimicke, 1998), or employ continuous improvement processes (Cohen and Eimicke, 1998). The customer label can be useful, particularly for organizations that need to improve their "customer service." In other situations, the customer language can actually be problematic. One danger is that focusing on a single "customer" may lead these organizations inadvertently to ignore other important stakeholder groups. Another danger is that the customer label can undermine the values and virtues of active citizenship that many nonprofit organizations are trying to promote (de Leon and Denhardt, 2000; Denhardt and Denhardt, 2000). In addition, many community-based nonprofit organizations and those relying on government funding also face very complex stakeholder environments.

The organizers of the planning effort should count on using several different techniques, including what I call the "basic stakeholder analysis technique" (Bryson, 2004a, 2004b). This technique requires the strategic planning team to brainstorm a list of who the organization's stakeholders are, what their criteria are for judging the performance of the organization (that is, what their "stake" is in the organization or its output), and how well the organization performs against those criteria *from the stakeholders' points of view.* If there is time, additional steps (perhaps involving additional analysis techniques) should be considered, including understanding how the stakeholders influence the organization, identifying what the organization needs from its various stakeholders (money, staff, political support), and determining in general how important the various stakeholders are. Looking ahead, a stakeholder analysis will help clarify whether the organization needs to have different missions and perhaps different strategies for different stakeholders, whether it should seek to have its mandates changed, and in general what its strategic issues are. Indeed, planners should expect to perform stakeholder analyses of various kinds at various points in the process as a way of understanding what stakeholders want or need and how stakeholder support can be generated (see Figure 8.1) (Bryson, 2004b).

Step 2: Identifying Organizational Mandates

The formal and informal mandates placed on the organization consist of the various "musts" it confronts, the requirements, restrictions, and expectations it faces. It is surprising how few organizations know precisely what they are—and are not—formally mandated to do. Typically, few members of any organization have ever read, for example, the relevant legislation, policies, ordinances, charters, articles, and contracts that outline the organization's formal mandates. Many organizational members also do not understand the informal mandates—which are primarily political in the broadest sense—that the organization faces. It may not be surprising, then, that most organizations make one, two, or all of three fundamental mistakes. First, by not articulating or learning what they must do, they are unlikely to do it. Second, they may believe they are more tightly constrained in their actions than they actually are. And third, they may assume that if they are not explicitly told to do something, they are not allowed to do it.

Step 3: Clarifying Organizational Mission and Values

An organization's mission, or purpose, in tandem with its mandates, provides the organization's raison d'être, the social justification for its existence. An organization's mission and mandates also point the way toward the ultimate organizational end of creating public value. For a nonprofit organization, this means that there must be identifiable social or political demands or needs that the organization seeks to fill in a way that accords with its nonprofit status (Bryce, 2000). Viewed in this light, nonprofit organizations must always be seen as a means to an end, not as an end in and of themselves. For a collaborative, it means identifying the collaborative advantage to be gained by working together—that is, what can be accomplished together that creates public value that cannot be achieved alone (Huxham, 2003).

Identifying the mission, however, does more than merely justify the organization's existence. Clarifying purpose can eliminate a great deal of unnecessary conflict in an organization and can help channel discussion and activity productively (Terry, 2001; Thompson, 2001; Nutt, 2002). Agreement on purpose also defines the arenas in which the organization will collaborate or compete and, at least in broad outline, charts the future course of the organization. Agreement on purpose thus serves as a kind of "primary framework" (Goffman, 1986; Bryant, 2003) that bounds the plausibility and acceptability of arguments. Agreement on purpose can go even further and provide a kind of premise control that constrains thinking, learning, and acting (Perrow, 1986; Weick, 1995) and even legitimacy (Suchman, 1995). Moreover, an important and socially justifiable mission is a source of inspiration and guidance to key stakeholders, particularly employees (Weiss and Piderit, 1999; Kouzes and Posner, 2002). Indeed, it is doubtful if any organization ever achieved greatness or excellence without a basic consensus among its key stakeholders on an inspiring mission (Collins and Porras, 1997; Light, 1998).

Some careful stakeholder analysis work should precede development or modification of a mission statement so that attention to purpose can be informed by thinking about purpose *for whom.* If the purposes of key stakeholders are not served, the organization may be engaging in what historian Barbara Tuchman (1984) aptly calls "folly." The mission statement itself might be very short, perhaps not more than a sentence or a slogan. But development of the mission statement should grow out of lengthy dialogue about the organization's identity, its abiding purpose, desired responses to key stakeholders, its philosophy and core values, and its ethical standards. These discussions may also provide a basic outline for a description of the organization in the future, or its "vision of success," described in step 8. Considerable intermediate work is necessary, however, before a complete vision of success can be articulated.

Step 4: Assessing the
Organization's External and Internal Environments

The planning team should explore the environment outside the organization to identify the opportunities and threats (or more euphemistically, the challenges) the organization faces (step 4a). It should explore the environment inside the organization to identify strengths and weaknesses (step 4b). Basically, "outside" factors are those not under the organization's control, while "inside" factors are those that are (Pfeffer and Salancik, 1978). Opportunities and threats are usually (though not necessarily) more about the future than about the present, whereas strengths and weakness are about the present and not the future (Nutt and Backoff, 1992).

Monitoring a variety of forces and trends, including political, economic, social, educational, technological, and physical environmental ones, can help planners and decision makers discern opportunities and threats. Unfortunately, organizations all too often focus only on the negative or threatening aspects of these changes and not on the opportunities they present, so care must be taken to ensure a balanced view (Dutton and Jackson, 1987; Borins, 1998; Nutt, 2001). In other words, attending to threats and weaknesses should be seen as an opportunity to build strengths and improve performance (Weick and Sutcliffe, 2001).

Besides monitoring trends and events, the strategic planning team also should monitor various important external stakeholder groups, including especially those that affect resource flows (directly or indirectly). These groups would include customers, clients, payers or funders, dues-paying members, regulators, and relevant policy bodies. The team also should attend to competitors, competitive forces, and possible sources of competitive advantage; as well as to collaborators, collaborative forces, and potential sources of collaborative advantage.

The organization might construct various scenarios to explore alternative futures in the external environment, a practice typical of much strategic planning in large private sector organizations. Scenarios are particularly good at demonstrating how various forces and trends are likely to interact, which are amenable to organizational influence, and which are not. Scenarios also offer an effective way of challenging the organization's "official future" when necessary. The official future is the presumed or taken-for-granted future that makes current strategies sensible. Organizations unwilling to challenge this future are the ones most likely to be blindsided by changes (Schwartz, 1991; van der Heijden and others, 2002).

Members of an organization's governing body (particularly if they are elected) may be better at identifying and assessing external threats and opportunities (especially present ones) than the organization's employees. This is partly due to a governing board's responsibility for relating an organization to its external environment and vice versa (Scott, 1987; Carver, 1997). Unfortunately, neither governing boards nor employees usually do a systematic or effective job of external scanning. As a result, most organizations are like ships trying to navigate troubled or treacherous waters without benefit of human lookouts, global positioning systems, radar, or sonar. All too often, the result is unwelcome surprises (Weick and Sutcliffe, 2001).

Because of this, both employees and governing board members should consider relying on a somewhat formal external assessment process to supplement their informal efforts. The technology of external assessment is fairly simple and allows organizations to cheaply, pragmatically, and effectively keep tabs on things that are happening in the larger world that are likely to have an effect on the organization and the pursuit of its mission. Clip services, discussion groups, and periodic retreats, for example, might be used to explore forces and trends and their potential impact. The key, however, is to avoid being captured by existing categories of classification and search, since they tend to formalize and routinize the past rather than open one to the surprises of the future (Mintzberg, Ahlstrand, and Lampel, 1998; Weick and Sutcliffe, 2001).

Attention to opportunities and threats, along with a stakeholder analysis, can be used to identify the organization's "critical success factors" (Johnson and Scholes, 2002). These may overlap with mandates, in the sense that they are the things the organization must do, or criteria it must meet, in order for it to be successful in the eyes of its key stakeholders, especially those in the external environment. Ideally, the organization will excel in these areas, and it must do so in order to outperform or stave off competitors.

To identify internal strengths and weaknesses, the organization might monitor resources (inputs), present strategy (process), and performance (outputs). Most nonprofit organizations, in my experience, have volumes of information on many of their inputs, such as salaries, supplies, physical plant, and full-time-equivalent personnel. Unfortunately, too few organizations have a very clear idea of their philosophy, core values, distinctive competencies, and culture, a crucial set of inputs for both ensuring stability and managing change.

Organizations also tend to have an unclear idea of their present strategy, either overall, by subunit, or by function. And typically, they cannot say enough about their outputs, let alone the effects, or outcomes, those outputs create for clients, customers, or payers, although this, too, is changing. The difficulties of measuring performance are well known (Osborne and Plastrik, 2000; Kaplan, 2001), but regardless of the difficulties, organizations are continually challenged to demonstrate effective performance to their stakeholders.

In this regard, some nonprofit organizations have been able to pull their input, process, and outcome measures together in the form of a "balanced scorecard" (BSC) that shows, in effect, the organization's "theory of action" and allows it to monitor how it is doing in terms of the theory's components (Kaplan, 2001; Niven, 2003). BSCs are likely to become far more widely used in the future by nonprofit organizations. Exhibit 8.1 presents a BSC for the United Way of Southeastern New England. The BSC identifies desired financial, customer, and internal process outcomes and strategic objectives designed to help produce the outcomes. Many BSCs also include a category of learning and growth outcomes (Niven, 2003).

A lack of performance information presents problems both for the organization and for its stakeholders. Stakeholders judge an organization according to the criteria *they* choose, which are not necessarily the same criteria the organization would choose. For external stakeholders in particular, these criteria typically relate to performance. If an organization cannot effectively meet its stakeholders' performance criteria, then regardless of its "inherent" worth, the stakeholders are likely to withdraw their support. An absence of performance information may also create—or harden—major organizational conflicts. Without performance criteria and information, there is no way to objectively evaluate the relative effectiveness of alternative strategies, resource allocations, organizational designs, and distributions of power. As a result, organizational conflicts are likely to occur more often than they should, serve narrow partisan interests, and be resolved in ways that don't further the organization's mission (Terry, 1993; Flyvbjerg, 1998).

A consideration of the organization's strengths and weaknesses can also lead to an identification of its "distinctive competencies" (Selznick, 1957), or what have been termed more recently "core competencies" (Prahalad and Hamel, 1990; Johnson and Scholes, 2002) or "capabilities" (Stalk, Evans, and Shulman, 1992). These are the organization's strongest abilities, or the most effective strategies and actions, or resources (broadly conceived), on which it can draw routinely to perform well. What makes these abilities "distinctive" is the inability of others to replicate them easily, if at all, because of the way they are interlinked with one another (Eden and Ackermann, 2000).

Exhibit 8.1. Balanced Scorecard for the United Way of Southeastern New England.

Outcomes	Strategic Objectives
Financial	
External growth	Increase net amount of funds raised
Internal stability	Balance internal income and expenses to maintain our 100 percent guarantee to others
Community building	Increase amount of funds that go to services
	Increase amount of funds that go to proprietary products
Customer	
Customer satisfaction	Recognition, ease of giving
Market growth	Products that customers care about and that will improve the community
Customer retention	Information on results; quality, timely service
Internal	
Key internal business processes	Improve key internal processes in the following areas:
	• Fundraising
	• Fund distribution
	• Community building
	• Information processing and communications
	• Pledge processing
	• Product development
	• Volunteer and staff development
	• Customer service
	• Interdepartmental communications
Innovative products	Develop a research and development process to come up with new, innovative products
Viable product line	Develop a consistent process for evaluating existing products and services

Source: Kaplan, 2001. Used with permission of United Way of Rhode Island (formerly United Way of Southeastern New England).

Step 5: Identifying the Strategic
Issues the Organization Must Face

Together the first four elements of the process lead to the fifth, the identification of strategic issues. *Strategic issues* are fundamental policy questions or critical challenges affecting the organization's mandates, mission and values, product or service level and mix, clients, users or payers, cost, financing, organization, or management. Finding the best way to frame these issues typically requires considerable wisdom, dialogue, and deep understanding of organizational purposes, operations, stakeholder interests, and external demands and possibilities. The first four steps of the process are designed deliberately to slow things down so that there is enough information and interaction for the needed wisdom to emerge. The process is designed, in other words, to "unfreeze" people's thinking (Lewin, 1951; Dalton, 1970) so that knowledge exploration, development, and learning might occur (March, 1991; Crossan, Lane, and White, 1999). This knowledge will be exploited in this and later phases.

Strategic planning focuses on achieving the best "fit" between an organization and its environment. Attention to mandates and the external environment can therefore be thought of as planning from the outside in. Attention to mission and organizational values and the internal environment can be considered planning from the inside out. Usually, it is vital that pressing strategic issues be dealt with expeditiously and effectively if the organization is to survive and prosper. An organization that does not respond to a strategic issue can expect undesirable results from a threat or a missed opportunity (or both).

The iterative nature of the strategic planning process often becomes apparent in this step when participants find that information generated or discussed in earlier steps presents itself again as part of a strategic issue. For example, many strategic planning teams begin strategic planning with the belief that they know what their organization's mission is. They often find out in this step, however, that one of the key issues their organizations faces is determining exactly what its mission ought to be. In other words, if the organization's present mission is found to be inappropriate, given the team members' new understanding of the situation the organization faces, a new mission must be selected and embraced.

Strategic issues, virtually by definition, involve conflicts of one sort or another. The conflicts may involve ends (what), means (how or how much), philosophy (why), location (where), timing (when), and who might be advantaged or disadvantaged by different ways of resolving the issue (who). For the issues to be raised and resolved effectively, the organization must be prepared to deal with the almost inevitable conflicts that will occur. Conflict, shifts in understanding, and shifts in preferences will all evoke participants' emotions (Weick, 1995; Bryant, 2003). It is therefore in this stage that the importance of emotion will become dramatically apparent, along with the concomitant need for "emotional intelligence" on the part of participants if the emotions are to be dealt with effectively (Goleman, 1995; Goleman, Boyatzis, and McKee, 2002; Heifetz and Laurie, 1997).

A statement of a strategic issue should contain three elements. First, the issue should be described succinctly, preferably in a single paragraph. The issue should be framed as a question that the organization can do something about. If the organization cannot do anything about it, it is best not to think of it as an issue for the organization; it is simply a *condition* (Wildavsky, 1979). An organization's attention is limited enough without wasting it on issues it cannot address effectively. The question also should have more than one answer, as a way of broadening the search for viable strategies. Too often organizations focus too quickly on a specific solution, without first learning more about the context within which the issue arose and without exploring the full range of possible responses (Eden and Ackermann, 1998; Nutt, 2002).

Second, the factors that make the issue a fundamental challenge should be listed. In particular, what is it about the organization's mandates, mission, values, internal strengths and weaknesses, and external opportunities and threats that make this a strategic issue for the organization? Listing these factors will become useful in the next step, strategy development. Every effective strategy builds on strengths and takes advantage of opportunities while minimizing or overcoming weaknesses and threats. The framing of strategic issues is therefore very important because it will provide much of the basis for the issues' resolution (Eden and Ackermann, 1998; Nutt, 2002; Bryant, 2003).

Finally, the planning team should prepare a statement of the consequences of failure to address the issue. This will help organizational leaders decide just how strategic or important various issues are. If no consequences will ensue from failure to address a particular issue, it is not a strategic issue (at least not yet). At the other extreme, if the organization will be destroyed or will miss a valuable opportunity by failing to address a particular issue, the issue is clearly *very* strategic and is worth attending to immediately. Thus the step of identifying strategic issues is aimed at focusing organizational attention on what is truly important for the survival, prosperity, and effectiveness of the organization.

Once statements of the issues are prepared, the organization will know what kinds of issues it faces and just how strategic they are. There are several kinds of strategic issues. *Developmental issues* have the potential to alter the organization and its "core business" but have no real precedent (Nutt, 2001). They involve a fundamental change in products or services, customers or clients, service or distribution channels, sources of revenue, identity or image, or some other aspect of the organization for which there is no real organizational precedent.

Nondevelopmental issues involve far less ambiguity because most of the aspects of the organization's overall strategy will not change. Most existing decision premises can be presumed still to apply (Nutt, 2001).

Then there are issues that require an immediate response and therefore cannot be handled in a more routine way. There are issues that are coming up on the horizon and are likely to require some action in the future or perhaps some action now; for the most part, these issues can be handled as part of the organization's regular strategic planning cycle. And finally, there are issues that require no organizational action at present but must be continuously monitored.

There are seven basic approaches to the identification of strategic issues. The *direct approach* goes straight from a discussion of mandates, mission, and SWOTs (strengths, weaknesses, opportunities, and threats) to the identification of strategic issues. The *indirect approach* begins with brainstorming about several different sets of options before identifying issues. The sets of options include actions the organization could take to meet stakeholders' performance expectations; to build on strengths, take advantage of opportunities, and minimize or overcome weaknesses and threats; and to incorporate any other important aspect of background studies or reports or present circumstances. Each option is put on a separate card or self-adhesive label. These options are then merged into a single set of potential actions, and the actions are regrouped into clusters, with each cluster representing a potential issue category. A category label is developed for each cluster that identifies the subject or theme of the cluster.

The *goals approach* starts with goals (or performance indicators) and then identifies issues that must be addressed before the goals (or indicators) can be achieved. And the *"vision of success" approach* starts with at least a sketch of a vision of success in order to identify issues that must be dealt with before the vision can be realized. This approach is probably necessary in situations involving developmental decisions—where fundamental change is needed but the organization lacks a precedent (Nutt, 2001). For example, development of a vision is often recommended for organizations about to engage in a serious way in e-commerce (Abramson and Means, 2001).

The *oval mapping approach* grew out of the Strategic Options Development and Analysis (SODA) method developed by Colin Eden, Fran Ackermann, and their associates (Eden and Ackermann, 2001; Bryson, Ackermann, Eden, and Finn, 2004). Oval mapping involves creation of word-and-arrow diagrams in which ideas about actions the organization might take, how it might take them, and why, are linked by arrows indicating the cause-and-effect or influence relationships between them (see Eden and Ackermann, 1998, and especially Bryson, Ackermann, Eden, and Finn, 2004). In other words, the arrows indicate that action A may cause or influence B, which in turn may cause or influence C, and so on; if the organization does A, it can expect to produce outcome B, which may in turn be expected to produce outcome C. These "maps" can consist of hundreds of interconnected relationships, showing differing areas of interest and their relationships to one another. The approach's name comes from the fact that ideas are usually written on oval-shaped pieces of paper, one idea per oval, and then placed on a flipchart-sheet-covered wall; arrows linking ideas are then drawn on the flipchart sheets.

Important clusters of potential actions may indicate strategic issues. A strategy in response would be to determine actions to undertake in the issue area, how to undertake them, and why (see step 6). The approach is particularly useful when participants are having trouble making sense of complex issue areas, when time is short, when the emphasis must be on action, and when commitment on the part of those involved is particularly important.

The *tensions approach* was developed by Nutt and Backoff (1992) and elaborated in Nutt, Backoff, and Hogan (2000). These authors argue that there are always four basic tensions around any strategic issue, in various combinations. These tensions involve human resources, especially *equity* concerns; *innovation and change*; maintenance of *tradition*; and *productivity improvement.* The authors suggest critiquing the way issues are framed using these tensions separately and in combination in order to find the best way to frame the issue. The critiques may need to run through several cycles before the wisest way to frame the issue is found. Finally, a *systems analysis approach* can be used to help discern the best way to frame issues when the system contains complex feedback effects and must be formally modeled in order to understand it (Senge, 1990; Sterman, 2000).

By stating that there are seven different approaches to the identification of strategic issues, I may raise the hackles of some planning theorists and practitioners who believe that one should always start with issues or goals or vision or analysis. I argue that what will work best depends on the situation and that the wise planner should choose an approach accordingly.

Step 6: Formulating Strategies and Plans to Manage the Issues

A *strategy* is defined as a pattern of purposes, policies, programs, actions, decisions, or resource allocations that define what an organization is, what it does, and why it does it. Strategies can vary by level, function, and time frame. Strategies are developed to deal with the issues identified in step 5.

This definition is intentionally broad in order to focus attention on the creation of consistency across *rhetoric* (what people say), *choices* (what people decide and are willing to pay for), *actions* (what people do), and the *consequences* of those actions. Effective strategy formulation and implementation processes link rhetoric, choices, actions, and consequences into reasonably coherent and consistent patterns across levels, functions, and time (Eden and Ackermann, 1998). They will also be tailored to fit an organization's culture, even if the purpose of the strategy or strategies is to reconfigure that culture in some way (Johnson and Scholes, 2002). Draft strategies, and perhaps drafts of formal strategic plans, will be formulated in this step to articulate desired patterns. They may also be reviewed and adopted at the end of this step if the strategic planning process is relatively simple and small-scale and involves a single organization. (Such a process would merge this step with step 7.)

A Five-Part Strategy Development Process. There are numerous approaches to strategy development (Holman and Devane, 1999; Bryson, 2001, 2003; Bryson and Anderson, 2000). I generally favor either of two approaches. The first is a fairly speedy five-part process based on the work of the Institute of Cultural Affairs (Spencer, 1996). The second can be used if there is a need or desire to articulate more clearly the relationships among multiple options, to show how they fit together as part of a pattern.

The first part of the five-part process begins with identification of practical alternatives and dreams or visions for resolving the strategic issues. Each option should be phrased in action terms; that is, it should begin with an imperative, such as *do, get, buy,* or *achieve.* Phrasing options in action terms helps make the options seem more "real" to participants.

Next, the planning team should enumerate the barriers to achieving those alternatives, dreams, or visions. Focusing on barriers at this point is not typical of most strategic planning processes, but doing so is one way of ensuring that any strategies developed deal with implementation difficulties directly rather than haphazardly.

Once alternatives, dreams, and visions, along with barriers to their realization, have been listed, the team develops major proposals for achieving the alternatives, dreams, or visions, either directly or else indirectly by overcoming the barriers. (Alternatively, the team might solicit proposals from key organizational units, various stakeholder groups, task forces, or selected individuals.)

After major proposals have been submitted, two final tasks remain in order to develop effective strategies. Actions to implement the major proposals that must be taken over the next two to three years must be identified. And finally, a detailed work program for the next six to twelve months must be spelled out to implement the actions. These last two tasks shade over into the work of step 9, but that is good, because strategies should always be developed with implementation in mind. As Mintzberg (1994, p. 25) explains, "Every failure of implementation is, by definition, also a failure of formulation." In some circumstances, steps 6 and 9 may be merged—for example, when a single organization is planning for itself. In addition, in collaborative settings, implementation details must often be worked out first by the various parties before they are willing to commit to shared strategic plans (Innes, 1996; Bardach, 1998; Bryant, 2003). In such situations, implementation planning may have to precede strategy or plan adoption.

Using Oval Mapping to Structure Relationships Among Strategic Options to Develop Strategies. Developing strategies using the oval mapping process builds on the oval mapping approach to strategic issue identification; if strategic issues were developed using the oval mapping method, the transition from issues to strategy development is quite easy (Bryson, Ackermann, Eden, and Finn, 2004).

The method involves making a list of multiple options to address each strategic issue, on which each option is again phrased in imperative, action terms. The options are then linked by arrows indicating which options cause or influence the achievement of other options. An option can be a part of more than one chain. The result is a "map" of action-to-outcome (cause-and-effect, means-to-an-end) relationships; the options toward the end of a chain of arrows are possible goals or perhaps even mission statements. Presumably, these goals can be achieved by accomplishing at least some of the actions leading up to them, although additional analysis and work on the arrow chains may be necessary to determine and clearly articulate action-to-outcome relationships. The option maps can be reviewed and revised, and particular action-to-outcome chains can be selected as strategies. Additional detail and numerous examples will be found in Bryson, Ackermann, Eden, and Finn (2004).

An effective strategy must meet several criteria. It must be technically workable and politically acceptable to key stakeholders, and it must fit the organization's philosophy and core values. Further, it should be ethical, moral, and legal and should further the creation of public value. It must also deal with the strategic issue it was supposed to address. All too often, I have seen strategies that were technically, politically, morally, ethically, and legally impeccable but did not deal with the issues they were presumed to address. Effective strategies thus meet a rather severe set of tests. Careful, thoughtful dialogue—and often bargaining and negotiation—among key decision makers who have adequate information and are politically astute is usually necessary before strategies can be developed that meet these tests. Some of this work must occur in this step, and some is likely to occur in the next step.

Step 7: Reviewing and Adopting the Strategies and Plan

Once strategies have been formulated, the planning team may need to obtain an official decision to adopt them and proceed with their implementation. The same is true if a formal strategic plan has been prepared. This decision will help affirm the desired changes and move the organization toward "refreezing" in the new pattern (Lewin, 1951; Dalton, 1970), where the knowledge exploration of previous steps can be exploited (March, 1991). When strategies and plans are developed for a single organization, particularly a small one, this step may actually merge with step 6. But a separate step will likely be necessary when strategic planning is undertaken for a large organization, network of organizations, or community. The SPCC will need to approve the resulting strategies or plan; relevant policymaking bodies and other implementing groups and organizations are also likely to have to approve the strategies or plan, or at least parts of it, in order for implementation to proceed effectively.

To secure passage of any strategy or plan, it will be necessary to continue to pay attention to the goals, concerns, and interests of all key internal and external stakeholders. Finding or creating inducements that can be traded for support can also be useful. But there are numerous ways to defeat any proposal in formal decision-making arenas. So it is important for the plan to be sponsored and championed by actors whose knowledge of how to negotiate the intricacies of the relevant arenas can help ensure passage (Bryson and Crosby, 1992).

Step 8: Establishing an Effective Organizational Vision

In this step, the organization develops a description of what it should look like once it has successfully implemented its strategies and achieved its full potential. This description is the organization's "vision of success." Few organizations have such a description or vision, yet the importance of such descriptions has long been recognized by well-managed companies, organizational psychologists, and management theorists (Collins and Porras, 1997; Kouzes and Posner, 2002). Such descriptions can include the organization's mission, its values and philosophy, basic strategies, its performance criteria, some important decision rules, and the ethical standards expected of all employees.

The description, to the extent that it is widely circulated and discussed within the organization, allows organizational members to know what is expected of them without constant managerial oversight. Members are freed to act on their own initiative on the organization's behalf to an extent not otherwise possible. The result should be a mobilization of members' energy toward pursuing the organization's purposes and a reduced need for direct supervision (Nutt, 2001).

Some people might question why developing a vision of success comes at this point in the process rather than much earlier. There are two basic answers to this question. First, it does not have to come here for all organizations. Some organizations are able to develop a clearly articulated, agreed-on vision of success much earlier in the process. And some organizations start with "visioning" exercises in order to develop enough of a consensus on purposes and values to guide issue identification and strategy formulation efforts. Figure 8.1 therefore indicates the many different points at which participants may find it useful to develop some sort of guiding vision. Some processes may start with a visionary statement. Others may use visions to help them figure out what the strategic issues are or to help them develop strategies. And still others may use visions to convince key decision makers to adopt strategies or plans or to guide implementation efforts. The farther along in the process a vision is found, the more likely it is to be more fully articulated.

Second, most organizations will typically not be able to develop a detailed vision of success until they have gone through several iterations of strategic planning—if they are able to develop a vision at all. A challenging yet achievable vision embodies the tension between what an organization wants and what it can have (Senge, 1990). Often several cycles of strategic planning are necessary before organizational members know what they want, what they can have, and the difference between the two. A vision that motivates people will be challenging enough to spur action yet not so impossible to achieve that it demotivates and demoralizes people. Most organizations, in other words, will find that their visions of success are likely to serve more as a guide for strategy implementation than for strategy formulation.

Further, for most organizations, development of a vision of success is not necessary in order to produce marked improvements in performance. In my experience, most organizations can demonstrate a substantial improvement in effectiveness if they simply identify and satisfactorily resolve a few strategic issues. Most organizations simply do not address often enough what is truly important; just gathering key decision makers to deal with a few important matters in a timely way can enhance organizational performance substantially. For these reasons, the step is labeled "optional" in Figure 8.1.

Step 9: Developing an Effective Implementation Process

Just creating a strategic plan is not enough. The changes indicated by the adopted strategies must be incorporated throughout the system for them to be brought to life and for real value to be created for the organization and its stakeholders. Thinking strategically about implementation and developing an effective implementation plan are important tasks on the road to realizing the strategies developed in step 6. For example, in some circumstances, direct implementation at all sites will be the wisest strategic choice, while in other situations, some form of staged implementation may be best (Joyce, 1999).

Again, if strategies and an implementation plan have been developed for a single organization, particularly a small one, or if the planning is for a collaborative, this step may need to be combined with step 7, strategy formulation. On the other hand, in many multiorganizational situations, a separate step will be required to ensure that relevant groups and organizations do the action planning necessary for implementation success.

Action plans should detail the following:

- Implementation roles and responsibilities of oversight bodies, organizational teams or task forces, and individuals
- Expected results and specific objectives and milestones
- Specific action steps and relevant details

- Schedules
- Resource requirements and sources
- A communication process
- Review, monitoring, and midcourse correction procedures
- Accountability procedures

It is important to build into action plans enough sponsors, champions, and other personnel—along with sufficient time, money, attention, administrative and support services, and other resources—to ensure successful implementation. You must "budget the plan" wisely if implementation is to go well. In interorganizational situations, it is almost impossible to underestimate the requirements for communication, the nurturance of relationships, and attention to operational detail (Huxham, 2003).

It is also important to work quickly to avoid unnecessary or undesirable competition with new priorities. Whenever opportunities to implement strategies and achieve objectives arise, they should be taken. In other words, it is smart to be opportunistic as well as deliberate. And it is important to remember that what actually happens in practice will always be some blend of what is intended with what emerges along the way (Mintzberg, Ahlstrand, and Lampel, 1998).

Successfully implemented and institutionalized strategies result in the establishment of a new "regime," a "set of implicit or explicit principles, norms, rules, and decision-making procedures around which actors' expectations converge in a given area" (Krasner, 1983, p. 2; see also Crossan, Lane, and White, 1999). Regime building is necessary to preserve gains in the face of competing demands. Unfortunately, regimes can outlive their usefulness and must be changed, which involves the next step in the process.

Step 10: Reassessing Strategies and the Strategic Planning Process

Once the implementation process has been under way for some time, it is important to review the strategies and the strategic planning process as a prelude to a new round of strategic planning. Much of the work of this phase may occur as part of the ongoing implementation process. However, if the organization has not engaged in strategic planning for a while, this will be a separate phase. Attention should be focused on successful strategies and whether they should be maintained, replaced by other strategies, or terminated for one reason or another. Unsuccessful strategies should be replaced or terminated. The strategic planning process also should be examined, its strengths and weaknesses noted, and modifications suggested to improve the next round of strategic planning. Effectiveness in this step really does depend on effective organizational learning, which means taking a hard look at what is really happening and being open to new information. As Weick and Sutcliffe (2001, p. 18) say, "The whole point of a learning organization is that it needs to get a better handle on the fact that it doesn't know what it doesn't know." Viewing strategic planning as a kind of action research can help embed learning in the entire process and make sure that the kind of information, feedback, and dialogue necessary for learning occur (Eden and Huxham, 1996).

TAILORING THE PROCESS TO SPECIFIC CIRCUMSTANCES

The Strategy Change Cycle is a general approach to strategic planning and management. Like any planning and management process, it must therefore be tailored carefully to the specific situation if it is to be useful (Christensen, 1999; Alexander, 2000). A number of adaptations—or variations on the general theme—are discussed in this section.

Sequencing the Steps

Although the steps (or occasions for dialogue and decision) are laid out in a linear sequence, it must be emphasized that the Strategy Change Cycle, as its name suggests, is iterative in practice. Participants typically rethink what they have done several times before they reach final decisions. Moreover, the process does not always begin at the beginning. Organizations typically find themselves confronted with a new mandate (step 2), a pressing strategic issue (step 5), a failing strategy (step 6 or 9), or the need to reassess what they have been doing (step 10), and that leads them to engage in strategic planning. Once engaged, the organization is likely to go back and begin at the beginning, particularly with a reexamination of its mission. Indeed, it usually does not matter where you start; you always end up back at mission.

In addition, implementation usually begins before all of the planning is complete. As soon as useful actions are identified, they are taken, as long as they do not jeopardize future actions that might prove valuable. In other words, in a linear, sequential process, the first eight steps of the process would be followed by implementing the planned actions and evaluating the results. However, implementation typically does not, and should not, wait until the eight steps have been completed. For example, if the organization's mission needs to be redrafted, then it should be. If the SWOT analysis turns up weaknesses or threats that need to be addressed immediately, they should be. If aspects of a desirable strategy can be implemented without awaiting further developments, they should be. And so on. As noted earlier, strategic thinking *and* acting *and* learning are important, and all of the thinking does not have to occur before any actions are taken. Or as Mintzberg, Ahlstrand, and Lampel (1998, p. 71) note, "Effective strategy making connects acting to thinking, which in turn connects implementation to formulation. We think in order to act, to be sure, but we also act in order to think." And learn, they might have added. Strategic planning's iterative, flexible, action-oriented nature is precisely what often makes it so attractive to nonprofit leaders and managers.

Making Use of Vision, Goals, and Issues

In the discussion of step 8, it was noted that different organizations or collaboratives may wish to start their process with a vision statement. Such a statement may foster a consensus and provide important inspiration and guidance for the rest of the process, even though it is unlikely to be as detailed as a statement developed later in the process. As indicated in Figure 8.1, there are other points at which it might be possible to develop a vision statement (or statements). Vision thus may be used to prompt the identification of strategic issues, guide the search for and development of strategies, inspire the adoption of strategic plans, or guide implementation efforts. The Amherst H. Wilder Foundation of Saint Paul, Minnesota, for example, has a current vision in its *2000–2005 Strategic Plan* of "a vibrant Saint Paul where individuals, families, and communities can prosper, with opportunities for all to be employed, to be engaged citizens, to live in decent housing, to attend good schools, and to receive support during times of need" (Amherst H. Wilder Foundation, 2000). It had a similar vision in each of its previous plans and used it to help identify issues to be addressed and to develop strategies to be used to realize the vision. The decision to develop a vision statement should hinge on whether one is needed to provide direction to subsequent efforts; whether people will be able to develop a vision that is meaningful enough, detailed enough, *and* broadly supported; and whether there will be enough energy left after the visioning effort to push ahead.

Similarly, as indicated in Figure 8.1, it is possible to develop goals in many different places in the process (Borins, 1998; Behn, 1999). Some strategic planning processes will begin with the goals of new boards of directors, executive directors, or other top-level decision makers. These goals embody a reform agenda for the organization or collaborative. Other strategic planning processes may start with goals that are part of mandates. For example, government agencies often require the nonprofit organizations on which they rely for policy implementation to develop plans that include results and outcome measures that will show how the intent of the legislation is to be achieved. A *starting* goal for these nonprofits, therefore, is to identify results and outcomes they want to be measured against that are also in accord with legislative intent. The goal thus helps these organizations identify an important strategic issue—namely, what the results and outcomes should be. Subsequent strategic planning efforts are then likely to start with the desired outcomes the organization thinks are important.

Still other strategic planning processes will articulate goals to guide strategy formulation in response to specific issues or to guide implementation of specific strategies. Goals developed at these later stages of the process are likely to be more detailed and more specific than those developed earlier in the process. Goals may be developed anytime they would be useful to guide subsequent efforts in the process *and* when they will have sufficient support among key parties to produce desired action.

In my experience, however, strategic planning processes generally start neither with vision nor with goals. In part, this is because in my experience, strategic planning rarely starts with step 1. Instead, people sense that something is not right about the current situation—they face strategic issues of one sort or another, or they are pursuing a strategy that is failing or about to fail—and they want to know what to do (Borins, 1998; Nutt, 2001). One of the crucial features of issue-driven planning (and political decision making in general) is that you do not have to agree on goals to agree on next steps (Innes, 1996; Bryant, 2003; Huxham, 2003). You simply need to agree on a strategy that will address the issue and further the interests of the organization or collaborative and its key stakeholders. Goals are likely to be developed once viable strategies have been developed to address the issues. The goals will typically be strategy-specific.

Articulating goals or describing a vision in this way may help provide a better feeling for where an agreed strategy or interconnected set of strategies should lead (Behn, 1999; Nutt, 2001). Goals and vision are thus more likely to come toward the end of the process than near the beginning. But there are clear exceptions—the Wilder Foundation, for example—and process designers should think carefully about why, when, and how—if at all—to bring goals and vision into the process.

Applying the Process Across Organizational Subunits, Levels, and Functions on an Ongoing Basis

Strategic thinking, acting, and learning depend on getting key people together, getting them to focus wisely and creatively on what is really important, and getting them to do something about it. At its most basic, the technology of strategic planning thus involves deliberations, decisions, and actions. The steps in the Strategy Change Cycle help make the process reasonably orderly to increase the likelihood that what is important will actually be recognized and addressed and to allow more people to participate in the process. When the process is applied to an organization as a whole on an ongoing basis (rather than as a one-shot deal), or at least to significant parts of it, it is usually necessary to construct a *strategic planning system.* The system allows the various parts of the process to be integrated in appropriate ways and engages the organization in strategic *management,* not just strategic planning (Poister and Streib, 1999). In the best circumstances, the system will include the actors and knowledge necessary to act wisely, foster systems thinking, and prompt quick and effective action, since inclusion, systems thinking, and speed are increasingly required of nonprofit organizations (Bryson, 2003; see also Schachtel, 2001).

The process might be applied across subunits, levels, and functions in an organization as outlined in Figure 8.2. The application is based on the "layered" or "stacked units of management" system used by many corporations. The system's first cycle consists of "bottom-up" development of strategic plans within a framework established at the top, followed by reviews and reconciliations at each succeeding level. In the second cycle, operating plans are developed to implement

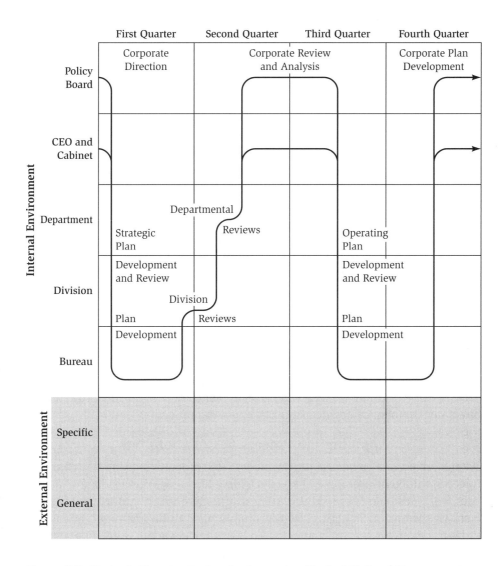

Figure 8.2. Strategic Planning System for Layered or Stacked Units of Management.

Source: Adapted from Bryson and Roering, 1987, p. 16.

the strategic plans. Depending on the situation, decisions at the top of the organizational hierarchy may or may not require policy board approval (which is why the line depicting the process flow diverges at the top). The system may be supported by a set of performance indicators and strategies embodied in a balanced scorecard (Kaplan, 2001); see Exhibit 8.1.

Strategic planning systems for nonprofit organizations are usually not as formalized and integrated as the one outlined in Figure 8.2. More typical is a "strategic issues management" system, which attempts to manage specific strategic issues without seeking integration of the resultant strategies across all subunits, levels, and functions. Tight integration is not necessary because most issues do not affect all parts of the organization, are subject to different politics, and are on their own time frame. Other common nonprofit strategic planning systems include the *contract model,* in which there is a contract or agreement between a "center" and related units, such as between a headquarters organization and local affiliates; the *goal model,* in which there are goals but little else to ensure implementation; the *portfolio model,* in which organizational subunits or programs are managed as part of an overall organizational portfolio; and *collaboration,* which itself can take a variety of forms (Gray, 1989; Huxham, 2003).

If the organization is fairly large, specific linkages will be necessary in order to join the process to different functions and levels in the organization so that it can proceed in a reasonably orderly and integrated manner. One effective way to achieve such a linkage is to appoint the heads of all major units to the strategic planning team. All unit heads can then be sure that their units' information and interests are represented in strategy formulation and can oversee strategy implementation in their unit.

Indeed, key decision makers might wish to form themselves into a permanent strategic planning committee or cabinet. I would recommend this approach if it appears workable for the organization, as it emphasizes the role of line managers as strategic planners and the role of strategic planners as facilitators of decision making by the line managers. Pragmatic and effective strategies and plans are likely to result. Temporary task forces, strategic planning committees, or a cabinet can work, but whatever the arrangement, there is no substitute for the direct involvement of key decision makers in the process.

Applying the Process to Collaboratives

When applied to a collaborative, the process will probably need to be sponsored by a committee or task force of key decision makers, opinion leaders, "influentials," or "notables" representing important stakeholder groups. Additional working groups or task forces will probably need to be organized at various times to deal with specific strategic issues or to oversee the implementation of specific strategies. Because so many more people and groups will have to be involved, and because implementation will have to rely more on consent than on authority, the process is likely to be much more time-consuming and iterative than strategic planning applied to an organization (Bardach, 1998; Bryant, 2003; Huxham, 2003).

Roles for Planners, Decision Makers, Implementers, and Citizens

Planners can play many different roles in a strategic planning process. In many cases, the planners are not people with the word *planner* in their job title but are in fact policymakers or line managers (Mintzberg, Ahlstrand, and Lampel, 1998). The people with the title of planner often act primarily as facilitators of decision making by policymakers or line managers or as technical experts in substantive areas. In other cases, planners operate in a variety of roles. Sometimes the planner is an "expert on experts" (Bolan, 1971) who eases different people with different expertise in and out of the process for different purposes at different times. At still other times, planners are "finders" of strategy, who do their job by interpreting existing actions and recognizing important patterns in the organization and its environment; "analysts" of existing or potential strategies; "catalysts" for promoting strategic thought and action; or "strategists" themselves (Mintzberg, 1994).

Since the most important thing about strategic planning is the development of strategic thought, action, and learning, it may not matter much which person does what. However, it does seem that strategic planning done by boards, executive directors, or line managers is most likely to be implemented. Exactly how people formally designated as planners contribute to that formulation is unclear. In any particular situation, they should be involved in a way that promotes strategic thought, action, and learning and enhances commitment to agreed-on strategies.

When a nonprofit organization is the principal focus of attention, few "outsiders" other than board members are ordinarily involved in the planning process. One reason may be that the organization may already possess the necessary knowledge and expertise in-house, so outsider involvement would be redundant and time-consuming. In addition, insiders are typically the chief implementers of strategies, so their ownership of the process and resultant decisions may be most crucial. Furthermore, participation by outsiders may not be necessary to legitimate the process because the board is directly involved and its members are seen as legitimate representatives of larger constituencies. The absence of participation by ordinary outsiders would parallel much private sector corporate planning practice. On the other hand, it is easy to be wrong about how much one "knows," or needs to know, and how much perceived legitimacy the process needs (Suchman, 1995; Nutt, 2002). Interviews, focus groups and surveys of outsiders, and external sounding boards of various sorts, such as advisory boards or councils, are often worth their weight in gold when they open insiders' eyes to information they have missed, add legitimacy to the effort, and keep insiders from reaching the wrong conclusions or making wrong decisions (Thomas, 1995; Feldman and Khademian, 2001). So a word of caution is in order, and that is to remember, as the Greeks believed, that nemesis always walks in the footsteps of hubris!

Program-focused strategic planning appears to be much more likely to involve outsiders, particularly in their capacity as clients or customers. Outsider involvement in program planning is thus roughly analogous to consumer involvement in private sector marketing research and development projects. Finally, planning on behalf of a collaborative almost always involves substantial participation, but who is inside and who is outside can be difficult to determine (Huxham, 2003).

SUMMARY

This chapter has outlined a process called the Strategy Change Cycle for promoting strategic thinking, acting, and learning in nonprofit organizations and collaboratives. Although the process is presented in a linear, sequential fashion for pedagogical reasons, it proceeds iteratively as groups continuously rethink connections among the various elements of the process, take action, and learn on their way to formulating effective strategies. In addition, the process often does not start with step 1 but instead starts somewhere else and then cycles back to step 1. The steps also are not steps precisely but are more like occasions for deliberation, decision, and action as part of a continuous flow of strategic thinking, acting, and learning; knowledge exploration and exploitation; and strategy formulation and implementation. Mintzberg, Ahlstrand, and Lampel (1998, p. 195) assert that "all real strategic behavior has to combine deliberate control with emergent learning." The Strategy Change Cycle is designed to promote just that kind of strategic behavior.

References

Abramson, D., and Means, G. *E-Government 2001*. Lanham, Md.: Rowman & Littlefield, 2001.

Ackerman, D. *Deep Play*. New York: Vintage Books, 1999.

Alexander, E. R. "Rationality Revisited: Planning Paradigms in a Post-Postmodernist Perspective." *Journal of Planning Education and Research*, 2000, *19*, 242–256.

Amherst H. Wilder Foundation. *Strategic Plan, 2000–2005*. Saint Paul, Minn.: Amherst H. Wilder Foundation, 2000.

Bardach, E. *Getting Agencies to Work Together*. Washington, D.C.: Brookings Institution Press, 1998.

Barzelay, M. *The New Public Management: Improving Research and Policy Dialogue.* Berkeley: University of California Press; New York: Russell Sage Foundation, 2001.

Baum, H. *The Organization of Hope: Communities Planning for Themselves.* Albany: State University of New York Press, 1997.

Behn, R. D. "Managing by Groping Along." *Journal of Policy Analysis and Management,* 1988, *7,* 643–666.

Behn, R. D. "The New Public-Management Paradigm and the Search for Democratic Accountability." *International Public Management Journal,* 1999, *1,* 131–165.

Behn, R. D. *Rethinking Democratic Accountability.* Washington, D.C.: Brookings Institution Press, 2001.

Bolan, R. S. "Generalist with a Specialty: Still Valid? Educating the Planner: An Expert on Experts." In American Society of Planning Officials, *Planning 1971: Selected Papers from the ASPO Conference.* Chicago: American Society of Planning Officials, 1971.

Borins, S. *Innovating with Integrity.* Washington, D.C.: Georgetown University Press, 1998.

Boyte, H. C., and Kari, N. *Building America: The Democratic Promise of Public Work.* Philadelphia: Temple University Press, 1996.

Bryant, J. *The Six Dilemmas of Collaboration: Inter-Organisational Relationships as Drama.* Chichester, England: Wiley, 2003.

Bryce, H. J. *Financial and Strategic Management for Nonprofit Organizations.* (3rd ed.) San Francisco: Jossey-Bass, 2000.

Bryson, J. M. "Strategic Planning." In N. J. Smelser, and P. B. Baltes (eds.), *International Encyclopedia of the Social and Behavioral Sciences.* Oxford, England: Pergamon, 2001.

Bryson, J. M. "Strategic Planning and Management." In B. G. Peters and J. Pierre (eds.), *Handbook of Public Administration.* Thousand Oaks, Calif.: Sage, 2003.

Bryson, J. M. *Strategic Planning for Public and Nonprofit Organizations.* (3rd ed.) San Francisco: Jossey-Bass, 2004a.

Bryson, J. M. "What to Do When Stakeholders Matter: Stakeholder Identification and Analysis Techniques." *Public Management Review,* 2004b, *6,* 21–53.

Bryson, J. M., Ackermann, F., Eden, C., and Finn, C. *Causal Mapping for Individuals and Groups: What to Do When Thinking Matters.* Chichester, England: Wiley, 2004.

Bryson, J. M., and Anderson, S. R. "Applying Large-Group Interaction Methods to the Planning and Implementation of Major Projects." *Public Administration Review,* 2000, *60,* 143–162.

Bryson, J. M., and Crosby, B. C. *Leadership for the Common Good: Tackling Public Problems in a Shared-Power World.* San Francisco: Jossey-Bass, 1992.

Bryson, J. M., and Roering, W. D. "Applying Private Sector Strategic Planning in the Public Sector." *Journal of the American Planning Association,* 1987, *53,* 9–22.

Carver, J. *Boards That Make a Difference: A New Design for Leadership in Nonprofit and Public Organizations.* (2nd ed.) San Francisco: Jossey-Bass, 1997.

Christensen, K. S. *Cities and Complexity: Making Intergovernmental Decisions.* Thousand Oaks, Calif.: Sage, 1999.

Cleveland, H. *Nobody in Charge: Essays on the Future of Leadership.* New York: Wiley, 2002.

Cohen, S., and Eimicke, W. *Tools for Innovators.* San Francisco: Jossey-Bass, 1998.

Collins, J. C., and Porras, J. I. *Built to Last: Successful Habits of Visionary Companies.* New York: HarperBusiness, 1997.

Crossan, M. M., Lane, H. W., and White, R. E. "An Organizational Learning Framework: From Intuition to Institution." *Academy of Management Review,* 1999, *24,* 522–537.

Dalton, G. W. "Influence and Organization Change." In G. W. Dalton, P. Lawrence, and L. Greiner (eds.), *Organization Change and Development.* Homewood, Ill.: Irwin, 1970.

de Leon, L., and Denhardt, R. B. "The Political Theory of Reinvention." *Public Administration Review,* 2000, *60,* 89–97.

Denhardt, R. B., and Denhardt, J. "The New Public Service: Serving Rather Than Steering." *Public Administration Review,* 2000, *60,* 549–559.

Dutton, J. E., and Jackson, S. E. "Categorizing Strategic Issues: Links to Organizational Action." *Academy of Management Review,* 1987, *12,* 76–90.

Eden, C., and Ackermann, F. *Making Strategy: The Journey of Strategic Management.* London: Sage, 1998.

Eden, C., and Ackermann, F. "Mapping Distinctive Competencies: A Systematic Approach." *Journal of the Operational Research Society,* 2000, *51,* 12–20.

Eden, C., and Ackermann, F. "SODA: The Principles." In J. Rosenhead and J. Mingers (eds.), *Rational Analysis in a Problematic World Revisited.* London: Wiley, 2001.

Eden, C., and Huxham, C. "Action Research for Management Research." *British Journal of Management,* 1996, *7,* 75–86.

Faragher, J. M. *Daniel Boone: The Life and Legend of an American Pioneer.* New York: Henry Holt, 1992.

Feldman, M. S., and Khademian, A. "Managing for Inclusion and Control: Balancing Control and Participation." *International Public Management Journal,* 2001, *3,* 149–167.

Feldman, M. S., and Khademian A. "To Manage Is to Govern." *Public Administration Review,* 2002, *62,* 541–554.

Flyvbjerg, B. *Rationality and Power: Democracy in Practice.* Chicago: University of Chicago Press, 1998.

Forester, J. *Planning in the Face of Power.* Berkeley: University of California Press, 1989.

Goffman, E. *Frame Analysis: An Essay on the Organizational Experience.* Boston: Northeastern University Press, 1986.

Goleman, D. *Emotional Intelligence.* New York: Bantam Books, 1995.

Goleman, D., Boyatzis, R., and McKee, A. *Primal Leadership: Realizing the Power of Emotional Intelligence.* Boston: Harvard Business School Press, 2002.

Gray, B. *Collaborating: Finding Common Ground for Multiparty Problems.* San Francisco: Jossey-Bass, 1989.

Hammer, M., and Champy, J. *Reengineering the Corporation: A Manifesto for Business Revolution.* New York: HarperBusiness, 1993.

Heifetz, R. A., and Laurie, D. L. "The Work of Leadership." *Harvard Business Review,* Jan.-Feb. 1997, pp. 124–134.

Holman, P., and Devane, T. E. *The Change Handbook: Group Methods for Shaping the Future.* San Francisco: Berrett-Koehler, 1999.

Huxham, C. "Theorizing Collaborative Practice." *Public Management Review,* 2003, *5,* 401–423.

Innes, J. E. "Planning Through Consensus Building: A New View of the Comprehensive Planning Ideal." *Journal of the American Planning Association,* 1996, *62,* 460–472.

Johnson, G., and Scholes, K. *Exploring Corporate Strategy.* (6th ed.) Upper Saddle River, N.J.: Prentice Hall, 2002.

Joyce, P. *Strategic Management for the Public Services.* Buckingham, England: Open University Press, 1999.

Kaplan. R. S. "Strategic Performance Measurement and Management in Nonprofit Organizations." *Nonprofit Management and Leadership,* 2001, *11,* 353–370.

Kouzes, J. M., and Posner, B. Z. *The Leadership Challenge: How to Get Extraordinary Things Done in Organizations.* (3rd ed.) San Francisco: Jossey-Bass, 2002.

Krasner, S. D. "Structural Causes and Regime Consequences: Regimes as Intervening Variables." In S. D. Krasner (ed.), *International Regimes.* Ithaca, N.Y.: Cornell University Press, 1983.

Letts, C. W., Ryan, W. P., and Grossman, A. *High-Performance Nonprofit Organizations: Managing Upstream for Greater Impact.* New York: Wiley, 1999.

Lewin, K. *Field Theory in Social Sciences.* New York: HarperCollins, 1951.

Light, P. *Sustaining Innovation: Creating Nonprofit and Government Organizations That Innovate Naturally.* San Francisco: Jossey-Bass, 1998.

Light, P. *Pathways to Nonprofit Excellence.* Washington, D.C.: Brookings Institution Press, 2002.

March, J. G. "Exploration and Exploitation in Organizational Learning." *Organization Science,* 1991, *2,* 71–87.

Mintzberg, H. *The Rise and Fall of Strategic Planning.* New York: Free Press, 1994.

Mintzberg, H., Ahlstrand, B., and Lampel, J. *Strategy Safari: A Guided Tour Through the Wilds of Strategic Management.* New York: Free Press, 1998.

Mitchell, R. K., Agle, B. R., and Wood, D. J. "Toward a Theory of Stakeholder Identification and Salience: Defining the Principle of Who and What Really Counts." *Academy of Management Review,* 1997, *22,* 853–886.

Moore, M. H. "Managing for Value: Organizational Strategy in For-Profit, Nonprofit, and Governmental Organizations." *Nonprofit and Voluntary Sector Quarterly,* 2000, *29*(suppl.), 183–204.

Niven, P. R. *Balanced Scorecard Step-by-Step for Government and Nonprofit Agencies.* New York: Wiley, 2003.

Nutt, P. C. "Strategic Decision-Making." In M. A. Hitt, R. E. Freeman, and J. S. Harrison (eds.), *Blackwell Handbook of Strategic Management.* Oxford, England: Blackwell Business, 2001.

Nutt, P. C. *Why Decisions Fail: Avoiding the Blunders and Traps That Lead to Debacles.* San Francisco: Berrett-Koehler, 2002.

Nutt, P. C., and Backoff, R. W. *Strategic Management of Public and Third Sector Organizations: A Handbook for Leaders.* San Francisco: Jossey-Bass, 1992.

Nutt, P. C., Backoff, R. W., and Hogan, M. F. "Managing the Paradoxes of Strategic Change." *Journal of Applied Management Studies,* 2000, *9,* 5–31.

Osborne, D., and Plastrik, P. *Banishing Bureaucracy: The Five Strategies for Reinventing Government.* Boston: Addison-Wesley, 1997.

Osborne, D., and Plastrik, P. *The Reinventor's Fieldbook: Tools for Transforming Your Government.* San Francisco: Jossey-Bass, 2000.

Perrow, C. *Complex Organizations.* New York: Random House, 1986.

Pfeffer, J., and Salancik, G. *The External Control of Organizations: A Resource Dependence Perspective.* New York: HarperCollins, 1978.

Poister, T. H., and Streib, G. D. "Strategic Management in the Public Sector: Concepts, Models, and Processes." *Public Productivity and Management Review,* 1999, *22,* 308–325.

Prahalad, C. K., and Hamel, G. "The Core Competence of the Corporation." *Harvard Business Review,* May-June 1990, pp. 79–91.

Schachtel, M.R.B. "CitiStat and the Baltimore Neighborhood Indicators Alliance: Using Information to Improve Communication and Community." *National Civic Review,* 2001, *90,* 253–265.

Schwartz, P. *The Art of the Long View: Planning for the Future in an Uncertain World.* New York: Doubleday Currency, 1991.

Scott, W. R. *Organizations: Rational, Natural and Open Systems.* (2nd ed.) Upper Saddle River, N.J.: Prentice Hall, 1987.

Selznick, P. *Leadership in Administration: A Sociological Interpretation.* Berkley: University of California Press, 1957.

Senge, P. M. "The Leader's New Work: Building Learning Organizations." *Sloan Management Review,* Fall 1990, pp. 7–23.

Spencer, L. *Winning Through Participation.* Dubuque, Iowa: Kendall-Hunt, 1996.

Stalk, G., Jr., Evans, P., and Shulman, L. "Competing on Capabilities: The New Rules of Corporate Strategy." *Harvard Business Review,* Mar.-Apr. 1992, pp. 57–69.

Sterman, J. D. *Business Dynamics: Systems Thinking and Modeling for a Complex World.* New York: McGraw-Hill, 2000.

Suchman, M. C. "Managing Legitimacy: Strategic and Institutional Approaches." *Academy of Management Review,* 1995, *20,* 571–610.

Terry, R. W. *Authentic Leadership: Courage in Action.* San Francisco: Jossey-Bass, 1993.

Terry, R. W. *Seven Zones for Leadership: Acting Authentically in Stability and Chaos.* Palo Alto, Calif.: Davies-Black, 2001.

Thomas, J. C. *Public Participation in Public Decisions: New Skills and Strategies for Public Managers.* San Francisco: Jossey-Bass, 1995.

Thompson, J. D. *Organizations in Action.* New York: McGraw-Hill, 1967.

Thompson, L. *The Mind and Heart of the Negotiator.* Upper Saddle River, N.J.: Prentice Hall, 2001.

Tuchman, B. *The March of Folly: From Troy to Vietnam.* New York: Knopf, 1984.

van der Heijden and others. *The Sixth Sense: Accelerating Organizational Learning with Scenarios.* Chichester, England: Wiley, 2002.

Weick, K. E. *The Social Psychology of Organizing.* Boston: Addison-Wesley, 1979.

Weick, K. E. *Sensemaking in Organizations.* Thousand Oaks, Calif.: Sage, 1995.

Weick, K. E., and Sutcliffe, K. M. *Managing the Unexpected: Assuring High Performance in an Age of Complexity.* San Francisco: Jossey-Bass, 2001.

Weiss, J. A., and Piderit, S. K. "The Value of Mission Statements in Public Agencies." *Journal of Public Administration Research and Theory,* 1999, *9,* 193–223.

Wildavsky, A. *Speaking Truth to Power: The Art and Craft of Policy Analysis.* Boston: Little, Brown, 1979.

CHAPTER NINE

Ethical
Nonprofit Management

Thomas H. Jeavons

I n the past decade, scandals in the nonprofit sector and the corporate world
have given rise to heightened concerns about ethics, accountability, credibility, and public trust for all types of organizations. Certainly, charitable organizations and the people who run them have sometimes behaved badly before now,
but they have probably never received such intense public scrutiny. And the moral
miscalculations of major corporations have regularly been front-page news, giving additional justifiable cause for public cynicism about major institutions.

The repercussions of such problems have been seen before. In the 1990s, following the United Way of America scandal, the public's faith in nonprofit institutions fell. Efforts to make nonprofits more accountable caused public trust
to rebound somewhat (INDEPENDENT SECTOR, 2002). But given the recent frauds,
abuses of power, and evasions of accountability that were so evident in the
cases of the New Era Foundation and the Catholic church, to cite just two
prominent examples, public faith in nonprofits is at risk of eroding again.

Such a decline in public trust for institutions could be widespread. It would
represent a significant problem for business and government but an even greater

I am indebted for the definition of *ethics* used in this chapter and for the formulation of much of
the material on ethical theory to Mike W. Martin, professor of philosophy at Chapman University.
His critical reading of an early draft of this chapter was immensely helpful.

one for nonprofits. Why? Because nonprofit organizations—at least those of the public benefit variety, the 501(c)(3)s—are especially dependent on the public's trust and goodwill to gain the support they need for the work they do. These organizations are sometimes described as "values-expressive," as being instrumental and indispensable in building social capital (a concept that centers on trust), and as being instruments of collective action for serving the public good (Payton, 1988; Lohmann, 1992; Putnam, 2000). If they are not perceived as organizations of integrity, organizations that are trustworthy, they will not be able to function effectively. Why would people want to give money or time to an organization if they have reason to doubt that the organization is representing itself and the work it does honestly and is using the contributions it receives for the purpose of fulfilling its stated mission?

The responsibility for ensuring the ethical behavior of a nonprofit organization resides, as recent scandals have made clear, with both the managers and the trustees or board members of nonprofits. The roles and responsibilities of governing boards are addressed elsewhere in this volume, so this chapter will focus primarily on the responsibilities of professional staff, the managers. The discussion here is about professional ethics.

There was a notable surge in interest in professional ethics following the Watergate scandal in the mid-1970s, after it was observed that the majority of the individuals involved were lawyers, and many of them came from the most prestigious law schools. One can see a similar surge of interest in ethics in light of the high-profile nonprofit and corporate scandals of the past few years. Yet in the responses of some commentators, some professionals, and some of the schools that train them, one can identify two troubling assumptions at work in the discussions.

The first assumption is that careful, skilled thinking about ethical matters is more the business of philosophers and academics than of practitioners. Although persons who are "training for the professions" may be required to take courses in or complete assignments relating to ethical issues of their particular profession, many involved—especially the students—assume that these courses and assignments are of secondary importance. Why would they assume that? Well, both practitioners and students can see (from observing their fields) that the skills one must "master" to have a successful career are the practical skills of their profession. And they can also see that often an inability to think clearly about and act appropriately on the ethical issues has not been a major stumbling block to professional advancement.

The second assumption is that ethical questions and issues can be dealt with as discrete concerns in professional practice, in isolation from others. This perspective can be seen in the tendency to have but a single course on ethics in a professional program or to have one or two sessions in courses on other subjects take up ethical issues, rather than trying to have the ethical implications of all subjects and of every aspect of professional practice dealt with wherever they might arise in a professional education.

I raise these assumptions at the beginning of this chapter because they are both, I believe, patently false. Both undermine the maintenance of appropriate ethical standards and behavior in the management and operation of nonprofit organizations. (Indeed, this is true for organizations of any kind.)

The analysis that follows builds, in fact, on two quite opposite assumptions. The first is that reflecting critically and actively on ethical issues is an obligation of every professional, including nonprofit managers. The capacity for and inclination toward socially responsive, historically grounded, critical, ethical judgment should be one of the outcomes of any sound professional education program and one of the capacities of a "professional" as "reflective practitioner" (Schön, 1983, 1990). The second is that a concern for the ethical implications of one's decisions and actions is salient in every aspect of professional practice and—in the context of the considerations of this volume—in relation to every facet of the life of nonprofit organizations.

Indeed, I will argue here, as the chapter title implies, that we are most likely to see consistently ethical behavior among nonprofit managers and organizations only in organizations with a deeply embedded emphasis on ethical values and behavior. So building and reinforcing that kind of organizational culture becomes a primary responsibility for those desiring that ethical practice be a hallmark of all the functions, including the management, of their organization.

OVERVIEW

The argument to be made in this chapter is that ethical behavior in and by nonprofit organizations cannot be ensured simply by employing encouraging rhetoric about ethics or by establishing specific rules for ethical behavior. This point can be readily demonstrated by examining the historical record and the common experience of most managers and organizational analysts. Almost anyone with significant experience in organizational life knows there is often a marked disparity between rhetoric and practice in organizational behavior. They also know that rules about ethics (and other matters) can be, and frequently are, followed "in the letter" while being totally ignored or violated "in the spirit."

Thus the claim argued here is that truly ethical behavior will be ensured only by creating an organizational culture in which key ethical ideals and expectations are incorporated in the organization's "core values" (Schein, 1985) and thus permeate its operations. This process will almost certainly involve the use of appropriate rhetoric about values. More important, though, it must involve modeling of the core values in the behavior of key individuals in the organization and reinforcement of those values through the organization's structures and reward systems.

I will further argue that because of the unique historical and social dimensions of their character and function, expectations about what constitutes ethical behavior in and by nonprofit, public-benefit charities differ from those placed on other organizations. Specifically, questions of trust and integrity go to the core of the reason for the existence of these organizations and their ability to satisfy public expectations. The existence of most charitable nonprofit organizations, their capacity to garner resources—and so to survive and carry out their missions—depends on their moral standing and consistency (see Hansmann, 1987; Douglas, 1987; Ostrander and Schervish, 1990; and Jeavons, 1992).

In this context, there is an implicit social contract supporting the presence and function of private, public-benefit nonprofits in our society. These organizations are given special standing and even certain legal advantages over other private organizations on the assumption that they will serve the public good. The public expects these organizations to be motivated by and adhere to such a commitment in their performance. The public also expects that these organizations will honor a set of widely accepted moral and humanitarian values—deriving from the organizations' historical and philosophical roots—and that they will not act in a self-serving manner.

Accordingly, if the managers of public-benefit nonprofits wish to ensure the ethical behavior of their organizations, staffs, and themselves, they need to create and maintain organizational cultures that honor, fundamentally, in practice a set of core values that are in keeping with the historical, philosophical, moral, and religious roots of the voluntary sector and that meet the public's current expectations. In this context, trust is the lifeblood of the nonprofit sector—trust that nonprofits will fulfill this implicit social contract. And to ensure that this trust is sustained, I will argue, five core values must permeate these organizations, shaping their ethics. These values are integrity, openness, accountability, service, and charity (in the original sense of that term).

To understand this argument, we must begin by considering what ethics are and are not. We will look at a number of definitions of ethics, with a particular eye toward the origins, character, and purposes of ethical norms or standards. Then we need to examine more closely the kinds of ethical norms that are usually applied to nonprofit, public-benefit organizations in American culture, the factors that have shaped these norms, and the purposes they serve.

Having formed a well-grounded perspective on the norms or standards for ethical behavior in and by nonprofit organizations, we next need to ask how such behavior can be ensured. What is the relationship between values and behavior? Assuming that an organization does subscribe to the "right" values, how can one help ensure that those values are captured and reflected in all aspects of its operations, by all its members?

In essence, this is to ask about the integrity of an organization, about how to make certain that it is—and will continue to be—what it claims to be. Specifically, how can one make certain that there will be continuity between the values an organization claims to represent and the purposes it says it intends to serve, on the one hand, and its actual operation, on the other? Finally, this chapter concludes with some specific suggestions about how a "culture of integrity" can be created and sustained in nonprofit organizations. For assuming that nonprofit organizations wish to act ethically, it is only by creating and sustaining such an organizational culture that this intention is likely to be fulfilled consistently. Let us begin, then, by examining the nature of ethics and ethical behavior.

WHAT ARE "ETHICS"?

As a field of study, *ethics* refers to the study of moral topics, including moral issues, moral responsibilities, and moral ideals of character. In a normative sense, ethics may be seen simply to refer to "justified moral standards"—which is to say, not just what people believe about how they should act but what they *should* believe. As this chapter is directed more to practitioners of management and other "laypeople" than to scholars and philosophers, however, we probably need to think more about more common uses of the term *ethics*.

Dictionaries define *ethics* as a "system or code of morals of a particular person, religion, group, or profession"; "the moral principles by which a person is guided"; and "the rules of conduct recognized in certain areas of human life." The word itself comes from the Greek *ethos,* meaning "custom, usage, manner, or habit." The derivation of the term and the differences we see in the dictionary definitions highlight two facets of the origins and purposes of ethics that it is useful to examine.

One set of issues involves the derivations of and justifications for specific ethical systems or values. To explore various types of ethical theories—rights ethics, duty ethics, utilitarianism, virtue ethics—might be fascinating. However, it is not helpful here, as it would divert us from our intended focus on questions about applied ethics in nonprofit management.

On the other hand, these definitions of ethics also remind us that much of what we typically think of as ethical principles or judgments, especially when our concern is application and practice, do not derive from philosophical absolutes but rather from the reference point of social or community standards. To play with the words, ethics (as we typically use the term) may be as much a matter of ethos—what is expected or socially acceptable, what is customary—as a matter of indisputable moral vision. Of course, these two aspects of ethics are often intertwined. What a particular community views as ethically acceptable will often be determined by what its members believe are required by some source of absolute moral authority (God, perhaps).

Understanding these things about the origins and meaning of *ethics* makes it clear that when we raise and examine questions about ethics—ethics generally, professional ethics, the ethics of nonprofit managers, or the ethics of the behavior of nonprofit organizations—there are two reference points we need always to bear in mind in our considerations. One is a point of moral absolutes; the other, of community standards and expectations. For our purposes, when we think about the ethics of nonprofit organizations and their management, I believe we should then be asking two kinds of questions. First, what are we morally obligated to do and not do? And second, what does society require or expect of us? Moreover, I believe that ethical questions should be considered in that order, giving preference to moral obligations over customary ones.

PROFESSIONAL ETHICS

One book claims that ethics are "a set of rules that apply to human beings over the totality of their interrelationships with one another and that take precedence over all other rules" (Gellerman, Frankel, and Ladenson, 1990, p. 41). If we accept this, then we need to ask, how are such rules more specifically defined by and applied to particular spheres of professional activity?

Some scholars claim that one of the elements that define a "profession" (as opposed to other kinds of work) is that every specific profession involves a commitment to a publicly articulated set of goals and social purposes for that profession's practice and to standards for and approaches to that practice that should be shared by all its practitioners. It is because they meet social needs with special expertise, it is argued, that professions are given certain privileges—such as self-regulation, control over standards for training and entry into practice, and thus control over their own markets and competition. These prerogatives are provided in exchange for the professions' commitment (implicit, at least) to meet public needs and serve the public good (see Bellah and others, 1985; Flores, 1988; Larson, 1977; and Van Til, 1988). Interestingly, here we have another implicit social contract. A classic paradigm for this is the medical profession and doctors with their Hippocratic Oath and the other specific expectations about their obligations to society in the provision of medical care.

Following this line of reasoning, one commentator on "professional values" argues that in our culture, "professionals are viewed as morally committed to pursuing the dominant value that defines the goals of their professional practice. . . . They are expected to pursue such goals on a social as well as individual level. . . . And they are expected to do so even when self-interest may have to be sacrificed in that pursuit" (Goldman, 1987, p. 48).

Now, it may not be immediately clear what the "dominant value" that defines the goals of the practice of management generally is (or should be). Still, it can be argued that the dominant value that should define the practice of management of public-benefit nonprofits is *morally responsible service.* Such organizations are (or were) usually created specifically to provide services, and as I will show, often in situations where the establishment of trust in the integrity and commitment of the service-delivering agency is a paramount concern.

In sum, the claim here is that the ethical operation of nonprofit agencies and ethical nonprofit management require the articulation and internalization of standards for behavior and ways of being for those agencies and their managers that adequately reflect the sector's origins in the moral spheres of our culture and that also meet the current, morally justifiable expectations of our society. Before moving on to look closely at those origins and expectations and the standards for behavior they necessitate, however, I want to comment briefly on how this perspective contrasts with some current views of the purposes of professional ethics—because those views are especially dangerous if they are adopted in the nonprofit world.

MISUNDERSTANDING PROFESSIONAL ETHICS

One commonly articulated rationale for ethical behavior in professional practice is that it is simply "good for business." This may be the case. It may be possible to demonstrate that it is generally true that honesty—and other ethical behavior—is the best policy. What is also clear, however, is that this utilitarian perspective does not provide an adequate underpinning for behaving ethically. Yet this is often the only, or at least the most prominent, rationale or motivation given for the development and practice of "sound business ethics."

Consider, for example, a long-running advertisement for a prestigious business school's seminars on ethics that said that the reasons for learning and, presumably, practicing "good business ethics" is to "build stable, profitable relationships; strengthen employee loyalty; . . . and avoid litigation." One would hope that all these results would ensue for the ethical organization. Still, we need to ask, how well does a focus on these goals hold up as the rationale or motivation for behaving ethically? What if lying about something that has recently occurred is likely to be more helpful in avoiding litigation than telling the truth would? Is lying acceptable then? What if misusing funds to provide extra perquisites for employees is more effective in gaining their loyalty than using funds properly? What if there are cases where "more stable, profitable relationships" can be better secured through bribery or deceit than through honest competition? The point here is that when commitments to or judgments about ethical behavior are based primarily on cost-benefit calculations, they will be weak indeed.

It is easy to argue for the practical benefits of ethical behavior as the primary justification for adhering to ethical standards. But as the examples just cited highlight, such a justification is easily undermined. Ironically, it is most easily undermined in just those situations where sound ethical choices may be the most difficult to discern and the most important to make.

One potential advantage of nonprofit, public-benefit organizations in this sphere is that they can—and should—root their judgments about commitments to ethical behavior in the moral traditions from which the nonprofit sector sprang. As one scholar reminds us, "Institutions that enunciate, transmit, and defend ethical values fall within the boundaries of our nonprofit sector. Educational, religious, and advocacy organizations constitute a majority of [the] membership and have shaped the form of the sector itself" (Mason, 1992b, p. 26). Put more plainly, as a monograph titled "Ethics and the Nation's Voluntary and Philanthropic Community" noted, "Those who presume to serve the public good assume a public trust" (INDEPENDENT SECTOR, 1991, p. 1).

Understanding that ethical judgments must be based on firmer moral and social considerations, let us look more closely at the particular ethical values— and the character of the public trust—that can and should shape the ethical perspectives of nonprofit managers, whatever the practical advantages (or disadvantages) of ethical behavior may be.

CORE VALUES AND THEIR ORIGINS IN THE VOLUNTARY SECTOR

Many explanations have been offered for the origins and use of the nonprofit organizational form. Scholars differ as to which explanations are most valid. (For useful discussions of this question, see Columbo and Hall, 1995; Douglas, 1987; Hansmann, 1987; Hopkins, 1998; O'Neill, 2003; Salamon, 1999; Van Til, 1988.) One of these explanations that holds substantial explanatory power revolves around two issues or dynamics that economists and organizational theorists call "market failure" and "contract failure" (or an "agency problem").

Too simply put, the market failure theory suggests that private nonprofits are (or were) created to provide services where agencies of governments cannot or will not provide the service for some reason, and the nature of the service needed is such that for-profit businesses cannot make a sufficient return on their investment to be induced to offer it. Contract failure and agency theory suggest that nonprofits are needed to provide services where the parties who want a service offered are not in a position to provide it themselves and also that the parties paying for the service are unable to judge the quality of that service because of the nature, location, or setting of the service to be provided. In such circumstances, it is argued, people create or use private nonprofit (rather than for-profit) organizations because they feel that nonprofit organizations will have less incentive to cheat consumers or supporters. That is, they think that this type of organization—acting as their agent—is less likely to skimp on the amounts or quality of services offered because its board and managers have less opportunity to enrich themselves by that behavior in this organizational structure.

Note that it is assumed in these cases that the people paying for the services are often not the consumers of the services. Often they are donors. This being so, they want to work through an organization that, as an agent, can be expected to provide that service in the manner in which the donors would provide it themselves if they could. Consequently, they seek an agent that they believe is highly committed to providing that service for others. Baldly put, they want an agent that is involved for the cause and not for the money.

A quick analysis of both these situations tells us what is likely to be the most important and desirable ethical quality of nonprofit organizations, at least in the public's eyes. In these circumstances, trust is a key consideration. That being so, we can project what operational and ethical values will need to be evident in organizations to earn and deserve the public's trust. Among the most central, as already noted, are integrity, openness, accountability, and service.

Also on that earlier list, though, is *charity,* in the original sense of the term— from the Latin *caritas,* "caring love," from a root meaning "beloved" or "dear." Obviously, there are some nonprofit organizations that would not be expected to be *charitable* as that word is often used—that is, to mean "openhanded, generous, eleemosynary." Most people do not expect these to be characteristics of trade associations, for example. Still, the majority of the organizations that populate the nonprofit or voluntary sector are service providers dependent in some way on the philanthropic traditions and practices of our society. Indeed, the majority are religious or have religious roots (Jeavons, 2003). And all these are expected in that context to be basically "caring" organizations, willing to put the public good and the welfare of others above their own private interests.

It is important to understand how this last expectation presumes a moral quality ascribed to such organizations deriving from their historical and sociological functions. The fact is that nonprofit philanthropic and service organizations occupy a distinctive place in American society because of their origins—largely in religious or other idealistic voluntary associations—and because they have traditionally been vehicles for preserving, transmitting, or promoting social values. Because of their historical development and their contemporary roles, these institutions carry much of the burden of mediating civic, moral, and spiritual values in the public realm and from one generation to the next (Curti, 1958; Parsons, 1960). The public therefore has special expectations that they will behave in morally honorable ways.

So there are ethical qualities or values that are intrinsic to the character and behavior of public-benefit nonprofits. These organizations are expected to—and should—demonstrate integrity, openness, accountability, service, and caring. And what is required of managers in this context is that they give attention to seeing that these ethical values are reflected in every aspect of these organizations. This requires that the managers model ethical qualities in their own behavior as well as articulate and foster them as ideals for others. Considering carefully the meaning of these values in organizational behavior should allow us to see better how managers can undertake these responsibilities and work toward creating a culture of integrity.

ETHICAL MANAGEMENT IN ETHICAL ORGANIZATIONS

It will be useful now to consider the key ethical attributes of nonprofit managers and their organizations more fully. In this process, we should undertake an analysis at two levels—the individual and the organizational—asking, for example, what does it mean for a manager to do his or her work with integrity and for an organization to operate with integrity?

It is important to say that I cannot, in this one section, make an exhaustive analysis or offer numerous illustrations of how these ethical qualities would be evident in each of the many aspects of the operations and management of nonprofit organizations. Authors of other chapters in this volume that address other aspects of nonprofit management discuss questions and offer considerations of ethical issues specifically relevant to different facets of the work of nonprofit organizations. At this point, my intention is to offer a broader context within which to think further in ethical terms about the material presented in the other chapters (and in real life). Ideally, the relationship between this chapter, focused specifically on ethics, and those addressing various facets of nonprofit management should lay the groundwork for a dialogue about ethical issues nonprofit managers face.

Integrity

It may be most useful to describe integrity as "honesty writ large." That is to say, integrity has to do with congruence between appearance and reality, between intention and action, between promise and performance, in every aspect of a person's or an organization's existence. If trust is essential to support the operation of charitable nonprofit organizations, and if the expectation these organizations will be "trustworthy" is one of the most basic expectations the public holds for them, then "integrity" in this sense becomes a fundamental ethical characteristic they must possess.

At the organizational level, integrity is most obviously demonstrated to be present or absent by comparing an organization's own literature—fundraising materials, reports, mission statements, and such—with its actual program priorities and performance. For instance, an organization that claims to exist to serve the poor but regularly spends extensive resources on enlarging itself, enhancing its own image before the public, or attending to the comfort of its staff must be suspect. So, too, one wonders about educational institutions that say they are devoted to providing the best education possible to students but spend more of their resources on things intended to improve their own status—image-enhancing athletics, high-profile research projects, or "star" faculty members—than on facilities and activities for teaching and learning.

This is not to say that staff in such organizations should not have reasonable salaries and benefits, that being in the public eye for fundraising purposes is not important to support the work to be done, or that an organization might not be able to improve its service delivery by growing. But it is to say that a careful examination of budgets, allocations of staff time, and the application of other resources too often show that nonprofit organizations that were created to serve the public good are giving more attention to caring for and improving themselves than others. Moreover, the public is highly sensitive to these issues. If we need proof of this, we would do well to recall the controversies involving United Way of America or some television ministries in the late 1980s and early 1990s.

In the late 1980s and 1990s, at a time when it could be argued greed was a socially acceptable value, the PTL Ministries, a nonprofit corporation involving an evangelical Christian broadcasting operation and theme park, became embroiled in an enormous controversy. Although the initial problems related to the sexual indiscretions of the organization's head, Jim Bakker, what finally brought the wrath of the public (and the Internal Revenue Service) down on the operation was the wanton waste, misdirection, and misuse of donated funds. The wildly excessive salaries and opulent lifestyle of Bakker and his wife, Tammy Faye, supported by donations from people who thought they were giving to a ministry of evangelism and service, were so embarrassing as to damage the credibility and fundraising efforts of a wide range of legitimate Christian ministries simply through guilt by association.

In an event even more injurious to the credibility of charities more generally, in the spring of 1992, it was revealed that the head of the United Way of America was receiving a salary of almost $500,000, traveling about the world in first-class accommodations, and setting up subsidiary organizations run by his friends and relatives. When the millions of small donors to local United Ways found out that a chunk of their gifts was going to support the lavish lifestyle of an executive of a charitable organization, most were outraged. Despite the massive efforts of local United Ways to explain that only a tiny portion of income went to the national organization, which was a legally separate entity, the giving to local United Ways (and hence to their member agencies) in the following year fell significantly. Once more, a great many ethical and efficient charitable organizations found themselves tarnished with guilt by association.

Dramatic disparities between the ethical promise (implicit or explicit) and the real performance of one charitable organization may precipitate difficulties for the entire nonprofit sector. As one economist studying the nonprofit sector has observed, "Whenever any nonprofit is found to have abused its trusted position, the reputation of trustworthy nonprofits also suffers. . . . Nonprofits that do not act opportunistically, as well as those who do, will find it increasingly difficult to obtain resources" (Weisbrod, 1988, p. 13). This observation seems only to grow truer as media scrutiny of nonprofits intensifies.

A specific example of the kind of behavior that raises such issues about integrity can be drawn from a study of relief and development agencies (Jeavons, 1994). One of the agencies studied engaged in practices that were not illegal but would certainly have raised questions in the minds of donors (and others) had they become aware of them. At least two practices were ethically questionable.

First, the agency sometimes used what are called "representational" images in its fundraising materials. That is to say, brochures told stories about a person or family in need, often desperate need, and included pictures of their plight that were quite striking. However, sometimes these stories were actually composites of stories of a number of people in the impoverished area, put together for maximum effect; or the pictures were not of the particular persons or family mentioned at all but were selected from a photo bank for their ability to pull on donors' heartstrings. The needs were real, and the stories and pictures conveyed the needs quite effectively; but the approach lacked integrity because the stories and pictures were not factually true.

Some persons would argue that this is morally wrong because it is a form of dishonesty, regardless of the fact that it raises money for a good purpose. Even some persons within the organization admitted that if donors became aware of this practice, there would have been problems. The donors' expectations of high moral standards—in this case, higher standards of truthfulness—for such an organization would have been violated.

Second, this same agency often made general appeals with brochures featuring projects for which it could most easily raise money, with the brochures giving a strong impression (though not a specific promise) that the money raised would go to those particular projects. But in fact, those projects were fully funded from other sources, and the donations were used for other purposes. Again, this was done in a way that ensured there was no illegality, but neither was there any integrity. (I should note that similar charges on a far larger scale were raised about the Red Cross's fundraising in the aftermath of the terrorist attacks on the United States on September 11, 2001, and caused that organization great embarrassment.)

One is left to wonder, in such an organizational climate, what other normal ethical standards were allowed to slide and how well the funds that were raised were being used. If one is inclined to think that these kinds of decisions can be seen purely as matters of strategic choice, one needs to see the contrast between this organization and other relief and development agencies studied.

In many other agencies, there were specific rules against using representational images and policies that required donors to be consulted before their gifts were used for projects other than the ones for which they were solicited. The managers in those agencies described their standards and policies as points of pride, as conscious choices made to uphold the ethical character of their organizations and their work. And those managers pointed out that it was vital to maintain the highest moral standards in all facets of their operations, lest the willingness to compromise at one point become the beginning of a lowering of standards more generally—the first step on the proverbial slippery slope. This, in fact, points us back to examining the meaning of integrity at the individual level for managers and management.

Integrity may have different meanings for different individuals, but in the context of professional ethics, it must mean doing one's job as honestly and as fully in adherence to one's professed principles as possible. Careful observers of organizational behavior have noted that managers and leaders in organizations, or particular parts of organizations, can have a significant effect in setting behavioral standards, either as a matter of personal influence or because of their control of reward systems.

The manager who wants employees to deal honestly with others had better deal honestly with them and, further, had better reward honesty and discourage the slightest dishonesty. If the manager is willing to cut corners, tell "little" lies, or act in self-serving ways, it becomes more likely that employees too will come to regard this as acceptable, at least in the work setting. So a manager who wants the organization to be known for its integrity and to be trustworthy must begin by being completely trustworthy in dealings with all who are part of the organization and make it clear that similar behavior is expected of all those people.

Put more simply, integrity must be one of the hallmarks of nonprofit management. It is an ethical obligation, both as a matter of morality, because it is right, and as a matter of social necessity, because the public expects nonprofit organizations to do these things. And as recent history shows, failing to uphold the highest standards for personal and organizational integrity can have enormous consequences for nonprofit managers and their agencies or institutions.

Openness

It would not be accurate to call the quality of openness a "moral" value, at least within the context of the most common value systems of American culture. So the claim to be made here about openness as an ethical value is not based so much on moral absolutes—as may be the case for integrity—as on social values and expectations. In this context, we might think of openness as a "derivative virtue." We might also note, however, that in businesses as well as nonprofits, efforts to make organizations more transparent to stakeholders are gaining ground as leaders in both spheres recognize that being trustworthy is often critical to success.

In any case, in the history of philanthropy in America, whenever an organization or individual tries to hide philanthropic endeavors from public view, the result—if they are discovered—has almost always been to raise profound skepticism about the motivation for and character of those endeavors. The public's attitude here has been, "If they are really doing good, why would they be reluctant (or embarrassed) to have us see what they are doing?"

This is especially true for organizations. It is possible to put forth a reasonable argument, even one based on religious grounds (see Matthew 6:2–4 or the Mishneh Torah), for individuals "doing good works" anonymously or in secret. However, organizations operating in the public sphere, especially in areas of service or advocacy that can have an impact on public policy or community life, find it hard to argue convincingly that there is value to any secrecy about how they make their choices and do their work. Indeed, it may be crucial for these organizations to conduct their business in a way that is open to public scrutiny.

One compelling reason for this is that openness undergirds other ethical behaviors. The organization that operates openly cannot afford to cut other ethical corners. If one looks at the case just considered of the relief and development agencies, it seems clear that the one that engaged in questionable tactics would not be able to operate in this way and retain its donor base if its practices were open to the scrutiny of outsiders.

Another reason for this is historical. Critical questions have long been raised about the roles philanthropic and service organizations play in shaping people's and communities' lives. (See, for instance, Griffin, 1957, or Nielsen, 1985.) One reason for this is that some of these organizations appear to have had ulterior motives—for example, intentions of "social control" or protection of the interests of the privileged—embedded in their work. It is clear, for instance, that some of the impetus for legislation regulating the operation of foundations (in 1969) came from supposedly philanthropic entities being formed and using their tax-exempt status as a way to protect family fortunes from taxation while still controlling family businesses (Bremner, 1988). And more recent scandals in the conduct of nonprofit organizations reinforce the case to be made for their being subject to public scrutiny.

In addition, observers who are concerned about the continuing vitality of nonprofit organizations and recognize that maintaining a climate of trust is essential to that vitality argue that operating openly is one of the best ways to build trust. Organizations that wish to engage people's support and good faith can find no better way to do so than to do good works well and then welcome the inquiries and inspection of anyone interested in their methods.

The same kind of logic applies to the leaders of these organizations, in terms of their leadership and management. In the effort to build the support and commitment of staff, volunteers, and donors, a manager's willingness to talk openly and honestly about rationales for programs, the reasons for and ways in which decisions are made, and approaches to problem solving can be invaluable. Furthermore, many nonprofits (as voluntary associations) come out of a populist democratic tradition in American culture. So it can be argued that they really ought to be operated in an open and democratic manner to represent and perpetuate that tradition—that this may be another significant part of their role and social obligation in this society. (For a very helpful discussion of these issues, see Lohmann, 1992; O'Neill, 2003; and Van Til, 1988.)

Finally, this means that openness in the business of decision making, in matters of raising and allocating resources, and generally in the manner of their operation should be seen as a key ethical value for nonprofit organizations and their managers. Moreover, openness is, of course, a necessary prerequisite to accountability, which is the next core value we should examine.

Accountability

Not only is it important for nonprofit, public-benefit organizations to be open about the things they do and how and why they do them, but it is also important that they be ready to explain and generally be accountable for their choices. This is an extension of the implicit social contract of privilege and trust that these organizations enjoy in our society. By accepting the privilege of tax exemption and the right to solicit tax-deductible contributions, public-benefit nonprofits also accept an obligation to be ready to answer for their behavior and performance—and not just to their membership but also to the communities they serve and to the broader public as well, for they are using financial resources that would otherwise have gone into the public treasury.

Looked at in contractual terms, we see that these organizations are granted the right to solicit tax-deductible contributions or are granted tax-exempt status on the assumption that they are serving the public good and will put their resources to work as directly and as efficiently as possible on behalf of the causes or people they claim to serve. Indeed, the character and language of the legal discourse about these issues—employing terms like "public benefit" or "mutual benefit" organizations—confirms these assumptions (see, for example, Simon, 1987). From this implicit social contract derives a clear ethical obligation to perform according to promise, to be subject to evaluation, and to be answerable for any failure to perform.

In fact, issues of nonprofits' accountability are very complicated, much more so than it may seem sometimes from the public discussions of it. To really understand these issues for different nonprofits, one must ask multiple questions. "To whom is a nonprofit accountable?" is only the first question. And the answer to this might be, "Multiple constituencies." In addition, one should also ask, "For what aspects of their operations should they be accountable, by whom will they be held accountable, and in what manner?" Some would argue that while all nonprofits should have some public accountability, the specifics of "to whom" and "how" are matters that should be thought about strategically and that need to be determined according to the stakeholders involved (Kearns, 1996).

All of this is to say that in social and contractual terms, all nonprofit organizations have an ethical responsibility to be accountable to their supporters, their members, and their donors; most of all, the public-benefit organizations have a larger responsibility to be accountable to the broader public for the ways in which they undertake to fulfill their philanthropic purposes. A confirmation of the growing public expectations in this regard (and some organizations' recognition of these expectations) can be found in the growth in recent years of "watchdog" groups like the Better Business Bureau's Wise Giving Alliance and groups formed to create mutual accountability in particular fields, like the Evangelical Council for Financial Accountability. In addition, more and more states are passing laws to mandate financial disclosure and regulate the fundraising practices of nonprofits.

How does this obligation of accountability extend to nonprofit managers? In much the same way as the obligations of integrity and openness do. First, if this is a quality that managers and leaders want to see reflected in their organization, it is one that they had better model in their own behavior. It then becomes an expectation that they can articulate credibly to others.

Second, managers can establish this commitment most firmly by making sure they hold themselves accountable to their organization's board and work to build a board that will hold them accountable for their performance. Executives who view themselves as free agents, trying to isolate their boards from full information about and active involvement in the work of the organization, and boards that hire an executive and then fall into a passive, "rubber-stamp" role in evaluation and governance have been two key contributing factors to poor performance and ethical problems in a number of nonprofits. The most useful literature on the board-executive relationship has pointed out that a full and vital partnership between executives and managers is essential for there to be effective leadership in nonprofit organizations (Drucker, 1990; Herman and Heimovics, 1991; Middleton, 1987).

Ironically, one of the things that this may require of an executive is that he or she encourage (or even teach) a board to play a more active role in evaluating the executive's—and the organization's—performance. Yet in this way, if the board is representative of, or at least in touch with, the needs and feelings of the larger community, the executive is soliciting oversight and potentially helpful feedback from those the organization should serve. In this the executive is also modeling a quality that he or she should hope to encourage in all staff—general accountability for performance and receptivity to constructive criticism.

Service

The grounds for the ethical obligation here are virtually identical to those for accountability. Nonprofit organizations, especially public-benefit organizations, exist and are granted specific privileges (as noted earlier) with the explicit understanding that they are committed in some way to serve the public good. Those that are classified as "mutual benefit" organizations—which include trade associations and fraternal organizations—are not beholden in the same way to serve "the public" in the broadest sense, but they are still expected to serve their membership. The point is that service, to people or to a cause, is at the heart of the reason these organizations exist.

The social contract extended to these organizations assumes that they will devote themselves primarily to service. In accepting the privileges they have been granted, these organizations incur the ethical obligation to be service-oriented. Moreover, in accepting the support—membership dues, donations, volunteers' time—of people who sustain them, these organizations reinforce their ethical obligations in this regard.

This ethical obligation to service should be manifest in the conduct of managers in a number of ways. This commitment to service should be apparent as managers make practical and strategic choices that give precedence to fulfilling the mission of their organization over possibilities for advancing their own status and careers. Often—one hopes most often—these two goals can go hand in hand. But there are situations in which executives can make a choice that yields a short-term gain for the organization and makes the executive look good—improving his or her chances for a better next job—even though that choice harms the organization in the long run.

Many people now make a career of work in the nonprofit sector, especially in the field of fundraising. We could not have a meaningful discussion, as we do in this book, of nonprofit management as a "profession" if people did not commit themselves to careers in this area. This creates the ground for our discussion of professional ethics. It also creates a context in which managers can easily work with more concern for their own advancement than for the people or cause their organization is supposed to serve—and that can be problematic.

Now, this is not to say that managers are required to sacrifice themselves—their health, their basic financial security, or their personal well-being—for the benefit of their organization. Nonprofit organizations, especially cause-oriented ones, are notorious for exploiting and burning out their staff in the name of noble ideals (see Greene, 1991). But the undergirding values of the nonprofit sector are altruistic, and while it is fine to be concerned for one's own career, it is never acceptable for managers to advance themselves at the expense of the people and causes they have promised to serve.

In addition, observation suggests that the willingness of managers and leaders to see themselves as servants of others may be crucial to focusing others in an organization on that organization's commitment to service. Here the notion of "servant leadership" (Greenleaf, 1977) takes on both profound significance and immediate salience.

Charity

Finally, the last but certainly not least important ethical obligation of nonprofit, public-benefit organizations is to charity, in the original sense of the term. As noted earlier, the word *charity* comes from the Latin *caritas*. This means more than giving to those in need. It was originally translated as "love"—not romantic love, but the love of neighbor and committed concern for the welfare of others illustrated in the parable of the Good Samaritan. It meant caring, putting the welfare of others on a par with one's own, being generous with one's own resources, not out of a sense of pity, but out of a sense of relationship with and concern for others.

It can surely be argued that for nonprofit organizations, an ethical obligation to charity in this sense derives from reciprocity. That is, many of these organizations depend on the generosity of their supporters for their existence and ought to display such generosity themselves. Furthermore, at least in the case of the nonprofit, public-benefit organizations, the motivation of most of their supporters rests in no small way on a belief that these organizations are committed to caring for others. As noted earlier in this chapter, the basis of many of these organizations' support is the expectation that they will be vehicles for building a better world or a more caring and just society.

This expectation is manifest in an interesting range of phenomena. For instance, the preference of many clients and supporters of social service agencies for private nonprofit groups appears to be based on an assumption that they will provide services in a more personal, more caring way than a government agency would. In industries where potential employees—for example, teachers, nurses, or social workers—might work for either government or private organizations, the preference of some for private nonprofits is often explained in terms of their expectation (or experience) of these organizations as more caring work environments. And this expectation is certainly confirmed by the public indignation that is often evident when an organization that is itself the beneficiary of charity turns around and acts in uncaring ways.

Once more, the way in which this expectation applies to the ethics of management seems obvious. An uncaring or mean-spirited manager can undermine the caring quality of an organization as fast as any negative influence imaginable. If one wants the participants in an organization to treat its clients (and one another) with love and respect, it is hardly likely that treating the participants coldly or unfairly will help that occur. Managers and leaders help set the tone of an organization's life—whether they intend to or not—and that tone is almost certainly going to be reflected in the way the organization and all its staff interact at every level with its various constituencies.

Finally, organizations in the nonprofit sector are often perceived to have a special role in transmitting civic, social, and ethical values in our society from one generation to the next. If that is true, we have yet another reason to insist that these organizations reflect the highest ideals for a caring society. And it is clear that some managers do see their responsibilities in this light. Discussing the kind of "witness" his organization wants to make to all those which deal with it, the president of a Christian relief and development agency said, "We have a major challenge in living up to our commitment [to care for people]; not just for children eight thousand miles away, but also for the people at our elbow" (quoted in Jeavons, 1994, p. 265).

FROM IDEALS TO OPERATIVE VALUES

If we can agree, then, that these five concepts or ideals—integrity, openness, accountability, service, and charity—describe key ethical qualities and obligations of nonprofit organizations and their managers, we are still left to ask how these ideals get translated into behavior.

At the individual level, this may be easy. If we assume that people can choose what to value and choose to embody those values in their actions, then for individuals, ethical behavior is primarily a matter of choice and will. If this is the case, then the managers of nonprofit organizations simply need to choose to act with integrity, to be open and accountable in their work, and to make commitment to service and charity a cornerstone for their decision making and interaction with others. They need to do these things because they are the right things to do; because that is what the public that supports (and can withdraw its support from) their organization expects (or even demands) of them; and because the failure to uphold these obligations can have very significant negative consequences for their organizations and others. However, this still leaves open the question of how these ethical ideals become the operational values of an organization as a whole.

At this point, we need to turn to the work that has been done on organizational culture, which adds valuable insights to our discussion. In particular, I want to draw heavily on the careful research and analysis Edgar Schein presented in *Organizational Culture and Leadership* (1985).

Some early thinking about organizational culture tended to focus, sometimes shallowly, on the "rites and rituals" of organizational life (see Deal and Kennedy, 1982; Peters and Waterman, 1982). Schein takes a different tack, arguing that an excessive focus on what he calls "the manifestations of culture" will obscure the fact that very similar rituals, conventions, or regular practices in various companies are undertaken for very different reasons. Therefore, he claims, to understand organizational culture, one must focus on the essential values these visible practices are meant to express. These values are "the substance of culture," in Schein's view.

Indeed, Schein argues that some values represent the basic assumptions of a group of people, like the membership of an organization, about the way the world is and how they, as a group, can function most successfully in it. These "core values" will shape the organization's behavior, not only by dictating what are right or acceptable responses to different kinds of situations, but even more fundamentally by shaping the way those situations are perceived and thereby influencing what people regard as important or unimportant information.

Schein's views are reinforced by other scholars of organizations who contend that the most effective (and "unobtrusive") controls on the behavior of individuals in organizations may be achieved by either selecting people who will come to the organization with certain (shared) basic understandings about organizational or professional goals and practices or by orienting them toward those understandings, goals, and practices once they arrive (Perrow, 1986).

In this vein, Schein argues that leaders or managers can shape the direction, character, and operations of an organization most fundamentally and effectively by shaping the core values of the participants within it or selecting new participants who share those values. Indeed, he claims that "there is a possibility— underemphasized in leadership research—that the only things of real importance that leaders do is to create and manage culture" (1985, p. 2). The implications of this for people who are concerned about creating and maintaining organizations that behave ethically are obvious.

Managers' capacities to create a culture of integrity take root in the connection between the ethical behavior of those managers and the maintenance of the highest ethical standards of behavior of their nonprofit organizations. This is a culture where the ethical ideals we have been discussing come to be accepted as givens and where the expectation that these ideals will be honored in the life and work of the organization permeates every participant's thinking. This can only occur where these ethical values are both articulated and modeled by those in positions of responsibility and leadership. In this way, leaders and managers can shape the core values of an organization as a whole—and the individuals in it—around these ethical ideals.

One place where such a dynamic can readily be observed is in some religious service organizations that maintain a strong commitment to honoring very clear and sometimes constricting ethical ideals in their operations while still competing successfully for donor support in a highly competitive market. (For a detailed description of such groups, see Jeavons, 1994.)

CREATING AND MAINTAINING
A CULTURE OF INTEGRITY

Finally, we must see that clear, strong commitments to ethical ideals and behavior on the part of managers is a prerequisite to creating organizational cultures of integrity in nonprofits that will enable the organizations to behave ethically. The importance of the example of leadership in this process cannot be overemphasized. As one commentator has observed, CEOs "are ultimately accountable for [their] organization's ethical posture. . . . No organization can rise above the ethical level of its manager" (Mason, 1992a, p. 30).

Clearly, a manager who tells others about the importance of behaving ethically while behaving otherwise is likely to have little positive influence on the organization. In fact, such a manager is likely to have a destructive influence, generating cynicism about and indifference to ethical concerns throughout the organization. And ultimately, a manager whose own behavior models all the best of these values but who does not talk about their significance for the organization's life may have a less positive influence than is needed.

Still, even if the management of an organization is consistent in both preaching and practicing the right values, more will probably be needed to solidify and sustain a culture of integrity. Organizational structures and reward systems must also support and encourage ethical behavior among all employees and volunteers. People's best intentions can be undermined or confused by organizational structures and processes that lead them to make choices that have negative ethical consequences.

One wonders, for instance, how often in nonprofit service agencies of various types, reports of problems with programs or relationships to their clients are stifled or mistakes that could reveal ways to improve their service are never mentioned because staff and volunteers are rewarded only for successes. As in many organizations that are hierarchically ordered, some nonprofits have a tendency to punish the bearers of bad news—and even reward the bearers of false news when it is good. Encouraging employees to be less than honest about policies and programs that are failing leaves an organization less able to perform its mission. The leadership and management of a nonprofit organization must put in place systems that reward participants for honesty in every form, even forms that lead to the revelation of difficulties and deficiencies.

Similarly, one has to wonder about organizations that constantly emphasize short-term goals and focus solely on raw numbers (of dollars raised) in evaluating development efforts, rather than asking questions about the quality of relationships with donors and other potentially positive effects of fundraising—such as its educational impact on constituencies they are trying to reach. Where narrower emphases and reward systems dominate, what is the impact on fundraisers' approaches to donors? Are they as honest and caring as they should be? What is the effect on individual and organizational reporting? Is the information about fundraising costs and results as complete and fully revealing as it should be? (For a fuller examination of these issues, see Jeavons and Basinger, 2000.)

These kinds of questions about the relationship between reward systems and structures and ethical behavior become even more complex, but no less important, when the behaviors at issue are not so simple or when more subtle matters are involved. For instance, what about a situation where questions are being asked about whether a "progressive nonprofit organization" is exploiting its employees or whether it is being true to the values it claims to represent in the ways it treats them?

By way of example, I once worked with an organization that claimed that one of the principles to which it was committed was that it "values people" and "does not permit the accomplishment of goals at the expense of people." However, the organization had a structure for and approach to fundraising that emphasized continually increasing the number of dollars raised and reducing administrative costs without consideration for the effects of such goals and policies on the relationships among staff or between donors and staff. Furthermore, rewards in the organization—both raises and promotions—were distributed in a highly competitive system according to an assessment of performance based almost solely on quantitative measures. The outcome was that managers tended to push staff to achieve "more impressive" results—that is, raise more money—without regard to the impact that pressure might have on either the donors they worked with or the staff themselves. This seemed a direct contradiction of articulated values and led to high staff turnover.

One could look as well at the famous United Way of America scandal, mentioned earlier. How did an organization that was formed specifically to serve and support local United Ways and to promote a philosophy of service, volunteering, and giving come to be an example of self-serving, empire-building management practices? In part, at least, this seems to have been a result of organizational structures that insulated the management from the constituencies they were supposed to be serving, making them less aware of and accountable to the people the organization most needs to hear—in this case, local United Ways' donors and clients.

In addition, the staff leadership, in its effort to gain support and resources, seemed to spend most of its time with business leaders and came to pattern itself after them. In the process, the United Way's leaders came to think like for-profit corporate executives and apparently adopted the belief that organizational growth was an end worth pursuing for United Way of America. They overlooked the fact that the strategies for attaining this end were undermining United Way's stated mission. The result was a misuse of donated funds, a clear abuse of public trust, and some erosion of the very spirit of giving and volunteering the organization was supposed to promote.

The point is that organizational structures and processes, and systems of rewards and disincentives, must be put in place and consciously maintained to reinforce whatever rhetoric about ethical values an organization puts forth. Moreover, all this must be supported by the managers and leaders of the organization demonstrating personal commitment to those ethical values in their own behavior. The creation and maintenance of an organizational culture of integrity—one where integrity, openness, accountability, service, and charity consistently predominate, one that will lead to consistently ethical behavior on the part of nonprofit organizations—cannot be achieved absent these elements in an organization's life.

SUMMARY

Ethical questions and issues must be primary concerns of all nonprofit managers, and these issues and questions are salient in all aspects of the operation of nonprofit organizations. The ethical values most important for nonprofit managers and organizations to honor and exhibit center on the qualities of integrity, openness, accountability, service, and charity. These particular ethical ideals are prescribed for nonprofit organizations by virtue of the distinctive history of the voluntary and nonprofit sector and the roles that these organizations play in American society. It is crucial that nonprofit organizations embody these ethical ideals in practice, both because ethical conduct is what moral duty requires—it is right—and because the public expects this of nonprofit organizations that say they are serving the public good. Only in this way can nonprofits fulfill the implicit social contract that supports their existence in our society.

It is important to note the educational implications of this. The past two decades have seen the emergence of a number of programs around the country to educate people specifically for the work of managing nonprofit organizations. How much attention do these programs give to helping those people understand the special history and unique roles and expectations that should shape the way these organizations function and are managed? Some observers would say not enough. The individuals being educated to take on the responsibilities of management and leadership in nonprofit organizations must be taught sound approaches to, as well as the profound importance of, careful, responsible reflection on the ethical issues embedded in the various facets of the life of these organizations.

Managing an organization so that key ethical values will be consistently embodied in the organization's life requires more than rhetoric. It requires that managers demonstrate these values in their own conduct in their professional lives and service. It also requires that they create and maintain organizational structures and dynamics by which ethical conduct is rewarded and unethical conduct, in any manifestation, is discouraged. This has to involve an examination of all organizational systems and structures, from fundraising strategies to human resource policies to accounting systems, to ensure that those structures and systems do not generate pressures on personnel to ignore or violate the standards and assumptions for ethical behavior espoused in broader contexts. Other chapters offer more illustrations of how ethical questions might arise in specific aspects of the work of nonprofit organizations and their managers.

The vital significance of these matters cannot be overemphasized. The lifeblood of the nonprofit sector is trust. Without trust on the part of donors, clients, and the larger public, nonprofit organizations will not be able to do the important work and fulfill the crucial roles they play in our society. And nothing erodes this foundation of trust—for the good nonprofits as well as the bad—as quickly as scandals involving unethical behavior by nonprofit organizations and their managers.

When the temptation to cut an ethical corner, tell a little lie, not bother with full disclosure, or let the ends justify the means arises, it is essential that the leadership and management of nonprofit organizations understand the implications of such actions and refuse to compromise on upholding rigorous ethical standards. We have to remember that ultimately noble ends are never served by ignoble means. Inevitably, our ethical chickens will come home to roost.

Nonprofit, public-benefit organizations have special responsibilities to serve the public good in our society, to do the right thing—for those in need and for important causes and those who care about them—because it is right. This represents the ethical and essential foundation of the nonprofit sector. Without this foundation intact, it is quite likely that the sector will, and perhaps should, disappear from our society. So attention to ethical concerns must continue to be a primary concern of every nonprofit manager.

References

Bellah, R. N., and others. *Habits of the Heart: Individualism and Commitment in American Life.* Berkeley: University of California Press, 1985.

Bremner, R. H. *American Philanthropy.* (2nd ed.) Chicago: University of Chicago Press, 1988.

Columbo, J. D., and Hall, M. H. *The Charitable Tax Exemption.* Boulder, Colo.: Westview Press, 1995.

Curti, M. "American Philanthropy and the National Character." *American Quarterly,* 1958, *10,* 420–437.

Deal, T. E., and Kennedy, A. A. *Corporate Cultures: The Rites and Rituals of Corporate Life.* Boston: Addison-Wesley, 1982.

Douglas, J. "Political Theories of Nonprofit Organization." In W. W. Powell (ed.), *The Nonprofit Sector: A Research Handbook.* New Haven, Conn.: Yale University Press, 1987.

Drucker, P. F. *Managing the Nonprofit Organization.* New York: HarperCollins, 1990.

Flores, A. (ed.). *Professional Ideals.* Belmont, Calif.: Wadsworth, 1988.

Gellerman, W., Frankel, M. S., and Ladenson, R. (eds.). *Values and Ethics in Organization and Human Systems Development.* San Francisco: Jossey-Bass, 1990.

Goldman, A. H. "Professional Values and the Problem of Regulation." *Business and Professional Ethics Journal,* 1987, *5*(2), 47–59.

Greene, S. G. "Poor Pay Threatens Leadership." *Chronicle of Philanthropy,* Mar. 26, 1991, pp. 28–31.

Greenleaf, R. K. *Servant Leadership.* Mahwah, N.J.: Paulist Press, 1977.

Griffin, C. S. "Religious Benevolence as Social Control, 1815–1860." *Mississippi Historical Review,* 1957, *44*, 423–444.

Hansmann, H. "Economic Theories of the Nonprofit Sector." In W. W. Powell (ed.), *The Nonprofit Sector: A Research Handbook.* New Haven, Conn.: Yale University Press, 1987.

Herman, R. D., and Heimovics, R. D. *Executive Leadership in Nonprofit Organizations: New Strategies for Shaping Executive-Board Dynamics.* San Francisco: Jossey-Bass, 1991.

Hopkins, B. R. *The Law of Tax-Exempt Organizations.* (7th ed.) New York: Wiley, 1998.

INDEPENDENT SECTOR. *Ethics and the Nation's Voluntary and Philanthropic Community.* Washington, D.C.: INDEPENDENT SECTOR, 1991.

INDEPENDENT SECTOR. *Keeping the Trust: Confidence in Charitable Organizations in an Age of Scrutiny.* Washington, D.C.: INDEPENDENT SECTOR, 2002.

Jeavons, T. H. "When Management Is the Message: Relating Values to Management Practice in Nonprofit Organizations." *Nonprofit Management and Leadership,* 1992, *2*, 403–421.

Jeavons, T. H. *When the Bottom Line Is Faithfulness: The Management of Christian Service Organizations.* Bloomington: Indiana University Press, 1994.

Jeavons, T. H. "The Vitality and Independence of Religious Organizations." *Society,* 2003, *40*(4), 27–36.

Jeavons, T. H., and Basinger, R. B. *Growing Givers' Hearts: Treating Fundraising as Ministry.* San Francisco: Jossey-Bass, 2000.

Kearns, K. P. *Managing for Accountability: Preserving the Public Trust in Public and Nonprofit Organizations.* San Francisco: Jossey-Bass, 1996.

Larson, M. S. *The Rise of Professionalism: A Sociological Analysis.* Berkeley: University of California Press, 1977.

Lohmann, R. *The Commons: New Perspectives on Nonprofit Organizations and Voluntary Action.* San Francisco: Jossey-Bass, 1992.

Mason, D. E. "Ethics and the Nonprofit Leader." *Nonprofit World,* 1992a, *10*(4), 30–32.

Mason, D. E. "Keepers of the Springs: Why Ethics Make Good Sense for Nonprofit Leaders." *Nonprofit World,* 1992b, *10*(2), 25–27.

Middleton, M. "Nonprofit Boards of Directors: Beyond the Governance Function." In W. W. Powell (ed.), *The Nonprofit Sector: A Research Handbook.* New Haven, Conn.: Yale University Press, 1987.

Nielsen, W. *The Golden Donors: A New Anatomy of the Great Foundations.* New York: Dutton, 1985.

O'Neill, M. *Nonprofit Nation: A New Look at the Third America.* San Francisco: Jossey-Bass, 2003.

Ostrander, S. A., and Schervish, P. G. "Giving and Getting: Philanthropy as a Social Relation." In J. Van Til and Associates, *Critical Issues in American Philanthropy: Strengthening Theory and Practice.* San Francisco: Jossey-Bass, 1990.

Parsons, T. *Structures and Process in Modern Societies.* New York: Free Press, 1960.

Payton, R. *Philanthropy: Voluntary Action for the Public Good.* Old Tappan, N.J.: Macmillan, 1988.

Perrow, C. *Complex Organizations: A Critical Essay.* (3rd ed.) New York: Random House, 1986.

Peters, T. J., and Waterman, R. *In Search of Excellence.* New York: HarperCollins, 1982.

Putnam, R. *Bowling Alone: The Collapse and Revival of American Community.* New York: Simon & Schuster, 2000.

Salamon, L. M. *America's Nonprofit Sector: A Primer.* New York: Foundation Center, 1999.

Schein, E. H. *Organizational Culture and Leadership.* San Francisco: Jossey-Bass, 1985.

Schön, D. A. *The Reflective Practitioner.* San Francisco: Jossey-Bass, 1983.

Schön, D. A. *Educating the Reflective Practitioner: Toward a New Design for Teaching and Learning in the Professions.* San Francisco: Jossey-Bass, 1990.

Simon, J. G. "The Tax Treatment of Nonprofit Organizations: A Review of Federal and State Policies." In W. W. Powell (ed.), *The Nonprofit Sector: A Research Handbook.* New Haven, Conn.: Yale University Press, 1987.

Van Til, J. *Mapping the Third Sector.* New Brunswick, N.J.: Transaction, 1988.

Weisbrod, B. *The Nonprofit Economy.* Cambridge, Mass.: Harvard University Press, 1988.

CHAPTER TEN

Nonprofit Lobbying

Bob Smucker

The importance of charity lobbying and advocacy has been addressed over the years by a number of the nation's leaders. The late philanthropic leader John W. Gardner said, "Virtually every far-reaching change in our history has come up in the private sector: the abolition of slavery, the reforms of populism, child labor laws, the vote for women, civil rights and so on" (Coalition, 1978, p. 13). A review of those issues indicates that all involved lobbying and advocacy at some point. Moreover, charities played a key role in organizing and conducting the lobbying that led to those reforms. Clearly, the nation is richer for having charities that speak out on issues in the public interest.

The noted religious leader Paul H. Sherry (1970) issued a pointed challenge to nonprofits about the importance of lobbying. He stated, "The primary role of voluntary associations in American life is not service delivery but to continually shape and reshape the vision of a just social order . . . , to argue for that vision with other contenders in the public arena, and to press for its adoption and implementation. For voluntary associations to do less than that is to abdicate their civic responsibility" (p. 3).

Recent remarks by Timothy E. Wirth (2003), former U.S. senator from Colorado, underscore the same point. He said, "If we believe in what we are funding and are hopeful about replicability, we have to work the system. That means we have to educate, persuade, and sometimes lobby our government. Good laws and good governance are essential to good public policy, and I for one want to help define what 'good' means."

Charities make an enormous contribution to our national life, often through "hands-on" services provided by the eighty-four million Americans who volunteer each year (INDEPENDENT SECTOR, 2002). Unfortunately, charities seldom organize those volunteers to contribute their time to perhaps the most important service they can provide—speaking out to policymakers about the people they serve and their organizations' missions. Instead, many charities view lobbying as irrelevant to their mission, inappropriate, or even illegal. This is a huge loss not only for the people and causes that charities serve but also for the nation as a whole: the right of citizens to petition their government is basic to our democracy, and charities are one of the most effective vehicles for allowing citizen participation to shape public policy. Our democratic system can only be strengthened by charities and their volunteers telling public officials about the needs as they see them—firsthand.

Most nonprofit programs are affected directly or indirectly by legislation. Whether a group's concern is conquering cancer, preserving the ozone layer, saving neighborhood schools, providing famine relief, or championing the rights of children, women, or minorities, decisions affecting those issues and programs are made by legislators in Washington, D.C., and in state capitals, city councils, and county governments throughout the nation. Their decisions affect not only public policy that is central to programs carried out by nonprofits but also the funding. It is a little-known fact that while private giving makes up 20 percent of all charitable income, government is the source of 31 percent, according to recent research by INDEPENDENT SECTOR and the Urban Institute (2002).

The importance of government decisions on nonprofit programs and the government funding of those programs argues strongly for the development by nonprofits of lobbying skills and knowledge of the laws governing nonprofit lobbying. However, managers of nonprofits and their boards of directors have been slow to recognize and act on this point. Many still doubt that lobbying is a proper and legal nonprofit activity. This is reflected in recent research, which indicated that 69 percent of nonprofits lobby only infrequently (OMB Watch, 2002). And of all the charities that report to the Internal Revenue Service, less than 2 percent report lobbying expenditures as defined by the IRS (Center on Nonprofits and Philanthropy at the Urban Institute, 1999).

The law is absolutely clear about the legality of lobbying. In fact, since 1919, the law has permitted some lobbying by nonprofits, although the amount permitted was originally ambiguous. In 1976, legislation was passed that clarified and vastly expanded the amount of lobbying nonprofits can conduct. Equally important, on August 31, 1990, the Internal Revenue Service promulgated regulations that supported both the spirit and the intent of the 1976 law. Together the law and the regulations provide more lobbying leeway than 99 percent of all nonprofits will ever need—or want.

That the law provides plenty of leeway for charities to lobby is evidenced by the fact that charities, on average, spend just $15,000 annually on lobbying, which is only a small fraction of the maximum permitted by the 1976 law. (See Table 10.1 later in this chapter for the lobbying expenditure limits.)

Although lobbying is both a legal and an essential nonprofit activity, volunteers and staff are often inclined to place lobbying at the very bottom of the list of abilities they want to develop. In addition to the question of legality, they may believe that it is too complex to master, perhaps a bit tainted, or they may assign it low priority simply because they already have a number of well-honed skills that they can immediately put to work for their organizations. Once involved in the process, however, most find that lobbying is not difficult to learn and that the organizing skills they possess are easily transferred to influencing legislation for the people they serve. And most discover that far from being disreputable or illegal, lobbying is a perfectly legitimate, reasonable, and personally rewarding way of fulfilling their organization's public purposes.

The primary purpose of this chapter is to provide information regarding the generous lobbying limits permitted to nonprofits under the law. The lobbying process and how-to-lobby information are described more briefly here but have been addressed exhaustively in other publications, including *The Lobbying and Advocacy Handbook for Nonprofit Organizations* (2002) by Marcia Avner, which focuses on shaping public policy at the state and local levels; *Real Clout* (1999) by Judith C. Meredith and Catherine M. Dunham, a how-to manual for community activists; and *The Dance of Legislation* (1973) by Eric Redman and *The Giant Killers* (1986) by Michael Pertschuck, both of which give lively descriptions of how nonprofits and other groups have successfully affected legislation. My own *Nonprofit Lobbying Guide* (Smucker, 1999) provides information on why lobbying is important, instructions on how to lobby, and answers, in lay language, to a number of technical questions regarding lobbying by nonprofits. Much of the material in this chapter is drawn from that book and is used here with the permission of INDEPENDENT SECTOR (www.IndependentSector.org).

LOBBYING AND ADVOCACY:
SIMILARITIES AND DIFFERENCES

People sometimes confuse the concepts of "lobbying" and "advocacy." The legal definition of *lobbying* usually involves attempting to influence legislation. *Advocacy* covers a much broader range of activities that might, or might not, include lobbying. One way of differentiating between the two is to understand that lobbying always involves advocacy but advocacy does not necessarily involve lobbying. For example, a group might picket or boycott a store to stop it from selling a particular product. That action is advocacy, and it might result in the store's discontinuing sale of the product. If that advocacy is not successful, the group might, as a next step, urge the city council to pass an ordinance prohibiting sale of the product. That action, to influence legislation, is lobbying.

Lobbying is only a small part of the advocacy carried out by charities. Almost all social change has started with nonlobbying advocacy but ended with major lobbying efforts. For example, the civil rights movement included sit-ins, marches, and other forms of protest, which were advocating for equal rights. Ultimately, that advocacy led to the enactment, through extensive lobbying, of the Civil Rights Act of 1964.

This kind of citizen action has been carried out repeatedly over the years by citizen groups working for the protection of women's rights, child labor laws, stricter laws against drunk driving and smoking, requirements for safe drinking water and clean air, disabled persons' rights, and many more. All these efforts initially combined a broad spectrum of nonlobbying advocacy activities, with lobbying added somewhat later to achieve the needed change in public policy.

A FEW BASICS ABOUT HOW TO LOBBY: AN INDIVIDUAL PERSPECTIVE

Sometimes individuals and organizations won't lobby because they're afraid they don't know how. They are staunch supporters of their cause, they recognize the importance of lobbying, and they know that it pays off. Yet they hold back on the mistaken notion that lobbying is only for experts.

Like anything else, the more you know about how to lobby, the better you will be at it. But if you can make a phone call or write a letter, you can lobby. All you need to be a lobbyist—and not just a lobbyist but an *effective* lobbyist—are three things:

- A few basic facts
- Belief in your cause
- Common sense

The most important single thing a lobbyist needs to know is his or her subject. What is the substance of the legislation you are proposing (or opposing)? Why is it so important? What will happen if it passes? What will happen if it does not pass? How much will it cost? Normally, the place to get these facts is the headquarters of your organization. Typically, whoever asks you to get involved in lobbying, perhaps the chair of your legislative committee or the executive director of your association, will provide these facts at the time of the call for action. No responsible organization is going to ask its volunteers or staff to lobby without arming them with the facts.

Know Your Legislators

It helps to know the legislator or legislators you contact. What are their interests? What are their backgrounds? What is their record of support? What positions do they hold in the legislature? Who is the chair of the committee that will consider your proposal? Who is the chief spokesperson for the opposition?

The good lobbyist also knows how the system works, what steps a proposed municipal ordinance or state law or federal appropriation bill goes through from introduction to enactment, and which committees will consider the legislation. All of this information should be provided by your staff and volunteer leadership. And before you know it, you may well be the one who's providing the information to the beginning lobbyist.

Facts alone are not enough. Without conviction, dedication to the cause, loyalty to the organization, and determination to see the job through no matter how long it takes (and it can indeed take long!), a lobbyist won't be very effective. It is far better to say no than to agree to lobby for something when your heart isn't in it.

Concentration Counts

Difficult as it is, keep your focus on just one issue. It's the only way you can successfully marshal all your resources and ultimately prevail in the tough environment you will face in any legislative fight.

Use Common Sense

The minimum principles you need to know when lobbying are these: be brief, be clear, be accurate, be persuasive, be timely, be persistent, and be grateful. These commonsense principles apply whether you're lobbying by telephone, by letter, or face to face. The only one that's a bit difficult for the beginner is timing. There are good times, better times, and best times, and until you've become an expert in your own right, your organization's staff or volunteer leadership should call the shots on timing.

Never promise a reward for good behavior or threaten retribution for a failure to support you. Be persuasive rather than argumentative or demanding. Don't knock your opponents—they probably believe in their position as sincerely as you believe in yours.

When you write, keep your letter or fax to a single page—literally. If you need more space, include an attachment elaborating on that one-page summary. Be absolutely sure you spell your legislator's name correctly, have the correct title, and get the address right. Falling short in those areas undermines the credibility of everything else in your letter. And of course, always personalize your letter. Get the facts from your organization, but use your own words on your own stationery.

Speak Face to Face

The first time you meet your United States senator—or for that matter, a city council member—you will probably have butterflies in your stomach. It would be unusual if you didn't. If you'd feel better having a few other people along, fine. Just be sure your companions can also speak to the matter at hand and are not just along for the ride. Keep the group size small. The fewer present, the more candid the legislator will be.

Always Be Brief

Again, when meeting as when writing, be brief. Make an appointment, be on time, state your case, and leave. Plan to cover your topic in five minutes if possible, ten minutes at the most. Don't linger unless your legislator chooses to prolong the meeting.

If you get hit with any questions you can't answer, admit it, say you'll find out, and provide the answers later. Don't bluff—it always shows. When you depart, hand your host a written summary—again, a one-pager—of your position and exactly what you want him or her to do about it.

Aides Are Influential

Do not be offended if you don't get to see the boss. Even if you had a firm appointment, you may be referred instead to an assistant. The demands on a legislator's time are unbelievable, and last-minute changes in schedule quite often simply can't be avoided.

Never underestimate the importance of an aide. Treat him or her just as you would your legislator, not only as a matter of courtesy but because the aide is in a position to advance—or sink—your cause.

Say Thank You!

When you get back home, after you've talked with your legislator by phone, or after he or she has voted your way or done something else to help you, send a thank-you letter. The vast majority of all mail a legislator gets is either asking for personal favors, complaining about something the government has or has not done, or blasting the legislator for something he or she has or has not done. A thank-you letter really scores. Besides, it's the polite thing to do.

Always Keep a Record

Report to your organization using any means that will get the information quickly to your group's government relations office, where the details can be kept on file. Whom did you see or talk with? What did you discuss? What was that person's position? Your reports and those of other staff or volunteers are indispensable to your leadership in planning strategy.

So yes, you can lobby. You'll learn a lot, and you'll be a real participant in this business called democracy. And not only will you help bring about that change you feel is so important, but you'll also get more satisfaction out of lobbying than you ever imagined.

ANYONE CAN LOBBY: AN ORGANIZATIONAL PERSPECTIVE

The personnel manager of a large midwestern manufacturing company once told me that job descriptions, even for junior executives, are often drawn up by well-intentioned but unknowing staff to include requirements so demanding that not even the president of the company could fulfill them. How-to information can suffer from the same problem. Often it doesn't distinguish between what you have to know and all the other things that could be helpful but are not absolutely essential.

All your organization needs as you start lobbying is a staff person or volunteer who has a little knowledge of lobbying techniques; has an elementary understanding of how the legislative process works in whatever body you are planning to lobby, whether Congress, the state legislature, county government, or the city council; can organize a government relations committee that will consider the legislative issues your organization may want to tackle; can organize volunteers to form a legislative network; and has a passing knowledge of the law governing lobbying by nonprofits.

Much of the information you need to start lobbying is available through Charity Lobbying in the Public Interest (CLPI) in Washington, D.C. The mission of CLPI is to educate charities about the important role lobbying can play in achieving their missions. CLPI resources include information on why lobbying is important, how to lobby, and the lobby law. It has a very comprehensive Web site, books, videos, brochures, curriculum guides, and twenty "one-pagers," all directed toward educating charities about lobbying.

Much of the information you need to start lobbying is probably also readily available in your own community. A number of nonprofits, civic organizations, and public-spirited citizens have been lobbying for years and would be complimented if your group asked them for help in understanding the areas just described. The League of Women Voters is one such organization; others include environmental organizations and most of the major health groups (such as the heart, lung, cancer, mental health, and mental retardation associations), whose staff members often have considerable lobbying knowledge and would probably have affiliates in your community.

LOBBYING LAW

Before you start lobbying, you should know a little about the law governing lobbying by nonprofits. The 1976 lobby law and regulations provide very generous lobbying limits. You should know what the law says about how much of your organization's annual expenditures can go for lobbying and what activities are defined as lobbying, but the most important point to keep in mind is that the law permits ample room for all the lobbying your group will probably want to undertake. It is very simple for a nonprofit to elect to come under the provisions of that law. If you don't elect to come under the 1976 law, you are under the "no substantial part" provision, which means that no substantial part of your organization's activities may be devoted to attempts to influence legislation. It is to the advantage of almost all charities, except perhaps those that are very large, to elect to come under the 1976 law.

If you have questions about whether the amount of lobbying you want to conduct is within the law, discuss it with other nonprofits that lobby extensively, as well as with your attorney. But remember that attorneys almost always err on the side of extreme caution in counseling nonprofits about lobbying. If you ask your lawyer for advice, be certain that he or she not only knows the lobby law well (only a few do), but, even more important, is also familiar with the experience of organizations that have lobbied under the law. Most groups have found plenty of legal latitude for lobbying without jeopardizing their tax-exempt status.

THE LEGISLATIVE PROCESS AND YOUR LOBBYIST

It is important to have a volunteer or staff person in your organization who knows the basics of how your legislature works, because you will need that information in order to focus your efforts. For example, you may be trying to block legislation averse to your group, help support pending legislation backed by your organization, or arrange the introduction of legislation vital to your group. In the typical legislature, to achieve any of these aims, you will have to gain the support of the committee designated to consider your issue. It follows that you will need to know something about the composition of that committee. For example, if you are seeking to have legislation introduced, it is usually possible to recruit a committee member to introduce your bill. But you won't want just any member. You will want a person of influence, and that usually means a senior committee member whose party is in the majority and therefore controls the committee.

It is, incidentally, helpful to know that many decisions on legislation are made in a last-minute frenzy as legislators prepare to adjourn the legislative session.

The lobbyist (whether a volunteer or a paid staff member) who is following your issue in the legislature should have enough understanding of how the legislative process works that your group can make the right move at the right place and time. Your lobbyist needs to recognize, for example, whether this is the last chance to modify your bill or if you still have a reasonable chance to effect the changes you want in the other house of the legislature. A lobbyist who knows (among other things) who would be the best legislators to introduce your bill and how and when decisions are made in your legislature is referred to as an inside lobbyist.

Having a seasoned insider available to your organization can save you enormous amounts of time and effort. Perhaps volunteers or staff people bring such experience to your group from their work with other nonprofits. If not, such groups as CLPI and the League of Women Voters can help your group develop an understanding of how your legislature really works. Former legislators or those currently in office can also be very helpful. Nationally, the Advocacy Institute, the Alliance for Justice, OMB Watch, and INDEPENDENT SECTOR, all in Washington, D.C., are among the organizations that can provide how-to information about lobbying by nonprofits.

If you have the funds, it is possible to hire a good, experienced lobbying consultant. If you choose that route, check with other nonprofits whose opinions you value highly and who have used consultants to lobby. The best way to be certain that you are getting the right person is to check his or her track record with other groups. Consultants should be pleased to give you the names of groups for which they have lobbied.

THE GOVERNMENT RELATIONS COMMITTEE
AND THE LEGISLATIVE NETWORK

Your organization will need to set up a government relations committee or similar group that can recommend public policy to consider how your group's program can be furthered by legislative initiatives. The committee will also establish legislative priorities and provide direction for the group's lobbying efforts. A strong government relations committee that represents a broad cross section of your community can add immeasurably to the impact of your lobbying efforts. In using a government relations committee, it is enormously important to hold firmly to one top legislative priority, rather than follow the more common route of trying to work on many issues at once.

A nonprofit's principal lobbying power resides in its ability to enlist as many of its members as possible in supporting its legislation. To achieve that objective, most groups set up a legislative network to mobilize their grassroots network. At the minimum, your network should assign one volunteer, capable of enlisting others in the community, as a contact person for each member of each legislative committee that will act on your bill. If there are twenty members of a legislative committee that will act on your bill, twenty contact persons should be recruited.

Establishing and maintaining the network takes time and commitment because it is tedious, time-consuming work. It is easy to put off establishing a network and even easier to neglect it once it is set up. A nonprofit neglects its network at great risk, however. Without a network, there may be no chance to mobilize broad support on short notice. That kind of quick mobilization may be needed repeatedly during a legislative campaign. Fortunately, e-mail provides an effective way of both recruiting and communicating with your networks, including alerting people when action is needed.

In short, you need very little to get started. As we have seen, it helps to know a little about the law governing lobbying and to have a volunteer or a staff person who has an elementary understanding of basic lobbying techniques and of the lobbying process, as well as some organizing skills. It's helpful to have a government relations committee or similar group and critically important to have a legislative network, and as in all activities that involve people, common sense helps immeasurably. Most important, don't be put off by the amount of technical information in this chapter. Just go ahead. Get started, and keep in mind that lobbying and the legislative process are not nearly as complicated or as difficult as lobbyists would have you believe.

THE 1976 LOBBY LAW AND THE 1990 INTERNAL REVENUE SERVICE REGULATIONS: AN OVERVIEW

The landmark legislation enacted into law in 1976 clarified and greatly expanded the extent to which nonprofits could lobby without jeopardizing their tax-exempt status. That legislation, section 1307 of Public Law 94-455, recognized lobbying as an entirely proper function of nonprofits and ended the long-standing uncertainty about the legality of lobbying by groups that are tax-exempt under section 501(c)(3) of the Internal Revenue Code. Briefly, 501(c)(3) nonprofit organizations are those that are organized for specific public-benefit purposes. These are the only U.S. nonprofit organizations that are both exempt from federal income taxes and to which contributions by individuals (and other taxpayers) may be deductible from their tax liability. Public Law 94-455 resulted in Internal Revenue Code sections 4911 and 501. Section 4911 includes information on how much can be spent on lobbying. Section 501 provides information on electing to come under the provisions of Public Law 94-455.

It took a full fourteen years for the Internal Revenue Service to issue final regulations under the 1976 lobby law, but the regulations were worth the wait. While there was some stormy debate between nonprofits and the IRS regarding earlier proposed regulations, the final version, issued on August 31, 1990, is faithful to the 1976 law. There is clear consensus in the nonprofit community that the regulations provide a framework that is both flexible and workable for charities' efforts on legislation. In every critical area, the regulations reflect responsiveness to (although not complete acceptance of) the criticisms and suggestions offered by nonprofits during the long process that led to the final outcome.

In understanding the 1976 lobby law, it helps to know that for a nonprofit electing to come under the law, lobbying is defined as the expenditure of money by the organization for the purpose of attempting to influence legislation. If there is no expenditure by the organization for lobbying, there is no lobbying by the organization. Therefore, lobbying by a volunteer for a nonprofit is not counted as a lobbying expenditure to the organization and hence is not lobbying. If, however, the volunteer is reimbursed by the nonprofit for out-of-pocket expenses, the reimbursed funds do count as a lobbying expenditure. But it's important to keep in mind the point that lobbying occurs only when there is an expenditure of funds for an activity that meets the other criteria for lobbying.

It is also helpful in understanding the 1976 law to recognize that it defines two kinds of lobbying: direct lobbying and grassroots lobbying. To oversimplify, *direct lobbying* refers to communication that your organization has about legislation (1) with legislators or government officials who participate in the formulation of legislation and (2) with its own members. Direct lobbying would include visiting a congressperson about a bill and being in touch with your organization's members and urging them to contact legislators. *Grassroots lobbying* refers to any attempt to influence legislation by affecting the opinion of the general public.

Sometimes groups confuse grassroots lobbying of the general public with urging their members to lobby. They mistakenly think that contacting their members (who may number in the hundreds of thousands) to urge them, in turn, to contact members of the legislature constitutes grassroots lobbying, simply because those members are at the grassroots level. Only when an organization is trying to reach beyond its members to get action from the general public does grassroots lobbying occur.

Don't be deterred by all the detail in the following description of the 1976 law. Keep in mind that the law is very generous. It provides all the lobbying latitude that ninety-nine out of a hundred groups will ever need. The details included here will help provide the assurance you may need that many of your activities in the legislative arena are not lobbying under the 1976 lobby law.

Virtually all of the information that follows is drawn from materials written for INDEPENDENT SECTOR by Walter B. Slocombe, formerly of Caplin & Drysdale,

Washington, D.C. It is an overview of the lobbying latitude permitted to 501(c)(3) organizations under the 1976 law and regulations.

Regulations Under the 1976 Lobby Law

The 1990 regulations were final on August 31, 1990. Public charities that have elected to come under the 1976 lobby law need to familiarize themselves with the regulations so that they will know what activities will and will not count against the statutory limits and so that they can correctly calculate the amounts they treat as spending for lobbying. Private foundations are affected. This is because the regulations (1) elaborate the standards that foundations must meet to comply with the general ban on lobbying by private foundations and (2) establish guidelines for grants by private foundations to public charities that elect to come under the law.

The general rule of section 501(c)(3), to which all organizations exempt under that provision are subject unless they elect to come under the 1976 lobby law, is that "no substantial part" of their activities may consist of attempting to influence legislation. Although the provision has been in the IRS code since 1934 and has occasionally been applied by the courts, there has never been a clear definition of the point at which lobbying becomes "substantial" or, indeed, of what activities related to public policy constitute attempts to influence legislation. In particular, the IRS position under the "no substantial part" test is that spending, as a share of budget, is far from the sole measure of whether a nonelecting group's lobbying is substantial; such factors as absolute amount spent, impact, public prominence, and unpaid volunteer work also enter into the determination.

To clarify and liberalize the rules for lobbying by charities, sections 501(h) and 4911 were added to the code in 1976, as a result of the enactment of the 1976 lobby law. In outline, the provisions permit most public charities (but not churches, their integrated auxiliaries, or a convention or association of churches) to elect to have their legislative efforts governed by the specific rules of sections 501(h) and 4911, instead of the vague "substantiality" standard. To that end, the 1976 legislation both sets financial limits for lobbying activities and defines clearly the activities that count against those limits.

Key Exclusions from Lobbying Under the 1976 Law

Critical to the 1976 law are the provisions declaring that many expenditures that have some relationship to public policy and legislative issues are not treated as lobbying and so are permitted without limit.

1. Contacts with executive branch employees or legislators in support of or opposition to proposed regulations is not considered lobbying. So if your nonprofit is trying to get a regulation changed, it may contact both members of the

executive branch as well as legislators to urge support for your position on the regulation, and the action is not considered lobbying.

2. Lobbying by volunteers is considered a lobbying expenditure only to the extent that the nonprofit incurs expenses associated with the volunteers' lobbying. For example, volunteers working for a nonprofit could organize a rally of volunteers at the state capitol to lobby on an issue, and only the expenses related to the rally paid by the nonprofit would count as a lobbying expenditure.

3. A nonprofit's communications to its members on legislation—even if it takes a position on the legislation—is not lobbying so long as the nonprofit doesn't directly encourage its members or others to lobby. For example, a group could send out a public affairs bulletin to its members in which it takes a position on legislation, and it would not count as lobbying if the nonprofit didn't ask its members to take action on the measure.

4. A nonprofit's response to written requests from a legislative body (not just a single legislator) for technical advice on pending legislation is not considered lobbying. So if requested in writing, a group could provide testimony on legislation in which it takes a position on that legislation, and it would not be considered lobbying.

5. So-called self-defense activity—that is, lobbying legislators (but not the general public) on matters that may affect the organization's own existence, powers, tax-exempt status, and similar matters—would not be lobbying. For example, lobbying in opposition to proposals in Congress to curtail lobbying by nonprofits or lobbying in support of a charitable tax deduction for nonitemizers would not be a lobbying expenditure. It would become lobbying only if you asked for support from the general public. However, lobbying for programs in the organization's field (health, welfare, environment, education, and so on) is not self-defense lobbying. For example, an organization that is working to cure cancer could not claim that campaigning for increased appropriations for cancer research was self-defense lobbying.

6. Making available the results of "nonpartisan analysis, study, or research" on a legislative issue that presents a sufficiently full and fair exposition of the pertinent facts to enable the audience to form an independent opinion would not be considered lobbying. The regulations make clear that such research and analysis need not be "neutral" or "objective" to fall within this "nonpartisan" exclusion. The exclusion is available to research and analysis that take direct positions on the merits of legislation, as long as the organization presents facts fully and fairly, makes the material generally available, and does not include a direct call to the reader to contact legislators. This exception is particularly important because many nonprofits that engage in public policy do conduct significant amounts of nonpartisan analysis, study, and research on legislation.

7. A nonprofit's discussion of broad social, economic, and similar policy issues whose resolution would require legislation—even if specific legislation on

the matter is pending—is not considered lobbying so long as the discussion does not address the merits of specific legislation. For example, a session at a nonprofit's annual meeting regarding the importance of enacting child welfare legislation would not be lobbying so long as the organization is not addressing the merits of specific child welfare legislation pending in the legislature. Representatives of the organizations could even talk directly to legislators on the broad issue of child welfare so long as there is no reference to specific legislation on that issue.

8. It's not grassroots lobbying if a nonprofit urges the public, through the media or other means, to vote for or against a ballot initiative or referendum. (This is direct lobbying, not grassroots lobbying, because the public in this situation becomes the legislature. Lobbying the public through the media is therefore considered a direct lobbying expenditure, not a grassroots expenditure. This is an advantage because nonprofits are permitted to spend more on direct lobbying than on grassroots lobbying.)

Permitted Levels of Spending for Lobbying

Another key element of the 1976 law is that it unequivocally declares that activities that do constitute active lobbying are permitted, provided only that they fall within the spending ceilings established by the law. The spending ceilings are based on percentages of the charity's budget for the year, beginning at 20 percent of the first $500,000 and ending at 5 percent of expenditures over $1.5 million. (Strictly speaking, the base is the charity's exempt-purpose expenditures, which include all payments for the organization's programs and exempt purposes but exclude costs of investment management, unrelated businesses, and certain fundraising costs.) There is an overall maximum ceiling of $1 million a year. The effect of the sliding-scale ceilings is that an organization reaches the maximum permissible ceiling when its exempt-purpose expenditures reach $17 million. Amounts spent on lobbying in excess of that level must be for direct lobbying—that is, for communications made directly to legislators and their staffs and to executive branch officials who participate in the formulation of legislation. As previously described, communications with an organization's members that urge them to contact legislators are also treated as direct, rather than grassroots, lobbying. The total and grassroots ceilings at various exempt-purpose expenditure levels are shown in Table 10.1.

Flexible Sanctions

Another important element of the 1976 legislation was the establishment of a new and more flexible system of sanctions, to replace the "death sentence" of loss of exemption as the principal sanction for violation of the "substantiality" standard. (Since 1976, Congress has added additional sanctions, beyond loss of exemption, for nonelecting organizations that violate that standard: a 5 percent

Table 10.1. Lobbying Ceilings Under the 1976 Lobby Law.

Exempt-Purpose Expenditures	Total Lobbying Expenditures	Amount of Total Allowable for Grassroots Lobbying
Up to $500,000	20% of exempt-purpose expenditures	5% of exempt-purpose expenditures
$500,000–$1 million	$100,000 + 15% of excess over $500,000	$25,000 + 3.75% of excess over $500,000
$1 million–$1.5 million	$175,000 + 10% of excess over $1 million	$43,750 + 2.5% of excess over $1 million
$1.5 million–$17 million	$225,000 + 5% of excess over $1.5 million	$56,250 + 1.25% of excess over $1.5 million
Over $17 million	$1 million	$250,000

excise tax on excessive lobbying spending and a similar tax on managers who willfully and unreasonably agree to lobbying expenditures knowing that these are likely to cause loss of exemption.) The initial sanction under the 1976 law for public charities that spend more than either the overall or the grassroots limit is a 25 percent excise tax on the lobbying spending in any year in excess of the ceiling. (If both ceilings are exceeded, the tax is on the greater of the two excess amounts.) Loss of exemption is an available sanction only if spending normally exceeds 150 percent of either the overall or the grassroots limit, generally determined by aggregating both spending and limits over a four-year period.

What spending counts against the expenditure limits? There is considerable uncertainty about which activities count against the "substantiality" standard, but the standard, under the 1976 lobby law, is strictly financial. The only factor that must be taken into account is the cost of communications for direct or grassroots lobbying, including the cost of preparing the communication (such as staff time, facilities, and allocable overhead).

Elements Required for a Lobbying Communication

To be a direct lobbying communication, and therefore to count against the direct lobbying dollar limits, a communication must refer to specific legislation and reflect a point of view on its merits. "Specific legislation" includes a specific measure that has not yet been introduced, but it does not include general concepts for solving problems that have not yet been distilled into legislative proposals.

To be a grassroots lobbying communication, in most cases, a communication must, apart from referring to specific legislation and reflecting a view on it, encourage recipients to contact legislators. Under the regulations, such a call to action exists only when the material directly tells its audience to contact legislators; provides a legislator's address, phone number, or similar information; provides a petition, postcard, or other prepared message to be sent to the legislator; or identifies one or more legislators as opposing the organization's views, being undecided, being recipients' representatives, or being a member of the committee that will consider the legislation. As mentioned earlier, under these rules, a public charity (except in the narrow case of "highly publicized legislation," to be discussed) can make any public statement it likes about a legislative issue without having the costs counted against its grassroots lobbying limit as long as it avoids calls to action.

Special Rules for Referenda, Initiatives, and Similar Procedures

In general, legislative messages aimed at the public as a whole are grassroots lobbying if they meet the "call to action" standard. The final regulations, however, recognize that in the case of referenda, initiatives, and similar procedures, the public is itself the legislature. Accordingly, communication to the public that refers to such measures and that takes a stand on them is treated as direct lobbying of a legislature, subject only to the higher ceiling. The effect of these rules is that communications (newspaper ads, for example) that refer to a ballot measure and reflect a view on it are direct lobbying, whether or not they explicitly tell people how to vote.

The rule gives public charities important flexibility to be active in referendum efforts, which would have been impractical if they had been forced to count against the lower grassroots lobbying limits.

WHEN DOES LATER USE OF MATERIALS CAUSE THEIR COSTS TO BE COUNTED AS LOBBYING?

The costs of a lobbying communication include the costs of the staff and facilities needed to prepare it, not just the costs of paper and ink or videotape. An issue of concern to many groups, especially those doing research on public policy issues, has been the possibility that research costs might be treated as costs of preparing to lobby if the published results of the research were later referred to and used in lobbying. The final regulations on this so-called subsequent use issue should greatly ease organizations' concerns that their lobbying spending will be boosted unexpectedly because materials they have prepared are later used in lobbying—whether the use is by the organization itself, by a related organization, or by a third party. This is because the costs of materials that are not themselves used for lobbying must be counted as lobbying support costs (on the basis of their later use in lobbying) *only* in cases in which all of the following conditions exist:

1. The materials both refer to and reflect a view on specific legislation. (They do not, however, in their initial format, include a call to action. If the materials do include such a call, their public circulation would itself be grassroots lobbying.) Materials—such as raw research data—that do not meet this test are entirely outside the "subsequent use" rules.

2. The lobbying use occurs within six months of payment for the materials. Therefore, lobbying use more than six months after a research project is complete cannot affect the organization's lobbying costs. In any case, only the most recent six months of spending potentially represents a lobbying cost. There is no risk that if some lobbying use is made of research results more than six months after a project is finished, years of accumulated research spending will be treated as lobbying costs.

3. The organization fails to make a substantial nonlobbying distribution of the materials before the lobbying use. If the materials are "nonpartisan, analysis, study, or research," a nonlobbying distribution qualifies as "substantial" (and therefore excludes all the costs from lobbying treatment) if it conforms to the normal distribution pattern for similar materials, as followed by that organization and similar ones. For other materials, the nonlobbying distribution must be at least as extensive as the lobbying distribution. This rule means that by seeing that research and analysis materials that take positions on legislation are first distributed to the public in normal ways, an organization can prevent their costs from being treated as lobbying costs, even if the materials are later used in lobbying by the organization itself or by an affiliate.

4. The organization's primary purpose in creating the materials was to use them in lobbying rather than for some nonlobbying goal. When the lobbying use is by an unrelated organization, not only must there be clear and convincing evidence of such a lobbying purpose, but that evidence must also include evidence of collusion and cooperation with the organization using the material for lobbying.

For private foundations making grants to public charities that spend the money on materials later used in lobbying, there is another layer of protection. Even if the grantee violates the "subsequent use" rules, the grantor foundation can be taxed on the grant as a lobbying expenditure only if the private foundation had a primary lobbying purpose in making the grant or if the grantmaking foundation knew or should reasonably have known of the grantee's lobbying purpose.

The cumulative effect of these safeguards is that a research organization can readily avoid any risk of unexpected lobbying expenses. As noted, *all* of the following have to occur for the organization to incur a lobbying expenditure. (1) Only costs that are less than six months old can be at issue. (2) Even in theory, the problem can arise only in the case of material that takes a position on specific legislation. (3) Even for such materials, there is a safe harbor for distributions that follow the normal patterns of dissemination. (4) In any event, an organization can avoid having costs for materials later used in lobbying treated as grassroots lobbying expenses if the primary purpose of incurring the cost was a nonlobbying objective. If the later use is by an unrelated organization, there must be clear and convincing evidence that the organization developed the research for the purpose of lobbying.

DOES ELECTING TO BE GOVERNED BY THE NEW REGULATIONS COMPLICATE RECEIVING GRANTS FROM FOUNDATIONS?

Private foundations may not elect to come under the 1976 law, and they remain absolutely prohibited from making expenditures for lobbying purposes. Therefore, some foundations have been concerned about their ability to make grants to nonprofits that explicitly adopt programs of lobbying by electing to come under the 1976 lobby law, and some nonprofits have worried that making an election under the 1976 law will scare off foundation funders.

The regulations—which codify and even liberalize long-established IRS policy—meet these concerns by setting up a highly protective system for grants by private foundations to public charities that elect to come under the 1976 law. Under these rules, a foundation may, without tax liability, make a general-purpose grant to a public charity that lobbies, whether or not the public charity has elected. A private foundation may also make a grant to support a specific project that includes lobbying as long as its own grant is less than the amount budgeted for the nonlobbying parts of the project. For example, if a specific project has a $200,000 budget, of which $20,000 is to be spent for lobbying, a private foundation can give the project up to $180,000 because that is the part of the project budget allocated to nonlobbying uses. The fact that other private foundations have already made grants for the project need not be taken into account in considering how much a private foundation can give.

The regulations make clear that a foundation can rely on statements by the prospective grantee regarding how much the project will spend on lobbying, unless the foundation knows or has reason to know that the statements are false. The regulations also make clear that as long as the granting foundation complies with these standards when it makes the grant, it will not be held to have made a taxable lobbying expenditure if the public charity violates the assurances it gave when seeking the grant.

WHEN WILL A PUBLIC CHARITY'S TRANSFERS TO A LOBBYING ORGANIZATION BE COUNTED AS LOBBYING EXPENDITURES?

If a public charity pays another organization or an individual to do lobbying for it, the payment counts against its direct or grassroots lobbying ceiling according to the nature of the work done. The regulations also seek to prevent evasion of the limits by public charities that provide funds to other organizations not subject to the section 501(c)(3) lobbying limits—such as, presumably, a related organization exempt under section 501(c)(4)—to increase the resources available for the recipient's lobbying efforts. In such a case, the funds transferred are deemed to have been paid for grassroots lobbying, to the extent of the transferee's grassroots lobbying expenditures; any remaining amount is treated as having been paid for direct lobbying, to the extent of the transferee's direct lobbying expenditures.

This rule is subject to some very important qualifications, however. There is no lobbying expenditure when a public charity makes a grant to a noncharity and the grant's use is expressly limited to a specific educational or otherwise charitable purpose and when records demonstrate that use. The regulations also make clear that the rule does not apply when the public charity is getting fair market value for the money it transfers. Thus if a 501(c)(3) organization pays rent at fair market value to a 501(c)(4) group or if the 501(c)(3) group pays a 501(c)(4) group its proper portion of the costs of a shared employee, the rule does not apply because the 501(c)(3) group is getting full value from the 501(c)(4) group.

These transfer rules protect public charities that engage in normal and legitimate transactions with related (or unrelated) entities. Such charities need only follow the substantive and accounting procedures that are required in any case for general tax purposes without regard to the special lobbying provisions.

WHAT ACCOUNTING IS REQUIRED FOR LOBBYING EXPENDITURES?

All section 501(c)(3) organizations—whether or not they elect to come under the 1976 lobby law—must report the total amount of their lobbying expenditures on their annual IRS Form 990. Both classes of organizations must maintain records to support the entries on the return—showing, for example, the basis for computing the overhead allocated to lobbying activities.

Organizations that have not elected are required to state whether they attempted to influence public opinion through the use of volunteers and if so, to give a detailed description of the activities. There is no such requirement for electing organizations, which should give substantial additional incentives to nonprofits to elect.

HOW ARE EXPENDITURES THAT HAVE BOTH LOBBYING AND NONLOBBYING PURPOSES TREATED?

Sometimes a public charity wants to distribute a communication that has both lobbying and nonlobbying messages, such as a mass mailing that calls for readers to contact legislators about pending legislation and also asks them for contributions to the organization. In general, the regulations permit allocation between the lobbying and nonlobbying aspects of such mixed-purpose communications, but to reflect the special solicitude that is extended to communications with members, treatment of such communications is more generous.

The details are beyond the scope of this overview, but the general situation is as follows. First, costs of communications with members may be allocated, as between lobbying and any other bona fide nonlobbying purpose (education, fundraising, or advocacy on nonlegislative issues), in any reasonable basis. An attempt to allocate to lobbying only the particular words actually urging legislative action—and not the material explaining the legislative issue and the organization's position—will be rejected as unreasonable. Second, costs for part-lobbying communications to nonmembers (including even the membership share, if the communications go primarily to nonmembers) can be allocated to nonlobbying purposes only to the extent that they do not address the "same specific subject" as the legislative message in the communication. The "same specific subject" is rather broadly defined to include activities that would be affected by legislation addressed elsewhere in the message, as well as the background and consequences of the legislation and activities affected by it. Nevertheless, fundraising and providing general information about the organization are not treated as being on the "same specific subject" as a legislative message. Therefore, expenses attributable to those goals would not be considered lobbying costs. Allocation of expenditures away from lobbying is also permitted for the parts of a communication that discuss distinct aspects of a broad problem, one feature of which would be affected by the legislation addressed elsewhere.

Organizations that have extensive and expensive direct mail operations aimed at current contributors (who are members) and prospects (who are not) will need to review their mailings to ensure that they do not inadvertently make large grassroots lobbying expenditures. Similarly, groups that routinely send legislative alerts to nonmembers may want to make them distinct publications, rather than combining them with general communications.

WHEN ARE SEVERAL NONPROFITS
TREATED ON AN AGGREGATE BASIS?

In general, ceiling determinations and lobbying expenditure calculations are made on a separate basis for each legally distinct 501(c)(3) organization. Only if two or more organizations are subject to common control through interlocking majorities on their boards (or to common control by a third organization) or if one organization is required by its governing instrument to follow the legislative decisions of another are the organizations aggregated under a single ceiling, with aggregate computations of expenditures. The requirement to follow legislative decisions must be expressed and not merely implied.

FOR FURTHER INFORMATION

The foregoing analysis is intended to give interested volunteers and staff members an overview, in lay language, of the 1976 lobby law. No guide, however, can adequately substitute for official information. If you wish to make your own analysis, you will find the following additional sources to be of value:

- U.S. Internal Revenue Code of 1986, as amended, especially sections 501(a), 501(c)(3), 501(h), and 4911

- Public Law 94-455, the Tax Reform Act of 1976, approved October 4, 1976 (specifically, section 1307, "Lobbying by Public Charities")

- House Report 94-1210, "Influencing Legislation by Public Charities," June 2, 1976, to accompany House Report 13500 (H.R. 13500 became section 1307 of Public Law 94-455)

- Senate Report 94-938, part 2, supplemental report on additional amendment to House Report 10612, July 20, 1976 (H.R. 10612 became Public Law 94-455)

- House Report 94-1515, conference report on House Report 10612, September 13, 1976

- "Final Regulations on Lobbying by Public Charities and Private Foundations," *Federal Register,* August 31, 1990, p. 35579.

ELECTION PROCEDURE FOR NONPROFITS

The process for electing to come under the 1976 lobby law (Public Law 94-455) is very simple, which no doubt partly accounts for the fact that as of 1999, about seventeen hundred nonprofits, large and small, have chosen to do so since 1976 (Center on Nonprofits and Philanthropy, 1999). Those eligible to so elect are nonprofits exempt from taxation under section 501(c)(3) of the Internal Revenue Code. The legislation does not apply to churches, their integrated auxiliaries, or a convention or association of churches. Private foundations also are not eligible, although they may make grants to nonprofits that do elect.

If a nonprofit does not elect to take advantage of the generous lobbying provisions under the 1976 lobby law, it remains subject to the vague "insubstantial" rule that has been in the tax code since 1934. Under that provision, if a charity engages in more than "insubstantial" lobbying, it loses its section 501(c)(3) status and its right to receive tax-deductible charitable contributions. Unfortunately, "insubstantial" has never been defined under the law, with the result that nonprofits that do lobby but have not elected to come under the 1976 law cannot be certain how much lobbying they may conduct without jeopardizing their tax-exempt status. Many nonprofits have followed the questionable guideline that the allocation of 5 percent of their total annual expenditures to lobbying is not substantial and is therefore within the law. They have assumed that 5 percent of their expenditures is permissible because of a 1955 Sixth Circuit Court of Appeals ruling to the effect that attempts to influence legislation that constitute 5 percent of total activities are not substantial.

There is good reason to doubt that the 5 percent test should be relied on. It was called into question by a 1972 ruling, which rejected a percentage test in determining what constituted substantial lobbying. In that case, the Tenth Circuit Court of Appeals supported a "facts and circumstances" test instead of a percentage test. In a 1974 ruling, the Claims Court stated that a percentage test was deemed inappropriate for determining whether lobbying activities are substantial. It was found that an exempt organization enjoying considerable prestige and influence could be considered as having a substantial impact on the legislative process solely on the basis of making a single official position statement—an activity that would be considered negligible if measured according to a percentage standard of time expended. It is clearly in the interest of every nonprofit that lobbies more than a nominal amount to consider electing to come under the provisions of the 1976 law.

The law makes the process for electing very easy. A nonprofit's governing body—that is, its executive committee, board of directors, other representatives, or total membership, according to the constitution or bylaws of the particular nonprofit—may elect to have the organization come under the law. An authorized officer or trustee signs the one-page Internal Revenue Service Form 5768 and checks the box marked "Election." Regardless of the actual date of election, the nonprofit is considered to have come under the provisions of the law as of the start of the tax year during which it files the election.

The nonprofit automatically continues under the provisions of the 1976 law unless it chooses to revoke that election. It can do that by having its governing body vote on revocation and by having an authorized officer or trustee sign another Form 5768. The revocation becomes effective at the start of the tax year that follows the date of the revocation. In other words, revocation can only be prospective.

A new nonprofit may elect to come under the lobby law even before it is determined to be eligible by the IRS and may start lobbying immediately. It simply submits Form 5768 at the time it submits its "Application for Recognition of Exemption" (Form 1023). The nonprofit's employer identification number, which is requested at the top of the form, is listed on the nonprofit's "Employer Quarterly Federal Tax Return" (Form 941).

One final important note: some nonprofits have been reluctant to come under the 1976 lobby law for fear that taking this action will serve as a red flag to the IRS and prompt an audit of lobbying activities. Fortunately, this is not the case. In a June 2000 letter to Charity Lobbying in the Public Interest, the IRS stated, "The Internal Revenue Service Manual specifically informs our examination personnel that making the election will not be a basis for initiating an audit." (Information letter is available at www.clpi.org. or by calling CLPI at 202-387-5048.) When Congress was debating the 1976 lobby law, before its enactment, there was clear evidence that Congress fully intended the law to encourage nonprofits to lobby and not to discourage them by singling them out for audit. These facts should reassure nonprofit groups that they will not be targeted for lobbying audits if they elect to be covered under the 1976 law.

SUMMARY

The programs and funding of services of particular interest to nonprofits are closely linked to the decisions of legislatures and government executive offices in Washington, D.C., and in state capitals, city councils, and county seats throughout the nation. It is very important, therefore, that volunteers and staff of nonprofits understand how to affect the outcome of those decisions and how lobbying can open that door.

To get started lobbying, you need to know only a little about the lobbying process, organizing your group's government relations committee, setting up a legislative network, and the law governing lobbying by nonprofits. Also, it is important to have the help of a volunteer or staff person who has at least a rudimentary understanding of basic lobbying techniques and the lobbying process as well as nonprofit organizing skills. A number of publications provide helpful information regarding the nonprofit lobbying process and the law affecting such lobbying.

The information provided in this chapter on the lobbying latitude under the law is somewhat complex and may tend to discourage those who think they must understand it before they start lobbying. In all candor, you really don't have to master the information. It is provided more as a useful resource than as a mountain you must climb before you can safely enter the lobbying arena. The main point is that the 1976 lobby law provides extraordinarily generous nonprofit lobbying limits—more than ninety-nine out of a hundred organizations that lobby will ever need or want. So don't be put off by the somewhat complex information regarding the law. Go ahead. Get started, and keep in mind that lobbying is often a nonprofit's best service.

References

Avner, M. *The Lobbying and Advocacy Handbook for Nonprofit Organizations.* Saint Paul, Minn.: Amherst H. Wilder Foundation, 2002.

Center on Nonprofits and Philanthropy at the Urban Institute. "Quick Facts on Lobbying Data for 501(c)(3) Nonprofit Organizations." [http://www.urban.org/advocacyresearch/data_findings.html]. 1999.

Coalition of National Voluntary Organizations (CONVO) and National Council on Philanthropy (NCOP). "Background Information and Initial Statements by John W. Gardner and Brian O'Connell." Press release, Nov. 29, 1978.

INDEPENDENT SECTOR. *Giving and Volunteering in the United States, 2001.* Washington, D.C.: INDEPENDENT SECTOR, 2002.

INDEPENDENT SECTOR and Urban Institute. *The New Nonprofit Alamanac and Desk Reference: The Essential Facts and Figures for Managers, Researchers, and Volunteers.* San Francisco: Jossey-Bass, 2002.

Meredith, J. C., and Dunham, C. M. *Real Clout: A How-To Manual for Community Activists Trying to Expand Healthcare Access by Changing Public Policy.* Boston: Access Project, 1999.

OMB Watch. "Strengthening Nonprofit Advocacy Project (SNAP): Overview of Findings: Executive Summary." [http://www.npaction.org/article/articleview/136/1/184]. May 31, 2002.

Pertschuck, M. *The Giant Killers.* New York: Norton, 1986.

Redman, E. *The Dance of Legislation.* New York: Simon & Schuster, 1973.

Sherry, P. H. "America's Third Force." *Journal of Current Social Issues,* 1970, *9,* 2–3.

Smucker, B. *The Nonprofit Lobbying Guide.* (2nd ed.) Washington, D.C.: INDEPENDENT SECTOR, 1999.

Wirth, T. E. "The Need for Philanthropic Advocacy." Paper presented at the Global Philanthropy Forum Conference on Borderless Giving, Stanford, Calif., June 6, 2003.

CHAPTER ELEVEN

Strategic Alliances

John A. Yankey
Carol K. Willen

T he last quarter of the twentieth century was a time of dramatic growth and change in the U.S. nonprofit sector. Between 1977 and 1997, nonprofit revenue increased at nearly twice the growth rate of the economy as whole, and the number of 501(c)(3) and 501(c)(4) organizations registered with the Internal Revenue Service rose 115 percent. Although government assistance accounts for a substantial portion of this income, fee and service-charge revenue was the primary source of growth (Salamon, 2002), for it was during this period that nonprofit organizations became more active in seeking commercial or earned income. During the same period, for-profit entities advanced more aggressively into areas that had traditionally been the preserve of nonprofits. Social service agencies and health care providers, the first wave of public-benefit organizations to undergo what Salamon (1993) has termed "marketization," soon found themselves engaged in intense competition with businesses, as well as with other nonprofits. Faced with these new economic realities, health and human service organizations began forming alliances in order to respond to community needs and ensure their own institutional viability (Bailey and Koney, 2000).

The authors gratefully acknowledge the assistance and technical expertise of Michelle Gayles.

The trend toward partnering that arose in these fields in the 1980s was the harbinger of a new era in the history of the nonprofit sector. Following the lead of health care providers and social service agencies, nonprofits in other subsectors soon adopted the practice of developing alliances as a way of addressing competitive forces and challenges in their own fields. New types of relationships began to emerge as organizations devised creative ways of building capacity; sharing costs, benefits, and risks; achieving synergies; competing successfully; accomplishing common goals; and fulfilling their individual missions. McLaughlin (1998), arguing that the focus of innovation in the nonprofit world is shifting from programs and services to management, perceives that for nonprofit organizations of all types, exploring and developing mergers and other alliances will be "the new strategic planning for the 21st century" (p. xxii). The implications of this change in managerial thinking transcend sectoral boundaries, as evidenced in Salamon's assessment of trends and challenges in the coming years. He calls for "an explicit acknowledgment of the modern reality of collaborative problem-solving, of *nonprofit organizations working collaboratively with government and the business sector to respond to societal needs*" (Salamon, 1999, p. 179, emphasis in the original).

DRIVING FORCES OF STRATEGIC ALLIANCE FORMATION

Strategic alliances come into being for a host of reasons, variously referred to as "driving forces," "drivers," or "motivations." Some authors emphasize conditions in the external environment that provide impetus for the formation of alliances, while others focus on the individual organization's internal rationale for seeking the benefits of partnering. Both sets of causes are important, and in some instances, an external force and an internal motive may be viewed as two ways of describing the same reality. Understanding the context for strategic alliance development requires examining *environmental* issues and trends as well as intraorganizational factors—*financial, managerial,* and *programmatic* considerations—for the kind of thinking required of nonprofit leaders and managers when contemplating an alliance is closely related to the process of strategic planning (Arsenault, 1998).

Environmental Drivers

Turbulent is a term frequently used to characterize the environment in which nonprofit organizations must operate. Powerful forces such as new technologies, globalization, regionalization, increased competition, the redefinition of performance, and the demand for greater accountability, along with other social, political, and cultural shifts, have affected government, business, and nonprofit organizations alike (Fosler, 2002). Besides competing for consumer attention and market share, nonprofits must vie for a limited, if not diminishing, pool of human and financial resources.

Changes in the funding climate are critically important environmental factors. The flow of public dollars has shifted, government support has diminished, and private funding for nonprofits has become harder to come by. The economic downturn of recent years has led to a shrinkage of foundation endowments and a drop in corporate profits, resulting in lower contribution levels and more intense competition for scarce resources. Both public and private funders, intent on achieving maximum impact with finite resources while simultaneously promoting nonprofit efficiency and effectiveness, have encouraged, or even pressured, organizations to form alliances.

Another driving force is the performance culture that arose in the business world and has since spread to the public and nonprofit sectors (Fosler, 2002). Government interest in managed care and the adoption of a system of outcome assessment by United Way of America are but two examples of the growing emphasis on results. Private funders, too, are calling for evidence of a return on investment, establishing evaluation criteria for grants and tying future allocation decisions to the attainment of performance standards.

Political pressures and other dynamics in the external environment may influence strategic alliance formation by causing organizations to reposition themselves. For example, proposed legislative, regulatory, or policy changes that may adversely affect a group of organizations, their funding, their tax-exempt status, or the population or cause that they serve can drive like-minded nonprofits to align themselves in coalitions so as to focus their advocacy efforts more effectively. Finally, real or perceived external threats, such as the discovery or the perception that funders are reevaluating their own strategic directions, may trigger preemptive actions on the part of nonprofits.

Internal Drivers

Because of the ominous implications of some of these external forces, it would not be difficult to conclude that alliance formation is tantamount to circling the wagons. However, by behaving *strategically*—that is, by joining together intentionally with one or more carefully selected partners—an organization can exercise a substantial measure of control over its own destiny. There are many benefits, both individual and collective, to be gained through involvement in such alliances. As positive motivations for alliance participation, these considerations provide the internal rationale that a nonprofit might use to explain or justify its actions to stakeholders. Yankey, Jacobus, and Koney (2001) categorize these driving forces as *financial, managerial,* or *programmatic.*

Financial drivers are among the most frequently cited reasons for pursuing a strategic alliance. By partnering, nonprofits can often achieve greater efficiency through economies of scale, gain access to increased (or more reliable or stable) external funding, leverage their strengths to increase purchasing power, obtain a better return on investment, improve cash flow, and enhance their bottom line.

Closely related to the financial forces that give impetus to alliance formation are the *managerial* drivers. Alliance participation enables nonprofits to acquire intellectual capital, expertise, and professional competencies, thus enriching their human resources. In addition, organizations can strengthen their strategic positions, solidify their service niche, gain increased visibility, and expand political influence.

The final set of organizational drivers is *programmatic* in nature. Here the focus is on the "deliverables"—the organization's products and services. Partnering enables participating organizations to improve the quality of their offerings, diversify or expand their product or service mix, and extend their geographical market. In this way, strategic alliances help organizations realize their missions and at the same time demonstrate a commitment to social responsibility (Bailey and Koney, 2000). Finally, such alliances offer the potential for significant public benefit, for they build community capacity as well as organizational capacity and provide a way of ensuring the survival and increasing the availability of valued and important programs and services.

STRATEGIC ALLIANCES DEFINED

Strategic alliances, the planned relationships discussed in this chapter, are generally understood to be capacity-building mechanisms that enable partnering entities to achieve results exceeding those that might be attained on the basis of each participant's individual resources and efforts. Within this broad context, the partners can align themselves in any number of ways and with varying degrees of integration—an array of possible models ranging from the loosely connected to the highly integrated.

The absence of a standard lexicon and a generally accepted theoretical base presents challenges for those who would seek to define and categorize such arrangements. *Strategic alliances* and *strategic restructuring* are names frequently applied to relationships between nonprofit partners working together toward a common goal, although some authors, such as McLaughlin (1998) and Mattessich, Murray-Close, and Monsey (2001) employ *collaboration* as the all-encompassing term. Austin (2000), focusing on partnering between nonprofits and businesses, speaks of both strategic alliances and strategic collaborations.

For some authors, the choice of the adjective *strategic* underscores the purposeful quality of relationships in which two or more entities come together to accomplish a mutually valued goal. For example, Bailey and Koney (2000), in defining strategic alliances, emphasize their intentional quality. Fosler

(2002), whose focus is *intersectoral* collaboration involving government, business, and nonprofit organizations, speaks of "consciously undertaken joint activity among entities that would not ordinarily be expected to work intentionally together" (p. 19).

However, just as there is no consensus on the selection of an all-encompassing name for partnering relationships, there is no common nomenclature for the types of arrangements or structures that can be formed. Identical terms are employed by various authors to mean different things. One author may have a narrow technical, legal, or financial definition in mind, while another may employ the same word as it is used in everyday parlance. Furthermore, a term used in an overarching sense by one author may, in the lexicon of another, refer to a specific strategic alliance type. For example, while McLaughlin (1998) and Mattessich, Murray-Close, and Monsey (2001) use *collaboration* as a general term encompassing the full array of alliance configurations, Bailey and Koney (2000) use it to refer to one of four different "strategic alliance processes," specifically, a process in which the partners are united by a common strategy, as in the case of consortia, networks, and joint ventures. For La Piana (1999), collaboration is *not* considered to be a form of strategic restructuring; moreover, in the Partnership Matrix (see Figure 11.1), "strategic alliance" simply refers to one of two primary kinds of strategic restructuring.

Conceptual variations underlie the linguistic issues that make efforts at comparison difficult. A number of researchers and practitioners have created frameworks for organizing and categorizing alliance arrangements by type, but these frameworks reflect somewhat different perspectives. What is most important at this juncture is the recognition that both within the nonprofit world itself and across the sometimes blurry boundaries of the nonprofit, corporate, and public sectors, entities of various types are partnering with increasing frequency in order to achieve mission enhancement and greater organizational effectiveness.

TYPES OF STRATEGIC ALLIANCES

As indicated, *strategic alliance, collaboration,* and *strategic restructuring* are terms frequently used by those who have conducted research in this area to describe intentional relationships aimed at maximizing the use of resources to advance the mission and goals of the organizational participants.

The various types of strategic alliances are typically arrayed along a continuum of progressively increasing levels of formalization or integration (Bailey and Koney, 2000) or mutual involvement (Girls Scouts of the USA, 1997). In their representation of strategic alliance options, Yankey, Jacobus, and Koney

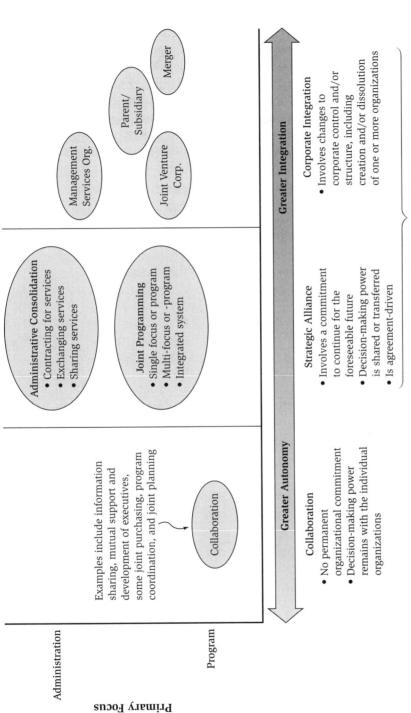

Figure 11.1. The Partnership Matrix.

Source: David La Piana. Copyright © 1999 by La Piana Associates, Inc.

(2001) associate the degree of autonomy relinquished with a concomitant level of risk, while Arsenault (1998), in a pyramid depicting what is termed the Consolidation Continuum, incorporates three factors: autonomy, risk, and cost.

Figure 11.2 is a useful device for graphically depicting and differentiating alliance types proposed by various authors along parallel continua. The range of mutual involvement described by the national organization Girl Scouts of the USA (1997) identifies a series of key elements that are represented in the strategic alliances continuum. As one moves to the right on the continuum, incremental changes occur along seven dimensions:

- The intensity, scope, and duration of the joint efforts increase.
- There is greater unity of mission and purpose.
- The legal linkage of the organizations tends to become more complex and permanent.
- A greater amount of authority is ceded to the alliance.
- A higher degree of trust is necessary.
- A greater measure of change is required.
- The potential for resistance increases.

Cross-sectoral strategic alliances can be characterized in a similar manner. Austin (2000, p. 35), writing of collaboration between nonprofits and businesses, depicts a continuum reflecting progressive movement along the following dimensions:

- Level of engagement
- Importance to mission
- Magnitude of resources
- Scope of activities
- Interaction level
- Managerial complexity
- Strategic value

Each of the frameworks shown in Figure 11.2 seeks to encompass virtually every type of strategic alliance. Due in large measure to the absence of a generally accepted terminology and classification system, each framework uses a somewhat different set of names for the types that are displayed. In instances where the same word or phrase appears in more than one framework, its placement on each of the continua may be different.

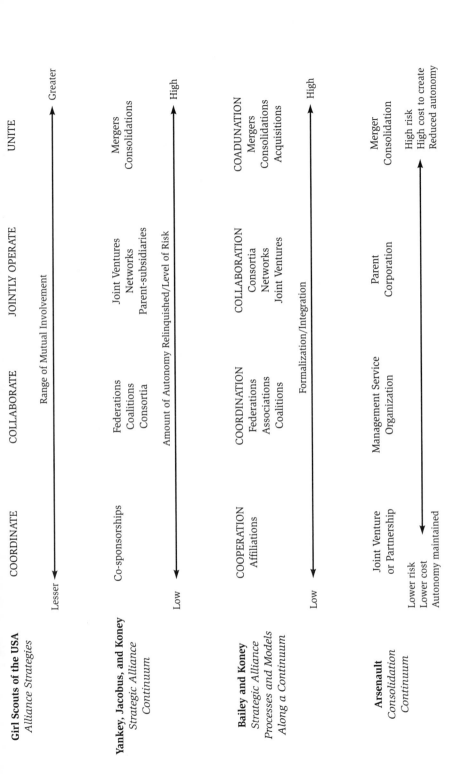

Figure 11.2. Strategic Alliance Continua.

Sources: Girl Scouts of the USA, 1997, pp. 13–14; Yankey, Jacobus, and Koney, 2001, p. 6; Bailey and Koney, 2000, pp. 9–10 (Copyright © 2000 by Sage Publications, Inc.); Arsenault, 1998, p. 34. Reprinted by permission of Sage Publications, Inc.

STAGES OF STRATEGIC ALLIANCE DEVELOPMENT

Despite the challenges posed by differences in language and taxonomy, one finds striking similarities among various descriptions of the stages of development of strategic alliances. Although scholars and practitioners who have written most recently on this topic have applied a variety of names to the evolutionary stages of alliance development—and have divided the process into differing numbers of steps—there is a consistency to the way in which they portray the sequence and nature of these stages. Commonalities among authors who envision a four-stage approach are apparent in Figure 11.3.

Every alliance, regardless of type, follows a "developmental path" that begins with one or more individuals conceiving of the possibility of partnering. Regardless of how it is labeled, the initial stage typically involves the following activities:

- Self-examination on the part of at least one organization (sometimes conducted in conjunction with a strategic planning process)

- A decision to explore the possibility of an alliance

	1	2	3	4
Girl Scouts of the USA	Exploration	Planning	Implementation and Integration	Evaluation
Yankey, Jacobus, and Koney	Making Decisions	Planning	Implementation	Reviewing or Evaluating
Bailey and Koney	Assembling	Ordering	Performing	Transforming
La Piana	Inspiration	Formalization	Operation	Institutionalization or Termination
Austin	Making the Connection	Ensuring Strategic Fit	Generating Value	Managing the Relationship

Figure 11.3. Stages of Strategic Alliance Development.

Sources: Girl Scouts of the USA, 1998, pp. 14–18; Yankey, Jacobus, and Koney, 2001, p. 17; Singer and Yankey, 1991, p. 358; Bailey and Koney, 2000, p. 33; La Piana, 2001, p. 7; Austin, 2000, pp. 41–146.

- Identification of potential partners
- Initial contacts between representatives of the organizations
- Efforts to assess the degree of mutual interest

Before the parties agree to form an alliance, they must learn more about each other. The process known as "side-by-side analysis" entails the joint development of full-blown organizational profiles (Yankey, Jacobus, and Koney, 2001). Dimensions investigated include mission, vision, values, organizational culture, governance, programs and services, human resources (both paid and volunteer), facilities and equipment, financial management, fund development, and communications. In less formal alliance types in which the parties surrender very little autonomy, prospective partners do not ordinarily take the time to scrutinize one another's operations in minute detail. However, the more highly integrated the proposed alliance type and the more permanent the relationship is intended to be, the more important it is to do a multifaceted examination of the potential partner's background, current situation, and future potential. Although the phrase "due diligence" is sometimes used to refer in a broad sense to the systematic examination of a potential partner's operations (McLaughlin, 1998), as if it were synonymous with "side-by-side analysis," the primary foci of a due diligence investigation are the legal status and financial condition of the organizations (Bailey and Koney, 2000). When viewed in this narrower context, due diligence represents the final step in the exploratory process and entails careful scrutiny by attorneys and accountants.

Although experts may differ in drawing the boundaries between the stages of development, the second stage generally begins when the organizations, having agreed to engage in a strategic alliance, begin to formalize their relationship. A negotiation process, often involving legal counsel, culminates in an agreement. Depending on the alliance type, this may be as simple as a memorandum of understanding or as complex as a full set of legal documents detailing the dissolution of a number of nonprofit corporations and the creation of a new one. In this stage, future partners also focus their attention on "operational issues involving the differentiation and integration of systems, strategies, and structure" (Bailey and Koney, 2000, p. 42) as they plan how the alliance will function. It is also important at this point that the partners determine the criteria and measures that will be used to gauge the success of the newly formed alliance.

The third stage of the four-stage process is marked by the transition from planning to action as the alliance begins to operate. This stage has been variously titled "implementation" (Singer and Yankey, 1991), "implementation and integration" (Girl Scouts of the USA, 1998), "performing" (Bailey and Koney, 2000), and "operation" (La Piana, 2001). Systems and procedures designed by the planners are now activated. As those who are performing the work of the alliance discover areas that require fine-tuning, modifications may be made.

During the implementation stage, the anticipated benefits of the alliance begin to accrue to the participants. Data gathered on activities and their outcomes will lay the groundwork for the next stage, which involves reflection and evaluation.

In the fourth and final stage, the partners assess the experience of the alliance to date and determine how to proceed in the future. If an evaluation of the track record shows that the alliance has been generally successful, the participants may agree to continue along established lines, or they may modify the nature of the arrangement to ensure even greater effectiveness, take measures to make it more permanent, or seek additional resources to expand it programmatically or geographically. Alternatively, this review may lead to the conclusion that the alliance has *not* achieved the anticipated results and should therefore be disbanded. La Piana, in *Real Collaboration* (2001), therefore refers to the final stage as "institutionalization or termination."

The work of Austin (2000), who examines strategic alliances between non-profit organizations and businesses, offers an interesting set of parallels to this four-stage process. In language characteristic of the field of *for-profit* management, he speaks of making the connection with the right organizational partner; ensuring strategic fit by aligning mission, strategy, and values and achieving environmental (as well as organizational) fit; generating value, thus providing benefits to the participants as well as to society as a whole; and managing the relationship to ensure sustainability through the continued generation of value (pp. 16–17).

Although this four-stage process provides a useful conceptual framework, it is not the only way to describe the sequence of steps in alliance formation. Although McCormick, in *Nonprofit Mergers* (2001), does not speak of stages per se, he suggests a similar sequence of activities through chapter titles such as "Deciding to Merge," "Selecting a Merger Partner," "Laying the Groundwork with Staff and Volunteers," "Negotiating and Determining Structure," "Transitioning to Merge," and "Evaluation and Stewardship."

Even among those who segment the process into a greater number of steps, the flow of activities is comparable. For example, McLaughlin (1998) identifies seven tasks of alliance development, referring to each activity as a stage. Fosler (2002), who explores boundary-spanning alliances involving government, business, and nonprofit organizations, identifies seven elements of cross-sector collaboration that in some respects parallel the tasks of alliance development cited by McLaughlin.

However helpful it may be to portray alliance formation as a series of stages, any linear representation is an oversimplification. As Bailey and Koney (2000) note, the process, although evolutionary, is also iterative, and "the fact that an alliance has been together for a long time does not necessarily mean that it will have reached a late phase of development" (p. 32). As in all human interactions, an element of unpredictability is ever-present, for the path taken by the participants as they journey toward alliance formation is influenced not only by environmental factors and intra- and interorganizational considerations but also by interpersonal dynamics. David Bergholz, the recently retired executive director of the George Gund Foundation, wisely observes that deliberations having to do with alliance exploration and development can be nothing short of high drama (personal communication, Aug. 4, 2003).

The complexity and challenge of these endeavors, particularly the intricacy and delicacy of interorganizational negotiations, should not be underestimated. Throughout the strategic alliance formation process, measures must be taken to build trust among the participants. Some phases require confidentiality, while others call for communication; and determining what to communicate, when, and to whom can be of critical importance. External assistance, which can be extremely valuable in a variety of areas, is virtually imperative in the more technical aspects of alliance development. Unbiased consultants with specialized expertise can be engaged to conduct research and gather data, facilitate the process, and offer advice on public relations and communication strategies. Professionals such as attorneys and certified public accountants, particularly those whose practice focuses on the nonprofit sector, can play an indispensable role, most notably during the due diligence step, in ensuring that the partnering organizations do not encounter avoidable problems of a legal or financial nature.

PARTNER SELECTION

Once a nonprofit organization has identified reasons to explore the possibility of forming a strategic alliance, the most critical decision to be made is the selection of one or more potential partners. In some instances, this may be a simple matter of turning to a known entity with which one's own organization has had a successful partnering experience. An existing arrangement can also evolve into one that is more fully integrated. For example, organizations engaged in a loose affiliation may decide to further intensify and more completely formalize their relationship—or to create a new one. Such variations in the prototypical alliance formation process help reinforce the point that any representation of a stage-by-stage linear sequence can only be considered a framework for understanding the vagaries of these interorganizational dynamics.

Yankey, Jacobus, and Koney (2001) explain how to initially assess the degree of fit between one's own organization and other nonprofits. Although the following set of considerations was developed for use in evaluating the attractiveness of potential merger partners, a number of items on this comprehensive checklist pertain to other forms of proposed alliances as well. Given the variability and distinctiveness of individual alliance situations, it must be emphasized that determining what makes for the most effective matches is not an exact science. These elements should therefore be regarded as considerations rather than criteria:

- History of previous relationships
- Mission and values compatibility
- Consistency of vision of future direction
- Receptivity to giving up some degree of autonomy
- Program strengths and weaknesses (The potential for success is enhanced when the strengths of one partner compensate for the weaknesses of another.)
- Organizational size (There is no convincing evidence of a positive correlation between the relative sizes of the prospective partners and the likelihood of alliance success; moreover, the optimal size relationship may vary from one type of strategic alliance to another.)
- Complementarity of organizational culture
- Board and trustee compatibility
- Organizational management and staff leadership
- Human resource integration complexities
- Potential for operating efficiencies
- Financial status (including endowments and cash reserves)
- Predicted long-term survival
- Funders' support of partnership
- Community and stakeholder perceptions
- Other special assets

McCormick (2001) also focuses on mergers when enumerating factors that bear on the choice of a potential partner. He articulates four possible types of connection that can help lay the foundation for future success: mission relatedness, organizational relatedness, constituency relatedness, and geographical relatedness.

Regardless of the type of strategic alliance being explored, there are ways in which the respective parties can ensure that their best interests, both individually and collectively, will be served. During exploratory negotiations, individual organizations should "read the signs," states Arsenault (1998), and use impressions gleaned by their representatives to "draw conclusions about the [potential] success of the relationship based on the observed behavior or unspoken messages from members of the other team" (pp. 101, 103). They can also make a conscious effort to build trust so that the potential partners are willing to discuss the proposed alliance and their qualifications for participation both candidly and completely. Underscoring the relationship between trust and the partner selection process, Yankey, Jacobus, and Koney (2001) observe that the level of trust between organizational leaders influences not only which organizations are approached as potential alliance partners but also the final decision about whether to proceed.

CHALLENGES TO STRATEGIC ALLIANCE FORMATION AND IMPLEMENTATION

Creating strategic alliances is both an art and a science. Although every situation is different—and the influence of intangibles is often difficult to anticipate— there are clearly identifiable challenges to the formation and implementation of alliances as well as a number of proven factors that foster success.

The literature reveals general agreement among authors with regard to the primary challenges facing organizations that elect to enter into a partnering relationship. These include the following:

• *Incompatible mission, vision, and values.* The conditions for alliance formation and operation are unfavorable when the parties are divided by substantial ideological differences, a history of disagreement, or debates that leave little room for flexibility.

• *Egos.* Both the egos of individual leaders and the generally positive tendency of group members to demonstrate pride in their own team can be sources of active or passive resistance to alliance formation (McLaughlin, 1998).

• *Turf issues.* Organizational "turf issues" can be a major obstacle. An agency that perceives itself to be preeminent in a specific domain because of its size, scope, or program quality may expect to play a dominant role in the new configuration and may be less likely to treat potential partners as equals. Failure to place the partners' shared mission and the good of the community above loyalty to one's own agency will imperil the alliance.

• *Cost: time required.* Alliance formation requires a significant amount of two precious commodities, time and money. Whereas less formal alliances can be mounted or disbanded fairly quickly, more complex alliances may require twelve to eighteen months from the moment of their conception to the date on which they become operational.

• *Cost: funds required.* The more integrated the alliance, the more expensive it will be to develop and implement. Expenditures will frequently be required for facilitation, organizational analyses, and due diligence (legal fees, financial auditing, and so on). The expenses do not stop there. Opportunity costs may be involved as well because substantial amounts of energy, attention, and time are likely to be directed to the development of the relationship between the partnering organizations, possibly at the expense of programmatic activities or adminis-trative functions. Once a merger or consolidation is up and running, costs may be incurred for any or all of the following: accrued salaries, severance pay, legal judgments, systems integration (management information systems, human re-sources, payroll, fund development, and so on), lease-related payments, mort-gage financing, new taxes, signage, printing, and promotional and public relations materials to reposition the entity in the marketplace.

• *Cultural differences.* The role of cultural differences between organizations is of major importance. Most of the authors writing about alliance formation and implementation emphasize both the importance and the magnitude of this challenge. Cartwright and Cooper (1996) have shown that rumors or an-nouncements of impending alliances raise concerns and cause stress for em-ployees as they begin to anticipate the changes in culture that they may experience and the impact of the new organizational structure on their careers. As Arsenault (1998) indicates, although certain parallels can be drawn between for-profit and nonprofit consolidations, cultural integration poses a special set of challenges for nonprofits. Because nonprofits typically use volunteers as well as paid personnel, human resource issues are more complex. Moreover, as value-driven entities operating in a world of intangibles, nonprofits employ many well-educated people in nonroutine jobs who perform their work with higher degrees of individual autonomy than their counterparts in the corporate world (Arsenault, 1998). Failure to correctly assess one's own organizational culture and that of potential partners, coupled with inattention to the need for cultural integration, can endanger board and staff morale and jeopardize the success of a strategic alliance.

Other concerns stem from fears of perceived threats to personal and profes-sional security or, at the institutional level, the potential loss of independence, control, identity, volunteers, funding, or public support. Such fears are often the result of misapprehensions or misperceptions. They rest on assumptions that are partly, if not completely, erroneous, such as the following:

• Organizational survival should be pursued at any cost.
• To be viable, an organization must remain totally independent.
• Joining an alliance is tantamount to going out of business.
• An organization loses everything by giving up its name.
• The safest course is to preserve the status quo.
• Reductions in force are inevitable.
• Public and philanthropic support will necessarily erode.

Accurate information is often the best way to dispel personal concerns and over-come sources of organized resistance.

FACTORS CONTRIBUTING TO ALLIANCE SUCCESS

The likelihood of alliance success is influenced by many factors, but there is broad agreement on those that appear to be among the most important. Although these consistently recurring themes are described in the literature in different terms, they include a shared vision, a sound process, open communication, an atmosphere of trust, effective leadership, and hard work.

Shared Vision

The possibility of success is greatly enhanced when there is clarity of purpose and a congruency of mission, strategy, and values (Austin, 2000). Strategic alliances enable the partnering organizations to harness their collective resources and capacities in the pursuit of a mutually desired outcome. Because organizations with varying missions may be drawn together for different reasons, it is vital that they agree on a shared vision and purpose and develop a set of concrete, attainable goals and objectives (Mattessich, Murray-Close, and Monsey, 2001). Both the aspirations and the limitations of the partnering arrangement must be clearly articulated and mutually understood.

Sound Process

The process through which the alliance is developed and operationalized has a significant impact on the likelihood of its success. Care must be taken to ensure that the strengths and contributions of all parties are recognized and validated and that more powerful organizations and individuals do not suppress the views of others. A skilled convener (Mattessich, Murray-Close, and Monsey, 2001) or an external facilitator can help create an environment that is conducive to success by streamlining management of the process and reducing feelings of anxiety and uncertainty (Arsenault, 1998). Based on their review of the research literature, Mattessich, Murray-Close, and Monsey (2001) recommend that alliance members share in both the process and the outcome, that clear roles and policy guidelines be developed, and that there be multiple layers of decision making. Continual learning, which Austin (2000) considers essential to the success of collaborations between nonprofits and businesses, is applicable to intrasectoral alliances as well.

Open Communication

Honest and open communication is consistently cited as a critical element of successful partnering (La Piana and Kohm, 2003; Yankey, Jacobus, and Koney, 2001; Mattessich, Murray-Close, and Monsey, 2001; Austin, 2000). The sharing of accurate and objective information by potential partners, including the disclosure of negative as well as positive features of each organization, enables board and staff members to make sound, reasoned, and clear-sighted judgments about the benefits and risks of entering an alliance. Creating and adhering to a communication plan will enable the prospective partners to keep key internal and external stakeholders apprised of developments in a timely fashion and will help ensure that an appropriate level of confidentiality is maintained.

Atmosphere of Trust

Trust, perceived by some as the "glue" of strategic alliances, is based on shared expectations, mutual obligations, and a commitment to accountability—as well as a recognition of possible risk (Yankey, Jacobus, and Koney, 2001). The establishment of trust promotes successful alliance development by helping lower the barriers between individuals and organizations, foster the growth of positive relationships, discourage hidden agendas, and promote good-faith negotiations. In a climate of mutual respect, understanding, and trust (Mattessich, Murray-Close, and Monsey, 2001), prospective partners are better able to take the leap of faith that entering into an alliance requires and better prepared to manage the challenges that will inevitably arise during implementation. Since trust involves disclosure and consultation, open and candid communication is essential to its development (McLaughlin, 1998).

Effective Leadership

Successful alliances cannot be created without strong and effective leadership on the part of at least one of the partnering organizations. Every alliance needs to be championed by individuals who are capable of articulating a vision and inspiring others to follow. Leaders set the tone for their coworkers and colleagues (including board members) by modeling such behaviors as mutual respect, candor, fairness, and flexibility. They convene and guide the teams that will develop and operationalize the alliance, continually promoting the concept of mission-focused rather than ego-based decisions (La Piana and Kohm, 2003).

Hard Work

The formation of a strategic alliance is a labor-intensive undertaking, and there is a great deal of hard work to be done at each stage of the process. The initial spark—the inspiration for partnering—may be kindled during the intensive organizational self-examination and thorough, extensive environmental scanning performed in conjunction with a strategic planning exercise. The exploration and assessment of various options, the identification of potential partners, and the investigation of their suitability through a side-by-side analysis and a due diligence examination are research steps that require considerable effort and care.

After the organizations agree to formalize their relationship, they must negotiate arrangements, define a structure, and resolve operational issues relating to systems and procedures. Personnel, facilities, and technology must be addressed, along with internal and external communications. Mutually understood expectations need to be articulated and an evaluation mechanism established. Once implementation begins, the delivery of programs and services must be monitored and evaluated so that a decision to maintain, modify, or terminate the alliance at some future time can be made on the basis of sound data.

In summary, throughout the process, either the prospective partners or their agents must perform essential activities such as research, analysis, planning, monitoring, and assessment. The hard work that is a necessary condition for strategic alliance success clearly demands energy and commitment as well as time and other resources.

LESSONS FROM THE FIELD

The key components of success—a shared vision, a sound process, open communication, an atmosphere of trust, effective leadership, and hard work—are important considerations for nonprofits that are contemplating the possibility of entering into a strategic alliance. In addition to the lessons implicitly contained in these success factors, much wisdom is to be gleaned from the experience and observations of practitioners. The following insights and recommendations, representing "a view from the field" (Yankey, Jacobus, and Koney, 2001), emerged from answers given by respondents from sixty-five organizations who participated in a national study of nonprofit strategic alliance development:

- There is no such thing as a "zero defects" strategic alliance.
- The size of a nonprofit organization is not correlated with its success.
- Organizations should proactively pursue strategic alliances rather than waiting to be pursued.
- Strategic alliances usually should not be presented as an approach or strategy that will yield short-term cost savings.
- The criteria and process for evaluating the success of a strategic alliance should be established prior to its implementation.
- Strategic alliances are often more successful when funders are partners and provide financial support for both planning and implementation.
- A change in leadership in one or more of the organizations may represent an opportune time for exploring a merger or consolidation.
- The challenges in creating a new corporate culture following a merger or consolidation can be more significant than the challenges presented in the exploring and planning phases of strategic alliance development.
- Merger and consolidation processes must include opportunities to grieve and to celebrate.

CONCLUSION

Strategic alliance development, implementation, and evaluation are fascinating and fertile areas for research and scholarly discourse that merit serious attention in the curricula of academic programs in nonprofit management as well as in executive education courses and leadership training. While the past decade has produced a virtual explosion of books and articles on nonprofit strategic alliances as well as a substantial body of work on partnering across sectoral boundaries, there is clearly a great deal more to be learned, particularly in the area of best practices. Agreement on a standard taxonomy—although it does not appear imminent—would foster the development of knowledge and facilitate its dissemination.

If strategic alliance formation is an accurate reflection of what Salamon (1999) has termed "the modern reality of collaborative problem-solving" in response to society's needs, there is every indication that the dynamic field of alliance development will continue to grow and evolve as leaders and managers seek creative ways of working together. New types of partnering arrangements will emerge, and the corpus of knowledge will expand as nonprofit organizations experiment with systems, structures, and strategies.

References

Arsenault, J. *Forging Nonprofit Alliances: A Comprehensive Guide to Enhancing Your Mission Through Joint Ventures and Partnerships, Management Service Organizations, Parent Corporations, and Mergers.* San Francisco: Jossey-Bass, 1998.

Austin, J. E. *The Collaboration Challenge: How Nonprofits and Businesses Succeed Through Strategic Alliances.* San Francisco: Jossey-Bass, 2000.

Bailey, D., and Koney, K. M. *Strategic Alliances Among Health and Human Services Organizations: From Affiliations to Consolidations.* Thousand Oaks, Calif.: Sage, 2000.

Cartwright, S., and Cooper, C. L. *Managing Mergers, Acquisitions, and Strategic Alliances: Integrating People and Cultures.* Oxford, England: Butterworth-Heinemann, 1996.

Fosler, R. S. *Working Better Together: How Government, Business, and Nonprofit Organizations Can Achieve Public Purposes Through Cross-Sector Collaboration, Alliances, and Partnerships.* Washington, D.C.: Three Sector Initiative, 2002.

Girl Scouts of the USA. *Exploring Strategic Alliances in Girl Scouting.* New York: Girl Scouts of the USA, 1997.

Girl Scouts of the USA. *Combining Our Strengths in Girl Scouting: Merger and Consolidation.* New York: Girl Scouts of the USA, 1998.

La Piana, D. "The Partnership Matrix." La Piana Associates [http://www.lapiana.org/defined/matrix.html]. 1999.

La Piana, D. *Real Collaboration: A Guide for Grantmakers.* New York: Ford Foundation, 2001.

La Piana, D., and Kohm, A. *In Search of Strategic Solutions: A Funders' Briefing on Nonprofit Strategic Restructuring.* Washington, D.C.: Grantmakers for Effective Organizations, 2003.

Mattessich, P. W., Murray-Close, M., and Monsey, B. R. *Collaboration: What Makes It Work.* (2nd ed.) Saint Paul, Minn.: Amherst H. Wilder Foundation, 2001.

McCormick, D. H. *Nonprofit Mergers: The Power of Successful Partnerships.* Gaithersburg, Md.: Aspen, 2001.

McLaughlin, T. A. *Nonprofit Mergers and Alliances: A Strategic Planning Guide.* New York: Wiley, 1998.

Salamon, L. M. "The Marketization of Welfare: Changing Nonprofit and For-Profit Roles in the American Welfare State." *Social Service Review,* 1993, *67,* 16–39.

Salamon, L. M. *America's Nonprofit Sector: A Primer.* (2nd ed.) New York: Foundation Center, 1999.

Salamon, L. M. (ed.). *The State of Nonprofit America.* Washington, D.C.: Brookings Institution Press, 2002.

Singer, M. I., and Yankey, J. A. "Organizational Metamorphosis: A Study of Eighteen Nonprofit Mergers, Acquisitions, and Consolidations." *Nonprofit Management and Leadership,* 1991, *1,* 357–369.

Yankey, J. A., Jacobus, B. W., and Koney, K. M. *Merging Nonprofit Organizations: The Art and Science of the Deal.* Cleveland, Ohio: Mandel Center for Nonprofit Organizations, 2001.

PART THREE

MANAGING OPERATIONS

I n developing programs and activities to achieve their missions, nonprofit leaders must organize exchanges with others, including (usually) volunteers, donors, clients or customers, and government officials. This range of exchanges represents the basic marketing relationships in which most nonprofit organizations engage. In Part Three, the first chapter describes the most important ways in which nonprofits can use marketing concepts and skills; two other chapters focus on the details of relationships with parties crucial to many nonprofit organizations. The chapter on volunteer programs examines the issues and choices nonprofit managers face in designing and carrying out volunteer service programs. The chapter on government contracting analyzes the effects of government contracting and describes ways in which nonprofit managers can more effectively manage exchanges with governments.

As various parties that engage in exchanges with nonprofit organizations have become increasingly concerned with accountability and evidence of performance, nonprofit organizations have been challenged to develop better ways to analyze program and organizational effectiveness. Though program and organizational effectiveness may frequently be related, they need not be. We think of program effectiveness as concerned with the extent to which a specific program (for example, increasing adult literacy or reducing child abuse) has had an effect. Organizational effectiveness is concerned with judgments about the overall performance of a nonprofit organization, typically including considerations of financial performance, community involvement, and other factors. One chapter in this part describes tools both to assess outcomes as well as more thoroughly evaluate programs. The chapter on organizational effectiveness reviews the substantial difficulties of organizational effectiveness evaluation as well as recent efforts to improve its practice, providing readers with a helpful assortment of approaches and cautions about the limitations of those approaches.

CHAPTER TWELVE

Marketing for Nonprofit Managers

Brenda Gainer
Mel S. Moyer

A ll around us we hear that consumers are changing, business is changing, the nature of work is changing, technology is changing, the economy is changing—the list goes on and on. Corporations are no longer making annual donations from a budget earmarked for charity but instead are looking for concrete evidence of a "return on their investment" in terms of sales and paying for this out of marketing budgets (Smith, 1994). Employees are changing too; more now work at home, change employers multiple times during their lives, and prefer to work as self-employed consultants. Individuals want more choice, more control, and more accountability, both in their capacity as users of the services of nonprofit organizations and as volunteers and donors. More people have access to and are comfortable with the Internet, opening opportunities for nonprofit organizations to cut communications costs but increasing their vulnerability to the importance of brand-name recognition in a crowded and increasingly competitive marketplace. Foundations and wealthy individuals are changing the way they do business with charities, adopting venture philanthropy models of seeking out opportunities to invest in new projects (Letts, Ryan, and Grossman,1997). Governments are cutting back funding that used to be transferred to nonprofit organizations at the same time as they cut back on welfare payments and other subsidies to the poor. New diseases, poverty, social problems, and environmental degradation continue to grow, increasing the demands on nonprofit organizations engaged in both service delivery and advocacy work.

In an era of increasing demand for service, crowded markets, declining sources of traditional support, and a rapidly changing social and economic environment, there is a growing interest in many nonprofit organizations in practices and ideas imported from the business sector (Siciliano, 1997). Nonprofit marketing, once considered controversial in the marketing literature and by many nonprofit managers, is now widely accepted as an effective management tool for nonprofit organizations (Sargeant, 2001). Most nonprofit organizations recognize the need to broaden their activities beyond the production of services or advocacy to focus on the clienteles they are trying to reach.

Nevertheless, while there is almost universal enthusiasm for the *idea* of marketing in the nonprofit sector, in many organizations, marketing continues to be understood primarily as "selling," and the activities associated with marketing continue to be mostly advertising, communications, and public relations tasks. Few organizations have an explicitly designated marketing department or director, and the marketing function continues to be divided among departments identified by such titles as communications, fundraising (development, advancement), public education, volunteer recruitment, or government relations, to name only a few. Despite the fact that marketing theory, research, and practice in the nonprofit sector have advanced considerably in the past decade, there is as yet little understanding in the nonprofit sector of the strategic, top-level role that marketing can play in achieving the overall goals of an organization through more explicit focus on its exchange relationships with its various stakeholders. It is the goal of this chapter to outline a basic theory of nonprofit marketing and then describe some of the marketing strategies and tactics that can lead to superior organizational performance in the nonprofit sector.

WHAT IS MARKETING?

For decades, marketing has been defined as the facilitation of exchange (Bagozzi, 1975). In this conceptualization, marketing is concerned with the relationships between, most obviously, an organization that produces products or services and the customers that pay for and use them. However, a focus on exchange also suggests that marketing is concerned with the relationships that link an organization to other publics such as donors, governments, media, taxpayers, other organizations, and—that most elusive market of all—"public opinion." In the nonprofit sector, marketing must be stretched to include relationships with all these key stakeholder groups.

Marketing is therefore understood not simply as the facilitation of the exchange of money for goods and services (its meaning in the private sector) but as the facilitation of exchanges that are often of a nonmonetary nature. This might, for example, involve an exchange transaction in which one party (donors, for example) offers money while the other offers something more amorphous or abstract like "a good feeling," a sense of community, or social prestige. Furthermore, the exchange could be nonmonetary in both directions, such as an organization involved in advocacy work that offers messages embodying new ideas to the public, some members of which change their attitudes and behaviors in return.

Moreover, nonprofit marketing encompasses not simply dyadic, or two-party, exchanges but multiparty exchange relationships that are much more complex than those characteristic of the private sector. A social service organization, for example, will exchange its services with a client group while another group of donors and funders provides the money to support the organization and its development of those services. Thus marketing for nonprofit organizations, unlike private sector marketing, which defines the market solely in terms of customers, is always focused on two major market constituencies, namely, the resource provision market (volunteers, donors, funders, government grantors) and the resource allocation market (clients, patients, students, legislators, the general public). An organization must manage its relationships in both of these basic markets simultaneously.

The complexity of an organization's marketing relationships in these markets will vary, depending on the organization's mission or mandate. For example, in social service organizations, marketing tasks might include attracting funding from government agencies and private donors as well as attracting clients for services and volunteers to help in service delivery. Arts and culture organizations will be concentrating on selling tickets to performances or exhibitions, attracting corporate sponsorships, raising funds from individuals, and obtaining government grants. Environmental organizations will be focused on persuading legislators to create or change laws while raising funds to pay for these advocacy efforts. Health care charities might be raising money from individuals while trying to interest scientists and medical researchers in a particular area of inquiry, advocating changes in public opinion or legislation, and perhaps attracting clients for services.

The focus on exchange as the basis of marketing has led a number of scholars to warn against interpreting this to mean a focus on individual transactions. In *transaction* marketing, the elements of the marketing mix are used to trigger an isolated transaction, whereas in *relationship* marketing, the long-term quality of the interface between the organization and the customer is paramount (Conway, 1997). It has been argued that transaction-based marketing and relationship marketing are ends of a continuum and that the particular characteristics of nonprofits mean that a focus on relationships is more appropriate (Brennan and Brady, 1999). Relationship marketing is based on the idea that a focus on the provision of continuous value to key constituencies will provide a more valuable set of exchanges with the organization over time than "losing" customers continually and having to develop new ones.

The most common application of this principle is in high-end fundraising, where relationships are assiduously cultivated and sustained, with the result that often extremely generous past donors make second and even third major gifts. This application of relationship marketing involves a great deal of personal contact, but an organization might apply the same principles to a direct mail fundraising campaign as well. Here there is not as much personal contact, but through personalization and continuous fostering of the relationship through newsletters, e-mails, or minor gifts between annual solicitations, a nonprofit can renew a donor at a fraction of the cost of the initial transaction. Relationship marketing would be equally effective applied to a service-providing nonprofit that wanted to build long-term goodwill in particular communities in which it wanted to locate halfway houses for released convicts, for example, or an advocacy organization that dealt with public issues where a loyal and strong public response would be needed on a frequent and immediate basis.

What marketing contributes to the management of all of these relationships is an understanding that they are based on mutually beneficial exchanges—and further that understanding the wants and needs of the exchange partners and being able to satisfy those needs, on a short- or long-term basis, is critical to a nonprofit organization's survival and success. The latter notion has been characterized as the marketing concept (Kotler and Armstrong, 1994).

The operationalization of the marketing concept in organizations has been described as a market orientation. Research in the private sector has demonstrated that higher levels of organizational orientation toward the market are associated with performance outcomes like return on investment (Narver and Slater, 1990; Kohli, Jaworski, and Kumar, 1993). Recent research on nonprofit sector organizations has shown that market orientation not only predicts success in attracting financial resources in nonprofit organizations but is also associated with other variables important in mission-driven organizations such as higher degrees of client satisfaction (Gainer and Padanyi, 2002). Sargeant, Foreman, and Liao (2002) have argued that although the marketing concept has relevance in the nonprofit sector, the characterization "societal orientation" is more accurate than "market orientation" when it comes to implementing marketing because nonprofit organizations must be oriented to many groups of key stakeholders as well as to society in general. Regardless of the terminology that is used, the marketing concept appears to be useful to nonprofit organizations by focusing attention on the importance of satisfying the needs of the multiple external constituencies with which they interact.

One of the problems with advocating the introduction of marketing theories and practice to nonprofit organizations, however, has traditionally been resistance on the part of employees and volunteers to the adoption of what they see as "Madison Avenue" values that are thought to conflict with the social, artistic, or environmental orientations of nonprofit organizations. Marketing has tended to be accepted faster in organizations that are heavily dependent on "sales revenue," such as the arts, or in the parts of organizations that are devoted to raising money, such as fundraising departments. One of the problems with this limited view of marketing, and the fact that marketing is often considered to be only a set of tactics with limited usefulness that might actually be dangerous if allowed to spread too widely within the organization, is that the potential value of thinking about satisfying multiple stakeholders needs at every level and in every department of the organization is lost. One of the purposes of this chapter is to demonstrate that marketing has strategic value to nonprofit organizations of all types in terms of enabling them to achieve goals that are much broader than the merely financial and are in fact intimately connected with the fundamental mandate of these mission-driven organizations. It will be seen that the adoption of a market orientation by nonprofit organizations is a way to *drive* the mission as opposed to detracting from it.

MARKETING STRATEGIES AND THE MARKETING MIX

To promote mutually beneficial exchanges with a large number of stakeholders, an organization must first understand its market or markets. Research, formal or informal, will be necessary to identify the potential groups the organization wants to interact with as well as to clarify what other organizations or alternatives may exist that also serve the needs of those clienteles. On the basis of this information and analysis, an organization will then be able to decide which groups it makes most sense to serve or to target, based on analysis of the possible clienteles, the alternatives that exist, the human and financial resources that are available to the organization, and its mission. Once these decisions have been made, an organization will then tailor its products, services, and messages, adjust its prices and delivery systems, and promote itself in ways that truly serve the exchange partners.

From this it can be seen that to create a fully professional marketing process, one conceived as the facilitation of exchange in all its dimensions, the nonprofit manager must develop a solid knowledge of the organization's external and internal capabilities and goals and must then blend its products, prices, promotions, and delivery systems into a "marketing mix" that meets the needs of both the organization and its target markets. (In what may be an excessive devotion to alliteration, marketers refer to "the four P's of the marketing mix"—"product, price, promotion, and place.")

THE ROLE OF MARKETING RESEARCH IN OUR UNDERSTANDING OF CONSUMER BEHAVIOR

If marketing is based on satisfying the needs of an organization's various clienteles, its plans must be grounded in a thorough understanding of these markets. Therefore, the manager must usually preface the crafting of marketing strategies by undertaking some form of marketing research.

Formal market investigations in nonprofit enterprises are quite rare. The reasons are several. One is management's belief that it already has an informed relationship with the populations it serves. This conviction is nourished by the fact that compared to private sector organizations, nonprofits often do seem to be closer to their clients or customers. For example, they tend to operate on a small scale in local markets (community centers, arts organizations, crisis counseling units), they frequently deal directly with end users rather than through intermediaries (vocational guidance programs, museums, religious organizations), and the interaction that results may furnish the service provider with substantial personal information about the clients (children's camps, marriage counseling, higher education). In these circumstances, marketing research may seem unnecessary.

And in other third-sector settings, market studies may appear unwarranted because the service deliverer seems to be in a better position than the user to specify the appropriate product. Thus when the "customer" is an emotionally disturbed child entering therapy, a recently released convict consigned to a halfway house, or a student confronting a curriculum, the service deliverer may see it as a right, even a duty, to prescribe what the other party should receive.

Understandable as these views may be, they are too flawed to allow professional nonprofit managers to bypass an earnest and open-minded exploration of their markets (Andreasen, 1982). For example, despite the widely held belief alluded to in the opening paragraph of this chapter that corporate donations are becoming more of an advertising "buy," research on corporations suggests that their primary motive for supporting charities is philanthropic (Sargeant and Stephenson, 1997). In service delivery situations, a perception that clients are unqualified to have opinions on the treatment they should receive can lead professionals to be inattentive to the legitimate wishes of those they intend to serve. It has been suggested that because clients and funders are separate constituencies in nonprofit organizations, there is no direct feedback loop as in business marketing, which can lead to poor-quality service over long periods of time (Connor, 1999). Moreover, when clients are ill-served, their remedies may be few and frail. Compared to shoppers in open markets, the customers of nonprofit organizations are often more likely to be disadvantaged and vulnerable or at least to have fewer opportunities to complain or to switch to other offerings. Therefore, despite their apparent closeness to their customers, many nonprofits are sufficiently insulated from and unresponsive to their clienteles as to need an open window on the market.

Moreover, market investigations need not be unsupportable in a nonprofit enterprise. Quite simple probes can produce highly profitable insights. For example, many organizations could easily collect and collate in a more systematic way information that they are already receiving through frontline staff such as receptionists, counselors, nurses, box office attendants, or community workers. Nonprofits may also find it more possible or more necessary to rely on publicly available secondary information, perhaps from the United Way or a municipality or a national statistical agency, in lieu of primary data from the proprietary in-house surveys that companies buy (Moyer, 1994). Nonprofits may also undertake joint projects with organizations with a common interest—say, in how to reduce vandalism or how to attract tourists to a city's arts festival. Indeed, the investigation may be a public exercise involving shared authority among diverse stakeholders, as in the case of a needs assessment focusing on the problems of a community's recent immigrants, unemployed youth, or people with disabilities.

SEGMENTATION AND TARGET MARKETING

Target marketing is the process whereby decisions are made about which groups an organization will choose to serve. It is achieved by first identifying the main population groups that might be addressed by the enterprise, then selecting those market segments that best fit the organization's objectives and abilities, and tailoring marketing programs to each chosen segment.

To the nonprofit manager, the process of choosing to "target" certain groups may seem a questionable, if not unacceptable, approach. The reason is that choosing some segments means not choosing others—which is to say that focusing on some people means not serving or communicating with others. In a field in which turning no one away or achieving mass social change is often a cherished norm, neglecting some possible clients as a matter of policy can seem to degrade fundamental organizational values.

Yet in many nonprofits, the case for target marketing is both strong and responsible. In an environment in which human needs are huge and escalating while resources are constrained and shrinking, no organization can reach all possible constituencies. The question then is not whether the enterprise will constrain its domain but how. Market segmentation allows nonprofit organizations to control whom they serve by choosing where it is most effective or most important, according to organizational mandate or mission, to spend limited resources, as opposed to letting the limits of their funding arbitrarily make that decision for them. Segmentation helps an organization focus its resources on the clienteles that best fit its mission, capabilities, and aspirations.

The first step in segmentation is to divide the total market into meaningful groups. There are many possible lines along which the manager may form clusters of potential clients. The most conventional divisions are demographic, geographic, and socioeconomic. These include age, sex, marital status, education, and income. Because available data are most often arrayed along these lines, marketers frequently define their target clienteles in these terms. Thus college recruiters will seek out people in defined areas, age brackets and educational levels, while the director of a YWCA life skills program will invoke dimensions such as sex, marital status, and income.

Against the operational convenience of segments bounded by demographics, the marketer must weigh the conceptual richness of segments defined by psychographics. Psychographic descriptors include lifestyles, values, attitudes, opinions, and personalities. Political parties often seek out supporters according to their attitudes toward government involvement in public life, advocacy bodies search for sympathizers on the basis of their positions on key issues, and arts organizations may estimate the market potential in a catchment area disaggregated into the "home-centered," the "sports followers," and the "culture seekers." Personality variables such as empathy and self-esteem have been suggested as useful segmentation variables for recruiting volunteers (Wymer, 1997).

One may also consider assigning marketing efforts to different groups segmented according to the benefits they seek. Some prospective volunteers for a seniors' center may wish to exercise their skills in crafts while others may need to earn credits toward a certificate and still others may find reward in befriending lonely people. A similar scheme is often used in fundraising—for example, an organization may deal with some donors who are motivated by public recognition while others are motivated by the concrete benefits awarded for "membership" donations. In the case of a public campaign to discourage smoking, some members of the public may be motivated by health concerns while others are more receptive to messages that emphasize peer pressure and social stigma. Benefit segmentation is attractive because it indicates to the marketer the types of products and appeals that will find favor with the other party. Put another way, benefit segmentation is efficacious because, being rooted in the fundamental notion of exchange, it not only identifies homogeneous client clusters but also is suggestive of the most relevant offer for each.

Populations can also be segmented according to how they behave with respect to the product or service being offered. Those that are heavy users can be especially propitious targets. Thus longtime subscribers to the ballet, excessive consumers of alcohol, frequent donors of blood, extravagant users of energy, or generous supporters of a church may justify specially designed marketing programs.

Finally, because marketing aims ultimately to consummate exchanges, the marketer may find it logical and advantageous to cluster consumers by how they respond to marketing variables. If younger college graduates are more budget-minded but more bonded to their alma mater than older ones, the alumni officer must ask whether they should not be approached as different segments in terms of product and price. Similarly, if some potential donors are moved by sympathy for people who have a given disease while others react to a warning that they may contract it, the fundraiser should consider whether it is feasible to mount separate appeals. In these cases, the decision will be made on the basis of whether the expected reward from appeals tailored more specifically to the needs of individual groups will outweigh the costs associated with developing multiple campaigns.

In choosing target markets, the manager may apply several criteria. Logically, the first is whether a candidate segment fits the mission of the enterprise. Because nonprofits must be mindful of many constituencies whose aims and values will not fully mesh, accommodating this criterion may be challenging. A church considering ministering to gays and lesbians, a girls' school planning to go coeducational, or an agency aiming to discontinue a camp for diabetic youngsters will need to enter into the exercise with care, patience, and sensitivity.

A second test is whether the segment aligns with the organization's present or potential capabilities. Here, too, discerning judgment can be called for. Human service organizations seek to build élan and combat burnout by celebrating the dedication and professionalism of their people. Conversely, they tend to downplay the capabilities, and even the existence, of alternative service providers. Both of these tendencies, while understandable, can be detrimental to clear-eyed organizational stock taking. This means that in appraising their goodness of fit with potential target markets, nonprofit managers must take care not to overvalue the capabilities of their organizations and underestimate the strengths of competitors.

A third criterion is whether the segment is sufficiently large to justify a special marketing treatment. Arriving at an answer can be less straightforward than in a business firm. In a commercial undertaking, projected return on investment is likely to be the dominant (though not the only) arbiter of acceptable segment size; in a charitable enterprise, unprofitably small segments are more likely to be selected as target markets because the organization has decided to override financial considerations. This is acceptable if the organization has other resources available to offset the loss associated with the program (for example, arts organizations may undertake tours to small, remote centers with the aid of government grants and donations), but not if the loss associated with serving a particular market endangers the survival of the organization and its ability to continue to serve its mission.

A segment is also an attractive choice to the extent that it can be measured and accessed. Senior citizens with suicidal tendencies or fathers who exhibit violent behavior are groups whose size is difficult to estimate and whose members are hard to reach. In addressing such targets, marketing-minded managers face several challenges. One is to measure the scope of the chosen segment, this being necessary for an informed budgeting of marketing programs. Another is to find promotional appeals that are powerful enough, nonmonetary costs that are low enough, and service delivery systems that are nonthreatening enough to bring the agency and the client together so that a beneficial transaction can occur. Ideally, the idea of targeting specific markets is to use a "rifle" approach in which only the specified clients are reached, but often it is necessary, and more economical, to use a "shotgun" campaign to a mass market, which leaves it to members of the target population to "come into the market" through a process of self-selection. Thus women who have experienced domestic violence, school dropouts, and obese citizens are urged to seek remedies through a marketing mix of low costs, empathic services, and mass advertising.

COMPETITION, POSITIONING, AND BRANDING

Competition is an idea that is often rejected in the nonprofit sector or at least understood to apply only to "commercial" markets, such as the market for donations or the performing arts market, which involve financial transactions. Adherents of economic theories of the nonprofit sector that consider these organizations to have developed out of market failure argue that nonprofit organizations respond to need and do not compete for clients. Often there is a philosophical aversion to the idea of competition on the part of nonprofit managers, who would prefer to think of their organizations as engaging in cooperative, as opposed to competitive, behavior.

Nevertheless, competition is a reality in the nonprofit sector (Oster, 1995). In many countries, the number of nonprofit organizations has exploded, and many of them have been founded specifically because they intend to provide alternative programs or philosophies to the offerings of existing organizations. Moreover, nonprofit organizations are always trying to influence behavior, and their clienteles always have choices about how they choose to act—even if it involves choosing not to avail themselves of services at all, as opposed to choosing the services of another agency (Andreasen and Kotler, 2003). There is no escaping the inevitability of competition.

Positioning refers to the place that an agency or its services or ideas occupy in the minds of the individuals in its target market (Trout and Rivkin, 1997). Thus it relates to a concept that is based on understanding how an organization and its offerings are evaluated in terms of the set of alternatives (or competitors) known to the potential clientele. The first step in positioning involves understanding the dimensions that the target market uses to compare organizations and alternatives, and the second seeks to place the alternatives along a continuum of these dimensions. For example, if potential customers evaluate organizations that offer services for immigrants along the dimensions of "multiple services" and "effectiveness in service outcomes," different settlement organizations would be placed in different positions on a grid formed with the two dimensions as axes (see Figure 12.1).

One of the troubling realities of positioning in the nonprofit sector is that the multiple constituencies with which organizations interact often evaluate both the dimensions that are used to compare agencies and the position of individual agencies differently. For example, wealthy potential donors may compare arts organizations in terms of the services and opportunities for recognition that they provide to their major patrons, while government granting agencies that support artistic work may compare the same organizations along different lines such as originality or creativity. It may also happen that different market constituencies use the same dimensions but evaluate competitors differently. Both clients and foundation officials may evaluate and compare social service agencies in terms of their effectiveness, but clients may evaluate a particular agency as highly effective while a funder may rate the same agency low on effectiveness. The key point is that positioning refers to the dimensions and the relative

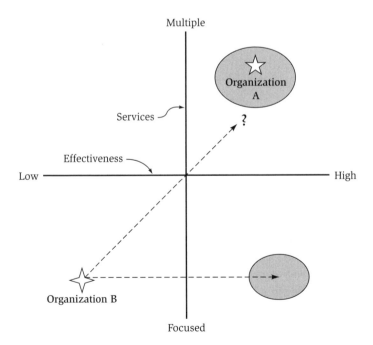

Figure 12.1. Positioning Map for Hypothetical Immigrant-Serving Agencies.

positions along those dimensions that are in the minds of *each* clientele in question. A nonprofit organization that serves several clienteles (donors, clients, foundation funders) will develop a unique map for each. These may form a series of grids in which the axes represent different dimensions that different clienteles use to evaluate alternatives or, if all groups use similar dimensions for comparison, a series of grids with the same axes in which the competitive organizations are placed differently along those axes. In either case, the positioning maps are unique for each market constituency and will dictate a unique strategy for each separate clientele.

Of course, the grids cannot be mapped unless the perceptions of the target markets are known, and the best way to collect this information is through some form of market research. However, even a dispassionate and objective "back of the envelope" grid can be mapped without expensive data collection if nonprofit managers are willing to talk to their potential audiences and listen to what they say about the evaluative dimensions that matter to them and how they see the alternatives in terms of these dimensions.

Once an organization has determined how it is positioned, the next step is to develop a positioning strategy. Positioning is based on the idea of differentiation—in other words, an organization is positioned on the grid on the basis of how it differs from its competitors on the dimensions of interest. The important thing to notice about Figure 12.1 is that even if an organization has given no thought to positioning and is not interested in the process, it is still positioned on the grid in the minds of its target market.

An organization may choose to maintain its current position by continuing to emphasize those factors that differentiate it in positive ways, or it may choose to emphasize characteristics that would differentiate it from the alternatives by moving it to a more advantageous position on the grid. In either case, it is important to keep in mind that not all competitors should plan to locate themselves in the same position on the grid (there may be potential customers elsewhere who prefer a different combination of attributes). The trick is to find a group of customers who want a particular combination of attributes and evaluate whether a particular organization has the capacity to serve them better than the alternatives.

For example, in Figure 12.1, we can see that Organization A is well positioned and Organization B is not. What should Organization A's strategy be? It should continue to emphasize the fact that it offers "one-stop shopping" (multiple services) and that it is effective in delivering desired outcomes. What should Organization B's strategy be? This organization has two choices: it must definitely improve the public perception of its effectiveness, but instead of adding more programs and services in order to move to the upper right quadrant, where it will have to compete directly with Organization A, it may find that there is a market interested in effective language training but that is not looking for job training, child counseling, or computer training. By improving and emphasizing its achievements in the area of language training, it may be able to move to the lower right quadrant and become very effective in serving a small niche market. Repositioning an organization is done through manipulating the elements of the marketing mix (changing programs or aspects of them, changing prices, changing program delivery or delivery locations, or changing the communication mix).

An important marketing idea related to positioning is branding. A brand is a shortcut means of identifying an organization, program, or cause in a way that differentiates it from alternatives. It will embody a set of organization or program characteristics that customers believe will be delivered consistently. It can convey the organization's position in the market, build trust between the organization and its clienteles, raise an organization's profile, and provide insulation from competition (Ritchie, Swami, and Weinberg, 1999).

Branding has recently become a popular concept among nonprofit organizations. There are particular challenges to branding in the third sector. First, branding can absorb considerable financial resources because of the advertising that is required to develop and sustain the brand. This is particularly difficult to justify when a rebranding exercise is undertaken while there are still plenty of old brochures, posters, leaflets, and banners in existence. Second, to create a successful brand, every element of the organization must support the ideas that the brand is trying to communicate. This means that "buy-in" across all functional areas and at all organizational levels must occur and that it must involve more than simple use of a logo or a tagline and include concrete attempts to change service delivery modes and program elements to be consistent with the brand image. Third, in organizations characterized by a large national office and multiple branches with a high degree of local autonomy, it can be very difficult to standardize not only advertising materials but also organizational cultures around the values inherent in the brand.

MANAGING PRODUCTS AND PROGRAMS IN THE NONPROFIT SECTOR

Having chosen target markets by means of thoughtful segmentation and determined a positioning strategy on the basis of competitive analysis, management is in a position to begin formulating the marketing mix. Among the four P's, the program is usually shaped first because the choice of "product" tends to set the bounds for decisions on place (distribution channels), price, and promotion (communications).

It should be noted that more often than not, the product under consideration will be substantially intangible. Some nonprofits do deal in physical goods, of course: a museum may have a gift shop, a social services agency may run a secondhand clothing store, an orchestra may sell compact discs, and an environmental agency may offer posters or tote bags. Generally, though, the third sector puts forth services, such as concerts, courses, counseling, recreation, or memberships, or advocates social ideas and behaviors, as when a citizens' group calls for compulsory helmets for cyclists, an antipollution group calls for recycling, or an AIDS group encourages the use of condoms.

The differences between marketing products, services, and social behaviors can be significant. Services and social behaviors have characteristics that call for different marketing treatments than conventional products. For example, services usually cannot be created in advance of consumption and then "inventoried," nor can they be "stored" if they are not consumed when produced. If live theater performances do not sell adequately to meet production costs, the theater company cannot sell the seats later. One cannot routinize or control the production and quality of services as easily. The care available at a hospital may vary widely from day to day and shift to shift, depending on staffing levels and personnel. Furthermore, customers are often unable to judge the quality of services for themselves and have to rely on atmospheric cues, such as the physical facilities in which marriage and family counseling takes place, or the reassurance of a well-known brand name, such as child care offered in a YMCA.

Social behaviors, in particular, are products that bring additional marketing challenges (Kotler and Roberto, 1989). Some are controversial (birth control information for teens, the ordination of gays and lesbians, the banning of "obscene" art). Others are deeply embedded in individuals' lives (speeding, overeating, discriminating against visible minorities). Others involve target markets that are entire populations (the ownership of handguns, the use of nonmetric measures, the vaccination of children).

Moreover, the successful marketing of new or different social behaviors may require changing pleasurable personal habits, even addictions, in favor of a larger and more remote public good. Examples of such behaviors are converting to more fuel-efficient vehicles, replacing air conditioners with ceiling fans, quitting smoking, or giving blood. All of this means that the nonprofit manager who would change social behaviors can expect a formidable task. Among other things, the successful marketer must usually find compelling incentives for individuals to "buy into" what is proposed, mobilize allied organizations to facilitate or even enforce the advocated ways of acting, and counter forceful opposition from determined adversaries.

Analyzing the Organization's Portfolio

To add to these, management will face other challenges in shaping its product lines. Because the pressure from rivals often seems weak, third-sector enterprises frequently have difficulty freeing up resources to scan the environment for new market opportunities. They may also lack the funds, or believe they do, to probe the wants and needs of potential clients and to develop prototypes of new offerings, as commercial firms routinely do. Furthermore, where a case can be made for upgrading or downgrading a program, management's deliberations can be complicated by the dedication of founders, directors, funders, staff, or volunteers to preserving or protecting certain programs at the expense of other priorities. Underlying all of these obstacles to timely and rational product line planning is the absence of a market mechanism to arbitrate disagreements as to the adding and dropping of nonprofit programs.

Nevertheless, nonprofit managers will have to establish the relative priorities to be given to the organization's programs, including potential new programs. That ranking will probably not be a straightforward exercise. Many nonprofits, especially larger ones, are an assemblage of enterprises. A social services agency may run a self-help group for the children of divorce, a social center for isolated seniors, a counseling program for substance abusers, a parenting program for teenage mothers, and an advocacy campaign to enhance the legal protections for people experiencing domestic violence. Similarly, a museum may offer major exhibitions, a permanent collection, educational workshops, public lecture series, a gift shop, a restaurant, concert series, and children's programming. Such organizations confront decisions not unlike those of a corporation that must determine which product lines to promote, maintain, or drop.

To settle these issues, a formal analytical process for prioritizing programs and for allocating limited resources among them can be useful. One such approach is portfolio analysis. Essentially, portfolio analysis identifies the main programs of an organization, establishes a set of criteria for judging the relative importance of these units, and evaluates each program against those criteria.

Several frameworks are available for conducting a portfolio analysis in a nonprofit setting. In them, individual criteria are clustered to produce a summary evaluation of each program on two or three key dimensions. For example, after being weighed on a number of subfactors, each faculty in a college or school may be placed in an overall classification according to its quality and reputation, the size and growth of its student market, and its centrality to the mission of the college (Andreasen and Kotler, 2003). A social services agency may use criteria such as congruency with the organization's mission, community need, and funding availability or likelihood of breaking even. These summary appraisals are usually pulled together in a grid in which each program is placed in its strategic space. The resulting portfolio matrix is a convenient visual representation of management's best judgment as to the importance of pursuing various options.

One portfolio framework developed for nonprofits over twenty years ago (MacMillan, 1983) is based on a three-way matrix in which the dimensions are program attractiveness, alternative coverage, and competitive position. Program attractiveness and alternative coverage can be categorized as high or low; competitive position, as strong or weak. Once the matrix is laid out, it will have eight cells representing all the possible combinations. Various programs and options can be clustered in the appropriate cells. This will aid in the development of effective marketing strategies in several ways.

First, the portfolio analysis will have signaled whether the enterprise is, in general, strong or weak, well positioned or in danger. For example, if most of the programs are in areas that are unattractive, that have strong alternative coverage, and where the organization does not have the facilities, budget, or human and knowledge resources to compete effectively, the enterprise's health is frail, and its future life is perilous.

Second, how its programs cluster in the matrix will indicate in turn whether the enterprise's marketing goals should be expansion or retrenchment and whether its existing programs should continue and grow or be discontinued and replaced. In particular, nonprofit managers should examine whether most, or an increasing number, of its programs are clustered in areas of great attractiveness but dense alternative coverage, which may signal that management has fallen into the habit of seeking easy funding wherever it may lie—a seductive strategy of drift. Such a diagnosis would indicate that at the very least, the board should reaffirm or revise the mission of the enterprise. A weak portfolio tends to narrow the organization's options; a healthy one gives management a wide choice of marketing strategies.

The portfolio analysis also aids the marketing manager by suggesting what strategies are appropriate for individual programs. For example, if a program falls in a cell representing an attractive field but one that fits poorly with the organization's mission and that is served by more capable alternative suppliers, a logical initiative might be to market the program to agencies better positioned to deliver it. Alternatively, a social services agency in a catchment area with a growing number of large single-parent families might see this as a highly attractive situation with low alternative coverage, leading it to add study areas, extend its hours, develop new recreational programs, and target youngsters needing a suitable place to go after school.

The Product Life Cycle

The offerings of nonprofits, as in the conventional marketplace, are subject to changing circumstances: a tilt in the balance of competition upon the entry of a new service or service provider, a shift in the market with the emergence of an unserved population, or a revision of the organization's position due to the loss of a funding source. This suggests that programs need to be constantly reappraised over the course of their lives and that marketing strategies may need to be revised as products age.

To assist in this process, the nonprofit manager can borrow and bend a tool that has been useful to the business executive: the concept of a product life cycle

(PLC). The life cycle is a widely observed phenomenon. Indeed, some marketing writers have commented on the similarity of the marketplace to an ecological environment, while others have compared the competition among products to the struggle among organisms. The analogy is not perfect, and in particular cases, the relevant life cycle may not be easy to define and apply, but the open-minded nonprofit manager should consider the usefulness of the concept.

Most verbal models of the PLC divide the product's evolution into stages of introduction, growth, maturity, and decline. These stages are defined and differentiated by the changing level of "sales" for the brand or product category. Graphical models depict an S-shaped curve in which inflection points in the curve represent shifts in the rate of sales or profits over time. In a nonprofit setting, this could be, for example, the value of ticket subscriptions sold, the number of voters registered, or the percentage of the population that adopts a new behavior or attitude.

Each phase of the PLC is described in terms of the consumer behavior and competitive actions that one tends to see at that point. These generalizations serve as suggestions for the manager who wants to anticipate future stages and adapt the marketing program to each. The PLC, of course, was developed for commercial products and even in that context has been criticized for being too formulaic and unrepresentative of the huge diversity of products and markets that exist. Nevertheless, the idea that markets evolve over the lifetime of an organization and its products or programs and the necessity for adopting different marketing strategies over that lifetime can be usefully applied in nonprofit settings. Refugee and immigrant settlement services were established in many large cities decades ago, and in the early (introductory) stages of the movement, the marketing task was focused on building awareness and support. As the value of these services became apparent, more "competitors" entered the market in the form of new settlement agencies, ethnospecific agencies, and large multiservice agencies that developed specific programs directed at newcomers (growth phase). In a market crowded with many agencies offering similar services (maturity), the marketing task shifts to distinguishing the value and quality of a particular agency's work and the effectiveness of its management in attracting the clientele and the funding that is needed to support the programs. A similar pattern of development can be seen in the market for the performing arts, where shifts in both consumer behavior (audiences, donors, and grantors) and competitive pressures can be seen over time (Gainer, 1989).

Adoption and Diffusion

In guiding products through their life cycles, particularly the "behavioral" products characteristic of social behavior marketing, marketers can also take advantage of what is known about how innovations are adopted. Scholars in several fields have been interested in how new ways of thinking and acting are accepted. What explains the pattern whereby farmers move to new strains of seed, physicians accept new kinds of drugs, and women adopt new styles of dress? The relevance for marketers is plain: by better understanding the diffusion of innovations, they can better manage the marketing of new products.

Such insights can also aid third-sector enterprises. An explanation of why some forms of contraception are more acceptable than others in developing countries can have implications for a nongovernmental organization (NGO), a profile of the kinds of people who lead in accepting environmentally friendly habits can provide an opening target for antipollution groups, and knowledge of the interpersonal connections through which drug use is sanctioned, accepted, and spread can assist agencies working with youth at risk.

These examples suggest some of the aspects of diffusion that can be especially useful to nonprofit marketers. One is the nature of the individuals who, within the life of innovations, play the roles of opinion leaders, early adopters, the majority, and the laggards. Special interest should be directed to finding and persuading those who are likely to be active and influential at the outset of the life cycle of a new idea or behavior. Rogers (1995) has generalized that compared to those who come along later, early adopters in a social system tend to be younger, of higher social status, financially better off, more plugged into impersonal and cosmopolitan information sources, and in closer contact with the origins of new ideas. This suggests that messages geared toward encouraging people to stop smoking, switch to less polluting vehicles, or become physically fit are more likely to be effective throughout a population if directed in the early stages to the people most likely to lead new trends as opposed to, say, those who are most seriously engaged in the negative behaviors the marketer wants to change. Once an idea becomes "fashionable" through adoption by opinion leaders, it is much more likely to diffuse to other groups that are the ultimate target than if those groups were approached initially.

By applying diffusion theory, the third-sector marketer can be assisted in two other product management tasks: estimating how quickly the organization's newly launched program will be accepted and accelerating that process. Six characteristics have been found to speed or impede the diffusion of a new idea or innovation. The first is its relative advantage: for example, is this new teen phone-in service less likely to alert one's parents than a walk-in center? The second is its compatibility with existing values and past experiences: will this parking-lot church service meet the traditional expectations of immobile seniors? Another is the innovation's complexity: how difficult is it for householders to sort out recyclable items from the regular trash? In addition, the marketer should consider its trialabilty or divisibility: can children in low-income neighborhoods attend day care programs on a drop-in basis, or must parents agree to pay for a full month at a time? A further consideration is the innovation's observability or communicability: if one makes the substantial personal investment to pass the docent course for the art gallery, will this accomplishment be celebrated in ways that are important to the prospective volunteer? Finally, the marketer must consider the risk as seen by the user (even if the marketer discounts that risk): if a person joins the movement against globalization, what does that person consider to be the odds of public embarrassment or physical harm?

PRICING, COSTS, AND VALUE

Too often in nonprofit organizations, prices (including no financial charge for services) are set in casual and arbitrary ways. Often there is a belief that services should be delivered free or that a target market cannot afford to pay anything when this is not necessarily the case. In an era of increasing cutbacks in government financial support for nonprofit organizations and growing competition for donated revenues, nonprofit organizations will have to revisit their pricing policies. They may find that they are accepting an unnecessary loss of revenue to the enterprise or a diminution of available benefits to customers. Moreover, as more and more nonprofit organizations address the revenue crisis through activities associated with social enterprise, they are going to be setting prices in a competitive marketplace. For these reasons, pricing decisions in the nonprofit sector need to be made in a logical, orderly, and analytical manner.

Reducing Nonfinancial Costs

The first thing a nonprofit organization must keep in mind is that the "price" of using a service or accepting an idea will include nonfinancial costs. Nonprofit organizations need to aggressively and creatively search out ways in which the organization might reduce the nonfinancial costs for their clientele. There are, potentially, a significant number of subtle but substantial barriers to patronage in many nonprofit offerings, including, for example, adopting recycling, wearing motorcycle helmets, attending symphony concerts, or using family counseling services. These consumer deterrents are, in effect, product costs. Reviewing them may lead the nonprofit manager, as part of a pricing exercise, to revisit the design of the offer.

Such nonfinancial costs might include social awkwardness or embarrassment, time costs such as missing work or having to travel to a difficult and remote location, ancillary financial costs such as having to pay for parking or for child care, or psychological costs associated with giving up familiar or pleasurable habits. A marketing perspective would argue that before putting resources into promoting a service or a behavior, one should search out opportunities to reduce each of these costs. A "value" approach to pricing suggests that customers compare the benefit they receive for the costs they incur. Lowering the costs to the clientele, including nonfinancial costs, can thus increase the value of the offering substantially. Increasing the value of a product by cutting social, psychological, and time costs may be particularly important in a situation where the organization is about to start charging for a service that has previously been free.

Establishing Pricing Objectives

After reducing nonfinancial costs, the next thing to establish is the pricing objectives. In pricing tickets for a fundraiser or gifts in a hospital shop, profit maximization may be a dominant goal; in establishing membership fees for a save-the-wetlands group or the tariff for a college reunion, expanding the base of supporters could override other aims; in setting the charges for respite care or the price per seedling in a tree-planting program, cost recovery may have the first claim; and in establishing a fee scale for a legal aid office or a day camp for children with disabilities, social equity might be the first pricing objective.

However, it will be observed that in each case, other desirable aims will lay some claim. The hospital gift shop will not want to appear to gouge people who are distressed, the wetlands group will want to generate a surplus to pay for lobbying, the tree-planting program would want to avoid charges of unfair competition from private nurseries, and the legal aid office will want to discourage frivolous consultations. At the outset, then, the marketing manager will have to find an acceptable balance among pricing objectives that are multiple and conflicting.

Having established pricing goals and their priorities, management must fashion a strategy for achieving them. In doing so, it should take account of three key considerations: *costs, demand,* and *competition.* Of these three, the least problematic may be costs. To calculate the cost per child for a day care center or the cost per unit for a proselytizing video will not be a difficult exercise. However, when an organization produces a number of services out of a common facility, as conglomerate nonprofits often do, management must make judgments as to the allocation of joint costs. To determine how much to charge a learned society for the use of summertime conference space, a university will have to decide how to apportion the year-round costs of operating its facilities. The same kind of decision will arise in pricing a church wedding, a visit to a hospital emergency ward, or a fee-for-service contract. As when diverse products come out of a single factory, management must arrive at a basis for allocating charges—by the percentage of total space used or total time taken, for example—that seems rational under the circumstances (see Chapter Twenty for details about cost allocation methods).

Pricing policies should be informed by break-even analysis. In settling on a price for a product or a program, a manager will want to take into consideration how many units would have to be sold at a given price in order to cover all costs. To determine this, one begins by separating expenses that vary with the number of participants from those that are fixed regardless of patronage. For example, the handout materials in a board management workshop cost, say,

$200, versus the instructor's stipend, say, of $1,750 plus rent charges of $750. The difference between the intended fee or revenue per unit (say, $250) and the variable cost per unit (the $200 for handouts) is called the "contribution per unit" because it is the amount ($50) that each sale contributes to covering the fixed costs. The number of units (registrations) necessary to break even, then, is the number of enrollments that will just cover all the fixed and variable costs. The calculation would be as follows:

$$\text{Break-even volume} = \frac{\text{Fixed costs}}{\text{Contribution per unit}}$$

$$= \frac{\text{Fixed costs}}{\text{Price} - \text{Variable cost per unit}}$$

$$= \frac{\text{Instructor's stipend} + \text{Rent}}{\text{Fee} - \text{Cost of handouts per person}}$$

$$= \frac{\$2,500}{\$250 - \$200} = 50 \text{ registrants}$$

If fifty registrants seemed more than could be expected, the workshop planners might ask, "With twenty-five participants, what fee would allow us to break even?" The calculation would be as follows:

$$\text{Break-even fee} = \frac{\text{Total cost}}{\text{Number of participants}}$$

$$= \frac{\text{Fixed costs} + \text{Variable costs}}{\text{Number of participants}}$$

$$= \frac{\$2,500 + (25 \times \$200)}{25} = \$300$$

The question then would be whether $300 is a price that the intended participants would pay. If that seemed unlikely, then the break-even analysis would help the workshop planners calculate their options for subsidizing the event or somehow reducing the variable costs.

Note that the marketer began with costs to calculate the break-even price but was soon led to ask how prospective buyers might respond to that price. The example thus illustrates another point about price making: cost analysis is linked to demand analysis.

In analyzing demand, a useful concept is that of elasticity. Essentially, price elasticity is the responsiveness of demand to changes in price. When a large change in the price of an offering causes a relatively small change in its sale, demand for it is said to be "price-inelastic." When small changes in price (up or down) have a relatively large effect on sales, its demand curve is said to be elastic at that point. In general, inelastic demand suggests that the marketer can increase total revenue and perhaps net profits by raising the price, whereas elastic demand tends to encourage management to avoid price increases and to expand patronage by lowering prices. Clearly, knowledge of the elasticity of demand can be helpful in deciding on user fees in a day when more and more charitable enterprises are using them.

In some situations, elasticity of demand varies significantly across market segments. That variability invites different prices in various segments. The differential pricing of various seat locations in an opera house, the offering of lower-priced student memberships by a political party, and the subsidization of some children in a YMCA computer camp all represent pricing schemes that recognize and respond to differing demand elasticities in component segments of a market. Of course, differential pricing involves ethical as well as economic issues, which nonprofit leaders must recognize, resolve, and defend.

Be aware that demand-oriented pricing requires that the seller estimate the value of the offer as perceived by the buyer. That has important implications for nonprofit administrators. Executives who are insulated from their markets may substitute their own appraisals of the worth of their offers—which may be too high or too low. In doing so, they risk inventing inaccurate pricing data. To illustrate, a social services agency aiming to offer employee counseling services in competition with private firms and assuming that "nonprofit" would be equated with "second-rate," opted for low prices and lean margins. Subsequent inquiries with corporate customers showed that the agency's long history, high profile, and nonprofit status invested it with a reputation for professionalism, dedication, and quality. That finding translated into an unforeseen opportunity for the manager of the employee assistance program to justify high prices. With that, the program became a cash cow that subsidized the expansion of counseling services to low-income individuals. Astute and fair pricing rests on accurate market inputs based on knowledge of the market rather than assumptions about what people will want to or be able to pay.

Along with costs and demand, the price maker should analyze competition. Pressed to keep up with the demand for their services, some nonprofit managers are inclined to dismiss competition as irrelevant to their own decisions. Yet the intended clienteles of most nonprofit enterprises do have alternatives to their patronage. The field of home health care and homemaking for seniors, for example, once dominated by nonprofit agencies, is being rapidly transformed by the entry of private sector firms. Even in less obviously competitive areas, however, customers have choices. A family considering joining an art gallery may see for itself a large number of acceptable suppliers, ranging across the arts, education, recreation, and entertainment fields. A couple with marital problems can likewise look in many directions for help: to religious organizations, legal firms, family service agencies, psychologists or social workers in private practice, self-help groups, phone-in shows, family, and friends. End users often define relevant competitors as those enterprises that offer equivalent benefits, rather than just similar-looking products; using this perspective, managers of nonprofit organizations, even ones that appear to be semimonopolies, may find that they do in fact have competition.

Appraising competition—the third element of pricing—can be useful in several ways. First, it will help identify the ceiling—the highest price the marketer can charge. Studying competitors' prices, both monetary and nonmonetary, can also reveal ways in which service deliverers can offer better products at lower prices. At the same time, however, nonprofit managers must consider the ethical implications of competitive pricing. Sometimes competitors, particularly private sector companies, are able to offer low prices through extremely low wage policies or by hiring less qualified service deliverers than nonprofit agencies are comfortable with. On the other hand, private sector competitors may feel on occasion that nonprofits are unfairly undercutting their prices because they don't have to pay income taxes on their profits. Thus while competitive analysis is an essential part of the pricing process, it must be examined in conjunction with costs, market demand, and social and ethical considerations.

DESIGNING MARKETING CHANNELS

Decisions about how best to distribute an offering to a market or designing suitable marketing channels can have a major effect on the fortunes of the offering itself. As in the private sector, a worthy and attractively priced product that is not effectively deployed may well fail. Thus when an agency offering services for immigrants and refugees employs receptionists and registration clerks who speak only English, the ultimate service becomes, for practical purposes, inaccessible to many of its intended users. Conversely, a part-time master's program in business administration might successfully connect with young professionals by locating its classrooms on commuter trains.

In some respects, the choice of channels can be more critical in the third sector than in the private sector. When the product is a service, it is often consumed at the same time and place that it is produced, thereby putting the nonprofit manager in direct contact with end users. Religious, psychological, health, and educational services tend to be of that sort. The buyer-seller contact may be inherently sensitive and intrusive, making the quality of the product-channel offering unusually crucial to a satisfactory outcome. Such is the case with marriage counseling and police services. Under such circumstances, the nonprofit marketer must be a consumer-oriented channel manager. It follows from this that the first step in channel design should be to analyze the requirements of the end user. How promptly must a police car arrive at the scene of a robbery in order to foil it? How far can a recreation center be from seniors and still attract them? How crowded can a subway become before the system loses regular users? In building a marketing channel, then, a basic building block is the user's specification of acceptable performance. That will require market knowledge.

In designing service facilities, management may find it useful to invoke a categorization common in retailing: that of convenience, shopping, and speciality goods. Convenience products are those that the shopper will not exert much effort to investigate, access, and buy. At the other extreme, speciality products will call forth considerable effort by the buyer. Shopping goods lie in between. These consumer-imposed definitions have implications for marketing logistics: convenience goods must be readily accessible, usually through broadcast distribution, while speciality goods can be successfully marketed through fewer and more remote outlets. Thus social marketing messages that advocate changes in behavior, such as an antismoking campaign, will not be sought out by the target market of teenage smokers. Campaigns directed at this target will have to be readily accessible and ubiquitous in order to reach the target because consumers cannot be expected to seek out this information or put effort into finding it. On the other hand, an organization that provides respite care for people with Alzheimer's disease can probably expect that their services will be sought out by families who are investigating the services and options that are available in their community.

Where alternative suppliers are absent, suppliers are inclined to design distribution systems that suit their convenience more than the end user's. Governments provide the most notorious examples. Locations and hours of service are often restricted. Public libraries, for example, are often open only on weekdays, when many people who would like to use their services are at work or in school, and are closed on Sundays, to give their employees a free day, when many potential users might prefer to access library services. Still, the marketer does have to balance the customer's desire for buying convenience with the service deliverer's need for operating efficiency. Secondhand goods outlets, opera houses, and lecture halls may demand minimum numbers of users if economies of scale and acceptable levels of service are to be enjoyed by both users and operators. This trade-off should be management's next consideration.

Organizations have found several ways to manage the trade-off (Lovelock and Weinberg, 1989). One is to decentralize the customer contact function while centralizing the technical operations, as when the Red Cross collects blood via bloodmobiles and processes it at a headquarters location. A national health care charity might, for example, centralize its direct mail fundraising operations while operating many small local chapters that provide service to patients. Another solution is to offer more limited services at branches than at the main site—a channel compromise commonly struck by post offices, hospitals, libraries, and large universities. Another is to join with providers of compatible products and services to form a larger meaningful assortment at a local site. Community information booths in shopping centers are, in effect, retailers of a broad line of complementary products distributed to them by governments and charitable organizations. Nonprofit theaters may also join forces to establish one ticket agency that plays the same kind of assortment role.

Related to the issue of a site's accessibility is the question of the kind and quality of the experience it will deliver. Concert halls are often criticized for their acoustics, but customers are equally affected by the number and convenience of washrooms, the location and price of parking or public transportation, and the quality and range of food and beverage services. In the past, museums and hospitals have attracted critical comment for their forbidding atmosphere. In contrast, an agency serving at-risk youth enhanced its service delivery by relocating from an aging and intimidating mansion in an out-of-the-way neighborhood to an economical loft, furnished with modern furniture, located near a subway stop. A settlement agency in a large city recorded its telephone answering message in four different languages—only a subset of the dozens actually represented by its clientele—in order to communicate a multilingual and multicultural atmosphere for callers contacting the agency for the first time. Nonprofits that distribute their services through immigration centers, courtrooms, employment offices, and other sites should consider shopping their own distribution systems in order to improve their "atmospherics" in this way.

Although many third-sector organizations market their programs directly to end users, and although there are substantial advantages in the short, controlled channels that result, some nonprofit managers, like some commercial marketers, find it necessary or advisable to take an indirect approach by using channel intermediaries. Channels handled by others may be cheaper, more quickly activated, more expert, and more accessible to end users. Thus nonprofit arts organizations will often buy the services of a large and well-known commercial ticket agency as opposed to developing and running their own ticketing services. In the 1960s, a famous example of this occurred when the government of India, committed to the mass distribution of condoms, engaged the vast distribution system of Lever Brothers of India, thereby reaching out to health clinics, barbershops, rural stores, and vending machines across the country (Demerath, 1967). The Canadian Post Office vends stamps and basic postal services out of booths in convenience stores and drugstores, and the Girl Guides and Boy Scouts build their channels around church halls and school gymnasiums.

Enterprises that seek changes in social behavior often collaborate with other players in order to complete the "sale." To illustrate, advocacy alone may persuade some smokers that they should quit, but their behavior may not change unless it is validated by medical judgments, mandated by laws, and supported by workplace regulations. Clearly, no organization acting alone can deliver all of those components. Out of such imperatives come marketing partnerships among hospitals, cancer societies, medical associations, school boards, industry associations, and government departments.

The experienced nonprofit manager will know that interinstitutional cooperation is anything but automatic, however. Even enterprises that want to collaborate will bring to the table not just potentially complementary competencies but also potentially competing values, goals, perceptions, and priorities. For this reason, the literature on distribution systems takes it as given that some channel conflict is inevitable, even useful, and that the management task is to keep it to levels that are workable rather than pathological. Because charitable enterprises are highly value-driven, imprinted with founders' visions, protective of their turf, and in competition with one another for scarce funds, they are probably just as liable as business firms to experience interorganizational conflict. Therefore, the third-sector administrator should be as assiduous as the private-sector executive in forging channel partnerships that work to the advantage of the distribution system as a whole, including the end user, and recognizing the need for continuous attention to the power relationships and their management that a complex channel requires. In the field of early intervention services for children with disabilities, for example, it has been suggested that neutral brokers may help parents or caregivers access the best services by resolving some of the channel conflict that clients may lack the power to resolve on their own (Fugate, 2000).

MANAGING COMMUNICATION PROGRAMS

It was observed earlier that third-sector managers often tend to equate marketing with advertising. Regrettably, those managers are then inclined to define all marketing challenges as "communication" problems; to rush to judgment about mounting promotional efforts; to overlook opportunities for improved products, prices, and channels; and as a consequence, to burden advertising with an unrealistically heavy part of the total marketing task—and unattainable goals.

To avoid charging advertising with more than it can accomplish, management should remember that the market is a clamorous place and that people develop built-in defenses against its noise. These filters include selective perception (an affluent alumnus may not open mail from his fraternity, or a pregnant drinker may ignore the advertising that highlights the effects that alcohol can have on the fetus) and selective retention (a driver who does not buckle up may remember particularly well accounts of traffic accidents in which the people killed were wearing seat belts). These common human coping mechanisms combine to present powerful barriers to successful communication.

So do the complexities of the communication process itself. How messages are encoded, transmitted, screened, decoded, stored, retrieved, and acted on can be modeled in the abstract, but they may be unfathomable in a particular situation. To open that black box may require market research. It will probably reveal that the final message the target receives and retrieves is very different from the message the advertiser intended to communicate.

The advertising program must flow logically from, and fit consistently with, the other parts of the overall marketing strategy. To accomplish that overall effect, management should begin with the embracing objectives of the total marketing effort. In an institute for the blind, the product, price, and place elements of the marketing program will be shaped in one way if the goal is to introduce a friendly visiting service to partially blind seniors and in quite another way if the aim is to raise funds to support research on the prevention and treatment of macular degeneration—and the role of advertising will then vary accordingly. Here one sees how reliant the promotional planner is on the goals and guidelines drawn from the mission, portfolio, and priorities of the enterprise as a whole.

To give further focus to the promotional effort, there should be a subset of targets for the advertising program in particular. A key question will be, what is the target audience? The answer should flow from earlier decisions as to the organization's target markets, as when a young people's theater concentrates its phone solicitation on upscale young families or an engineering faculty targets promising high school women.

However, within the organization's natural client group, further choices remain. A smoking cessation program with a wide mandate may target teenage girls because they are taking up the habit at a particularly high rate or longtime smokers because they are especially at risk, and a hospital bequest program may focus on nearby seniors because they are likely customers or on recent patients because they may want to express their gratitude.

An often relevant way to define target groups for promotional purposes is according to their "readiness." The notion is that on the way to engaging in the desired behavior, an audience moves through various stages. People in one or more of these states may then be targeted by the advertiser. Subdividing the market in this way helps sharpen advertising's goals, clarify its tasks, and shape its strategy. For example, the goal of advertising would be to create *awareness* if the audience has never heard of the organization or the cause, to *inform* if the target market is not convinced or still undecided, and to *persuade* if the audience is aware and informed but has not yet decided to take the desired action.

These kinds of communication objectives set the stage for the next step, which is setting the promotional budget. Without clearly stated goals, management may simply imitate what others spend or may allocate an arbitrary percentage of the organization's revenue. Both approaches are essentially mindless.

The most appropriate method is to work back from the promotional goals to the level of spending that would seem to be necessary to their accomplishment. Operationally, this approach will not be easy. Forecasting audience response to various advertising outlays will be daunting, especially if there is no track record to consult. And when the necessary spending has been estimated, it may be unaffordable, in which case the original objectives have to be revised. Despite these difficulties in practice, the essential point is that outcomes and budget outlay are positively related—a point often forgotten in nonprofit marketing environments.

There follows the question, what essential message is to be conveyed? The answer will be suggested in the prior choice of target audiences and in the statement of communications objectives, but at this stage, the central themes and copy platforms must be articulated with more precision. Are prospective foster parents to be appealed to on the basis of compassion or compensation? How will an international development agency solicit donations: on the basis of pity or empowerment? Should the opera be portrayed as a fabulous "special occasion" grand event or as an "everyday" entertainment experience?

Related to the advertising's themes is its style and tone. A political candidate can make the same point by invoking revered symbols in a respectful way, by enumerating proposed polices in a businesslike way, by attacking opponents in a dismissive way, or by citing the record in a proud way. A range of choices will also be available to persuade at-risk youth to stay in school, to urge construction workers to follow safety rules, and to sign people up for a marathon.

Each promotional medium has its own strengths and limitations. Direct mail can deliver messages customized for different market segments but may be lost in the daily shuffle; television can demonstrate through action but leaves no record for later reference; billboards can command attention but only momentarily; the Internet offers interactivity, but its use relies on the target market's seeking access. Public service announcements are free, but one should remember that the advertiser has little control over whether they will be aired at appropriate times.

Evaluating the results of advertising is a worthy but tricky undertaking. One reason is that the final transaction is brought about by the combined action of many marketing strategies and tactics, not simply the advertising, plus the effect of external variables such as competition, legislation, and the economy. Even where the results are strongly governed by promotion alone, as in the case of lobbying, there remains the problem of disentangling the effects of speeches, position papers, petitions, media campaigns, and personal solicitations. Moreover, the advertiser must try to take account of the time lag between the stimulus and the response: taking action to become a volunteer for Big Brothers Big Sisters, enter an addiction program, or switch churches normally follows a protracted period of persuasion and deliberation.

Despite these difficulties, a number of techniques are available for testing alternative messages, media, and spending levels. They range from the simple (a split-sample direct mailing) to the sophisticated (test markets in different cities). Part of effectively managing promotional programs is being aware of the means for evaluating advertising's impact and determining which tests are justified under the circumstances (Andreason and Kotler, 2003).

CURRENT ISSUES

As stated earlier, there are few nonprofit managers who are unaware that resources are becoming scarcer and that competition is growing. This is most obvious in the market for financial resources and thus in the area of fundraising, particularly in large nonprofits, where we have seen the rapid adoption of sophisticated marketing systems and thinking. But in the competitive markets for the services and social ideas and behaviors that nonprofit organizations offer or advocate, experience has been more mixed. Managers in large mainline cultural organizations (the opera, the ballet, the symphony) typically moil in markets that are vulnerable to consumer preferences and competitive thrusts. Accordingly, they see themselves as arts marketers (Kotler and Scheff, 1997; Colbert, 1994), and their operations, outlooks, and attitudes are not much different from those of executives in business firms. By contrast, leaders in less popular enterprises (modern dance groups, fringe theater companies, new music organizations) are more dependent on financial grants and are relatively less reliant on revenues from sales and private donations.

In nonprofits that deal in social services, the influence of the market may be even less evident. In these areas, the demand for services often outstrips supply. Competition is sometimes further restricted or managed by government fiat (the Charities Commission in the United Kingdom, for example, might restrict start-ups in areas with an existing service provider) or by mutual consent (in Toronto, Canada, organizations in the children's mental health field agreed to focus their activities in particular geographical areas). Where the need is vast and the supply of services is limited, rationing is construed to be the central management task, and marketing can seem a gratuitous exercise.

These deterrents to marketing, largely external, lead to others that are essentially internal. To be fully effective, a marketing mix must be integrated. That is most readily accomplished when the marketing executive, like a product manager in a consumer packaged-goods company, has substantial authority over all of the four P's (product, price, promotion, and place). In a nonprofit organization, this does not happen—nor should it.

Generally, the promotion task is assigned to marketing specialists: public relations and communications specialists in social service agencies, publicists in advocacy organizations, and development directors in universities. Fundraisers and volunteer administrators are widely used in the third sector and are consigned major responsibilities for promoting charitable organizations and their needs to specific publics. Pricing policies may also be open to discussion across several jurisdictions in a nonprofit enterprise—in an arts organization, this area may be consigned specifically to marketing, while in a social services agency, it may be consigned to a marketing specialist charged with social enterprise development but fees for client services may be set by a combination of financial officers, social work managers, and marketers.

The same is not true for decisions about programs and how they are delivered. In a live performing arts company, the repertoire is largely chosen by the artistic director; in a family service agency, the programs to be mounted are primarily determined by professional social workers or psychologists; in a university, the curriculum is mostly shaped by faculty; in a public art gallery, decisions about acquisitions lie primarily with curators; and in a hospital, the specialties to be emphasized are governed by physicians, nurses, and other health care workers.

These customary organizational arrangements are highly significant for anyone who would champion marketing within a nonprofit organization. They testify to the fact that in many parts of the nonprofit sector, key decisions about the most pivotal parts of the marketing mix are not made solely by marketing professionals but by experts who, in their training and their experience, have little exposure to, curiosity about, or regard for marketing. Moreover, marketing managers must accept that in mission-driven organizations, this is as it should be. Whereas the primary purpose of commercial organizations is to make money for their owners or shareholders and thus it is appropriate for marketing managers to have control over much of the production of these organizations, the primary purpose of nonprofit organizations is to serve the public good through the production of goods, services, and ideas that are generated on the basis of expert knowledge and not on the basis of market demand.

However, once it has been accepted that expert knowledge is critical to achieving the mission of nonprofit organizations, it is also essential to recognize that facilitating mutually advantageous exchanges between the organization and key elements of its environments is equally critical. A dance company that produces great art to empty houses is not achieving its mission; nor is a social services agency with programs that are not attractive to at-risk youth or ineffective in the minds of funders, an environmental advocacy group whose message does not reach the public, a mental health charity whose services are difficult to access by those in need, or a religious congregation whose membership is confined to elderly people.

Nonprofit organizations achieve their mission not merely through producing services and advocacy but also by ensuring that this production is adequately funded and that their services and ideas are "consumed" by those for whom they are produced. Marketing's fundamental purpose in the nonprofit sector is the facilitation of these funding and consumption exchanges by focusing on the clienteles that the organization seeks to serve. Healthy organizations are fully responsive to their environments. Lacking unambiguous feedback from a conventional market mechanism, nonprofits must find other ways to ensure that they respond effectively to clients' wants and needs. Without such measures, nonprofit mangers, like business executives, risk working hard in wrong directions. Marketing can help avoid that. How? By sharing in monitoring the environment, undertaking market research, communicating the changing wants and needs of key client groups, participating in portfolio analysis, suggesting suitable target markets, branding the organization in the public's mind, participating in the mounting of the organization's offer, fostering the relationships that are crucial to survival, and appraising client satisfaction levels. Marketing actions contribute to a healthy relationship between a nonprofit enterprise and its most significant others. And it is through long-term, healthy relationships with clients, donors, corporations, the media, governments, legislators, and the public that nonprofit organizations will survive and continue to contribute to the quality of our lives and the public good.

References

Andreasen, A. R. "Nonprofits: Check Your Attention to Customers." *Harvard Business Review,* May-June 1982, pp. 105–110.

Andreasen, A. R., and Kotler, P. *Strategic Marketing for Nonprofit Organizations.* (6th ed.) Upper Saddle River, N.J.: Prentice Hall, 2003.

Bagozzi, R. P. "Marketing as Exchange." *Journal of Marketing,* 1975, *39,* 32–39.

Brennan, L., and Brady, E. "Relating to Marketing? Why Relationship Marketing Works for Not-for-Profit Organisations." *International Journal of Nonprofit and Voluntary Sector Marketing,* 1999, *4,* 327–337.

Colbert, F. (with J. Nantel and S. Bilodeau). *Marketing Culture and the Arts.* Montreal, Canada: Morin, 1994.

Connor, R. "How Responsive Are Charities to Market Needs?" *International Journal of Nonprofit and Voluntary Sector Marketing,* 1999, *4,* 338–348.

Conway, T. "Strategy vs. Tactics in the Not-for-Profit Sector: A Role for Relationship Marketing?" *International Journal of Nonprofit and Voluntary Sector Marketing,* 1997, *2,* 42–51.

Demerath, N. J. "Organization and Management Needs of a National Family Planning Program: The Case of India." *Journal of Social Issues,* 1967, *4,* 179–193.

Fugate, D. L. "Channel Design for Early Intervention Services: Is There a Role for Brokers?" *Journal of Nonprofit and Public Sector Marketing,* 2000, *7*(4), 3–15.

Gainer, B. "The Business of High Art: Marketing the Performing Arts in Canada." *Service Industries Journal,* 1989, *9,* 143–161.

Gainer, B., and Padanyi, P. "Applying the Marketing Concept to Cultural Organizations: An Empirical Study of the Relationship Between Market Orientation and Performance." *International Journal of Nonprofit and Voluntary Sector Marketing,* 2002, *7,* 182–193.

Kohli, A. K, Jaworski, B. J., and Kumar, A. "MARKOR: A Measure of Market Orientation." *Journal of Marketing Research,* 1993, *30,* 467–477.

Kotler, P., and Armstrong, G. *Principles of Marketing.* Upper Saddle River, N.J.: Prentice Hall, 1994.

Kotler, P., and Roberto, E. L. *Social Marketing: Strategies for Changing Public Behavior.* New York: Free Press, 1989.

Kotler, P., and Scheff, J. *Standing Room Only: Strategies for Marketing the Performing Arts.* Boston: Harvard Business School Press, 1997.

Letts, C. W., Ryan, W., and Grossman, A. "Virtuous Capital: What Foundations Can Learn from Venture Capitalists." *Harvard Business Review,* Mar.-Apr. 1997, pp. 2–7.

Lovelock, C., and Weinberg, C. B. *Marketing for Public and Nonprofit Managers.* (2nd ed.) Redwood City, Calif.: Scientific Press, 1989.

MacMillan, I. C. "Competitive Strategies for Not-for-Profit Agencies." *Advances in Strategic Management,* 1983, *1,* 61–68.

Moyer, M. S. "Marketing for Nonprofit Managers." In R. D. Herman and Associates, *The Jossey-Bass Handbook of Nonprofit Leadership and Management.* San Francisco: Jossey-Bass, 1994.

Narver, J. C, and Slater, S. F. "The Effect of a Market Orientation on Business Profitability." *Journal of Marketing,* 1990, *54,* 20–35.

Oster, S. M. *Strategic Management for Nonprofit Organizations: Theory and Cases.* New York: Oxford University Press, 1995.

Ritchie, R., Swami, S., and Weinberg, C. B. "A Brand New World for Nonprofits." *Journal of Nonprofit and Voluntary Sector Marketing,* 1999, *4*(1), 26–42.

Rogers, E. *The Diffusion of Innovations.* (4th ed.) New York: Free Press, 1995.

Sargeant, A. " Preface." *Journal of Nonprofit and Public Sector Marketing,* 2001, *9*(4), xiii–xv.

Sargeant, A., and Stephenson, H. "Corporate Giving: Targeting the Likely Donor." *Journal of Nonprofit and Voluntary Sector Marketing,* 1997, *2*(1), 64–79.

Sargeant, A., Foreman, S., and Liao, M. "Operationalizing the Marketing Concept in the Nonprofit Sector." *Journal of Nonprofit and Public Sector Marketing,* 2002, *10*(2), 41–45.

Siciliano, J. "The Relationship Between Formal Planning and Performance in Nonprofit Organizations." *Nonprofit Management and Leadership,* 1997, *7,* 387–403.

Smith, C. "The New Corporate Philanthropy." *Harvard Business Review,* May-June 1994, pp. 105–116.

Trout, J., and Rivkin, S. *The New Positioning: The Latest on the World's #1 Business Strategy.* New York: McGraw-Hill, 1997.

Wymer, W. W., Jr. "Segmenting Volunteers Using Values, Self-Esteem, Empathy, and Facilitation as Determinant Variables." *Journal of Nonprofit and Public Sector Marketing,* 1997, *5*(2), 3–28.

CHAPTER THIRTEEN

Designing and Managing Volunteer Programs

Jeffrey L. Brudney

One of the most distinctive features of the nonprofit sector is its ability to harness the productive labor of literally millions of citizens in service to organizational goals, without benefit of remuneration. Government organizations at the federal, state, and local levels also rely on substantial volunteer labor to pursue their public purposes. This remarkable achievement does not just happen spontaneously as a consequence of compelling agency missions, although, certainly, the desire to help people by donating time to a worthwhile cause is a powerful motivation for most volunteers. The credit belongs, instead, to the volunteer program, which allows citizens to realize the helping impulse as a well as a variety of other motives through work activities designed by the organization with the volunteer in mind to meet its needs and objectives. The volunteer program may be part of an organization that also has paid staff, or it may consist of a group or organization staffed entirely by volunteers.

An organized volunteer program provides a structure for meeting certain requisites: volunteers must be recruited; they must be screened and given orientation to the agency; they must be assigned to positions and afforded training as necessary; they must be supervised, motivated, and accorded appropriate recognition; and they should be evaluated to assess the efficacy of their placement for themselves as well as for the organization. This inventory focuses too narrowly on the volunteer, however, and overlooks the groundwork the organization must first lay for an effective program. The agency must determine its reasons for enlisting voluntary assistance and how it plans to involve and integrate citizen participants. Based on that philosophy, it must develop job descriptions for volunteer positions and arrange for orientation and training for employees expected to work with nonpaid staff. The agency should make clear the importance of collaborating with volunteers and hold these employees accountable for doing so. Given the infrastructure that must be created to have an effective volunteer program, an agency must exhibit or reach a certain state of readiness (Brudney, 1995).

The volunteer program is a vehicle for facilitating and coordinating the work efforts of volunteers and paid staff toward the attainment of organizational goals. The core program functions that make this achievement possible can be grouped as follows:

- Establishing the rationale for volunteer involvement
- Involving paid staff in volunteer program design
- Integrating the volunteer program into the organization
- Creating positions of program leadership
- Preparing job descriptions for volunteer positions
- Meeting the needs of volunteers
- Managing volunteers
- Evaluating and recognizing the volunteer effort

This chapter elaborates the essential components of the volunteer program and offers suggestions for increasing their effectiveness. Several caveats with respect to coverage are in order. First, "volunteer recruitment" would ordinarily merit inclusion in any listing of program functions; indeed, in surveys and interviews with those who administer volunteer programs, recruitment and retention are usually cited as the most important responsibility and, often, the greatest difficulty. Because recruitment is the subject of another chapter in this handbook (Chapter Twenty-Two), however, it is treated here only in passing. Second, in the decade since the publication of the first edition of this book, risk management for volunteers and volunteer programs has become a much greater concern (Herman and Jackson, 2001). Again, this topic is the focus of another chapter in the handbook (Chapter Twenty-One) and will not be covered here.

Second, this chapter concentrates on "service" volunteers, individuals who donate their time to help other people directly, rather than on "policy" volunteers, citizens who assume the equally vital role of sitting on boards of directors or advisory boards of nonprofit organizations (see Chapter Six). Although the demands of managing the performance and incorporating the benefits into the agency of these two types of volunteer activity are quite distinct, some overlap does exist. Service volunteers can bring a wealth of practical experience and knowledge that might prove a great asset to an advisory board; similarly, experience in direct service might usefully shape or sharpen the observations and insights of board members. Yet service volunteers may not always possess the breadth of perspective and background important to effective policymaking or an interest in this pursuit, while board members may lack the immediate skills or motivation to perform well in a service capacity. As a result of such trade-offs, a great variety of practices governs the relationship between service and policy volunteering across the nonprofit sector. Some organizations encourage service volunteers to become board members, others permit the interchange, and still others prohibit it. The term *volunteer program* conventionally refers to the organization and management of service volunteers for best results. This topic forms the core of the present chapter.

ESTABLISHING THE RATIONALE FOR VOLUNTEER INVOLVEMENT

No matter how overburdened an agency is, how constrained its human and financial resources may be, how eager it is for fresh input and innovation, and how enthusiastic it is about the potential contribution of citizens, its efforts to incorporate volunteers should not begin with recruitment. Unfortunately, well-intentioned but premature calls for (ordinarily undifferentiated) help can breed apprehension among paid staff and frustration among volunteers and can exacerbate the very problems volunteerism was intended to solve. Because this scenario would reinforce negative stereotypes about volunteers and undermine their credibility as a vital service resource, it must be avoided. In fact, Susan J. Ellis begins *The Volunteer Recruitment (and Membership Development) Book* with the admonition that "recruitment is the third step" (2002, p. 5.). The first step, treated in this section, is to determine why the organization wants volunteers; the second, discussed later in this chapter, is to design valuable work assignments for them (Ellis, 2002). The agency must resist the temptation to "call in the volunteers" until the groundwork for their sustained involvement has been put in place. The foundation for an effective volunteer program rests, instead, on a serious consideration by the agency of the rationale for citizen involvement and the development of a philosophy or policy to guide this effort. The initial step in planning the program should be to determine the purposes for introducing the new participants into the organization. For what reasons are volunteers sought?

Especially in times of fiscal exigency, top organizational officials will often express "cost savings" as the primary reason for enlisting volunteers. Yet the claim is misleading. In the first place, while the labor of volunteers may be "free" or donated, a volunteer program requires expenditures for orientation, training, reimbursement, promotion, materials, and so forth. In the second, for volunteers to finance cost savings (rather than extend agency resources), cutbacks must be exacted somewhere in the agency budget. If cutbacks are to be visited on paid staff, officials risk the kinds of resentments and antagonisms that have scuttled many a volunteer program.

A more accurate description of the economic benefits that volunteers can bring to an agency is "cost-effectiveness." When a volunteer program has been designed to supplement or complement the work of paid staff with that of citizens, volunteers can help an agency hold costs down in achieving a given level of service or help it increase services for a fixed level of expenditure (Brudney, 1990; Karn, 1982; Moore, 1978). From the perspective of organizational efficiency, what volunteers offer is the capacity to make more productive application of existing funds and "person power." With a relatively small investment of resources, volunteers have the potential to increase the level and quality of services that an agency can deliver to the public. Though costs are not spared in this situation, to the degree that volunteers improve the return on expenditures, they extend the resources available to an agency to meet pressing needs for assistance and services.

Additional or different purposes may drive a volunteer program. The leadership of a nonprofit organization may decide to enlist volunteers to interject a more vibrant dimension of commitment and caring into its relationships with clients. Or the goal may be to learn more about the community, nurture closer ties to citizens, and strengthen public awareness and support. Volunteers may be needed to reach clients inaccessible through normal organizational channels, that is, to engage in "outreach" activities (see, for example, May, McLaughlin, and Penner, 1991; Dorwaldt, Solomon, and Worden, 1988; Young, Goughler, and Larson, 1986). They may be called on to provide professional skills, such as computer programming, legal counsel, or accounting expertise, not readily available to an agency. The purpose may be to staff an experimental program otherwise doomed to financial austerity. Enhancing responsiveness to client groups may offer still another rationale.

Volunteers also make excellent fundraisers. Because the public tends to perceive them as neutral participants who will not directly benefit from monetary donations to an agency, organizations frequently enlist citizens for this task. According to the 1996 *Giving and Volunteering in the United States* survey undertaken by the INDEPENDENT SECTOR, the most common job assignment reported by volunteers in the past month was fundraising; in earlier surveys, this assignment also ranked at or near the top in frequency (Hodgkinson and Weitzman, 1996).

That the list of possible purposes for establishing a volunteer program is lengthy attests to the vitality of the approach. Before seeking volunteers, agency leaders should settle on the ends for their organization. An explicit statement of goals advances several important facets of program design and functioning. First, it begins to define the types of volunteer positions that will be needed and the number of individuals required to fill these roles. Such information is at the core of eventual recruitment and training of volunteers. Second, it aids in delineating concrete objectives against which the program might be evaluated once it is in operation. Evaluation results are instrumental to strengthening and improving the program.

Finally, a statement of the philosophy underlying volunteer involvement and the specific ends sought through this form of participation can help alleviate possible apprehensions of paid staff that the new participants may intrude on professional prerogatives or threaten job security. Clarifying the goals for voluntary assistance can dampen idle, typically negative, speculation and begin to build a sense of program ownership on the part of employees—especially if they are included in planning for the volunteer program.

It should be acknowledged that simply stating the mission or goals for volunteer involvement (or for other organizational endeavors) is insufficient. Without follow-through or commitment, even the most laudable purposes can fall easy victim to failure and frustration. Worse, rhetorical support can breed cynicism and lack of trust that can be particularly difficult to overcome. In the wake of the tragic events of September 11, 2001, for example, President Bush seemed to have the moment and the oratory to galvanize the citizenry toward greater volunteerism, self-sacrifice, and responsibility for common purposes. A year later, editorialists began to question whether the social, moral, and political capital that grew out of that terrible day had already evaporated. "Mr. Bush continues to extol the virtues of voluntary service, and this is admirable. But it is hardly enough to resist the erosion in the level of public engagement as people return to everyday routines" ("An Uncertain Trumpet," 2002).

INVOLVING PAID STAFF IN VOLUNTEER PROGRAM DESIGN

Although the support of top-level organizational officials is crucial to the establishment and vitality of a volunteer program (Ellis, 1996; Valente, 1985; Farr, 1983; Scheier, 1981), they are not the only ones who should be involved in defining the mission, philosophy, and procedures of this effort. Paid staff—and volunteers, if they are already known to the agency or can be identified—should also be included in these meetings and discussions.

A precept in the field of organizational development is to include groups to be affected by a new policy or program in its design and implementation. Involvement adds to the knowledge base for crafting policy and inculcates a sense of ownership and commitment that can prove very beneficial in gaining acceptance for innovation. Because the incorporation of volunteers into an agency can impose dramatic changes in work life, the participation of paid staff is especially important (Graff, 1984). The sharing of needs, perspectives, and information among agency leadership, employees, and prospective volunteers that ensues plays a pivotal role in determining how the volunteer program might be most effectively designed, organized, and managed to further attainment of agency goals. At the same time, the process helps alleviate any concerns of paid staff regarding volunteer involvement and its implications for the workplace.

A primary purpose of the planning meetings and discussions is to develop policies and procedures governing volunteer involvement endorsed by all parties. Agency guidelines need not be lengthy, but they should address all major aspects of volunteer participation (see McCurley and Lynch, 1996). Important aspects include the following:

- Definition of volunteer
- Screening procedures
- Assignment of volunteers
- Performance evaluation
- Benefits of service
- Length or term of service
- Grievance procedures
- Reimbursement policies
- Use of agency equipment and facilities
- Confidentiality requirements
- Disciplinary procedures
- Record-keeping requirements

In all areas, these policies should be as comparable as possible to pertinent guidelines for employees.

Although some may lament the formality of conduct codes for volunteers as somehow inimical to the spirit of help freely given, this device is associated with positive results. Explicit policies for volunteers demonstrate that the agency takes their participation seriously and values their contribution to goal attainment. By setting standards as high for volunteers as for paid staff, an agency builds trust and credibility, increased respect and requests for volunteers from employees, a healthy work environment, and perhaps most important, high-quality services (McCurley and Lynch, 1989, 1996; Goetter, 1987; Deitch and Thompson, 1985; Wilson, 1984). A seasoned volunteer administrator advises, "One should not have different qualifications for staff than one has for volunteers doing the same work" (Thornburg, 1992, p. 18). These guidelines and expectations greatly facilitate organizing the volunteer program, handling problem situations, protecting rights, and managing for consistent results.

Some authorities go farther to argue that "nonprofits should treat volunteers as if they were paid employees" (Stoolmacher, 1991). They contend that the standard elements of volunteer administration, such as an interview, screening, placement, job description, orientation, supervision, ongoing training, performance review, maintenance of records, recognition, and fair and professional treatment, reduce the possibility for confusion and frustration on the part of volunteers that can result in an unsuccessful experience for both them and the organization. The "volunteers as unpaid staff" model is not without detractors (for example, Ilsley, 1990), and the approach should be amply leavened to take into account the needs, perspectives, and circumstances of volunteers so that volunteers are matched to missions and jobs for which they have interest, ability, skills, and input. Other scholars maintain that this "program" model of volunteer management may work well in certain circumstances (for example, in a larger volunteer program or in a program operated by a government agency or a large nonprofit) but not in all, such as in a membership-based organization or a small cooperative (Meijs and Hoogstad, 2001).

Explicit policies for the volunteer program help solidify the "psychological contract" linking volunteers to the agency and thus may reduce withdrawal and turnover. In one study, Jone L. Pearce (1978) found that organizations that were most successful in clarifying the volunteer-agency relationship suffered the lowest rates of turnover. These agencies distributed notebooks with all written policies, formal job descriptions, and training manuals to citizen participants. By contrast, the organization with the highest turnover in Pearce's sample provided none of this information to volunteers.

In more recent research, Steven M. Farmer and Donald B. Fedor (1999) investigated the effects of the psychological contract in a survey of 451 executive committee volunteers working in the chapters of a large national nonprofit fundraising health advocacy organization. Similar to the results of Pearce's study, Farmer and Fedor found that fulfillment (or violation) of the psychological contract affected the level of volunteer participation. Volunteers who reported that the organization had met their expectations participated more in the organization and perceived greater levels of organizational support for their involvement. In turn, perceived organizational support not only increased levels of participation but also reduced volunteers' turnover intentions. In another study, Matthew Liao-Troth (2001) found the attitudes of paid workers and volunteers holding similar jobs in a single hospital setting to be quite similar, including the psychological contract (with the exception of psychological contracts regarding benefits). He concludes, "Volunteers may believe that they have made certain agreements with the organization as to what they will provide the organization and what the organization will provide them. If a manager is not aware of her or his volunteers' psychological contracts, then he or she may unintentionally violate the volunteers' psychological contracts, which can have negative consequences in terms of job performance" (p. 437). Although volunteers may not be involved in initial discussions concerning volunteer program planning and design, once this effort is launched and in operation, they need to have input into major decisions affecting the program. Just as for paid employees, citizens are more likely to invest in and commit to organizational policies, and provide useful information for this purpose, if they enjoy ready access to the decision-making process. Participation in decision making is a key element of "empowerment" in volunteer administration, which is thought to result in increased ownership of the volunteer program by participants and hence greater commitment and effectiveness (for a full discussion, see Scheier, 1988a, 1988b, 1988c; Naylor, 1985). Formerly, the term *empowerment* seemed to center on citizen volunteers and expressed the idea that they should enjoy greater say in these programs, as well as greater recognition for the time, skills, and value they contributed. More recently, the term seems to have shifted to the administrators of these programs and expresses the conviction that they should have positions, influence, authority, and status in host organizations commensurate with their performing a very difficult but highly productive managerial task (see, for example, McCurley and Ellis, 2003a; Ellis, 1996).

INTEGRATING THE VOLUNTEER PROGRAM INTO THE ORGANIZATION

As these comments suggest, the volunteer program must be organized to respond to the motivations and requirements of volunteers and employees. With respect to volunteers, the program should have mechanisms for determining the types of work opportunities sought and meeting those preferences and for engendering an organizational climate in which volunteers can pursue their goals with the acceptance, if not always the avid endorsement, of paid personnel. From the perspective of staff, the program must have structures and procedures in place to assume the task of volunteer administration and to generate a pool of capable citizens matched to the tasks of participating offices and departments.

To accomplish these goals, the volunteer program must be linked to the structure of the nonprofit or government host organization. A small nonprofit may accommodate volunteers with a minimum of structural adaptations, but larger agencies need to consider alternative structural configurations for integrating volunteers into their operations (Brudney, 1995; Valente and Manchester, 1984). In order of increasing comprehensiveness, these arrangements consist of ad hoc volunteer efforts, volunteer recruitment by an outside organization with the agency otherwise responsible for management, decentralization of the program to operating departments, and a centralized approach. Each option presents a distinctive menu of advantages and disadvantages.

Volunteer efforts may arise spontaneously in an ad hoc fashion to meet exigencies confronting an organization, especially on a short-term basis. Normally, citizens motivated to share their background, training, skills, and interests with organizations that could profit by them are the catalyst. Financial stress, leaving an agency few options, may quicken the helping impulse. The Service Corps of Retired Executives (SCORE), an association of primarily retired businesspersons who donate their time and skills to assist clients of the U.S. Small Business Administration (SBA), began in this way in the early 1960s; retired business executives approached the SBA to offer assistance with its huge constituency (Brudney, 1986). The responsiveness and alacrity with which an ad hoc effort can be launched and operating is inspiring: within six months of its inception, SCORE supplied two thousand volunteers to the SBA. Crisis and emergency situations can provoke an even more spectacular response, mobilizing huge numbers of volunteers in a remarkably short time.

Spontaneous help from citizens can infuse vitality (and labor) into an agency and alert officials to the possibilities of volunteerism. Offsetting these benefits, however, is the fact that only selected parts or members of the organization may be aware of an ad hoc citizen effort and thus be able to take advantage of it. In addition, because energy levels and zeal wane as emergencies are tamed or fade from the limelight of publicity or attention, the ad hoc model of volunteer involvement is very vulnerable to the passage of time. A volunteer program requires not only a different type of ongoing, rather than sporadic, commitment from citizens but also an organizational structure to sustain their contributions and make them accessible to all employees. Unless the agency takes steps to institutionalize participation, it risks squandering the long-term benefits of the approach. Almost from the start, the SBA and the SCORE volunteers worked to develop an appropriate structure. In 2004, they celebrated the fortieth anniversary of a partnership that has brought a continuous stream of volunteers to the agency (10,500 in 2003 alone) and advice and assistance to an estimated 6 million aspiring entrepreneurs and small business owners (SCORE, 2003).

A second option sometimes open to nonprofit agencies is to rely on the expertise and reputation of an established organization, such as the United Way and its affiliates, or a volunteer center or clearinghouse, to assist in the recruitment of volunteers while retaining all other managerial responsibilities in-house. Since recruitment is the most fundamental program function and, arguably, the most problematic, regular professional assistance with this task can be highly beneficial, particularly for an agency just starting a volunteer program. Some private business firms seeking to develop volunteer programs for their employees have extended this model: they find it advantageous to contract with local volunteer centers not only for help with recruitment but also other main pro- gram functions, such as volunteer placement and evaluation (Haran, Kenney, and Vermilion, 1993). A large national network of more than four hundred vol- unteer centers affiliated with the Points of Light Foundation offers these services to nonprofit and government agencies (Brudney, 2003). When this model is used, quality control presents a necessary caution, just as it does in the dele- gation of any organizational function. Recruiters must be familiar with the needs of the nonprofit agency for voluntary assistance, lest volunteers be referred who do not meet the desired profile of backgrounds, skills, and interests. A recruiter may also deal with multiple client organizations so that the priority attached to the requests of any one of them is unclear. More important, trusting recruitment to outsiders is a deterrent to developing the necessary capacity in-house, which is an essential aspect of a successful volunteer program. By all means, organi- zations should nurture positive relationships with agencies in the community to attract volunteers and for other purposes. But they must avoid being totally dependent on external sources and endeavor to implement recruitment mech- anisms of their own.

The volunteer program can also be decentralized in individual departments within a larger nonprofit organization. The primary advantage offered by this approach is the flexibility to tailor programs to the needs of specific organiza- tional units and to introduce volunteers where support for them is greatest. Yet duplication of effort across several departments, difficulties in locating sufficient expertise in volunteer management to afford multiple programs, and problems in coordination—particularly, restrictions on the ability to shift volunteers to more suitable positions or to offer them opportunities for job enrichment across the organization—are significant liabilities.

In the public sector, the selective approach can unwittingly generate disin- centives for managers to introduce volunteers (Brudney, 1989). Top agency offi- cials may mistakenly equate nonpaid work with "unimportant" activities, to the detriment of a department's (and a manager's) standing in the organization, or they may seize on the willingness to enlist volunteers as an excuse to deny a unit essential increases in budget and paid personnel. Such misunderstandings must be eliminated prior to the introduction of volunteers.

Despite the limitations, the decentralized approach may serve an agency quite well in starting a pilot or experimental program, the results of which might guide the organization in moving toward more extensive volunteer involvement. Alternatively, a lack of tasks appropriate for volunteers in some parts of the agency or perhaps strong opposition from various quarters may confine volun- tary assistance to selected departments.

The final structural arrangement is a centralized volunteer program serving the entire agency. With this approach, a single office or department is responsi- ble for management and coordination of the volunteer program. The volunteers may serve exclusively in this unit, or they may be deployed and supervised in line departments throughout the organization. The office provides guidelines, technical assistance, screening, training, and all other administration for volunteer activity throughout the agency. The advantages of centralization for averting duplication of effort, assigning volunteers so as to meet their needs as well as those of the organization, and producing efficient and effective voluntary services are considerable. However, the program demands broad support across the organization, especially at the top, to overcome issues that may be raised by departmental staff and any limitations in resources. When such backing is not forthcoming, the other structural arrangements may serve the nonprofit agency quite well.

CREATING POSITIONS OF PROGRAM LEADERSHIP

Regardless of the structural arrangement by which the volunteer program is integrated into agency operations, this component requires a visible, recognized leader. All program functions, including those discussed to this point (developing a rationale for the volunteer effort, involving paid staff in program planning and design, housing the volunteer program), benefit from the establishment and staffing of a position bearing overall responsibility for management and representation of the volunteers. The position goes by a variety of names (for example, "volunteer coordinator"); we shall call it the "director of volunteer services" (DVS) to signify the importance of the role.

James C. Fisher and Kathleen M. Cole (1993) elaborate two approaches that organizations typically take in designing the volunteer management function: personnel management and program management. The personnel management approach is most common in organizations in which volunteers are deployed in several or many units or departments and have many different responsibilities throughout the organization. In this configuration, the volunteer program manager works with the line departments in all facets of volunteer administration and supports the line departments. However, the principal accountability of the volunteer is to the paid staff (or other) supervisor in the unit where the volunteer is housed. The volunteer administrator does not directly supervise the volunteer or provide training or evaluation. By contrast, in the program management approach, the volunteer administrator normally supervises the volunteers, who are housed in a single unit under her or his leadership. As Fisher and Cole explain, "In the program management approach, the volunteer administrator is a program developer as well as the leader of volunteer efforts integral to the organization's program delivery. In the personnel management approach, the volunteer administrator recruits, selects, and places volunteers and trains paid staff to work with them. In both approaches, the responsibilities of the volunteer administrator usually include job design, recruitment, interviewing, orientation, and recognition" (p. 18).

The manner by which the office of the director of volunteer services is staffed sends a forceful message to employees regarding the significance of the volunteer program to the agency and its leadership. Organizations have experimented with an assortment of staffing options for the post, including volunteers, personnel with existing duties, and employee committees. None so manifestly demonstrates a sense of organizational commitment and priorities as a paid DVS position. Establishing the office as close to the apex of the agency's formal hierarchy as feasible conveys a similar message of resolve and purposefulness. Unfortunately, the evidence suggests that agencies do not always attend to supports for the position (for a review, see Brudney, 1992).

The DVS should enjoy prerogatives and responsibilities commensurate with positions at the same level in the organization, including participation in relevant decision making and policymaking and access to superiors. In this manner, the incumbent can represent the volunteers before the relevant departments or the organization as a whole, promote their interests, and help prevent officials from taking their contributions for granted. A part-time or full-time paid position, as appropriate, lodges accountability for the program squarely with the DVS; presents a focal point for contact with the volunteer operation for individuals inside as well as outside the organization; implements a core structure for program administration; and rewards the officeholder in relation to the success of the volunteers.

In addition to these roles, the DVS has important duties that further substantiate the need for a dedicated position (Ellis, 1996). The DVS is responsible for volunteer recruitment and publicity, a critical function requiring active outreach in the community and highly flexible working hours. The incumbent must communicate with department and organizational officials to ascertain workloads and requirements for voluntary assistance. Assessing agency needs for volunteers, enlarging areas for their involvement, and educating staff to the approach should be seen not as a onetime exercise but as an ongoing DVS responsibility. The DVS interviews and screens all applicants for volunteer positions, maintains appropriate records, places volunteers in job assignments, provides liaison supervision, and monitors performance. The office must coordinate the bewildering variety of schedules and backgrounds volunteers bring to the agency. The DVS also bears overall responsibility for the orientation and training, evaluation, and recognition of volunteers. Since employees may be unfamiliar with the approach, training may be appropriate for them as well; the DVS is the in-house source of expertise on all aspects of volunteer involvement and management. Finally, as the chief advocate of the program, the DVS endeavors not only to express the volunteer perspective but also to allay any apprehensions of paid staff and facilitate collaboration.

As volunteer programs increase in size, the DVS will likely have to share leadership duties with volunteers or paid staff (or both), but the functions must be performed. Given the scope of the job tasks, clerical and other support for the position is highly advisable.

PREPARING JOB DESCRIPTIONS FOR VOLUNTEER POSITIONS

The essential building block of a successful volunteer program is the job description. Paradoxically, no intrinsic basis exists to create (or classify) a position as "paid" or "volunteer." Even among agencies that have the same purpose or mission or that work in the same substantive or policy domain, a given position can be classified differently (examples include business counselor, computer programmer, day care provider, receptionist, and ombudsperson). Within an agency, moreover, job definitions are dynamic, meaning that volunteers can be succeeded by paid service professionals in some areas (Ellis and Noyes, 1990; Park, 1983; Schwartz, 1977; Becker, 1964) and take over from them in others (Brudney, 1986).

Without an intrinsic basis to designate a task or position as "volunteer" or "paid," the process by which work responsibilities are allocated assumes paramount importance. As just elaborated, the most enduring basis for an effective volunteer program is for top agency officials and employees (and if possible, volunteers) to work out, in advance of program implementation, explicit understandings regarding the rationale for the involvement of volunteers, the nature of the jobs they are to perform, and the boundaries of their work (Ellis, 1996; Graff, 1984; Brown, 1981; Wilson, 1976). This agreement should designate (or provide the foundation for distinguishing) the jobs assigned to volunteers and those held by paid staff.

The second critical step in the job design process consists of surveying employees, or perhaps conducting personal interviews with them, to ascertain key factors about their jobs and to make them aware of the potential contributions of volunteers. At a minimum, a survey should seek to identify the aspects of the job that employees most enjoy performing, those that they dislike, and those for which they lack sufficient time or expertise; the survey should also ascertain any activities or projects that employees would like to do but never find the time to perform. Since employees may lack background information regarding the assistance that volunteers might lend to them and to the agency, the survey or interview (or alternatively, in-service training) should provide resource material regarding volunteers, such as a listing of the jobs or functions that unpaid staff are already performing in their agency or in similar organizations, new initiatives undertaken by volunteers beyond the time or expertise of paid staff, and skills and descriptions of available volunteers (see McCurley and Lynch, 1989, 1996).

Popular stereotypes to the contrary, not all volunteer positions need be in supportive roles to employee endeavors. In some Maryland counties, for instance, paid staff have facilitated and supported the activities of volunteers in delivering recreation services, rather than the reverse (Marando, 1986). In the Court Appointed Special Advocates (CASA) and Big Brothers Big Sisters programs, paid staff also facilitate and support the core work performed by volunteers. Many organizations rely on donated labor for highly technical professional tasks, such as accounting, economic development, and computer applications, that are not provided by employees and that they could not otherwise obtain. More important is that the delegation of tasks takes into account the unique capabilities that staff and volunteers might bring toward meeting organization needs.

To allocate work responsibilities among employees and volunteers, Susan J. Ellis (1996) suggests that an agency reassess the job descriptions of the entire staff. Prime candidates for delegation to volunteers are tasks with the following characteristics:

- Those that might be performed periodically, such as once a week, rather than on a daily or inflexible basis
- Those that do not require the specialized training or expertise of paid personnel
- Those that might be done more effectively by someone with specialized training in that skill
- Those for which the position occupant feels uncomfortable or unprepared
- Those for which the agency possesses no in-house expertise
- Those that might be performed "episodically," that is, on an occasional basis using very short time intervals
- Those that might be performed "virtually" or through computer technology such as e-mail or the Internet

The culmination of the task analysis should be a new set of job descriptions for employees and a second set for volunteers that are sensitive to prevailing organization conditions. Paid staff are primarily assigned to the most important daily functions, while volunteers handle work that can be done on a periodic basis or that makes use of the special talents for which the volunteers have been recruited (Ellis, 1996). The intent is to achieve the most effective deployment of both paid and nonpaid personnel. The respective tasks should be codified in formal job descriptions for not only paid but also nonpaid workers, with the stipulation that neither group will occupy the positions reserved for the other.

A pioneer in the field, Harriet H. Naylor, insisted, "Most of the universally recognized principles of administration for employed personnel are even more valid for volunteer workers, who *give* their talents and time" (1973, p. 173; emphasis in original). Her insight into the parallels between the administration of paid staff and volunteers is especially pertinent with respect to job specifications, placement, and orientation. Studies undertaken by the International

City/County Management Association on volunteer programs in local governments indicate that "volunteer job descriptions are really no different than job descriptions for paid personnel. A volunteer will need the same information a paid employee would need to determine whether the position is of interest" (Manchester and Bogart, 1988, p. 59). Specifications for volunteer positions should include (McCurley and Lynch, 1996, p. 30):

- Job title and purpose
- Benefits to the occupant
- Qualifications for the position
- Time requirement (for example, hours per week)
- Proposed starting date (and ending date, if applicable)
- Job responsibilities and activities
- Authority invested in the position
- Reporting relationships and supervision

The parallels to paid administration noted by Naylor (1973) and others continue beyond the job description to other key functions of the volunteer program. Applicants for volunteer positions should be screened for relevant competencies and interests, as well as pertinent background and qualifications. Especially for positions that call for contact with vulnerable populations such as youth and the infirm, reference or background checks should be conducted for volunteers. Volunteers should be interviewed by officials from the volunteer program and the agency to ensure a suitable fit of citizen and organizational needs. These new members will require an orientation to the agency and its volunteer component. Among the topics that orientation activities should address are the overall mission and specific objectives of the organization, its traditions and philosophy, its operating rules and procedures, the rationale and policies of the volunteer program, and the roles and interface of paid and nonpaid staff members. Finally, as needed, training should be provided to volunteers to assume the organizational tasks assigned to them. (Chapter Twenty-Three of this book treats these important elements of an effective volunteer program in the depth and richness they deserve.)

EMERGING JOBS FOR VOLUNTEERS: VIRTUAL VOLUNTEERING AND EPISODIC VOLUNTEERING

As mentioned briefly in the listing of organizational tasks that might be delegated to volunteers, virtual volunteering and episodic volunteering are emerging forms. Virtual volunteering refers to volunteering "at a distance" through electronic technology, including the Internet or e-mail (Murray and Harrison, 2002a, 2002b). In the 1999 edition of the INDEPENDENT SECTOR survey *Giving and Volunteering in the United States,* just 1 percent of respondents had learned about volunteering via the Internet, a finding that prompted the authors to conclude, "Few charities are maximizing the possibilities of the Internet to stimulate giving and volunteering" (Kirsch, Hume, and Jalandoni, 2000, p. 16). By the time of the 2001 *Giving and Volunteering* survey, however, 3.3 percent of a national sample of U.S. volunteers reported that they had learned about a volunteering opportunity via an Internet advertisement or responded to a solicitation over the Internet (Toppe, Kirsch, and Michel, 2002, p. 41). Also in the 2001 survey, among volunteers with Internet access, about 13 percent reported that they had used the Internet to search for or learn about volunteer opportunities. About 4 percent of volunteers with Internet access reported that they had volunteered over the Internet during the past year, performing such activities as mentoring, tutoring, or Web site development (p. 41). The USA Freedom Corps, an umbrella organization for coordination of volunteer programs in the U.S. federal government, relies on the nonprofit, online virtual volunteer service VolunteerMatch (http://www.volunteermatch.org) for much of its initial recruitment and information gathering. VolunteerMatch claims to have helped more than twenty thousand community service organizations receive nearly eight hundred thousand volunteer referrals.

A study of virtual volunteering in Canada conducted by Vic Murray and Yvonne Harrison in 2001–2002 yielded similar findings. Murray and Harrison (2002a, 2002b) found that only about 4 percent of a sample of 1,747 potential volunteers who had used the online Volunteer Opportunities Exchange said that they had done any virtual volunteering in the past year. Of the 494 managers of volunteer resources surveyed across Canada as part of the study, only one-third reported having any openings for virtual volunteering, and over 70 percent of them reported making fewer than five such placements in the previous year. The study showed that the top three types of virtual volunteer assignments reported by mangers of volunteer resources were desktop publishing, Web site development and maintenance, and research. Despite the limited use of virtual volunteering found in their study, Murray and Harrison (2002a, p. 9) conclude, "Even though the demand for virtual volunteers may not be large at present, it is likely to grow in the future."

Interestingly, Murray and Harrison (2002a, pp. 9–10) attribute the relatively low incidence of virtual volunteering in Canada in 2001–2002 not to a lack of potential volunteers or "supply" but to a lack of organizational readiness or "demand." They observe that this form of volunteering may require a review of all current volunteer (and possibly paid staff) positions to determine if the work could be reorganized to become virtual rather than on-site. In addition, other major organizational changes to accommodate virtual volunteers that will likely prove necessary can also occasion reluctance, if not outright resistance. Once virtual volunteer jobs have been identified, defined, and posted, for example, training, supervision, recognition, and communication systems will likely need to be redesigned to support the new kinds of volunteers.

Although the nature of virtual volunteering appears to be well understood, no universally accepted definition of episodic volunteering exists. Nancy Macduff (1995) characterizes episodic volunteers as those who give service that is short in duration (temporary) or at regular intervals for short periods of time (occasional). "A rule of thumb is that the episodic volunteer is never around longer than six months" (p. 188). Michele A. Weber (2002) defines episodic volunteers as those who contribute their time sporadically, only during special times of the year, or consider it a onetime event. These volunteers give time without an ongoing commitment, often in the form of self-contained and time-specific projects. Weber contrasts these volunteers with "periodic" volunteers, who give time at scheduled, recurring intervals, such as daily, weekly, or monthly.

The trend data made available by INDEPENDENT SECTOR in its biennial national surveys illustrate the scope of episodic volunteering in the United States (Kirsch, Hume, and Jalandoni, 2000). Over the period 1987–1998, reported rates of volunteering among the American public generally increased, with some perturbations. Yet the total number of hours contributed annually remained fairly constant (within the range of 19.5 to 20.5 billion), meaning that the average number of hours donated by volunteers on a weekly basis diminished over that decade. And the decline was substantial, a 25 percent decrease, from an average of 4.7 hours contributed per week and 244.4 hours per year in 1987 to 3.5 hours weekly and 182.0 hours annually in 1998. Michele Nunn (2000, p. 117) speculates, "This could be the result of broader participation levels of individuals who did not regularly volunteer"—in other words, episodic volunteers.

Given the vagaries of definition, estimates of the extent of episodic volunteering are not precise—although, as suggested by the comparative data, unquestionably substantial. According to the 1999 INDEPENDENT SECTOR survey, which assessed giving and volunteering behavior retrospectively for 1998, some 39 percent of volunteers preferred to volunteer at a regularly scheduled time, weekly, biweekly, or monthly. By contrast, "For 41 percent of volunteers, serving is a sporadic, one-time activity"; another 9 percent reported volunteering only at special times of the year such as holidays or festivals (Kirsch, Hume, and Jalandoni, 2000, p. 5). If Weber's distinction between periodic and episodic volunteering is accepted, 69 percent of volunteers could be classified as "periodic" in 2001, meaning that they volunteered at scheduled times recurring at regular intervals (for example, daily, weekly, monthly). The other 31 percent were "episodic volunteers" who contributed their time sporadically, during special times of the year, or regarded it as a onetime activity (Toppe, Kirsch, and Michel, 2002). With regard to the preference among potential volunteers for shorter-term, episodic engagements, McCurley and Ellis (2003b, p. 1) insist, "You can find similar data in Canada, Australia, the United Kingdom, and practically every other country that's done even a casual survey of volunteer attitudes."

McCurley and Ellis (2003b) argue that given the rising trend in short-term, episodic volunteering, the field is in danger of "using the wrong model" to design volunteer jobs, manage and supervise volunteer involvement, and integrate these vital human resources into host organizations. In light of changing volunteer attitudes, preferences, demographics, and availability, the traditional "volunteer as unpaid staff" model that conceived of volunteers as holding long-term, continuous jobs, albeit for many fewer hours than paid staff, may well be in need of refinement for large numbers of potential volunteers. Host organizations that wish to attract episodic volunteers must overcome several barriers, such as possibly antagonistic attitudes of long-term volunteers and paid staff regarding the value of episodic volunteering, agency preferences for continuous service, general resistance to change, and legal liabilities (Macduff, 1995). To start or accommodate an episodic volunteer program, volunteer jobs will need to be shorter in duration; have a clearer, more limited focus; avoid areas in which legal liability could be an issue (for example, direct contact with vulnerable populations); and have less intensive administrative procedures, such as the extent of screening, interviewing, and training required for the job. An organization need not choose between having an episodic volunteer program and a more traditional one based on long-term volunteer involvement: the programs can exist side by side. In fact, Macduff believes that "supervision of short-term volunteers can be done quite effectively by long-term volunteers" (p. 201), a factor that would carry benefits for both parties as well as the organization.

Virtual volunteering and episodic volunteering increase the demands on agencies and their directors of volunteer services to design positions creatively to integrate new forms of productive labor and to make attendant changes in the workplace—as well as to overcome the organizational and personal hurdles and obstacles likely to result. In a volunteer world in which traditional sources of recruitment are lagging, competition for recruits is keen, new forms of participation are gaining popularity, and agency workloads are expanding, organizational investment in these emerging forms of volunteering may well be worth the effort.

MEETING THE NEEDS OF VOLUNTEERS

To this point, the analysis has focused primarily on the demands of the nonprofit organization for attracting, structuring, and managing volunteer labor. Agency needs constitute only half of the equation for a successful volunteer program, however. The other half consists of meeting the needs of volunteers. An effective volunteer program marries organizational demands for productive labor with the disparate motivations that volunteers bring for contributing their time.

The theme of voluntary action gives to the study of nonprofit institutions much of its characteristic identity. Most nonprofit organizations are vitally dependent on volunteers to carry out missions and objectives. Accordingly, voluminous research has been concerned, directly or indirectly, with the motivations that spur volunteers. A basic conclusion emanating from this research is that these motivations are complex and multifaceted and that they may serve a variety of functions for the individual volunteer, along values, understanding, career, social, esteem, and protective dimensions (Clary, Snyder, and Stukas, 1996; Clary, Snyder, and Ridge, 1992). As Gil Clary and his colleagues point out, an understanding of volunteer motivations and the functions that they perform for individuals will assist nonprofit and government organizations in recruiting and retaining volunteers—as well as lead to more satisfying experiences for these citizen participants (Clary, Snyder, and Stukas, 1996).

Although the reasons for volunteering are diverse, several large national surveys extending for more than a quarter of a century reveal a markedly consistent (and interpretable) pattern of professed motivations. Table 13.1 displays the reasons for involvement in volunteer work expressed most often by representative samples of Americans over time in seven surveys between 1965 and 1991. More recent surveys of volunteers' professed motivations have been based on different items. The survey results summarized in Table 13.1 offer the longest and most consistent set of items available regarding volunteer motivation. The length of the series reinforces the reliability of the responses.

According to the data presented in Table 13.1, the most common stimulus for volunteering is to "do something useful to help others" (or to "help people"), manifested by the highest number of respondents in every survey and often by substantially more of the respondents in each successive survey. In addition, approximately one in four people mentioned "religious concerns." About 10 percent of volunteers, rising to 17 percent in 1991, stated as a motivation that they had previously benefited from the activity; perhaps their volunteer work was motivated by a desire to "give something back" for the services or attention they had received. Even allowing for the possibility of some socially desirable responses, the attention that such altruistic motivations seem to command is impressive. Although such professed altruistic motivations appear to drive a great amount of volunteering, more instrumental motivations are common as well. For example, in the survey findings summarized in Table 13.1, approximately 30 to 40 percent of the volunteers gave as reasons that they "enjoy doing volunteer work" or they "had an interest in the activity or work." A substantial number of volunteers (22 to 29 percent) also said that they have a friend or relative either involved in the activity in which they volunteer or who would benefit from it.

Table 13.1. Motivation for Involvement in Volunteer Work, 1965–1991 (percentages).

Motivation	1965[a]	1974	1981	1985	1987	1989	1991
Help people	38	53	45	52	—	—	70
Do something useful	—	—	—	—	56	62	61
Enjoy doing volunteer work	31	36	29	32	35	34	39
Interest in activity or work	—	—	35	36	—	—	—
Sense of duty	33	32	—	—	—	—	—
Religious concerns	—	—	21	27	22	26	31
Could not refuse request	7	15	—	—	—	—	—
Friend or relative received service[b]	—	22	23	26	27	29	29
Volunteer received service	—	—	—	—	10	9	17
Learning experience[c]	—	3	11	10	9	8	16
Nothing else to do, free time	—	4	6	10	9	10	8
Thought work would keep taxes down	—	—	5	3	—	—	—

Notes: The percentages do not sum to 100 because respondents were permitted multiple responses. A dash indicates that this option was not presented to respondents. In the 1965 and 1974 surveys, volunteers were asked about the reason for doing their first "nonreligious" volunteer work. In the 1981, 1985, 1987, 1989, and 1991 surveys, the motivations also pertained to "informal" volunteer work, that is, work that did not involve a private sector association or formal organization.

[a]In the 1965 survey, the question regarding motivations for volunteering was presented to respondents open-ended. The responses were coded into the categories shown in the table. In the other surveys, the respondents were presented with a list of possible motivations for volunteering and were asked which were motivations for them (see U.S. Department of Labor, 1969, p. 9).

[b]In 1974, this category referred exclusively to respondents' children; in 1989, the category stated that a family member or friend would benefit.

[c]In the 1974 study, this category referred to the idea that volunteer work can lead to a paid job.

Sources: U.S. Department of Labor, 1969; ACTION, 1974; Gallup Organization, 1981; Hodgkinson and Weitzman, 1986, 1988, 1990, 1992.

In the surveys conducted in the 1980s, another 8 to 11 percent of respondents identified volunteering as a "learning experience" (16 percent in the 1991 survey). The educational or training benefits afforded by this opportunity are especially important to individuals who seek entry or reentry into the job market but lack requisite competencies or experience. According to one volunteer coordinator and consultant, "*Any* marketable skills can be strengthened and brought up to date in a well-structured volunteer setting" (O'Donald, 1989, p. 22; emphasis in original).

The data in Table 13.1 suggest that many people seem to hold both other-directed and self-directed motivations for volunteering simultaneously. To capture some of the richness of these motivations, the national surveys allowed multiple responses, and indeed, in each survey, the cumulative percentages surpass 100 percent. Volunteering thus appears to spring from a mixture of altruistic and instrumental motivations. Volunteers can—and most likely do—pursue both types of rewards simultaneously: One can certainly help others, derive strong interest and satisfaction in the work, learn and grow from the experience, and enjoy the company of friends and colleagues in the process. These rewards emanate from the quality and meaning of the volunteer experience. As Jon Van Til (1988) observes, volunteering is helping behavior deemed beneficial by participants, even though this action "may contribute to individual goals of career exploration and development, sociability, and other forms of personal enhancement" (p. 8). That is, volunteering is "prosocial" rather than self-sacrificial; it is activity intended to benefit others but not restricting possible benefits to the volunteers as well.

It is also worth noting in Table 13.1 what the volunteering impulse is not: very few citizens apparently engage in this activity with the motivation to spare organizational funds or the conviction that their "work would keep taxes down" (only 3 to 5 percent of volunteers).

How might these motivations evolve as individuals join organizations and engage in volunteer work? Strong altruistic or service motivations could reasonably lead individuals to seek productive outlets for donating their time. As might be expected, however, once they have begun to assist an organization, the immediate rewards of the work experience—such as the social aspects of volunteering and the characteristics of the job they are asked to perform—tend to rise in salience.

For example, based on a study of diverse work settings, Jone L. Pearce (1983) discovered that volunteers stated that they joined the organization for predominantly service reasons but that friendships and social interaction became more influential in their decision to remain with it. While the long-range rewards of helping others, supporting organizational goals, and making a contribution decreased in importance to them (albeit the scores remained at high levels), the rewards of meeting people and enjoying the company of friends and colleagues increased. Similarly, in a study of volunteers to local government, the importance attached by participants to doing something useful or benefiting a family member or friend diminished over time, but interest in or enjoyment of the work grew as a motivation (Sundeen, 1989).

Pearce (1983) concludes, "The rewards individuals expected from volunteering are often not the rewards most salient to them once they have become volunteers" (p. 148). If not anticipated and addressed, this shift in the expected rewards from the experience can result in rapid and ruinous turnover of volunteers. The volunteer program must be designed to counteract this possibility; fortunately, many options are open.

To reinforce volunteers' initial emphasis on service motivations, they might be placed in positions where they can contribute directly to organizational goals, for example, through contact with clients or participation in policy activities. Agencies should also offer entry-level counseling and careful placement to assist volunteers in reaching their personal goals and attempt to foster a work environment conducive to their efforts. Training programs and orientation sessions should present an accurate picture of the rewards of volunteering so that citizens—and the organizations they serve—do not fall prey to unrealistic expectations of the experience.

Agencies also need to respond to changes in the motivations of volunteers. An organization may have a standard set of activities designed to recruit volunteers, but retaining them is not easy to standardize; it is a dynamic process of reviewing performance, growth, and aspirations with the volunteer and modifying work assignments accordingly. Thus in addition to the methods we have already discussed, organizations may, to motivate the continued involvement of volunteers, have to offer a variety of inducements, depending on individual circumstances. These include a progression of steps toward greater responsibilities; participation in problem solving and decision making; opportunities for training; supportive feedback and evaluation; and letters of recommendation documenting work performed.

MANAGING VOLUNTEERS

Managing volunteers is different from managing employees. Volunteers are much less dependent on the organization to which they donate their time than paid staff members, who must earn their livelihood from it. Volunteers can usually leave the organization and find comparable opportunities for their labor with far less effort and inconvenience than employees can. As a result, nonprofit managers and supervisors do not have as much control over volunteer workers.

These differences in control help explain some oft-noted characteristics of volunteers in the workplace. Volunteers can afford to be more selective in accepting job assignments. They may insist on substantial flexibility in work hours. They may not be as faithful in observance of agency rules and regulations, particularly those they deem burdensome or consider "red tape." Part of the reason may stem from the fact that nearly all who volunteer do so on a part-time basis and thus can be expected to have less information about organizational policy and procedures. Also, many regard these aspects of the job and agency as inimical to the spirit and practice of help freely given and so choose to evade or even ignore them. Social interaction is part of the fun and spark of volunteering, and participants may place high value on this feature of the experience.

Given the relative autonomy of volunteers, a heavy-handed approach to supervision can be expected to elicit antagonism and turnover rather than productivity and compliance. Standard organizational inducements for paid employees, such as pay, promotion, and perquisites, are not operative for volunteers. Conventional organizational sanctions are likely to prove unavailing. For example, referring a problem to hierarchical superiors for resolution or disciplinary action (or threatening to do so) is far less apt to sway volunteers than employees.

These considerations may leave the impression that volunteers cannot be "managed," but that conclusion is unfounded. In reviewing certain "myths" that people sometimes have about volunteers, I debunk this notion, as well as the view that volunteers cannot be terminated or "fired" (see Brudney, 2002). Instead, I prescribe a reasonable course for the manager to take should a serious problem arise and persist with a volunteer: ascertain the facts of the situation, be firm in explaining both the problem and the consequences of further violation, and follow through according to agency policy if the problem continues. Management authority Peter F. Drucker (1990, p. 183) agrees that in cases of egregious misconduct, volunteers "must be asked to leave." Countenancing the transgression sends the wrong message to employees, other volunteers, and agency clients that staff (paid or nonpaid) are free from organizational direction and oversight.

The message for management is decidedly more positive: the foundation for the effective management of volunteers rests on applying different techniques and incentives than are commonly used for paid employees to motivate and direct work behaviors toward agency goals. Managerial investment in building trust, cooperation, teamwork, challenge, growth, achievement, values, excitement, and commitment have proved to be much more effectual strategies for this purpose than the conventional methods. In their influential study *In Search of Excellence,* Thomas J. Peters and Richard H. Waterman (1982) maintained that "America's best-run companies" use the same approach for paid employees—with enviable results. Although a common admonition in this literature is to manage volunteers as if they were employees (see Stoolmacher, 1991), the research suggests that it is equally persuasive to recommend "managing employees as if they were volunteers" (Smith and Green, 1993).

Based on a careful examination of a volunteer program serving a large, urban public library system, Virginia Walter (1987, p. 31) found that administrators who embraced this style of "management-by-partnership" enjoyed greater success in dealing with volunteers and meeting objectives than officials intent on control. In a major study of the volunteer SCORE program sponsored by the U.S. Small Business Administration, I arrived at a similar conclusion (see Brudney, 1990). The volunteer business counselors who assisted the SBA sometimes fit the stereotypes attributed to volunteer workers. For example, they displayed low tolerance for necessary government paperwork and "bureaucracy," uneven knowledge of SBA rules and procedures, and keen interest in deciding what cases they would accept or reject for counseling. Yet SBA staff rated the performance of the volunteers as comparable to their own on signal dimensions, including quality and timeliness of services to clients and dependability in work commitments. Like Walter, I attribute these beneficial results to the partnership approach to managing the volunteer program practiced by the SBA and SCORE.

A successful volunteer program must do more than advance changes in managerial style. It must also institute a framework or infrastructure to facilitate successful volunteer integration and involvement in the organization. To channel volunteer talents and energies productively, agencies must elucidate the behaviors expected from unpaid staff. Probably no factor aids more in supervising volunteers (and paid staff) than placing them in positions where they can put their strongest motivations and best skills to work. The procedures discussed earlier in this chapter offer a viable means to elaborate and promote mutual understanding of the volunteer-agency relationship. Developing a coherent philosophy for volunteer involvement, preparing guidelines for the volunteer program, creating formal positions for volunteers, preparing the relevant job descriptions, interviewing and screening applicants and placing them in mutually satisfactory work assignments, and presenting orientation and training are potent means to define what volunteer service means to the agency and to citizens and to coordinate the needs and motives of both parties. Jean Baldwin Grossman and Kathryn Furano (2002, p. 15) similarly identify three elements as "vitally important to the success of any volunteer program": screening potential volunteers to ensure appropriate entry and placement in the organization, orientation and training to provide volunteers with the skills and outlook needed, and management and ongoing support of volunteers by paid staff to ensure that volunteer time is not wasted but is used as effectively as possible.

Effective management of volunteers thus calls for more than changes in managerial style, although these adjustments are certainly important. The volunteer program must also provide an infrastructure to impart a shared conception of volunteer service. Absent such a framework, managerial adaptations in themselves are likely to prove insufficient. As Grossman and Furano (2002, p. 15) aptly summarize, "No matter how well intentioned volunteers are, unless there is an infrastructure in place to support and direct their efforts, they will remain ineffective at best or, worse, become disenchanted and withdraw, potentially damaging recipients of services in the process."

EVALUATING AND RECOGNIZING THE VOLUNTEER EFFORT

Researchers contend that the evaluation function is carried out less often and less well than the other central elements of a volunteer program (see Allen, 1987; Utterback and Heyman, 1984). Samples of volunteer programs in government bear out this contention. In a study of 534 cities with populations greater than 4,500 people that enlisted volunteers in the delivery of services, Sydney Duncombe (1985, p. 363) found that just a handful (62, or 11.6 percent) had made an evaluation study; a study of 189 state agencies reported a comparable rate (13.6 percent) (Brudney and Kellough, 2000, p. 123). Understandably, organizations that rely on the assistance of volunteers may be reluctant to appear to question through evaluation the worth or impact of well-intentioned helping efforts. In addition, officials may be apprehensive about the effects of an evaluation policy on volunteer recruitment and retention and on public relations. Nevertheless, for individual volunteers and the paid staff who work with them, as well as for the volunteer operation as a whole, evaluation and recognition activities are essential program functions.

Evaluation of Volunteers and Employees

The fears of organizational leadership notwithstanding, volunteers have cogent reasons to view personnel assessment in a favorable light. A powerful motivation for volunteering is to achieve worthwhile and visible results; evaluation of performance can guide volunteers toward improvement on this dimension. No citizen contributes his or her time to have the labor wasted in misdirected activity or to repeat easily remedied mistakes and misjudgments. That an organization might take one's work so lightly as to allow such inappropriate behavior to continue is an insult to the volunteer and an affront to standards of professional conduct underlying effectiveness on the job. Clients and host organizations suffer the brunt of these lapses. Evaluation of performance, moreover, is actually a form of compliment to the volunteer (Ellis, 1996). A sincere effort at appraisal indicates that the work merits review and that the individual has the capability and will to do a better job. For many who contribute their time, volunteering offers an opportunity to acquire or hone desirable job skills and to build an attractive résumé for obtaining paid employment. To deny constructive feedback to those who give their time for organizational purposes and who could benefit from this knowledge and hope to do so is a disservice to the volunteers.

Open to nonprofit organizations are an assortment of procedures for carrying out evaluation of volunteer performance. Often the employee to whom the volunteer reports will prepare the appraisal. Or the responsibility may rest with the director of volunteer services or with the personnel department in larger organizations. A combination of these officials might also handle the task. To complement this agency-based perspective, volunteers might evaluate their own accomplishments and experience in the agency, as suggested by some authorities (for example, Manchester and Bogart, 1988; McHenry, 1988). The assessment should tap volunteer satisfaction with important facets of the work assignment, including job duties, schedule, support, training, and opportunities for personal growth. The self-assessment is also a valuable tool to obtain feedback on the management and supervision of volunteers; employees should learn from the process as well. Regardless of the type of evaluation, the goal ought to be to ascertain the degree to which the needs and expectations of the volunteer and the agency are met so that job assignments can be continued, amended, or redefined as necessary.

Agency officials might recognize and show their appreciation to volunteers through a great variety of activities: awards or social events (luncheons, banquets, ceremonies), media attention (newsletters, newspapers), certificates (for tenure or special achievement), expansion of opportunities (for learning, training, management), and personal expressions of gratitude from employees or clients. A heartfelt "thank you" can be all the acknowledgment many volunteers want or need. Others require more formal recognition. The director of volunteer services should make letters of recommendation available to all volunteers who request them. Recognition is a highly variable activity that should ideally be tailored to the wants and needs of individual volunteers.

Some agencies choose to recognize volunteers who evince especially strong potential and who seek paid employment with the agency by considering them for such positions when they become available (for example, police auxiliaries). One volunteer administrator refers to this process as a "try before you buy" opportunity for paid staff (Thornburg, 1992, p. 20). The advantages offered by this procedure notwithstanding, volunteering should not be seen as a necessary credential or requirement for paid employment with a nonprofit or governmental organization.

In general, volunteer-based services require the participation of not only volunteers but also paid staff. If organizational officials are committed to having employees and volunteers work as partners, program functions of evaluation and recognition should apply to both members of the team. Though frequently neglected in job analysis, employees expected to work with volunteers should have pertinent responsibilities written into their formal job descriptions. Equally important, performance appraisal for the designated positions must assess requisite skills in volunteer management. Just as demonstrated talent in this domain should be encouraged and rewarded, an employee's resistance to volunteers or poor work record with them should not be overlooked and hence implicitly condoned in the review. As necessary, the organization should support training activities for paid staff to develop competencies in volunteer administration.

Similarly, recognition activities for volunteer programs normally focus on citizen participants rather than on both members of the team. Employees value recognition as well, especially when award ceremonies, social events, media coverage, agency publications, and the like bring their efforts and accomplishments with volunteers to the attention of organizational leadership. In addition, feedback on employee achievement from volunteers and the director of volunteer services belongs in agency personnel files. By taking seriously the evaluation and recognition of paid staff with regard to their collaboration with volunteers, nonprofit and government officials provide incentives for an effective partnership.

Evaluation of the Volunteer Program

The overriding goal of a volunteer program ought to be to exert a positive effect on the external environment or to better the life circumstances of agency clients. Periodically, agencies that mobilize volunteers for such purposes should undergo evaluation of the impact or progress they have registered in ameliorating the conditions or problems identified in their mission statements. Too often what passes for "evaluation" of the volunteer program is a compilation of the number of volunteers who have assisted the organization, the hours they have contributed, and the number of client contacts or visits they have made.

A highly recommended but more complicated evaluation procedure is for agencies to calculate the total "equivalent dollar value" of all the jobs or services performed by volunteers, based on the market price for the labor the organization would otherwise have to pay employed personnel to accomplish the same tasks (Ellis, 1996; Karn, 1982, 1983). Anderson and Zimmerer (2003) demonstrate that estimating the dollar value of volunteer work can be done in a variety of ways: at least five methods are available, based on the average wage, the average nonagricultural wage rate (as released annually by the Bureau of Labor Statistics and used by INDEPENDENT SECTOR), a "living wage" (based on dollars required to subsist or cost of living aligned with the federal poverty line), comparable worth (equivalent dollar valuation), and minimum wage. Fringe benefits ranging from 10 to 12 percent may also be included in the calculation.

Impressive and significant though these data may be—normally documenting tremendous levels of contributed effort and monetary value across nonprofit and public institutions—they tap the inputs or resources to a volunteer program, rather than its results or accomplishments. Some researchers complain, too, that this approach slights the monetary costs associated with the volunteer program, for example, for paid staff supervision, reimbursement for expenses, training of volunteers, and use of organizational resources and facilities (Quarter, Mook, and Richmond, 2003; Utterback and Heyman, 1984). To correct for this problem, in my analysis of the SCORE program (Brudney (1990), I applied a cost-effectiveness model in which both the equivalent dollar value of volunteer services and the costs or expenses associated with the volunteer program are taken into account, thus resulting in a cost-effectiveness ratio. For every dollar the Small Business Administration invested in support of the SCORE program, the agency garnered volunteer services worth from $1.11 to $1.86 (p. 48). Katharine Gaskin (1999a, 1999b, 2003) similarly proposed a "volunteer investment and value audit" (VIVA) in which a cost-benefit analysis is performed, based on the ratio of the comparative market value of the functions performed by volunteers to the organization's expenditures on volunteers. In an evaluation of volunteer programs cross-nationally, Gaskin (2003, p. 46) reports very high cost-benefit ratios or returns on the investment in volunteers, ranging from 1:1.3 to 1:13.5, a finding that indicates that for every pound sterling (or dollar) invested in volunteers, the "return" varied from 1.3 to 13.5 pounds (or dollars). Nonprofit organizations should consider additional forms of evaluation of the volunteer program. Much as they might be expected to do for any other operational unit, at regular intervals, agency officials should assess the outcomes of the volunteer program against its stated goals or mission. Volunteer activity is other-directed; it should do more than gratify citizen participants and accommodate employees. Officials need to review the aggregate performance of the volunteers in assisting clients, addressing community problems, expediting agency operations, and meeting further objectives. Not only does the assessment yield information that can improve functioning of the program, but it also reinforces for all concerned—citizens, paid staff, and agency clients alike—the importance the organization places on the volunteer component. Smith and Ellis (2003) propose, conceptually, an ambitious evaluation of volunteer programs to incorporate their contribution to economic capital, physical capital, human capital, social capital, and cultural capital. Although such a methodology has not yet been developed, these authors point out that a concentration on the economic impacts of volunteering to the exclusion of impacts in these other areas not only gives "a very partial picture of the total value of volunteering" but also is potentially damaging in that it serves to "reinforce the notion that volunteering is all about saving money" (p. 52).

A second type of evaluation, also recommended, pertains to assessing the processes of a volunteer program. Officials should determine that procedures to meet essential program functions discussed in this chapter are in place and that they are operating effectively. In addition, the evaluation should attempt to gauge the satisfaction of volunteers and paid staff members with the program, as well as their perceptions concerning its impact on clients and the external environment. Continuing struggles with, for example, recruiting suitable volunteers, arresting high rates of volunteer burnout and turnover, relieving staff antagonisms, and reaching mutually agreeable placements point to flaws in program design that must be addressed. By diagnosing such difficulties, a process evaluation can enhance progress toward achievement of program objectives.

Recently, Jack Quarter, Laurie Mook, and Betty Jane Richmond (2003) have extended the evaluation of volunteer programs—as well as the evaluation of the activities of nonprofit organizations and cooperatives—by placing them in the broader context of "social accounting." These authors focus on valuing the contributions of volunteers to the organization and its clients and the larger social impacts of these organizations—for example, their effects on clients, the community, and the environment, as well as on the volunteers themselves. As

Quarter and colleagues note, conventional accounting practices overlook these aspects, despite the fact that they are among the most important effects of nonprofit organizations: "Even though volunteers in the United States and Canada contribute the equivalent full-time work of almost 10 million people per year . . . the value of this work, estimated to be over $250 billion, is not recognized in conventional accounting" (p. 131). Quarter, Mook, and Richmond introduce new types of accounting statements intended to assess the social impacts of nonprofit organizations and volunteers, including the "socioeconomic impact statement," the "socioeconomic resource statement," the "expanded value-added statement," and the "community social return on investment model."

SUMMARY AND CONCLUSION

According to the 2001 *Giving and Volunteering in the United States* survey (Toppe, Kirsch, and Michel, 2002), conducted for INDEPENDENT SECTOR, 44 percent of adults over the age of twenty-one volunteered with a formal organization in 2000. On average, they volunteered fifteen hours in the prior month. Of these formal volunteers, 69 percent reported they volunteered on a regular basis, monthly or more often. In the month prior to the survey, 27 percent had volunteered, averaging twenty-four hours of time donated in that month. In all, an estimated 83.9 million adults formally volunteered approximately 15.5 billion hours in 2000. The formal volunteer workforce represents the equivalent of over 9 million full-time employees, with an estimated value of $239 billion.

The key to integrating this staggering volume of talent and energy into nonprofit and government organizations is the volunteer program. This chapter has elaborated the central elements of a successful organizationally based volunteer effort:

- The program should begin with the establishment of a rationale or policy to guide volunteer involvement.
- Paid staff must have a central role in designing the volunteer program and creating guidelines governing its operation.
- The volunteer program must be integrated structurally into the nonprofit organization.
- The program must have designated leadership positions to provide direction and accountability.
- The agency must prepare job descriptions for the positions to be held by volunteers, as well as see to the related functions of screening, orientation, placement, and training.

- The volunteer program must attend to the motivations that inspire volunteers and attempt to respond to them, with the goal of meeting both these needs and those of the organization.

- Managing volunteers for best results typically requires adaptations of more traditional hierarchical approaches toward teamwork and collaboration.

- All components of the volunteer effort—citizens, employees, and the program itself—benefit from evaluation and recognition activities.

This list is ambitious, but well within the reach of the nonprofit organization. So, too, are the advantages to be derived from an effective volunteer program.

References

ACTION. *Americans Volunteer, 1974.* Washington, D.C.: ACTION, 1974.

Allen, N. J. "The Role of Social and Organizational Factors in the Evaluation of Volunteer Programs." *Evaluation and Program Planning,* 1987, *10,* 257–262.

Anderson, P. M., and Zimmerer, M. E. "Dollar Value of Volunteer Time: A Review of Five Estimation Methods." *Journal of Volunteer Administration,* 2003, *21*(2), 39–44.

Becker, D. G. "Exit Lady Bountiful: The Volunteer and the Professional Social Worker." *Social Service Review,* 1964, *38,* 57–72.

Brown, K. "What Goes Wrong and What Can We Do About It?" *Voluntary Action Leadership,* Spring 1981, pp. 22–23.

Brudney, J. L. "The SBA and SCORE: Coproducing Management Assistance Services." *Public Productivity Review,* Winter 1986, pp. 57–67.

Brudney, J. L. "The Use of Volunteers by Local Governments as an Approach to Fiscal Stress." In T. N. Clark, W. Lyons, and M. R. Fitzgerald (eds.), *Research in Urban Policy,* Vol. 3. Greenwich, Conn.: JAI Press, 1989.

Brudney, J. L. *Fostering Volunteer Programs in the Public Sector: Planning, Initiating, and Managing Voluntary Activities.* San Francisco: Jossey-Bass, 1990.

Brudney, J. L. "Administrators of Volunteer Services: Their Needs for Training and Research." *Nonprofit Management and Leadership,* 1992, *2,* 271–282.

Brudney, J. L. "Preparing the Organization for Volunteers." In T. D. Connors (ed.), *The Volunteer Management Handbook.* New York: Wiley, 1995.

Brudney, J. L. "Supplanting Common Myths with Uncommon Management: The Effective Involvement of Volunteers in Delivering Public Services." In S. W. Hays and R. C. Kearney (eds.), *Public Personnel Administration: Problems and Prospects.* (4th ed.) Upper Saddle River, N.J.: Prentice Hall, 2002.

Brudney, J. L. (with D. Kim). *The 2001 Volunteer Center Survey: A Report on Findings and Implications.* Washington, D.C.: Points of Light Foundation, 2003.

Brudney, J. L., and Kellough, J. E. "Volunteers in State Government: Involvement, Management, and Benefits." *Nonprofit and Voluntary Sector Quarterly,* 2000, *29,* 111–130.

Clary, E. G.; Snyder, M., and Ridge, R. "Volunteers' Motivations: A Functional Strategy for the Recruitment, Placement, and Retention of Volunteers." *Nonprofit Management and Leadership,* 1992, *2,* 333–350.

Clary, E. G.; Snyder, M., and Stukas, A. A. "Volunteers' Motivations: Findings from a National Survey." *Nonprofit and Voluntary Sector Quarterly,* 1996, *25,* 485–505.

Deitch, L. I., and Thompson, L. N. "The Reserve Police Officer: One Alternative to the Need for Manpower." *Police Chief,* 1985, *52*(5), 59–61.

Dorwaldt, A. L., Solomon, L. J., and Worden, J. K. "Why Volunteers Helped to Promote a Community Breast Self-Exam Program." *Journal of Volunteer Administration,* 1988, *6*(4), 23–30.

Drucker, P. F. *Managing the Nonprofit Organization: Practices and Principles.* New York: HarperCollins, 1990.

Duncombe, S. "Volunteers in City Government: Advantages, Disadvantages and Uses." *National Civic Review,* 1985, *74,* 356–364.

Ellis, S. J. *From the Top Down: The Executive Role in Volunteer Program Success.* (rev. ed.) Philadelphia: Energize Books, 1996.

Ellis, S. J. *The Volunteer Recruitment (and Membership Development) Book.* (3rd ed.) Philadelphia: Energize Books, 2002.

Ellis, S. J., and Noyes, K. H. *By the People: A History of Americans as Volunteers.* (rev. ed.) San Francisco: Jossey-Bass, 1990.

Farr, C. A. *Volunteers: Managing Volunteer Personnel in Local Government.* Washington, D.C.: International City/County Management Association, 1983.

Farmer, S. M., and Fedor, D. B. "Volunteer Participation and Withdrawal: A Psychological Contract Perspective on the Role of Expectations and Organizational Support." *Nonprofit Management and Leadership,* 1999, *9,* 349–367.

Fisher, J. C., and Cole, K. M. *Leadership and Management of Volunteer Programs: A Guide for Volunteer Administrators.* San Francisco: Jossey-Bass, 1993.

Gallup Organization. *Americans Volunteer, 1981.* Princeton, N.J.: Gallup Organization, 1981.

Gaskin, K. "Valuing Volunteers in Europe: A Comparative Study of the Volunteer Investment and Value Audit." *Voluntary Action,* 1999a, *2*(1), 35–49.

Gaskin, K. *VIVA in Europe: A Comparative Study of the Volunteer Investment and Value Audit.* London: Institute for Volunteering Research, 1999b.

Gaskin, K. "VIVA in Europe: A Comparative Study of the Volunteer Investment and Value Audit." *Journal of Volunteer Administration,* 2003, *21*(2), 45–48.

Goetter, W.G.J. "When You Create Ideal Conditions, Your Fledgling Volunteer Program Will Fly." *American School Board Journal,* 1987, *194*(6), 34–37.

Graff, L. L. "Considering the Many Facets of Volunteer/Union Relations." *Voluntary Action Leadership,* Summer 1984, pp. 16–20.

Grossman, J. B., and Furano, K. "Making the Most of Volunteers." Public/Private Ventures [http://www.ppv.org]. 2002.

Haran, L., Kenney, S., and Vermilion, M. "Contract Volunteer Services: A Model for Successful Partnership." *Leadership,* Jan.-Mar. 1993, pp. 28–30.

Herman, M. L., and Jackson, P. M. *No Surprises: Harmonizing Risk and Reward in Volunteer Management.* Washington, D.C.: Nonprofit Risk Management Center, 2001.

Hodgkinson, V. A., and Weitzman, M. S. *The Charitable Behavior of Americans: A National Survey.* Washington, D.C.: INDEPENDENT SECTOR, 1986.

Hodgkinson, V. A., and Weitzman, M. S. *Giving and Volunteering in the United States: Findings from a National Survey.* Washington, D.C.: INDEPENDENT SECTOR, 1988.

Hodgkinson, V. A., and Weitzman, M. S. *Giving and Volunteering in the United States: Findings from a National Survey.* Washington, D.C.: INDEPENDENT SECTOR, 1990.

Hodgkinson, V. A., and Weitzman, M. S. *Giving and Volunteering in the United States: Findings from a National Survey.* Washington, D.C.: INDEPENDENT SECTOR, 1992.

Hodgkinson, V. A., and Weitzman, M. S. *Giving and Volunteering in the United States: Findings from a National Survey.* Washington, D.C.: INDEPENDENT SECTOR, 1996.

Ilsley, P. J. *Enhancing the Volunteer Experience: New Insights on Strengthening Volunteer Participation, Learning, and Commitment.* San Francisco: Jossey-Bass, 1990.

Karn, G. N. "Money Talks: A Guide to Establishing the True Dollar Value of Volunteer Time, Part I." *Journal of Volunteer Administration,* 1982, *1*(2), 1–17.

Karn, G. N. "Money Talks: A Guide to Establishing the True Dollar Value of Volunteer Time, Part II." *Journal of Volunteer Administration,* 1983, *1*(3), 1–19.

Kirsch, A. D.; Hume, K. M.; and Jalandoni, N. T. *Giving and Volunteering in the United States: Findings from a National Survey.* (1999 ed.) Washington, D.C.: INDEPENDENT SECTOR, 2000.

Liao-Troth, M. A. "Attitude Differences Between Paid Workers and Volunteers." *Nonprofit Management and Leadership,* 2001, *11,* 423–442.

Macduff, N. "Episodic Volunteering." In T. D. Connors (ed.), *The Volunteer Management Handbook.* New York: Wiley, 1995.

Manchester, L. D., and Bogart, G. S. *Contracting and Volunteerism in Local Government: A Self-Help Guide.* Washington, D.C.: International City/County Management Association, 1988.

Marando, V. L. "Local Service Delivery: Volunteers and Recreation Councils." *Journal of Volunteer Administration,* 1986, *4*(4), 16–24.

May, K. M., McLaughlin, R., and Penner, M. "Preventing Low Birth Weight: Marketing and Volunteer Outreach." *Public Health Nursing,* 1991, *8,* 97–104.

McCurley, S., and Ellis, S. J. "Is Volunteer Management Superior to Employee Management?" *e-Volunteerism,* 2003a, *3*(2) [http://e-volunteerism.com].

McCurley, S., and Ellis, S. J. "Thinking the Unthinkable: Are We Using the Wrong Model for Volunteer Work?" *e-Volunteerism,* 2003b, *3*(3). [http://e-volunteerism.com].

McCurley, S., and Lynch, R. *Essential Volunteer Management.* Downers Grove, Ill.: VMSystems and Heritage Arts, 1989.

McCurley, S., and Lynch, R. *Volunteer Management: Mobilizing All the Resources in the Community.* Downers Grove, Ill.: Heritage Arts, 1996.

McHenry, C. A. "Library Volunteers: Recruiting, Motivating, Keeping Them." *School Library Journal,* 1988, *35*(8), 44–47.

Meijs, L.C.P.M., and Hoogstad, E. "New Ways of Managing Volunteers: Combining Membership Management and Programme Management." *Voluntary Action,* 2001, *3*(3), 41–61.

Moore, N. A. "The Application of Cost-Benefit Analysis to Volunteer Programs." *Volunteer Administration,* 1978, *11*(1), 13–22.

Murray, V., and Harrison, Y. "Virtual Volunteering: Current Status and Future Prospects." Canadian Centre for Philanthropy [http://www.nonporfitscan.ca]. 2002a.

Murray, V., and Harrison, Y. "Virtual Volunteering in Canada." Canadian Centre for Philanthropy [http://www.nonporfitscan.ca]. 2002b.

Naylor, H. H. *Volunteers Today: Finding, Training, and Working with Them.* Dryden, N.Y.: Dryden Associates, 1973.

Naylor, H. H. "Beyond Managing Volunteers." *Journal of Voluntary Action Research,* 1985, *14*(2–3), 25–30.

Nunn, M. "Building the Bridge from Episodic Volunteerism to Social Capital." *Fletcher Forum of World Affairs,* 2000, *24,* 115–127.

O'Donald, E. "Re-Entry Through Volunteering: The Best Jobs That Money Can't Buy." *Voluntary Action Leadership,* Fall 1989, pp. 22–27.

Park, J. M. *Meaning Well Is Not Enough: Perspectives on Volunteering.* South Plainfield, N.J.: Groupwork Today, 1983.

Pearce, J. L. "Something for Nothing: An Empirical Examination of the Structures and Norms of Volunteer Organizations." Doctoral dissertation, Yale University, 1978.

Pearce, J. L. "Participation in Voluntary Associations: How Membership in a Formal Organization Changes the Rewards of Participation." In D. H. Smith and J. Van Til (eds.), *International Perspectives on Voluntary Action Research.* Washington, D.C.: University Press of America, 1983.

Peters, T. J., and Waterman, R. H., Jr. *In Search of Excellence: Lessons from America's Best-Run Companies.* New York: Warner Books, 1982.

Quarter, J., Mook, L., and Richmond, B. J. *What Counts: Social Accounting for Nonprofits and Cooperatives.* Upper Saddle River, N.J.: Prentice Hall, 2003.

Scheier, I. H. "Positive Staff Attitude Can Ease Volunteer Recruiting Pinch." *Hospitals,* 1981, *55*(3), 61–63.

Scheier, I. H. "Empowering a Profession: Leverage Points and Process." *Journal of Volunteer Administration,* 1988a, *7*(2), 50–57.

Scheier, I. H. "Empowering a Profession: Seeing Ourselves as More Than Subsidiary." *Journal of Volunteer Administration,* 1988b, *7*(1), 29–34.

Scheier, I. H. "Empowering a Profession: What's in Our Name?" *Journal of Volunteer Administration,* 1988c, *6*(4), 31–36.

Schwartz, F. S. "The Professional Staff and the Direct Service Volunteer: Issues and Problems." *Journal of Jewish Communal Service,* 1977, *54,* 147–154.

SCORE. "A Historical Look at SCORE, 'Counselors to America's Small Business'" [http://www.score.org/history.html]. 2003.

Smith, A. C., and Green, F. B. "Managing Employees as if They Were Volunteers." *SAM Advanced Management Journal,* 1993, *58*(3), 42–46.

Smith, J. D., and Ellis, A. "Valuing Volunteering." *Journal of Volunteer Administration,* 2003, *21*(2), 49–52.

Stoolmacher, I. S. "Non-Profits Should Treat Volunteers as if They Were Paid Employees." *Chronicle of Philanthropy,* July 16, 1991, pp. 34–35.

Sundeen, R. A. "Citizens Serving Government: Volunteer Participation in Local Public Agencies." In INDEPENDENT SECTOR, *Working Papers for the Spring Research Forum.* Washington, D.C.: INDEPENDENT SECTOR, 1989.

Thornburg, L. "What Makes an Effective Volunteer Administrator? Viewpoints from Several Practitioners." *Voluntary Action Leadership,* Summer 1992, pp. 18–21.

Toppe, C. M., Kirsch, A. D., and Michel, J. *Giving and Volunteering in the United States, 2001: Findings from a National Survey.* Washington, D.C.: INDEPENDENT SECTOR, 2002.

"An Uncertain Trumpet." *New York Times,* Sept. 8, 2002, p. 21.

U.S. Department of Labor. *Americans Volunteer.* Washington, D.C.: Manpower Administration, U.S. Department of Labor, 1969.

Utterback, J., and Heyman, S. R. "An Examination of Methods in the Evaluation of Volunteer Programs." *Evaluation and Program Planning,* 1984, *7,* 229–235.

Valente, C. F., and Manchester, L. D. *Rethinking Local Services: Examining Alternative Delivery Approaches.* Washington, D.C.: International City/County Management Association, 1984.

Valente, M. G. "Volunteers Help Stretch Local Budgets." *Rural Development Perspectives,* 1985, *2*(1), 30–34.

Van Til, J. *Mapping the Third Sector: Voluntarism in a Changing Social Economy.* New York: Foundation Center, 1988.

Walter, V. "Volunteers and Bureaucrats: Clarifying Roles and Creating Meaning." *Journal of Voluntary Action Research,* 1987, *16*(3), 22–32.

Weber, M. A. "What Can Be Learned About Episodic Volunteers from a National Survey of Giving and Volunteering?" Paper presented at the annual meeting of the Association for Research on Nonprofit Organizations and Voluntary Action. Montreal, Canada, Nov. 14–16, 2002.

Wilson, M. *The Effective Management of Volunteer Programs.* Boulder, Colo.: Johnson Publishing, 1976.

Wilson, M. "The New Frontier: Volunteer Management Training." *Training and Development Journal,* 1984, *38*(7), 50–52.

Young, C. L., Goughler, D. H., and Larson, P. J. "Organizational Volunteers for the Rural Frail Elderly: Outreach, Casefinding, and Service Delivery." *Gerontologist,* 1986, *26,* 342–344.

CHAPTER FOURTEEN

Evaluating the Effectiveness of Nonprofit Organizations

Vic Murray

I n the first edition of *The Jossey-Bass Handbook of Nonprofit Leadership and Management,* a decade ago, the gist of this chapter was simple:

• Increasingly, nonprofit organizations are under pressure from funders, clients, and others to "prove" that they are achieving their missions effectively and efficiently. Aside from these external pressures, well-trained managers and board members are more likely to want better information on how the organization is performing. All this means an increased demand for more and better evaluation.

• However, formal evaluation at the level of the organization as a whole is a complex and costly task. Furthermore, it is usually very difficult to carry out in a way that is completely objective. Thus there is a political element to it that requires evaluators, evaluatees, and other interested parties to "negotiate" the process and how its results are to be interpreted and used.

• In spite of the problems with formal evaluation systems, the process of evaluation always goes on. Decisions are constantly being made about the introduction or change of programs, funding allocations, and a myriad of policy matters. To some extent, these are based on an assessment (however subjective) of past performance. Therefore, there are always new tools and guidelines for evaluation being offered to nonprofit leaders to make their decisions better.

In this new edition of the handbook, the question is, What has changed in ten years? We will look at developments in the demand for organizational evaluation in the sector, new research into the processes of organizational evaluation as they actually occur, and new tools and so-called best practices that have emerged to help practicing decision makers to obtain, interpret, and use evaluation information.

In a nutshell, it will be seen that the demand for more and better evaluation has continued to grow, and although there has been ongoing research into the reality of evaluation processes, it has served mainly to confirm the conclusions of past research regarding its essentially subjective and political nature. However, there has been a great increase in the number of new tools and "how-to" writings aimed at helping willing parties to the evaluation process do a better job of it. The implications of the former conclusion for the latter will be discussed.

But first we need a recapitulation of the basics of organizational effectiveness evaluation.

WHAT IS ORGANIZATIONAL EFFECTIVENESS EVALUATION?

Evaluation is the process of gathering information on the results of past activities for the purpose of making decisions about them. Organizational effectiveness evaluation (OEE) occurs when this process is applied to assessing the state of the organization as a whole. Typically, this refers to how well it is achieving its stated mission and involves looking at its goal attainment as well as how efficiently it has performed. (This is different from program evaluation, where the focus is on one specific part of the organization. It is discussed in Chapter Sixteen.)

Evaluation can occur in a formal, systematic way through the application of a professionally designed evaluation program, or it can be carried out with varying degrees of informality, ranging from gathering a few reports to completely impressionistic estimates about how things have been going.

WHY EVALUATE? THE CONTEXT OF OEE

Why evaluate? The obvious answer is to obtain information to make better decisions. Sometimes decision makers are interested in evaluating their *own* activities (this is called self-evaluation), but more often they seek to evaluate the activities of others. Thus there are distinct role differences: the users of evaluation information and the parties who obtain this information both play the role of evaluators, and the subjects of evaluation are the evaluatees. Even when the focus of evaluation is ostensibly "the organization," it still boils down to looking at the results of the actions of many units and individuals. Evaluators' desire to assess evaluatees is the focus of this chapter.

Ever since the beginning of the most recent movement to make government organizations more efficient and responsive (see Osborne and Gaebler, 1992), pressure has been growing for nonprofit organizations to do so also. This general tendency has sometimes been called the "accountability movement" and refers to the belief that nonprofits, and the people who run them, should be more "accountable" to those they are created to serve and those who provide the money to operate them. It is this pressure from the environment of the sector—funders, clients, regulators, and other stakeholders—that has been the primary cause of the growing interest in organizational evaluation.

Before providing some illustrations of these recent pressures, it is necessary to first clarify what the concept means. In essence, accountability is "the obligation to render an account for a responsibility which has been conferred" (Cutt and Murray, 2000, p. 1). This definition presumes the existence of at least two parties, one who allocates responsibility and one who accepts it and undertakes to report on the way it is being discharged. It is also necessary to understand that there are two basic forms of accountability: "legal" and "moral." Legal accountability occurs when the parties formally and officially accept their relationship and commit to some form of explicit reporting. Moral accountability exists when reporting is not legally required but the parties believe there is an obligation for one to be accountable to the other (see Chapter Nine for further consideration of the ethics of accountability). For example, the board of directors of a nonprofit organization may not be legally accountable to the organization's clients; however, clients may expect, and the board may agree, that it should report to clients on how well the organization is serving them. Conversely, a funder who stipulates in a grant agreement the nature of the reports it expects regarding how its money is used would be an example of a legal accountability relationship.[1]

The demand for both legal and moral accountability has been growing significantly in the period since the first edition of this book. One recent study (Cutt and Murray, 2000) reported that in 1998, there were at least eighteen organizations calling for more and better evaluation in the nonprofit sector in the United States and Canada, all of which had emerged since 1990. Some of these simply offered various tools and frameworks to aid evaluators (to be discussed later), while others had set themselves up as watchdogs offering "report cards" on charities primarily in terms of their financial probity and administrative and governance soundness (see, for example, the Better Business Bureau's Wise Giving Alliance at http://www.give.org, the American Institute for Philanthropy at http://www.charitywatch.org, the Charities Review Council of Minnesota at http://www.crcmn.org, and the Canadian Council of Christian Charities at http://www.cccc.org).

Within the sector itself, umbrella organizations such as the United Way of America (1996), INDEPENDENT SECTOR (Morley, Vinson, and Hatry, 2001), and the Aspen Institute (Light, 2000; Fine, Thayer, and Coglan, 1998) have felt the need to respond to what they perceived as growing public concern over inefficient or unethical charities by launching major initiatives aimed at improving and increasing evaluation, especially emphasizing the measurement of outcomes (to be defined shortly). In Canada, sector leaders in 1998 created a high-profile body known as the Panel on Accountability and Governance in the Voluntary Sector for the very same reasons. It traveled the country gathering information on the sector's accountability practices and produced an influential report before it disbanded (Panel on Accountability and Governance in the Voluntary Sector, 1999).

As for why these external pressures have been growing so substantially, one of the best explanations comes from Light (2000), who looks at the phenomenon in terms of institutional theory (Di Maggio and Powell, 1983). This theory posits that a great deal of organizational behavior can be accounted for by the pressure put on the organization by others (stakeholders, allies, competitors, regulators). These pressures can be coercive (involving the use of power), mimetic (acting on the tendency to want to conform by imitating what others do), or normative (unconsciously adopting group norms). All three of these pressures can be seen in the accountability movement, with funders and regulators applying coercive pressure ("evaluate or you won't be funded"), business corporations becoming models to imitate ("we must be more businesslike"), and professional and trade associations creating normative pressure.

To summarize, the call for more and better evaluation in accountability relationships has been growing steadily, along with the availability of tools for helping with this process. What is not known are the answers to three very important questions:

1. Have these developments led to more organizationwide evaluation actually taking place?

2. To what extent is the information generated by evaluations being used in an effort to improve the performance of nonprofits?

3. To the extent that it is being used, how much are nonprofits being improved as a result?

Before looking at these questions, however, we must first briefly review how the evaluation process works in theory and practice.

THE IDEAL EVALUATION PROCESS AND ITS PROBLEMS

In an ideal world, the process of evaluating the impact of an organization's efforts in the voluntary sector would be rational and objective. All parties involved—those asking for the evaluation, those carrying it out, and those being evaluated—would be seeking valid information so that they could make better decisions for the benefit of them all. The only problem might be the occurrence of some technical difficulties in developing the measurement instruments, which top-notch, professionally trained evaluators should be able to overcome.

Unfortunately, the world is far from ideal, and the fact is that the evaluation process is rarely rational and objective. And once matters become subjective, they quickly become political.[2]

Why Politics Is Inevitable in Evaluation

Politics is inevitable in evaluation because there is so much room for subjectivity that differences can easily arise between the parties involved. All evaluation processes go through four distinct stages, and at each stage, decisions are required that evaluators, evaluatees, and other interested stakeholders may disagree about, thus giving rise to political behavior. These stages and the trigger questions that lead to differences are discussed here.[3] The bases of these disagreements lie in inherent problems with the technical elements of evaluation methods and very common frailties in many human beings, such as inevitably seeing events from their own point of view.

The Design Stage. The key question here is, what is the purpose of organizational evaluation? The usual answer is to learn more about the strengths and weaknesses of the organization in order to make better decisions in the future. But what if the evaluatees believe that the real purpose is to increase efficiency by uncovering ways to cut costs by eliminating jobs?

Then there is the question of what, exactly, will be measured—inputs, activities or processes, outputs or outcomes?

The Implementation Stage. Once the evaluation has been designed, it must be carried out. Implementation raises the question of how the information will be gathered—for example, by collecting statistics, administering questionnaires, conducting focus groups, or carrying out a series of one-on-one interviews? Differences galore can arise over whether the methods chosen will accurately get at what they are supposed to get at.

The Interpretation Stage. Once information has been gathered, there arises the question of how to interpret it. What will be considered a "success" or a "failure"? Even more important, if an evaluation measure reveals problems, there is the question of drawing conclusions about *why* these occurred in order to make decisions about the future. Was it because those being evaluated were poorly selected or trained? Was it due to poor management? Or was it due to a series of external events that were beyond anyone's control? Most evaluation systems are not sophisticated enough to "prove" what caused what, which leaves all interested parties free to come up with their own differing explanations.

The Application Stage. This is the "so what?" question. Given that evaluations produce reports, statistics, and other information on how something worked out, there remains the question of how that information will be used in subsequent decision making. The more it is used to make tough decisions, such as whether to keep, drop, or change programs, increase or decrease funding, or terminate, promote, or transfer staff, the greater the chances will be that one or more of the involved parties will disagree with the decisions.

Clearly, then, differences can arise between evaluators, evaluatees, and other interested parties around many decision issues. There are two reasons that make it almost inevitable that one or more of these differences will in fact occur. One is because of technical problems, and the other because of human foibles.

Technical Problems of Evaluation Methods

There would be few problems if all evaluations clearly measured the results of whatever they were supposed to measure and led to unambiguous conclusions about what changes are needed for the future. But that is rarely the case. Here are some of the places where evaluations have technical weaknesses and therefore give rise to the differences that lead to political behavior.

Evaluation works best when the measurements can be compared to clearly stated goals, objectives, or standards that a given organization is trying to achieve. But often goals are vague and ambiguous. How does one measure the goal of an art gallery to "enliven and enrich the human spirit through the appreciation of the visual arts"? How does one evaluate the goal of the Scout movement to develop the potential in youth and create better citizens? It is not *impossible* to measure such goals, but it is easy to see how any given set of measures might be seen to be inadequate. And developing valid measures of these kinds of things is technically challenging, costly, and subjective.

Then there is the question of deciding what to focus the evaluation on. The work of individuals, programs, or organizations proceeds in a recurring cycle. It begins with an objective—the reason for the work being done. This leads to the first phase of the cycle—obtaining the resources needed to carry out the work (commonly called inputs). It then proceeds to the actual production of goods or services. This is called the process, activity, or output phase. The cycle concludes with the work actually having some kind of impact on the objectives. This is the outcome phase. Some evaluation systems just measure inputs (for example, how much money was invested, and how was it spent?). Some systems measure the numbers of activities that were engaged in (for example, number of clients served, number of interviews carried out, number of staff training sessions held). These are called process or output measures. Finally, some systems focus on the actual impact that the program or organization has had, that is, the extent to which it achieved its objectives. These are outcome measures.

A good evaluation system will always attempt to make explicit the underlying assumptions (or "logic model," as it is called by professional evaluators) that link one part of the cycle to the others. This articulation of assumptions need not be elaborate or complex. The main thing is to make them explicit before the evaluation gets under way so that potential conflicts can be identified before it is too late. Regrettably, few evaluation systems articulate their logic models. This leads to situations in which one stakeholder, say, a funder, may want to see outcome information, for example, while others inside the organization think that information on the need for funds (inputs) and the numbers to be served (outputs) should make it "obvious" that funds should be supplied.

Another common technical problem in design is that of measuring one level of an organization but generalizing to another. Again, this causes problems when no logic model has been worked out showing the links between the performance of individuals, programs, or functions and the organization as a whole. It is assumed that organizations are performing well if it can be shown that individuals are performing well or that specific programs are performing well. At the organizationwide level of analysis, a unique problem is how to compare the results of one program to those of another. When programs have different goals, this becomes a problem of comparing apples and oranges, and it raises immense technical difficulties (Cutt and Murray, 2000).

Even when everyone focuses on outcomes and agrees on what should be evaluated, there are inevitable difficulties over the extent to which outcome measures really capture the goals they are intended to measure. Take, for example, an organization created to teach English to recent immigrants as a second language. An outcome measure in its evaluation system might be the number of its clients who achieve a certain level on a standard test of English proficiency at the end of the program. Is this a clear, unambiguous indicator of the organization's mission? What if the people in charge of this organization, in an effort to score well on this indicator, select only clients who are already quite proficient in English or who have certain characteristics that make it more probable that they will succeed in the program? Some might argue that this is a distortion of the "real" mission, which is to provide this service to all in need of it, not just those who are most likely to pass a test.

Finally, as noted earlier, most evaluation systems are unable to provide conclusive analyses of why the results came out as they did. Most outcomes have multiple causes, and opinions can easily differ over which are the most important ones.

Human Foibles in Evaluation Processes

In addition to the inevitable technical difficulties that make it easy for differences to arise among those involved in evaluation, there are several common psychological tendencies that increase the likelihood of political game playing. These are the "LGAB," "SIR," and trust factors (Cutt and Murray, 2000).

Most people prefer to succeed, and if there is a failure, they prefer not to be seen as responsible for it. This is the "look good and avoid blame" (LGAB) mind-set. Managers embarking on a formal evaluation process often proclaim that it is not being carried out for the purpose of judging the parties responsible. The intent is simply to reveal any problems that might exist and provide information to help resolve them. The difficulty is that in spite of all the assurances to the contrary, many evaluatees believe in their hearts that if an evaluation reveals problems, they will be blamed or, conversely, that if the evaluation results are positive, they can take the credit. The behavior of elected officials when there are reports of economic conditions improving or worsening is only one of the more vivid examples of this tendency.

Therefore, when an LGAB attitude prevails, the evaluation process will likely be a political one. The evaluatees will focus on whatever the evaluation indicators are and will do what they can to show the desired results. Or if the results look bad in spite of their efforts, they will go to whatever lengths are necessary to explain them as being beyond their control.

The other key psychological tendency that creates major problems for evaluation systems is called the "subjective interpretation of reality" (SIR) phenomenon. It arises when evaluation data must be interpreted and explained. We have already seen how frail most logic models are. When it comes to analyzing almost any aspect of human behavior, there are too many variables and too little control over those variables to permit solid conclusions about causal connections. For every human behavior, there are usually many theories that can be presented to explain it, few of which can be proved conclusively. This is one of the reasons for the constant flow of new ideas in fields such as child rearing, managing people, education, welfare dependency, and the treatment of mental illness.

In spite of the lack of fully proven theories, however, decisions about complex social problems must be made. The people who make such decisions usually say that they make them on the basis of empirical evidence, but since such evidence is inevitably inconclusive, they also base them on their preexisting beliefs and attitudes about "what works." In other words, most evaluation results are interpreted subjectively, and different people can interpret the same data in many ways.

One additional factor is vital in triggering both the LGAB and SIR phenomena in evaluation: the extent to which the parties involved in the evaluation process trust one another (Ring and Van de Ven, 1994). Trust is the feeling that one can rely on others. In the context of evaluation and accountability, it is the belief that others will not intentionally do them harm. It is a complex concept with many levels, ranging from total distrust through varying degrees of partial trust (for example, trusting someone only in certain circumstances or about certain matters) to full trust in all things. The lower the level of trust, the more likely that the LGAB and SIR phenomena will result in political game playing during evaluation activities.

RECENT RESEARCH INTO
REAL-LIFE EVALUATION EXPERIENCES

It would be a pleasure to report that in the past decade, a number of large-scale studies of nonprofit organizational evaluation activities have been carried out, studies providing data from many different kinds of nonprofits with a wide range of missions that tell us how their performance was measured, what responses occurred during and after these assessments, and the nature and extent of any improvements that occurred as a result of these evaluations. Unfortunately, such large-sample, comparative, longitudinal studies have not yet been attempted, though one recently completed study comes close (more on this shortly).

What has appeared instead is a series of smaller studies, usually of one or a few organizations, often based on case study methodology. This makes it difficult to generalize across the whole nonprofit sector, but when most report similar findings, it is tempting to start drawing some tentative conclusions about what is likely to happen when organizational evaluation occurs under various circumstances.

The Large-Scale Study

The one large-scale study of evaluation practices was carried out in Canada in 2002 (Hall, Phillips, Meillat, and Pickering, 2003). This research was based on a stratified random sample of 1,965 voluntary sector organizations of all types and sizes from across the country. In addition, 322 funders of these organizations were surveyed. They included various government bodies, federated funding organizations, and private foundations. The study produced a number of very interesting findings. Among them are the following:

• Forty-one percent of funders reported that they expected more evaluation-based information from their fundees than three years earlier, and 50 percent said they wanted more outcome-based information than three years before. This confirms the assertion at the beginning of this chapter regarding the increased pressure for evaluation from the environment of the nonprofit sector.

• Though expectations may be higher, just under half of the funders said they provide their fundees with tools or resources to help them with this process (53 percent provided no funding and did not allow their funds to be used to pay for the costs of evaluation). Sixty percent claimed they offered "evaluation advice," but only 38 percent of the nonprofit organizations reported actually receiving such advice. (A similar point is made by Light, 2000).

• Though 77 percent of the nonprofit organizations surveyed said that they had carried out some type of evaluation in the previous year, only 18 percent reported that the evaluation was focused on "organizational goals and objectives," that is, on the performance of the organization as a whole. The other foci of evaluation were programs and projects (25 percent), staff or volunteer performance (14 percent), services or products such as workshops and courses (12 percent), client or community satisfaction (10 percent), and events and activities such as fundraising (11 percent).

• Of the organizations that reported carrying out some kind of evaluation in the previous year, 73 percent claimed that they evaluated outcomes. However, postsurvey follow-up interviews with a small sample of respondents revealed that "when asked how they actually measured outcomes, many gave examples of output measures" (Hall, Phillips, Meillat, and Pickering, 2003, p. 100).

• In spite of this, the great majority (95 percent) of respondents claimed that they were satisfied with their evaluation efforts and that they used the results of evaluations in making a variety of decisions. By contrast, less than half (47 percent) of the funders reported making effective use of the evaluation information provided to them in evaluation reports. More than a third (36 percent) said that the information they received was not what they had asked for, and more than a quarter (26 percent) reported that they had no capacity to review the information they received.

• Though overall satisfaction with evaluation practices was high, this did not keep both funders and the nonprofits themselves from admitting that it could be better and identifying several barriers that prevent them from improving. Chief among them were "lack of internal capacity, such as staff or time" (61 percent of voluntary organizations, 81 percent of funders), "unclear expectations from funders about what is wanted in an evaluation" (31 percent and 64 percent), and "lack of skills and knowledge in conducting evaluations" (31 percent and 64 percent). Note that funders identified all barriers as posing problems to a greater extent than voluntary organizations did, which suggests that funders may have greater concerns about evaluation (Hall, Phillips, Meillat, and Pickering, 2003, pp. x–xi).

The Smaller Studies

Turning now to the more in-depth case studies of the past decade, they can be roughly categorized in terms of those that tried to follow the entire evaluation process through all the stages discussed earlier in this chapter, those that focused primarily on the design and interpretation stages, and those that focused primarily on the application stage.

Overall Process Studies. When researchers attempt to observe the behavior of evaluators, evaluatees, and other interested stakeholders over time, the results all seem to support the "social constructionist" model (Herman and Renz, 1997). Time and again, we see the parties bringing their own attitudes, perceptions, values, and agendas to the process and engaging in some form of negotiation of their differences at each stage of the process. For example, Herman and Renz (forthcoming) conducted one of the more sophisticated studies in that it looked at forty-four nonprofit organizations in a single community at two points in time (1993 and 1999). At both times, they found that key stakeholders such as funders or client groups all had opinions as to how the studied nonprofits were doing but all had differing criteria for judging and used different "data" to make up their minds about this.

In a similar vein, Cutt and Murray (2000) reported a series of case studies of eight nonprofit organizations in two Canadian cities (see also Tassie, Murray, Cutt, and Bragg, 1996; Cutt and others, 1996). They too focused on the relationship between funders and fundees. While both the funders and nonprofit managers subscribed wholeheartedly to the rhetoric of evaluation—that there should be more of it, that it should be objective and emphasize outcomes—in fact they behaved quite differently. Funders did not demand much in the way of formal evaluation data; what was provided rarely attempted to measure outcomes, and both funders and fundees attempted to influence one another's behavior in many informal ways outside of the evaluation process. In the end, funders came to definite conclusions about the performance of the organizations they funded, but these were heavily influenced by their preexisting values and an organization's informal reputation in the funder's broader information network. And in spite of these opinions, their eventual decisions about whether to increase, decrease, or terminate funding to these organizations was scarcely influenced at all by their evaluations. Other matters such as economic conditions and political pressures to favor one set of social issues over another proved much more important. Similar conclusions to these were reached by Forbes (1998) and Scotch (1998).

Studies of Evaluation Design and Interpretation Processes. Several case studies have looked in detail at the questions of what will be evaluated, how it will be done, and how the results will be interpreted. For example, Campbell (2002) studied eight local economic development projects in Northern California with an emphasis on the negotiations over evaluation criteria between funders and project leaders. Lindenberg (2001) reported on a detailed case study of the efforts of the head of CARE, the international relief and development organization, to implement a variety of modern management practices drawn from business. Among them was the practice of benchmarking. Ebrahim (2002) looked at efforts by funders of two major nongovernmental organizations in India to control the information coming to them and the resistance they encountered. Ospina, Diaz, and O'Sullivan (2002) documented even more complex patterns of negotiation between organization leaders, funders, and clients in four successful Latino nonprofits in the New York City area.

Finally, in a most important book, Paton (2003) described a wide range of evaluation practices in twenty-seven "social enterprises," primarily in Britain.

Among them are ten organizations required to report administrative cost to expenditures (ACE) ratios to external evaluation bodies, five organizations that implemented various forms of total quality management systems, four that subjected themselves to external performance audits such as ISO 9000, three that attempted to implement outcome measurement systems, and one that conducted a social audit to assess its impact on the community it served.

The conclusions from all of these studies are neatly summarized by Paton (2003, p. 160):

> The limitations, difficulties, and pitfalls associated with the various forms of performance measurement are very clear, if hardly a great surprise. Thus, it is probable that, if taken literally, outcome measurement will be impracticable for many social enterprises. More generally, the features that managers hope to find in measurement systems—such as both focus and comprehensiveness, or reliable validity and non-intrusive simplicity—are incompatible and so cannot be realized simultaneously. Moreover, for both internal and external reasons, "measurement churn" seems increasingly to be a fact of life in social enterprises, as it is elsewhere. So the stability on which much of the logic of measurement depends is unlikely to be realized.

Studies of the Use of Evaluation Data. When evaluators do obtain information on organizational performance by whatever means, there is the question of what they will do with it—the extent to which it will be considered in making decisions about the future. Managers and boards of directors must make decisions about internal policy matters such as whether to drop, add, or change programs or introduce new management systems or structures. Funders, of course, must decide whether to increase, decrease, or eliminate funding to recipients, and government bodies must make decisions about policies that affect the organization's clients and mission. In theory, formal evaluations of what has worked and how efficient a nonprofit organization has been *should* play a prominent role in the making of these kinds of major decisions. The question is, do they?

Research into this question remains skimpy, but what there is suggests that it often has only a minimal influence at best, except when the evaluation was carried out as part of a special investigation of a crisis situation. Gebelmann, Gilman, and Pollack (1997), Cutt and Murray (2000), Holland (2002), and Miller (2002) all report studies revealing that many boards of directors in particular are prone to not proactively seeking more and better evaluation systems and ignoring or willfully misinterpreting evaluation information that presents bad news until a crisis arises. The same tendencies are probable among CEOs, though, surprisingly, there is much less research available on them. A similar pattern also prevails when looking at funders as revealed in the work of Hall, Phillips, Meillat, and Pickering (2003), Cutt and Murray (2000), and Lohmann (1999).

The results of the past decade of research into "what actually happens" in organizational effectiveness evaluation tend to confirm the conclusions reached in the first edition of this book: that OEE is a subjective, political process involving a negotiated interpretation of reality by all interested parties.

In spite of these conclusions, several matters must be remembered:

• The people who make the decisions affecting an organization will continue to make them, and they often wish for more information. Sometimes they genuinely feel that they don't know what to do and want information that is as objective as can be obtained to shed light on the problem. But at other times, what they really want is information that will back up what they already believe to be the truth so that it will help them "tell their story" to influential stakeholders.

• At times, both the users of evaluation information and those being evaluated may manage to agree that carrying out a formal evaluation is a desirable thing and both want to find a process that is as thorough, fair, and objective as is possible.

• An occupational group of professional evaluators has developed over the past half-century, many of whom are always looking for more useful and valid evaluation systems to offer their clients. The universities and colleges who offer training in evaluation methods do the same.

What all this means is that new evaluation tools are constantly being developed and being welcomed by nonprofit managers. Therefore, the final section of this chapter will look briefly at some of the better-known evaluation tools that have achieved prominence over the past ten years. The chapter will conclude with a few remarks aimed at practicing executives regarding what can be done to give these new tools a chance of succeeding in the real-world politics of evaluation.

RECENT TOOLS FOR IMPROVING OEE

Too many evaluation tools have been developed in the past ten years to be able to report on all of them here (for one useful attempt to do this, see Bozzo and Hall, 1999; Cutt and Murray, 2000, offer a similar review, though of fewer tools). What I have done instead is select a few of the best-known and highest-potential developments as a sample of what is available.

Program Outcomes: The United Way Approach

The United Way evaluation system (http://www.unitedway.org/outcomes) focuses exclusively on the identification and measurement of program outcomes for United Way–funded agencies. The system starts by evaluating results at the program level; these are then supposed to be aggregated at the organizational level by member agencies to report on their effectiveness.

The outcome information is intended to be used by the United Way to help member agencies improve program performance, to identify and achieve United Way priorities (funding allocation criteria), and to broaden the base of financial and volunteer support (fundraising).

Implementation of the outcome measurement system is divided into six stages:

1. Building agency commitment and clarifying expectations

2. Building agency capacity to measure outcomes

3. Identifying outcomes, indicators, and data collection methods

4. Collecting and analyzing outcome data

5. Improving the outcome measurement system

6. Using and communicating outcome information

The United Way has developed a set of guiding principles and specific steps to help the member agencies complete each stage of the implementation process. Rather than advocate one particular way to develop outcomes or to collect outcome data, the United Way uses a checklist approach to encourage agencies to think more broadly and critically about its measurement processes. For example, agencies are asked to think about their proposed data collection methods in terms of their validity, reliability, sensitivity to client characteristics, and ability to capture longer-term results, but they are not told which methods to use.

The outcome measurement system does not specify the types of evaluation standards to be used but does suggest that target-based absolute standards and time-based relative standards are best. Agencies are not expected to establish targets until they have at least one year of baseline data. The system discourages the use of benchmark-based relative standards or those that involve comparison with similar programs that are considered exemplary until accurate outcome data are available. It is generally understood that in the first few years of an outcome measurement system, the data often say more about what is wrong with the evaluation system than about what is taking place in the programs.

Recent research reported on the United Way Web site suggests that there is general satisfaction with the six-stage process it recommends and its approach to developing an outcome measurement system. Of all those reviewed, this tool is also the most sensitive to the importance of the implementation process.

The Balanced Scorecard

The balanced scorecard (http://www.balancedscorecard.org) is a multiattribute system for conceptualizing and measuring performance designed originally for business organizations and currently being adapted for nonprofit organizations (Kaplan, 2001). In its original form, it assumes that the primary goal of a business is long-run profit maximization. It argues that this will be achieved through a "balanced scorecard of performance attributes" grouped around four "perspectives":

- The *financial perspective,* measuring various financial performance indicators of primary interest to shareholders
- The *customer perspective,* comprising measures of customer satisfaction
- The *internal business perspective,* which measures internal efficiency and quality
- The *innovation and learning perspective,* which attempts to measure the organization's ability to adapt to changes required by a changing environment

In the case of nonprofit organizations, their mission statement, rather than the profit statement, becomes the endpoint to be reached through these perspectives. The process starts with defining what that is and identifying outcome indicators that will reveal the extent to which it is being achieved. "Customers" must be replaced by "clients" or "users" of the organization's services, and the "financial perspective" becomes that of the funders or potential funders.

CCAF/FCVI Framework for Performance Reporting

The CCAF/FCVI framework (http://www.ccaf-fcvi.com) is the most significant Canadian effort at tackling the "value for money" issue in both the public and nonprofit sectors. It puts forward twelve "attributes of effectiveness," suggesting that organizations can be audited in terms of how well they manifest these attributes. In this sense, it can be focused at either the organizational or the program or function level and is intended to help evaluators get a clear picture of how effectively and efficiently goals are being achieved. It is similar in many ways to the balanced scorecard; however, the details of implementation are more thorough.

The system involves developing indicators for the following attributes of effectiveness:

1. *Management direction*—the extent to which programmatic objectives are clearly stated and understood
2. *Relevance*—the extent to which the organization or program continues to make sense with respect to the problems or conditions to which it was intended to respond
3. *Appropriateness*—the extent to which the design of the organization or program and the level of effort are logical in relation to their objectives
4. *Achievement of intended results*—the extent to which the goals and objectives have been achieved

5. *Acceptance*—the extent to which the stakeholders for whom the organization or program is designed judge it to be satisfactory

6. *Secondary impacts*—the extent to which significant consequences, either intended or unintended and either positive or negative, have occurred

7. *Costs and productivity*—the relationship between costs, inputs, and outputs

8. *Responsiveness*—the capacity of the program or organization to adapt to changes in such factors as markets, competition, available funding, and technology

9. *Financial results*—accounting for revenues and expenditures and for assets and liabilities

10. *Working environment*—the extent to which the organization or program provides an appropriate work environment for staff and to which staff have the information, capacities, and disposition to serve the objectives

11. *Protection of assets*—the extent to which the various assets entrusted to the organization or program (physical, technological, financial, and human) are safeguarded

12. *Monitoring and reporting*—the extent to which key matters pertaining to performance and organizational or program strength are identified, reported, and monitored

The system encompasses both process and outcome elements, though the former are dominant. As Cutt and Murray (2000) point out in their extensive discussion of this approach, it lacks an overall conceptual framework. Interestingly, the twelve dimensions of effectiveness can be fairly easily placed within the balanced scorecard approach, a move that would enhance the value of both tools. Again, there is no publicly available information on how effective this evaluation system is.

Another approach related to the balanced scorecard model is that presented recently by Rob Paton of the Open University in Britain (2003). Called the "Dashboard for Social Enterprises," it is more specifically designed for nonprofit organizations. The Dashboard is based on asking two sets of questions about the organization's activities: "Do they work?" and "Are they well run?" These questions are then asked in two contexts: the short-term, operational context and the longer-term, strategic context.

Best-Practice Benchmarking

One of the most frequently cited tools of the past decade is the application of benchmarking to the evaluation of nonprofit organizations (see especially Letts, Ryan, and Grossman, 1999). Benchmarking is a system that compares the organization's practices with those of others doing similar things but who are deemed to be doing it better. It is usually applied to specific programs or functions of the organization, so it is not, strictly speaking, a tool for evaluating the organization as a whole. However, its advocates assume that a thorough program of benchmarking will "roll up" to provide a good indicator of how well the organization is doing overall.

Paton (2003) is one of the few who have actually carried out research into how well benchmarking works for nonprofits in practice. He found that although there was considerable enthusiasm for the idea of benchmarking, it was not actually implemented very frequently (in Britain, at least). In part, this is because it is extremely time-consuming and costly. It may also be because in the nonprofit sector, it is particularly difficult to identify the better-performing organizations with whom to compare oneself (unlike the situation in many industries, where trade associations facilitate the exchange of information about who is succeeding and why). There is also a problem with what Paton calls "measurement churn"—the tendency to change measurement tools so frequently that rarely are the same data gathered over long periods, making it difficult to compare performance with others over time. A final difficulty with comparisons of "best practices" is that there is no way of knowing if they are the reason for other organizations' being more successful. It is possible that practices that work for one organization may not work for one's own due to unique situational characteristics of history, culture, personalities, economic conditions, and so on.

Charity Rating Services

There are also several evaluation systems developed in the United States to help funders and the public decide how effective various charities are (see, for example, the Better Business Bureau's Wise Giving Alliance at http://www.give.org, the American Institute for Philanthropy's Charity Rating Guide at http://www.charitywatch.org, and the Charities Review Council of Minnesota at http://www.crcmn.org).

All of these systems offer generic "standards" that will reveal how well a nonprofit organization is managed. For example, they may report on various aspects of a charity's finances, public availability of audit reports, how fundraising is conducted, and the presence of certain policies for its board of directors, such as conflict-of-interest policies.

Paton (2003) also reports on research into the value of more generic systems that attempt to audit the performance of organizations of all types. One of these is the International Standards Organization's 9000 series (ISO 9000), a set of procedural standards for quality management systems. Organizations that meet these standards (as measured by ISO inspectors) are deemed to be well run and hence are expected to perform at a high level. Paton's research, and that of others, reveals, however, that it is difficult to adapt the ISO standards, which were originally developed for manufacturing businesses, to the world of nonprofit service organizations. This leads to many differences between the various stakeholders who get involved in the process either as evaluatees or evaluators.

The problem with all these rating services is that in trying to compare organizations with so many different missions, the standards make no reference to outcomes. They also do not attempt to explicitly reveal the implicit measurement or logic models they are built on. Instead, they assume that organizations that meet their process standards will be more likely to be effective in achieving their goals. Regrettably, there is little or no published research that supports these assumptions, though it may be that organizations that most severely violate the standards they measure are less likely to be effective. Whether those that best meet or surpass these standards are comparatively more effective, however, is unknown (Murray, 2002).

Another problem with all of the evaluation tools except the United Way approach is that very little attention is paid to how the evaluation system is to be implemented. As previously noted, a great deal of research has concluded that unless all those to be affected by an evaluation system have a strong voice in its design and accept the final product, there is a high probability that the system will fail (Cutt and Murray, 2000; Mark, Henry, and Julnes, 2000; Sonnichsen, 2000).

To summarize, it appears that there is still a long way to go before there will be available a tried and tested evaluation system that can be applied by most nonprofit organizations to provide a valid picture of how well the organization is performing. Some would argue there is no point in trying; yet decisions are made every day based on untested assumptions and idiosyncratic perceptions of performance. Therefore, the goal of trying to improve the dialogue around this process in a way that takes account of the research into the everyday reality of OEE processes discussed in this chapter is worthwhile pursuing.

CONCLUSION

How can nonprofit organization leaders make practical use of the tension between the results of the empirical research and the promises of the new tools? I have argued in this chapter that politics in evaluation is almost inevitable because of the frailties in evaluation techniques and simple human foibles—the LGAB, SIR, and trust phenomena. Many of the political games can be destructive in that they distort the information produced or result in its being ignored or misused in the way it is applied to future decision making. They can also create major motivational problems among the evaluatees that can, paradoxically, damage their productivity.

Since one cannot avoid the political dimension in evaluation, therefore, attention has to be focused on what can be done to make the differences among the parties constructive rather than destructive. Conflict is not inevitably bad. Indeed, when handled constructively, it can often result in a product that is better than if there had been no conflict at all.

In an ideal world, each stage of the evaluation process—its design, implementation, interpretation, and application—would be characterized by open discussions among all interested parties during which differences would be aired and resolved by mutual consensus. Unspoken beliefs and assumptions would be made explicit in logic models and standards. Even if some people cannot change their beliefs to make them congruent with the other parties', at least all parties would be conscious of the other parties' stances and why they hold the positions they do. This could lead to greater understanding, if not acceptance, of these positions. What has to be done to move toward this ideal of constructive conflict resolution?

Trust Building

The basic secret for creating openness is the creation of an atmosphere of trust among the interested parties. If one of them believes the other is concerned only with its own interests, there is little chance of avoiding destructive game playing. The only approach then becomes one of trying to win the games more often than the opponents.

How is this trust built? Unfortunately for those seeking a "quick fix," it is usually built over time through many encounters between the parties. During these interactions, each must show concern for the other, each must commit fully to communicating reasons for its actions, each allows the other to have a voice in decisions that affect it, and each keeps its word when actions are promised or provides explanations if its word cannot be kept. Paradoxically, though trust takes time to build, it can be destroyed in an instant with only one or two violations of the rules.

If a prior relationship of trust does not exist before evaluation begins, it must consciously be worked on as the process is developed. This means involving all interested parties in that process, particularly those who are to be evaluated. All must have a voice in deciding the following six questions:

1. What is the purpose of the evaluation?
2. What should be measured?
3. What evaluation methods should be used?
4. What standards or criteria should be applied to the analysis of the information obtained?
5. How should the data be interpreted?
6. How will the evaluation be used?

Is there a time when this kind of consultation is *not* advisable? Probably the only occasion is when there is strong evidence of malfeasance or willful ineptitude among the evaluatees. This would suggest that there is a high probability that they will consciously suppress or distort information. In such cases, external evaluation by professionals trained in looking for reporting errors (forensic accountants, for example) would have to be used.

Logic Model Building

Many evaluations founder in destructive politics simply because the people designing them fail to articulate the underlying logic models. This allows all parties to unconsciously apply their own answers to the six questions, which gives rise to differences that are not confronted. Two basic logic models need to be discussed among the parties: one that is measurement-based and one that is level-based. These are illustrated in Figures 14.1 and 14.2.

Measurement logic models (see Figure 14.1) try to articulate the links between inputs, activities or outputs, outcomes, and goals. They recognize that inputs create the basis for how much and what kinds of outputs will occur but that other influences can also affect this linkage, so it is not possible to argue,

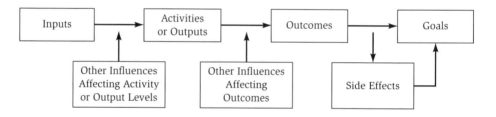

Figure 14.1. Generic Measurement-Based Logic Model.

Source: Cutt and Murray, 2000, p. 36.

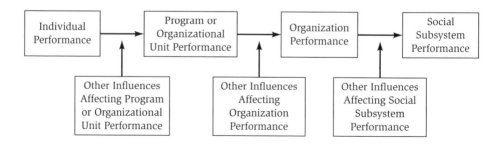

Figure 14.2. Generic Level-Based Logic Model.

Source: Adapted from Cutt and Murray, 2000, p. 37.

for example, that more inputs alone will improve performance. Similarly, they lay out the connections between activities or outputs and outcomes, again trying to consciously identify what else can affect outcomes. Finally, they recognize that the link between outcome measures and the actual objectives they are trying to measure is not always perfect and that unanticipated side effects can occur when a program or organization is trying to reach a given objective. Effort should be made to look out for these in the evaluation system.

A logic model based on the level of evaluation is illustrated in Figure 14.2. It attempts to articulate the links between the performance of individuals, programs or units within the organization, the organization as a whole, and (if this is of interest) the organization and any system of organizations of which it is a part. It also tries to identify the other influences that intervene between these links so that no one will try to argue simplistically that good or bad evaluations of individuals reveal how well a program is doing or that good or bad evaluations of a program reveal how well the organization is doing.

The time to develop such logic models is during the design phase of the evaluation process. For example, if the top management of an organization wants to evaluate how well the organization is performing, it would sit down with representatives of those who are on the front line of program delivery and representatives of program users to discuss the six questions. When it comes to the question of what to measure and how (methods), the outline of the measurement-based logic model could be distributed and these kinds of questions asked: Can we measure outcomes, and if so, how? How well will outcome information reveal goal achievement? Is there any chance that the organization's activities might be causing unanticipated side effects beyond the stated goals, and should we try to look for them? Assuming that we can get good indicators of program outcomes, how will we decide what caused those outcomes? Do we also need some activity and output measures and some way of tracking other factors that could influence the outcomes?

Similarly, the level-based logic model could be used as the basis for discussing the links between individuals, programs or organizational units, and the organization as a whole. Applying it, these kinds of questions could be raised: If we are focusing on program evaluation and it reveals problems with a program, what implications does this have for the organization as a whole? Do we need to reconsider the strategic priorities of the organization? To what extent are problems with a program due to performance problems of individuals or other influences such as funding levels? How do we compare the evaluations of very different programs in order to get a sense of their contribution to the organization's overall mission?

By raising these kinds of questions with the aid of logic model frameworks, it is possible to surface a lot of potentially conflicting assumptions and beliefs before they can cause problems once the evaluation process gets under way.

The resulting design will usually be stronger and better supported by all interested parties.

Some Practical Problems in Certain Relationships

The general guidelines of trust building, participant involvement, and logic model creation will help create constructive political climates in evaluation. However, they are more or less difficult to apply, depending on the identities of the evaluators and the evaluatees. The most straightforward situation is where the evaluator is the management of the organization (or some part of it) and the evaluatees are the individuals running a particular program, function, or department within it. Evaluation in this situation is known as internal evaluation (Love, 1991; Sonnichsen, 2000). The decisions about the evaluation process are under the control of the management, who, if so desired, can ensure that consultation with evaluatees occurs and logic models are thought through before the process starts.

But what if the evaluator is the organization's board of directors? This group is legally responsible for seeing that the organization achieves its mission, so the management team is accountable to the board. As the earlier discussion of empirical research shows, however, many boards make little time for carrying out evaluations and feel they have no skill in doing so. Many also do not know what to evaluate and feel that probing too deeply into how the organization is doing would suggest that they do not trust the executive director (who is usually well known to them and is often considered a friend). As a result, many boards fail badly in their fiduciary duty to hold management accountable for its actions. Special effort must be devoted to training boards in these duties and providing them with the expertise they need to develop evaluation systems that meet their information needs (Cutt and others, 1996). However, if the board wants to minimize political game playing with management, the guidelines presented here suggest that the design process should be consultative. In most situations, the best approach would be to have a board task force on evaluation work together with staff representatives and a professional evaluator (if possible).

An even more difficult relationship exists when the evaluator is an external funder or contractor (United Way, community foundation, government department). Usually funders or contractors have *many* organizations as their clients. How can they follow the recommended participative model in developing systems for evaluating the performance of these clients? They often express the wish for more and better accountability reporting from them, but the participative approach takes time and involves intense face-to-face interactions that are difficult to arrange when there are so many clients. Because of this, as the review of the empirical literature shows, many of these external organizations go to one of two extremes. Some require little or no evaluation other than regular budget and financial reports on how money was spent. As a result, they get no real idea what impact their funds have had.

Other funders and government contractors arbitrarily impose requirements for complex and numerous progress reports as well as final reports. Since many evaluatees in this situation don't see the point in this reporting, a climate of frustration and cynicism develops, along with incomplete or inaccurate reporting practices. The only way to overcome these kinds of problems is for those who seek better accountability to invest the time and money needed to bring their clients together to design mutually satisfactory accountability frameworks.

In practical terms, this means that whenever a funding arrangement is made, the discussion of it should include a detailed look at the evaluation system that will be used in reporting results. The recipient organization needs to know what kind of information the funder wants, and if, for example, it wants only statistics that obscure important outcomes that can only be assessed qualitatively, the fundee should have an opportunity to influence that decision. It also should have the opportunity to raise beforehand the question of how reported information will be interpreted or used. For example, if measurements reveal low levels of participation or higher than expected costs, will there be an opportunity to conduct research into the reasons for this?

One of the more innovative approaches to conducting open dialogues between the parties in an evaluative process is known as appreciative inquiry (AI). This is not specifically a model of evaluation but rather a model for organizational change developed initially by David Cooperrider and Suresh Srivasta (Srivasta, Cooperrider, and Associates, 1990; Cooperrider and Whitney, 2000). It posits an alternative to the conventional "problem-solving approach" that lies at the base of traditional evaluation methods. The AI approach focuses exclusively on appreciating the best of "what is," envisioning "what might be," and conducting a dialogue on "what should be." Emphatically a collaborative process, it requires the involvement of all stakeholders in an organization's future. In the context of evaluation, it would require those involved to focus first on what they have been doing well and their vision for the future. The assessment of performance occurs only later during the process of thinking how to overcome barriers that might exist in moving from the current to the future desired state. Framed this way, evaluation might become less threatening to the evaluatees. As with so many of the newer tools of evaluation, this approach has not been itself carefully evaluated as to its impact beyond the level of numerous case studies of success reported by its adherents.

To summarize, organizational evaluation will never be free of politics. In the final analysis, there will always be a subjective element that will lead to differences among the parties involved. It is only when these differences can be confronted and talked through in a nonthreatening, trusting environment that we can avoid destructive game playing and realize the benefits that can be obtained from a well-designed evaluation process.

Notes

1. In an accountability relationship, much of the information produced is derived from formal evaluations of past activities. However, it must be noted that this is not the only source of information. Those expecting accountability reports from others might also want, for example, reports on planned future activities.

2. The term *political* as used here does not refer to government-style politics—parties, campaigning, and so forth. *Politics* here refers to behavior that occurs when conflict is perceived to exist by at least one party in a relationship (Tassie, Murray, Cutt, and Bragg, 1996). Once differences are seen to exist, any subsequent actions taken to deal with them can be called "political." These actions can bring the perceived differences out into the open and try to resolve them (overt politics), or other parties can be kept unaware of them (covert politics). Applied to the world of evaluation, whenever one of the parties involved disagrees with the reasons for the evaluation, the type of evaluation to be undertaken, the methods used, the interpretation of the results, or the way the results are used, there will be a political element to the evaluation.

3. The following discussion is from my paper titled "Evaluation Games: The Political Dimension in Evaluation and Accountability Relationships," posted on the Web site of the Voluntary Sector Evaluation Research Project at Carleton University (http://www.vserp.ca).

References

Bozzo, S. L., and Hall, M. H. *A Review of Evaluation Resources for Nonprofit Organizations.* Toronto: Canadian Centre for Philanthropy, 1999.

Campbell, D. "Outcomes Assessment and the Paradox of Nonprofit Accountability." *Nonprofit Management and Leadership,* 2002, *12,* 243–260.

Cooperrider, D., and Whitney, D. *Collaborating for Change: Appreciative Inquiry.* San Francisco: Barrett-Koehler, 2000.

Cutt, J., and Murray, V. *Accountability and Effectiveness Evaluation in Non-Profit Organizations.* London: Routledge, 2000.

Cutt, J., and others. "Nonprofits Accommodate the Information Demands of Public and Private Funders." *Nonprofit Management and Leadership,* 1996, *7,* 45–68.

Di Maggio, P., and Powell, W. W., Jr. "The Iron Cage Revisited: Institutional Isomorphism and Collective Rationality in Organizational Fields." *American Sociological Review,* 1983, *48,* 147–160.

Ebrahim, A. "Information Struggles: The Role of Information in the Reproduction of NGO-Funder Relationships." *Nonprofit and Voluntary Sector Quarterly,* 2002, *31,* 84–114.

Fine, A., Thayer, C., and Coglan, A. *Program Evaluation in the Nonprofit Sector.* Washington, D.C.: Aspen Institute, 1998.

Forbes, D. P. "Measuring the Unmeasurable." *Nonprofit and Voluntary Sector Quarterly,* 1998, *27,* 183–202.

Gebelman, M., Gilman, S. R., and Pollack, D. "The Credibility of Nonprofit Boards." *Administration in Social Work,* 1997, *21*(2), 21–40.

Hall, M. H., Phillips, S. D., Meillat, C., and Pickering, D. *Assessing Performance: Evaluation Practices and Perspectives in Canada's Voluntary Sector.* Ottawa: Centre for Voluntary Sector Research and Development, Carleton University, 2003.

Herman, R. D., and Renz, D. O. "Multiple Constituencies and the Social Construction of Nonprofit Organization Effectiveness." *Nonprofit and Voluntary Sector Quarterly,* 1997, *26,* 185–206.

Herman, R. D., and Renz, D. O. "Doing Things Right and Effectiveness in Local Nonprofit Organizations." *Public Administration Review,* forthcoming.

Holland, T. P. "Board Accountabilities: Lessons from the Field." *Nonprofit Management and Leadership,* 2002, *12,* 409–428.

Kaplan, R. S. "Strategic Performance Measurement and Management in Nonprofit Organizations." *Nonprofit Management and Leadership,* 2001, *11,* 353–370.

Letts, C., Ryan, W. P., and Grossman, A. *High-Performance Nonprofit Organizations: Managing Upstream for Greater Impact.* New York: Wiley, 1999.

Light, P. *Making Nonprofits Work.* Washington, D.C.: Aspen Institute/Brookings Institution Press, 2000.

Lindenberg, M. "Are We at the Cutting Edge or the Blunt Edge? Improving NGO Organizational Performance with Private and Public Sector Strategic Management Frameworks." *Nonprofit Management and Leadership,* 2001, *11,* 247–270.

Lohmann, R. A. "Has the Time Come to Reevaluate Evaluation?" *Nonprofit Management and Leadership,* 1999, *10,* 93–101.

Love, A. J. *Internal Evaluation: Building Organizations from Within.* Thousand Oaks, Calif.: Sage, 1991.

Mark, M. M., Henry, G. T., and Julnes, G. *Evaluation: An Integrated Framework for Understanding, Guiding, and Improving Policies and Programs.* San Francisco: Jossey-Bass, 2000.

Miller, J. "The Board as a Monitor of Organizational Activity." *Nonprofit Management and Leadership,* 2002, *12,* 429–450.

Morley, E. E., Vinson, E., and Hatry, H. P. *A Look at Outcome Measurement in Nonprofit Organizations.* Washington, D.C.: Urban Institute, 2001.

Murray, V. "The State of Evaluation Tools and Systems for Nonprofit Organizations." In P. Barber (ed.), *Accountability: A Challenge for Charities and Fundraisers.* New Directions for Philanthropic Fundraising, no. 31. San Francisco: Jossey-Bass, 2002.

Osborne, D., and Gaebler, D. A. *Reinventing Government: How the Entrepreneurial Spirit Is Transforming the Public Sector.* New York: Plenum Press, 1992.

Ospina, S., Diaz, W., and O'Sullivan, J. F. "Negotiating Accountability: Managerial Lessons from Identity-Based Nonprofit Organizations." *Nonprofit and Voluntary Sector Quarterly,* 2002, *31,* 5–31.

Panel on Accountability and Governance in the Voluntary Sector. *Building on Strength: Improving Governance and Accountability in Canada's Voluntary Sector.* Ottawa, Canada: Voluntary Sector Roundtable, 1999.

Paton, R. *Managing and Measuring Social Enterprises.* London: Sage, 2003.

Ring, P., and Van de Ven, A. H. "Developmental Processes of Cooperative Interorganizational Relationships." *Academy of Management Review,* 1994, *19,* 90–118.

Scotch, R. K. "Ceremonies of Program Evaluation." In *Conference Proceedings.* Indianapolis, Ind.: Association for Research on Nonprofit Organizations and Voluntary Action, 1998.

Sonnichsen, R. C. *High-Impact Internal Evaluation.* Thousand Oaks, Calif.: Sage, 2000.

Srivasta, S., Cooperrider, D., and Associates. *Appreciative Management and Leadership.* San Francisco: Jossey-Bass, 1990.

Tassie, B., Murray, V., Cutt, J., and Bragg, D. "Rationality and Politics: What Really Goes On When Funders Evaluate the Performance of Fundees?" *Nonprofit and Voluntary Sector Quarterly,* 1996, *25,* 347–363.

United Way of America. *Measuring Program Outcomes: A Practical Approach.* Alexandria, Va.: United Way of America, 1996.

CHAPTER FIFTEEN

Managing the Challenges of Government Contracts

Steven Rathgeb Smith

In the past thirty years, a major restructuring of the provision of public services has occurred; increasingly, public services are provided by nonprofit service agencies through government contracts (Smith and Lipsky, 1993; Grønbjerg, 1993; Grønbjerg and Smith, 1999; De Hoog, 1984; Kramer, 1983). Consequently, nonprofit managers are on the front lines in government's response to major social problems, including AIDS, homelessness, chronic mental illness, and drug and alcohol abuse. Government funding can often be a boon to nonprofit agencies struggling with resource constraints because it can allow nonprofit agencies to expand services and improve quality. However, government contracts also mean that nonprofit managers are intertwined with government. Nonprofit managers who are used to working with boards of directors now face meeting the demands and expectations of public contract managers, the legislature, the governor, and even social policy advocacy groups. Contracting exposes nonprofit agencies to government budgetary politics and complex funding issues, such as rate setting, fee-for-service clients, and cost reimbursement contracts. Funding delays, political interference in contract negotiations,

The author would like to acknowledge the support of the Nancy Bell Evans Center of Nonprofit Leadership at the Daniel J. Evans School of Public Affairs at the University of Washington and the Center for the Study of Philanthropy and Voluntarism at the Sanford Institute of Public Policy, Duke University. Helpful comments on earlier versions of this chapter were provided by Charles T. Clotfelter and Robert Herman.

and uncertainty about future agency revenues are only a few of the many new concerns for nonprofit managers due to the growth of contracting.

Contracting also tends to precipitate internal changes within the organization, including greater formalization and professionalization. New internal accountability structures need to be created, and the board's role in agency oversight tends to become more focused on long-term strategic issues rather than on operational concerns. The efficient allocation of resources becomes a much more pressing concern as the extent and duration of contracting increases.

The central focus of this chapter is an examination of the dilemmas posed by contracting for nonprofit management and the implications of contracting for future nonprofit managers and boards of directors. The chapter is based on extensive research on the impact of government contracting on nonprofit health and social welfare organizations. Although this chapter concentrates on nonprofit service organizations, the effects of contracting and the management recommendations are applicable to other types of nonprofit organizations receiving public contracts, such as arts and cultural organizations.

THE RISE OF GOVERNMENT CONTRACTING WITH NONPROFIT SERVICE AGENCIES

Prior to the 1960s, nonprofit service agencies were overwhelmingly dependent on private funds, primarily endowment income, client fees, and charitable contributions. However, many nonprofit and public organizations faced mounting criticism in the late 1950s and early 1960s for their failure to adequately serve the poor and disenfranchised. In response, the federal government sharply increased its role in addressing social problems. New federal initiatives included neighborhood health centers, community mental health centers, community action agencies, and greatly increased discretionary spending on social services.

This new federal role was reflected in the rapid rise in federal spending on social services. Federal expenditures for social welfare services almost tripled between 1965 and 1970, from $812 million to $2.2 billion. Federal funding continued to expand throughout the 1970s. By 1980, federal funds accounted for 65 percent of total government spending at all levels on social welfare services, compared to 38 percent in 1965. State and local spending also rose, spurred in part by the increase in federal spending. Total spending at all levels of government (in constant 1995 dollars) for social welfare services rose from $45.20 in 1965 to $104.79 in 1980 (Bixby, 1999, pp. 92–93). A large percentage of the increase in public funding of social services was channeled through nonprofit agencies in the form of government contracts. In 1977, twenty-five states used half or more of their state human service expenditures for contracts with nonprofit agencies (Kettner and Martin, 1985, p. 8). In Massachusetts, the Department of Welfare increased its contracting with nonprofit agencies from $36 million (380 contracts) to $84 million (over 1,000 contracts) between 1977 and 1980 (Gurin, Friedman, Ammarell, and Sureau, 1980, p. 137). Many state agencies relied almost exclusively on nonprofit agencies to provide services, especially new and innovative services such as community residential programs, respite care, and day treatment (Smith and Lipsky, 1993).

The Reagan administration came to power in 1981 with a commitment to reduce federal spending. During his first year in office, President Reagan successfully achieved the enactment of the Omnibus Budget Reconciliation Act (OBRA). Key features of the legislation included an approximate 20 percent reduction in federal spending on social services, the consolidation of many different categorical federal social programs into block grants, and the decentralization of administrative responsibility for the expenditure of federal funds to state and local governments (Gutowski and Koshel, 1982).

The impact of these Reagan administration policy changes on public social expenditures is evident in the shifts in federal and state funding. Total federal spending on social welfare services through a variety of block grant and categorical spending programs declined from $8.8 billion in 1980 to $7.5 billion in 1985 (in current dollars). During this period, state and local spending rose from $4.8 billion to $6 billion (Bixby, 1999, p. 90).

But somewhat surprisingly, federal funding of social services began to rise again in the late 1980s and 1990s through a variety of changes to existing law as well as new program initiatives. States and localities and nonprofit agencies refinanced services and tapped into Medicaid and to a lesser extent Medicare for funding. New federal programs were created in child welfare, workforce development, and welfare to work, to name just a few of these new initiatives. Federal housing and correctional programs, for example, expanded to include a social service component. These funds were often distributed to nonprofit agencies through government contracts (Smith and Lipsky, 1993; Grønbjerg and Smith, 1999; Smith, 2002). This increase in funding spurred the growth of more contracting for services and many new nonprofit agencies.

But recent cutbacks at the federal level and the fiscal crisis of many states signal a shift to a much tighter funding environment. The fiscal crisis in many states severely limits the ability of state governments to substitute state funds for reduced federal funds. Sources of private funding for nonprofit agencies such as the United Way and private foundations have limited capacity to substitute for declining government funds. And private foundations have been hurt by the downturn in the stock market, and United Way chapters face increased demand for funding at the same time that many chapters are facing declines in their annual campaigns.

This competitive and austere funding climate, though, is likely to encourage continued reliance on government contracting with nonprofit agencies. State and local governments, eager to save money, view contracting as a less costly way of providing needed public services. Indeed, the major public policy response to the serious problems of homelessness, hunger, AIDS, child abuse, and domestic violence in recent years has been through government contracting with nonprofit organizations. Moreover, the percentage contribution of government revenues of many nonprofit organizations remains high (examples include residential programs for developmentally disabled adults, emotionally disturbed children, or drug and alcohol treatment). Further, President George W. Bush's Faith Based and Community Initiative—even if it is not enacted into law—is already leading to an increase in government support for faith-based service agencies.

THE CONTRACTING REGIME
AND ITS MANAGEMENT IMPLICATIONS

The growth of contracting has created patterned relationships and expectations between government and nonprofit agencies that can be characterized as a "contracting regime." A regime is a "set of principles, norms, rules, and decision-making procedures around which actor expectations converge in a given issue area" (Krasner, 1982, p. 185). This concept has been most fully developed by analysts in international relations, who used the regime concept to characterize the relatively stable relationships that appear to exist between countries, despite the absence of a single entity to act with authority in managing the relationship. Thus countries can develop certain formal and informal rules and expectations about their interactions, even though the countries may not be bound by legal agreements.

The nonprofit-government contracting relationship is similar to the regime in the following respects. First, regimes tend to have accepted means of resolving disputes and addressing particular problems. This is evident in the tendency today to use nonprofit organizations funded by government to address current social problems and in the accepted norms governing the interaction between nonprofit organizations and government. Second, the regime concept is helpful in illuminating the regularized patterns of interaction between government and nonprofit agencies, even when these nonprofit organizations are opposed or resistant to government regulations and mandates. Third, participants in regimes are mutually dependent and marked by continuity. And if participants depart from the regime norms, they are penalized, either by the dominant party or by third parties. Fourth, regimes are usually sustained and dominated by a powerful party. In international relations, this role is performed by a country whose policies and norms are accepted by other countries in the regime. The government-nonprofit relationship is similar because despite the mutual dependency of government and nonprofit organizations, government tends to be the more powerful in the relationship. Thus nonprofit organizations are often in the position of accepting or following the norms and policies of government (Smith and Lipsky, 1993).

The implications of the contracting regime for nonprofit management are profound. Managers of nonprofit agencies receiving government contracts are not free agents but are linked in an ongoing relationship with government, which at once constrains their behavior and provides certain incentives for managerial action. The dilemma for nonprofit managers is that the process of government contracting may undermine a nonprofit's financial stability while encouraging nonprofit organizations to move away from their own distinctive mission and reflect more closely the priorities and goals of the government administrators. The following sections provide more detail on the specific problems posed by the uncertainties of contracting for nonprofit managers.

Public attention to contracting has often focused on strategies to ensure the accountability of nonprofit organizations for the expenditure of government funds. Also, many scholars and practitioners worry that government contracts may change the mission of a nonprofit agency. But much less attention has been given to the many ways in which government contracts can greatly complicate the management of nonprofit service agencies even in situations where government and nonprofit agencies may initially agree on the purpose and intent of a contract. I will focus here on two specific aspects of contracting that can produce profound uncertainties and management challenges for nonprofit agencies: the cash flow problem and contract renewal and negotiation.

Cash Flow and Resource Development

Nonprofit service organizations can face serious problems generating adequate cash flow and revenue, especially in times of government fiscal austerity. The roots of this problem reflect the unique role played by nonprofit organizations in social service delivery. Nonprofit agencies, especially grassroots community agencies, such as battered women's shelters, poverty agencies, and youth organizations, emerge through the collective efforts of like-minded individuals interested in addressing a particular social problem. Typically, these organizations are dependent on a mix of small cash and in-kind donations. As a result, they tend to be significantly undercapitalized. Overcoming the capitalization dilemma is hampered by the preference of private donors for specific programs and projects. Many banks further exacerbate the situation by their reluctance to loan money to nonprofit agencies, especially smaller programs.

The constraints on building an adequate capital base make it difficult to weather disruptions in cash flow. When nonprofit organizations are young and small, a cash flow interruption may represent a minor problem. The sole paid staff member skips a paycheck. Or a board member steps in to make up the difference. Or a creditor agrees to forgive a bad debt.

But when a nonprofit becomes involved in a contractual arrangement with government, the implications of cash flow disruptions become more serious, since contracting means more resources for the agency, hence much greater cash flow demands. Perhaps one of the best examples of how agencies can change is provided by many associations of retarded citizens (ARCs) across the country. These ARCs typically started very small and often existed for many years without a full-time executive. The revenue demands were very small. Over time, ARCs began to provide contracted services. During the 1980s, state governments looked to ARCs to provide community-based services to deinstitutionalized persons with developmental disabilities through the Intermediate Care Facilities for the Mentally Retarded program funded through Medicaid (Bradley, 1981; Braddock and others, 1998). This program is very costly, often requiring ARCs to generate tens and sometimes hundreds of thousands of dollars every month to pay the bills of participants in the programs. Shortfalls in client censuses, management miscues, payment delays, or unexpected expenses can often prove fatal for an organization with such high revenue needs. The same problems affect smaller organizations whose programs are less costly.

The cash flow problem is exacerbated by a common characteristic of the contracting regime: the inability of the contract to cover all an agency's costs under the contract requirements. This serious problem can be due to several factors. The nonprofit manager may underestimate the costs of implementing the contract. Through no fault of the manager, agency expenses may rise when unexpected increases in the cost of doing business occur in such areas as insurance, utilities, and staff salaries. The contract amount, although adequate at the start of the contract, may over the years lose ground to inflation and state budget cutting. In these situations, the nonprofit manager is often put in the position of either giving up the contract, with its implications for staff layoffs and shrinkage of the agency, or continuing with the contract, albeit an underfunded one. Since nonprofit executives are rarely rewarded for staff layoffs and the accompanying organizational turmoil, most nonprofit executives keep the contract and try to make the best of a difficult situation.

In short, the cash flow problem is not an idiosyncratic occurrence or primarily due to mismanagement; rather, it is built in to the very structure of the contracting regime. Cash flow problems are to be expected. Nonprofit managers are in the position of coping with chronic cash flow concerns. Managers respond with a variety of strategies. They may delay their payments to their vendors, ask their bankers for easier terms on their loans, request that staff take unpaid leave or vacation time, temporarily lay off employees, or freeze hiring, even in cases of staff members leaving. In particularly serious cases, agency executives may forgo some of their salary or decide to suspend payment of the agency's payroll taxes.

Nonprofit executives facing these difficult management decisions often try to obtain additional revenues for the agency from government. They may try to obtain a line of credit or increase their credit line. Or they may seek private donations from individuals and companies or tap into the principal of their endowments. These strategies, however, are complicated and challenging, especially in times of fiscal austerity. Moreover, the number of nonprofit agencies has grown substantially in the past twenty years; indeed, the number of nonprofit social welfare agencies has more than tripled since the late 1970s (Smith, 2002). This growth has been disproportionately rapid among smaller agencies. Hence intense competition exists for private donations and government contracts in many service categories. Public and private funders are also expecting contract agencies to be much more performance-oriented, placing additional demands on the capacity of agencies to provide services.

The difficulty of raising or gaining access to sufficient revenue to compensate for revenue shortfalls is one reason that government administrators often prefer to contract with large agencies. Only the large agencies have the credit lines, the endowments, or the fundraising capacity to compensate for the inevitable cash flow problems experienced by nonprofit agencies.

The contract renewal and negotiation process has also become more complicated owing to the advent of managed care in many government-funded social and health services. Managed care has been widely employed with hospital services since the 1970s. Basically, a third party for-profit or nonprofit firm such as a health maintenance organization "manages" the health care for a population of patients with the goal of improving the efficiency and delivery of care. In the 1990s, many state and local governments started to contract with managed care firms to manage the services provided by government in a particular service category such as child welfare or mental health. For instance, a county government that had previously contracted directly with local nonprofit agencies for community mental health services now gives a fixed sum of money to a managed care firm that is responsible for administering services for a specified number of clients for their community mental health needs. The managed care firm then subcontracts with local nonprofit (and for-profit) service agencies to provide the actual community mental health services. For the nonprofit agency, this arrangement introduces greater funding uncertainty and less ability to reliably predict cash flow and revenue possibilities.

Contract Renewal

The ongoing and enduring cash flow problems of nonprofit agencies are often intensified by the uncertainties that accompany contract renewal. When government contracts with a nonprofit agency, it has a vested interest in the sound and smooth operation of the agency. Nonetheless, it frequently undermines the operations of the agency through debilitating delays and unpredictability in naming and providing contract renewal awards—circumstances that make it extremely difficult for nonprofit contract agencies to adequately plan and manage their affairs.

Delays in contract renewal occur for many reasons. The state legislature may be deadlocked, requiring that the state agencies suspend final action on contract renewals until the potential amount available for contracts is known. Key administrators at the government agency contracting with nonprofit agencies may have left or been replaced. An election may be under way, generating uncertainty among government administrators as to their future, with resultant ripple effects on the contracting process.

Other reasons for delay may be more strategic from the standpoint of the government contract administrators. State administrators may want to delay the process of contract renewal in order to gain greater compliance by nonprofit agencies to contract terms and expectations. For example, a contract administrator may have found the nonprofit agency resistant to accepting certain government client referrals. Delaying renewal may, in the eyes of the government administrator, make it more likely that the agency will soften its position in a direction more amenable to the government's position.

Alternatively, government administrators may use their ability to expedite the contract renewal process, to at least some degree, as a way of currying favor with nonprofit contract agencies. This debt may then be useful in future negotiations with nonprofit contract agencies.

The renewal process can be a highly uncertain process despite the high rate of contract renewal. Most contracts are renewed. A battered women's shelter awarded a contract in 1995 is likely to still have the contract in 2005, barring any major shocks to the provider system. But the high rate of renewals masks the regular dilemmas faced by nonprofit agencies during the contract renewal process. Nonprofit managers may be unclear as to the exact amount of the new contract. Given cutbacks in state governments, a renewed contract might well be for a lower amount than the previous one. Also, the state may decide to rewrite the contract upon renewal. A child welfare agency might have a contract for several years to provide counseling services to children. But a change in political priorities might lead state administrators to use contract renewal as an opportunity to restructure the agreement so that the child welfare agency, if it wants to keep the contract, would be required to provide intervention services to abused and neglected children. Other examples of substantive changes in contracts by state officials include requiring nonprofit agencies to serve a larger geographical area, giving part of a contract to another agency, reducing the administrative costs allowed on the contract, and requiring that client referrals be screened by government program staff.

Nonprofit managers, at least theoretically, have the option of refusing to rewrite the terms of the contract or to abide the long delays often accompanying contract renewal. But this strategy can be problematic. First, the proliferation of nonprofit (and for-profit) service agencies has greatly increased the service options of government program staff. In the past, many nonprofit agencies enjoyed a monopoly position in their geographical area, giving them substantial leverage with government administrators in a contract situation. Most agencies, except for very specialized services, have lost this status. Now nonprofit managers know that if they resist the renegotiation of a contract, many agencies are waiting in line to take the contract on the terms stipulated by government.

Second, competition for private charitable funds, which might serve as alternatives to contract funds, is fierce. Moreover, most foundation grants are unable to replace lost contract funds because they tend to be short-term and for much smaller amounts than contract funds. As noted, United Way funds are difficult to obtain. And raising private funds with appeals to individuals is a long-term project that cannot substitute for lost government funds. Agencies that have lost contracts are rarely able to approach the level of contract funding using private donations. As a result, these agencies often merge with other agencies or shrink drastically. In extreme cases, agencies go out of business.

Third, nonprofit agencies often find that the only way they can fulfill their mission to address a particular problem, such as juvenile delinquency or child abuse, is through government funding. Private funding is either unavailable or inadequate to the agency's needs.

STRATEGIC MANAGEMENT IN THE AGE OF CONTRACTING

The cash flow crisis and the uncertainties of contract renewal create enduring challenges for nonprofit managers. Responding to these challenges is complicated when contracting precipitates changes within the organization. Strategies exist, however, that can help nonprofit executives and board members adequately manage their agencies through difficult times. I will detail these changes here and outline specific initiatives to enhance the capacity of nonprofit service agencies to effectively manage the challenges of government contracting.

A New Role for the Board of Directors

The ideal nonprofit organization is governed by a volunteer board of directors who serve as the connecting link between the organization and the local community. This board role is especially critical if community-based service agencies are to effectively represent their communities and the users of their services.

But contracting poses serious problems for many boards. Most board members tend to be unfamiliar with contracting and the intricacies of the contracting process. It is often difficult for board members to exercise oversight over contracts and the management of contracts by executives. Further, the executive is usually the person within the organization who is knowledgeable about contracting opportunities and potential sources of new revenues for the agency.

Also, contracting requires the agency to develop new systems of accountability to track expenditures and clients. Inevitably, these new systems require greater staff specialization and a more formal organization of the agency. A full-time bookkeeper may be hired. New program managers may be necessary. Additional secretarial support may be needed to process forms and requests for information about clients and agency spending. As the paid staff expands and the demands on the agency's resources grow, the board may find itself less capable of setting the agenda for the agency, especially if the agency is highly dependent on contract revenues. The board may be relegated to a position of supporting the executive's initiatives rather than the executive implementing the board's directives and policies.

The danger for the organization inherent in this kind of shift is that the board may encounter some unpleasant surprises. The executive, in the pursuit of contract revenues, may obligate the agency to contracts that are underfunded or ill-advised. Board involvement in the agency may wither as board members find that they are severely limited in terms of the types of input sought by the executive. As board involvement declines, management mistakes or morale problems may go undetected until a crisis develops.

Other types of management problems may develop due to conflicts over agency mission. For example, the board may be made up of the founding members of the organization, who have a commitment to a specific mission. They may feel that the executive is trying to take the organization in a direction that violates the agency's spirit as originally defined by the board. The result may be protracted negotiations between the board and staff about the agency's future. Sometimes the outcome is the resignation of some board members or the ouster of the executive as the board and staff try to define the agency's mission.

The executive may have the key role in agency governance until a crisis develops, such as inadequate cash flow, staff discontent, or lost contracts. In response, the board may exert greater control and oversight over agency operations. Yet the board often withdraws to its previous role as the crisis eases. In other cases, the board may simply be unable to find an appropriate executive director, so the board retains an important role in day-to-day agency management and the overall agenda setting for the organization.

The shift in power from the board to the executive director and his or her staff is a general tendency among nonprofits, although the extent of this change will differ with organizations' individual circumstances. This kind of change—and the organizational problems created by this new staff role—is most visible in new community-based organizations that emerge out of the informal helping system of community members, neighbors, and social movements. For these agencies, professional management often represents values and policies antithetical to the original purposes of the organization (Wilson, 1973; Smith and Lipsky, 1993).

To a certain extent, the enhanced role of the executive is part of the process of organizational growth and development (Wilson, 1973). The board and the organization as a whole, however, can take steps to minimize the extent to which the board's role in agency oversight is unduly altered. First, the board can recruit individuals with knowledge of contracting for board membership. Second, the board can institute procedures that require the executive director and his or her staff to submit timely reports on various programmatic and financial aspects of the agency. Third, the board should tour agency facilities and programs on a regular basis, to learn in detail about agency activities and consumers. Fourth, depending on the agency, the board should include consumer or community representatives. These individuals can supply useful feedback to the rest of the board on agency performance and provide very valuable advice and input on agency mission and goals. Indeed, community participation is increasingly being viewed as critical to strong management and governance (Crosby, 2003).

Finding the Right Executive

When contract funds are on the rise, management miscues in nonprofit agencies can be overlooked by board members or masked by new contracts. Especially for nonprofit agencies providing valued public services, government contract managers can have an incentive to spend dollars quickly in order to develop new services. For example, in the late 1990s, many state and local governments had a lot of new funds to spend on workforce development programs and welfare-to-work programs. But in the current era of budget scarcity, the environment for contracting is quite different. Contract managers are now in a very demanding mode, and funding is in decline. Even a relatively small management mistake can create a financial crisis for the agency.

This new environment places significant pressure on the executive director to manage the internal operations and the external network of public and private funders. Ideally, agency executives should be comfortable with government contracting procedures and financial management as well as be sensitive to the agency's mission.

Given the multiple pressures on executive directors and nonprofit agencies, the process of selecting an executive director may lay bare some of the underlying differences within the organization on the agency's future. For this very reason, nonprofit agencies can find themselves mired in controversy as a newly hired executive takes the agency in a direction perceived to be contrary to its original mission. This is a particularly common problem in the current contracting environment because many individuals with the credentials necessary to cope with the management complexities of contracting may not be well attuned to the subtleties of the agency's approach to its surrounding community or consumers. Or financial viability may require the agency to move into new directions that are opposed by many staff. The financial problems of nonprofit agencies lead many boards of directors to hire individuals who would operate the agency as a business, prompting internal feuds over agency mission and direction.

Given these management challenges, the ideal type of executive for a nonprofit service agency cannot be determined without reference to the particular characteristics and needs of the organization. And while it may no longer be sufficient to have a respected clinician with relatively little management training or experience as an executive, it is equally true that a board of directors would be in error if it simply sought an executive whose primary qualification was a management background in another agency or organization. Although individuals with a business background may bring a new focus on efficiency to an agency, over the long run, costs may be very high in terms of staff turnover, morale, and client dissatisfaction. An agency needs to strike a balance between the concern for the efficient utilization of resources, due in part to the demands of the contracting regime, and the commitment to agency mission that exists outside market-driven imperatives.

Enlarging the Agency Constituency

Nonprofit agencies, as noted, often represent at their founding the efforts of like-minded people to address a particular problem. Often these organizations are not representative of their community as a whole; many agencies are directed by people from a particular political, ideological, ethnic, or income group in a community. Indeed, nonprofit organizations are valued in part because of their ability to represent specialized or minority constituencies (Weisbrod, 1988; Smith and Lipsky, 1993). This narrowness can become a handicap as an agency develops and becomes involved in a contracting relationship with government. Cash flow problems and the uncertainties of the contract process are part of contracting. But they may be addressed or alleviated through the support or intervention of community notables, politicians, consumers, and board members. Consequently, a crucial part of nonprofit management today is the diversification or enlargement of the organization's constituency.

Several strategies to achieve this goal are possible. First, an agency may create an affiliate organization that can help with fundraising, community support, and program visibility. Typically, these organizations are directed by the paid staff of the parent organization but are operated primarily by volunteers. Second, the organization may alter the composition of its board in order to bring interested supporters directly into an oversight and governance role for the organization. Third, the agency might join community organizations, such as the

Chamber of Commerce. The regular presence of a nonprofit contract agency at Chamber meetings can go a long way toward creating a role for the agency as a vital and important member of the community.

Fourth, the agency may alter its rules for membership. Many nonprofit organizations were established by a relatively small number of people who formed the core of the initial board of directors; no official membership in the organization apart from the board and staff may have existed. In such agencies, the board of directors was frequently self-perpetuating rather than elected by the membership. Later, however, an agency can change the rules to allow interested community supporters or financial contributors to be eligible for membership. This may give important friends of the organization a stake in it that would be very useful for purposes of political and financial support. It may also give the organization greater leverage in its relations with government contract administrators.

Fifth, agencies can create new advisory councils (or other more informal governance structures) as complements to the board of directors. These advisory councils can be especially helpful for specialized purposes such as strategic planning and a new capital campaign for the organization (Saidel, 1998).

Enlarging the agency's constituency through these new initiatives or governance structures is not without risks. New members or supporters may try to change the agency's mission and lead it in new directions. An agency may trade dependency on state contract administrators for dependency on a powerful donor or group of donors. More community members may make the organization more risk-averse. For example, a community residence program for the developmentally disabled might shy away from developing an innovative apartment program if it knew that substantial community opposition might develop. Consequently, clarity about an organization's mission and the role of new constituency groups is absolutely critical if an agency is to avoid organizational instability.

STRENGTHENING POLITICAL ADVOCACY AND ASSOCIATIONAL ACTIVITY

Prior to the advent of widespread contracting, nonprofit service agencies tended to be quite separate from the political process. Dependent primarily on private revenues, management decisions and the fate of the organization were relatively disconnected from decisions made by state and local legislatures, the federal government, or governors and mayors. Contracting has changed this situation. Nonprofit management is now inextricably connected to the political process. Important political decisions, legislation, and administrative rulings can have a profound impact on the success of nonprofit managers. If the legislature refuses to allocate sufficient funds for a contract rate increase, the nonprofit executive may be forced to lay off personnel, with the accompanying implications for morale and program quality. Accountability requirements instituted by the legislature or administrators may have a major impact on how a nonprofit executive spends his or her time. Funding cutbacks may require agencies to merge or go out of business entirely. Cash flow problems and the contract renewal process can create severe management difficulties for nonprofit agencies. The success of nonprofit managers now hinges, at least in part, on decisions made in the political arena. This changed relationship between nonprofits and the political world requires nonprofit executives and their boards to adopt new strategies in order to manage their organizations effectively.

Enhancing the Agency's Political Presence

Nonprofit executives and their boards need to increase their agency's political visibility and support. The executive should strive to enlist the support of local political figures, including municipal leaders and state legislators. This goal can be accomplished in part by enlisting key politicians or friends of politicians as agency board members. Also, a nonprofit executive can significantly help the agency's image by making local leaders aware of agency activities through mailings, articles in the local newspaper, and letters. Over time, these sometimes minor efforts can create a positive public image of the agency and garner favorable political support in the community.

This enhanced local political presence is especially important given the numerous local issues confronted by nonprofit service agencies. Many nonprofits need special zoning permits in order to house their facilities. Other nonprofits receive various cash and in-kind subsidies from municipalities. Nonprofit child welfare agencies are often required to have close connections with local school districts. And many nonprofit clients and consumers use local public transportation. Consequently, if an agency does not have good relations with its surrounding community and its political leaders, implementing the agency's programs may prove very difficult.

A nonprofit agency can also encounter political difficulties if it disagrees with a major decision of a state or local contracting agency. The state contract administrators may want to refer different types of clients to the agency. Or the state may want to restrict or curtail certain contract expenditures. Or the state may want to end the contract altogether and award it to another agency. Personal appeals by the executive, letters from the board of directors, or intervention by community political supporters may produce a reversal of unfavorable rulings. But many nonprofit agencies, especially smaller or newer agencies, lack the political clout to get these decisions overturned. Furthermore, many nonprofits, even the large ones, are averse to aggressive political action out of concern that such efforts may alienate government contract officials and lead to retribution against the agency at a later date. For this reason, it is also crucial for nonprofit executives to try to work together through nonprofit associations to create a strong political base. Broadening the political support for the agency through new governance initiatives may also be helpful. These actions may not ensure that unfavorable rulings will be overturned, but it may make it more difficult for government administrators to implement arbitrary or ill-advised policies.

In addition, nonprofit executives and their boards need to be much more aware of the legal issues surrounding advocacy and lobbying. Many nonprofits are very wary of advocacy because they fear that advocacy might spur scrutiny from the Internal Revenue Service or other government regulators, perhaps leading to threats to their tax-exempt status or serious fines (Berry, 2003). In reality, though, most nonprofit service agencies with government contracts can engage in far more advocacy than they currently do without risking legal complications (see Chapter Ten for more information about advocacy). Consequently, the boards and staff of nonprofit service agencies need to be much more active politically while educating themselves on the legal issues and regulations pertaining to permissible advocacy and lobbying.

The Role of Nonprofit Associations

Associations can fulfill a number of valuable functions for nonprofit managers, in addition to providing a means for collective influence with government. Many nonprofit agencies have participated in associations for decades. The Child Welfare League of America and the Alliance for Families are just two of the many national associations of nonprofit organizations. However, these organizations have not generally been involved in issues of contracting. More recently, though, many nonprofit associations have been founded at the state and local levels. These organizations have tended to be more directly involved in government contracting policies.

The new associations tend to be of two types. First, service-specific associations exist, such as the North Carolina Association of Home Care Agencies and the Massachusetts Association of Community Mental Health Centers. Second, statewide associations of different types of nonprofit agencies have been established. Good examples include the California Association of Nonprofits and the Maryland Association of Nonprofits. Indeed, thirty-four states and the District of Columbia now have associations of nonprofit organizations that advocate for their members with state legislatures (National Council of Nonprofit Organizations, 2004). Furthermore, the National Council of Nonprofit Organizations advocates for the state associations at the federal level and around the country.

Both types of organizations can be helpful to nonprofit managers on key policy issues relating to agency contracts, including rates, funding levels, service priorities, and contracting procedures. At times these associations may also be helpful in advocating for agencies in specific disputes between the state and individual organizations.

Statewide associations can also be very helpful in a number of other areas of direct concern to nonprofit managers. These statewide associations are able to call attention to the organizational difficulties nonprofits face. This may be particularly helpful as state policymakers deliberate on issues pertaining to nonprofits. These associations can also assist member agencies with more practical concerns, such as insurance, liability issues, human resource problems, and bulk purchasing.

Many nonprofit associations must contend with internal issues that constrain their advocacy role on behalf of nonprofit contract agencies. Some associations are forced to be very cautious in their advocacy work because of their members' concerns about alienating government policymakers. Other associations are divided on such issues as appropriate funding levels, contract requirements, and rates. Some associations with diverse memberships may also need to focus on issues of concern to every nonprofit, such as the local property tax questions or higher wages for employees. Nonetheless, in an era when state and local governments are increasingly important in the funding and monitoring of nonprofit programs, these nonprofit associations can be very helpful to nonprofit managers.

CONTRACTING REFORM AND NONPROFIT MANAGEMENT

The management challenges of contracting have led to calls for reform from policymakers, administrators, and nonprofit executives. This reform effort has focused on three areas. First, during the 1980s and 1990s, many states and localities experimented with simplifying the contracting process by expediting contracting renewal and the initial application process. Government officials have also tried in some instances to deregulate contracting to ease the administrative burden on nonprofit agencies.

Second, government officials and nonprofit agencies have tried to change the reimbursement process. One strategy has entailed trying to address the cash flow dilemmas noted earlier. For example, in 1984, New York State enacted "prompt payment" legislation to address the cash flow problems of nonprofit contract agencies. Under this legislation, the state is required to pay interest on any overdue payments to vendors. Although this law helped ease the cash flow problem somewhat, nonprofit agencies still complained of cash flow difficulties related to delays in contract renewal and approval. In response, new legislation was passed in 1991. The Prompt Contracting Law contains a number of innovative provisions, including time targets for the renewal of continuing contracts and new or onetime contracts and a legislation appropriation, to be managed by the Office of State Comptroller, for interest-free loans to contract agencies experiencing cash flow problems (Grossman, 1992).

Another reform with potential implications on cash flow is component pricing. Basically, this system establishes uniform costs for various "components" of nonprofit agency operation, such as social workers' and psychologists' fees, space rental, and reporting costs. A cost range is determined for all providers of these components. Negotiated contracts then contain these cost ranges, allowing greater discretion on the part of nonprofit managers to move money from one category to another, depending on agency needs (Koch and Boehm, 1992). With greater managerial flexibility, it is hoped that nonprofit managers will be in a better position to prevent cash flow or more general financial problems.

More recently, the drive to simplify the contracting process has been joined with much greater concern with outcomes and accountability, spurred in part by the fiscal problems of government and the movement to reinvent government to make it more effective and responsive (Behn, 2002; Smith, 2003; Osborne and Gaebler, 1992). The result has been not only more government contracting with nonprofit agencies but also a restructuring of reimbursement systems to tie payment to nonprofit agencies to specific outcomes. For example, Oklahoma instituted a system in the late 1980s and 1990s that tied reimbursement in a supported work program for the disabled to the attainment of specific outcomes (Kennedy School of Government, 1998). This type of reimbursement system— often called performance contracting—has been widely replicated with many different services, including welfare-to-work, mental health, workforce development, and counseling.

Depending on the structure of implementation, performance contracting can reduce the administrative burdens on nonprofit agencies by reducing the need for extensive documentation on billable services. However, in practice, performance contracting in the current environment has often meant much greater attention to outcomes without the reduction in paperwork and time. As a consequence, many nonprofit agencies find themselves with ever-rising demands for accountability. These challenges can also be compounded by low payment rates for nonprofit services and cutbacks in government funding support.

Given the current emphasis on performance and outcomes, combined with the tight fiscal realities, government policymakers and nonprofit managers need to approach the contracting relationship as a long-term investment. Government policymakers and administrators should avoid short-term contracts and constant bidding and rebidding of contracts. Instead, government and nonprofit organizations should craft longer-term contracts that balance the need for accountability with the recognition that frequent turnover in contracts (or the threat of turnover) can be destabilizing for nonprofit agencies and can undermine the quality of services.

Nonprofits, for their part, should strive to invest in their administrative and programmatic infrastructure, including new technology and qualified administrative staff. This effort could also include new or innovative ways to infuse the board and local community members with specific expertise in support of the organization. Nonprofits can also help themselves in building their administrative capacity and infrastructure by creating or initiating ongoing private fundraising initiatives in the community. Many nonprofit contract agencies have tended to neglect community fundraising, especially as contract funds have risen. To be sure, fundraising may not produce large benefits for the organization in the short term, but in the long term, it can be very helpful as a way of cross-subsidizing programs supported by inadequate contract funds.

Government policies and programs to support nonprofit agencies with their capital costs are also a very positive reform strategy. In many states and localities, government officials have provided low-cost loans to nonprofits, including access to bond funds, to help them with their capital expenses, such as the purchase and renovation of their facilities and new equipment. To the extent that nonprofits can improve their capital position, they will be in a better position to manage their cash flow effectively and be able to develop productive relationships with government contract officials.

SUMMARY

Widespread government contracting has remade the management of nonprofit social and health agencies. It has allowed many nonprofit agencies and managers to expand their services, client bases, and geographical jurisdictions. But cash flow problems, government cutbacks, and higher administrative and regulatory compliance burdens remain persistent issues for nonprofit managers. Moreover, contracting alters the balance of power within nonprofit agencies. With the goals of many service contracts set outside the agency, the agency board may be less than assertive in monitoring the financial and programmatic operations of the agency. Contracting also pushes nonprofit agencies into the world of lobbying, political associations, legislative politicking, and appeals to the mayor and governor, either directly or indirectly.

Nonprofit service agencies receiving government contracts are now part of the nation's public service system. As a result, the management of nonprofit agencies is more diffuse, with more diverse constituencies and with important linkages to political leaders, interest groups, and the political process in general. The task of defining a nonprofit agency's mission and its future direction is more complicated because the fate of the agency is at least in part determined by political decisions made outside the agency. While nonprofit agencies may influence these decisions, the extent of their influence will be affected by many factors, including state and local budgetary politics. The mission of a nonprofit contract agency is no longer strictly private but includes a substantial public dimension. As nonprofit executives and board members try to navigate an increasingly complex and challenging fiscal and political environment, they will have to carefully balance their public and private responsibilities if they are to preserve the vital role of nonprofits as alternatives to government agencies while at the same time maintaining the financial and programmatic health of their agencies. Government, for its part, needs to recognize that effective nonprofit management hinges at least in part on adequate funding and an appropriate regulatory framework that reflects the vital role of nonprofit service agencies in providing valued public services to citizens in need.

References

Behn, B. *Rethinking Democratic Accountability.* Washington, D.C.: Brookings Institution Press, 2002.

Berry, J. M. *A Voice for Nonprofits.* Washington, D.C.: Brookings Institution Press, 2003.

Bixby, A. K. "Public Social Welfare Expenditures, Fiscal Year 1995." *Social Security Bulletin,* 1999, *62*(4), 86–94.

Braddock, D., and others. *The State of the States in Developmental Disabilities.* Washington, D.C.: American Association of Mental Retardation, 1998.

Bradley, V. "Mental Disabilities Services: Maintenance of Public Accountability in a Privately Operated System." In J. J. Bevilacqua (ed.), *Changing Government Policies for the Mentally Disabled.* Cambridge, Mass.: Ballinger, 1981.

Crosby, A. "Community Purpose Means Community Involvement." *Nonprofit Quarterly,* 2003, *10*(3), 24–28.

De Hoog, R. H. *Contracting Out for Human Services: Economic, Political, and Organizational Perspectives.* Albany: State University of New York Press, 1984.

Grønbjerg, K. A. *Understanding Nonprofit Funding: Managing Revenues in Social Services and Community Development Organizations.* San Francisco: Jossey-Bass, 1993.

Grønbjerg, K. A., and Smith, S. R. "Nonprofit Organizations and Public Policies in the Delivery of Human Services." In C. T. Clotfelter and T. Ehrlich (eds.), *Philanthropy and the Nonprofit Sector.* Bloomington: Indiana University Press, 1999.

Grossman, D. A. *Paying Nonprofits: Streamlining the New York State System.* Albany, N.Y.: Nelson A. Rockefeller Institute of Government, 1992.

Gurin, A., Friedman, B., Ammarell, N., and Sureau, C. *Contracting for Services as a Mechanism for the Delivery of Human Services: A Study of Contracting Practices in Three Human Service Agencies in Massachusetts.* Waltham, Mass.: Florence Heller School of Advanced Studies in Social Welfare, 1980.

Gutowski, M. F., and Koshel, J. J. "Social Services." In J. L. Palmer and V. Sawhill (eds.), *The Reagan Experiment.* Washington, D.C.: Urban Institute, 1982.

Kennedy School of Government. *Oklahoma's Milestones Reimbursement System: Paying for What You Get.* Cambridge, Mass.: Kennedy School of Government, Harvard University, 1998.

Kettner, P. M., and Martin, L. L. "Purchase of Service Contracting and the Declining Influence of Social Work." *Urban and Social Change Review,* 1985, *18*, 8–11.

Koch, D. S., and Boehm, S. *The Nonprofit Policy Agenda: Recommendations for State and Local Action.* Washington, D.C.: Union Institute, 1992.

Kramer, R. *Voluntary Agencies in the Welfare State.* Berkeley: University of California Press, 1983.

Krasner, S. D. "Structural Causes and Regime Consequences: Regimes as Intervening Variables." *International Organization,* 1982, *36,* 185–205.

National Council of Nonprofit Organizations. "State Association Directory" [http://www.ncna.org/index.cfm?fuseaction = Page.viewPage&pageID = 342]. Apr. 2004.

Osborne, D., and T. A. Gaebler. *Reinventing Government: How the Entrepreneurial Spirit Is Transforming the Public Sector.* New York: Plenum Press, 1992.

Saidel, J. R. "Expanding the Governance Construct: Functions and Contributions of Nonprofit Advisory Groups." *Nonprofit and Voluntary Sector Quarterly,* 1998, *27,* 421–436.

Smith, S. R. "Social Services." In L. M. Salamon (ed.), *The State of Nonprofit America.* Washington, D.C.: Brookings Institution Press, 2002.

Smith, S. R. "Street-Level Bureaucracy and Public Policy." In B. G. Peters and J. Pierre (eds.), *Handbook of Public Administration.* London: Sage, 2003.

Smith, S. R., and Lipsky, M. *Nonprofits for Hire: The Welfare State in the Age of Contracting.* Cambridge, Mass.: Harvard University Press, 1993.

Weisbrod, B. *The Nonprofit Economy.* Cambridge, Mass.: Harvard University Press, 1988.

Wilson, J. Q. *Political Organizations.* New York: Basic Books, 1973.

CHAPTER SIXTEEN

Outcome Assessment and Program Evaluation

John Clayton Thomas

Nonprofit organizations need to know how effectively they are performing their jobs. Are their programs achieving the desired results? How could programs be modified to improve those results? Because the goals of nonprofit programs are often subjective and not readily observable, the answers to these questions may be far from obvious.

These questions have grown in urgency in recent years as a consequence of new external pressures. Funders of nonprofit programs increasingly demand evidence of program effectiveness, as illustrated by the United Way of America's outcome measurement initiative of the past decade (1996). In addition, "The Government Performance and Results Acts of 1993 . . . place a renewed emphasis on accountability in federal agencies and nonprofit organizations receiving federal support" (Stone, Bigelow, and Crittenden, 1999, p. 415). Yet research on contemporary practice indicates that many nonprofit agencies still perform relatively little assessment of program performance (Morley, Hatry, and Cowan, 2002).

To address these needs, nonprofit organizations need, at a minimum, to engage in systematic outcome assessment, that is, regular measurement and monitoring of how well their programs are performing relative to the desired outcomes. (The terms *outcome assessment* and *performance assessment* will be used interchangeably in this chapter.) Nonprofit executives may want, in addition, to employ the techniques of program evaluation in order to define the specific role their programs played in producing any observed beneficial changes. Used

391

appropriately, outcome assessment and program evaluation can inform a wide range of decisions about whether and how programs should be continued in the future and satisfy funder requirements at the same time.

This chapter introduces the techniques of outcome assessment and program evaluation as they might be employed by nonprofit organizations. These techniques are not designed for more general evaluations of organizational effectiveness (but see Chapter Fourteen in this volume). The emphasis here is on how these tools can be useful to organization executives by providing information relevant to decisions those executives must make. To make that case, I will provide a step-by-step description of how to conduct outcome assessment before explaining how that assessment can be incorporated into more advanced program evaluations.

PLANNING THE PROCESS FOR OUTCOME ASSESSMENT

For outcome assessment to have maximum value, the process for that assessment must be well planned and executed. The first step in that regard is for the organization's leaders to be committed to the effort. Ideally, an initiative of this kind will begin with the chief executive of the nonprofit organization, but in any event, that chief executive and the organization's board should understand and support the initiative. Support includes recognizing and accepting that outcome assessment could uncover unwelcome truths about program performance. There is no point in taking the time to develop and obtain performance data if the people in charge are not committed to looking at those data.

Assuming that support is assured, outcome assessment should be undertaken on a program-by-program basis. For a nonprofit organization with multiple programs, that guideline means that each program will require separate outcome assessment planning. A specific individual should be assigned primary responsibility for the planning for each program, perhaps as part of a small team. (The following discussion will use the term *decision makers* to encompass both possibilities.)

Regardless of whether a team is used, the planning process should entail extensive involvement of staff and perhaps even clients who are connected with the program. That involvement serves at least two functions. First, it assists in information gathering. The individuals most involved with a program know the program from the inside and hence can offer valuable intelligence on the program's desired outcomes and possible means for measuring their achievement. Second, involvement can also build ownership in the outcome assessment process. If the people involved with a program are given some say in how it will be assessed, they are more likely to buy into the eventual results of that assessment.

Finally, the process should also be linked to the organization's information technology. Improved information technology, by facilitating the recording and analysis of performance data, is a major factor underlying the recent push for better performance assessment in both the nonprofit and public sectors. Building the strongest performance assessment system requires that the system be planned in conjunction with the organization's technology.

DEFINING PROGRAM GOALS

Outcome assessment is a goals-based process in that programs are assessed relative to the goals they are designed to achieve. Defining those goals can be a difficult task, with the project leader or team required to define and differentiate several types of goals while at the same time navigating the sometimes difficult politics of goal definition. I will first explain the several goal types and then discuss how to define them in a political context.

Types of Goals

A first type of goal refers to the ultimate desired program impact. *Outcome goals* are the final intended consequences of a program for its clients or society. An outcome goal has value in and of itself, not as a means to some other end, and is usually people-oriented because most public and nonprofit programs are designed ultimately to help people.

Activity goals, by contrast, refer to the internal mechanics of a program, the desired substance and level of activities within the program. These specify the actual work of the program, such as the number of clients a program hopes to serve. How the staff of a program spend their time—or are supposed to spend their time—is the stuff of activity goals.

The distinction between outcome and activity goals can be illustrated through a hypothetical employment counseling program. An activity goal for this program might be "to provide regular employment counseling to clients," with an outcome goal being "to increase independence of clients from public assistance." The activity goal refers to the work of the program, the outcome goal to what that work is designed to achieve. As this example also suggests, outcome goals tend to be more abstract, conceptual, and long-term; activity goals are more concrete, operational, and immediate.

Understanding the distinction is crucial if outcome assessments are to resist pressures to evaluate program success in terms of activity rather than outcome goals. Program staff often push in that direction, for several reasons. First, activity goals are easier for them to see: they can more readily see their day-to-day work than what that work is designated to achieve at some time in the future. Second, activity goals tend to be more measurable; it is easier to measure the "regularity" of counseling than "independence from welfare." Finally, activity goals are also usually easier to achieve. Police working in a crime prevention program, for example, can be much more confident of achieving an activity goal of "increasing patrols" than an outcome goal of "reducing crime."

Outcome assessment planning can often sidestep pressures of this kind by including both types of goals in the goal definition. As a practical matter, both outcome and activity goals are important in most outcome assessments in order to elucidate how different parts of a program link to eventual program outcomes.

Sometimes a program will have so many activity goals that it could be too much work to attempt to define all of them as part of the outcome assessment system. A good guideline in such cases is to define activity goals only for key junctures in the program, that is, only at the major points in the program sequence where information is or might be wanted.

Falling between activity and outcome goals are *bridging goals,* so named because they supposedly connect activities to outcomes (Weiss, 1972). Bridging goals, like outcome goals, relate to intended consequences of a program for society, but bridging goals are an expected route to the final intended consequences, rather than final ends in themselves. In an advertising campaign designed to reduce smoking, for example, a bridging goal between advertising (activity) and reduced smoking (outcome) might be "increased awareness of the risks of smoking." That increased awareness would be a consequence of the program for society, but instead of being the final intended consequence, it is only a bridge from activity to outcome.

Bridging goals can be important for outcome assessment systems for a variety of reasons. For one thing, because they are often essential links in a program's theory—the hypothesized process by which program inputs lead to outcomes—their achievement may be a prerequisite to demonstrating that program activities have produced the desired outcomes. Thus to confirm that a program works, it may be necessary to establish that the bridging goal is achieved before the outcome goal. For another thing, bridging goals can provide a means to obtain an early reading on whether a program is working. Effects may be observable on a bridging goal when it is still too early to see any impact on final outcome goals.

Outcome assessment systems may also occasionally incorporate *side effects.* Side effects, like outcome and bridging goals, are also consequences of a program for society, but they are *unintended* consequences. They represent possible results other than the program's goals. For example, an effective neighborhood crime prevention program may displace crime to an adjacent neighborhood, producing the side effect of increased crime in the latter neighborhood. A side effect can also be positive, as when a neighborhood street cleanup program induces residents to spruce up their yards and homes too.

The outcome assessment system of a nonprofit agency should incorporate side effects only if the chief executive, staff, or other stakeholders view specific possible side effects as an important aspect of the program. Is there an interest in examining a possible negative side effect, perhaps with an eye toward changing the program so as to reduce or eliminate that result? Agency decision makers must make that judgment based on what data they believe are necessary for a full outcome assessment. In most cases, given a principal interest in activity and outcome goals, the executive may not want to spare limited resources to monitor possible side effects too. On occasion, however, possible side effects may loom as so important that they must be addressed.

Whatever the type of goal, its definition must satisfy three criteria. (1) Each goal should contain only one idea. A goal statement that contains two ideas (for example, "increase independence from welfare through employment counseling") should be divided into two parts, each idea expressed as a distinct goal. (2) Each goal should be distinct from every other goal. If goals overlap, they may express the same idea and so should be differentiated. (3) Goals should employ action verbs (for example, *increase, improve, reduce*), avoiding the passive voice.

Goal definitions can be derived from two principal sources: (1) program documentation, including initial policy statements, program descriptions, and the like, and (2) the personnel of the program, including program staff, the organization's executive, and possibly other stakeholders, including clients. These personnel should always be asked to react to draft goals before they are finalized.

The Politics of Goals Definition

Understanding the different types of goals and where to find them may be the easy part of goal definition. The difficult part can be articulating that definition in a manner satisfactory to all the important stakeholders. To do that may require overcoming the difficult politics of goal definition.

As a first difficulty, many programs begin without clearly defined goals. Initial program development may have focused on where money should be spent to the neglect of what the program should be designed to achieve. Second, as programs adapt to their environments, goals sometimes change, perhaps departing from the program's original intent. "Policy drift" can result when programs move away from that original intent and once-distinct goals become fuzzy or inconsistent (Kress, Springer, and Koehler, 1980).

More difficulties can arise when planning for outcome assessment begins. The common perception of any kind of assessment as threatening may prompt some program staff, when they are asked, to be evasive about goals. Or staff or other stakeholders at different places inside and outside the program may simply have different perspectives, resulting in conflicting opinions about a program's goals.

A variety of techniques are available to cope with these problems. Fuzzy or inconsistent goals may be accommodated by including all of the different possible goals in a comprehensive goals statement. If some perspectives appear too contradictory to fit in the same statement, a goal clarification process might be initiated (Kress, Springer, and Koehler, 1980). Working with staff and stakeholders to clarify the goals of a program could be the most important contribution of an outcome assessment planning process by building a cohesiveness previously lacking in the program.

Disagreement over goals can also sometimes be sidestepped as irrelevant. Patton (1997) recommends asking stakeholders what they see as the important *issues* or questions about the program. These issues, because they represent areas where information might be used, should be the focus of most eventual data analysis anyway. And there may be more agreement about issues than about goals. Outcome assessment decision makers might then be able to express these issues in terms of the types of goals outlined earlier.

The agency's chief executive can play several roles in the definition of program goals. At a minimum, the executive should oversee the entire process to ensure the necessary participation, lending the authority of her or his position as necessary. Second, the executive should review proposed goals as they are defined, both for clarity and for conformity to the agency's overall concerns. Finally, if conflicts over goals arise, the executive may need to intervene to achieve resolution.

The Impact or Logic Model

As part of the process of goal definition, the several types of goals should be combined into a visual impact or logic model—an abstracted model of how the various goals are expected to link to produce the desired outcomes (see also Rossi and Freeman, 1993). Such a model should have several characteristics. First, it should be an abstraction, removed from reality but representing reality, just as the goals are. Second, the model should simplify, reducing substantially the detail of reality. Third, as the "logic" component, the model should make explicit significant relationships among its elements, showing, for example, how activity goals are expected to progress to outcome goals. Fourth, the model may involve formulation of hypotheses—the suggestion of possible relationships not previously made explicit in program documents or by program actors. Indeed, a principal benefit of model development often lies in how program stakeholders are prompted to articulate hypotheses they had not previously recognized. Exhibit 16.1 shows an impact model for a hypothetical nonprofit training program.

The model links the various goals from the initial activity goals through the bridging goals to the ultimate outcome goals. As the model illustrates, bridging goals sometimes fall between two activity goals but still serve as links in the chain from activity goals to outcome goals. This model may be atypical in that the goals follow a single line of expected causality, whereas the more common model may fork at one or more points (for example, if different types of executives received different kinds of training).

**Exhibit 16.1. Impact Model for a Training Program
for Executives of Local Branches of a National Nonprofit.**

1. Determine developmental needs of local executives. (A)

2. Develop training materials to address these needs. (A)

3. Screen and select executives for training. (A)

4. Conduct training of executives. (A)

5. Executives formulate individualized plans for development of their organizations. (B)

6. Executives attend follow-up training. (A)

7. Local organizations increase volunteer membership. (O)

8. Local organizations increase volunteer giving. (O)

Note: (A) = activity goal; (B) = bridging goal; (O) = outcome goal.

Development of an impact model can help staff and stakeholders clarify how they expect a program to work and what questions they have about that operation, in the process perhaps suggesting how to use assessment data once they become available. Should staff or stakeholders disagree about the likely impact model, decision makers must determine whether the disagreement is sufficiently important to require resolution before further outcome assessment planning can proceed.

MEASURING GOALS

Once the goals have been defined, attention must turn to how to measure them. Before thinking about specific measures, decision makers should become familiar with some basic measurement concepts and with the various types of measures available.

Concepts of Measurement

Measurement is an inexact process, as suggested by the fact that social scientists commonly speak of "indicators" rather than measures. As the term implies, measurement instruments indicate something about a concept (that is, about a goal) rather than provide perfect reflections of it. So crime reported to police constitutes only a fraction of actual crime, and scores on a paper-and-pencil aptitude test reflect the test anxiety or cultural background of test taker as well as his or her aptitude.

The concepts of *measurement validity* and *measurement reliability* rest on recognition of the inexactness of measurement. Measurement validity refers to whether or to what extent a measure taps what it purports to measure. More valid measures capture more of what they purport to measure. Measurement reliability refers to a measurement instrument's consistency from one application to another. Reliability is higher if the instrument produces the same reading when applied to the same phenomenon at two different times (or when applied by different observers to the same phenomenon at the same time). Obviously, evaluators prefer measures that are more valid and more reliable.

Executives and staff of nonprofit agencies need not know a great deal about how to assess the validity and reliability of measures, but two points should be kept in mind. First, given the fallibility of any particular measure, multiple measures—two or more indicators—are desirable for any important goal, especially any major outcome goal. (One measure each may prove sufficient for many activity goals.) Once data collection begins, the different measures should then be compared to see if they appear to be tapping the same concept. Second, if there are concerns about reliability, taking multiple observations is recommended. Any important measure should, if possible, be applied at a number of time points to see if and how readings might fluctuate. (Multiple observations are also useful for other aspects of research design, as I will explain.)

Decision makers must also consider *face validity,* that is, whether measures appear valid to key stakeholders. Measurement experts sometimes discount the importance of face validity, arguing that measures that appear valid sometimes are not. However, the appearance of validity can be crucial to the acceptance of specific measures as really reflecting program performance. These considerations imply two guidelines for outcome assessment planning: (1) decision makers should consider whether recommended measures appear valid, and (2) they should consider whether any seemingly attractive measures might actually *not* tap the relevant goal.

At the same time, the ability of program staff to assess measurement validity should not be underestimated. By virtue of their experience with the program, program staff often have unique insights into the merits of specific measures, insights that trained outside experts might miss.

Types of Measures

Outcome assessments can employ several types of measures and to achieve the benefit of multiple measures will typically use two or more of the types. The different types are briefly introduced here in terms of what nonprofit executives and staff may need to know about each.

Program Records and Statistics. An obvious first source for data is the program itself. Records can be kept and statistics maintained by program staff for a variety of measures. Almost every evaluation will employ at least some measures based on program records.

These measures must be chosen and used with caution, however. For one thing, program staff ordinarily should be asked to record only relatively objective data, such as numbers of clients served, gender and age of clients, and dates and times services are delivered. Staff can usually record these more objective data with little difficulty and high reliability, whereas they cannot be expected, without training, to record more subjective data, such as client attitudes or client progress toward goals.

In a similar vein, program records can serve as an excellent source of measures of activity goals—the amount of activity in the program—but should be used only sparingly as outcome measures and probably never as the *sole* outcome measures. Program staff are placed in an untenable position if they are asked to provide the principal measures of their own effectiveness, especially if those measures include subjective elements.

That concern notwithstanding, the staff who will record the measures should be involved in defining the measures. In addition to offering insights about measurement validity, staff can speak to whether the demands of the proposed record keeping have been kept reasonable. The requirements of record keeping should not be so great that staff must choose between the evaluation and the program. If that happens, either the evaluation will interfere with the program because staff give too much time to record keeping, or the measures will produce poor data as staff slight record keeping in favor of more time for the program.

Client Questionnaire Surveys. Any program serving client populations, including most nonprofit programs, should include as part of outcome assessment some measures of client perceptions and attitudes. These perceptions could include ratings of the program's services and service providers, client self-assessments, and other basic client information. The obvious means for obtaining these measures is a questionnaire survey, of which there are several forms, each with its own advantages and disadvantages (see also Rea and Parker, 1997).

Phone surveys can produce good response rates (that is, responses from a high proportion of the sample), assuming that respondents are contacted at good times (usually in the evening) and interviewed for no more than ten to fifteen minutes. However, phone surveys can be expensive due to interviewer costs. In addition to actual interview time, multiple phone calls will be required to reach many respondents.

The desire for a lower-cost procedure often leads to consideration of *mail surveys*. Questionnaires are mailed to respondents, who are asked to complete and return them by mail. Any reduction in costs through using a mail survey can be more than offset, however, by the frequent poor response rate, typically lower and less representative than with a phone survey. Questions on mail surveys must also be structured more simply since no interviewer is available to guide the respondent through the questionnaire. Mail surveys work best when sent to groups that are both highly motivated to respond (as sometimes with clients of nonprofit programs) and willing and able to work through written questions independently. Even then, obtaining a high response rate usually requires sending one or two follow-up mailings to nonrespondents.

E-mail surveys are a contemporary variation on the mail survey. Relatively inexpensive online options are now available, too, for recording and summarizing responses. Obviously, though, this technique will work only with a computer-literate population.

The best choice for many programs is the so-called *convenience survey,* a survey of respondents who are available in some convenient setting, as when they receive program services. A program can capitalize on that availability by asking clients, while on site, to complete and turn in a brief questionnaire. As with mail surveys, the questionnaires must be kept simple and short to permit easy and rapid completion. To reassure respondents about the confidentiality of their responses, ballot box–like receptacles might be provided for depositing completed questionnaires. A well-planned convenience survey can produce a good response rate and at a cost lower than that of any of the alternatives.

Construction of any kind of questionnaire requires some expertise. Agency executives wishing to economize here might share the construction process with an outside consultant. The outcome assessment planners might draft initial questions for the consultant to critique and polish before another review by staff and again by the consultant. This collaborative procedure can both reduce the organization's costs and provide training in questionnaire construction to program staff.

Formal Testing Instruments. With many programs, the outcomes desired for clients—self-confidence, sense of personal satisfaction—are sufficiently common that experts elsewhere have already developed appropriate measurement instruments. Some formal testing instruments are available free in the public domain; others may be available at a modest per-unit cost. In either case, it is often both wiser and more economical to obtain these instruments than to develop new measures.

Trained Observer Ratings. These ratings can be especially useful for outcomes "that can be assessed by visual ratings of physical conditions," such as physical appearance of a neighborhood for a community development program (Hatry and Lampkin, 2003, p. 15). As that example suggests, these ratings work best for subjective outcomes that are not easily measured by other techniques. These ratings can be expensive in terms of both time and money, however, since their use necessitates development of a rating system, training of raters, and a plan for oversight of the raters. It can also be difficult in a small or moderate-sized nonprofit agency to find raters who do not have a personal stake in a program's effectiveness.

Qualitative Measures. Outcome assessment will typically be enhanced by some use of qualitative measures, measures designed to capture nonnumerical in-depth description and understanding of program operations. After long disdaining these measures as too subjective to be trusted, most experts now recognize that programs with subjective goals cannot be evaluated without qualitative data.

Qualitative measures can be obtained through two principal techniques, observation and in-depth interviews. Observation can provide a sense of how a process is operating, as, for example, in evaluating how well group counseling sessions have functioned. By observing and describing group interaction, an evaluator could gain a sense of process unavailable from quantitative measures.

In-depth interviews have a similar value. In contrast to questionnaire surveys, these relatively unstructured interviews are composed principally of open-ended questions designed to elicit respondents' feelings about programs without the constraints of the predefined multiple-response choices of structured questionnaires. These interviews can be extremely useful as, for example, in assessing the success of individualized client treatment plans.

Still, nonprofit agencies should use qualitative measures with caution, taking care to avoid either too much or too little reliance on them. Evaluation of most nonprofit programs calls for multiple measures, including both quantitative and qualitative measures. Outcome assessment planners must be sure that both perspectives are obtained.

Finally, outcome assessment planners should be prepared for the possibility that discussion of measures may rekindle debate about goals. Perhaps staff paid too little attention to the earlier goal definition, or perhaps thinking about measures prompts staff to see goals differently. When that happens, planners should be open to a possible need to reformulate goals.

DATA COLLECTION, ANALYSIS, AND REPORTING

Once the necessary measures have been defined, decision makers should address several issues around data collection, analysis, and reporting. They must ensure first that procedures are established for recording observations on the measures. They must also determine how the new data collection can be incorporated into the agency's information technology, including whether new software will be needed for the effort.

Before putting the full outcome assessment in place, the agency should pilot-test the measures and the data collection procedures to see how they work. Measures sometimes prove not to produce the anticipated information. Convenience surveys, for example, sometimes elicit incomplete responses from program clients, which could require either improving or abandoning that instrument.

Problems can also arise in the recording of data, perhaps necessitating rethinking the recording procedures.

Decision makers, certainly including the agency's chief executive, should also establish a schedule for regular reporting and review of the data. Depending on agency preferences and perceived needs, reviews might be planned as frequently as weekly or as infrequently as annually. Or less intensive reviews might be planned more often—on a weekly or monthly basis—with more intensive reviews scheduled on a quarterly or annual basis.

The details of that schedule are probably less important than that a schedule is established and observed. Judging from the findings of one study (Morley, Hatry, and Cowan, 2002), many nonprofit agencies that currently collect outcome information do not systematically tabulate or review the data, instead "leaving it to supervisors and caseworkers to mentally 'process' the data to identify patterns and trends" (p. 36). Agencies unnecessarily hamstring themselves when they make such choices. If systematic outcome data are available, agencies need to ensure that the data are tabulated and reviewed.

Actual review of the data can go in any number of directions, depending on what the data look like and what questions the agency has about the programs. At the outset, initial data on any new measures can be at once the most interesting and yet the most difficult to interpret. Novelty accounts for the likely high interest: agency executives and staff may be looking at outcome readings they have only been able to guess at before. However, with initially only one data point to analyze, those readings may seem uninterpretable. Interpretation becomes easier as readings accumulate over time, permitting comparisons of current performance to past performance.

The focus of the interpretation depends on a variety of factors. If the data show an unexpected pattern—such as an unanticipated decline on an outcome measure from one quarter to the next—attention may focus on explaining that pattern. More generally, though, the analysis of the data may be driven by the questions and concerns of the agency. Is there a concern about whether a program is working at all? Or might there be a concern instead whether a new program component is bringing desired improvements?

At the same time, care must also be taken not to *overinterpret* outcome data. In particular, these outcome data should not by themselves be taken to imply causality; that is, one must not assume that any observed changes resulted from a specific program or programs. Such changes could have resulted from other factors (a turnaround in the economy, for example) that are wholly independent of the program. Outcome assessment data by themselves answer questions of whether progress is being made on key agency objectives but do not reveal the part the agency played in inducing those changes.

When questions about program performance turn in this direction, agency executives may want to take a step beyond outcome assessment to conduct a program evaluation, too. Program evaluations, in essence, start from a foundation of strong outcome assessment, adding the techniques of comparison and control necessary to address more definitively the role of specific programs in producing desired outcomes.

TWO APPROACHES TO PROGRAM EVALUATION

Program evaluation can seem a frightening prospect, raising the specter of outside experts "invading" the organization, seeking information in a sometimes mysterious and furtive manner, and ultimately producing a report that may contain unexpected criticisms. Such fears are not ungrounded. The traditional approach to program evaluation, which I call the *objective scientist approach,* often proceeds along those lines.

Borrowed from the natural sciences, the objective scientist approach entails several elements. To begin with, objectivity is valued above all else. To achieve that objectivity, the evaluator must maintain a critical distance from the program being evaluated, thereby minimizing possible influence by program staff, who may be biased in the program's favor. The objective scientist also strongly prefers quantitative data, viewing qualitative data as subjective by definition—the antithesis of objectivity. Finally, the usual purpose of an evaluation by an objective scientist is to determine whether or to what extent the program has achieved its goals. Is the program sufficiently effective to be continued, or should it be terminated? The objective scientist takes little interest in how a program's internal mechanics are functioning.

Two decades of experience have revealed frequent failings in this approach. Evaluators who insist on keeping their distance miss the special insights staff often have about their programs. Disdaining qualitative data further limits the ability to assess a program because the goals of most public and nonprofit programs are too subjective to be measured only by quantitative techniques. Finally, the insistence on critical distance combined with an exclusive focus on program outcomes can result in evaluations that fail to answer the questions decision makers have.

Recognition of these problems led to the development of an alternative approach, what Michael Patton (1997) has termed *utilization-focused evaluation.* This approach begins with a goal of balance rather than objectivity. Whereas objectivity implies taking an unbiased view of a program by observing from a distance, balance recommends viewing program operation from up close as well as from afar, thus to discern important details as well as broad patterns. Achieving balance also requires both qualitative and quantitative data because quantitative data alone are unlikely to capture all that is important about programs whose goals are subjective. A balanced assessment necessitates multiple perspectives.

The balanced approach also rejects outcome assessment—did the program work?—as the only purpose of an evaluation. A utilization-focused evaluation seeks information for use in modifying programs, too. Getting close to the program helps by putting the evaluator in contact with the program administrators who have questions about how programs should be modified as well as the authority to make changes.

The balanced approach is not appropriate for every program, every evaluator, or every nonprofit executive. In getting close to a program, an evaluator can risk being "captured" by the program—that is, becoming only a mouthpiece for the parties who are vested in the program. For that reason, if there are serious questions about the quality of a program or about the competence of its staff, the nonprofit executive may prefer an evaluation performed from the critical distance of the objective scientist.

For the most part, however, nonprofit executives will find that the utilization-focused evaluation approach promises both a more balanced assessment and information more likely to be useful in program development. The following discussion assumes a utilization-focused approach to evaluation.

WHO DOES THE EVALUATION?

A first question when planning a program evaluation is who should conduct the evaluation. Here the principal options are (1) an internal evaluation performed by the organization's staff, (2) an external evaluation performed by outside consultants, and (3) an externally directed evaluation with extensive internal staff assistance.

An internal evaluation is possible only if the organization has one or more staff members with extensive training and experience in program evaluation. Unlike outcome assessment, full-scale program evaluation is too technical a task to attempt without that expertise. An internal evaluation also requires that the nonprofit executive give essentially free rein to the evaluation staff. Since inside evaluators may face strong pressures to conform their findings to the predispositions of program staff, standing up to those pressures is possible only if the nonprofit executive has made an unequivocal commitment to an unbiased evaluation.

As a practical matter, most nonprofit organizations lack sufficient in-house expertise to perform internal evaluations. They will need to find outside assistance from private sector consulting firms, management assistance agencies for the nonprofit sector, or university faculty, usually in public administration, education, or psychology departments.

Hiring an outside consultant carries its own risks. Perhaps the greatest risk is that the evaluation may be conducted with insufficient concern for the organization's needs if the external evaluators, perhaps trained in the objective scientist tradition, refuse to get close to the program. A preference for critical distance may blind them to the questions and insights the agency has about the program.

To minimize this risk, the nonprofit executive should discuss at length with any prospective evaluators how the evaluation should be conducted, including whether they are capable of taking a utilization-focused approach. It is also wise to negotiate a contract that specifies in detail how the nonprofit organization will be involved in the evaluation.

Perhaps the best means for conducting an evaluation is through a combination of outside consultants and internal staff. Here outside consultants provide technical expertise plus some independence from internal organizational pressures, while internal staff perform much of the legwork and collaborate with the consultants in developing the research design, collecting data, and interpreting findings.

The advantages of this approach are several. First, it provides the necessary technical expertise without sacrificing closeness to the program. Second, greater staff involvement should produce more staff commitment to the findings, increasing the likelihood that the findings will be utilized. Third, the evaluation can be used to train staff to serve a greater role in future evaluations. Finally, having staff do much of the legwork should reduce the out-of-pocket costs for the outside consultants. This reduction is possible, however, only if care is taken that working with the staff does not require too much of the consultants' time.

That time commitment can be limited by creating a small advisory committee to oversee the evaluation. This committee should include the outside evaluators, the nonprofit executive (or the executive's personal representative), and a few (at least one to three) other staff members in the nonprofit organization. The committee should serve as the central mechanism to which the evaluators report, reducing the time necessary for working with program staff. Keeping its size small, in the range of four to seven members, makes it easier for the committee to provide clear and prompt feedback to the evaluation process. A committee of this kind is probably desirable for wholly internal or external evaluations too.

The only way to ensure that the chief executive's concerns about the program are addressed is for that executive to be personally involved in the evaluation, optimally as a member of the evaluation advisory committee. In addition, as the literature on organizational change attests (see, for example, Rodgers and Hunter, 1992), programmatic change is unlikely to occur through an evaluation unless the chief executive is involved and committed to the process.

The goal of this involvement should not be to obtain the "right" answers—answers that conform to the executive's predispositions—but to ensure that the right *questions*—the questions crucial to the program's future—are asked. The chief executive should emphasize this distinction to the evaluators up front and then monitor to be sure the distinction is observed as the evaluation proceeds.

DETERMINING THE PURPOSE OF THE EVALUATION

The first task of an evaluation is to define its purpose. What sort of information is desired and why? How will the information be used? Answers to these questions will be crucial in determining the other elements of the evaluation.

Discussion of evaluation purposes typically begins with a dichotomy between summative and formative purposes (Scriven, 1967). A *summative* purpose implies a principal interest in program outcomes, in "summing up" a program's overall achievements. A *formative* purpose, by contrast, means that the principal interest is in forming or "re-forming" the program by focusing the evaluation on how well the program's internal mechanics are functioning. In reality, though, the purposes of evaluations are much more complex than a dichotomy can convey. Saying that an evaluation has a formative purpose, for example, does not indicate which of the program's internal mechanisms are of interest.

An evaluation's purpose should reflect the concerns key stakeholders have about the program. The process of defining this purpose should therefore begin with the nonprofit organization's executive: What questions does she or he have about how the program is working? What kinds of information might aid anticipated decisions about the program? Opinions of other stakeholders, including funders, may also be solicited.

In the end, any of a wide variety of purposes is possible, depending on the perceptions of stakeholders and the specific program. An evaluation performed primarily for funders will often have a summative purpose, given their likely interest in whether the program is having the desired impact. By contrast, a program that has only recently been implemented may be a poor candidate for a summative evaluation because more time may be necessary to produce an observable impact, but it may be a good candidate for an *implementation assessment*—an evaluation of how the program has been put into operation. Evaluations designed mainly for program staff are likely to have principally formative purposes to help staff in modifying the program.

Because this purpose will guide decisions at all subsequent steps in the evaluation, a mistake here can hamper the entire effort. The nonprofit executive should consequently review this purpose, making certain that it reflects his or her concerns as well as the concerns of other key stakeholders. It is also true, though, that an evaluation's purpose may become clearer as the evaluation progresses. Stakeholders may be able to articulate their questions about programs only as they consider program goals and measures. Evaluators should be open to this possibility.

Evaluators and nonprofit executives must also be alert to the possibility of so-called *covert purposes,* unvoiced hidden purposes for an evaluation (Weiss, 1972). Program managers, for example, sometimes have an unspoken goal of "whitewashing" a program by producing a favorable evaluation. The responsible chief executive should reject such an evaluation as unethical as well as incapable of producing useful information.

It is at this stage that the evaluator and the organization's chief executive should also consider whether the evaluation is worth doing. Revelation of a dominant covert purpose would provide one reason to bow out. Or it may be impossible to complete an evaluation in time to inform an approaching decision about the program. The resources necessary for a program evaluation are difficult to justify unless the results can be meaningful and useful.

OUTCOME EVALUATION DESIGNS

Most program evaluations will be concerned to some extent with assessing program impact—whether or to what extent a program has produced the desired outcomes. To achieve that end, evaluators can employ a number of outcome evaluation designs. Ordinarily, nonprofit executives and staff will neither need nor desire to become experts on these designs, but they should understand their basic structure and underlying principles in order to participate intelligently in the evaluation process. I will first explain those principles and then briefly survey the most important of the designs. (For a more detailed recent discussion of these designs, see Rossi and Freeman, 1993, ch. 5–8.)

Causality

The goal of any outcome evaluation design is to demonstrate causality— whether a program has caused the desired changes. To do that, the evaluation design must satisfy three conditions:

- *Covariation:* Changes in the program must covary with changes in the outcomes. Changes in outcome measures should occur in tandem with changes in program effort.

- *Time order:* Since cause must come before effect, changes in the program must *precede* changes in the outcome measures.

- *Nonspuriousness:* The evaluator must be able to rule out alternative explanations of the relationship between the program and outcome. The evaluator must demonstrate that the relationship is not spurious, that is, not the result of a joint relationship between the program, the outcome, and some third variable.

An evaluation design has *internal validity* to the extent that it satisfied these three conditions. Internal validity, in other words, refers to how accurately a design describes what the program actually achieved or caused.

Evaluation designs can also be judged for their *external validity:* the extent to which the design's findings can be generalized to contexts beyond that of the program being evaluated. Ordinarily, however, nonprofit organizations will have little or no concern for external validity. Internal validity must have first priority anyway; we must be sure that findings are accurate before considering at all how they might be generalized. In addition, nonprofit executives will usually be interested only in how their program works, not in how the program might work elsewhere. External validity becomes a major concern only if, for example, a program is being run as a pilot to test its value for possible broader implementation.

Threats to Internal Validity

The difficulties of satisfying the three conditions for causality can be illustrated relative to three so-called preexperimental designs, designs that are frequently but often carelessly used in program evaluations (X refers to treatment, 01 to a first observation on the experimental group, and 02 to a second observation—on the comparison group in the posttest-only design and on the experimental group in the pretest-posttest design):

- One-shot case study: X 01 (treatment group)
- Posttest only with comparison group: X 01 (treatment group) 02 (nonrandom comparison group)
- One-group pretest-posttest: 01 X 02 (treatment group)

The one-shot case study can satisfy none of the conditions of causality. As the most rudimentary design, it provides no mechanism for showing whether outcomes and program covary, much less for demonstrating either time order or nonspuriousness.

The posttest only with comparison group design can establish covariation. The comparison of a program group to a nonprogram group will show whether outcomes and program covary. However, this design can tell us nothing about time order; we cannot tell whether any outcome differences occurred *after* the program's inception or were already in place beforehand.

The one-group pretest-posttest design can satisfy the first two conditions for causality. Taking observations before and after a program's inception tests for covariation and time order. The weakness of this design—and it is a glaring weakness—lies in its inability to establish nonspuriousness.

Take, for purposes of illustration, a rehabilitation program for substance abusers as evaluated by the one-group pretest-posttest design. This design can establish covariation, whether substance abuse decreases with program involvement, and it can establish time order, since substance abuse is measured both before and after the program intervention. But it does not control for such threats to nonspuriousness as the following:

- *Maturation.* Decreased substance abuse could have resulted from the maturing of participants during the time of the program, a maturation not caused by the program.

- *Regression.* Extreme scores tend to "regress toward the mean" rather than become more extreme. If program participants were selected on the basis of their extreme scores (that is, high levels of substance abuse), decreased abuse could be a function of statistical regression rather than a program effect.

- *History.* Events concurrent with but unrelated to the program can affect program outcomes. Perhaps a rise in the street price of illegal drugs produced a decline in substance abuse, which could mistakenly be attributed to the program.

These flaws make the preexperimental designs undesirable as the principal outcome designs in most evaluations. Stronger designs are necessary to provide reasonable tests of the conditions of causality.

Experiments

Experimental designs offer the strongest internal validity. The classic experimental design takes this form:

$$R\ 01\ X\ 02$$
$$R\ 03\quad 04$$

R refers to *randomization,* meaning that subjects are assigned by chance—for example, by lot or by drawing numbers from a hat—to the experimental or control group in advance of the experiment.

Randomization is a crucial defining element of experimental designs. With the intergroup and across-time components of this design testing for covariation and time order, randomization establishes the final condition of causality, nonspuriousness, by making the experimental and control groups essentially equivalent. As a consequence of that equivalence, the control group provides a test of "change across time"—the changes due to maturation, regression, history, and so forth, that could affect program outcomes. Comparing the experimental and control groups can thus separate program effects from other changes across time, as this simple subtraction illustrates:

$$\text{Program effects} + \text{Change over time } (02 - 01)$$
$$-\text{ Change over time } (04 - 03) = \text{Program effects}$$

Unfortunately, many practical problems work against the use of experimental outcome designs in evaluations. In particular, randomization poses a number of difficulties. First, it must be done prior to the beginning of an intervention;

participants must be randomly assigned before they receive treatment. Second, ethical objections may be raised to depriving some subjects of a treatment that other subjects receive, or political objections may be raised to providing treatment on anything other than a first come, first served basis.

Experiments can also be costly, given the need to establish, maintain, and monitor distinct experimental and control groups. Many programs are still changing as they begin operation, which can make it impossible to maintain the same program structure throughout the length of the experiment, as a valid experiment requires.

At the same time, these difficulties can be exaggerated. The need for prior planning can sometimes be surmounted by running an experiment not on the first cohort group of subjects but on a second or later cohort group, such as a second treatment group of substance abusers. Ethical and political objections can often be overcome by giving the control group a traditional treatment rather than no treatment. That choice may make more sense for the purpose of the evaluation since the ultimate choice is likely to be between the new treatment and the old, not between the new treatment and no treatment. In short, experiments should not be too quickly eliminated as possible evaluation designs.

Quasi-Experiments

If an experimental design cannot be used, the evaluator should consider one of the so-called *quasi-experimental designs.* These designs are so named because they attempt, through a variety of means, to approximate the controls that experiments achieve through randomization. The strongest of these designs come close to achieving the rigor of an experiment.

A first quasi-experimental design is the *nonequivalent control group:*

$$01 \ X \ 02$$
$$03 \quad 04$$

Here, in lieu of randomization, a comparison group is matched to the experimental group in the hope that the pretest-posttest comparison of the two groups will furnish an indication of program impact.

This design is as strong—or weak—as the quality of the match. The goal of matching is to create a comparison group that is as similar as possible to the experimental group, except that it does not participate in the program. A good match can be difficult to achieve because the available comparison groups often differ in crucial respects from the experimental group.

Consider a hypothetical job-training program for the unemployed that takes participants on a first come, first served basis. The obvious candidates for a comparison group are would-be participants who volunteer after the program has filled all of the available slots. The evaluator might select from those late volunteers a group similar to the experimental group in terms of race, sex, education, previous employment history, and the like—similar, in other words, on the extraneous variables that could affect the desired outcome of employment success.

The difficulty arises in trying to match on all of the key variables at once. Creating a comparison group similar to the experimental group on two of those variables—say, race and gender—may be possible, but the two groups are unlikely then to also have equivalent education levels, previous employment histories, and other similar characteristics. In addition, the two groups may differ on some unrecorded or intangible variable. Perhaps the early volunteers were more motivated than late volunteers, accounting for their having volunteered sooner. If that difference were not measured and incorporated into the analysis, the program could erroneously be credited for employment gains that actually stemmed from differences in motivation. In cases such as this, no match is preferable to a bad match.

A second kind of quasi-experimental design is the *interrupted time series* design, diagramed as follows:

$$01\ 02\ 03\ X\ 04\ 05\ 06$$

The defining elements of this design are three or more observations recorded both before *and* after the program intervention. These multiple observations are important because they provide a reading on trends, thereby controlling for most of the changes over time (maturation, regression, and so on), which randomization controls for in an experimental design. Those controls give this design relatively good internal validity.

History is the principal weakness of this design, with respect to internal validity. The design contains no control for any events that could affect program impact by virtue of occurring at the same time as the program. A program to improve the situation of the homeless could be affected, for example, by an economic upturn (or downturn) that began at about the same time as the program.

Obtaining the necessary multiple observations can also prove difficult. On the front end, preprogram observations may be unavailable if measurement of key outcome indicators began only when the program itself began. On the back end, stakeholders may demand evidence of program impact before several postprogram observations can be obtained.

The strongest of the quasi-experimental designs is the *multiple interrupted time series:*

$$01\ 02\ 03\ X\ 04\ 05\ 06$$
$$07\ 08\ 09\quad 010\ 011\ 012$$

The strength of this design results from combining the key features of the interrupted time series and the nonequivalent group design. The time series dimension controls for most changes across time; the nonequivalent control group dimension controls for the threat of history.

The potential problems with this design are the weakness of its component parts. A bad match can provide a misleading comparison; the lack of longitudinal data can rule out use of this design at all.

Other Designs and Controls

The realities of many programs preclude the use of either experimental or quasi-experimental designs. Perhaps no one planned for an evaluation until the program was well under way, thereby ruling out randomization and providing no preprogram observations. Finding a comparison group may also prove too difficult or too costly.

Under such conditions, the evaluator may be forced to rely on one or more of the preexperimental designs as the principal outcome evaluation design, leaving the evaluation susceptible to many threats to internal validity. Fortunately, means are available to compensate for, if not to eliminate, these design weaknesses.

A first possibility is to use *statistical controls.* If their numbers and variability are sufficient, the subjects of a program can be divided for comparison and control. For example, a one-group pretest-posttest might be subdivided into those receiving a little of the program (x), and those receiving a lot (X). The resulting design becomes more like the stronger nonequivalent control group design:

$$01 \ X \ 02$$
$$03 \ x \ 04$$

There remains the question of whether the two groups are comparable in all respects other than the varying program involvement. If that comparability can be shown, the design can provide a reading on whether more program involvement produces more impact, substituting for the unavailable comparison of program versus no program.   The option to strengthen designs through statistical controls can also be useful with quasi-experimental and experimental designs. When a nonequivalent control group design is used, the evaluator may want to subdivide and compare subjects on variables on which the matching was flawed. If the two groups were matched on race and gender but not on education, the experimental and control groups might be compared while statistically controlling for education. Or where a time series design is employed, additional data might be sought to control for threats of history. In a study of how the 55-mile-per-hour speed limit affected traffic fatalities, researchers examined data on total miles traveled to test an alternative explanation that fatalities declined as a consequence of reduced travel amid the 1974–1975 energy crisis and not as a consequence of reduced speed (Meier and Morgan, 1981). The data added to the evidence that reduced speed was the cause.

Combining several outcome evaluation designs can also add to the strength of the overall design. Many evaluations will employ multiple designs, each for a different measure. Stronger designs on some measures might then help compensate for the weaker designs necessary for other measures.

Assuming an outside evaluator is involved, these design decisions will be made principally by that individual. Still, to the extent that executives and staff understand these basic principles of evaluation design, they may be able to advise evaluators on these decisions.

The nonprofit executive can perform an even more important role by monitoring the design planning to ensure its fit to the purposes of the evaluation. The most rigorous design will be of no use unless it addresses the issues of concern to the organization's executive or stakeholders. It is up to the executive to ensure that the evaluation remains relevant and appropriate to the organization's needs.

PROCESS EVALUATION

With most program evaluations, nonprofit executives will want to evaluate the program process as well as its ultimate impact. Outcome evaluation designs usually indicate only whether a program is working, not why. Process evaluation may be able to discern what steps in a program's process are not working as intended, perhaps pointing to ways in which a program can be changed to increase its effectiveness. These suggestions will often prove the most useful.

The techniques of process evaluation are both simpler and less systematic than those for outcome evaluations (see also Thomas, 1980). In essence, process evaluation entails examining the internal workings of a program—as represented largely through activity goals—both for their functioning and for their role in producing the desired outcomes.

The executives and staff of nonprofit organizations should be key actors in any process evaluation. In particular, they should attempt to define at the outset what specific questions they have about the program's process. Conceivably, they may already feel adequately informed about performance as it pertains to some activity goals and so may not desire new information there. They will then want to be certain that the evaluation includes the questions they do have about program process.

The basics of a process evaluation can be illustrated by the case of an affirmative action program designed to increase the hiring of minority firefighters by a municipal government. The activity goals of interest in this evaluation included the following:

1. Increase the number of minority applicants.
2. Increase the success rate of minority applicants on the written examination.
3. Increase the success rate of minority applicants on the physical examination.

These activity goals are designed to lead to this outcome goal (among others):

4. Increase the proportion of minority firefighters in the fire department.

The several activity goals can illustrate how a process evaluation can be useful. Data on these various activities could indicate where, if at all, the program might be failing. Are too few minorities applying? Or are minorities applying only to be eliminated disproportionately by written or physical exams? Answering these questions could help a program administrator to decide whether, or how, and where to change the program.

A good process evaluation can often compensate for weaknesses in the outcome evaluation designs. As explained earlier, the difficulty of controlling for all threats to internal validity in outcome evaluation designs can leave unanswered questions about the linkage of program to outcomes. A process evaluation provides an additional test of this linkage by indicating whether the program activities have occurred in a manner consistent with the observed outcomes. If, for example, an impact evaluation shows significant gains on the outcome measures *and* the process evaluation shows high levels of program activities, the evaluator can argue more convincingly that the program caused the impact. By contrast, evidence of low activity levels in the same scenario would raise doubts about whether the program could be responsible for outcome gains.

Most program evaluations should contain some form of process evaluation. Though less systematic than outcome designs, process evaluation techniques will often provide the more useful information for nonprofit executives.

DATA DEVELOPMENT, REPORT WRITING, AND FOLLOW-UP

Nonprofit executives should plan to involve themselves and the program staff extensively in analysis and review of evaluation findings. This involvement is necessary first for accuracy: staff review of data and reports minimizes the risk of outside evaluators' reporting inaccurate conclusions. Staff are also more likely to make use of the findings and implement recommendations that they helped develop.

Assuming outside evaluators, the best approach to this involvement may be to ask for the opportunity to review and comment on interpretations and reports while also indicating that the evaluators retain final authority on the substance of reports. Most evaluators will welcome this arrangement for self-protection; no evaluator wants to go public with conclusions that are subsequently shown to be erroneous. Staff might also be involved in basic data interpretation, as, for example, by meeting with evaluators to review data printouts (for other techniques, see Patton, 1997).

The chief executive must also decide what final written products to request. A comprehensive evaluation report is usually desirable, both for the historical record and as a reference if questions arise, along with a brief executive summary of one to three pages for broader distribution and readership. Other reports may be desirable for particular clienteles.

The job of the outside evaluator customarily concludes at this point, but the agency's chief executive and program staff still need to consider if and how the program should be changed in light of the evaluation. A program evaluation can provide both a direction and an impetus for change, but often with a limited window of opportunity. The agency's chief executive should take advantage of that window by discussing the evaluation with staff and, where appropriate, developing plans for what changes are to be made and when. Since the evaluation data presumably came from the agency's outcome assessment system, this is also a good time to consider any need to change that system. Only through such efforts can a nonprofit agency gain the full value of a program evaluation.

SUMMARY

Nonprofit agencies are confronting ever-greater demands to demonstrate that their programs work. To meet these demands, contemporary nonprofit agencies must engage in systematic outcome assessment, measuring and monitoring the performance of their programs. In some cases, these agencies must take the additional step of subjecting certain of their programs to systematic program evaluation.

Outcome assessment data can reveal whether progress is being made on key agency objectives. As a result, every nonprofit agency, if it has not already done so, should consider if and how it can develop, collect, and analyze these data on a continuing basis.

Outcome assessment data alone *cannot* speak to issues of causality, that is, to whether any observed changes resulted from a specific agency program or programs. Agency executives who wish to investigate those kinds of causal connections should consider taking a step beyond outcome assessment to conduct a program evaluation too. Program evaluations build from a foundation of strong outcome assessment, adding the techniques of comparison and control necessary to address the role of specific programs in producing desired outcomes.

Succeeding in these efforts requires a delicate balancing of analytic and scientific expertise with group process skills. For the former, nonprofit executives and staff should acquire at least a basic expertise, which they supplement, as necessary, with the talents of skilled consultants. For the latter, nonprofit executives must ensure that any outcome assessment planning or program evaluation is planned and executed with extensive participation of the agency's stakeholders, including at least the program staff and funders. Achieving that balance can give the executives and staff of nonprofit organizations the knowledge necessary to make their programs better.

References

Hatry, H. P., and Lampkin, L. M. *Key Steps in Outcome Management.* Washington, D.C.: Urban Institute, 2003.

Kress, G., Springer, J. F., and Koehler, G. "Policy Drift: An Evaluation of the California Business Enterprise Program." *Policy Studies Journal,* 1980, *8,* 1101–1108.

Meier, K. J., and Morgan, D. P. "Speed Kills: A Longitudinal Analysis of Traffic Fatalities and the 55-mph Speed Limit." *Policy Studies Review,* 1981, *1,* 157–167.

Morley, E., Hatry, H. P., and Cowan, J. *Making Use of Outcome Information for Improving Services: Recommendations for Nonprofit Organizations.* Washington, D.C.: Urban Institute, 2002.

Patton, M. Q. *Utilization-Focused Evaluation: The New Century Text.* (3rd ed.) Thousand Oaks, Calif.: Sage, 1997.

Rea, L. M., and Parker, R. A. *Designing and Conducting Survey Research: A Comprehensive Guide.* (2nd ed.) San Francisco: Jossey-Bass, 1997.

Rodgers, R., and Hunter, J. E. "A Foundation of Good Management Practice in Government: Management by Objectives." *Public Administration Review,* 1992, *52,* 27–39.

Rossi, P. H., and Freeman, H. E. *Evaluation: A Systematic Approach.* (5th ed.) Thousand Oaks, Calif.: Sage, 1993.

Scriven, M. "The Methodology of Evaluation." In R. W. Tyler, R. M. Gagné, and M. Scriven (eds.), *Perspectives of Curriculum Evaluation.* Skokie, Ill.: Rand McNally, 1967.

Stone, M., Bigelow, B., and Crittenden, W. "Research on Strategic Management in Nonprofit Organizations: Synthesis, Analysis, and Future Directions." *Administration and Society,* 1999, *3,* 378–423.

Thomas, J. C. "'Patching Up' Evaluation Designs: The Case for Process Evaluation." *Policy Studies Journal,* 1980, *8,* 1145–1151.

United Way of America. *Measuring Program Outcomes: A Practical Approach.* Washington, D.C.: United Way of America, 1996.

Weiss, C. H. *Evaluation Research: Methods of Assessing Program Effectiveness.* Upper Saddle River, N.J.: Prentice Hall, 1972.

PART FOUR

DEVELOPING AND MANAGING FINANCIAL RESOURCES

Nonprofit management continues to be seen by some as mainly a matter of fundraising. No doubt fundraising is a major leadership and management task, and fundraising has become more competitive and sophisticated. Nonetheless, nonprofit organizations do not (or should not) exist to raise money. They exist (or should exist) to pursue a mission or cause that benefits some part of the public (or future generations). The first chapter in Part Four emphasizes how to develop the fundraising effort so that it fits with and flows from the mission and culture of the organization. Those seeking details on the techniques will find the suggestions for further reading at the end of that chapter helpful. The extent to which nonprofit organizations rely on donations varies substantially. For many nonprofit organizations, earned income has become a bigger source of revenues. The second chapter in this part shows how nonprofit organizations can make better decisions about enhancing various types of earned income, including ventures that generate unrelated business income.

Although fundraising is sometimes overemphasized as at the heart of nonprofit management, the principles, practices, and uses of accounting are often underemphasized. In recognition of their significance for effective nonprofit management, this part of the handbook includes two extensive chapters on accounting and control. Chapter Nineteen, on financial accounting and management, describes how nonprofit managers can use various financial ratios and other accounting tools to improve financial and program management. Chapter Twenty, on management accounting, shows various managerial uses of cost accounting data. The final chapter in this part provides up-to-date and thorough guidance for improving risk management in nonprofit organizations.

CHAPTER SEVENTEEN

Designing and Managing the Fundraising Program

Robert E. Fogal

F undraising is essential to charitable organizations. Boards and senior management give substantial attention to resource development and income generation. This chapter provides a guide to thinking about fundraising and addresses ways to *integrate fundraising into an organization's life.* These emphasized words are central to the perspective called "philanthropic fundraising," understood as the philosophy and practice that fosters voluntary giving to achieve public good. This author supports the view that philanthropic fundraising will substantially assure the future of nonprofit organizations and the good work that they aim to accomplish. Three themes will amplify this view: fundraising as a management concept, fundraising as a management process, and issues in fundraising management.

FUNDRAISING AS A MANAGEMENT CONCEPT

Fundraising is important to nonprofit leaders for many reasons. The first, the most obvious and most practical, is that fundraising generates essential income for charitable organizations. The 2002 *Nonprofit Almanac* reported the following illuminating facts: "in 1997, private contributions . . . accounted for 19.9 percent of total revenue for the independent sector, down from 22.9 percent in 1987. These private contributions represented 4.0 percent of total revenue in

419

health services (down from 5.4 percent in 1987); 13.4 percent in education and research (compared to 13.0 percent in 1987); 19.6 percent in social and legal services (down from 24.8 percent in 1987); 35.2 percent in civic, social, and fraternal organizations (up from 33.0 percent in 1987); and 43.5 percent in arts and cultural organizations (up from 40.2 percent in 1987)" (Weitzman, Jalandoni, Lampkin, and Pollak, 2002, pp. 98–99).

An equally important but typically less obvious reason for fundraising to be a priority for nonprofit leaders is that fundraising success measures the degree to which an organization's purpose is affirmed. Donors' support for a particular organization or institution reflects their perception of that entity as an effective vehicle in meeting a community or human need. The responsibility of a nonprofit's board and senior managers to clearly articulate their organization's mission and document its effectiveness in fulfilling that mission—that is, to provide a strong case for support—is critical to successful fundraising. Through their contributions, donors show their acceptance of an organization's mission and respect for the organization's leadership. Low response to fundraising appeals can suggest that an organization and its mission are little known or poorly understood—in short, that its prospective donor constituencies have not accepted the nonprofit's purposes.

An organization's need for gift income and its style in engaging prospective donors results in diverse attitudes toward fundraising. Henry A. Rosso, the founding director of The Fund Raising School (which is now a program at the Center on Philanthropy at Indiana University), developed a succinct grid that characterizes these organizational attitudes (see Exhibit 17.1). Rosso titled this grid "Three Stages of Fundraising Development" because it represents the steps through which nonprofits often progress in developing their fundraising programs. The idea is that most begin at the formative stage, when fundraising is a new activity. Organizations potentially reach the integrative stage when fundraising is a fully developed component of an organization's life and work.

Exhibit 17.1. Three Stages of Fundraising Development.

	Stage 1: Formative	Stage 2: Normative	Stage 3: Integrative
Who	Vendor	Facilitator	Strategist
What	Product	Relationships	Growth partnerships
Skills	Selling	Soliciting	Building and maintaining philanthropic relationships
Result	Making sales	Relationships with donors	Assured organizational growth

Source: H. A. Rosso, personal communication; terminology adapted by the author.

The *formative stage* views fundraising as an appendage to organizational life—something we do because we have to, a "necessary evil." It is characterized by an emphasis on fundraising techniques that generate needed income, such as mass appeals through direct mail and telephone solicitation. Fundraising in the formative stage is motivated primarily by the nonprofit's need to have more money. The objective is to "sell" the organization and what it does (the products) to donors who want to "purchase" the idea or service that the nonprofit represents. Success is measured by how often asking for gifts results in "making a sale." In this stage, fundraising is commonly carried out by personnel who are hired to perform as a sales staff, with their primary role being to interact with prospective donors and persuade them to contribute to the nonprofit. If volunteers participate in this style of fundraising, they also view their work as sales activity.

The *normative stage* understands fundraising in terms of family, applying fundraising techniques largely to prospective donors whose connections to the nonprofit have been established through some other relationship, such as those who receive services (clients, students, audience members, or patients) or volunteer leaders and workers. Leaders and managers typically concentrate on the operation of the institution. Fundraising in this stage is commonly staff-centered also, with a small number of others, usually the chief executive and a handful of volunteers, participating selectively in the process of engaging a prospect's interest, soliciting a contribution, and maintaining good relationships with donors.

The *integrative stage* places philanthropy at the center of who we are and what we do—that is, it is central to the building of a human community that achieves a common good. Donors are regarded as thoughtful participants in the organization's life and work, filling a role that is appropriate to them and essential to the well-being of the nonprofit. In the integrative stage, volunteer leaders are vocal advocates of the nonprofit and its work, and they participate fully in the process of building constituencies who can financially support the organization.

In addition, senior staff, board members, and other volunteer leaders work at sustaining healthy relationships (or growth partnerships) with those who have made philanthropic commitments to the organization, responding to donors' needs and interests that relate to the nonprofit and its activity. There is a high level of communication between the nonprofit and those who make "leadership gifts." These donors know the organization well. Their gifts reflect values that are important to them. Furthermore, because they are known for their generous commitments, their views are valued by others, and they are often articulate advocates of the organization. In the integrative stage, organizational leaders are capable of looking at their institution or agency from the perspective of important donors whose views may help assure an organization's continued growth.

The three stages are not mutually exclusive. Fundraising principles and techniques are important to all three. But how they are used reflects the organization's style of management and institutional philosophy. Philanthropic fundraising strives to achieve the integrative stage of fundraising practice, which incorporates voluntary giving as one of the nonprofit's core values.

FUNDRAISING AS A MANAGEMENT PROCESS

Classic management practice consists of five activities: analysis, planning, execution, control, and evaluation. Fundraising as a management process utilizes all these activities. The most effective fundraising staff are managers who ensure that discipline based on the five activities is applied to the fundraising process.

Through *analysis,* a nonprofit assesses whether or not it is ready for fundraising. Analysis is guided by questions like these: What is the fundraising history? How many donors contributed at what levels? Are constituencies and gift markets well defined and responsive? Are internal resources adequate to meet the costs of fundraising? Is the case for support valid and compelling?

An essential tool in analyzing fundraising performance is the gift range chart, which organizes information about past giving by the number of philanthropic gifts and grants received at defined dollar levels. Consider, for example, a human services organization with a $2.5 million budget. In the past fiscal year, the organization received $299,500 in gifts and grants, with the balance of revenue derived from government contracts and service fees. Table 17.1 shows that the distribution of gifts and grants reflects a well-established fundraising effort: two-thirds of gift revenue came from about 10 percent of donors, another 24 percent was contributed by 42 percent of donors, and the final 10 percent of gifts came from 48 percent of the donors. (Such a distribution of dollars and donors is typical of an established fundraising program.) This information is essential to answering the kinds of questions articulated in the preceding paragraph.

Planning grows out of analysis. Too little planning impedes success; too much planning leads to inaction. Good planning encourages prudent risk taking and helps nonprofits respond to opportunities that will advance their purposes. Answers to the following questions will facilitate good planning: How should the case for support be articulated? How many gifts in what amounts are needed? From whom? How should donor prospects be solicited? By whom? When should the gift be solicited? What training is required for volunteers to engage prospects and ask for gifts? How much money should be invested to accomplish fundraising objectives?

As in analysis, the gift range chart undergirds fundraising planning by focusing the attention of staff and volunteers on the number and size of gifts needed to reach a fundraising goal. (Gift range charts were used historically

Table 17.1. Gift Range Chart Analyzing the Previous Year's Giving.

Gift Level ($)	Number of Gifts	Subtotal ($)	Cumulative Total ($)
25,000	1	25,000	25,000
10,000	2	20,000	45,000
5,000	5	25,000	70,000
2,500	12	30,000	100,000
1,000	30	30,000	130,000
500	75	37,500	167,500
250	120	30,000	197,500[a]
100	350	35,000[b]	232,500
50	720	36,000[b]	268,500
25	1,240	31,000[c]	299,500
		Grand total	299,500

[a]Sixty-six percent of the total philanthropic gifts and grants received ($197,500) is from 244 donors, or about 10 percent of the 2,554 donors (those who gave $250 or more).

[b]Twenty-four percent of the total gifts and grants received ($71,000) is from 1,070 donors, or about 42 percent of total donors ($50 and $100 donors).

[c]Ten percent of the gifts and grants received ($31,000) is from 1,240 donors, or 48 percent of total donors (those who contributed $25).

only for capital campaigns, but their use is now commonly accepted in annual campaigns for funds as well.) Continuing with the example of a $2.5 million human services organization, Table 17.2 is an example of a planning gift range chart to reach an annual giving goal of $500,000.

The planning gift chart, when compared with current patterns of voluntary contributions, helps nonprofit leaders understand the potential of the donor base (and the work that will be required to grow giving) by comparing "what is" with "what we want to be achieve." Comparing the charts (Tables 17.1 and 17.2) makes clear how many new prospective donors at what gift levels need to be identified, and how many additional donors at each level have to be successfully invited to give, to reach the desired fundraising goal of $500,000. Planners can assess if the desired goal is feasible by identifying the prospects for each gift level.

For example, presuming that the two donors of $10,000 gifts in the previous year (Table 17.1) renew their giving at the same level, the planning chart (Table 17.2) requires three more gifts or grants at this level (a total of five gifts of $10,000 each) than the analysis chart indicates to reach the $500,000 goal. Since four prospects for each donor are suggested for this level (the planning chart

Table 17.2. Gift Range Chart for $500,000 Annual Fundraising Goal.

Gift Level ($)	Number of Gifts	Number of Prospects	Subtotal ($)	Cumulative Total ($)
25,000	2	10	50,000	50,000
10,000	5	20	50,000	100,000
5,000	10	40	50,000	150,000
2,500	20	60	50,000	200,000
1,000	50	150	50,000	250,000
500	100	300	50,000	300,000
250	200	600	50,000	350,000[a]
100	500	1,500	50,000[b]	400,000
50	1,000	3,000	50,000[b]	450,000
25	2,000	5,000	50,000[c]	500,000
			Grand total	500,000

Note: The arithmetic for creating an annual giving gift chart is based on the top gift range typically being 5 percent of the goal, with two gifts required at that level. Subsequent gift levels are simply defined as conventional gift amounts that donors are accustomed to considering. Subtotals for each range are usually the same amounts or amounts that do not vary widely. The number of donors required for each gift level is determined by calculating how many are needed at each level to achieve the desired subtotal (in this example, the subtotal of $50,000).

The number of prospects for each gift level varies. At the higher levels, more prospects are required for each gift simply because these gifts and grants are usually more difficult to obtain. Since gifts at the lower levels are easier to obtain, fewer prospects are required. Also, many prospects at higher gift levels may give at lower levels, thus adding to the prospective donor pool at lower levels.

Gift charts for capital campaigns are built on the same principles, with the difference that the top gift range is at least 10 percent of the goal and may even equal 20 to 25 percent, with only one gift anticipated at the top level. Capital campaigns are typically characterized by a fairly small number of donors committing to substantially larger gift pledges that are paid over three to five years.

[a]Seventy percent of the goal ($350,000) is projected from 387 major or leadership gifts, or 10 percent of the 3,887 donors (those who will give $250 or more).

[b]Twenty percent of the goal ($100,000) is projected from 1,500 donors, about 40 percent of total donors (those who will give $50 and $100).

[c]Ten percent of the goal ($50,000) is projected from 2,000 donors, about 50 percent of total donors (those who will give $25).

indicated twenty prospects for the five gifts desired), the organization needs to identify twelve additional prospects for $10,000 gifts or grants to ensure the likelihood of obtaining the three additional gifts. Implementing this planning process for all gift levels will determine whether or not the $500,000 is feasible. It may be that only four $10,000 gifts are likely but enough prospects for seven or more $5,000 gifts are identifiable, thus compensating for the lower number of $10,000 donors. In this way, fundraising managers and volunteer leaders can prepare a planning gift chart that provides a sound basis for the year's fundraising activity.

Effective planning requires that a nonprofit's leaders, both board and staff, take ownership of fundraising activities. Given the importance of planning, it is also important to recognize that plans can be changed, and should be, to take advantage of giving opportunities when they occur or to respond to other unanticipated situations.

Execution means carrying out the plan. Tasks are assigned and responsibilities are accepted, individuals are trained and empowered, timelines are established and respected, and follow-up ensures that tasks have been completed. A high-performance fundraising executive is guided by the following question: "What can I do to ensure that everyone who is involved in our fundraising is successful?" Fundraising managers have the challenge of directing the energy and activity of people to whom they are responsible (senior staff, board members, and other volunteers) in their fundraising tasks. This requires a high level of mutual respect and a firm commitment from all participants to their common success.

Control depends on information systems that enable fundraising staff to implement the plan. A multitude of details and tasks must be monitored and coordinated. Gift processing must be timely, gift records must be accurate, and gifts must be acknowledged. Reports must be generated. Volunteer and staff time must be used effectively. Timelines should be honored. Budgets have to be well utilized. Interpersonally, fundraising executives have to exercise control on a daily basis by diplomatically asserting their leadership to ensure that tasks are accomplished and the fundraising plan is fulfilled.

Evaluation enables a nonprofit, its leaders, and its staff to grow and become more effective. The key question for fundraising is this: What enabled or prevented us from meeting our objectives for each level in the planning gift chart? It is as important to assess what worked well and why as it is to determine how to improve. By reflecting on its fundraising practices as well as all its management and programs, a nonprofit's leadership determines whether or not resources are maximized, constituents' needs are served, and the mission is fulfilled. Good evaluation depends on a spirit of cooperation and a sense of common purpose. It combines objectivity and sensitivity and fosters organizational integrity that leads to a more productive future. As a result, voluntary giving in support of the nonprofit's mission will be enhanced.

In addition to these classic areas of management, fundraising for nonprofits is substantially enhanced by a solid *professional stance* that is distinguished by integration and integrity. First, sound fundraising is highly integrated and synergistic. For example, effective direct mail solicitations broadly promote an organization's mission and help create the climate for engaging leadership giving. Also, major donors are typically leaders in many areas of community life, and their support includes their gifts as well as their advocacy on behalf of the organizations they support. While such dynamics occur in ways that are distinctive to each organization, fundraising leaders need to foster a sense of connection among fundraising practices so that all participants focus on a shared outcome—accomplishing the organization's mission—that is greater than the sum of the parts.

Connecting the parts also produces feelings of integrity that have immeasurable value in a philanthropic organization. An organizational sense of wholeness or completeness—a shared purpose—energizes everyone from board members and other volunteers to every employee on the payroll. Such cohesiveness communicates to prospective donors that the organization has its act together, adding value to the community and meriting philanthropic support.

Nonprofits that are successful in philanthropic fundraising apply all these activities to the three dimensions of institutional life: at the department level, throughout the organization, and in its interaction with the environment that surrounds it. In each dimension, specific management fundraising activities are required. Exhibit 17.2 shows how the tasks of fundraising pertain in all three dimensions.

Within the fundraising office or department, fundraisers implement several technical tasks for which they are solely responsible. Alongside these are several organizational tasks that fundraising staff may foster and coordinate but that involve other staff and board leadership and may require some compromise to accomplish. Finally, a number of activities are directed beyond the nonprofit and require that fundraising managers exercise considerable judgment and negotiation in their realization. The responsibilities and tasks listed in Exhibit 17.2 are not mutually exclusive. Nor does the exhibit list all possibilities. It does indicate, however, how the management of philanthropic fundraising intersects with various dimensions of a nonprofit's life.

ISSUES IN FUNDRAISING MANAGEMENT

The three stages of fundraising development suggest several issues that are central to philanthropic fundraising. The first focuses on the various roles that board members, other volunteers, and staff play in fundraising.

Exhibit 17.2. Fundraising Management Grid.

Fundraising Management Tasks	Organizational Dimensions		
	Departmental	Organizational	External
Analysis	Fundraising history/ gift range chart Gift vehicle productivity Data systems Office space Staff resources	Communicating the case for support	Market needs and social needs Constituencies and gift markets Volunteer resources Feasibility study
Planning	Fundraising budget Gift range chart Gift market identification Gift vehicle selection Timelines	Fundraising goals Internal case statement Gift vehicles and donor markets Expressing the case for support Public information	Leadership training Gift solicitation: to whom, by whom, how much, when Gift incentives
Execution	Communication: letters, phone Staff relationships and tasks	Marketing fund-raising internally Staff relationships Staff solicitation	Expressing the case for support Volunteer and donor relationships Donor engagement and solicitation Public information
Control	Gift processing Gift acknowledgment Gift records Gift reports Fundraising costs	Gift reports	Volunteer recognition Donor recognition Timelines Major donor prospect system
Evaluation	Gift vehicles Fundraising budget Staff performance	Effectiveness of programs being supported	Gift markets Volunteer leaders Effectiveness of the case for support
Professional stance	Integrity of judgment about fundraising practices and information reported	Integrity of leadership among program and administrative colleagues in meeting organizational commitments	Integrity of mission in achieving public good

Volunteer Leadership and Giving

Fundraising will be most successful, and the "integrative stage" most readily attained, when leadership for fundraising is shared among many people. Core leadership includes the board chair, the chair of the development committee, the chief staff officer, and the chief fundraising officer, working together to develop fundraising policies and plans. Their leadership sets the tone for the entire organization and its commitment to building effective partnerships with leadership donors whose gifts (as illustrated in the gift chart) are major contributions.

The involvement of board members and other key volunteers reinforces the philanthropic character of nonprofit organizations. Their voluntary service demonstrates their commitment to the values that the nonprofit serves, providing an example and setting the standard for others' participation as volunteers and as donors. If board members, who are the volunteers most closely related to the organization, do not support it financially, it is unrealistic to expect others to contribute to the nonprofit's mission and work. When board members are recruited to serve, expectations regarding their financial support should be made clear. One of the most effective statements of standards for board giving is the following: "After your contributions to your religious community, we expect that our organization will be among your charitable priorities." This allows for people of differing financial ability to demonstrate their commitment in the manner most appropriate for them while still emphasizing that their giving is an essential responsibility of being a board member. This standard also encourages broad diversity on a board, along with the philanthropic commitments of time, service, and money.

It is worth noting that volunteer service has a direct relationship to contributions. INDEPENDENT SECTOR studies show that people who volunteer are more generous in their giving. In the biennial 2001 survey, households that both gave and volunteered averaged annual giving of $2,295, or 4.0 percent of household income. In contrast, households that only contributed and did not volunteer gave an average $1,009, or 2.4 percent of income (Toppe, Kirsch, and Michel, 2002, p. 107).

Organizational Readiness

As noted earlier, nonprofits too often pursue fundraising solely on the basis of their need for additional revenue. When this occurs, fundraising is characterized by the use of techniques designed to acquire as much money as possible in the shortest possible time. To succeed in the long-term development of philanthropic support, nonprofits must be internally prepared for fundraising. Leaders and managers must fully understand and be able to articulate the case for support. A compelling statement of the case for support will draw prospective donors to an organization's mission by answering the following questions persuasively (Seiler, 2003, p. 25):

1. Why does the organization exist? The answer lies in the human or social problem or need addressed by the nonprofit. This is the organization's mission, its raison d'être.

2. What services or programs does the nonprofit provide to meet the need or solve the problem?

3. Why should prospective donors (individuals, corporations, foundations) provide gifts, and what benefits accrue to donors who make gifts?

The answers to these questions will clarify the value of an organization to the community it aims to serve. They will explain how community life is enhanced because the nonprofit meets community needs; what specific goals, objectives, and programs the nonprofit plans to implement in response to the needs it identifies; and what constituencies will be served by those who support the organization. A nonprofit cannot exist in isolation from its environment. Its programs and activities must be valued, not only by the clients it serves but also by potential donors who view the nonprofit as contributing to the quality of community life. Fundraising success will depend on how well a nonprofit responds to its environment, adapts to changing conditions in the environment, and builds constituencies who believe in its value. An effective case is the basis for building philanthropic support.

Stewardship and Investment

The cost of raising money and the effectiveness of fundraising programs are critical issues for nonprofit leaders. Donors have the right to know that the nonprofits in which they invest are credible. Nonprofits that merit philanthropic support are able to justify fundraising costs. Standards of fundraising costs are not widely established, although experienced fundraisers increasingly accept certain guidelines as reasonable (see Table 17.3). These guidelines are best understood in the context of a nonprofit's own giving history.

Table 17.3. Suggested Guidelines for Fundraising Costs.

	Cost per Dollar Raised
New donor acquisition	Up to $1.50
Special events	Up to $0.50
Donor renewal (general donor programs)	Up to $0.25
Major gifts and capital campaigns	Up to $0.10
Planned giving	Up to $0.15[a]
Corporate and foundation grantseeking	Up to $0.20

[a]After at least five years of initial investment.

A well-established program will likely have costs that are lower than a new fundraising program. Introducing a new component of fundraising will be more expensive than maintaining a program component. The guidelines in Table 17.3 demonstrate that different fundraising strategies require different levels of investment. The more expensive forms of fundraising reflect the need to constantly renew the donor base with large numbers of smaller gifts. The less expensive strategies involve smaller numbers of larger gifts, commonly received from donors who have long giving histories with an organization. These people—whose donations are variously identified as "major gifts," "leadership gifts," and "strategic gifts"—provide important credibility for an organization through the example they set for others.

Another important consideration in budgeting for fundraising is efficiency (the cost per dollar raised) versus effectiveness (the net total amount raised). One nonprofit, for example, might raise an annual fund of $400,000 with a fundraising budget of $100,000. The annual fund nets $300,000 by spending $0.25 for each dollar raised. Another nonprofit might raise $600,000 with a fundraising budget of $200,000, netting $400,000 at a cost of $0.33 per dollar raised. The first organization would be considered more efficient because it spent less money per dollar raised, but the second would be considered more effective because it raised more money. The balance between fundraising efficiency and effectiveness is an issue that nonprofit boards must consider when setting their organizational budgets. Occasionally boards must decide to increase their fundraising investment so that their organizations can achieve higher levels of philanthropic giving. Fundraising managers are responsible for showing how such investment can yield new levels of contributions.

Stewardship and Providing Public Benefit

Stewardship, defined as how we exercise ethical accountability in the use of resources, applies to an organization's general success in fulfilling its mission as much as it does to its fundraising. Nonprofit boards carry ultimate responsibility for the fiduciary well-being of their organizations. This includes ensuring that all resources are used both efficiently and effectively. The board of directors has the right to be fully informed by staff about how resources are being used. Along with program evaluation, which is an essential part of this process, fundraising managers have a key role to play in helping volunteer leaders meet their stewardship responsibilities.

Obtaining the status of a 501(c)(3) nonprofit in the United States requires that the organization be committed to and demonstrably provide a public benefit. This requirement challenges the trend among many nonprofits to meet revenue needs by operating "more like a business" and focusing on service areas that will generate greater earned income. Earned income is certainly critical, but sound judgment among institutional leaders calls for a careful balance between generating operating margins and sustaining the core mission. One consequence of this trend is that the organization's mission may unintentionally become diverted or diluted. If commercialization of its services becomes a dominant priority, nonprofits run the risk of losing their identity as agents for community good and stewards of community resources.

Other potential distortions that can result from using business metaphors to characterize nonprofits are that "(a) donors are spoken of as customers; (b) fundraising is spoken of as marketing; and . . . (c) donors are likened to stockholders" (Clohesy, 2003, p. 134). Certain technical aspects of each of these perspectives may relate to fundraising practice: sales techniques in gift solicitation, opinion gathering to position a nonprofit's message, and the notion of investing in a nonprofit's cause. The fundamental fallacy in all these, however, is that the imagery presupposes a private interest or a private gain, which contrasts with the public benefit and common good that are the hallmarks of philanthropy and of nonprofit organizations and institutions.

Ethics in Fundraising

Nonprofits play a special role in our country because they address diverse public needs and enable people to participate in meeting those needs. Fundraising managers play a critical role in both of these outcomes. Their work leads to additional resources by helping articulate the good that is to be achieved and by facilitating donors' contributions. They ask donors "to become engaged in an activity of great importance to specific people in their community or somewhere in the world. . . . Donors are invited to act publicly, to make a difference, and to enjoy the satisfaction that comes with public action on behalf of a worthwhile cause" (Clohesy, 2003, p. 136).

In the daily activity of fundraising, unfortunately, evaluation is too often based on the precept that "what works is what is right." As indicated at the beginning of this chapter, fundraising can be narrowly regarded as a strategy for obtaining needed support. In fact, how a nonprofit raises funds is a powerful index of the degree to which its leaders grasp the moral dimensions of the nonprofit's purposes. We all live according to the customs, traditions, and values that have been handed down to us, and we apply this heritage to the decisions we make each day. The advances of technology and the challenges of a changing world, however, increasingly cause people to reflect on their purposes and think about how they should conduct their lives. Nonprofit leaders who think about philanthropic fundraising, the integrative stage of fundraising, organizational readiness, the case for support, and efficiency and effectiveness in fundraising will very likely find themselves reflecting on ethical matters on behalf of their organizations.

The most comprehensive statement on ethics in fundraising is the Association of Fundraising Professionals (AFP) Code of Ethical Principles and Standards of Professional Practice. Members of the AFP agree to abide by these standards, and nonprofits who hire the AFP's members should expect to support the standards as well. Nonprofits whose fundraising staff do not belong to the AFP will do well to apply these principles as guidelines for professional performance. The complete text of the society's principles and standards appears in the Appendix to this chapter.

The AFP principles and standards imply that fundraising staff bring appropriate technical and managerial competency to their responsibilities. Such competency, and the commitment to continually strengthen it, is an ethical condition of fundraising that is an integral part of staff professionalism. Successful nonprofit organizations will serve as vehicles for fundraising that is ethical and professional.

SUMMARY

"Fund raising is an essential part of American philanthropy; in turn, philanthropy—as voluntary action for the public good—is essential to American democracy" (Payton, Rosso, and Tempel, 1991, p. 4). This observation affirms the reality that fundraising cannot be an isolated activity in a successful nonprofit organization. Fundraising practices reflect what we are as organizations. The values, style, and commitment that undergird fundraising will likely be the same as those that characterize the rest of an organization's work.

Philanthropic fundraising is mission-driven. That is, funds are sought to enable a nonprofit to serve the community good that the organization addresses. Philanthropic fundraising is also volunteer-centered. Over the long term, the involvement of volunteers in governance, advocacy, and giving is essential to healthy nonprofits.

Successful fundraising is also the result of disciplined management. When fundraising professionals provide leadership to other staff and to volunteers, a productive collective effort results. Just as disciplined fundraising management is important to obtaining resources, it is also important in exercising accountability for resources. Nonprofits must ensure that they use contributed income for the purposes for which it was sought. Although they are privately controlled, mission-driven nonprofits are publicly accountable.

The public good that fundraising supports is essential to the well-being of our communities and our nation. Weaving philanthropic fundraising into the fabric of their existence is integral to the moral purpose of ethical nonprofits.

Appendix:
Association of Fundraising Professionals
Code of Ethical Principles and Standards of Professional Practice

Code of Ethical Principles

The Association of Fundraising Professionals (AFP) exists to foster the development and growth of fundraising professionals and the profession, to promote high ethical standards in the fundraising profession, and to preserve and enhance philanthropy and volunteerism.

Members of AFP are motivated by an inner drive to improve the quality of life through the causes they serve. They serve the ideal of philanthropy; are committed to the preservation and enhancement of volunteerism; and hold stewardship of these concepts as the overriding principle of their professional life. They recognize their responsibility to ensure that needed resources are vigorously and ethically sought and that the intent of the donor is honestly fulfilled. To these ends, AFP members embrace certain values that they strive to uphold in performing their responsibilities for generating charitable support. AFP members aspire to:

- Practice their profession with integrity, honesty, truthfulness, and adherence to the absolute obligation to safeguard the public trust.
- Act according to the highest standards and visions of their organization, profession, and conscience.
- Put philanthropic mission above personal gain.
- Inspire others through their own sense of dedication and high purpose.
- Improve their professional knowledge and skills, so that their performance will better serve others.
- Demonstrate concern for the interests and well-being of individuals affected by their actions.
- Value the privacy, freedom of choice, and interests of all those affected by their actions.
- Foster cultural diversity and pluralistic values, and treat all people with dignity and respect.
- Affirm, through personal giving, a commitment to philanthropy and its role in society.
- Adhere to the spirit as well as the letter of all applicable laws and regulations.
- Advocate within their organizations adherence to all applicable laws and regulations.
- Avoid even the appearance of any criminal offense or professional misconduct.
- Bring credit to the fundraising profession by their public demeanor.
- Encourage colleagues to embrace and practice these ethical principles and standards of professional practice.
- Be aware of the codes of ethics promulgated by other professional organizations that serve philanthropy.

Standards of Professional Practice

Furthermore, while striving to act according to the above values, AFP members agree to abide by the AFP Standards of Professional Practice, which are adopted and incorporated into the AFP Code of Ethical Principles. Violation of the Standards may subject the member to disciplinary sanctions, including expulsion, as provided in the AFP Ethics Enforcement Procedures.

Professional obligations

1. Members shall not engage in activities that harm the members' organization, clients, or profession.

2. Members shall not engage in activities that conflict with their fiduciary, ethical, and legal obligations to their organizations and their clients.

3. Members shall effectively disclose all potential and actual conflicts of interest; such disclosure does not preclude or imply ethical impropriety.

4. Members shall not exploit any relationship with a donor, prospect, volunteer, or employee to the benefit of the members or the members' organizations.

5. Members shall comply with all applicable local, state, provincial, and federal civil and criminal laws.

6. Members recognize their individual boundaries of competence and are forthcoming and truthful about their professional experience and qualifications.

Solicitation and use of charitable funds

7. Members shall take care to ensure that all solicitation materials are accurate and correctly reflect their organization's mission and use of solicited funds.

8. Members shall take care to ensure that donors receive informed, accurate, and ethical advice about the value and tax implications of potential gifts.

9. Members shall take care to ensure that contributions are used in accordance with donors' intentions.

10. Members shall take care to ensure proper stewardship of charitable contributions, including timely reports on the use and management of funds.

11. Members shall obtain explicit consent by the donor before altering the conditions of a gift.

Presentation of information

12. Members shall not disclose privileged or confidential information to unauthorized parties.

13. Members shall adhere to the principle that all donor and prospect information created by, or on behalf of, an organization is the property of that organization and shall not be transferred or utilized except on behalf of that organization.

14. Members shall give donors the opportunity to have their names removed from lists that are sold to, rented to, or exchanged with other organizations.

15. Members shall, when stating fundraising results, use accurate and consistent accounting methods that conform to the appropriate guidelines adopted by the

American Institute of Certified Public Accountants (AICPA)* for the type of organization involved. (*In countries outside of the United States, comparable authority should be utilized.)

Compensation

16. Members shall not accept compensation that is based on a percentage of charitable contributions; nor shall they accept finder's fees.

17. Members may accept performance-based compensation, such as bonuses, provided such bonuses are in accord with prevailing practices within the members' own organizations, and are not based on a percentage of charitable contributions.

18. Members shall not pay finder's fees, commissions, or percentage compensation based on charitable contributions and shall take care to discourage their organizations from making such payments.

Source: Association of Fundraising Professionals, 1964, amended Oct. 1999.

References

Clohesy, W. H. "Fund-Raising and the Articulation of Common Goods." *Nonprofit and Voluntary Sector Quarterly,* 2003, *32,* 128–140.

Payton, R. L., Rosso, H. A., and Tempel, E. R. "Toward a Philosophy of Fund Raising." In D. F. Burlingame and L. J. Hulse (eds.), *Taking Fund Raising Seriously: Advancing the Profession and Practice of Raising Money.* San Francisco: Jossey-Bass, 1991.

Seiler, T. L. "Plan to Succeed," In H. A. Rosso, *Achieving Excellence in Fund Raising.* San Francisco: Jossey-Bass, 2003.

Toppe, C. M., Kirsch, A. D., and Michel, J. *Giving and Volunteering in the United States in 2001.* Washington, D.C.: INDEPENDENT SECTOR, 2002.

Weitzman, M., Jalandoni, N. T., Lampkin, L. M., and Pollak, T. H. *The New Nonprofit Almanac and Desk Reference.* San Francisco: Jossey-Bass, 2002.

Additional Reading

Dove, K. E. *Conducting a Successful Capital Campaign.* San Francisco: Jossey-Bass, 2000.

Fischer, M. *Ethical Decision Making in Fund Raising.* New York: Wiley, 2000.

Greenfield, J. M. *Fund Raising: Evaluating and Managing the Fund Development Process.* New York: Wiley, 1999.

Jordan, R. R., and Quynn, K. L. *Planned Giving: Management, Marketing, and Law.* New York: Wiley, 2000.

Kelly, K. S. *Effective Fund-Raising Management.* Mahwah, N.J.: Erlbaum, 1998.

New, A. L. *Raise More Money for Your Nonprofit Organization: A Guide to Evaluating and Improving Your Fund Raising.* New York: Foundation Center, 1991.

CHAPTER EIGHTEEN

Enterprise Strategies
for Generating Revenue

Cynthia W. Massarsky

S ince the beginning of what we now call the *nonprofit* or *third sector,* nonprofit organizations have created and implemented important programs while at the same time facing the difficult task of soliciting financial support to pay for them. In essence, the fate of the majority of nonprofit organizations in this country was, and still is, in the hands of their funders—foundations, corporate giving offices, government agencies, and individual donors. Today, as in the past, nonprofits create a host of programs in concert with their mission and then seek grant monies to support them. When programs are fresh and innovative, the fundraising task is easier. But as programs become more commonplace, regardless of their need and importance, the task gets more difficult.

The environment for receiving special-project grants is getting more and more competitive every day, and general support grants are even more difficult to come by. Privatization is growing. Government retrenchment continues. Corporate monies are available, but in shorter supply, and an increasing number of mergers and acquisitions means that there are fewer entities to tap. Many individual givers, usually reached via direct mail campaigns, are finding it more difficult to repeat donations made in previous years. Yet nonprofits must balance their budgets. Foundation and public funding agencies do not appreciate deficit spending. So what is a nonprofit organization to do?

One solution is to explore the potential for generating earned income by charging fees for service; selling products; the development, sale, and lease of buildings and land; and "soft" property or income-earning assets such as copyrights, patents, and trademarks. With an earned income venture, a nonprofit creates a business and, if successful, provides its organization with an additional stream of revenue or support. Earned income ventures are sexy. They are in vogue. But they are serious endeavors that require a significant amount of research and planning. And they usually require a change or shift in attitude among board and staff as well.

During the past twenty years, we have seen a blurring of the distinction between nonprofit and private sector practices. Nonprofit organizations are becoming more business- and marketing-oriented as they learn the rewards of selling, as opposed to giving away, their products, services, or other assets. And the business community is discovering new market opportunities in areas that were once the exclusive domain of nonprofits. From within these two roles, a third scenario has surfaced as well—the corporate-nonprofit joint venture. Nonprofits are working with the business community in a variety of innovative ways to accomplish their own goals and often those of their partners too.

NEW DEVELOPMENTS IN THE FIELD

Since the first edition of this book was published a decade ago, we have seen a number of developments in the practice of income generation itself. I shall examine a number of them here.

Greater Interest and Participation Among Nonprofits

Nonprofits have clearly shown greater interest in income generation as a potential source of new revenue and hence greater visibility and acceptance, especially when the nonprofit's business is tied closely to the mission and strengths of the parent organization. In a groundbreaking study I conducted with Samantha L. Beinhacker for the Pew Charitable Trusts (Massarsky and Beinhacker, 2002), one in four of the 519 nonprofits responding to a survey reported that they were already operating earned income businesses, nearly three-quarters of them in the service-related arena. Examples include at-home elder care services and educational classes and workshops. Just under half are operating product-related enterprises and sell merchandise. About a quarter are running real estate properties, such as parking garages and office space for lease, that generate income. About 15 percent are engaged in cause-related marketing with the private sector, such as licensing their logo for use in a join marketing campaign. The research pointed out that the greater the size of its budget, the more likely the organization is to operate an earned income venture. Nonprofits operating earned income ventures also tend to be older and more experienced and assert that they are entrepreneurial. We also found a number of reasons, besides a desire for financial return, why nonprofits engage in nonprofit enterprise, most notably because it serves their clients by providing employment and training opportunities, generates positive community relations, and helps revitalize the neighborhood and community. A significant number also said their ventures have had a number of "halo effects" on the parent organization, including improving the nonprofit's reputation, allowing for better delivery of products and services, sharpening the nonprofit's mission, and contributing to the building of an entrepreneurial culture.

Although we cannot assume that the survey results were representative of all nonprofits because respondents were not based on a random sample, the Pew Charitable Trusts nevertheless believed that the study demonstrated a significant interest and involvement among nonprofits. So they joined forces in September 2001, along with Yale University and the Goldman Sachs Foundation, to form the Yale School of Management–Goldman Sachs Foundation Partnership on Nonprofit Ventures. The Partnership on Nonprofit Ventures educates nonprofits about nonprofit enterprise, serves as a mechanism for capitalizing promising profit-making ventures with financial support, and provides intellectual capital to build the practice of social entrepreneurship in the nonprofit sector at large.

New Players in the Field

The field has also produced an association and a number of national and local groups whose mission is to educate about and otherwise support nonprofit enterprise. These offer various forms of assistance in areas such as education and training, business development, technical assistance, consulting, and venture philanthropy and other types of financing. They provide educational resources, organize annual conferences, publish materials, and in some cases make financial awards and donate consulting services to winners of annual competitions.

For example, Social Enterprise Alliance (SEA; http://www.socialenterprise alliance.org) is a membership organization that mobilizes nonprofit organizations, practitioners, and investors to advance earned income strategies and provides support through an annual conference and other learning opportunities and resources. Practitioner members include both early-stage entrepreneurs seeking the nuts-and-bolts knowledge to start and run a social purpose venture and established practitioners seeking an opportunity to exchange ideas with other pioneers in the field. The Center for Social Innovation (CSI; http://www .gsb.stanford.edu/csi) at the Stanford Business School, works to bring entrepreneurship to the social arena. CSI pursues this goal by promoting rigorous, practice-oriented research; adopting an interdisciplinary approach; and reaching out to engage academics and leading practitioners in a process of mutual education. Its new journal, the *Stanford Social Innovation Review,* is devoted

exclusively to this topic. The Cause Marketing Forum Inc. (CMFI; http://www
.causemarketingforum.com), founded in 2002 to help advance and expand
cause marketing in America, has undertaken four major initiatives: a conference, the Cause Marketing Halo Awards, a resource center, and a series of one-
day workshops.

A new breed of consultants has entered the field as well. The Partnership on
Nonprofit Ventures' Web site (http://www.ventures.yale.edu/relatedorganiza
tions.asp) lists a number of consultants that specialize in nonprofit enterprise.
Its membership includes more than 665 consultants and consulting firms. Community Wealth Ventures (http://www.communitywealth.org), a for-profit subsidiary of the nonprofit Share Our Strength, provides consulting services in all
aspects of entrepreneurial wealth creation for nonprofit, corporate, and foundation clients. Rolfe Larson Associates (http://www.RolfeLarson.com) helps
nonprofits start and grow earned income projects. The firm provides support
for strategic planning and board development and also prepares feasibility studies, marketing plans, and business plans. Rolfe Larson is the author of *Venture
Forth! The Essential Guide to Starting a Moneymaking Business in Your Nonprofit Organization* (Amherst H. Wilder Foundation, 2002). Located in Connecticut, Brody-Weiser–Burns (http://www.brodyweiser.com) helps nonprofits
develop strategic and business venture plans, assists foundations with structuring and managing program-related investments, and facilitates partnerships
between businesses and nonprofits. Virtue Ventures (http://www.virtueven
tures.com) and principal Kim Alter specialize in bringing business practices to
nonprofit organizations and helping them manage the delicate balance between
their social mission and financial objectives—their double bottom line. She is
also the author of *Managing the Double Bottom Line: A Business Planning Reference Guide for Social Enterprises* (Pact Publications, 2000).

Other new players in the field include a growing number of nonprofits that
are bringing in executives from the business world to join their boards, are operating more than one enterprise, or are hiring outside expertise from the private sector to run them. For example, Zoo Atlanta recently retained a former
marketing executive from Coca-Cola to run its operations. A Harvard Business
School graduate, he was responsible for promoting several well-known brands
and eventually oversaw Coca-Cola Europe (Klineman, 2003).

Increased Interest Among the Funding and Investment Communities

Today, we also see more involvement among funders and social investors. Although the field has yet to capture data about grantmakers and others giving financial support to nonprofit enterprise, undoubtedly someone will begin to track
this soon. Grantmakers for Effective Organizations (http://www.geofunders.org)
devotes a part of its programming to informing its members about nonprofit

enterprise. Nonprofits that manage loan funds, particularly community development financial institutions such as the Nonprofit Finance Fund (http://www .nonprofitfinancefund.org) also offer loans and other services in support of nonprofit enterprise. And of course, private foundations and social investor groups provide various levels of funding for nonprofit enterprise through instruments such as grants, loans, investments, and program-related investments (PRIs). Some, like New Profit Inc. (http://www.newprofit.com), Seedco (http://www .seedco.org), the Goldman Sachs Foundation (http://www.gs.com/foundation), Common Good Ventures (http://www.commongoodventures.org), and Social Venture Partners International (http://www.svpinternational.org), are adapting the venture capital model and taking a more participatory role in the enterprises they support. In fact, this whole new category, called "venture philanthropy," is receiving more and more attention as grantmakers and investors consider how they can best influence nonprofit enterprise.

New Terms

The field has spawned a wealth of new terms to describe the practice of generating income—along with an often heated debate among supporters as to the correct terms to use under various circumstances. For example, a number of terms that describe the practice, from *social enterprise* and *affirmative business* to *nonprofit business venture* and *nonprofit enterprise,* are cropping up in a variety of contexts. Even the term *income generation* takes on a different meaning, depending on where you view it from. Although the terminology may be uncertain, the concept is not. For our purposes in this chapter, I will use the term adopted by the Partnership on Nonprofit Ventures and refer to any nonprofit engaged in generating earned income, as opposed to contributed income, as a *nonprofit enterprise.* This includes traditional fees for service—such as ticket sales and school tuitions—that represent perhaps the greatest source of revenue for nonprofits. I define *nonprofit enterprise* as "business ventures initiated by nonprofit organizations for the purpose of generating net income to support their mission and programs or to provide employment and other benefits to their clients" and use the term *business* universally and without regard to whether the business is located within the nonprofit or is a freestanding spin-off or subsidiary of the nonprofit.

Evolution of Business Plan Competitions for Nonprofits

Another way in which nonprofits are sharpening their business skills and finding financial support for their ventures is by entering one or more business plan competitions. The National Business Plan Competition for Nonprofit Organizations (run by the Partnership on Nonprofit Ventures, http://www.ventures.yale.edu), the Global Social Venture Competition (run jointly by Columbia School of Business, the Haas School of Business, and the London School of Business, http://

www.socialvc.net), and Social Stimulus (http://www.socialstimulus.org) are just three competitions that offer the reward of intellectual and financial capital to nonprofit venturers. In fact, the term *business plan* has become so common these days that when nonprofits ask funders to support their enterprise or even their grant-based programs, many funders respond in a more businesslike fashion and request that nonprofits submit their proposals in a business plan format.

Access to New Research, Publications, Workshops, and Course Offerings at Colleges and Universities

Within the past year in particular, a lot of buzz about nonprofit enterprise has been emanating from chat rooms, listservs, and sites on the Internet, as well as from lectures, workshops, and special events on college campuses and at industry conferences. We have witnessed a significant increase in the quantity and quality of research on the subject, as well as the number of publications available in the marketplace. For example, Community Wealth Ventures has developed an electronic directory of social enterprises and in July 2003 issued *Powering Social Change: Lessons on Community Wealth Generation for Nonprofit Sustainability,* a report that provides insights on how some of the country's most innovative nonprofit leaders are initiating business ventures and partnerships to better deliver their missions. Jed Emerson, senior fellow at the William and Flora Hewlett Foundation and the David and Lucile Packard Foundation, has completed a project that takes inventory of the people and organizations involved in corporate social responsibility, social enterprise, social investing, and strategic philanthropy (see http://www.blendedvalue.org). Kim Alter, an independent consultant who has written extensively in the field, has designed a typology that classifies and labels the different forms, operational models, and structures of nonprofit enterprise (http://www.virtueventures.com). The Partnership on Nonprofit Ventures collects data on its members and entrants in its National Business Plan Competition and also conducts longitudinal studies of award winners in its competition. Jossey-Bass, offering perhaps the greatest number of titles devoted to the nonprofit sector, is the leader in publishing on the subject, and currently has hundreds of books in print. Other publishers highlight this topic as well.

Debate About Accountability and Return on Investment

Perhaps as a result of the increased number of organizations operating nonprofit enterprises, we have seen a concurrent swell of debate focusing on how nonprofit entrepreneurs should account for the social and financial return on investments in their businesses. Is it necessary that a nonprofit enterprise include a social return on investment component, such as employing the clients of its parent organization in some aspect of the business? Is it legitimate to say that if a nonprofit enterprise is serving a social mission by driving revenues back to its nonprofit parent, this qualifies as a social return on investment? What is the best way to measure social return on investment and to incorporate it in financial statements? And further, if a nonprofit quantifies and incorporates a social return in its calculations, does that improve the profitability picture of the enterprise when compared to the nonprofit that does not incorporate a social return? That is, can an enterprise that incorporates a social return but makes less money overall be considered as profitable as one that does not incorporate a social return and makes more money overall?

During the past few years, several organizations have wrestled with these theories, most notably the Roberts Enterprise Development Fund (REDF) in San Francisco (http://www.redf.org). REDF has written extensively on the subject, and along with its former president, Jed Emerson, and director Melinda Tuan, has broken new ground in developing an approach for measuring social return on investment.

TYPES OF ENTERPRISE STRATEGIES

How, then, does a nonprofit organization go about the task of considering enterprise as a strategy for generating revenue? Over the years, I've spoken with a number of nonprofit executives who are already generating earned income and, by my definition, involved in enterprise yet don't think of it in these terms. These include performing arts organizations that sell tickets to their shows, educational programs that charge fees for their classes, and health clinics that require payments for office visits. Often nonprofits can significantly increase the net income they derive from selling their products and services merely by analyzing how they price these offerings and setting fees based on market rates or opportunities rather than strict cost recovery. Other nonprofits can become more familiar with earned income by examining whether there is a market that will pay for their products or services and starting to charge for them when this is appropriate.

BUSINESS VENTURES

Business ventures exist in many forms and sizes, from the traditional fee-for-service charges discussed earlier to full-scale commercial activities. But regardless of form or size, because it is generally believed that ventures have a greater chance of succeeding if they are related to their nonprofit's mission, we will begin with a focus on these.

Business ventures are best categorized according to the product or service being sold.

Program-Related Products

Program-related products are those that are closely identified with the organization and promote the organization's mission as well as earn money. San Francisco–based CompuMentor operates DiscounTech, a business that distributes donated and discounted technology products to other nonprofits at the lowest possible cost. This enterprise offers these high-demand products by working closely with leading technology companies to donate or steeply discount their products especially for the nonprofit sector and earns income by charging an administrative fee for each item sold.

The nonprofit Scojo Foundation combines a number of strategies in its business. Scojo's enterprise distributes high-quality, low-cost near-vision ("reading") glasses to women-run microenterprises in India. These women then sell the reading glasses to a portion of the more than 200 million people in India who need glasses to accomplish tasks such as reading a ledger, threading a needle, mending a shoe, or fixing a radio. To meets its mission, Scojo markets the reading glasses to one group of its constituents so that they can "see up close" and to another so that they can earn enough money to support their families.

Still other nonprofit organizations provide job training for their clients and employ them in their business to manufacture a product or supply a service in the commercial arena. These enterprises are often called "affirmative" businesses. Rochester Rehabilitation Center is a nonprofit organization in Rochester, New York, that helps people with disabilities. Its business, Parrett Paper, employs the clients of the parent organization and provides them with meaningful work experience. Parrett Paper manufactures, packages, markets, and distributes unique die-cut greeting cards, gift tags, and holiday cards.

El Puente Community Development in El Paso, Texas, runs a business that employs its constituents, low-income Mexican immigrant women and their families who have been adversely affected by global restructuring. El Puente's enterprise, Deseños Mayapan, operates a facility that manufactures customized medical scrubs to meet the increasing demand for affordable, attractive uniforms for the health, child care, and medical professions in the El Paso and West Texas area.

Program-Related Services

Ancillary services provided to members, friends, and alumni, as well as to the general public, can enhance the tax-exempt mission of the organization. Museum gift shops, parking lots, and cafés are typical examples. Nonprofits market other types of services too. Some nonprofit organizations involved in economic and community development offer mortgage brokerage services, environmental organizations run landscaping businesses, and social services agencies offer everything from duplicating documents to retrofitting homes to make them handicapped-accessible.

The Guthrie Theater and the Children's Theatre Company in Minneapolis formed a unique business partnership to capture additional value from the costumes designed for individual productions. CostumeRentals enables schools, theaters, corporations, and individuals to rent costumes at reasonable prices. Their combined inventory of more than 17,500 costumes offers a broad selection of periods and styles, designed by the country's leading theatrical costume designers.

In another type of program-related service, nonprofits market the expertise of their staff members. For example, Benhaven, a Connecticut-based nonprofit agency, has been providing services to children, adolescents, and adults with autism for 35 years. To support school system personnel in developing their capabilities to serve students with autism effectively, Benhaven established a consulting practice called Benhaven's Learning Network. The practice markets consultation and technical assistance to special education programs in public schools throughout Connecticut.

Hard Property

The sale, lease, development, and rental of land and buildings—sometimes referred to as "hard property"—offer ways of making use of an organization's downtime. Unlike the business activities cited earlier, these are not always related to the mission of the nonprofit organization. Colleges and universities, for example, often rent excess dormitory, cafeteria, gymnasium, and field space during slack summer months to such groups as professional sports teams and summer camps. Other nonprofits rent their facilities for conferences and meetings, some develop housing, and still others have sold the "air space" above the buildings they own to private developers. In Washington, D.C., the Harmon Central Kitchen is a commercial kitchen owned and operated by Nation's Capital Child and Family Development. This nonprofit runs Make A Difference Catering, a business that leverages Harmon's unused kitchen capacity to market food services to licensed child care and elder care programs.

Soft Property

"Soft property" is a form of income generation that exploits income-earning assets such as copyrights, patents, trademarks, and even art and artifacts. In this category, nonprofit organizations can generate earned income in several ways, including cause-related marketing and licensing.

Cause-Related Marketing. Cause-related marketing, also called joint-venture marketing, links a for-profit organization with a nonprofit organization for their mutual benefit. For some nonprofits, cause-related marketing can offer new sources of financial support and increased public exposure. For their corporate partners, cause-related marketing can provide an opportunity to increase product sales and gain public recognition while supporting the causes they care about. Chicago-based International Events Group (IEG) projects that corporate spending on cause-related marketing will hit $921 million in 2003, a 10.3 percent increase over 2002. If double-digit growth continues, the figure will top $1 billion in 2004.

Since American Express helped launch the Statue of Liberty–Ellis Island campaign in 1981, the use of this strategy has proliferated. As part of the campaign, American Express made a donation to the Statue of Liberty–Ellis Island Foundation every time one of its customers used its credit card. In 1983, American Express helped raise $1.7 million for the foundation and claimed a dramatic 28 percent increase in card usage for itself (Josephson, 1984).

Today, many organizations have taken the cause-related marketing effort a step further. Some nonprofits work with companies on "transactional programs" wherein the corporate partner agrees to make a contribution to a designated cause based on consumer activity such as buying a specific product, redeeming a coupon, registering at a Web site, or shopping at a particular retail chain. Procter & Gamble's "Inspire Greatness" campaign sent a ten-page insert to sixty million households in support of the Special Olympics, urging consumers to get involved. Donations linked to coupon usage and retail fundraising events enabled the program to raise $4.8 million for the Special Olympics in 2002 (Cause Marketing Forum, 2003).

Over the years, General Mills has also been involved in numerous cause-related marketing campaigns, at both the corporate and the brand level. Its largest and longest-running transactional program is Box Tops for Education, through which the company donates as much as $20,000 per school annually by giving 10 cents per box top coupon redeemed from more than eight hundred General Mills products. Recent additions to the program enable consumers to raise similar amounts by shopping online in the Box Tops for Education Marketplace and charging with their Box Tops for Education Visa card. This campaign raised more than $23 million for seventy-seven thousand schools in the 2002–03 school year, bringing the total generated to more than $90 million (Cause Marketing Forum, 2003).

Other nonprofits work with companies on "joint messaging" programs. This type of promotional campaign raises awareness of a cause's message (for example, to fight skin cancer or to participate in an environmental cleanup) while building a positive association with the corporate sponsor or its brands. One example is Ford Motor Company and the National Center for Missing and Exploited Children's Blue Oval Certified Commitment to Kids program. In this campaign, Ford was looking for a way to attract customers to its dealerships. The Commitment to Kids program invited parents to visit dealerships to receive free, personalized child identification kits, complete with a photograph and set of fingerprints—key information in cases of child abduction. Overall, the program resulted in the photographing and fingerprinting of more than 850,000 children and garnered 700 million public service announcement impressions and 153 million editorial impressions (Cause Marketing Forum, 2003).

A second example of joint messaging is National SAFE KIDS Week, a program of Johnson & Johnson and the National Safe Kids Campaign. In May 2002, these two launched one of the largest helmet safety programs ever, "Use Your Head, Wear A Helmet." It included national media, hundreds of grassroots community events, a freestanding Sunday paper insert, point-of-purchase merchandising, and a donation of $1 million worth of bicycle helmets. The campaign was a tremendous success, garnered 170 million media impressions; was the impetus for more than fifteen hundred events; and reached more than 1.5 million persons (Cause Marketing Forum, 2003).

Still other cause-related marketing programs extend a partnership beyond annual or even quarterly promotions. In some instances, corporate employees become involved as volunteers. In others, they help recruit volunteers. In the fall of 2003, Habitat for Humanity International premiered its volunteer recruitment and training program sponsored by DIY, the how-to cable television network, where it aired a five-part workshop providing an in-depth look at building a Habitat for Humanity house. The partnership also released training videos with house-building instructions to use in recruiting volunteers among Habitat for Humanity's seventeen hundred affiliate offices. In yet other examples, corporations such as McDonald's work with nonprofit social services agencies to hire people with disabilities.

Clearly, the push for companies to demonstrate that they are politically and socially "correct" is coming from all angles—employees, consumers, stockholders, and social and political organizations. Cause-related marketing has offered business an ideal vehicle for achieving a healthier bottom line and a better public image, particularly among health-related causes. The Susan G. Komen Breast Cancer Foundation has been a leader in this. Its "Race for the Cure" and other cause-marketing campaigns garner millions of dollars annually for breast cancer research. In 2003 alone, the Komen Foundation partnered with more than a dozen corporations, from Ford Motor Company, Lee Jeans, and Sherwin Williams to KitchenAid, the WNBA, and Saatchi & Saatchi Public Relations.

One of the more recent types of corporate-nonprofit collaborations, and a twist on the previous examples, is one in which the nonprofit organization helps market the products or services of the corporation in return for a donation or a percentage of sales. Corporations view this supplemental sales force or distribution arm as another vehicle to enhance their marketing efforts. For corporations, this approach also helps improve brand image and increase awareness. Nonprofit organizations view this approach as a way to increase and diversify their revenue, as well as to enhance the ways in which they are viewed by potential contributors and other important groups.

One way in which this happens is when a corporation secures the permission of nonprofit management to offer its products or services to the members of the nonprofit. Here the nonprofit organization makes various plans available to its members and receives a commission from the corporation in return for sales to members. For example, AARP (formerly the American Association of Retired Persons) offers numerous benefits to its members, including life insurance policies and discounts on travel.

Another example of a member-related service is through supermarket chains such as Stop & Shop or Pathmark. A nonprofit organization purchases Stop & Shop or Pathmark "scrip" in block amounts and at a discount and then resells the scrip to its members. Members then use the scrip when purchasing groceries at these stores. As a result of this program, the supermarkets are able to make advance bulk sales and potentially reach new customers, the nonprofit organization keeps the difference between the purchase and resale amount (usually 5 to 10 percent), and its members purchase in the way they normally do while helping the nonprofit at the same time.

A final model of cause-related marketing in which the nonprofit helps market the corporation's products and services is in the financial services area, with the use of affinity cards. Affinity cards provide an effortless way for people to contribute to a favorite charity or organization. Once a growth area, this approach may be nearing the saturation point, perhaps due to the number of private label cards offered by companies that range from banks to department stores. Nevertheless, to date, the Working Assets card has raised $40 million for progressive causes (Working Assets, 2004). Its new MBNA Bank card pays 10 cents for each use to groups working for peace, human rights, economic justice, education, and the environment. And still, a number of colleges and universities take advantage of this approach as well, marketing their cards to alumni and friends of their institutions. Most of these cards feature a logo or some symbol of the nonprofit group. The financial arrangements vary and include receipt of a percentage of all charges made by cardholders, a donation for each new cardholder, or a percentage of each annual fee. Some banks pay a percentage of charges incurred, while others pay a fee per transaction.

Licensing. *Licensing* is the term commonly used for the legal agreement whereby one party authorizes a second party to use its name, logo, characters, or products. In the case of corporations and their nonprofit partners, it is typically the nonprofit that grants a license to a corporation, for which the nonprofit receives a royalty based on sales. When licensing arrangements are well targeted, both licenser and licensee benefit financially, as well as in increased publicity.

For example, the Save the Children Federation licenses the rights to its children's designs to companies that manufacture greeting cards, calendars, eyeglasses, and decor for children's rooms. Other nonprofit organizations, such as the U.S. Fund for UNICEF, permit the use of their name in return for a licensing fee. Still other nonprofits license the right to reproduce their collections of art, artifacts, and furniture. For example, the nonprofit National Trust for Historic Preservation has licensed Valspar to produce a line of paints for Lowe's. All the paint colors in the line are based on colors found in historic homes, and both Valspar and Lowe's have found this to be a strong selling point. So has the Metropolitan Museum of Art, based in New York City, which has earned substantial income by licensing artistic designs from its collections to textile companies. Finally, perhaps one of the best-known example of licensing is between Sesame Workshop (formerly Children's Television Workshop, or CTW), the nonprofit organization that originated *Sesame Street,* and many toy, video, book, record, and clothing manufacturers, including Hasbro, Playskool, Western Publishing, and JC Penney. Sesame Workshop grants rights to these and many other companies to reproduce the characters, sets, and music from its television show.

QUESTIONS NONPROFITS TYPICALLY ASK ABOUT BUSINESS VENTURING

Typically, nonprofit organizations that are in the process of investigating potential income-generating ventures ask four main questions:

- We need money quickly. What's a good business to go into that will net us enough in six months to cover our deficit and then some?
- Is this legal? We're a nonprofit. Doesn't that mean that we aren't allowed to earn money?
- Might we lose our tax-exempt status if we are successful?
- Why don't we just try out an idea and see if it works?

Although these are good questions, they are not the heart of the issue. If a nonprofit organization looks for a quick fix, it will surely be disappointed. Just as it takes time to mount a fundraising campaign, it takes time to explore whether earning income is an appropriate way to "make ends meet." Finding a business that satisfies the needs of the organization and returns significant revenue to it is not like looking through a catalogue of office furniture and selecting between vertical- and lateral-file cabinets. The investigation process and business planning, the decision making that occurs every step of the way—not to mention the typical business start-up that doesn't break even for eighteen months—can take well over two years to accomplish. Moving ahead without proper analysis—that is, trying out an idea to see if it works—can frustrate staff, anger members, confuse supporters, and put a nonprofit in debt.

Initially, however, time is not well spent in being overly concerned about legalities and tax issues. By law, nonprofit organizations are permitted to earn income—to operate a business and generate profits. What they cannot do is pass along profits to equity owners. In this regard, an organization's tax-exempt status is not jeopardized as long as net earnings are not turned to the advantage of persons in their private capacities.

One legal and tax issue that nonprofits should consider is whether the business is related to the mission of the organization and hence whether the nonprofit will incur unrelated income tax. To put this in the simplest terms, if a business is deemed unrelated to the mission of the organization (a determination made by various rules and "tests"), it will probably incur a tax. Many nonprofit organizations pay unrelated business income taxes. Nonetheless, tax liability should not be the determining factor in deciding to engage in business venturing. If the business is viable, it should have the capacity to support a tax. However, it is generally held that organizations receiving in excess of 15 to 20 percent of their revenue from unrelated activities might attract continuing scrutiny regarding to their tax-exempt status, to ensure that they are organized and operated primarily for exempt purposes (Heritage and Orlebeke, 2004).

A second legal and tax issue that concerns nonprofits is whether the business should become a part of the nonprofit entity or should be spun off as a separate nonprofit or as a for-profit subsidiary that then drives back revenue to the nonprofit to support its mission-related programs. These decisions are further complicated when a nonprofit decides to operate its business as part of a joint venture either with another nonprofit or with a private sector concern. Because the interpretation of IRS rules depends on the specific nature of the business (that is, what the organization intends to do and how it intends to do it), legal and tax counsel cannot adequately assess these two issues until the nonprofit has made certain key decisions. Once the organization has determined its business concept, conducted a feasibility study, and decided to proceed in earnest, it can then seek the counsel of legal and tax specialists whose business it is to advise on structuring nonprofit business ventures, even if the organization already retains other counsel for its regular operations.

In spite of the foregoing, keep in mind that the IRS remains on the lookout for organizations that are operating businesses under their nonprofit umbrella when they should not, either because they are jeopardizing their tax-exempt status or because they should be paying taxes on profits. Clearly, it is important for nonprofits engaged in enterprise to consult a knowledgeable tax attorney to determine the most appropriate form of business and tax structure given the goals of both the venture and its nonprofit parent.

QUESTIONS NONPROFITS
SHOULD ASK ABOUT BUSINESS VENTURING

The important questions that nonprofits *should* ask are those that require taking a long, hard look at the organization—its mission, strengths and weaknesses, and financial wherewithal. Answers to such questions as the following will help a nonprofit determine whether it is ready to operate a profit-making business:

- What is our current and projected financial status, and how will earned income help us?

- Are we feeling desperate?

- Is business venturing consistent with our mission? Do we feel comfortable with the idea of selling a product or service?

- Will business venturing distract us from what we were founded to do? What are the potential risks and returns in terms of our finances, organization, and reputation?

- If we design and operate a business, will we have the support of our staff, board, funders, members, and others?

- How will a profit-making business fit into the overall structure of our organization? What priority will it have among staff? Among senior management?

- Are we prepared to allocate the staff to investigate possible ventures and get one up and running or to hire someone to do it for us? Do we have a "champion" among us who will take responsibility for the work and who has the influence and authority to move forward?

- Are we prepared to allocate the time necessary to conduct proper analysis, planning, and start-up to meet the demands of the marketplace?

- Do we have the financial resources to put toward the process of identifying a business and starting it up? Do we have access to other sources of capital?

- Do we really have a product or a service that people would be willing to pay for?

HOW NONPROFITS CAN FIND
THE ANSWERS TO THEIR QUESTIONS

To obtain complete and useful answers to the questions just listed, nonprofit organizations are advised to proceed through a series of steps, making a go or no-go decision after each one.

Step 1: Designate a Team to Explore the Issues

The team can include staff, board members, close friends, and others who would offer both a current and historical perspective. Some nonprofits have found it helpful to bring in a consultant to keep the discussion on track and to provide an unbiased opinion.

Perhaps the most difficult questions are those involving ethical considerations. It is crucial that you and your key constituents feel comfortable with the notion of business venturing. To some people, the idea may sound quite exciting. They may envision creative ways to incorporate a business and see how it enhances the mission of the organization. Others may see it as mercenary and contrary to what nonprofits are all about.

Often business venturing requires that staff and board redirect their thinking or alter their attitudes about what they do and how they do it. They need to move

- From being *reactive* to being *proactive*
- From being *reliant* to being *self-reliant*
- From being *traditional* to being *entrepreneurial*
- From being *conservative* to being *innovative*
- From being *risk-averse* to being *risk-taking*
- From being *mission-driven* to being *market-driven*

If these ideas present significant obstacles that cannot be overcome, it is probably best not to proceed.

Step 2: Conduct an Organizational Audit

As is true with several other steps in the process, when your nonprofit conducts an organizational audit, it benefits from exploring not only how its assets might be useful in business venturing but also how healthy your organization is as a whole, what its strengths and weaknesses are, and where it might want to make some improvements. Further, the discipline involved in "writing it down" forces careful thought, clarity of purpose, and communication and coordination among all the relevant players—staff, management, board of directors, members, and others. These are important ingredients for any well-run organization. They are critical ingredients for yours if you intend to create and sustain an earned-income venture.

An organizational audit is a systematic examination and accounting of the assets of your nonprofit—from the expertise and skills of your staff to the scope and quality of your programs, from the nature of your physical plant to the status of your financial portfolio. Equally important, an organizational audit tallies responses to the issues discussed in step 1, such as staff commitment and board or trustee support.

Although it can be a difficult task, your nonprofit should conduct an honest review of its organizational weaknesses as well. Some might significantly affect the success of a business venture, but if they are recognized early on, they can be reversed or ameliorated. If, for example, the organization is particularly weak at record keeping, it might contract with an outside firm to maintain data on its customers. If the weakness is one that your nonprofit cannot contract for and the new business cannot do without, you might eliminate that type of enterprise from your list of possibilities.

Often nonprofits find it difficult to begin the process. They are not used to describing or even thinking about strengths and weaknesses but tend rather to relate lists of particular programs and activities they offer. To be effective, participants in an organizational audit should try to characterize the quality of what their organization has, is, and does, in addition to making straightforward lists. You should look at the number and types of current constituents (clients, members or subscribers, supporters, and others) to see not only what they do for your organization but also how well you serve them. One way to begin is to proceed through the following sequence of questions:

Organization, Management, and Personnel

- Where is our organizational expertise? (What is our specialty? What do we know how to do? How well do we do it?)

- What particular talents do our staff have? (What is our breadth of knowledge and experience about specific subjects? What is our ability to communicate with various audiences? How well do we communicate internally with one another? Are we "team players"? How interested are we in exploring and implementing new ideas? Do we have a sense of business?)

- What level of support do we have for business venturing? (How comfortable with the idea are our clients, staff, board of directors, members, funders, and other constituents? How does each of us feel about our exempt goals?)

Program

- What specific activities and products do we offer?

- Who wants to use our products and services? (Why do they want them? What needs would we meet? Do the users pay for what we offer?)

- How do we make our products and services known to others? (Do we publish any material? Do we conduct public relations or direct mail campaigns?)

Finances

- What is our financial status? (How has our budget grown or declined over the past five years? Are we "desperate" for operating capital?)

- Are our sources of revenue diversified? (What percentage of our monies do we get from grants from government, foundations, corporations, individuals? From membership fees, program fees, earned income, investments? From other sources?)

- Are we likely to gain or lose support in any of these areas over the next five years?

- Do we have capital or access to capital for earned income venturing? (If so, how much? How difficult would it be to obtain it? Do we have credit or borrowing power? Do we have monies for start-up as well as working capital?)

Equipment and Facilities

- What type of equipment do we own or rent, and what is its state of repair? (What do we have in the way of furniture, specialized equipment or machinery, kitchen equipment, computers, software, telephone system, library?)

- Do we have a management information system (MIS) in place? (Is it manual? Computerized?)

- What characterizes our building or offices and grounds? (How many square feet do we have? How many offices do we have? On what floors are we located? Do we have elevators, air conditioning, storage space? What is our outdoor space like? Do we rent or own? Do we have excess capacity?)

- Where are we located? (In the building? In the neighborhood? Is storefront space available?)

- Are we close to public transportation? Are there parking facilities? Are there loading docks?

- How attractive are our facilities? In what state of repair are they?

Other Assets

- What is our reputation? (Who has opinions about us? How solid are those opinions? Are we considered an authority?)

- Do we have a following? (Among whom? How stable is it?)

- Do we have a network of contacts on whom we can rely? (Who are they? How might they be used?)

- Do we own a trademark or copyright?
- Do we have a mailing list? (Who is on it? Are there duplicates?)
- Do we have a toll-free number? A Web site?

Step 3: Brainstorm Ideas

In step 3, the nonprofit moves from determining whether it is ready for an earned income venture and listing its organizational assets to brainstorming ideas. Here the task is to find connections between what the nonprofit "brings to the table" and potential businesses with which it feels comfortable. In brainstorming to list potential businesses, your organization should think about its interests and capabilities, the degree to which it desires a business that is related to its mission, the size and scale of business it can handle, and its desired geographical outreach. It should consider the monies it wishes to earn, how labor-intensive it wishes the business to be, and its ability to capitalize the costs of various start-up and ongoing operations.

The best way to do this brainstorming is to call a meeting of the team and any others who have an entrepreneurial spirit. They can include staff, board members, friends of the nonprofit, current clients and constituents, and even trusted outsiders who have great ideas. Before the session begins, lay down some ground rules. The ones I like to set are the following:

1. Participants will sit facing each other. Everyone will have an opportunity to speak. Participants should feel free and comfortable to suggest any ideas they may have.

2. Group leaders will act as facilitators and will refrain from offering suggestions or opinions. They will guide the discussion, help determine speaking order, and take notes.

   There will be three rounds of brainstorming:

   - Idea generation—including brief descriptions of what each product or service might be and how it would work (no playing "devil's advocate" allowed here)

   - Discussion of pros and cons—including a review of the suggestions made and group feedback on the advantages and disadvantages of each

   - Narrowing of the list and priority setting—including a consensus of the areas most worthy of further investigation

Typically, participants find it helpful to concentrate on the enterprise categories discussed earlier (products, services, hard and soft property), thinking in terms of the enterprise's current and potential customers, who they are, and what they are willing to pay for. The following questions are helpful in defining these factors:

- What do we currently give away to our constituents that we might sell to them instead?
- What do we currently give away to our constituents that we might sell to a new group of customers?
- What new product or service might we develop and market to our current constituents?
- What new product or service might we develop and market to new customers?
- Which nonprofit organizations or private sector corporations might we partner with to market a new or current product or service?

In addition, it is useful to set some parameters by asking questions such as these:

- Which industries should we consider (high-tech, garment, food, recycling, real estate, others)? What are the "good" businesses to get into, and which ones should we avoid?
- Should the venture be located within our current facility or off site?
- Should the venture operate as a wholesaler or as a retailer of its product or service?
- Should we start our venture in a market where there is a lot of competition (possible benefit that it is a known quantity) or where there is little competition (possible drawback that there are barriers to entry or the potential for others to copy)?
- Where should the product or service be in terms of its product life cycle?
- Should we look for a business venture that is labor-intensive? That relies on large inventories? That relies on strict quality control? That is a margin versus a volume business? That is credit-oriented? That requires limited capitalization?

Step 4: Conduct One or More Feasibility Studies

Step 4 begins with the list of potential businesses that result from the brainstorming session: select two or three businesses on which to conduct feasibility studies, and designate a project leader or champion to shepherd the process. A feasibility study is a formal and systematic analysis that explores a number of issues critical to the success of the business and determines whether it can succeed at the level required by the principals. Because a feasibility study is the tool that is used most often to make the final go or no-go decision about a particular business venture, nonprofits are advised to be exacting. When you conduct your feasibility study, your team should ask all the questions you would want answered if this were someone else's business proposal and the team members were conducting a serious evaluation of it or were considering whether to invest a significant amount of their own money in this new venture. One of the best ways to do this is to take an adversarial position, that is, to ask the question, "What is wrong with this idea?" and to find honest and acceptable answers.

It is important to note here, however, that the purpose of a feasibility study is to explore, in detail, whether or not an idea for a business is really viable. Although it is very exciting to get a positive result from a feasibility study, nonprofits must be prepared to learn that the result indicates that you should not proceed. This is not an indication of failure; it is an indication that you have done a good job at investigating all aspects of the business and that you have the good sense to make an objective decision to look in other directions.

A feasibility study usually involves a significant amount of market research, but many nonprofit organizations assume that they know all there is to know without conducting any. A typical statement, for example, usually sounds something like this: "This is a perfect business for us to go into because we know there is a need for a service that renovates apartment buildings and makes them suitable for the handicapped." But in the commercial world, there is a fundamental difference between a need and a demand for a particular product or service. It is not enough, or even relevant, to say that a need exists because this service is important to the health and safety of disabled people. Although this may be true, a successful business cannot be based on need alone. People must demand the service in sufficient quantity and be willing to pay for it at a price that will generate net income for the business. If these conditions are not met, this will just be another program for which the nonprofit must go out and raise funds.

To demonstrate demand, it is usually necessary to conduct consumer-oriented market research. In simple terms, this means investigating what consumers want and are willing to pay for, not what you want to do and are willing to provide. It means analyzing the marketplace in terms of the following factors:

- The size and status of the market (economic, social, technological, political, and business environments; dollar and volume sales over time; growing, declining, or stable industry; seasonality; future projections; barriers to entry)

- Typical consumers and their buying habits (demographics, affiliations, purchasing motivation, willingness to pay)

- Your competitors (who they are, their size of operation and geographical outreach, products and services offered, pricing, general competitive advantage, experience of those who are no longer in business)

- Product or service attributes and production and delivery process (product or service description, typical pricing strategies, typical or innovative manufacturing or service delivery systems, retailing versus wholesaling, distribution channels)

It also means developing a general marketing strategy by specifying the following factors and tasks:

- Product or service creation and positioning
- Market segmentation and target marketing (relevant buyer groups, buyers versus end users)
- Product or service pricing
- Promotion (including personal selling, print advertising, direct mail, newsletters, collaborations with related associations and organizations, mail stuffers or inserts, conferences, workshops and special meetings, special projects, and public relations)
- Evaluation, tracking, and monitoring (management information system)

The operating plan, another essential tool, involves the clear delineation of the following:

- Requirements for daily operations (major tasks and responsibilities)
- Management and personnel
- Business location and physical features of the facility
- Type, quality, and quantity of inventory required
- Capital equipment requirements

The nonprofit must also set up a financial plan and legal structure that cover the following aspects of doing business:

- Estimated revenues and expenses
- Capitalization requirements
- Options for legal structure (nonprofit program, for-profit subsidiary, and so on)

This vast amount of information usually takes a period of three to six months to gather. Some nonprofits choose to collect it themselves, while others contract with consultants who specialize in conducting feasibility studies and putting the results in a format that is most useful to the nonprofit and potential funders.

Regardless of who performs the task, you should look first to see what information already exists. This can be accomplished by compiling and analyzing in-house data, conducting library searches for books and articles on the subject, contacting relevant associations and industry groups for any studies or reports that have been generated, and performing a competitor analysis by making blind telephone calls or actually purchasing various products or services.

There are many sources for this information, including your nonprofit's organizational records, lists, and surveys; federal, state, and local government agencies; the Internet and the library; the telephone book; corporate annual reports; associations; suppliers and vendors; bankers; real estate offices; colleagues; and the competition. Researchers should pay attention to how dated information sources are, however, since political, social, and technological development can change the picture dramatically in a very short period of time.

To supplement information that already exists, you can design (or have outside professionals design) e-mail, postal, telephone, or face-to-face surveys. You can conduct personal interviews and focus groups. You can begin to track telephone inquiries or solicit specific information when people call or visit. Your organization may want to actually develop your new product or service and test-market it with a limited, representative sample of people.

Step 5: Secure an Organizational Commitment

In step 5, your nonprofit reviews the results of the feasibility studies and lists the risks and returns associated with each business. The risks you should consider are those that affect your organization as well as the new enterprise, including risks to your organization's financial position, reputation, and relationships with clients and funders. When your team is satisfied that you have a contingency plan to mitigate any serious risk, you are then in a position to select the enterprise you want to pursue and to secure an organizational commitment from your board of directors. Although this sounds like a relatively simple step, it is not as simple as it seems. At this point, you have yet another opportunity to make a go or no-go decision, but this time you have much more information at hand. Because each feasibility study details the exact nature of the business venture and the risk-return trade-offs associated with it, your nonprofit can reevaluate its position, asking questions such as these:

- Are staff, management, and board still as committed to the idea of earning income as they were when discussions began? Why or why not?

- Is this particular earned income venture worth the investment of time and money that is required? Will it actually serve the purposes for which it would be created?

- Does this particular business venture show significant market potential? Do we have a competitive advantage? Do we have the skills to produce and market the product or service, or can we purchase them? Can we capitalize the business through our own sources, or do we have sufficient access to others?

- Are there any lingering conflicts between this business and the mission of our organization? Does it fit our style and values?
- Should other ideas be investigated?

If the answers to these questions and others particular to the organization can be given to the satisfaction of those involved in the decision-making process, the nonprofit should obtain a formal organizational commitment and move forward to the business planning stage.

Step 6: Develop the Business Plan

Step 6 involves writing a business plan that describes what the business will do, how it is going to do it, and why. The business plan is one of the most important tools for developing a business. It forces careful thinking, encourages discipline, forges internal communication, and enhances coordination and clarity of purpose among managers and investors. Because it is the written document that outlines the venture and the amount of capital required, it is an ideal vehicle for securing any financial support that may be required. Once the business is operating, the plan provides management with a yardstick against which to define and measure progress.

A business plan differs from a feasibility study in its degree of detail. Where a feasibility study examines the key business categories in a broad sense, a business plan delves into the specifics of each category. For example, the section on promotion in a feasibility study would investigate and list various types of promotional activities that the business *might* undertake, whereas a business plan would provide specific details about each activity it *will* undertake—the target market, time and event schedule, schedule of tasks, staff responsibility, anticipated expenses, and projected results.

One person can take responsibility for researching and writing the business plan, or several can participate in a team effort. In determining who should write the business plan, the three most important considerations are who has the requisite skills, the available time, and a clear understanding of the relationship and interplay between the business and the exempt mission of the organization. When a business venture involves different kinds of expertise in separate areas, it is not unusual to find various sections of a plan delegated to several people, each with a particular area of expertise. For example, it is common to find a financial manager writing the financial plan, a marketing manager writing the marketing plan, and an operations specialist writing the operating plan. This can work very well, provided that those involved in the process communicate with one another, make few assumptions, and ask questions in sufficient detail that all aspects of the business are considered. It is critical that all members of the research and writing team realize that their areas are interconnected and that most of what they decide will have a direct impact on the plans of the others.

Numerous books written for the private sector provide guidance to the novice in writing a business plan. Although the sequence and details may differ, most provide outlines for covering the same general categories. Writers need not conform to any one particular format, so long as the plan is comprehensive. The selection of a format should depend on the specific business involved and the most useful way in which to present it.

Fortunately, there are now a number of books on the market that were written specifically for nonprofit enterprise. These are particularly useful because they contain several sections that are not typically found in traditional business plans. They include a description of the mission of the nonprofit, its purpose and goals in business venturing, and the operational, financial, and legal relationships between the nonprofit and the new business venture (see Massarsky, 1988, and a searchable annotated bibliography at http://www.ventures.yale .edu/bibliography.asp).

A table of contents for a nonprofit enterprise might look something like this:

I. Executive Summary
II. Description of the Business (including a mission statement)
III. Industry and Market Analysis
IV. Marketing Plan
V. Management Plan
VI. Operations Plan
VII. Financial Plan for the Business Venture (including legal structure, relationship to the nonprofit parent, and performance measurement or milestones)
VIII. Risk Assessment and Contingency Plan
IX. Appendix (supporting documents)

Step 7: Seek Capitalization

In step 7, the nonprofit seeks any capitalization required for its new venture. It is rare to find a nonprofit organization that does not need some financial assistance in capitalizing its business, although depending on the extent of the need, some may be fortunate enough to have some of their own monies available. There are a number of sources of capital for nonprofit business venturing, although the appropriateness of each source depends, in part, on the legal structure of the business. If your business is to remain a part of your nonprofit organization, that is, as a program within your nonprofit, you can solicit funds from outside sources in the form of grants, gifts, and donations and can also borrow funds (obtain loans) from banks and others. If you spin off the business as a for-profit subsidiary, you may also raise funds through the sale of equity in the business. This is not possible with a nonprofit corporation, since it is illegal for a nonprofit to offer an equity position. Both types of legal forms, however, have access to venture capital, bank or insurance company loans, loans from social lenders, joint-venture financing (nonequity for the nonprofit), loans or credit from suppliers or vendors, and program-related investments, which are favorable-term, low-interest loans made by foundations for social purposes. Other new approaches to securing financial support include syndicated funding, revolving lines of credit, and revolving loan funds collateralized on future receivables.

Depending on need, nonprofits can try to secure funding at various times during the life cycle of their business. Typically, there are four stages in the business life cycle: the conceptual stage, the development stage, the growth stage, and the mature stage. Obviously, the type of capital that you might need will differ with each stage, as will the source. At the conceptual stage, it is difficult to obtain either debt or equity capital. At this point, most nonprofits subsidize their business ventures themselves or seek foundation, corporate, or government grants to conduct feasibility studies.

At the development stage, equity capital is easier to obtain, but a significant amount of ownership might have to be given up. Debt is harder to secure at this stage unless the borrower is willing to pay high rates and relinquish some management control. As in the conceptual stage, grant monies are still available here. At the growth stage, it is easiest to obtain both equity and debt capital, provided there is strong evidence that growth will continue, and grant monies are harder to come by. At the mature stage, the business is less attractive to equity investors and grantors but most attractive to lenders. As mentioned earlier in this chapter, a significant number of nonprofits have entered business plan competitions with the goal of securing prize money to seed their businesses. Although the odds of winning are not the best, many say that the process of entering a competition and the business planning and discipline required can have other benefits as well, such as improving the overall management and diligence of the parent organization.

One of the first questions that a lender or investor will ask is what type of financing is needed. To such parties, the purpose of the loan, the availability of collateral, the probability of repayment, and the amount of time it will take to recover the loan or investment are of primary concern. In structuring a capitalization plan, you must determine the answers to these questions, regardless of whether you seek seed capital (to conduct a feasibility study or provide for start-up expenses), cash flow financing (to cover expenses in anticipation of revenues), bridge financing (usually in the form of a loan), mortgage or permanent financing (usually long-term and for real property), construction or equipment financing, or working capital financing (as through a line of credit).

Having a good understanding of capital sources and the logic of lenders and investors can make the difference between capitalizing a business and not. It is critical that your nonprofit understand that unlike some grantmaking organizations, investors and lenders will not provide assistance simply on the virtues of an organization or cause. In fact, they may be more scrupulous in their analysis because the request comes from a nonprofit organization. Nothing takes the place of (1) a well-researched, well-written business plan that takes every contingency into account and (2) the presence of an articulate and well-informed negotiating team. Although it is certainly advisable to leverage any financial commitment you might receive, your nonprofit is advised not to proceed with business operations or commit the business in any way until funds are in hand.

LESSONS LEARNED FROM SUCCESS AND FAILURE

In spite of all the new developments in nonprofit enterprise, some things about revenue generation have not changed. Many nonprofit organizations have succeeded in creating and sustaining business ventures—particularly the ones that have carried out the proper market research and proceeded in a serious, formal, and calculated way—while others have not. Here are a few of the lessons learned by this new breed of entrepreneur:

1. **Nonprofit enterprise is not for everyone.**

This statement is crystal clear, perhaps now more than ever before. In spite of all the interest, all the literature on the subject, and all the training in business planning, nonprofit enterprise is just not right for every organization. Designing and running a business is complicated, particularly for an organization that is not used to thinking about how much money its "customers" are willing to spend for a product or service or paying attention to whether or not it turns a profit. Nonprofit enterprise involves operating with a different mind-set, one in which you feel very comfortable mixing mission and money, perhaps paying higher wages to enterprise personnel than to program staff, taking on greater risk, and recognizing and accepting that you might fail. Now that the sector has logged in some valid experience in revenue generation, if you're thinking about nonprofit enterprise, it behooves you to determine if this practice is right for your organization, and before proceeding, make certain that you sit down with your staff, board, and key influencers to hash out the tough questions and make certain you have their full commitment and support.

2. **There is no substitute for analyzing your marketable assets and conducting thorough research and planning for your business.**

History has shown that running a business that plays off the strengths of an organization's assets is more likely to succeed than one that does not. It is critical that a nonprofit lay a strong foundation by taking the time to find an excellent match between what it knows or does well and what people are willing to pay for. Nonprofit leadership must make certain that it doesn't begin business operations before it researches the market and tests all the angles, because this may be a prescription for disaster that can come not only in the form of lost dollars but lost reputation and goodwill as well. There is also no substitute for writing a business plan, because in putting its business intentions on paper, the venture team is forced to conduct appropriate due diligence and the nonprofit parent to demonstrate a solid commitment to the enterprise.

3. Develop a market-driven, full-cost pricing strategy.

Develop a market-driven strategy that responds to what customers want and are willing to pay for—not what you think they need and you are willing to provide. Develop a full-cost pricing strategy—don't price your product or service the way you price your programs. Remember that your business will be operating in the commercial arena alongside other businesses and competitors that will not care about the good works of your nonprofit parent. And in spite of the value you believe your nonprofit brings to its product or service, the ultimate test is whether or not consumers are going to buy it in sufficient quantities to allow your business to meet its goals, thrive, and grow.

4. Strong management is the first of the two most important keys to success.

Most people, particularly those who invest in small business, will say that this will never change. Investors who consider making a loan to, or taking an equity position in, a private sector concern look at the quality of the people who will run the business. In fact, some pay little attention to anything else, because they believe that management expertise will make or break most businesses. Many experts in nonprofit enterprise will tell you that transferring dedicated but unqualified staff from the nonprofit parent to the nonprofit enterprise or sharing staff between the two is generally not the best way to go. They preach that there is no substitute for engaging management with the expertise and track record to make the business a success. It's fine to look for people who are sensitive to the work your nonprofit does, but make certain that you hire management and personnel who have the knowledge and experience to run the business, and be prepared to pay them market rates, even if their salaries are higher than those of the staff at your nonprofit.

5. Acquiring sufficient capital is the second of the two most important keys to success.

It is also very risky to move from the planning to the implementation stage before having acquired sufficient capital to run the business. Don't begin business operations if you are not fully capitalized. Without the assurance that funds will be available when needed, a nonprofit enterprise runs the risk of falling into a hole from which it may never emerge. For decades, nonprofit organizations have learned to manage without knowing for certain, year by year, if grantors will fully fund their programs. But nonprofit enterprise cannot work that way and survive, even in the short term. If the main purpose of going into business in the first place is to drive back revenue to the nonprofit parent, it's antithetical for the parent to operate a business that constantly requires an infusion of capital to keep it going. If the purpose of going into business is to employ the clients of the parent nonprofit and to drive revenue to its coffers, then although the venture may be partially subsidized with grant money, it still needs to ensure that it has the necessary capitalization to keep it afloat.

6. Borrow some key marketing strategies that are used in the private sector.

One strategy is to presell and sell wholesale, as opposed to retail, whenever possible. That is, instead of making a large number of sales of a very small number of units to buyers who are purchasing for their own use, make a smaller number of very large sales at a wholesale price to intermediaries, such as distributors, who can then resell your product or service to their customers. Another win-win strategy is to cross-market your products or services, using every opportunity to market your wares—for example, by putting notices about your new business in your organization's newsletter and brochures in your direct mail fundraising appeals.

7. Think through each step in operating your business, yet expect to adapt to changes in your organization and in the marketplace.

Create an action plan that delineates each task, the person responsible, the budget, and so on, as well as a calendar with sufficient time to cover the various stages of concept, development, and start-up. Rushing to begin before key components are in place can lead to failure. Think about the risks associated with your business, and formulate practical contingency plans for various scenarios—loss of key managers, weaker sales than expected, higher expenses than expected, increased competition, stronger sales than expected and insufficient capacity to fulfill, and so on. In conducting a risk assessment, you may find that you can institute changes to mitigate some of the risks so that they do not occur, but at the very least, you will have a plan for dealing with them successfully if they do.

SUMMARY

During the past decade, nonprofit organizations have begun to view business venturing as a viable way to obtain revenue to support program budgets. Many have experimented and succeeded in creating businesses that offer various products and services to the public and have coventured with the private sector in cause-related marketing campaigns and licensing agreements.

Although many nonprofits are eager to plunge into earning income, they should not do so without thoroughly exploring the risks and returns associated with business venturing. Creating successful enterprise is hard work. It is not for everyone, and it is not a quick fix.

Before beginning to think about specific businesses, a nonprofit is advised to take a critical look at whether nonprofit enterprise is compatible with its organization's culture and mission. A nonprofit should explore how earning income will fit into the overall structure of the organization, and it should secure the support of staff and other key constituents.

When these issues and answers are resolved satisfactorily, a nonprofit can move on to conducting an organizational audit, examining and accounting for all the assets of the organization in order to pinpoint its strengths and weaknesses. Once it has determined that it is ready for earned income venturing and has listed its assets, the nonprofit can begin to brainstorm ideas—to find connections between what it has to offer and potential businesses with which it feels comfortable.

Next, the nonprofit takes the list of potential businesses from the brainstorming session, selects two or three on which to conduct feasibility studies, and designates a project leader or champion to shepherd the process. The extensive investigation and analysis explores the marketplace and develops a marketing strategy, operating plan, financial plan, and legal structure for each business contemplated. With the selection of the most promising venture and an organizational commitment secured once again, the nonprofit is able to develop its business plan and seek the capitalization required for start-up and ongoing operations.

References

Cause Marketing Forum. "2003 Cause Marketing Halo Award Winners" [http://www.causemarketingforum.com/page.asp?ID = 77]. 2003.

Heritage, W. H., Jr., and Orlebeke, T. "Legal and Tax Considerations," In S. M. Oster, C. W. Massarsky, and S. L. Beinhacker (eds.), *Generating and Sustaining Nonprofit Earned Income.* New York: Wiley, 2004.

Josephson, N. "American Express Raises Corporate Giving to Marketing Act." *Advertising Age,* 1984, *55*(4), 10–11.

Klineman, J. "New Zoo Chief Hopes to Lure More Humans to See the Animals." *Chronicle of Philanthropy,* Sept. 18, 2003, p. 34.

Massarsky, C. W. "Business Planning for Nonprofit Enterprise." In E. Skloot (ed.), *The Nonprofit Entrepreneur.* New York: Foundation Center, 1988.

Massarsky, C. W., and Beinhacker, S. L. "Enterprising Nonprofits: Revenue Generation in the Nonprofit Sector" [http://www.ventures.yale.edu/docs/Enterprising_Nonprofits.pdf]. 2002.

Working Assets. "More About the Working Assets Visa Credit Card" [http://www.workingassets.com/creditcard.cfm]. 2004.

CHAPTER NINETEEN

Financial Accounting and Financial Management

Robert N. Anthony
David W. Young

There are two types of accounting information. *Management accounting* deals with information that is useful to an organization's managers. *Financial accounting* deals with financial information published for use by parties outside the organization. This chapter focuses on financial accounting and extends the discussion to include several important financial management decisions that affect an organization's financial statements.

FINANCIAL ACCOUNTING

Financial accounting is guided by established rules.[1] There are three rule-making agencies in the United States. The Financial Accounting Standards Board (FASB) develops rules for businesses and nonprofit organizations. The Governmental Accounting Standards Board (GASB) develops rules for state and municipal organizations. The Federal Accounting Standards Advisory Board (FASAB) develops rules for federal agencies.

The principal reason for having rules is to provide comparability across organizations. Without the same rules for preparing financial statements, it would not be possible to compare the financial statements of one organization with those of another. Even with the best rules, however, the reports of two or more organizations cannot be exactly comparable since so much of what happens in them is too complicated to permit direct comparisons.

The Financial Accounting Statements

Most organizations publish three financial statements annually. One is a statement of the organization's status as of the last day of its fiscal year. The other two are statements of flows of financial amounts within the fiscal year: one on an accrual basis and one on a cash basis. In business entities, the status report is called the *balance sheet,* the accrual flow report is called the *income statement,* and the cash flow report is called the *statement of cash flows.* In nonprofit organizations, they have different titles, as will be described, but in general the differences are only in the labels for the items.

The Balance Sheet. The balance sheet has two sections. The upper (sometimes the left) section lists assets, which are the resources owned or controlled by the organization. The lower (sometimes the right) section lists the sources of the funds used to acquire these resources. The lower section contains both liabilities (the amounts obtained from nonowner sources) and equity (the amounts obtained from contributors of capital and from the organization's operations).

The totals of the two sections must balance; that is, assets must equal liabilities plus equity. There is no exception to this equality. If assets do not equal liabilities plus equity, there is something wrong with the organization's record keeping. At the same time, the equality does not mean that performance was good or bad; it simply is a fundamental characteristic of accounting.

The Income Statement. The income statement reports changes in equity during the accounting period. The bottom line, "Net income," is the difference between revenues and expenses. Revenues are amounts earned from the sale of goods and services, contributions for operating purposes, and certain gains relating to the sale of assets. Expenses are resources consumed during the period and certain losses.

Statement of Cash Flows. The statement of cash flows (SCF) reports the receipts and disbursements of cash. These flows are organized into three categories: operations, investing (generally the acquisition or sale of assets), and financing (generally the receipt or payment of loans, the receipt of capital contributions, or the payment of dividends).

The operations portion of the SCF can be prepared using either the " direct" or the "indirect" method. The direct method shows how much cash was collected from customers (as opposed to how much revenue was earned) and how much cash was paid out to suppliers and employees (as opposed to how much expense was incurred). The indirect method begins with organization's net income or loss and reconciles it to the change in cash.

The main advantage of the direct method is that relatively unsophisticated readers of financial statements find it intuitively more understandable than the indirect method. They can understand the idea of cash received from customers and cash paid to suppliers and employees, for example, whereas they typically have difficulty understanding the adjustments that are needed to reconcile net income with the change in cash under the indirect method.

The main advantage of the indirect method is that it allows readers to reconcile the organization's net income to the change in cash. That is, since the indirect method begins with net income and ends with the change in cash, the reasons for the difference between the two are readily apparent. The direct method does not include this reconciliation. It is perhaps because each method has some important advantages that many organizations prepare both rather than choosing one over the other.

Nonprofit Differences. There are only two fundamental differences between for-profit and nonprofit organizations. First, for-profit businesses have transactions with shareholders, whereas nonprofit organizations do not. Second, nonprofit organizations receive contributed capital, which businesses do not.

Important Concepts and Principles

Accounting rules are developed and promulgated by standards-setting bodies, such as the FASB. *Accounting concepts and principles,* by contrast, provide general guidance for determining the rules. Several of the most important concepts and principles are discussed here.

The Historical Concept. The amounts reported on the balance sheet are the amounts as of the end of the period. The income statement and statement of cash flows report the activities during the period; they are not estimates of future activities or future status or performance. Some estimates of future performance are necessary, but these are kept to a minimum.

Example: Accounts receivable is an asset that states the amounts customers *probably* will pay. The amount actually owed is reduced by an estimate of the portion that will not be collected, called an allowance for doubtful accounts. If the accountants did not make this reduction, the accounts receivable amount would overstate the actual asset.

The Monetary Concept. All the numbers on the financial statements are monetary. Without this common denominator, they could not be added or subtracted from one another. This point is obvious, but its significance sometimes is not recognized.

Example: The real assets of an organization include its skilled employees, its managerial capabilities, its reputation with the public, and the value of products being developed. These amounts are taken into account by analysts in judging the value of an organization, but they are not stated in the financial statements.

The Realization Principle. Revenue is recognized when goods are delivered to customers, when services are performed, or when contributions are made that are related to the period. Cash may be received either prior to or following the realization of revenue.

Example: The receipt of a grant to conduct a project in the future is not revenue in the period when it was received. Instead, it is a liability at the time of receipt. Its revenue will be realized in the period or periods when the associated work is done.

The Matching Principle Expenses are incurred in the period in which the related work is performed. In effect, they are "matched" to the revenue that was earned during the period. This does not mean that the expenses need to be equal to the revenue but rather that any expenses incurred in conjunction with the revenue that was realized must be included on the same income statement.

Example: Claims expense in a managed care organization must be matched against the premium revenue received during the period. In almost all managed care organizations, there are some claims that have been incurred but that have not yet been received by the organization at the time it prepares its financial statements. The matching concept requires that the accountants estimate the amount of claims incurred but not received and include this amount on the same income statement that contains the premium revenues.

Standards for Private Nonprofit Organizations

Until 1980, there were separate standards for four different types of private nonprofit organizations: colleges and universities, health care organizations, voluntary health and welfare organizations, and all others.[2] There were many inconsistencies among these standards. In 1980, the FASB accepted jurisdiction for all nonprofit organizations except governmental ones.

The important FASB standards are No. 93 ("Accounting for Depreciation"), No. 95 ("Statement of Cash Flows"), No. 116 ("Accounting for Contributions Received and Contributions Made"), No. 117 ("Financial Statements of Not-for-Profit Organizations"), and No. 124 ("Accounting for Certain Investments Held by Not-for-Profit Organizations"). These standards required radical changes in the accounting numbers developed using the earlier rules. Their requirements are discussed next.[3]

Transaction Classes. FASB Financial Accounting Standard No. 116 (FAS 116) requires that transactions in nonprofit organizations be reported in one of three classes: unrestricted, temporarily restricted, or permanently restricted. Unrestricted items are resource inflows that can be used for any purpose; that is, they are not legally restricted. Expenses of the period are also unrestricted. The other two classes include donations to the organization. A temporarily restricted donation, as the name implies, is for use in a specified future period or for a specific purpose, such as a donation for a new building. Permanently restricted donations—often called *endowments*—last forever. They include major financial contributions (usually $1 million or more), works of art and other museum objects, and other long-lived assets. Temporarily and permanently restricted donations are always maintained as specified by the donor; that is, they cannot later be moved from one class to another except with permission from the donor. Nonprofit organizations keep detailed accounting records of the purposes for which each of these donations was made, and the published financial statements are a summary of these detailed records.

Financial Statement Presentation. FAS 116 and 117 require organizations to publish a *statement of activities* that shows separately the inflows and outflows for each of the three classes during the accounting period. Inflows to all three classes are called *revenues.* Outflows are called *expenses* and are reported in the unrestricted class only. Exhibit 19.1 is a sample statement of activities that abides by the new rules. Note that it includes an operating (income) statement in the unrestricted class. FAS 116 permits organizations to report an operating statement within the statement of activities but not as a separate statement.[4]

FAS 117 requires nonprofit organizations to prepare a balance sheet that shows the assets, liabilities, and equity for the organization as a whole—that is, without showing the details of each class separately. The equity section of the balance sheet reports each class's "net assets" (or equity), however, as is shown in Exhibit 19.2. Each is discussed here.

Permanently Restricted Net Assets. This class contains any amounts whose use the donor has restricted permanently and any fixed assets that do not depreciate, such as land and most art and museum objects.

Unless the donor specifies that the gift of art or a museum object can be sold and the proceeds used for operating purposes, the contribution is reported in the permanently restricted class. The amount reported on the balance sheet is the fair market value of the asset at the time of the contribution. The asset is not depreciated unless it has a limited life, which would be unusual. The donor may permit the organization to sell the object and reinvest the proceeds in similar assets, but this is not the same as allowing the proceeds to be used for operating purposes.

Temporarily Restricted Net Assets. As indicated previously, this class is used when donors place temporary restrictions on the way an organization may use their contributions. This class includes *term endowments* (endowments that are used up within a time period specified by the donor, which may span several years), *annuities* (contributions that provide a return to the contributor for a period of several years and then revert to the nonprofit organization), advance payments for work to be performed in future years, and any donated fixed assets (unless the organization selects the alternative of including them in the unrestricted fund).

Unrestricted Net Assets. This class includes all equity that is not restricted by the donor. It therefore includes equity items related to the regular operations of the organization. It also includes contributions intended for purposes other than ongoing operations that were not legally restricted by the donor. Unless donors make their intentions clear, their contributions must be included in the unrestricted category.

Unrestricted Revenues and Expenses. Several types of revenues and expenses are unrestricted.

Revenues from Services. Revenues in nonprofit organizations should be recognized in accordance with the realization concept, just as in business entities. Fees charged to patients in a community health center, for example, are revenues of the period in which the patient received the center's services, even though this is not necessarily the same period in which the patient (or a third-party payer) was billed or when payment was actually received. The amount of revenue recognized is the amount that is highly likely to be received. If some patients are unlikely to pay their bills, the organization should include an estimate of bad debts. Similarly, if third-party payers disallow certain items on a bill, revenue is the amount billed less these "contractual allowances."[5]

Membership Dues. Some nonprofit organizations, such as industry or professional associations, have members who pay dues. These dues are revenues of the membership period, whether they are collected prior to (as is often the case), during, or after the period. If fees are not collected until after the period, the asset shown as *dues receivable* must be adjusted downward at the end of the period to allow for the amount that may not be received. If the collection of dues is fairly uncertain (as in an organization with high membership turnover), these dues are recorded as revenues only when cash is received.

Lifetime membership dues present a special problem. Conceptually, a part of the total should be recorded as revenue in each year of the member's expected life. As a practical matter, this calculation is complicated and requires

Exhibit 19.1. Sample Statement of Activities for Anderson College
for the Year Ended June 30, 2003, with Comparative Figures for 2002 (in thousands).

	Unrestricted	Temporarily Restricted	Permanently Restricted	Total 2003	Total 2002
Operating Activities					
Operating Revenues					
Tuition and fees	$20,064			$20,064	$18,291
Student aid	(4,340)			(4,340)	(3,873)
Net tuition and fees	15,724			15,724	14,418
Contributions	983			983	989
Endowment used for operations	2,498			2,498	2,242
Other investment income	462			462	310
Auxiliary enterprises	6,793			6,793	6,455
Equity released from restrictions	1,292			1,292	1,000
Other revenue	457			457	450
Total operating revenues	28,209			28,209	25,864
Expenses					
Instruction and research	10,477			10,477	9,740
Academic support	2,622			2,622	2,386
Student services	4,667			4,667	4,341
Institutional support	3,510			3,510	3,282
Auxiliary enterprises	6,237			6,237	5,856
Total operating expenses	27,513			27,513	25,605
Operating surplus	696			696	259

Nonoperating activities

Contributions	564	$4,087	$2,371	7,022	12,400
Investment income	766	2,042	146	2,954	2,484
Net realized and unrealized gains	3,473	6,650	1,068	11,191	9,399
Endowment used for operations			(2,498)	(2,498)	(2,242)
Other revenue		11	1	12	31
Capital campaign expenses	(333)			(333)	(349)
Investment expenses	(294)			(294)	(269)
Other expenses	(334)			(334)	(138)
Net change in annuity and life income funds		(867)	25	(842)	(391)
Equity released from restriction (Note 15)	10,472	(11,764)		(1,292)	(1,000)
Equity reclassified to permanently restricted	(876)	(99)	974	(1)	
Change in equity from nonoperating activities	13,438	60	2,087	15,585	19,925
Cumulative effect of change in accounting for land, buildings and equipment (Note 13)	(2,655)			(2,655)	
Total change in equity	11,479	60	2,087	13,626	20,184
Equity, beginning of year	65,796	14,962	35,715	116,473	96,289
Equity, end of year	$77,275	$15,022	$37,802	$130,099	$116,473

Exhibit 19.2. Sample Balance Sheet for Anderson College as of June 30, 2003 and 2002 (in thousands).

	2003	2002
Assets		
Cash and cash equivalents	$2,038	$1,664
Accrued income receivable	39	104
Accounts receivable	574	429
Funds held by trustee	664	561
Inventories	257	453
Prepaid expenses and deferred charges	354	345
Notes receivable	3,140	3,211
Pledges receivable and bequests in probate	6,775	7,403
Investments, endowment	78,140	67,783
Investments, annuity and life income funds	6,269	4,811
Investments, funds held in trust by others	5,048	4,687
Investments, other	4,126	3,550
Total investments	93,583	80,831
Land, buildings, and equipment (less allowance for depreciation of $10,194 in 2002 and $11,678 in 2001)	37,102	34,861
Total assets	$144,526	$129,862
Liabilities		
Accounts payable and accrued liabilities	$3,094	$2,204
Student deposits	664	898
Government advances for student loans	2,072	1,976
Annuity obligations	2,423	1,880
Bonds payable	5,925	6,303
Obligation under capital lease	77	128
Postretirement benefit obligation	172	
Total liabilities	14,427	13,389
Equity		
Unrestricted	77,275	65,796
Temporarily restricted	15,022	14,962
Permanently restricted	37,802	35,715
Total equity	130,099	116,473
Total liabilities and equity	$144,526	$129,862

considerable record keeping. Many organizations therefore take the simple solution of recording life memberships as revenues in the year received.

Pledges. In accordance with the basic revenue concept, pledges of support of
the current year's operating activities are revenues in the current year, even if
the cash is not received in that year. Unpaid pledges are adjusted downward to
allow for estimated uncollectible amounts, just as is done with other accounts
receivable. Some people argue that the basic revenue concept should not apply
to pledges because unlike accounts receivable, they are not legally enforceable
claims. Others maintain that it is so difficult to estimate the amount of uncollectible pledges that a revenue amount incorporating such an estimate is unreli-
able. Neither group would count unpaid pledges as revenues.[6]

Endowment Earnings. FAS 124 requires that the earnings on endowment, including increases in the fair market value of the investment principal (both
realized and unrealized), be reported in the unrestricted class. For some organizations, especially large universities, this results in a huge amount of unrestricted earnings, compared with the practice prior to FAS 124, in which they
transferred only a portion of the endowment earnings to the unrestricted class.

In effect, FAS 124 requires nonprofits to use the total return method to assess the earnings on their endowments. In the total return method, an organization computes the gain on its investments by summing its interest revenue,
dividend receipts, and the realized and unrealized gains on the fair market value
of its securities. This contrasts with using only interest revenue and dividend
receipts to calculate the gain on investments.

Although FAS 124 requires that the total earnings on a nonprofit's investments be recognized as unrestricted revenue, it does not require the organization to *spend* that amount in a given year. Indeed, although they may use the
total return method to measure the earnings on their investments, most nonprofits use only a fraction of that return for operations, that is, for spending purposes. To do so, they use a *spending rate.* The spending rate is usually about 5
or 6 percent of the average market value of the endowment, generally using a
moving average over a period of three to five years. The remainder of the total
return stays in the principal of the endowment (even though, under FAS 124, it
technically has been transferred to the unrestricted class).

There are two reasons for using a spending rate. First, if all endowment earnings were used for operating purposes, the purchasing power of the endowment
fund would decrease because of inflation. A spending rate of 6 percent assumes
that if there were no inflation, invested funds would earn 6 percent. Earnings
in excess of 6 percent are implicitly expected to approximate the rate of inflation and are added to the principal of the endowment fund to maintain its purchasing power. Second, the spending rate provides the organization's senior

management with a reasonably predictable flow of operating revenues for annual budgeting purposes.

Contributed Services. Volunteers donate their services to many nonprofit organizations. Although these services are valuable, they are recognized as revenues only if they (1) create or enhance nonfinancial assets, such as helping in the construction of a building, or (2) require specialized skills that the volunteers possess and that the organization would need to purchase in the absence of volunteers. When one of these conditions is met, the services are measured at the going wage rate. If it counts services as revenues, however, the organization also must report an equal amount as an expense, so there is no net effect on the bottom line.

Expenses. Nonprofit organizations report most expenses according to generally accepted accounting principles (GAAP) for businesses; that is, they record expenses when resources are consumed or otherwise used up. Some organizations do not follow this principle. For example, they report *purchases* of inventory as expenses. With minor supplies, the approach can be justified on grounds of materiality. Otherwise, the practice is inconsistent with GAAP. Similarly, some small nonprofits use a cash-basis accounting system; that is, they report cash disbursement and receipts rather than expenses and revenues. This also is not in accordance with GAAP, but in organizations that have small fixed assets and mostly cash transactions, the difference may not be great.

When fixed assets are sizable, there is a problem with the cash-based method. By definition, fixed assets provide service for several years after the organization has purchased them, and GAAP requires that depreciation be used to recognize the associated expenses in the year they provide service. If depreciation is not used, net income is understated in the year the asset is purchased and overstated in succeeding years. Nevertheless, some nonprofits do not depreciate their fixed assets, arguing that the practice of expensing an asset in the year of purchase is conservative. This is not consistent with GAAP.

Donated Long-Lived Assets. Donated long-lived assets are a special case. When an asset is donated, FAS 93 requires that it be recorded at its fair market value at the time it was received (even though its cost to the organization was zero) and depreciated over its useful life. Some organizations object to this requirement. They argue that because a fixed asset was donated, the organization did not—and never will—require the use of revenues to finance it. Therefore, the inclusion of a depreciation component as an expense item on the operating statement would result in understating the amount of income earned through operating activities. FAS 93 is based on the premise that fixed assets are used for operating purposes, and therefore omitting depreciation would understate the organization's real operating expense.

FAS 116 added a further complication to the accounting effort. For contributed long-lived assets or for assets acquired with contributed funds, an organization may take either of two approaches: (1) it may report the cost of the asset as unrestricted revenue in the year it is placed in service and depreciate this cost over the asset's useful life, or (2) it may report the asset as restricted initially and then report depreciation as an operating expense in each year of the asset's economic life while reporting an equal amount as revenue in each of those years. With the former approach, there will be a large positive impact on the organization's bottom line in the year of the asset's acquisition and small negative effects in each year of the asset's economic life. With the latter, there is no net effect on the bottom line from either acquisition or depreciation of the asset.

Equity. Although nonprofit organizations report assets and liabilities in essentially the same way as their for-profit counterparts, they report equity quite differently. Specifically, because nonprofit organizations have no investors, their balance sheets have no "paid-in capital" amount. Some nonprofits receive contributions, however, and many generate earnings from their operations, both of which increase equity. Since they are legally prohibited from paying dividends, equity ordinarily decreases only through operating losses. On some occasions, however, equity can also decrease through a reduction in the market value of the endowment fund's invested assets.

Contributed Capital. There are two general types of contributed capital: contributions for endowment and contributions for plant. As described earlier, only the earnings on the endowment or some fraction thereof are used for operating purposes; the principal is not used. Similarly, when a donor contributes money to acquire a building or other plant item, this contribution must be used for the specified purpose; it is not available to finance operating activities.

Standards for State and Local Governments

State and local governments collectively are the largest category of nonprofit organizations.[7] They are subject to a variety of external forces and political influences and therefore have difficult management control problems. Traditionally, they have used an accounting system called "fund accounting," a system that was designed to regulate spending. In this system, each type of activity is a separate fund with its own statement of financial status and statement of financial flows. Each fund was established by appropriated amounts from some other source. When the total additions were spent, no more could be spent.

Generally, in state and local governments, revenues are not directly related to services provided to clients. Although the person whose house is on fire is a client in one sense, the fire department's main function is to protect the whole community. Specific programs proposed to state and local government agencies are often political in nature and frequently not subject to economic analysis. The objectives of these organizations are difficult to define in ways that permit measurement of attainment. What is "adequate" fire or police protection, for example, is inherently difficult to determine.

Because management control in state and local governments is so difficult, good accounting systems are especially necessary. With a few notable exceptions, such systems do not now exist in most government units. Tradition has greatly hampered the development of adequate systems. Many government units keep their accounts solely on a cash receipts and disbursements basis, for example, a practice that has been obsolete since the nineteenth century. Only recently has pressure for change begun to emerge—primarily due to public dissatisfaction with rising taxes and revelations of poor management. There are also pressures from the federal government to implement revenue-sharing programs. Moreover, the Governmental Accounting Standards Board has made substantial improvements in governmental accounting systems.

The GASB was established in 1979 to take a fresh look at the system that should be used for government accounting. During its first year, it issued a concepts statement that differs drastically from fund accounting. The statement contained two principal concepts: accountability and interperiod equity. *Accountability* meant that the organization should account for all its resources. *Interperiod equity* meant that the taxpayers in the current year should pay for all the resources used in that year; in other words, current taxpayers should not put the burden for this year's services on taxpayers in future years. (This general concept actually permitted averaging over several periods.)

In 1999, the GASB issued Statement No. 34, which described the required accounting system. This statement called for two sets of financial statements: (1) governmentwide statements that are similar to the financial statements used by businesses and (2) a set that is essentially the same as the fund-accounting statements.

Governmentwide Statements. The two primary governmentwide financial statements are called the *statement of net assets* and the *statement of activities.*

Statement of Net Assets. The statement of net assets is a "status" statement similar to a business balance sheet, with some modification to take into account the special conditions of some government assets. It contains information for all the units in the reporting government, such as a municipality. Like a business balance sheet, it has assets in one section and liabilities plus net assets in

another. *Net assets* means the same as equity in a business. The statement conforms to the equation *Assets = Liabilities + Net Assets*—just like a business
balance sheet.

There is one column for the primary government and another column for
component units, such as schools, parks and recreation, and cemeteries. There
is a third column for businesslike activities—activities financed by revenues
from services rendered, such as water, sewer, and electrical services.

The rules for reporting most assets are the same as those in business. Capital
assets (long-lived assets) are reported at cost less depreciation. If the asset was
donated, it is reported at its fair value as of the time of acquisition.

Capital assets that are stationary, that have an extremely long life, and that
meet certain other conditions are called *infrastructure assets* and are not depreciated. They include roads, bridges, tunnels, dams, and sewer systems.
Works of art and historical treasures are also reported at cost or fair value when
donated and are not depreciated.

Statement of Activities. The statement of activities reports revenues and expenses for the year. In general, the rules for recognition and measurement are
the same as those for the business income statement. There are special rules
for items unique to government, however, such as taxes and contributions.

Revenues and expenses are reported separately for principal government functions (public safety, public works, health, sanitation, and so on). They are also
reported separately for each business-type activity (such as water and sewer).

Revenues are defined approximately the same as in business—that is, they
are the inflows of resources from operating activities during the period. There
are specific definitions for revenues from taxation and for contributions. Expenses are reported at the cost of resources consumed during the period, as in
business. Extraordinary items—items that are unusual or that occur infrequently—are reported at the bottom of the statement of activities, as in business.

The controller general has audited these statements and as of 2003 refused
to state that they are in accordance with GAAP.

Fund Financial Statements. Governmental accounting systems consist of a
number of separate funds, each of which is a self-balancing set of accounts.
The general fund, which accounts for governmental operating transactions, and
enterprise funds, which account for businesslike activities, such as public utilities, are the principal funds. Many governmental organizations also have some
special-purpose funds.

General Fund. The items in the general fund are essentially the same items as
those in the government's operating budget and form the basis for controlling
the organization's operating activities.[8] In preparing this budget, the organization

generally estimates revenues from nontax sources and then computes taxes as the difference between them and total operating expenses.[9]

Revenues. Revenues are the amounts received from taxes, grants and contracts, fines, parking meters, and other sources. In cases where estimates are difficult or impossible to make, revenues are measured in terms of cash received during the period. This is true for a state's income tax revenue, where there is considerable difficulty estimating in advance the revenues that the taxes will generate, as well as for fines and other miscellaneous sources of revenue.

In general, however, revenues are measured by the accrual concept.[10] For example, property tax revenue is the amount of the tax applicable to the current period (not the period in which the bills were sent out, which frequently is an earlier period), less an allowance for uncollectable amounts. Similarly, the amount for grants and contracts is the revenue earned from the grant or contract work done during the period, not the amount of cash received during the period for new grants and contracts.[11]

Expenditures. Resource outflows reported in the general fund differ from those reported in business accounting in two respects: (1) they are expenditures rather than expenses,[12] and (2) they do not include noncurrent transactions. In the case of supplies, operations for the current period are charged with the cost of goods *received* during the period, rather than the goods that were *used.*

Pension costs and other postemployment benefits are special cases. Historically, they were treated as expenditures in the period when the payments were made, which was a much later period than when the expenses were incurred. This practice seriously understated the cost of operating government organizations, sometimes by millions or even billions of dollars. In 1996, for example, the District of Columbia had an unfunded pension benefit of $4.7 billion. These benefits are recorded in the period in which employees work and thereby become entitled to them. This change, implemented in 1998, makes government practice consistent with the private sector's treatment of these benefits.[13]

The current practice reflects the fact that governments tend to acquire major long-lived assets by borrowing an amount that is approximately equal to the asset's acquisition cost. Often the terms of a bond issue or other form of borrowing require that annual payments be made to retire the debt over the useful life of the assets acquired. The annual payments, called *debt service,* include both the interest on the amount of the loan outstanding and a portion of the principal. Under GAAP, interest on the loan is properly an expense of the period, but the principal payment is not.

If, however, the loan is for the full cost of the asset and the term of the loan and the economic life of the asset are about equal, each year's principal payment will approximate the annual amount of depreciation that otherwise would have been charged as an expense. Under these circumstances, treating principal as an expenditure will have roughly the same effect on the government's surplus as using depreciation. The validity of such treatment depends, of course, on how closely the principal payments come to the amount that would have been charged as depreciation.

In summary, general fund transactions are limited to revenues and expenditures that are strictly related to governmental activities. In addition, these transactions are limited to current items as contrasted with capital ones. All other activities are accounted for in some other fund.

Enterprise Funds. Some governments operate electric, gas, water, sewer, and other utilities or have other units that generate substantial amounts of revenue, such as a subway, toll bridge, lottery, or hospital. Accounting for these enterprise funds is basically the same as accounting for business entities. The bottom line on the operating statement for such a fund is equivalent to a business organization's net income.

An enterprise fund is one type of what are called proprietary funds. Another type is the *internal service fund,* which is used for governmental units that sell goods and services to other units; a maintenance garage is an example. In business accounting, the sale of these services is handled by direct charges to the organizational units that receive them, rather than by creating a separate fund.[14]

Other Funds. Separate funds are used for each type of resource inflow wherein spending is limited to a specified purpose. For example, a government does not account for the acquisition of capital assets in the general fund. Instead, it uses a *capital projects fund* for this purpose. Authorized capital expenditures are described in a capital budget. As noted earlier, *debt service funds* are used to record borrowing and the associated principal and interest payments. *Special revenue funds* record the revenues and related expenditures for work on projects that are not included in the general fund, such as the cost of building a road that is to be paid by the developer of the property. *Fiduciary funds* account for assets that the governmental unit holds as a trustee or agent for another party. Federal tax withholding amounts are an example.

Account Groups. In addition to funds, there are two account groups, one for fixed assets and the other for long-term debt. Because the transactions for these items are recorded in one of the funds just discussed, the account groups serve only as "memorandums" or single-entry groups. They do not appear on the balance sheet of the government organization.

Federal Government Accounting

Several commissions have recommended that the federal government shift its accounting system from a focus on obligations to a focus on expenses. Legislation to this effect was enacted in 1984, but nothing actually happened for several years thereafter.

Federal Accounting Standards Advisory Board. In 1990, the Federal Accounting Standards Advisory Board issued its first pronouncement. The FASAB consisted of executives from the three agencies that set rules for federal accounting: the Department of the Treasury, the General Accounting Office, and the Office of Management and Budget. The rules are applicable both to the overall financial statements of the federal government and to individual agencies. They therefore apply to financial accounting, as described earlier, and also to management accounting.

The FASAB requires three principal financial statements: a balance sheet, a statement of operations and changes in net position, and a statement of net cost.

The balance sheet reports assets, liabilities, and "net position" (equity). It does not by any means report all the assets owned by the government. The items omitted are described in a separate section of the financial report. Examples include more than 700 million acres of land used for forests, national parks, grazing areas, and wildlife refuges; "heritage assets," such as buildings of historical significance and battlefields; Social Security and retirement funds, for which the government is in effect a trustee; military and space hardware; and mineral resources located on the continental shelf. Although the balance sheet reports a negative net position, taking the omitted assets into account would surely make it a strong positive.

The statement of operations and net position is a form of the income statement; it includes revenues and expenses for the government as a whole. The statement of net cost reports costs for each major program.

In businesses, private nonprofit organizations, and governmental organizations, the single most important number on the financial statements is the difference between revenues and expenses for a period. This is the bottom line, called *net income (loss)* in a business and *surplus (deficit)* in other organizations.

This is not the case for the federal government as a whole. Instead, it can and usually does operate at a deficit. Within limits, there is no cause for concern, because of the government's unique power to print money.[15] The focus of financial accounting in the federal government as a whole, therefore, is not on the measurement of net income or its equivalent.

Management Accounting. The rules for the overall financial statements also apply to financial statements prepared by each government agency. The FASAB has published additional rules for these statements; for example, there is a section on cost accounting. Standards for businesses and nonprofit organizations do not go into this level of detail.

This generalization applies to the federal government as a whole. Individual agencies, however, may have quite different circumstances. Some, such as the Internal Revenue Service, generate tax revenues that are far greater than their expenses. Others, such as the United States Postal Service and the Tennessee Valley Authority, are essentially businesses whose expenses are financed by their revenues (and in some cases by a government subsidy). Most agencies have little or no revenue; their activities are financed by congressional appropriations.[16] Nevertheless, all agencies need an accounting system that measures and controls their expenses and, where relevant, measures and controls their revenues. In addition, the system must control capital expenditures in all agencies.

Because of these multiple needs, the federal government has two accounting systems. One, the *budgetary system,* provides the information used to prepare the budget and to control spending. The other, the *federal accounting system,* is in most respects similar to the accounting systems used by many private nonprofit organizations.

Budgetary System. The budget is the primary financial planning and control tool of the government. Government managers and members of Congress are interested mainly in financial reports that show how much an agency actually spent compared with what it was authorized to spend.

The rules for these reports are given in OMB Circular A-34. They differ in two respects from expenses as this term is used in the governmentwide system: in terms of (1) time and (2) the responsible party.

For example, a contract for widgets written by the contracting office at Meriden Supply Center in 2005 is an "obligation" of the center. If the widgets are used at the Clavis base in 2006, they are an expense in 2006 of the Clavis base. If a contract to paint a building is signed in 2005, it is an obligation in 2005. If the building is painted in 2006, it is an expense in 2006. An employee's pay is an obligation of the unit showing the employee on its payroll even if the employee actually works in another unit.

Expenses are a better measure than obligations of resources used. Expenses permit comparisons with a prior period, and they can often measure efficiency, that is, the cost per unit of work. Because of this, the budgetary accounting system—which reflects the "power of the purse"—is much more important than the federal accounting system.[17] It starts with appropriations, which are the authority that Congress grants to spending agencies. There are several types of appropriations, each requiring somewhat different accounting procedures.

Annual Appropriations. The operating activity of most agencies, including their authority to make certain types of grants and contracts, is financed by annual appropriations. An annual appropriation, sometimes called *budget authority,* is the authority to obligate funds during the fiscal year. An agency obligates funds by such activities as writing contracts and grants or hiring employees. Since agencies lose any annual appropriations that are not fully obligated by September 30, they tend to write many contracts and grants shortly before this date.[18] In business accounting, there is no counterpart to the obligation activity.

No-Year Appropriations. Appropriations for the acquisition of major items, such as buildings, ships, airplanes, and equipment, are "continuing" or "no-year" appropriations. They grant authority to spend a specified amount of money on the particular project rather than in a particular year. If a project turns out to be more costly than originally anticipated, either an additional appropriation is made or the project stops. Stories about cost overruns do not mean that more than the appropriated amount was spent on the project; they usually mean that the amount originally appropriated was too low and that additional appropriations were subsequently made.[19]

Entitlement Programs. Amounts spent for entitlement programs are governed by formulas set by Congress. These include Social Security, Medicare, Medicaid, and most subsidies. Agencies have the authority to spend whatever the formula permits, and the amounts set forth in the approved budget are estimates rather than ceilings that cannot be exceeded.

Cost Accounting. Government grants and contracts prescribe the types of costs that the government will reimburse for a given program. The recipients of these grants and contracts must keep records of costs incurred according to principles established by the granting agency, the Cost Accounting Standards Board (CASB), or the Office of Management and Budget (OMB) in the Executive Office of the President. The CASB, located in the Office of Federal Procurement Policy, publishes federal acquisition regulations, which prescribe detailed rules for all cost-type defense contracts and for many contracts made by other agencies.

Implementation. New federal accounting rules require substantial educational programs, for both accountants who must provide the information and, more important, users of the information. The federal system was required by law to be operational in 1997. The system did produce a financial report for 1997 and has done so for every year thereafter, but none of these reports have met the minimum requirements established by the American Institute of Certified Public Accountants.

The changes require new software programs, and the market for these programs is huge. Some developers for federal programs have invested more than $100 million each in developing the software.

Providing the necessary resources for the FASAB program is especially diffi-cult, but this program must compete with the budgetary program already in ex-istence, which has the power of the purse. It is highly unlikely that a satisfactory system will be implemented in the next few years.

FINANCIAL MANAGEMENT

The purpose of financial statement analysis is not to determine how well or poorly an organization has followed generally accepted accounting principles.[20] Nevertheless, prior to undertaking an analysis of a set of financial statements, it is important to identify any accounting issues that would affect the analysis.

Distinction Between Accounting and Financial Management Issues

The distinction between accounting and financial management issues, though frequently ignored, is extremely important. There is little use in calculating a current ratio in the normal fashion, for example, if there is evidence to suggest that the organization has misclassified either its current assets or its current li-abilities. Similarly, calculating a profit margin is of little value if the organiza-tion has some significant estimated expenses for which the estimate may be either unduly high or unduly low. In either case, the profit margin will be quite misleading. Similar problems can exist for other ratios as well.

Identifying Accounting Issues. An important step in the process of financial statement analysis, then, is to identify accounts on the balance sheet and the operating statement that might have misleading numbers. Frequently, these will be accounts whose totals are derived via estimates. The following accounts are candidates for having misleading numbers:

- Bad debts, contractual allowances, and the allowance for doubtful ac-counts. These accounts rely on estimates that will affect both the profit margin and the net accounts receivable figure.

- Inventory. Obsolescence, spoilage, or other forms of shrinkage may mean that the *salable* inventory is much less than the reported figure.

- Depreciation and accumulated depreciation, where choices about eco-nomic lives and residual values of fixed assets affect both accounts.

- Any asset where amortization is involved and where the amortization schedule can lead the book value for the asset to diverge considerably from its market value.

- Any other asset or liability account involving estimates, where the esti-mates affect both the surplus on the operating statement and the size of the asset or liability account on the balance sheet.

Example: An estimated expense on an operating statement that affects a liability account on the balance sheet is the expense associated with an insurance claim *incurred* during an accounting period but not yet received by the insurer. As discussed earlier, this is a typical account for a managed care organization or other health insurer, such as Blue Cross. Since the insurer has earned premium revenue during the accounting period, it must match the associated expenses to that revenue, one of which is the claims that have been incurred but not yet received. In this respect, the estimate of expenses for claims incurred but not received is quite similar to the estimate of bad debt expenses.

Notes to the Financial Statements. An important source of information concerning accounting estimates and their effects on the associated accounts is the notes to the financial statements. The notes are the means by which an organization's independent auditors describe some of the underlying detail in the financial statements, disclose important accounting policies, and identify any special or unusual accounting practices that the organization has followed in preparing its financial statements. The notes should be read with care since they provide an analyst with a reasonably good idea of the kinds of accounting problems and issues the organization faces and how they affect the financial statements.

Example: In a community mental health center, the notes might contain a description of the organization's different types of payers and the expectations for payment from each group. If an analyst were assessing the accounts receivable collection period for the center, he or she might see that there are some extended payment plans for certain clients. The analyst might also find that the percentage of the total that each third-party payer comprises had changed over time and would therefore expect to see the accounts receivable collection periods shifting in conjunction with the shift in payers.

Frequently, the notes give a fair amount of information about the organization's debt structure, which can facilitate an analysis of long-term solvency. They also explain the reasons for "extraordinary items," activities that occur outside an organization's normal course of operations and that affect its financial statements. For example, an expense associated with a major fire in an organization would affect its surplus (or deficit) from operations. But this would not be included as part of ordinary operations. Rather, it would be identified separately, listed below the surplus from operations, and discussed in the notes.

Making Adjustments. Once significant accounting issues have been identified, an analyst can take one of three actions: (1) adjust the accounts to provide more appropriate totals, (2) ignore the accounting issues, or (3) keep them in mind when drawing conclusions. The first is risky since it rarely is possible to obtain enough information to make appropriate adjustments. Even if it were possible to obtain the information, the analyst would then need to be consistent in comparing the resulting totals to prior years or to other organizations.

The second option would be appropriate if the accounting issues were relatively minor or if they affected accounts that were relatively unimportant in conducting the rest of the analysis. If this is not the case, then the third option is probably the most reasonable. That is, when ratios are calculated, the analyst would need to keep in mind that a more accurate accounting effort would result in slightly (or significantly) different ratio results.

Analytical Techniques

Having identified the significant accounting issues and having made any necessary adjustments to the financial statements, an analyst can then undertake an assessment of the organization's financial management. As indicated earlier, the distinction between accounting and financial management is an important one: the accounting issues relate to the *accuracy* of the figures on the financial statements, whereas financial management focuses on the *meaning* of those figures. Properly analyzed, with appropriate allowances made for any inaccuracies, the operating statement, balance sheet, and statement of cash flows can convey a great deal of information about an organization's operations and financial management.

In general, conducting an analysis of an organization's financial management requires undertaking ratio analysis, assessing the statement of cash flows, and relying on whatever other information is available. Each of these activities is discussed in this section.

Ratio Analysis. One technique used to assess an organization's financial management is ratio analysis, which focuses on mathematical comparisons between or among the accounts on a set of financial statements. Ratios allow an analyst to look at the relationships among various parts of a single statement, such as the balance sheet, or to look at the relationships between elements on two different statements, generally the statement of activities and the balance sheet. The *current ratio*—which examines the relationship between current assets and current liabilities—is an example of the former; the *return on assets ratio*—whereby the surplus (or increase in net assets from the statement of activities) is compared with assets (from the balance sheet)—is an example of the latter. For readers unfamiliar with ratio analysis, the Appendix to this chapter provides a brief description of the technique and discusses some of the more common ratios.

The principal purpose of ratio analysis is to allow us to look closely at four categories of financial management: profitability, liquidity, asset management, and long-term solvency. Indeed, although dozens of ratios can be used for purposes of analyzing a set of financial statements, most fall into one of these four categories. Some of the more important questions that ratios can help answer are discussed here, by category.

Profitability. An organization's profitability—its surplus or change in net assets on its operating statement—can be thought about along two dimensions:[21]

- How large was the surplus relative to revenue? Is this amount about right or too small?
- What were the returns on assets and equity? Are these about right, given the risks that the organization faces in doing business, or are they too low?

Liquidity. The issue of liquidity is essentially one of cash availability and use. Among the questions we might ask are the following:

- How well is the organization using its cash? Does it have enough cash on hand to meet its current obligations? Does it have too much cash sitting idle?
- How well is the organization managing its accounts receivable? Are collection periods too long? Are they lengthening?
- How well is the organization managing its inventory? Does it have too much, thereby tying up cash in an otherwise unproductive asset, or does it have too little inventory?

Asset Management. Assessing an organization's assets requires examining both the current and noncurrent sections of the left side of the balance sheet. The current sections were looked at under the heading of "Liquidity." With regard to noncurrent assets, several questions emerge:

- What is the nature of fixed assets? Are they appropriate to the organization's strategy?
- How well are assets being utilized? For example, how much revenue is being generated for every dollar of assets?
- How old are the fixed assets? Are they in need of replacement? If so, does the organization have funds available to replace them or plans in place to obtain the funds?

Long-Term Solvency. To determine if the organization has made good financing decisions and has thereby provided for its solvency over the long term, we must look at the right side of the balance sheet as well as the operating statement, attempting to answer the following sorts of questions:

- How well have current liabilities been managed? Will the organization be able to meet these obligations when they become due?
- How much long-term debt is there relative to the amount of equity? Is this about right? Is there too much debt, given the inherent riskiness of

the organization's operations? Could the organization take on more debt without jeopardizing its ability to repay both the new and existing debt?

Standards for Comparison. Although ratios can assist us in analyzing a set of financial statements, they do not provide all the answers. One important question that emerges in the use of ratios is the standard to which each ratio should be compared. For example, the current ratio should give us some indication of an organization's liquidity and can therefore assist us in assessing the way the organization is managing its current assets.

Suppose we calculate the current ratio and find that it is below 2.0, the customary norm. Is this too low? Are there circumstances that would make it acceptable? Is it possible that under some circumstances a ratio below 2.0 might be too high? Answering these questions requires that we have some standard for comparison. In general, three possible standards exist: industry, historical, and managerial.

Industry Standards. Industry standards are popular and can form an easy basis for assessing the quality of an organization's financial ratios. However, industry standards can also be misleading. Typically, we have several concerns when using industry standards. The first is whether the organization we are analyzing is truly a member of the industry for which the standards have been developed. For example, considerable work has been expended developing industry norms for hospitals, and yet within this so-called industry there may be a number of subindustries that are more relevant for analysis. There are teaching hospitals and community hospitals, rural hospitals and urban hospitals, investor-owned hospitals and nonprofit hospitals, hospitals in the Southwest and hospitals in the Northeast.

For a variety of reasons, including regulatory requirements and regional payment patterns by insurance companies, a hospital in a particular region of the country may, by necessity, have a ratio that diverges from the so-called norm. Certainly, we would expect the financial ratios for a nonprofit teaching hospital in an urban setting in the Northeast to be somewhat, if not considerably, different from those of an investor-owned, rural community hospital in the Southwest.

Second, industry norms have generally been derived from published data, and it is important to ascertain that the ratios for both the organization under analysis and the industry have been calculated in the same, or approximately the same, way. With some ratios, there is only one method of calculation, and there are no problems. With others, there may be several ways the ratio can be calculated, each of which is legitimate but each of which will produce slightly different results.

Finally, we must be certain that the ratios are for roughly the same time period. This is particularly important if there have been changes in the organization's environment or its strategy. In short, an industry norm is not necessarily the right level for a ratio, and managers should view industry norms with considerable skepticism.

Historical Standards. Historical standards avoid many of the problems associated with industry norms. Since they consist of ratios calculated over time for the same organization, there is no question that the industry is the same (unless the organization has had a major strategic shift and moved into a new industry). It is also quite easy to avoid the problem of calculating the ratios in different ways.

The weakness of historical ratios, of course, is that they have no external validation. For example, an organization's accounts receivable collection period may have remained at sixty days for a number of years, but management may be unaware of a technique that other similar organizations in the same industry are using to accelerate collections to, say, thirty days. Without some sort of external validation, management may continue to think that a sixty-day collection period is appropriate.

Managerial Standards. Industry ratios are not the only way an organization's management learns of practices in its industry. For example, consider again the situation in which a sixty-day collection period was thought to be reasonable when other organizations in the industry had achieved a thirty-day period. It should not be necessary to bring information of this sort to management's attention via an industry norm for an accounts receivable collection period. Managers generally engage in a variety of activities that make them aware of how other organizations in their industry are being managed. It would be a rare case indeed for the manager of an organization with a sixty-day collection period not to be aware of the fact that many other organizations in the same industry were achieving payment in thirty-days, even if no published industry data were available.

Because of the availability of external information, and because different organizations have different strategic objectives, an organization's senior management may establish certain standards that deviate from historical patterns but are consistent with its chosen strategic directions and its own sense of how the organization's balance sheet needs to be managed. It is even possible, of course, that where industry norms are available, management will decide that it wishes to deviate from these norms for one reason or another.

The Need for Judgment. In summary, the use of ratio analysis to make comparisons among similar organizations must be done with great care. Not all organizations, even those in the same industry, prepare their financial statements in the same way or incorporate the same information into accounts with similar names. Thus when ratios are used to compare two or more organizations, even if the ratios included in the comparison use very specific accounts on the financial statement, the results should be viewed with some skepticism.

Even when ratios are calculated historically for the same organization, however, changes in the organization's environment, strategy, or managerial tactics may invalidate the comparisons. In short, an external analyst must exercise considerable caution in interpreting an organization's ratios. About all the analyst can do is raise questions about the quality of the organization's profitability, liquidity, asset management, and long-term solvency decisions; it is difficult to be critical or judgmental without some understanding of the organization's environment, strategy, and overall management.

Role of the SCF. Apart from ratios, the statement of cash flows can be a very powerful tool for understanding the kinds of financing decisions that management has made during an accounting period, as well as for assessing management's ability to make effective and efficient use of the organization's assets. In particular, the SCF can be used to determine the extent to which an organization is financing itself appropriately (using short-term debt to finance its seasonal and other short-term needs and long-term debt and equity to finance its fixed assets).

Compiling Other Information. Many nonprofit organizations publish annual reports or promotional literature that provide descriptive information about their operations. This can be quite helpful to the analyst in determining the nature of the organization's activities, its environment, its strategy, and other matters relevant to the quality of its financial statements. Of course, if the analyst has an opportunity to interview the organization's management, he or she may be able to determine other factors that bear on the financial management decisions being made and the reasoning behind them. All of these factors are important ingredients in a thorough analysis of an organization's financial statements. Taken together, they give the analyst some indication of the organization's financial management goals and constraints and therefore some basis for identifying and analyzing the quality of management's performance in achieving these goals.

Two Fundamental Financial Management Issues

Beyond the use of ratios and a reliance on supplemental information, such as the SCF and the notes to the financial statements, an analyst also must have an understanding of some of the fundamental financing issues that almost all organizations face. Two of these issues in particular stand out as significant: leverage and the role of surplus. They relate to two questions that must be addressed in any good analysis of an organization's financial management: (1) How much debt (or leverage) is appropriate for this organization? and (2) How large a surplus (or change in net assets) must the organization have?

Leverage. Leverage is a subject of great concern to managers of many organizations. One measure of leverage is the ratio of assets to equity. Therefore, according to the basic accounting equation (*Assets* = *Liabilities* + *Equity*), if an organization had no debt whatsoever, its assets and equity would be equal. Its leverage ratio would therefore be 1. As an organization begins to rely on debt to finance its assets, the ratio increases. Exhibit 19.3 illustrates this phenomenon with a simple example, beginning with a balance sheet in which assets and equity are equal and moving to a situation in which total debt and equity are equal. As can be seen, the ratio increases to a level of 2.0 under these circumstances.

As Exhibit 19.3 shows, leverage allows an organization to finance more assets than would be possible if it relied only on its own equity. Note that equity has remained unchanged in this example while assets have doubled. In a very real sense, the organization is using its equity as a "lever" to obtain funds from outsiders and thus to expand its asset base. This, in turn, allows it to deliver more services (or to produce more goods) than would otherwise be possible and therefore to earn more revenue.

Drawbacks to Leverage. Leverage is not entirely free of drawbacks. Funds borrowed must be repaid, and generally there is an interest charge. Organizations that rely heavily on borrowed funds spend considerable time and effort pre-

---

Exhibit 19.3. Examples of Leverage.

Situation 1: No debt

Assets	Liabilities	Equity
1,000	0	1,000

Leverage = 1,000 ÷ 1,000 = 1.0

Situation 2: Debt of $500

Assets	Liabilities	Equity
1,500	500	1,000

Leverage = 1,500 ÷ 1,000 = 1.5

Situation 3: Debt of $1,000

Assets	Liabilities	Equity
2,000	1,000	1,000

Leverage = 2,000 ÷ 1,000 = 2.0

---

dicting and managing their cash flows so as to ensure themselves of sufficient cash on hand to meet their debt service obligations.

Financial Risk Versus Business Risk. One way to think about leverage is in terms of the *financial risk* it creates as compared with the organization's overall *business risk*. Financial risk and leverage are synonymous. That is, other things being equal, the higher an organization's leverage, the higher its debt service obligation and the greater the risk that the organization will be unable to meet this obligation.

Business risk, by contrast, refers to the certainty of an organization's annual cash flows. Specifically, organizations that have a relatively high business risk have a high degree of *uncertainty* about their cash flows. An example of an organization with high business risk is a social services agency that relies on one or two large government grants for much of its revenue. An example of an organization with low business risk is a child care center located in a neighborhood with many two-income families. The social services agency quite likely would face a great deal of uncertainty about its annual cash flows from one year to the next, whereas the child care center would operate in almost completely certainty.

The combined effect of financial and business risk is illustrated in Figure 19.1. As it suggests, other things being equal, an organization with low business risk can have a fairly high financial risk. Assuming that the organization does not take on more debt service obligations than its cash flow can support, the relative certainty of its annual cash flows gives it some reasonable assurance that it will be able to meet these obligations from one year to the next. By contrast, an organization with a high business risk would generally find it unwise to have high financial risk, that is, a great deal of leverage. Since debt service obligations remain constant from year to year, the organization could quite easily find itself in a situation where, because of events beyond its control, cash

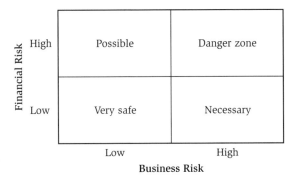

Figure 19.1. Business Risk Versus Financial Risk.

flows were not sufficient to meet these obligations. The result could be detrimental to the organization's continued existence as a financially viable entity.

The Role of Surplus. Economists frequently cite profit as the fundamental characteristic of capitalism. According to them, it motivates, measures success, and rewards. Indeed, economists see an adequate profit as a legitimate cost of operating an organization. It is excess profits (greater than a normal return) that provide an impetus for new organizations to enter a market. In the purely competitive model, excess profits entice new organizations to enter a market and increase the supply of goods and services. This goes on until prices fall to a level at which all organizations can earn a normal profit. At that point, the market is in *equilibrium*.

Surplus and Fixed Assets. Accountants and managers see profit somewhat differently from economists. In the first place, profit is simply the numerical difference between revenues and expenses. Second, in addition to providing a return to the owners of an organization, one of profit's principal purposes is to finance asset acquisitions. In fact, a basic financial management maxim is that an organization should finance its fixed assets with some combination of long-term debt and equity. For nonprofits, direct contributions by donors and retained earnings from operations are the sources of equity.

The financing role of profits is an important one. Museums, libraries, universities, hospitals, port authorities, and other institutions that must add to plant capacity, purchase new and more sophisticated equipment, or upgrade their facilities have large fixed-asset bases that require large amounts of financing. But even service and small nonprofit organizations, which must add office equipment, computers, and other small assets as they develop and grow, have financing needs. Moreover, any organization that wishes to remain in a steady state must provide for the replacement of assets, since inflation, however slight, effectively serves to erode an organization's asset base.

Organizations could avoid the need for profits (or surpluses) by relying exclusively on long-term debt. In general, however, this is not an adequate approach. Many organizations, for example, have increased their debt to the maximum prudent levels, where annual cash flows are about equal to debt service obligations. For these organizations, equity is the only additional source of funds.

Surplus and Growth. Independent of its need for fixed assets, an organization experiencing growth in its revenues also requires increasing amounts of cash. For example, because of the time lag inherent in collecting accounts receivable, an organization that is both growing and extending credit to its clients has an increasing amount of cash tied up in accounts receivable. Moreover, for organizations that require a sizable inventory, the time that passes between acquiring inventory and either selling or using it also requires cash.

The key idea is that an organization must finance the cash outflows that take place between the acquisition of inventory or the provision of service and the subsequent collection of accounts receivable. If managers of growing organizations use debt to finance these increases in inventory and receivables, the organization's indebtedness will continue to expand until growth slows or stops.

While a variety of financing or strategic options other than debt exist for a rapidly growing organization, the five that have the greatest impact are slowing growth, shortening the collection period for accounts receivable, shortening the inventory holding period, extending the period for paying accounts payable, or generating equity via either surplus or additional contributions. For managers to rely on debt—either long-term or short-term—instead of relying on one or more of these other options will ordinarily not suffice. The debt will not be repayable until management invokes one of the five options.

How Much Surplus Is Needed? Because these two uses of surplus—asset replacement and growth—are so different, managers need to take different approaches to assess how much surplus is sufficient for each. The first is related to the financing of fixed assets; the second concerns provision of adequate cash to cover the cash needs associated with growth.

Financing Fixed Assets. Most organizations, including many nonprofits, establish selling prices to provide for the desired amount of surplus so that retained earnings can help meet capital needs. The organization's price, then, becomes one element of the "profit formula," a formula that includes both volume and cost. Further, the required surplus level is generally related to the organization's desired return on equity (ROE).

ROE is closely related to another ratio of concern to managers: return on assets (ROA). Indeed, if an organization does not obtain a sufficiently high ROA, it will be unable to sustain itself over the long term. That is, as assets wear out or become technologically obsolete, management must replace them, and because of inflation, doing so requires more funds than depreciation provides.

One way of analyzing this problem is with a combination of several ratios, as demonstrated in Exhibit 19.4. The equations shown highlight some key managerial concerns. In particular, two important questions emerge from a careful analysis of the distinction between ROA and ROE: (1) Which is the preferable measure? and (2) How much is enough? The first question is not trivial. By using leverage, an organization can transform a low ROA into a high ROE. A high ROE, however, is no guarantee that assets can be replaced as they wear out. Indeed, if an organization is highly leveraged, and if managers wish to replace assets without a decline in ROE, they must maintain their organization's

Exhibit 19.4. A System of Ratios.

$$\frac{\text{Surplus}}{\text{Revenue}} \times \frac{\text{Revenue}}{\text{Assets}} = \frac{\text{Surplus}}{\text{Assets}}$$

Profit margin $\times$ Asset turnover $=$ Return on Assets (ROA)

$$\frac{\text{Surplus}}{\text{Assets}} \times \frac{\text{Assets}}{\text{Equity}} = \frac{\text{Surplus}}{\text{Equity}}$$

ROA $\times$ Leverage $=$ Return on Equity (ROE)

leverage at the initial level, but they often cannot either obtain more debt or refinance existing debt. As a result, it may not be possible to provide for asset replacement.

The second question can be answered by recognizing that other things being equal, in an inflationary economy, an ROA equivalent to the rate of inflation is necessary to replace assets as they wear out. Therefore, the desired ROA figure needs to be at least as high as the rate of inflation—and higher if the organization is expanding its asset base.

Once a desired ROA figure has been selected, it can be attained by using a variety of combinations of margin and asset turnover. In general, the easiest approach to take is to determine a reasonable asset turnover level—based on, say, past performance—and to use it, in conjunction with the desired ROA figure, to calculate the necessary profit margin percentage. This, in turn, can be used to set *desired* prices at an appropriate level above expenses. While market forces and third-party payers will clearly affect the prices an organization can actually charge, such an approach nevertheless provides a starting point. Moreover, it allows a manager to determine which services are priced below their desired level and therefore to better manage the needed cross-subsidization from other services.

Provision of Cash Needs. The need for cash arises from a combination of three factors: profit margin, changes in current assets (especially accounts receivable and inventory), and changes in current liabilities (especially accounts payable). Exhibit 19.5 illustrates why organizations need additional cash. The exhibit looks at a situation where there is no profit. It shows the resulting effect of growth on cash that arises *only* out of the time lag in collecting accounts receivable. Although additional cash requirements will result from the difference between the growth rate of remaining current assets and that of current liabilities, the most significant factor in many growing nonprofit organizations is generally accounts receivable.

As this exhibit indicates, under the assumed set of circumstances, there is a constant need for cash. As a result, if managers use debt to finance their cash

Exhibit 19.5. Cash Needs Associated with Growth.

Assumptions

1. Growth in revenue and expenses of approximately 2 percent a month.

2. Accounts receivable collection lag of two months.

3. Accounts payable paid immediately.

4. Inventory, prepaid expenses, and other current assets grow at same rate as revenue.

5. Current liabilities (other than payables) grow at same rate as inventory, prepaid expenses, and other current assets.

	Month					
	1	*2*	*3*	*4*	*5*	*6*
Operating statement						
Revenue	100	102	104	106	108	110
Expenses	100	102	104	106	108	110
Surplus	0	0	0	0	0	0
Cash flow						
Cash collections[a]	96	98	100	102	104	106
Cash payments[b]	100	102	104	106	108	110
Change in cash	(4)	(4)	(4)	(4)	(4)	(4)
Cumulative change	(4)	(8)	(12)	(16)	(20)	(24)

[a]From revenue earned two months ago that went into accounts receivable.
[b]Same as expenses due to assumptions 3, 4, and 5.

needs, they will not be able to repay the debt unless the growth rate slows or they take other measures (such as accelerating the collection of accounts receivable or delaying the payment of expenses) to lessen their need for cash. Therefore, under these circumstances, managers generally consider debt an undesirable alternative. As with the purchase and replacement of fixed assets, a surplus is needed. In the simplified example in Exhibit 19.5, a surplus figure equivalent to the "Change in cash" line would be satisfactory.

The Analytical Process

Most people develop their own process for analyzing a set of financial statements. Some begin by immediately calculating some ratios. Others begin with a careful reading of the notes to the financial statements. Regardless of the sequence of steps taken, three general categories of activities are necessary:

(1) assessment of the organization's strategy, (2) analysis of the significant accounting issues, and (3) analysis of the significant financial management issues. Each is discussed in turn.

Strategic Assessment. Understanding an organization's overall strategy is helpful if the analyst is to put the financial statements into a context. Doing so includes assessing the organization's environment and determining, for example, (1) the relevant competitive and regulatory forces, (2) the nature of the organization's clients or customers, and (3) possible changes in client needs in the future. In conducting this analysis, the analyst is typically attempting to answer two sets of questions:

- What are this organization's critical success factors? That is, what must the organization do well to succeed? How, if at all, will these factors show up on the financial statements?

- What are the important and tricky accounting issues for this organization? Does it need to estimate an expense for claims incurred but not received, for example? Does it have volatile accounts receivable, such that the bad-debt expense estimate is tricky?

Accounting Issues. In assessing the accounting issues the organization faces, many analysts focus on the notes to the financial statements. What accounting issues do the notes mention? How important do they seem? One fairly easy technique to use in assessing the importance of an accounting issue is to identify the relatively large numbers on the financial statements and then ask whether a change in accounting policies would affect any of these numbers in a significant way. For example, if accounts receivable comprise 50 percent of assets, the analyst would no doubt want to know about the process for estimating bad debts.

Clearly, there are gray areas, meaning that it is not possible to say with total certainty how one goes about determining significance. In general, however, the steps to follow are as follows:

1. Read the notes to the financial statements. What accounting issues do they suggest are present?

2. Look for the large numbers on the financial statements. Are any of them influenced by estimates? What do the notes say about the estimates?

3. Are any of the assets influenced by a distinction between book value and market value? What do the notes say about this distinction? What does intuition say? If, for example, the organization purchased a building in Beverly Hills, California, in 1970, the chances are good that the market value exceeds the book value.

4. How valid is the surplus figure? Was it based on real numbers or on estimates? For example, was there an estimate of bad debts, and if so, is any information available on its accuracy? If there is a depreciation expense, does it appear to be a reasonably accurate representation of the consumption of the associated assets?

5. What is the nature of the organization's liabilities? Are they truly obligations that must be repaid, or are they the result of higher-than-appropriate estimates? Have some liabilities, such as pensions, been underestimated such that there may be unanticipated drains on cash in the future?

Financial Management Issues. In assessing the significant financial management issues, many analysts conduct their investigation by using ratios, the SCF, and other information to support the analysis. A set of questions for each of the four ratio areas was given earlier in the text. Some further considerations are given here.

Profitability. Profitability analysis relies primarily on the set of ratios shown in Exhibit 19.4 and focuses on the following questions:

- How does this organization generate a surplus? Selling many units of relatively low-margin items, or selling a fewer units of relatively high-margin items?

- How do the ratios compare to the conclusions from the strategic analysis?

- Is the organization earning a sufficiently high return on assets to counteract the forces of inflation? If not, what steps has it taken to correct for the deficiencies? What else might be done?

Liquidity. Liquidity analysis relies on both the statement of cash flows and some liquidity ratios. Some questions are as follows:

- Is this organization generating cash from operations? If not, why not?

- What other sources of cash does the organization have? Are these likely to continue into the future? How have these other sources of cash been managed historically?

- What is the business risk of this organization? Are its cash flows fairly predictable and certain from year to year (low business risk), or is there considerable uncertainty (high business risk)?

Asset Management. Asset management analysis uses the investing portion of the statement of cash flows, two asset management ratios, and the accounts receivable and inventory turnover ratios. It attempts to answer the following questions:

- Does the asset turnover ratio seem about right for this organization, given its industry? For example, is this an industry with low profit margins where high asset turnover is key to success, and if so, how is this organization doing?

- How is the organization managing its current assets, particularly accounts receivable and inventory? Have these turnover rates been improving or worsening over the time period for which financial statements are available? Why?

Long-Term Solvency. Solvency analysis uses the financing portion of the statement of cash flows and some of the long-term solvency ratios. It focuses on the following questions:

- How has this organization structured its debt? Has it done a good job of matching the term of its debt to the life of its assets?

- How much leverage does this organization have? Does it have too much financial risk compared to its business risk (in other words, is it in the "danger zone" in Figure 19.1)?

- What kind of debt service coverage does the organization have? Is there a reasonable margin for safety given its business risk?

- What does an environmental assessment indicate about the future for this organization? Are any of the circumstances surrounding its business risk likely to change? If so, how will they affect it? What does this suggest for its debt?

SUMMARY

This chapter has provided an overview of some important aspects of financial accounting and financial management. With a few important exceptions, financial accounting is essentially the same for private nonprofit organizations as it is for for-profit companies. By contrast, financial accounting in state and local governments, as well as in the federal government, has some important differences.

An analysis of financial management consists of assessing the quality of an organization's financial statements—and thus its overall financial performance—through the use of ratio analysis, the statement of cash flows, and other related information. The SCF, although not always used as fully as it might be by analysts, provides some valuable insight into the way an organization has financed its activities over the course of the most recent accounting period.

Financing considerations inevitably result in the need to pay some attention to the issue of leverage and the advantages and risks of using debt. Indeed, one of the most important aspects of financial management is the management of debt, or leverage. Further, however, managers must be aware of the need to earn a sufficiently large surplus to provide for both asset replacement and the cash needs associated with growth, since to incur debt for these activities is to flirt with serious financial difficulties.

Appendix:
A Primer on Ratio Analysis

To understand ratio analysis and its use, one must recall that the asset side of the balance sheet contains those items that an organization owns or has claim to, while the liability and equity side shows how the assets were financed. Since the balance sheet is the result of all of the organization's historical financial activities viewed at a given point in time, it provides what might be thought of as the "long-run" view of an organization's asset acquisition and financing decisions.

This long-run view can be supplemented by an analysis of the statement of cash flows, which shows management's specific financing choices and activities over the course of a given accounting period (usually a year). Recall that the SCF gives specific information concerning the sources of funds during a year and the uses to which those funds were put. Thus by using the SCF, a reader of financial statements can determine the extent to which an organization acquired more fixed assets or current assets during a year and how those assets were financed (through, for example, operations, short-term debt, long-term debt, or annual contributions). Consequently, the SCF and the balance sheet together provide some indication of the financing decisions made by an organization's management, both over time and during the course of the most recent accounting period.

By contrast, the operating statement lets one look at the quality of the organization's *profitability* during a given accounting period. Ratios involving both the operating statement and the balance sheet can help us assess relationships among surplus, assets, and liabilities.

Role of Ratios

Imagine yourself with, say, $1,000 to invest in one of two companies, Company A or Company B. You are given the following information about each company:

	Company A	Company B
Profit last year	$100,000	$1,000,000
Current assets as of the end of last year	50,000	$500,000

In which company would you invest your $1,000? Is there any additional information from the financial statements you would like to have before making your decision?

Before answering the question, let's ask another question. Suppose you now were given the following information about the two companies:

	Company A	Company B
Shareholders' equity as of the end of the last year	$500,000	$100,000,000
Current liabilities as of the end of last year	25,000	$10,000,000

Would this make any difference in your investment decision? Why or why not?

In effect, the additional information has told us about two factors that might be of considerable importance to an investor: the relationship between profit and equity and the relationship between current assets and current liabilities. Each is important for different reasons. If, for example, you are interested in investing in a company that will earn the highest return possible on your $1,000, you would presumably prefer to have it invested in Company A, where profit is 20 percent of equity ($100,000 ÷ $500,000), rather than Company B, where profit is only 1 percent of equity ($1 million ÷ $100 million). Of course, these are the figures for last year only, and the future may be quite different from the past. Nevertheless, the notion of a return on investment would lead you in a quite different direction than simply looking at profit in isolation.

Similarly, if you are interested in investing in a company that can meet its current obligations when they come due, you would presumably be somewhat more concerned about Company B than Company A. That is, Company B has $10 million of liabilities that are current (will be due and payable sometime in the next year) and only $500,000 of current assets at the moment to provide the cash needed to meet those obligations. Company A, by contrast, while having only $50,000 in current assets, has only $25,000 in current liabilities. Thus it seems to have a comfortable margin of safety.

Clearly, there are many other factors you would consider in making an investment decision. The purpose of this example is only to illustrate that the absolute dollar amounts, by themselves, tell you relatively little about an organization's financial strength. Moreover, if we are to make comparisons of any sort—between two or more organizations or between different years of operations for the same organization—we must use something other than flat dollar amounts. Ratios allow us to do this. For a variety of reasons, many of which are discussed in the chapter text, even ratios have limitations, and we must move beyond them if we are to fully understand and analyze an organization's financial statements. Nevertheless, by permitting us to move beyond the absolute magnitude of the numbers on the financial statements to a *set of relationships between and among the numbers,* ratios can assist us greatly in the analytical effort.

Ratios can be classified into four categories for purposes of discussion: profitability, liquidity, asset management, and long-term solvency. Each is discussed here. Exhibit 19.6 summarizes the ratios and the items used in their computations.

Profitability Ratios

Profitability ratios attempt to measure the ability of an organization to generate sufficient funds from its operations to both sustain itself and, in the case of a for-profit entity, provide an acceptable return to its owners. The former aspect is important to both for-profit and nonprofit organizations. That is, over the long term, all organizations must generate enough funds from operations to allow them to (1) replace fixed assets as they wear out, (2) purchase new fixed assets as revenues grow, (3) service debt, and (4) provide for the cash needs associated with growth. Profitability ratios provide some partial evidence of how well an organization is satisfying these requirements.

Exhibit 19.6. Summary of Ratio Computations.

Profitability Ratios

$$\text{Profit margin} = \frac{\text{Surplus}}{\text{Operating revenues}}$$

$$\text{Return on assets} = \frac{\text{Surplus}}{\text{Total assets}}$$

$$\text{Return on equity} = \frac{\text{Surplus}}{\text{Equity}}$$

Liquidity Ratios

$$\text{Current ratio} = \frac{\text{Current assets}}{\text{Current liabilities}}$$

$$\text{Quick ratio} = \frac{\text{Cash + Marketable securities + Net accounts receivable}}{\text{Current liabilities}}$$

$$\text{Average days receivable} = \frac{\text{Net accounts receivable}}{\text{Revenue} \div 365}$$

$$\text{Average days inventory} = \frac{\text{Inventory}}{\text{Cost of goods sold} \div 365}$$

Asset Management Ratios

$$\text{Asset turnover} = \frac{\text{Revenue}}{\text{Total assets}}$$

$$\text{Fixed-asset turnover} = \frac{\text{Revenue}}{\text{Net fixed assets}}$$

Long-Term Solvency Ratios

$$\text{Debt-equity} = \frac{\text{Total liabilities}}{\text{Equity}}$$

$$\text{Leverage} = \frac{\text{Total assets}}{\text{Equity}}$$

$$\text{Long-term debt-equity} = \frac{\text{Noncurrent liabilities}}{\text{Equity}}$$

$$\text{Debt service coverage} = \frac{\text{Surplus + Depreciation + Interest payments}}{\text{Principal payments + Interest payments}}$$

$$\text{Times-interest-earned} = \frac{\text{Surplus + Interest payments}}{\text{Interest payments}}$$

Exhibit 19.6. Summary of Ratio Computations (continued).

Some Additional Ratios

$$\text{Gross margin percentage} = \frac{\text{Gross margin}}{\text{Sales revenues}}$$

$$\text{Earnings per share} = \frac{\text{Surplus} - \text{Dividends to preferred shareholders}}{\text{Average shares of common stock outstanding for the year}}$$

$$\text{Price-earnings ratio} = \frac{\text{Average market price of common stock}}{\text{Earnings per share}}$$

$$\text{Return on permanent capital} = \frac{\text{Surplus} + \text{Interest} + \text{Taxes}}{\text{Equity} + \text{Noncurrent liabilities}}$$

$$\text{EBIT margin} = \frac{\text{EBIT}}{\text{Sales revenues}}$$

$$\text{Capital turnover} = \frac{\text{Sales revenue}}{\text{Equity} + \text{Noncurrent liabilities}}$$

The first profitability measure is *profit margin.*

$$\text{Profit margin} = \frac{\text{Surplus}}{\text{Revenue}}$$

This ratio effectively measures how much of each dollar in revenue received by the organization ultimately becomes surplus. Profit margins tend to vary widely from one industry to the next. An organization in an industry with commoditylike product will tend to have a relatively low profit margin; it earns a surplus by having a high volume of sales relative to its assets. By contrast, an organization in an industry that is highly capital-intensive, such as a port authority, will tend to have a larger profit margin; its sales volume tends to be much lower relative to assets than, say, a museum.

A second profitability ratio is *return on assets.*

$$\text{Return on assets} = \frac{\text{Surplus}}{\text{Total assets}}$$

Since depreciation recognizes the expense associated with the using up of an asset, it is based on the historical cost of the asset and in no way compensates for the effects of inflation. Although there are a variety of other factors to consider with respect to the replacement of assets, the return-on-asset ratio provides at least a rudimentary indication of whether an organization—nonprofit or for-profit—is earning a sufficiently large excess of revenues over expenses to maintain itself in a steady state. Accordingly, one would hope to see a return-on-asset ratio that is at least as high as the rate of inflation in an organization's service area.

The final profitability measure is *return on equity.*

$$\text{Return on equity} = \frac{\text{Surplus}}{\text{Total equity}}$$

This ratio, abbreviated ROE (or sometimes ROI, for *return on investment*), is perhaps the most commonly used indicator of profitability. In the for-profit world, it allows investors or potential investors to compare the earnings on their investment in one organization with a variety of alternative uses (such as savings certificates or treasury notes) of the investment funds. It is of less value in the nonprofit world.

Liquidity Ratios

As the name implies, liquidity ratios measure the extent to which an organization has an ability to convert its noncash assets into cash (that is, to "liquidate" its assets). Liquidity ratios are generally computed with some portion of an organization's current assets, occasionally comparing them with its current liabilities. Recall that current assets are those assets that will be, or have a reasonable expectation to be, converted into cash within a year; current liabilities are those obligations that must be paid within a year. Consequently, the most commonly used liquidity ratio is the *current ratio.*

$$\text{Current ratio} = \frac{\text{Current assets}}{\text{Current liabilities}}$$

Although many considerations govern the appropriate size of this ratio for any given company, and there tend to be wide variations across industries, a figure of 2.0 is often used as an appropriate level. That is, current assets should be roughly twice as large as current liabilities.

A variety of other liquidity ratios can be computed to measure some portion of the current ratio. The most frequently used is the *quick ratio* (sometimes called the *acid-test ratio*).

$$\text{Quick ratio} = \frac{\text{Cash} + \text{Marketable securities} + \text{Net accounts receivable}}{\text{Current liabilities}}$$

The purpose of the quick ratio is to eliminate those current assets that for one reason or another may not be readily or fully convertible into cash. In particular, the quick ratio excludes inventory and prepaid expenses. If a quick ratio is below 1.0, it suggests that the organization may encounter some difficulties in meeting its current liabilities when they come due.

Although included in both the current and quick ratios, accounts receivable can frequently be a somewhat questionable asset. Both ratios attempt to compensate for this uncertainty by using a *net* accounts receivable figure (gross accounts receivable less the allowance for doubtful accounts). Nevertheless, more detail on accounts receivable is frequently helpful. A third liquidity ratio, *average days receivable,* allows us to make an assessment of how quickly, on average, an organization is collecting its accounts receivable.

$$\text{Average days receivable} = \frac{\text{Net accounts receivable}}{\text{Revenue} \div 365}$$

The denominator of this ratio gives us the average revenue earned per day (ideally using credit sales only). When this figure is divided into net accounts receivable, we have an estimate of the average number of days of revenue that are included in the net accounts receivable figure, which serves as a rough estimate of the average number days needed to collect an account receivable. This figure can be compared with the organization's payment policies to determine how well clients (or third parties on behalf of clients), on average, are abiding by the organization's payment expectations.

A final liquidity ratio is one that is comparable to the average days receivable ratio: *average days inventory.*

$$\text{Average days inventory} = \frac{\text{Inventory}}{\text{Cost of goods sold} \div 365}$$

As with revenue in the average days receivable ratio, cost of goods sold, divided by 365, gives the average cost of goods sold per day. When this is divided into inventory, the result is the average number of days that inventory remains on hand before being sold.

Most nonprofit organizations do not sell their inventory. Rather, they use up an inventory of supplies (such as office supplies) during the conduct of their business. In these cases, there will be no cost of goods sold figure. When this happens, total expenses (or better yet, total expenses less salaries and depreciation) can be used in place of cost of goods sold. Although some precision is lost, such a ratio, used in a comparative way over several years, may point up potential weaknesses in inventory management.

Asset Management Ratios

The average days receivable and average days inventory ratios lie at the intersection of liquidity and asset management, since they have aspects of each included in them. Asset management ratios help us assess how effectively an organization is using its assets (which include accounts receivable and inventory). In addition to average days receivable and average days inventory, a commonly used asset management ratio is *asset turnover.*

$$\text{Asset turnover} = \frac{\text{Revenue}}{\text{Total assets}}$$

This ratio allows us to determine how many dollars of revenue the organization has earned for each dollar it has invested in assets. Organizations that have an asset base consisting largely of accounts receivable and inventory would be expected to have a relatively high asset turnover; that is, each item in the asset base is used up and replaced many times a year, and revenue is earned each time an inventory item is sold and a new account receivable is created. By contrast, organizations with a high proportion of fixed assets, such as plant and equipment, would generally have a low asset turnover, since it takes several years for a fixed asset to be used up (via depreciation) and replaced.

If an organization is fairly capital-intensive, as is the case for a hospital, a university, or a port authority, a modified ratio may shed more light on the quality of its asset management; this is the *fixed-asset turnover ratio.*

$$\text{Fixed-asset turnover} = \frac{\text{Revenue}}{\text{Net fixed assets}}$$

In a rough sense, this ratio permits us to assess the relative productivity of new plant and equipment, compared to plant and equipment assets that are highly depreciated. One would expect that as assets depreciated (and hence as *net* fixed assets fell), the ability of those assets to earn revenue would also fall. The magnitude of this fall can be assessed by use of this ratio. A comparison might be made to the organization's past performance (when the assets were newer), for example, or to other organizations with relatively new assets.

Long-Term Solvency Ratios

Long-term solvency ratios provide an indication of the way an organization has financed its assets over the long term (the period extending beyond one year). Generally, two issues are of concern here. First is the balance between debt and equity financing. Debt consists of loans, mortgages, bonds, and similar instruments; equity financing consists of contributions and retained earnings. Second is the ability of the organization to meet its debt obligations.

In looking at the balance between debt and equity, the most commonly used ratio is the *debt-equity ratio.*

$$\text{Debt-equity} = \frac{\text{Total liabilities}}{\text{Equity}}$$

The higher this ratio, the greater the organization's "leverage," that is, the more it has used external funds (debt) to supplement its internal funds (equity).

Several other measures of leverage exist. One of the most common is *leverage,* obtained by dividing total assets by equity.

$$\text{Leverage} = \frac{\text{Total assets}}{\text{Equity}}$$

Effectively, this ratio is the same as the debt-equity ratio plus 1.[22]

Because of the need to make both short- and long-term assessments, analysts frequently distinguish between short- and long-term debt (that is, between current and long-term liabilities). This gives rise to a modified—and more frequently used—version of the debt-equity ratio: the *long-term debt-equity ratio.*

$$\text{Long-term debt-equity} = \frac{\text{Noncurrent liabilities}}{\text{Equity}}$$

Looked at over time, this ratio can reveal the extent to which an organization is relying increasingly on long-term debt to finance asset acquisition.

As indicated earlier, debt—either long- or short-term—gives rise to a debt service obligation, consisting of the payment of both principal and interest. An organization's ability to meet its debt service obligation in a timely way can be measured by a ratio called *debt service coverage.*

$$\text{Debt service coverage} = \frac{\text{Surplus} + \text{Depreciation} + \text{Interest payments}}{\text{Principal payments} + \text{Interest payments}}$$

The numerator of this ratio is a rough estimate of the cash available to meet debt service obligations; the denominator is the debt service obligation itself. Depreciation is included in the numerator because it is a noncash expense (for the same reason, we add it back to surplus when preparing the SCF). Interest payments are included because we want to determine the funds available to meet principal *and* interest payments, and surplus measures the funds left *after* interest payments have been made; therefore, we must add interest payments back. Thus the ratio provides some indication of the extent to which the debt service obligation is covered by available cash, subject, of course, to the caveat that not all of the surplus is available in cash.

Because principal payment amounts are frequently not known to individuals outside an organization (although they can usually be found on the SCF), a surrogate ratio, called *times-interest-earned,* is occasionally used by outside analysts in lieu of debt service coverage.

$$\text{Times-interest-earned} = \frac{\text{Surplus} + \text{Interest payments}}{\text{Interest payments}}$$

Since it does not include the principal payments on the debt, this ratio can be a misleading measure of an organization's ability to meet its debt service obligations. To illustrate this phenomenon, consider the following situation:

Surplus (*S*)	$20
Depreciation (*D*)	5
Interest (*I*)	2
Principal payment (*P*)	8

Under these circumstances, the organization's debt service coverage ratio is 2.7:

$$\frac{S + D + I}{P + I} = \frac{27}{10} = 2.7$$

Its times-interest-earned ratio, by contrast, is 11.0:

$$\frac{S + I}{I} = \frac{22}{2} = 11.0$$

Thus even though the organization has earned enough cash to cover its interest payment eleven times, it can cover its *debt service* obligation only about three times. Since *all* debt service payments must be made (not just interest), this discrepancy can be of some concern.

From a cash management perspective, we are most interested in debt service coverage. Yet unless we have information on principal payments (which we frequently do not), we cannot calculate the debt service coverage ratio. However, as the example suggests, to calculate only the times-interest-earned ratio could give a misleading sense of comfort about the organization's ability to meet its debt service obligations.

Even when the debt service ratio is used, we must bear in mind that most organizations have many more cash obligations than debt service. It is therefore extremely important that the debt service coverage ratio (or the times-interest-earned ratio) be analyzed in the context of other related ratios, notably those relating to liquidity.

Some Additional Ratios

As indicated previously, there are many other ratios that could be calculated. For completeness, several of these are discussed next. Interested readers can find more information on ratio calculations and ratio analysis in books dedicated specifically to those topics.[23]

$$\text{Gross margin percentage} = \frac{\text{Gross margin}}{\text{Sales revenues}}$$

This is a variation on profit margin, looking only at sales revenue and only at gross margin, which is sales revenue minus the cost of goods sold. It is a measure of profitability before the inclusion of operating expenses, sales and administrative expenses, interest, and taxes.

$$\text{Earnings per share} = \frac{\text{Surplus} - \text{Dividends to preferred shareholders}}{\text{Average shares of common stock outstanding for the year}}$$

$$\text{Price-earnings ratio} = \frac{\text{Average market price of common stock}}{\text{Earnings per share}}$$

Earnings per share computations are required on the operating statements of all publicly traded for-profit companies. The price-earnings ratio is used frequently by the investment community to judge whether a stock price is appropriate in light of a company's earnings. Neither of these is appropriate for a nonprofit organization.

$$\text{Return on permanent capital} = \frac{\text{Surplus} + \text{Interest} + \text{Taxes}}{\text{Equity} + \text{Noncurrent liabilities}}$$

This ratio is a variation on return on equity. It, like return on equity, sometimes is called ROI. Recall that permanent capital is defined as equity plus long-term debt (or noncurrent liabilities). Therefore, this ratio measures the earnings on all sources of long-term financing (debt and equity). It also does so before taxes and interest are deducted. Interest is added back because we are interested in the return on debt capital as well as equity capital. Therefore, we must include the earnings before the interest payment (the cost of the debt capital). For for-profit organizations, adding back taxes allows us to look at how well the company performed despite its particular tax situation.

The numerator of this ratio is frequently is called *earnings before interest and taxes,* or EBIT. The acronym EBIT is used quite frequently in finance and by the investment community.

$$\text{EBIT margin} = \frac{\text{EBIT}}{\text{Sales revenues}}$$

This is another variation on profit margin, using EBIT instead of surplus. Again, however, its use for nonprofit organizations is limited.

$$\text{Capital turnover} = \frac{\text{Sales revenue}}{\text{Equity} + \text{Noncurrent liabilities}}$$

This ratio is a variation on asset turnover, but it uses only permanent capital (equity and noncurrent liabilities) instead of total assets.

A Disclaimer

There is no general agreement that the four categories of ratios discussed in this chapter are the most appropriate ones. In addition, some writers and analysts would classify some of the ratios into categories differently than is done here. Still others would calculate the ratios themselves somewhat differently. They would use different numerators or denominators, for example, or they would use averages rather than ending amounts for balance sheet items.

You should be aware of these different approaches to ratio analysis. But more important, you should not lose sight of the fundamental thrust of ratio analysis. Its purpose is not to arrive at the "right" ratio or the "right" classification of a ratio. Rather, the purpose is to help us analyze a set of financial statements so that we can understand how an organization is being managed financially. In this regard, the goal is to see what sort of story a *set* of ratios tells about the company. In general, greater precision in calculating certain ratios or reclassifying some of the ratios into different categories will not change that story much, if at all. We thus must beware of the trap that many analysts fall into of worrying about the precision of specific ratio calculations and classifications rather than the overall story itself.

Notes

1. Our discussion in this section is very brief and is designed to serve only as a refresher. Readers who are not familiar with accounting principles may want to read Robert N. Anthony and Leslie Breitner, *Essentials of Accounting,* 8th ed. (Upper Saddle River, N.J.: Prentice Hall, 2003).

2. The discussion here is brief. For additional details, see Malvern J. Gross, Richard F. Larkin, and John H. McCarthy, *Financial and Accounting Guide for Not-for-Profit Organizations,* 6th ed. (New York: Wiley, 2000); Richard F. Larkin and Marie Ditommaso, *Wiley Not-for-Profit GAAP 2001: Interpretation and Application of Generally Accepted Accounting Standards for Not-for-Profit Organizations, 2001* (New York: Wiley, 2001); and Randall W. Luecke and David T. Meeting,

"FASB Statement No. 136 Clarifies Transfer of Assets," *Healthcare Financial Management,* Mar. 2000, pp. 70–73.

3. For a criticism of the standards, see Robert N. Anthony, "The Nonprofit Accounting Mess," *Accounting Horizons,* June 1995, pp. 44–53, and Robert N. Anthony, "Coping with Nonprofit Accounting Rules," *CPA Journal,* Aug. 1996, pp. 50–52.

4. The FASB also requires nonprofit organizations to prepare a statement of cash flows similar to that published by business organizations. Since the SCF has this similarity, and since it does not make a distinction among the three classes of funds, we do not show an example here.

5. Nonprofit organizations sometimes use the term *income* instead of *revenue,* as in *patient care income* or *interest income.* This usage is incorrect and potentially confusing. Income is the difference between revenues and expenses—not the revenues themselves.

6. Note that this paragraph relates only to pledges for the current year. Pledges for future years are described in FAS 116.

7. For a more extensive discussion of accounting in governmental entities, see John Engstrom and Paul A. Copley, *Essentials of Accounting for Governmental and Not-for-Profit Organizations* (New York: McGraw-Hill, 2000); Joseph R. Razek, *Introduction to Governmental and Not-for-Profit Accounting* (Upper Saddle River, N.J.: Prentice Hall, 2000); and Michael H. Granoff, *Government and Not-for-Profit Accounting: Concepts and Practices* (New York: Wiley, 2000).

8. Since 1997, the GASB has been considering a drastic change in the governmental model. Because no decision had been made as of the date this chapter was written, discussion of it in this section would be highly speculative.

9. This section of the general fund is labeled "expenses" in some entities and "expenditures" in others. Usually, it is a mixture of both types of outflows (see note 12).

10. Because some revenues are reported on a cash basis, the GASB describes its requirement as a modified revenue concept. Actually, most business organizations with similar uncertainties also would report these items on a cash basis.

11. See GASB Statement No. 24, "Accounting and Financial Reporting for Certain Grants and Other Financial Assistance," for the rules pertaining to grants and contracts and also concerning food stamps and payments of certain fringe benefits and salaries.

12. For a description of the difference between expenditures and expenses, see Gross, Larkin, and McCarthy, *Financial and Accounting Guide.*

13. See GASB Statement No. 27, "Accounting for Pensions by State and Local Governmental Employees." GASB Statements No. 25 and No. 26 have other requirements for pensions and postemployment benefits.

14. This charge is called a *transfer price.* It is discussed in Chapter Twenty. For additional details, see Robert N. Anthony and David W. Young, *Management Control in Nonprofit Organizations,* 7th ed. (Burr Ridge, Ill.: Irwin, 2003), ch. 8.

15. The expression "within limits" is key here. There have been many instances throughout history when the irresponsible printing of money led to high rates of inflation.

16. Some of these agencies have units within them that generate revenues from sales to the outside world or other government agencies, but in general, these are small. The Passport Office in the State Department, for example, generates revenue from the sale of passports.

17. FASB Statement of Recommended Accounting Standards No. 7, issued April 1996, paragraph 75.

18. Although rarely the case, an individual who overobligates an appropriation is subject to a fine or other penalty under the Antideficiency Act (31 U.S.C. 665).

19. As with annual appropriations, if more than the appropriated amount is spent, the person responsible can suffer the penalties of the Antideficiency Act, but this rarely happens.

20. For additional discussion of this topic, see Steven A. Finkler, *Financial Management for Public Health and Not-for-Profit Organizations* (Upper Saddle River, N.J.: Prentice Hall, 2000), or Adrian Randall and Paul Palmer, *Financial Management in the Voluntary Sector: An Introduction* (New York: Routledge, 2001).

21. The term *surplus* is used here. Alternative terms include *change in net assets* and *excess of revenue over expenses.*

22. This is true by virtue of the fundamental accounting identity: Assets = Liabilities + Equity. If this is so, then dividing each element by Equity gives Assets/Equity = Liabilities/Equity + Equity/Equity. Any value divided by itself equals unity, so assets divided by equity (leverage) equals liabilities divided by equity (debt-equity) plus 1.

23. One of the most popular books is Erich A. Helfert, *Techniques of Financial Analysis: A Guide to Value Creation,* 10th ed. (Burr Ridge, Ill.: Irwin, 1999).

CHAPTER TWENTY

Management Accounting

David W. Young

As noted in Chapter Nineteen, management accounting is concerned with the information needs of individuals within an organization, principally its managers, planners, and staff analysts. Much of the focus in management accounting is on costs and cost behavior. With *full cost accounting,* the concern is with each service's or each program's fair share of the organization's costs. By contrast, *differential cost accounting* focuses on how costs change as circumstances change (as when a program or a service is eliminated). With *responsibility accounting,* costs are analyzed from the perspective of the individuals in an organization who can control them.

Because of these different approaches, the central theme of this chapter is that *different costs are used for different purposes.* There is nothing illegal or unethical about looking at costs differently for different purposes. Rather, as managers' decision-making needs change, so do the costs that are relevant for a particular decision.

FULL COST ACCOUNTING

The question "What did it cost?" is an important one for nonprofit managers to answer, even when their organizations' prices or overall revenues are determined by third-party payers or governmental agencies. Indeed, whether their organizations are "price setters" or "price takers," managers must be able to determine if each of their various programs is financially viable.

Arriving at an answer to the "What did it cost?" question is more difficult than it might first appear. Obviously, it is rather easily answered if we are discussing the purchase of inputs (supplies, labor, and so on) for the service delivery process. Even calculating the full cost of a unit produced—whether it is the education of a high school student or fifty minutes of psychotherapy—is relatively easy as long as the organization is producing goods or services that are completely homogeneous. Complications arise when an organization offers multiple goods and services that require different kinds and amounts of resources.

Uses of Full Cost Information

Managers typically use full cost information for one or three purposes: pricing, profitability assessments, and comparative analyses. These purposes are appropriate at different times and under varying decision-making scenarios.

Pricing. One of the basic functions of full cost information is to assist management in setting prices. Organizations such as museums, private schools, and port authorities are price-setting nonprofits. By contrast, most health care organizations and some social services agencies are price-taking nonprofits; they must accept whatever price or pricing formula has been set by a third-party payer or a governmental agency. For price setters, full cost information helps inform the pricing decision; for price takers, it facilitates determining which programs are subsidizing which others.

An important variant of pricing based on full cost is cost-based (or cost-plus) pricing. With cost-based pricing, a purchaser agrees to pay full cost (with cost-plus, the purchaser also agrees to pay an increment, usually a percentage). For example, some health care insurance companies pay hospitals and other providers on a full cost basis. In research financed by the federal government, by contrast, the government pays direct costs plus an agreed (and audited) supplement for overhead costs, called an "indirect rate." This rate can be quite significant for some organizations, especially universities.

Example: Some years ago, Stanford University announced that its indirect rate—already one of the highest in the country—would be increasing from 74 percent to 84 percent. Many faculty were concerned that such a high rate would impede their ability to obtain federal research grants.[1]

Profitability Assessments. As noted, even organizations that are price takers must calculate full costs if management is to know whether a particular program is financially viable. If a program is not covering its full costs, it is by definition a "loss leader." Since an organization cannot have all its programs be loss leaders, full cost accounting serves to highlight where the cross-subsidization among them is taking place. This allows senior management to assess whether that cross-subsidization is consistent with the organization's overall strategy.

Comparative Analyses. Many organizations can benefit from comparing their costs with those of similar organizations delivering similar programs or services. In so doing, however, there can be a variety of complexities.[2]

Example: A university wishing to compare its cost per student with the per-student cost in other universities would need to consider such potential comparability problems as average class size, the existence of specialized programs (such as athletics, art, and music), the provision of special services (such as career counseling), whether it wishes to include room and board costs in the comparison, whether it wishes to include the cost of its library in the comparison (and if so, the method used to calculate the library's cost), and a variety of similar issues.

As this example suggests, even the definition of what is to be included in a "full cost" computation requires a managerial decision. Indeed, because there is such a wide range of choices embedded in an organization's cost accounting system, managers frequently find it difficult to compare costs between their organization and others where the choices may have been made differently. Instead, many simply make comparisons over time for their own organization, knowing that the methodology has remained consistent from one year to the next.

Role of Senior Management

If senior management does not wish to use full cost information for pricing, profitability assessment, or comparative analysis, it does not need to become involved in the effort to calculate full costs. Rather, it can delegate the cost accounting responsibility to the accounting staff. For example, Medicare and many third-party payers require hospitals to prepare a full cost report. Other than assuring that these external reporting requirements are met, senior management does not need to become involved in the full cost accounting effort.

Example: When the government contracts with a university to do research, the university's cost accounting must be in accordance with the principles set forth in the Office of Management and Budget's *Circular A-21: Cost Principles for Educational Institutions.* These principles provide for direct costs plus "an equitable share" of overhead costs. Overhead costs include a use allowance for depreciation of buildings and equipment, operation and maintenance of plant, general administration, departmental administration, student administration and services, and library.[3] Senior management's involvement in these computations is usually minimal.

If, on the other hand, senior management sees a need for full cost information, it can compute costs in a variety of ways, many of which can be defended as valid but each of which can produce quite different results. Therefore, if senior management has decided to calculate full costs, it must work with its accounting staff to select an appropriate methodology.

Because the issues are complex, the decisions are not ones that can be delegated completely to the organization's accounting staff. Rather, senior management must be intimately involved in setting the ground rules for the cost accounting effort and in guiding the accounting staff's work. Because there are no cost accounting rules similar to the generally accepted accounting principles (GAAP) in financial accounting, managers with differing needs will set different ground rules and make cost accounting decisions in different ways. Indeed, the decisions may change at various times in the life of the organization as managers' needs change. Consequently, the key question is "What does management find useful?" It is this question that must drive the full cost accounting effort.

Resource Usage: A Conceptual Framework

The fundamental issue that cost accounting addresses is the *use of resources*. At the most fundamental level, these resources are the classic ones of the economist: land, labor, and capital. These resources are shown schematically in Figure 20.1.

Land. Land consists of the site or sites where the organization offers its services. Some portion of this resource will be devoted to professional activities and some to administrative ones, but in general, there is nothing especially complicated about it.

Labor. Labor in most nonprofit organizations can be classified into either *professional* (sometimes called *mission*) or *administrative* (sometimes called *support*). Professional labor comprises the individuals who actually deliver the organization's services—the people who are directly associated with the organization's main mission. Administrative labor consists of everyone else in the organization. It can be divided between *professional support* and *general support*.

Professional support consists of the administrative activities that take place within any given *service department* (scheduling clients, for example, or providing secretarial support for a research project). General support can be related to program services, or it can be part of general administration. If the former, it includes centralized functions that assist the organization's professional departments but are organized separately from them, such as central maintenance or cleaning. General administration consists of the organization's central office staff activities, which typically are not directly related to specific professional departments. These activities include computer operations, payroll, purchasing, legal work, and billing.

Basic Category	Subclassifications				Cost Measure
	1	2	3	4	

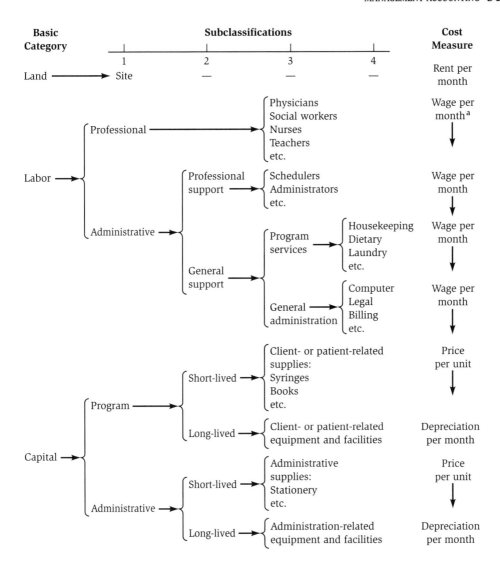

Figure 20.1. Resource Usage: A Conceptual Framework.

[a]Could also be wage per procedure, wage per visit, and so on, depending on the nature of the compensation arrangement (salary versus fee for service).

Capital. Capital can also be looked at as either professional (or mission) or administrative. The former includes all capital resources needed to provide direct support to the service delivery activity. It can be divided between *short-lived* (used up in one year or less) and *long-lived* (used up over several years).

Short-lived mission capital is sometimes called *direct* material. It comprises the items in a service delivery effort that are related to clients. The items range from textbooks in a school to floss in a dental clinic.

Long-lived mission capital includes equipment and facilities used in service-related activities. An organization's plant, equipment, and other fixed assets are included in this category.

Administrative (or support) capital can also be either short- or long-lived. It consists of those items that provide general support rather than being directly associated with service delivery. Supplies used in the executive director's or controller's office would be examples of short-lived administrative capital. Similarly, equipment such as centralized photocopying machines, fax machines, or a computing center would be considered long-lived administrative capital.

Units of Measure. Land is rather easily measured in terms of rent per unit of time (such as a month) or depreciation on a building. Labor is measured by wages—either per unit of time (such as an hour) or per unit of activity (class session, visit, and so on). Short-lived capital—program or administrative—is usually measured in terms of the factor price per unit, that is, what the organization paid to obtain the item. Long-lived capital is typically measured in terms of depreciation per unit of time.

Limitations. The conceptual framework in Figure 20.1 serves to put cost accounting into its broader economic context. However, although the categorization of costs in Figure 20.1 may be useful conceptually, its managerial utility in many organizations is limited by an incomplete understanding of the factors that influence the use of resources—and hence costs. Thus we need to find a way to bridge the gap between the economist's broad overview and the accountant's need to measure resource consumption. This is the role of the cost accounting methodology.

The Cost Accounting Methodology

Nonprofit organizations that have several programs or deliver a variety of services, each requiring different amounts of land, labor, and capital, need to make several decisions to determine full cost: (1) define a cost object, (2) determine cost centers, (3) distinguish between direct and indirect costs, (4) choose bases for allocating overhead costs, (5) select an allocation method, and (6) choose between a process and a job order system. Together these six decisions constitute the cost accounting methodology.[4]

Decision 1: Defining the Cost Object. The cost object is the service unit for which we wish to know the cost. Generally, as the cost object becomes more specific, the methodology needed to account for the associated costs becomes more complex. In some acute care hospitals, for example, the cost object is a day of care. When the day is "all-inclusive" (that is, when it includes surgical procedures, nursing care, laboratory tests, radiological exams, pharmaceutical usage, and all other care provided), determining the cost of a day of care is simply a matter of dividing total costs by total days.

In most hospitals, the cost object is more specific than an all-inclusive day of care. In some instances, for example, the day of care is for "routine" activities only (typically, room, dietary, and nursing costs), and separate cost objects exist for other activities, such as surgical procedures and laboratory tests. Obviously, various other combinations are possible, and even the routine versus nonroutine distinction is not implemented in a uniform way among similar institutions.

It is also possible to consider a totally different cost object from a day of care, such as a discharge or an episode of illness. If the cost object is a discharge, we would include all costs associated with the patient's entire stay in the hospital (that is, for all days of care rather than just an average single day). If we chose an episode of illness as our cost object, we would then include costs for all admissions associated with a particular illness for a given patient and perhaps incorporate outpatient and home care as well.

In general, depending on the particular cost object chosen, we would have a need for either different kinds of cost information or different ways of analyzing and presenting that information. As a result, the choice of a cost object can have a significant effect on the answer to the question "What did it cost?" In effect, the cost object defines the *it* in the question.

A final cost object typically is the unit that fits with the service provided to a client, whereas intermediate cost objects are smaller units that are summed to produce the final cost object.

Example: Homecare Human Services (HHS) delivers services to homebound clients. The agency's services include shopping, bathing, feeding assistance, and assistance with exercising. The cost for services is calculated on an hourly basis. Last year, the organization had total costs of $525,000 and delivered 30,000 hours of services.

If we define the cost object as an hour, we can say that the organization delivers a single service—an hour of care. The cost accounting process, therefore, is quite simple: $525,000 ÷ 30,000 hours = $17.50 per hour of service.

Unfortunately, the choice of an hour as the cost object poses a problem in that clients will most likely want to know the price for an entire visit (such as a trip to the grocery store or a trip to a home to provide some care). Therefore, the visit becomes the final cost object, and an hour is an intermediate cost object. In this regard, an important question is whether the cost of an hour is always the same or whether it changes depending on the kinds of services provided and the salary levels of the people who provide them.

Decision 2: Determining Cost Centers. The choice of cost centers affects how cost data will be accumulated. Cost centers can be thought of as categories (or "buckets") used to collect cost information. An organization such as HHS may divide itself into several cost centers—professional services, administration, housekeeping, and the like—for the cost accounting effort. If this is done, the cost of a particular cost object will be the sum of the costs attributed to it in each of the cost centers.[5]

Example: HHS uses three cost centers: housekeeping, administration, and client services. Its costs look like this:

| | Cost Centers | | | |
Cost Items	Housekeeping	Administration	Client Services	Total
Salaries	–	$120,000	$255,000	$375,000
Supplies	–	43,275	76,725	120,000
Contracted services	$30,000	–	–	30,000
Total	$30,000	$163,275	$331,725	$525,000
Cost per hour	$1.00	$5.44	$11.06	$17.50

Note that the total cost per hour remains $17.50. This must be the case, since total costs ($525,000) and total hours (30,000) are unchanged. What value, then, derives from the extra effort associated with separating the agency into three cost centers?

There are two related answers to this question: an accounting-oriented one and a management-oriented one. From an accounting perspective, costs are better understood and more easily computed if they are for relatively homogeneous groupings of activities. For this reason, senior management's choice of cost centers is ordinarily based on homogeneity; that is, the ideal cost center includes a collection of identical activities.[6]

Example: If a museum's photocopy center had an extremely sophisticated machine (for reproducing paintings, for example) and an extremely simple one (for everyday work), it would most likely want to create two cost centers, one for each machine. The sophisticated machine was no doubt more costly to purchase (and hence has higher depreciation), is more costly to service and repair, and perhaps requires a more highly skilled (and hence higher-salaried) operator. To calculate the average cost of a photocopy—by lumping together the two machines, their operators, and their other costs—would produce misleading cost figures. The average would overstate the cost of a copy on the simple machine and understate it on the sophisticated machine.

The management-oriented answer is that the choice of cost centers depends largely on senior management's plans for using the information. For example, the triple cost center structure may be helpful to management in comparing its costs with those of other agencies, thereby assisting with cost control. A comparison between HHS's administrative costs and those of other similar organizations, for example, could reveal areas of potential inefficiency and assist management in an effort to improve the efficiency of the agency's administrative operations.[7]

Another potential managerial use of the multiple cost center structure is for pricing. If each program (or service) offered by an agency were represented by a cost center, the costs of that center could be used as the basis for setting the appropriate prices.

In a multiple cost center structure, an organization's cost centers are generally divided into two broad categories: mission centers and service centers. Mission centers are associated with the organization's main focus (or mission); normally, they charge for (or are reimbursed for) their activities and are sometimes called "revenue centers."

Service centers, by contrast, contain the costs of the activities the organization carries out to support its mission centers. In our example, housekeeping and administration would be considered service centers, and client services would be a mission center. In a larger institutional setting, institutionwide depreciation, human resources, maintenance, and the like are generally service centers, while programs and client service departments are treated as mission centers. The cost for a given cost object then depends on (1) the mission center or centers in which a client received services, (2) the number of units of service received in each, and (3) the cost per unit of service, where the cost per unit of service in each mission center depends, in part, on that center's "fair share" of the organization's service center costs.

Example: Let's assume that in addition to the cost center decision described in the last example, HHS has decided to establish a client education program and to treat the program as a separate mission center. To do so, it hired a social worker at an annual salary of $60,000. The supplies for the program totaled $15,000. The social worker provided 1,250 hours of education during the year. The agency's costs now look like this:

| | Service Centers | | Mission Centers | | |
| | Housekeeping | Administration | Client Services | Client Education | Total |
Cost Items					
Salaries	—	$120,000	$255,000	$60,000	$435,000
Supplies	—	43,275	76,725	15,000	135,000
Contracted services	$30,000	—	—	—	30,000
Total	$30,000	$163,275	$331,725	$75,000	$600,000

At this point, the cost per hour in each mission center becomes somewhat more difficult to calculate, since it now relies on some further decisions. We will therefore defer the per-unit calculations until those decisions have been discussed. Note, however, that our total costs have increased to $600,000 as a result of the additional $75,000 for client education.

Decision 3: Distinguishing Between Direct and Indirect Costs. *Direct costs* are those costs that are unambiguously associated with or physically traceable to a specific cost center. *Indirect costs* are those costs that apply to more than one cost center and hence must be distributed among them.

The distribution of indirect costs can be carried out in one of two ways: (1) by developing techniques that measure their usage in considerable detail or (2) by establishing formulas that distribute them as fairly as possible into the appropriate cost centers.

Example: Let's assume that the social worker in the client education program at HHS is supervised by someone whose salary at present is included in the client services cost center. Since the supervisor's salary applies to activities in both the client services and client education cost centers, it is an indirect cost and must be distributed between the two cost centers.

There are several techniques we might use to distribute the salary to the two centers. We might ask the supervisor to maintain careful time records, which could then be used to distribute the salary. If we do this, we would in effect have converted the indirect cost into a direct cost, since we would have created a situation in which the cost (time) is physically traceable to each cost center. Alternatively, we might simply establish a distribution formula, using, say, salary dollars or number of personnel in each cost center as the distribution mechanism.

Example: Assume that the supervisor's salary is $75,000 and that we have decided to use hours of service as the distribution mechanism. The salary would be distributed as follows:

Cost Center	Hours of Service	Percent	Assigned Supervisor's Salary	Percent
Client services	30,000	96.0	$72,000	96.0
Client education	1,250	4.0	3,000	4.0
Total	$31,250	100.0	$75,000	100.0

The cost centers would then have the following costs:

Cost Center	Cost	
Housekeeping	$30,000	
Administration	163,275	
Client services	328,725	(331,725 − 3,000 for supervisor)
Client education	78,000	(75,000 + 3,000 for supervisor)
Total	$600,000	

Of the $75,000 salary, $72,000 is now in the client services cost center and $3,000 is in the client education cost center.

Decision 4: Choosing Allocation Bases for Service Center Costs. The hourly cost of client services and the hourly cost of client education include more than the direct and distributed indirect costs of those activities. The hourly cost also includes each mission center's *fair share* of the organization's service center costs. As you might imagine, the notion of what is fair can be highly debatable in cost accounting, just as in other aspects of life.

Because of the need to allocate service center (sometimes called "overhead") costs, the fourth decision in the cost accounting process is the choice of *bases of allocation.* We must select for each service center a metric that measures its use by the other cost centers as accurately as possible. In this regard, we are seeking the *activity* that gives rise to a service center's costs.

In summary, before we can allocate service center costs, we must (1) determine the direct costs of each cost center, (2) distribute indirect costs to the appropriate cost centers, and (3) choose a basis of allocation for each service center.[8] We are then ready to allocate service center costs to the mission centers. So we now must choose an allocation basis for each service center (housekeeping and administration in this case).

Let's begin with housekeeping. Our goal is to find a basis of allocation that measures as accurately as possible the use of the housekeeping resource by the other cost centers. Although a number of allocation bases may be available, one that seems to be quite appropriate is square feet of floor space. That is, the more floor space a cost center uses, the greater will be its share of the housekeeping expense.

Example: Assume that the following information on square footage is available to us:

Cost Center	Square Footage
Administration	2,500
Client services	4,500
Client education	1,000
Total	8,000

This means that the housekeeping cost per square foot is $3.75 ($30,000 of house-keeping divided by 8,000 square feet of floor space). As a result, the housekeeping allocation would look as follows:

Cost Center	Square Footage	×	Rate	=	Allocation
Administration	2,500	×	$3.75	=	$9,375
Client services	4,500	×	3.75	=	16,875
Client education	1,000	×	3.75	=	3,750
Total	8,000				$30,000

There are three items of importance here. First, housekeeping has not been allocated to itself; that is, we do not calculate the cost of cleaning the house-keeping department. Second, housekeeping has been allocated to the adminis-tration cost center as well as to the client services and client education cost centers; that is, in this approach, a service center's costs have been allocated to other service centers as well as to mission centers. Third, there are other ap-proaches. Depending on the cost allocation method in use, service center costs may be allocated only to mission centers and not to other service centers.

Given the approach we are using, we now must allocate the costs of the ad-ministration cost center to the remaining cost centers. To do so, we must choose an appropriate allocation basis. There are several alternative bases, such as number of personnel, salary cost, or number of visits. Assume that the agency decides to use salary cost as the allocation basis and that the following infor-mation is available:

Cost Center	Initial Salary Costs	Costs After Supervisor Salary Assignment	
Client services	$255,000	$252,000	($3,000 removed for supervisor)
Client education	60,000	63,000	(3,000 added for supervisor)
Total	$315,000	$315,000	

Determining the allocation rate per salary dollar for administration is some-what more complicated than it was for housekeeping, since total costs in the administration cost center have been increased by the housekeeping allocation. When we include the housekeeping allocation, the total costs in the adminis-tration cost center are $172,650, calculated as follows:

Direct costs	$163,275
Housekeeping allocation	9,375
Total costs to be allocated	$172,650

Since the administration costs are to be allocated to the remaining cost centers (client services and client education) and since the basis of allocation is salary dollars, we need to determine the allocation rate, that is, administration dollars per salary dollar.

Example: Using the figures given in the text, the amount of administration per salary dollar would be calculated as follows:

Total costs to be allocated	$172,650
Divide by salary dollars in *receiving* cost centers	$315,000
Equals rate of administrative costs per salary dollar (rounded)	$0.55

As a result, the amount of administration allocated to each cost center would be calculated as follows (the $0.55 rate is actually carried out to several decimal places so that there are no rounding errors):

Cost Center	Salary Dollars	×	Rate	=	Allocation
Client services	$252,000	×	$0.55	=	$138,120
Client education	63,000	×	0.55	=	34,530
Total	$315,000				$172,650

With this information, we can determine the full costs of each of our mission centers, as follows:

Cost Center	Direct + Distributed Costs	Housekeeping Allocation	Administration Allocation	Total Costs
Client services	$328,725	$16,875	$138,120	$483,720
Client education	78,000	3,750	$34,530	116,280
Total				$600,000

Note that our total costs of $600,000 remain the same as they were prior to the allocation of service center costs. We have now fully allocated the housekeeping and administration costs to the two mission centers. We did so by first allocating the housekeeping service center costs to the administration service center as well as the two mission centers and then allocating the administration service center costs (with its housekeeping allocation included) to the two mission centers.

In summary, the total costs in a given mission center are (1) its direct costs, (2) the indirect costs distributed to it, plus (3) the costs that have been allocated to it from the service centers. In this example, our bases of allocation were square footage and salary dollars, but an allocation basis could be almost anything that can be measured relatively easily and that has an apparent cause-and-effect relationship with the use of a service center's resources.

Decision 5: Selecting an Allocation Method. Several methods of varying complexity and accuracy are available for allocating service center costs to mission centers: (1) the *direct,* or single-stage, method; (2) the *stepdown,* or two-stage, method; and (3) the *reciprocal* method.

Direct Method. With the direct allocation method, service center costs are allocated to mission centers only and not to other service centers. This is the simplest method of the three and is used by many organizations. It is the least precise of the three, however, in that it does not include the cost effects associated with one service center's use of another service center.

Stepdown Method. The stepdown method, which was used in the last example, sequentially "trickles down" service center costs into the other service centers and mission centers. This stepping-down process begins with the first service center in the sequence, spreading its costs over the remaining cost centers (both service centers and mission centers). The distribution is based on each cost center's use of the service center's services as determined by the chosen allocation basis. This process is followed for all remaining service centers.

Because it allocates service centers to other service centers as well as to mission centers, the stepdown method is more complicated than the direct method, but it is also more precise in that it includes the cost effects associated with one service center's use of another service center. However, once a service center's costs have been allocated, it cannot receive an allocation; thus the stepdown method does not include the cost effects of a given service center's use of a service center that comes later in the allocation sequence.

Because of this feature, the sequence followed in allocating the service centers can affect the costs in each mission center. The sequence will not affect total costs, however, which will remain the same under all sequences ($600,000 for HHS). Occasionally, however, the effect of the sequence decision on a particular mission center can be significant.

In general, the approach to choosing a sequence is to allocate service centers in order of their use by other service centers. That is, the service center that uses other service centers the *least* is allocated *first,* and the service center that uses other service centers the *most* is allocated *last.* Clearly, considerable judgment is required to determine this sequence. At HHS, for example, management's judgment was apparently that the housekeeping department uses the administration department less than the administration department uses the housekeeping department. With regard to mission centers, since there is no allocation *out of* mission centers, their sequence is unimportant.

Reciprocal Method. With the reciprocal method, the most complex technique, all service centers both make and receive allocations to each other, as well as to mission centers. Because all service centers can both make and receive allocations, the reciprocal method is the most accurate of the three. The main problem with the reciprocal method is its complexity—it requires a computer program to solve the several (frequently as many as twenty) simultaneous equations representing the various service centers.[9]

Because of its precision, the reciprocal method is preferred by the Cost Accounting Standards Board (CASB). Nevertheless, many organizations find that the stepdown method strikes about the right balance between accuracy and ease of use. It is the most commonly used method for health care organizations, for example, and is used by many other nonprofit organizations as well.

Decision 6: Attaching Costs to Cost Objects. A final decision in the full cost accounting methodology concerns the way mission center costs are *attached* to an organization's cost objects. The choices range from a *process system,* which is typically used when all units of output are roughly identical, to a *job order system,* which is used when the units of output are quite different. Organizations that have production lines tend to use a process system, whereas those that do custom work use a job order system.

Job order and process systems are discussed at length in most cost accounting textbooks.[10] In both systems, there is a need for one or more overhead rates, which can be tricky to compute and use. Nevertheless, it seems clear that HHS, in setting up two mission centers, has moved along the spectrum toward a job order method. Further movement along the spectrum could take place by incorporating travel time into the number of hours, thereby reflecting a higher cost for clients who live farther away, or by calculating different costs for different categories of employees within each program, or even by separating a mission center into, say, two mission centers, each of which contains a more homogeneous collection of activities. Client services, for example, might be divided into shopping and in-home services. Or client education might be divided between individual and group education.

Effect of the Cost Accounting Methodology on Pricing Decisions

The cost accounting decisions discussed in the previous section can be expected to affect an organization's pricing decisions. This is especially true in situations where prices are based almost exclusively on full costs.

Example: If we assume for the moment that HHS's management wants a 10 percent markup over costs when pricing its services, the multiple cost center approach will give a very different pricing structure than the single cost center approach. To illustrate, assume that a potential client has asked HHS for a bid on a weekly home visit, which the manager estimates will require three hours. Another potential client has asked for a bid on educating an elderly relative, which the manager estimates will require one hour a week. The prices HHS proposes to these potential clients would be computed as follows:

Cost per Hour

One cost center: $600,000 ÷ 31,250 hours = $19.20
Multiple cost centers:
   Client services: $483,720 ÷ 30,000 = $16.12
   Client education: $116,280 ÷ 1,250 = $93.02

Price per Hour

One cost center: $19.20 + $1.92 = $21.12
Multiple cost centers:
   Client services: $16.12 + $1.61 = $17.73
   Client education: $93.02 + $9.30 = $102.32

The cost-based prices proposed to the client for the two jobs would be as follows:

One Cost Center

Client services: 3 hours @ $21.12 = $63.36
Client education: 1 hour @ $21.12 = $21.12

Multiple Cost Centers

Client services: 3 hours @ $17.73 = $53.19
Client education: 1 hour @ $102.32 = $102.32

Note that with the multiple cost center approach, the price for client services falls by about 15 percent and the price for client education increases by almost 500 percent. If we assume that the multiple cost center approach gives us a more homogeneous collection of activities in each mission center, then the cost on which the price is based comes closer to reflecting the true consumption of resources needed for each job. As a result, the multiple cost center approach helps eliminate the cross-subsidization that would take place in the single cost center approach.

Some Cautionary Notes

The primary purpose of full cost accounting is to help management measure the resources devoted to a particular cost object and to use that information internally for pricing, profitability analysis, or cost comparisons. However, full cost accounting has some important limitations. In particular, whether a cost is direct or indirect says little about its actual *behavior* as the volume of activity in a mission center increases or decreases. Cost behavior is discussed in the next section.

DIFFERENTIAL COST ACCOUNTING

Recall from the introduction to the chapter that *different costs are used for different purposes.* The full cost accounting methodology discussed in the first part of this chapter is not appropriate for several types of decisions that managers frequently must make, called *alternative choice decisions.* These decisions include (1) keeping or discontinuing an unprofitable program, (2) making or buying (for example, hiring personnel to clean the facilities or contracting with a cleaning vendor), or (3) accepting or rejecting a special request (such as selling a service below full cost so as to use a certain amount of otherwise unused capacity).

The key accounting question asked in the context of an alternative choice decision is "How will costs (and sometimes revenues) change under the alternative arrangements?" If a program or service is discontinued, for example, some costs and revenues will be eliminated. In a make-or-buy decision, by contrast, certain costs will be eliminated but other costs will be incurred. In the special-request situation, certain revenues will be received, but costs will not change in accordance with the indications of a full cost analysis.

As discussed in this section, using of full cost information as a basis for deciding which costs will change or how costs will change under alternative arrangements can lead managers to make decisions that are financially detrimental to the organization. For alternative choice decisions, the appropriate information is differential costs.

The Nature of Costs

Fundamental to any discussion of differential cost analysis is the question of cost behavior. In the first part of the chapter, we distinguished between mission center costs and service center costs. Differential cost analysis relies on a different view of costs, dividing them between fixed and variable. This distinction lets us see more clearly how a change in the volume of activity of a given cost center will affect the center's costs. We also need to include the refinements of semivariable and step-function costs. The four types of costs are shown in Figure 20.2.

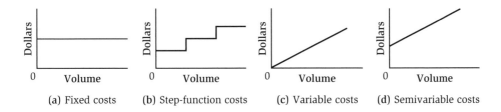

Figure 20.2. Types of Cost Behavior.

Fixed Costs. Fixed costs are independent of the number of units produced. Whereas no costs are fixed if the time period is long enough, the *relevant range* for fixed costs (that is, the span of units over which they remain unchanged or the time period within which they are considered) is generally quite large, so they can be viewed graphically as shown in panel (a) of Figure 20.2.

A good example of a fixed cost in most organizations is rent. Regardless of the number of units produced or other volume of activity, the amount of rent will remain the same.

Step-Function Costs. Step-function costs are similar to fixed costs in nature, except they have a much narrower relevant range. As such, they do not change in a smooth fashion but are added in "lumps" or "steps." The result is that, graphically, they take the form shown in panel (b), where the dotted lines represent discontinuous jumps.

A good example of a step-function cost in most organizations is supervision. As the number of workers increases, supervisory personnel must be added. Since it is difficult for most organizations to add part-time supervisory help, supervisory costs will tend to behave in a step-function fashion.

Variable Costs. Variable costs behave in a roughly linear fashion with changes in volume. That is, as volume increases, variable costs will increase in some constant proportion. The result is a straight line, the slope of which is determined by the amount of variable costs associated with each unit of output, as shown in panel (c).

An example of variable costs in many nonprofit organizations is client supplies, which will increase in almost direct proportion to increases in the number of client visits. Some organizations will have relatively high variable costs per unit, resulting in a line that slopes upward quite steeply; other organizations will have variable costs that are relatively low for each visit (or more generally, for each unit of output), such that the variable-cost line slopes upward more slowly.

Semivariable Costs. Semivariable costs (sometimes called *mixed* or *semifixed* costs) share features of both fixed and variable costs. There is a minimum level of costs that is fixed, but the cost line then increases with increases in volume. The result is a line that begins at some level above zero and then slopes upward in a linear fashion, as shown in panel (d).

A good example of a semivariable cost is electricity. Typically, there is some base cost each month for electricity that an organization must incur even if it uses no electricity at all. Costs then increase in a linear fashion in accordance with the number of kilowatt-hours used. Similar cost patterns exist for telephone, gas, water, and other utilities.

Relation of Cost Behavior to Full Cost Accounting. The analysis of differential costs would be simplified if, as is occasionally assumed, all service center costs were fixed and all production center costs were variable. Unfortunately, this is almost never the case. Figure 20.3 contains an illustration of four different cost types and their fixed versus variable and mission center versus service center distinctions. The example refers to the costs of Homecare Human Services, the organization discussed in the section on full cost accounting.

Cost Behavior in Organizations. Costs in most organizations can be classified without too much difficulty as fixed, step-function, variable, or semivariable. Doing so requires analyzing the actual or expected behavior of each cost item and determining how it will change with changes in the volume of activity.

Example: The Hawthorne Dental Clinic currently provides two thousand patient visits each month. At this level of activity, it incurs the following costs:

Hygienists	$21,000
Cleaning supplies (such as toothpaste)	8,000
Other supplies (such as aprons)	2,000
Utilities	1,000
Rent	6,000
Total	$38,000

Each of these costs can be classified into one of the four cost categories. Hygienists are probably step-function costs—they will remain fixed until the number of visits increases by some fairly sizable number. Cleaning supplies, by contrast, are most likely variable costs—they will change in direct proportion to a change in the number of visits. Other supplies are a little tricky, but since they probably vary with the number of personnel, they could be thought of as step-function costs.

	Fixed	Variable
Mission Center Costs	Supervisor's salary in the client services mission center	Client supplies in the client services mission center
Service Center Costs	Portion of CEO's salary that is allocated to the client services mission center	Cleaning supplies (which are costs of housekeeping) that are allocated to the client services mission center

Figure 20.3. Fixed and Variable Costs Versus Mission Center and Service Center Costs.

Utilities are most likely semivariable costs; the clinic probably pays a fixed amount each month with a variable component based on usage. Usage is probably proportional to the number of hours the clinic is open, which is somewhat related to the number of visits. Rent, on the other hand, is probably fixed (although with some ceiling on the number of visits—once they reach a certain level, the clinic will need to rent a larger facility).

Estimating Cost-Volume Relationships. Classifying costs is only the first step. The next step is to estimate how the costs will change with changes in volume and to develop a formula to indicate the relationship between volume and the amount of a cost item. To do this, several estimates are needed. We must decide if our rent truly is fixed, for example, or if there is some level of patient volume at which we will need to rent a larger facility. This is usually relatively easy to determine. Similarly, an estimate of the variable cost per unit of service is pretty easy in this example—with $8,000 in cleaning supplies and 2,000 visits, the variable cost per visit is $4.00. Step-function costs are more of a managerial decision; at what level of activity will the clinic need to hire another hygienist?

Semivariable costs are somewhat trickier to estimate, since we need to separate the fixed and variable components. To make the separation, we need at least two historical or projected data points. With two data points, we can draw a straight line between them and determine where the line intersects the vertical axis of a graph, which will give its fixed-cost component. The variable cost component is the line's slope (height of vertical rise per one horizontal unit).

Example: Assume we used 10,000 kilowatt-hours (kwh) of electricity in June and 12,000 kwh in July. The June electric bill was $1,500; the July electric bill was $1,700. To compute the fixed and variable components of the cost line, we take the following steps:

1. Compute the difference in total costs: $1,700 − $1,500 = $200
2. Compute the difference in volume: 12,000 kwh − 10,000 kwh = 2,000 kwh
3. Compute the variable cost per unit by dividing the two: $200 ÷ 2,000 kwh = $0.10 per kwh
4. Compute total variable costs for one data point: June = 0.10 per kwh × 10,000 kwh = $1,000
5. Compute fixed costs for the same data point: $1,500 − $1,000 = $500 fixed costs
6. Describe the line: Total cost = $500 + (0.10 ÷ kwh)
7. Test the line with the second data point: $500 + (0.10 ÷ 12,000 kwh) = $1,700

The Differential Cost Concept

With an understanding of costs according to the fixed, step-function, variable, or semivariable nature of their behavior, we are in a position to undertake a differential cost analysis. Differential cost analysis attempts to identify the behavior of an organization's costs under various scenarios related to the type of alternative choice decision under consideration.

Example: Clearwater Transportation Service operates two vans for transporting the elderly. It charges $2.00 a mile for each mile driven. Last year, van 1 drove 60,000 miles and van 2 drove 30,000 miles. The variable cost per mile (gasoline, tires, wear and tear) for each van was 40 cents. Each driver was paid a salary of $40,000 per year. Rent and administration were fixed costs totaling $60,000; they were allocated to each van on the basis of the number of miles driven. Under these circumstances, Clearwater's operating revenues and costs were as follows:

Item	Van 1	Van 2	Total
Revenue	$2.00 × 60,000 = $120,000	$2.00 × 30,000 = $60,000	$180,000
Expenses			
Variable costs	0.40 × 60,000 = 24,000	0.40 × 30,000 = 12,000	36,000
Drivers	40,000	40,000	80,000
Overhead costs (rent and administration)	40,000	20,000	60,000
Total expenses	$104,000	$72,000	$176,000
Profit (loss)	$16,000	$(12,000)	$4,000

While it might appear that the financial performance of Clearwater could have been improved if van 2, which lost money, had been discontinued at the beginning of the year, this is not the case. To see why, we need to structure the same information in terms of differential costs. The question is not whether van 2 lost money on a *full cost* basis (as it did) but rather the nature of its differential costs and revenues; that is, how Clearwater's revenues and costs would have changed if van 2 had been discontinued.

Although the data are not as good as we might like, we can nevertheless see that discontinuing van 2 would have eliminated its revenue and its variable costs as well as the fixed cost of the driver. From all indications, however, the overhead costs (rent and administration) would have continued (in other words, they are not differential). The result would have been a shift from a surplus of $4,000 to a loss of $4,000, as the following analysis indicates:

Item	Van 1
Revenue ($2.00 × 60,000)	$120,000
Expenses	
Variable costs (0.40 × 60,000)	24,000
Driver	40,000
Overhead costs (rent and administration)	60,000
Total expenses	$124,000
Profit (loss)	$(4,000)

This example illustrates several important principles.

Principle 1: Full Cost Information Can Be Misleading. The kind of information available from most full cost accounting systems can produce misleading results if used for alternative choice decisions—in this instance, a keep or discontinue decision. Here, the full cost data would seem to indicate that we could increase Clearwater's surplus by dropping van 2, but this clearly was not the case.

Principle 2: Differential Costs Can Include Both Fixed and Variable Costs. Although perhaps counterintuitive, you should note that differential costs can include *both* fixed and variable costs. In our example, the driver was a fixed cost of van 2, and yet the elimination of van 2 eliminated this fixed cost. The key point is that as long as we operate the van, we have the fixed cost of the driver's salary; it does not fluctuate in accordance with the number of miles driven. But when we eliminate the van, we also eliminate this cost in its entirety; thus it is differential in terms of the alternative choice decision we are making.

Principle 3: Assumptions Are Essential. Differential cost analysis invariably requires assumptions. Although the analysis of the Clearwater situation focused on what would have happened in the prior year, the real intent of the analysis is to assist management in a decision that it must make concerning the future. The assumption that underlay our analysis, therefore, was that next year's prices, costs, volume, and so forth would be the same as last year's.

Of course, it is not true that next year will be just like last year. Inflation will affect our costs, and it may be possible to raise our prices. The general state of the economy, along with a wide variety of other factors, will affect our volume next year such that it will quite likely be different from last year's. This raises some important concerns about the reliability of our analysis.

Despite these concerns, since we do not have perfect knowledge of the future, we must speculate about how costs will behave. In the Clearwater example, we made two important assumptions that went beyond the general ones just mentioned: (1) the number of miles driven by van 1 will not increase with the elimination of van 2, and (2) we will not be able to reduce or eliminate any rent or administrative costs with the elimination of van 2. Changes in either of these assumptions would have an impact on the new surplus (or loss) figure and might in fact actually make it financially beneficial to eliminate van 2.

Principle 4: Causality Must Be Determined. A key aspect of differential analysis is causality. Specifically, for an item to be included in a differential analysis, it must be *caused* by the alternative under consideration. For example, if we assume that there will be an increase in the miles driven by van 1, that increase would have to be *caused* by the elimination of van 2. If van 1 would have driven more miles anyway, then the increased mileage is irrelevant for the differential analysis. If, however, we assume that the elimination of van 2 means that some people who would have used it now will use van 1 instead, then the increased mileage is relevant for the differential analysis. We would need to include that additional mileage in computing van 1's revenue and variable expenses under the alternative scenario.

The same issue must be considered for rent and administrative costs. If we were planning to decrease our administrative costs with or without van 2, then the change is irrelevant for the differential analysis. If, on the other hand, the elimination of van 2 will allow us to decrease our administrative costs (such as by eliminating a portion of the dispatcher wage expense), then we would need to include this decrease in the differential analysis.

Principle 5: Sensitivity Analysis Can Be Helpful. Because assumptions play such a crucial role in a differential analysis, it is important to identify and document them as completely as possible. Furthermore, it is important to explore how changes in the assumptions would affect the conclusions of the analysis. This latter activity is called *sensitivity analysis.* If we were doing a sensitivity analysis for Clearwater, we might try to determine how many more miles van 1 would have to drive for the organization to maintain its $4,000 surplus. Or if we thought we might be able to reduce our rent and administrative costs by eliminating van 2, we might ask by how much they would need to fall to maintain the $4,000 surplus. We would follow this sensitivity analysis with an assessment of whether managerial action could be taken that would allow the assumptions to become reality.

The Concept of Contribution

One way to structure differential cost information to facilitate decision making is in terms of *contribution.* As the Clearwater example indicates, an important question is the behavior of overhead (or service center) costs. Ordinarily, an analysis of differential costs is most easily performed when the direct fixed and variable costs of a program are analyzed separately from the organization's overhead costs.

An analysis that separates costs in this way is usually structured in terms of the contribution of the particular program to the organization's overhead costs. The term *contribution* refers to the amount left after a program's direct costs have been deducted from its revenue. Direct costs include a program's variable, semivariable, fixed, and step-function costs. The amount left after deducting these costs *contributes* to the coverage of overhead costs.

The cost data for Clearwater Transportation Service can be structured in terms of a *contribution income statement.* An example of such a statement is presented in Exhibit 20.1.

Exhibit 20.1. Contribution Income Statement for Clearwater Transportation Service.

Item	Van 1	Van 2	Total
Revenue	$120,000	$60,000	$180,000
Less: Variable costs	24,000	12,000	36,000
Equals: Margin (for fixed and overhead costs)	$96,000	$48,000	$144,000
Less: Production center fixed costs (drivers)	40,000	40,000	80,000
Equals: Contribution (to overhead costs)	$56,000	$8,000	$64,000
Less: Overhead costs			60,000
Equals: Profit (loss)			$4,000

As Exhibit 20.1 indicates, both van 1 and van 2 are contributing to the coverage of overhead costs. Consequently, eliminating either van will reduce this contribution and will either reduce the organization's surplus or increase its loss. In fact, it was the $8,000 that van 2 was contributing that led to the change from a $4,000 profit to a $4,000 loss.

Sunk Costs

One of the most difficult aspects of differential cost analysis concerns the role of *sunk costs*. The term refers to an expenditure that was made in the past and that results in an expense on a full cost report but that is inappropriate for future considerations because the expenditure already has been incurred and the decision cannot be reversed. Consequently, the amount should be excluded from a differential cost analysis (which is concerned only with the future).

The classic example of a sunk cost is depreciation, an accounting technique used to spread the cost of an asset over its useful life. Although depreciation (a noncash expense) will appear on a full cost report, accountants have traditionally considered it inappropriate for a differential cost analysis because it will not change regardless of the alternative chosen. To examine this idea, let's look first at the accounting view of sunk costs and then examine them in a more strategic context.

The Accounting View. Accountants typically consider sunk costs from a relatively nonstrategic perspective. This means that they ignore the book value of any assets that are involved in an alternative choice decision. Because of this, the accounting view ordinarily excludes consideration of any decision to replace the assets once they wear out.

The Strategic View. Although depreciation is a sunk cost and therefore a non-differential item in any alternative choice decision, there is a question of how depreciation should be treated if the perspective extends beyond the remaining years of an asset's economic life. The strategic view thus asks a slightly different question from the accounting view, namely, what the costs and revenues will be over an *indefinite* time period. When this is the case, depreciation is a relevant item to include.

Stated somewhat differently, when the time horizon is short, the financial perspective is generally a cash-maximizing one. When the time horizon is long (extending beyond the economic life of the asset), the decision becomes more strategic. When this is the case, senior management tends to include depreciation in the analysis.

The strategic perspective occurs in almost all alternative choice decisions. To illustrate, let's look at the analysis we might do in a contracting-out situation. In this type of decision, we are unconcerned with revenue. Instead, senior management needs to compare costs under two scenarios: (1) to make the item or provide the service ourselves or (2) to hire another organization to make the item or provide the service.

Example: Energy International (EI), a nonprofit organization, manufactures a wide variety of energy-saving devices, which it sells at a small markup to developers of low-income housing. One of its products contains a thermostat. The thermostats are made in a department that uses some highly specialized equipment. The annual full costs of the thermostat department are as follows:

Direct labor	$150,000
Materials	70,000
Department manager	50,000
Depreciation	30,000
Allocated overhead	20,000
Total	$320,000

EI has received an offer from a local firm that specializes in thermostats to manufacture the same annual volume of thermostats at an annual cost of $280,000. The contract is for five years. If EI accepts this offer, it will be able to totally eliminate the thermostat department. In this regard, management has determined the following:

1. Although the machines used in the department have five years of depreciation remaining, they are technologically obsolete and have no market value (they can be removed at no charge, but that is all). However, they can last for another five years before they need to be replaced.
2. No inflation is expected.

3. The department manager is willing to accept early retirement (at no additional cost to the company) if the department closes. That is, her salary will be eliminated, and she will draw her retirement income from the company's pension fund, which is a separate entity.

4. None of the allocated overhead is differential; that is, it will be reallocated to other departments if the thermostat department is eliminated.

5. The expected number of thermostats needed for each of the five years of the contract is well known and will be the same as it was during the year in which the current figures were computed.

6. The local firm making the offer has an excellent reputation for quality and delivery.

If we adopt the traditional approach to this analysis, we would use the following costs:

Savings If We Subcontract

Direct labor	$150,000
Materials	70,000
Department manager	50,000
Depreciation (sunk)	0
Allocated overhead (nondifferential)	0
Total	$270,000
Less: Cost of contract	280,000
Net financial benefit	($10,000)

If we adopt a more strategic perspective and include depreciation in the analysis (even though it is a sunk cost), we would use the following costs:

Savings If We Subcontract

Direct labor	$150,000
Materials	70,000
Department manager	50,000
Depreciation	30,000
Allocated overhead (nondifferential)	0
Total	$300,000
Less: Cost of contract	280,000
Net financial benefit	$20,000

In effect, the traditional approach, which excludes sunk costs, would lead us to reject the offer, since we would save only $270,000 in expenses and spend $280,000 for the contract. From a longer-term, strategic perspective, however, our focus shifts to what might be called "steady state" operations. This focus recognizes that at some point we will need to replace the equipment and therefore includes depreciation in the analysis. Under these circumstances, we would accept the offer, since it improves our financial performance over the long term.

Ideally, of course, we would wait for five years to accept the contract. Much could change in the interim, however, that would affect our decision. More important is the fact that that option is not available.

Traditionally, the strategic perspective was used only when an organization was deciding whether to purchase replacement equipment. At that time, management would look at the annual cash flows associated with the proposed investment in new assets and compare their present value with the amount of the proposed investment. The problem with this approach was that it rarely considered alternatives such as contracting out. Instead, the decision was made in relative isolation.

In an effort to correct for this incremental approach to strategic decision making, senior management must ask the strategic question whenever an opportunity to contract out presents itself. To do so, many managers will include depreciation in the cost analysis because its inclusion provides a good approximation of the company's costs from a steady-state perspective. That is, an analysis that includes depreciation shows what the "typical year" would look like.

Nonquantitative Considerations

The strategic perspective also includes nonquantitative considerations. In any alternative choice decision, there are a variety of factors that cannot be quantified but that can easily tip the balance in one direction or another, frequently overriding the financial analysis. This is especially true if the financial analysis indicates that the two approaches have roughly similar cost and revenue implications.

In the decision to keep or drop a program or service line, for example, nonquantitative considerations might include program interdependencies, that is, the extent to which revenue from some of the organization's programs are dependent on use of the program being considered for elimination. In many hospitals, for example, the pediatrics program loses money, but most of these hospitals would find it unwise to eliminate the program. This is because the use of many of the hospital's other (and more financially viable) programs is based on parental familiarity with the hospital, which comes about as a result of their experiences in the pediatrics department.

In a contract-out decision, nonquantitative considerations typically include factors such as quality, service, delivery, and reputation of the vendor. They may also include market considerations, such as the difficulty and cost of switching from one vendor to another if a particular relationship does not work.

In a highly competitive market, an organization that is dissatisfied with one vendor can simply hire another. If the market is more oligopolistic, however, it may be difficult to find a new vendor. A nonprofit organization that contracts for snow-plowing services for its parking lot, for example, typically has an easy time switching from one vendor to another. In contrast, a state agency that contracts for some highly specialized computer services may have a difficult time switching vendors, as the market for such vendors may be quite small.

Another nonquantitative consideration in contracting out is the cost of switching back to internal provision of the service. Once a organization contracts out, it may eliminate its facilities, equipment, and trained personnel. Leasing or purchasing new facilities and equipment and training new personnel may be quite costly. Moreover, if the organization has eliminated its capacity for internal service provision, it may find itself at the mercy of its vendor. Rarely is this desirable.

Cost-Volume-Profit Analysis

An important technique used in differential cost situations is cost-volume-profit (CVP) analysis. The purpose of CVP analysis is to determine (1) the volume of activity needed for an organization to achieve its surplus goal, (2) the price that an organization needs to charge to achieve its surplus goal, or (3) the cost limits (fixed, variable, or both) that an organization needs to adhere to in order to achieve its surplus goal.

CVP analyses usually are done for a particular activity within an organization—such as a program or service line. A CVP analysis thus begins with the fundamental equation

$$\text{Surplus} = \text{Total revenue (TR)} - \text{Total costs (TC)}$$

Total revenue for many activities is easy to calculate. If we assume that an organization's price is represented by the letter p and its volume by the letter x, then total revenue is price times volume, or

$$\text{TR} = px$$

Total costs are somewhat more complicated. CVP analysis requires a recognition of the different types of cost behavior in a organization: fixed, step-function, variable, and semivariable. Let's begin with the simplest of cases, in which there are no step-function or semivariable costs. In this instance, the formula would be quite simple:

$$\text{Total costs} = \text{Fixed costs} + \text{Variable costs}$$

Fixed costs are generally represented by the letter a, and variable costs per unit by the letter b. Thus total variable costs can be represented by the term bx, where, as before, x represents volume. The resulting cost equation looks like this:

$$\text{TC} = a + bx$$

This means that the fundamental surplus equation can be shown as

$$\text{Surplus} = px - (a + bx)$$

Graphically, we can represent the formula as shown in Figure 20.4. Point x_1, where $px = a + bx$, is the *break-even volume*—the point at which total revenue (px) equals total costs ($a + bx$). At a volume above x_1, the organization earns a surplus; below x_1, it incurs a loss.

To illustrate how this formula can be used, let's assume that an organization wishes to determine its break-even volume. If we know price, fixed costs, and variable costs per unit, we can solve the formula algebraically for x, which would be our break-even volume.

Example: Littleton Public Radio publishes a monthly newsletter on its upcoming programs and details of some of its stories from the prior month. The agency incurs fixed costs of $100,000 a month for its newsletter and variable costs per newsletter of $0.80. It charges $1.80 per newsletter. To compute its break-even volume (number of newsletters per month), we can begin with the cost-volume-profit formula and drop in the known elements. We then solve for the unknown, which in this case is volume, or x.

$$\text{Profit} = px - (a + bx)$$

At break-even, profit equals zero; therefore,

$$px = a + bx$$
$$1.80x = 100,000 + 0.80x$$
$$1.00x = 100,000$$
$$x = 100,000$$

Break-even is 100,000 newsletters.

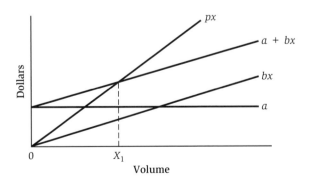

Figure 20.4. Graphic Representation of Revenue, Fixed Costs, and Variable Costs.

Unit Contribution Margin. An important aspect of CVP analysis is the concept of *unit contribution margin*. This is the contribution to fixed costs that comes about as a result of each additional unit sold. In effect, the unit contribution margin is the difference between price and unit variable cost, or $p - b$. By rearranging the terms of the CVP formula, we can see that break-even volume is simply fixed costs divided by unit contribution margin, as follows:

$$px = a + bx$$
$$px - bx = a$$
$$x\,(p - b) = a$$
$$x = \frac{a}{(p - b)}$$

In effect, price minus unit variable cost tells us how much each unit sold contributes to the recovery of fixed costs. When we divide this amount into fixed costs, we arrive at the volume (number of units of activity) needed to recover all our fixed costs. This is our break-even volume.

To illustrate, the Littleton Public Radio's newsletter has a unit contribution margin of $1.00 ($1.80 − $0.80). When we divide this amount into the newsletter's fixed costs of $100,000, we arrive at its break-even volume of 100,000 newsletters.

Incorporating Other Variables into a CVP Analysis. In the Littleton example, we used CVP analysis to solve for the break-even volume. Clearly, if we knew how many units of our product we were likely to sell, our fixed costs, and our unit variable costs, we could then determine the price we would need to charge to break even. Similarly, if we were in an environment where price was market-driven and we knew about how many units we could sell at that price, we could set up either fixed costs or unit variable costs as the unknown and solve for it.

We also can incorporate the need for a surplus into a CVP analysis. The easiest way to do this is to add the amount of desired surplus to our fixed costs and then to calculate a break-even point with that new level of "fixed costs."

Special Considerations in Cost-Volume-Profit Analysis

There are a number of special considerations that can complicate a CVP analysis: Three of the most significant are the presence of semivariable costs, the behavior of step-function costs, and the existence of more than one program.

CVP Analysis with Semivariable Costs. Incorporating semivariable costs into a CVP analysis is relatively easy. Since they have a fixed component and a variable component, we simply need to add the fixed component to the fixed cost total and add the unit variable cost amount to the existing unit cost figure.

CVP Analysis with Step-Function Costs. Ideally, for any given relevant range, we would like to be able to add the step-function costs to fixed costs to obtain total applicable fixed costs. We then could use the break-even formula. Unfortunately, the process is not quite that simple, as the following example illustrates.

Example: In addition to the $100,000 in fixed costs stipulated earlier, Littleton has supervisory costs. These costs behave as follows:

Volume	Costs
0–50,000	$10,000
50,001–100,000	20,000
100,001–150,000	30,000
150,001–200,000	40,000

If we attempt to solve the break-even formula at the first level of fixed costs, we get the following:

$$1.80x = (100,000 + 10,000) + 0.80x$$
$$1.00x = 110,000$$
$$x = 110,000$$

The problem with this solution is that whereas the break-even volume is 110,000 newsletters, the relevant range for the step-function costs was only 0–50,000 newsletters. Thus a break-even of greater than 50,000 newsletters is invalid. Only when we get to the third level do we encounter a valid solution:

$$1.80x = (100,000 + 30,000) + 0.80x$$
$$1.00x = 130,000$$
$$x = 130,000$$

In short, incorporating step-function costs into a CVP formula requires a trial-and-error process to reach the break-even volume.

CVP Analysis with Multiple Products or Services. Thus far we have made all of our CVP calculations in situations where there was only one program. When there are two or more programs involved in the calculation, and where the individual contribution margins are quite divergent, the analysis becomes considerably more complicated. Indeed, a break-even figure computed for an organization with multiple programs, each of which has a quite different contribution margin, is very unstable—as the organization's program mix changes, so will the break-even figure.[11]

Because of this instability, CVP analysis tends to be used relatively little on an ongoing basis in organizations with multiple programs. It is frequently used in conjunction with an analysis of the possible introduction of a new program, however. Indeed, it is an essential aspect of a good marketing analysis for a new program.

On an ongoing basis, managers tend to be much more interested in contribution. When this is the case, each program is assessed in terms of its contribution to the organization's overhead costs, such as we saw with the Clearwater Transportation Service in Exhibit 20.1.

RESPONSIBILITY ACCOUNTING

Increasingly, senior managers in nonprofit organizations are encouraging their professionals as well as their line managers to engage in cost management. To move from improved cost *measurement* (which was the subject of the first two sections of this chapter) to improved cost *management,* a nonprofit needs to focus on the individuals who control its costs. It must also structure its departments and programs in such a way as to provide line managers with incentives to engage in cost control. These matters are the subject of responsibility accounting.

Responsibility Accounting Defined

The goal of responsibility accounting is to help ensure the effective and efficient use of an organizations' resources. In practice, one finds a wide variety of responsibility accounting systems in nonprofit organizations. Sometimes the system consists of highly formal procedures and regularly scheduled activities, and sometimes it is quite informal and sporadic. Sometimes the system involves a great deal of time on the part of senior management, and sometimes senior managers are only marginally involved. Sometimes a great deal of decision-making autonomy is delegated to divisional, departmental, or program managers, and sometimes these middle managers have almost no authority or responsibility in decisions concerning the use of resources.

In large part, these differences arise because the precise characteristics of an organization's responsibility accounting system are highly situational. Moreover, because the principles of responsibility accounting are concerned with the behavior of people, the motivation of managers and professionals, and the role of information, they do not lend themselves to experiment or "proof." Nevertheless, they provide a way of thinking about some important management problems and can be extremely useful for planning and controlling resource usage.

In short, though principles exist, there is no *single correct way* to design a responsibility accounting system. As with any system, however, a responsibility accounting system consists of both structure and process. Structure is what the system *is;* process is what it *does.* In studying the human body, for example, students learn about anatomy (its structure) and physiology (its process). Similarly, a responsibility accounting system can be thought of as having an anatomy and a physiology.

The Responsibility Accounting Structure

The structure of a responsibility accounting system can be assessed in terms of groups of individuals working together toward some common purpose. Each group is called a "responsibility center" and is led by a manager. Responsibility centers can take a wide variety of forms. The development office of a university is a responsibility center. So is a museum's curatorial department. A laboratory in a hospital is a responsibility center. A substance abuse program in a community center is a responsibility center as well.

Organizational units with some sort of responsibility exist in almost all organizations. Therefore, the central question is not whether there are responsibility centers but rather whether their design facilitates the organization's ability to achieve its goals in an efficient fashion. There are many examples of organizations where (1) responsibility centers have overlapping goals and objectives that frequently come into conflict, (2) some of the organization's important goals and objectives have not been assigned to any particular responsibility center, or (3) managers of particular responsibility centers are not given appropriate incentives to achieve the center's objectives.

Types of Responsibility Centers. There are five main types of responsibility centers: revenue centers, standard expense centers, discretionary expense centers, profit centers, and investment centers. The principal factor guiding the selection of one type over another is the kind of resources controlled by the responsibility center manager. These choices are shown in Exhibit 20.2.

Exhibit 20.2. Types of Responsibility Centers.

Type of Responsibility Center	Responsibility
Revenue center	Revenue earned by the center
Standard expense center	Expenses *per unit of output* (but not total expenses) incurred by the center
Discretionary expense center	Total expenses incurred by the center
Profit center	Total revenues and expenses of the center
Investment center	Total revenues and expenses of the center, computed as a percentage of the assets used by the center; this is the center's return on assets (ROA)

As Exhibit 20.2 indicates, if a manager has a great deal of control over revenue, as is ordinarily the case in a development office or a grant-writing office, the manager's department would be considered a revenue center. This is true even though the responsibility center incurs some expenses. That is, the manager's *performance* is evaluated in terms of the *revenue generated* by his or her department. On the other hand, if a manager has a great deal of control over a department's expenses but no ability to generate revenue, the department would ordinarily be an expense center.

There are two types of expense centers: standard and discretionary. A standard expense center is appropriate when a manager can control the expense *per unit* of output but not the *number of units* of output. The laundry department of a hospital, for example, might be a standard expense center—the manager of the laundry would be responsible for controlling the expense per pound washed but not for the total expenses of the department. This is because total expenses depend on the number of pounds washed, which is not under the manager's control.

A discretionary expense center, by contrast, has no easily measurable unit of output. This is the case in, say, a legal or accounting department. Under these circumstances, the department would simply receive a fixed budget, negotiated with senior management but not tied to any units of output. The manager would be expected to adhere to this budget during the budgetary period.

If the manager has control of both revenue and expenses, the center would ordinarily be a *profit center* (a term used in both nonprofit and for-profit organizations). Increasingly, over the past several years, many large and even some small nonprofit organizations have instituted profit centers in an attempt to give their managers incentives to both control expenses and consider ways to generate additional revenues.

Finally, it is possible that a manager also exerts some control over the acquisition and management of certain assets, such as equipment, accounts receivable, or inventory. If this is the case, the manager is expected to control the productivity of those assets in addition to the center's revenue and expenses. This would imply designation as an investment center, where the manager is responsible for the center's surplus as a percentage of its assets (that is, the center's return on assets).

Large organizations frequently have a complicated hierarchy of responsibility centers, such as units, sections, departments, branches, and divisions. Except for activities at the lowest levels of the organization, each responsibility center generally consists of aggregations of smaller responsibility centers. A significant activity for senior management in any organization, regardless of its size, is to design, coordinate, and control the work of all of these responsibility centers.

Design of Responsibility Centers. The issue of importance for designing the structure of a responsibility accounting system is capsulized in the question "For what financial results is the center responsible?" Senior management's objective is to design the organization's responsibility centers in such a way that managers are held responsible for those financial results over which they exercise a reasonable amount of control. This simple-sounding task is frequently quite complicated in practice.

In considering the design of responsibility centers, senior management begins with the premise that the organization itself is an investment center. This is true for both nonprofit and for-profit organizations. As discussed in Chapter Nineteen on financial accounting and financial management, a nonprofit organization must obtain a sufficiently high return on assets (ROA) to allow it to replace its assets as they wear out and to provide the working capital needed to finance growth. This means that a fundamental design question for a responsibility accounting system is how to decentralize that investment responsibility among the various organizational units.

In some instances, the ability of a given manager to control certain elements of ROA is quite clear, and in others, there is considerable ambiguity. When ambiguity is present, senior management must be extremely careful to select a responsibility center that corresponds to the control and decision-making authority of the middle manager in question. If this does not happen, middle managers will quite likely feel that they are being held responsible for resources they cannot control, which can lead to considerable stress within the organization.

In short, there is no one "right" answer to the problem of responsibility center design. Each organization is unique in terms of its strategy, management philosophy, programs, and a wide variety of other characteristics. The guiding principle is that of aligning responsibility and control, but no clear-cut prescriptions can be given. As a result, senior management in many organizations spends a considerable amount of time debating the most appropriate responsibility center structure for a given strategy and organizational structure. Moreover, when either strategy or organizational structure shifts, as they frequently do, senior management must reconsider its responsibility center structure.

In a nonprofit organization, responsibility center design issues extend beyond the question of which *financial* resources a manager controls to include *programmatic* results as well. Indeed, in most nonprofit organizations, financial objectives are frequently viewed as constraints on a manager's ability to achieve a desired set of programmatic results. In essence, then, programmatic results must be measured separately from financial ones and attained if possible in the context of the limited financial resources available.[12]

The Responsibility Accounting Structure and Motivation. A responsibility accounting structure can provide a powerful motivating force for middle- and lower-level managers, as well as for the organization's professionals. It is therefore extremely important for senior management to consider the incentives the structure provides to the affected individuals. Indeed, in designing a responsibility accounting system, senior management must ask a very fundamental question: "Does the responsibility center structure that is in place motivate managers and professionals to take actions that are in the best interest of both their individual responsibility centers and the organization as a whole?" If the answer is yes, *goal congruence* has been achieved, and an appropriate responsibility center structure most likely exists.[13] If the answer is no, there is an absence of goal congruence, and a redesign effort is necessary.

A lack of goal congruence frequently arises in situations where several responsibility centers in a large organization buy and sell services from each other. For example, a school of communication in a university may "buy" maintenance and repair work from the university's building services department, or it may buy food and beverages for its recruiting functions from the university's dining services department.

When intraorganizational transactions of this sort happen, the main question concerns the prices—called "transfer prices"—at which these transactions take place. Indeed, if an organization contains a number of responsibility centers that are not completely independent of one another, they almost certainly will engage in "buying and selling" transactions among themselves. As a result, the transfer prices become important elements of the responsibility accounting structure.[14]

Role of Full Cost Information. It is desirable to have the system for accumulating full cost information also be the system for responsibility accounting. For this to happen, the accounting department has to pay careful attention to the differing needs of the two types of accounting. Consider, for example, the cost of a day of inpatient care in a hospital. From a full cost accounting perspective, we would wish to add together the various resources that went into that day: room, board, nursing care, medications, and so on.

By contrast, from a responsibility accounting perspective, we are concerned with the individuals who control those resources. For example, physicians carry a major responsibility for the use of resources: they decide on the level of nursing care; order tests, procedures, and medications; and determine a discharge date. A nursing director or supervisor, who determines the staffing and efficiency of nurses, carries some additional responsibility. A director of housekeeping, who is responsible for the efficiency and quality of the cleaning effort, also has some responsibility. And so on.

As a result, the accounting system must be able to resort and reclassify the full cost information into responsibility centers and to eliminate costs that responsibility center managers cannot control (such as allocated overhead). If there are profit centers, the system needs to combine the cost information with the revenue earned by the center in such a way that the resulting reports are of use to the responsibility center managers. Unfortunately, this rarely happens. To gain a perspective on the challenges facing the accounting staff in developing the appropriate responsibility accounting information, we need to examine the responsibility accounting process.

The Responsibility Accounting Process

Much of the responsibility accounting process is informal. Meetings, ad hoc memoranda, and hallway and lunchtime conversations, all can serve to influence managers' decisions about the use of resources. Nevertheless, in most organizations, a more formal process also exists. This formal process usually consists of a regularly scheduled set of activities during which decisions are made about the kinds and quantities of outputs the organization expects during an upcoming accounting period (such as a fiscal year) and the kinds and amounts of resources it will use to generate those outputs. During the accounting period, the organization keeps records on actual results (outputs and inputs) and prepares reports on these results that senior and middle managers can use as a basis for determining whether corrective action of some sort is needed. These activities comprise four separate phases—programming, budgeting, operating and measuring, and reporting and evaluating—that recur in a regular cycle and build on each other, as indicated in Figure 20.5.

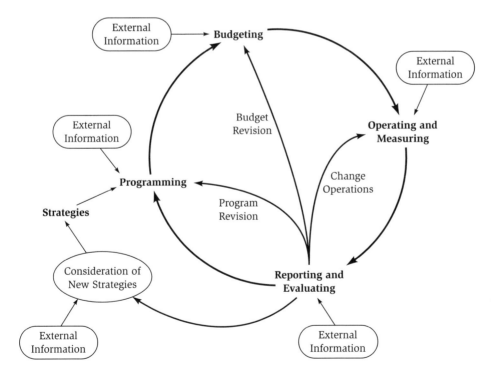

Figure 20.5. Phases of the Responsibility Accounting Process.

Programming. In the programming phase of the cycle, managers make a variety of decisions of a long-term nature. These decisions concern both the kinds of programs the organization will engage in and the kinds and amounts of resources it will devote to each. In general, as Figure 20.5 indicates, these decisions are made in the context of the organization's overall strategy, coupled with whatever information is available concerning new opportunities, increased competition, new or pending legislation that might affect the organization's efforts, and other external inputs.

The programming phase of the responsibility accounting process frequently looks ahead by as much as five or ten years. The program planning document in a large nonprofit organization is often lengthy, describing each proposal in detail, estimating the resources necessary to accomplish the program, and calculating the expected social and financial returns from the effort. Nevertheless, many benefits are difficult to quantify, and that complicates the decision making.

Because many of the benefits of new program proposals are difficult to quantify and because profit center managers will tend to be quite optimistic about their program proposals, a new program bias often finds its way into the programming phase. Senior management tends to counteract this bias by using its own staff to analyze proposals submitted by responsibility center managers, and as might be imagined, this occasionally causes friction between the planning staff and these managers and gives the entire process a political overtone. Managing this friction and the political aspect so that the final result is the selection of an appropriate set of new programs is perhaps one of the most challenging tasks senior management faces in the programming process.

Budgeting. In contrast to the programming phase, which looks ahead several years, the budgeting phase generally looks ahead only one year. It accepts programs as given and attempts to determine the revenues and expenses that will be associated with each. In many organizations, programs fall neatly into responsibility centers such that each responsibility center manager can be charged with preparing a budget for each of his or her programs. Sometimes a program and a responsibility center are identical, but in most organizations, the fit between programs and responsibility centers is not so neat, and a more complicated budgeting process is necessary.

The need for a more complicated budgeting process arises when the organization's programs cut across several responsibility centers. For example, in many health care organizations, medical records is a responsibility center that serves all the organization's programs, but it is generally not thought of as a "program." Similarly, nursing is an example of an activity that might either stand alone as a responsibility center serving a variety of programs or departments in a hospital or be viewed as an activity that can be divided among the organization's programs in such a way that each program manager's responsibility extends to the supervision and management of several nurses. By contrast, a substance abuse program might function as a stand-alone program in a mental health agency.

Although each organization must develop a budgeting process that meets its individual needs, a good budgeting process is typically characterized by several elements:

- A set of guidelines that are developed by senior management and communicated to line managers. This is ordinarily the first step in the annual process. It is usually done in writing and sets forth a timetable for the rest of the process.

- A participatory element in which managers at the lowest levels have an opportunity to prepare budgets for their responsibility centers and discuss them with their superiors.

- A central staff (usually in the controller's office) responsible for co-ordinating the activities, carrying out many of the technical aspects of the process, and occasionally providing analyses that serve as "checks and balances" against projections by responsibility center managers.

- A hierarchy of information, beginning with the smallest responsibility center and accumulating budget information by successively larger re-sponsibility centers, eliminating excessive detail at each step.

- A negotiation phase during which, if necessary, each responsibility cen-ter manager can defend his or her budget against anticipated reductions or otherwise argue why it should be retained as originally prepared.

- A final approval and sign-off by senior management authorizing respon-sibility center managers at each level to carry out the budget as agreed in the preparation and negotiation phases.

In general, final approval constitutes a commitment between each responsi-bility center manager and his or her superior that the budget will be adhered to unless there are "compelling reasons" to change it. Compelling reasons include large and unanticipated changes in volume, a lengthy strike, fuel shortages and resulting large price increases, a fire in the main building, and any number of similarly significant or catastrophic events.

As anyone who has participated in a budget preparation effort knows, the process often has a certain gamelike quality to it. This, in part, is the reason se-nior management uses staff analyses in addition to the information submitted by responsibility center managers. The principal intent of this effort is to elim-inate any slack in the budget so that the final budget estimates the future as re-alistically as possible. Overall, the budget for each responsibility center should be relatively difficult to attain, but attainable nevertheless.

Operating and Measuring. Once programs have been established and a budget has been agreed on, the organization commences operating during the budget year. This is, of course, an oversimplification, since all organizations except newly established ones operate continually. However, if some new programs have been approved or if new funds have been made available for existing programs, it is quite likely that a variety of new or different types of activities will also commence at the beginning of a new budget year.

From a responsibility accounting perspective, new or different types of operations have important implications. Specifically, if the budget is to be adhered to, managers must receive information concerning their responsibility center's performance compared to budgeted objectives. Consequently, new as well as ongoing activities must be measured. More specifically, data must be collected about both financial and nonfinancial activities, and this information must be incorporated into the responsibility accounting system. The operating and measurement phase of the process, then, is one of putting plans into effect and measuring the relevant inputs and outputs.

Role of the Accounting System. If the measurement aspect of this phase of the responsibility accounting process is to be effective, the organization must have a well-developed accounting system. The accounting system must be designed so that it can both keep records of revenues and expenses and permit the information to be used for (1) preparing financial statements in accordance with the rules and guidelines of outside agencies; (2) preparing full cost analyses, in which overhead is allocated to programs and services for purposes of analyzing costs and establishing prices or reimbursement rates; (3) distinguishing between fixed and variable costs where necessary; and (4) classifying both revenues and expenses by programs and responsibility centers for purposes of measuring the performance of the managers of these centers.

Need for Integrated Information. Although the information has multiple uses, it must be integrated. That is, although data collected for one purpose may differ from those collected for another, or certain data elements will sometimes be reported in a detailed fashion and sometimes in summaries, in all instances the data should be reconcilable from one report to another. This requires careful and thoughtful design of the information coding structure at the outset and a cautious, systematic process for including new data elements when the system must be modified.

In designing and modifying the accounting system, the organization's accounting staff must be carefully managed to ensure that they consider the information's potential multiple uses. In addition, the system is ordinarily built on a financial base because monetary units are generally the easiest to collect, maintain, and integrate. Nevertheless, managers frequently wish to see a variety of nonmonetary measures, such as minutes per visit, number of clients, percentages, and client outcomes. These nonmonetary items also are part of the *measurement system*, which is thus somewhat broader than the accounting system.

Changing Information Needs of Managers. The role of the measurement phase—to determine and gather the appropriate information to meet the decision-making needs of responsibility center and program managers—is complicated by two factors: (1) different managers in an organization make different kinds of decisions, and (2) all managers make a variety of decisions depending on the particular circumstances they face at various times in the operating year. These factors require that the measurement phase of the responsibility accounting process be flexible and dynamic. In any growing or evolving organization, the information needed by senior and middle managers not only will differ from one responsibility center or program to the next but also will be changing constantly.

Reporting and Evaluating. The final phase of the responsibility accounting process entails the presentation of information to program and responsibility center managers. The information collected in the measurement phase of the cycle is classified, analyzed, sorted, merged, totaled, and finally reported to these managers. The resulting reports generally compare planned outputs and inputs with actual ones and thereby allow both operating managers and their superiors to evaluate performance during the period. This information, along with a variety of other information (from conversations, informal sources, industry analyses, and the like), generally leads to one of three possible courses of behavior, as indicated in Figure 20.5.

Change Operations. If the operating manager or his or her supervisor is not satisfied with the results shown on the reports, action of some sort may be necessary to correct the situation. This action can include examining sources of supply to attempt to obtain lower material prices, asking supervisors about the use of overtime, and speaking with the agency's professionals (such as social workers, curators, teachers, physicians, or nurses) about client satisfaction or dissatisfaction with the organization's services. Action can also include praise for a job well done, constructive criticism, reassignment, or, in extreme cases, termination.

Revise the Budget. In some instances, certain aspects of a responsibility center are not under the control of the center's manager. For example, because the volume and mix of activity in a hospital laboratory are determined exclusively by the test orders submitted by physicians, the laboratory manager has no ability to control either the number or the kinds of tests the laboratory must process.

Similarly, if supply prices are the responsibility of the purchasing department or if wage rates are determined by senior management in its negotiations with labor unions, managers of the affected responsibility centers will generally have little control over variations from the budget. Moreover, the effect of a strike or a natural disaster may mean that it is all but impossible for a responsibility center manager to meet the budget. In these instances, some organizations will revise the budget.

Revise a Program. The reports can also be used as a basis for program evaluation and revision. For any of a number of reasons, an organization's programming decisions may not be optimal. The anticipated demand for the program or service may not exist; competition may be stronger than anticipated; technological improvements may have made the program or service obsolete; the organization may not be able to develop the skills necessary to run the program well. In extreme situations, the reports may indicate a need not only to revise or discontinue one or more of the organization's programs but to change the organization's overall strategy as well.

Because the reporting and evaluation phase has this feedback characteristic, Figure 20.5 shows a closed loop. As a consequence, the process tends to be rhythmic—it follows a similar pattern every year. Managers learn this pattern and adjust their activities to it.

The Role of Cost Drivers in Responsibility Accounting

Over the past ten or fifteen years, many nonprofit organizations have begun to think about cost control in terms of a series of *cost-influencing* factors, or *cost drivers,* coupled with the individuals who control them. Cost drivers thus have some important responsibility accounting implications.

Cost Drivers Defined. A cost driver is an activity that takes place in an organization that can be directly linked to a change in costs. In some nonprofit organizations, cost drivers are rather easy to identify. Certain costs in a museum, for example, arise as a result of the number of visitors. Others arise as a result of the number and complexity of the exhibitions.[15]

Clearly, the number and nature of cost drivers will vary considerably from one organization to the next. Nevertheless, in most client-serving nonprofit organizations, there are the following six cost drivers:

- Type of client—sometimes called "case type"
- Volume, the number of clients of each type
- Client needs, which dictate the resources used by a particular type of client

- Efficiency of resource delivery
- Factor prices—the cost per unit of each resource
- Programs—the fixed costs incurred so as to be ready to serve clients

Exhibit 20.3 gives examples of these variables in a hospital setting.

Managerial Focus. When cost drivers are used in the responsibility accounting effort, management's focus moves beyond responsibility centers to include the factors that influence the kinds and amounts of resources a client or a program consumes. Regardless of the number or nature of cost drivers, the key thrust of the approach is to shift managers' thinking away from the traditional line item view of costs to a focus on the activities that generate costs. Frequently, some of these activities transcend traditional responsibility center boundaries. Indeed, the concept of cost drivers allows us to bridge the gap between the broad overview of costs in Figure 20.1 and potential managerial actions to influence and control costs, which is the concern of a responsibility accounting system.

Cost Drivers and Responsibility Accounting Systems. To move the cost driver idea into the realm of responsibility accounting, senior management must identify the forces that control each cost driver. This allows the alignment of responsibility with control, a key aspect of the responsibility accounting structure.

Exhibit 20.3. Examples of Cost Drivers in a Hospital.

Cost Driver	Examples
Case type	Myocardial infarction; pneumonia; appendicitis
Volume	10 cases of myocardial infarction; 50 cases of pneumonia; 30 cases of appendicitis
Patient needs	For myocardial infarctions: 2 days hospital care in coronary care unit; 4 days hospital care in ward; 3 days Level III nursing care; 2 days Level II nursing care; 12 laboratory tests; 7 X-rays
Efficiency of resource delivery	Actual nursing hours per patient versus standard nursing hours per patient at each level of nursing care; actual time and supplies per radiological procedure versus standard per procedure; actual time per lab test versus standard time per test
Factor prices	Hourly nursing wage; hourly technician wage; price per unit of radiological film
Programs	The fixed costs needed to run programs such as open-heart surgery, renal transplant, or alcohol detoxification

Nonprofit organizations that have begun to develop improved responsibility accounting systems have recognized that responsibility center managers and professionals control different resources. By incorporating cost drivers into their responsibility accounting systems, they have begun to manage the number and kind of resources used for a given type of client differently from the way they manage the cost of providing each of those resources. Making this distinction allows them to use *professional protocols* to address resources per client and *administrative protocols* to address the efficiency of resource provision.

Changes to Budget Preparation. By focusing on cost drivers, many nonprofit organizations have been able to revise the way they prepare their budgets. When cost drivers and their responsible agents have been identified, an organization can ask each group to prepare estimates for the cost drivers that it controls. Moreover, by using a model that permits members of each group to estimate their own cost drivers, many organizations have found that they can simulate program plans and budgets under different strategic alternatives, as with different programs or different client mixes within a program.

CONCLUSIONS

Good full cost accounting, differential cost accounting, and responsibility accounting systems are essential to a nonprofit organization's achievement of its strategic goals. Indeed, nonprofit organizations need to distinguish between full cost and differential cost accounting (where the accounting staff improves the measurement system) and responsibility accounting (where senior management becomes involved to shift the focus from cost and revenue measurement to their management). These different systems and their characteristics are summarized in Exhibit 20.4.

Many nonprofits attempting to improve their responsibility accounting systems have begun to identify cost drivers, thereby requiring responsibility center managers to focus their cost control efforts on groups of clients with similar characteristics. Moreover, by incorporating cost drivers and the individuals who control them into their responsibility accounting systems, these nonprofits have found that they can assign and monitor responsibility for cost changes. As a result, they have a much greater ability to control their costs. In particular, this effort can lead to a set of professional and administrative protocols that give them an opportunity to link cost drivers to budgets. Such an approach can be a powerful tool for nonprofit managers concerned about maintaining client services at acceptable levels in an era of rapidly escalating costs and shrinking public and private resources.

Exhibit 20.4. Nonprofit Management Accounting: A Summary.

Goal	Parties Responsible	Information Used	Key Activities Performed	Managerial Uses
Full Cost Accounting				
Improving the full cost system	Accounting staff	Direct and indirect costs	Choice of cost object	Product line profitability
			Assignment of costs to cost centers	Strategic decisions (programs, facilities, personnel needed to support chosen product lines)
			Choice of allocation bases	
			Allocation of service center costs to revenue centers	
Differential Cost Accounting				
Assessing cost behavior	Accounting staff	Fixed and variable	Analyses of costs	Decision making on such matters as offering a special price, contracting out for services, and retaining or discontinuing an unprofitable program
			Contribution analyses	
Management Control Systems				
Controlling costs	Senior management	Client and responsibility center costs	Determining cost drivers	Cost control
			Budgeting using cost drivers	Motivation
			Determining responsibility	Performance measurement
				Involvement of professionals in cost management centers
				Assigning responsibility to controlling agents

Notes

1. Marcia Baringa, "Stanford Erupts over Indirect Costs," *Science,* Apr. 20, 1990, p. 292.

2. For a discussion of the sorts of issues that an organization must consider, see David W. Young, "Cost Accounting and Cost Comparisons: Methodological Issues and Their Policy and Management Implications," *Accounting Horizons,* 1988, 2(1), 67–76.

3. Robert N. Anthony and David W. Young, *Management Control in Nonprofit Organizations,* 7th ed. (Burr Ridge, Ill.: Irwin, 2003).

4. For a more extensive discussion, see Anthony and Young, *Management Control in Nonprofit Organizations.*

5. The distinction between an intermediate cost object and a cost center is occasionally quite subtle. On occasion, both can be viewed as "purposes" for which costs are collected; for this reason, cost centers are sometimes called intermediate cost objects.

6. Complete homogeneity is rarely possible, and even if it were, the cost of making the requisite computations might be prohibitive. Compromises are therefore frequently necessary.

7. In undertaking an analysis of this sort, we would need to be aware of potential comparability problems (for example, whether the organizations with which we are comparing ourselves measure their costs in the same way we do).

8. This terminology can be confusing, since *allocation* is occasionally called *apportionment* and vice versa. Moreover, the terms *distribution, allocation,* and *apportionment* are sometimes used interchangeably. In addition to these terminology differences, service center costs that are allocated to mission centers are sometimes called *indirect costs.* As a result, one must be careful to understand the process that is at work rather than attempt to decipher the meanings of the terms.

9. For an illustration of the reciprocal method, see David W. Young, *Management Accounting in Health Care Organizations* (San Francisco: Jossey-Bass, 2003), app. to ch. 1.

10. For a discussion of their use in a health care context, see Young, *Management Accounting in Health Care Organizations,* ch. 3.

11. For additional discussion of this point, see Young, *Management Accounting in Health Care Organizations,* ch. 2.

12. There has been considerable discussion of this issue in the literature in terms of what has been called the "balanced scorecard." For details on the balanced scorecard, see Robert S. Kaplan and David P. Norton, *The Balanced Scorecard* (Boston: Harvard Business School Press, 1996). For a discussion of nonfinancial measures in nonprofit organizations, see Anthony and Young, *Management Control in Nonprofit Organizations,* ch. 12.

13. *Goal congruence* is a concept borrowed from social psychology. In this context, it is defined as a situation in which the goals of individual managers and profession-

als, based on senior management's expectations for their responsibility centers, are consistent with the overall goals of the organization.

14. Transfer pricing has been the subject of many academic treatises. For a description of its role in nonprofit organizations, see Anthony and Young, *Management Control in Nonprofit Organizations*, ch. 8. For a description in health care organizations, see Young, *Management Accounting in Health Care Organizations*, ch. 5. The practice case at the end of this chapter illustrates how transfer prices can create a goal congruence problem.

15. Considerable work done in the for-profit sector around the concept of cost drivers has culminated in the concept of "activity-based costing" (ABC). In a for-profit firm, however, ABC relates to the attachment of overhead to products rather than to the drivers of all costs. For a discussion of how the principles of ABC can be applied to a nonprofit context, see Anthony and Young, *Management Control in Nonprofit Organizations*, ch. 5. For a discussion of its role in some health care organizations, see Young, *Management Accounting in Health Care Organizations*, ch. 4. The practice case at the end of this chapter illustrates how ABC might be used in a hospital's dietary department.

CHAPTER TWENTY-ONE

Risk Management

Melanie L. Herman

During the past decade, nonprofit leaders have acquired increasingly sophisticated skills in various management disciplines, including fundraising, finance, and others addressed in this book. Yet most nonprofit leaders today continue to express concern that their knowledge of risk management principles is inadequate. Responsibility for this knowledge gap in the nonprofit sector rests in part with the risk management and insurance industries. The risk management industry has done a poor job overall of welcoming professionals from other fields as students of educational programs. The insurance industry has remained archaic, clinging to the use of confusing and easily misunderstood terminology while surrounded by fields of study that have moved comfortably into the twenty-first century.

Despite the fact that a growing number of nonprofit leaders recognize the importance of risk management to the health and sustainability of their organizations, educational opportunities in this arena are not being seized by nonprofit personnel. Many leaders continue to view risk management as a luxury their nonprofits cannot afford. Others are intimidated by the technical aspects of the discipline, including its relationship to finance. And some nonprofit managers have been "turned off" by the business-oriented language and analysis found in traditional risk management texts.

The challenge for educators in the risk management field include more effectively describing the tangible and intangible benefits of risk management to nonprofit organizations and succinctly presenting methods for integrating risk management that respect the enormous financial and time demands facing today's nonprofit leaders.

BENEFITS OF RISK MANAGEMENT

Developing a risk management plan in a nonprofit organization requires, at a minimum, a commitment of time and human resources. In some organizations, the implementation of some strategies outlined in the plan will require the expenditure of financial resources. What benefits can be realized by integrating risk management into the operations of a small, mid-sized, or large nonprofit?

The benefits of risk management range from truly intangible benefits such as increased confidence in the nonprofit's service delivery to quantifiable cost savings such as dollars saved due to skilled negotiation of the organization's insurance renewal. The benefits differ from one nonprofit to the next, based on the circumstances the organization faces, the degree to which risk management efforts and activities are accepted or undermined, and whether risk management activities are ad hoc or coordinated.

Intangible Benefits

The intangible benefits of a risk management program include the following:

- Increased confidence on the part of volunteer and staff leaders about the degree to which the organization has planned for potential downside and upside risks
- Nonprofit's managers' knowledge that the organization has set aside or arranged for the availability of resources to compensate persons (such as clients or volunteers) inadvertently harmed during the delivery of the organization's services
- Improved morale among paid and volunteer staff members, who believe that they work for an organization committed to safety in its service delivery
- Additional resources available for mission-related programs and services that would otherwise be spent paying for accidents and incidents
- Support from key stakeholders, who see the nonprofit taking visible steps to protect clients from harm
- Greater confidence among key funders, who appreciate the nonprofit's risk management efforts designed to prevent the erosion of financial and other assets

Tangible Benefits

The potential tangible benefits of risk management in a nonprofit organization include the following:

- Fewer accidents and incidents that distract the nonprofit's staff from mission-related activities

- Lower insurance costs due to fewer claims and better loss experience

- Lower insurance costs due to greater sophistication on the part of the personnel at the nonprofit who are responsible for procuring insurance for the nonprofit

- Increased enrollment in client and member programs due to the reputation of the nonprofit as an organization that takes safety seriously

- Less personnel time required to market the nonprofit's insurance program, due to the fact that several insurers view the nonprofit as a desirable risk

STARTING A RISK MANAGEMENT PROGRAM

The starting point for developing and sustaining a risk management program in a nonprofit is assigning responsibility for the development, implementation, and monitoring of the program.

Assigning Responsibility for Risk Management

There are two contrasting "schools of thought" with respect to assigning responsibility for risk management activities in a nonprofit. According to the first school of thought, it is important to assign responsibility for risk management to a single paid or volunteer staff member who can coordinate the organization's risk management efforts, provide periodic reports to the board on the success or failure of ongoing loss prevention efforts, and serve as the point of contact for contract personnel engaged to assist the nonprofit. Using this approach, a nonprofit can hold a single person accountable for the development of risk management activities.

The second school of thought suggests that a nonprofit is best served by involving a diverse group of people in the design and implementation of a risk management program. According to this school of thought, bringing a diverse group of people together early in the process not only increases the creativity of the risk identification and strategy development but also creates a road map for obtaining buy-in from key personnel. In some organizations, this approach is selected through the designation of a risk management committee, while other nonprofits add responsibility for various risk management tasks to the job descriptions of a handful of employees. Most nonprofits that have made a commitment to risk management fashion an approach that contains elements of both schools of thought. For example, a nonprofit social services agency might decide to create a volunteer risk management committee consisting of staff members, outside professionals, and representatives of the board, client community, and corps of volunteers. The committee might be staffed by the nonprofit's chief financial officer, who serves as coordinator of the group's activities.

Small, all-volunteer or principally volunteer nonprofits are most likely to rely solely on a volunteer risk management committee, while large, established, and mature nonprofits are more likely to add the position of risk manager to their organizational charts. The vast majority of nonprofits will select a strategy for staffing risk management that is compatible with the organization's culture. At a minimum, however, a decision about who will coordinate the design and implementation of risk management activities should be made before the nonprofit launches a vigorous risk identification exercise. Consider people with expertise in a broad area as you form the team or group that will coordinate risk management in your nonprofit. Some excellent candidates:

- People with working knowledge of the risks the nonprofit encounters on a day-to-day basis, such as representatives in the human resources, technology, service delivery, maintenance, and finance areas
- Outside advisers who bring expertise in finance, legal matters, and insurance
- Volunteers who have expressed concerns about safety or liability issues

A nonprofit's risk management committee is often responsible for all phases of an organization's risk management program, from development through implementation and monitoring. In a committee with wide-ranging responsibility, a work plan may include any or all of the following:

- Developing, for board approval, an organizational risk management policy that affirms the organization's commitment to safeguarding its assets
- Establishing the nonprofit's risk management goals (for example, ensuring its survival, maintaining essential operations, or providing humanitarian services)
- Identifying the organization's risks and establishing the risk management priorities
- Selecting the best risk management techniques (avoidance, modification, retention, or sharing) for the priority risks
- Recommending appropriate risk financing alternatives

- Communicating the agency's risk management plan and loss control procedures to the board of directors, employees, volunteers, clients, and the other stakeholders

- Selecting an insurance adviser (broker, agent, or consultant) and negotiating insurance arrangements

- Overseeing loss prevention and control activities

- Providing an annual risk management report to the board of directors

Once a nonprofit's leaders have decided who will coordinate the organization's risk management activities, these key designees can begin the process of developing a program that suits the nonprofit's unique circumstances, exposures, concerns, and resources. This work should generally begin with a discussion of the nonprofit's goals and aspirations for its risk management effort.

Risk Management Goals

As in other disciplines, it is important for a nonprofit to establish goals before moving too far along with any effort to realize changes in attitudes and outcomes. Establishing goals before engaging in risk identification and strategy development will provide the nonprofit with a yardstick against which it will be able to measure its results.

Although there are common threads in the risk management goals of diverse nonprofits, each organization should take the time to articulate what it hopes to accomplish by integrating risk management into its operations. Here are some examples of risk management goals:

- Reducing the frequency and severity of injuries suffered by volunteers working on home rehabilitation projects

- Planning appropriately for communitywide disasters to enable a nonprofit food bank to resume mission-critical operations within two days of a crisis

- Ensuring the adequate protection of a nonprofit association's financial assets by implementing a balanced investment policy, developing and instituting thoughtful internal controls, and ensuring periodic review by an active finance and audit committee

Although taking a broad approach is admirable, establishing narrow goals for a nonprofit's first risk management program increases the odds of success. An overly ambitious program is more likely to fail over time because the task at hand is disproportionate to the resources the nonprofit is able to marshal.

Finding Risk Management in Current Programs

Many nonprofits report that they have few, if any, risk management activities in place. Yet even a small, all-volunteer program is likely to have risk management policies and safeguards—including some activities that the nonprofit's leaders regard as "common sense" or simply good management. These existing assets should be recognized and noted by the risk management committee as it goes through the risk management process described in the next section. As the risk management effort matures, the committee will be encouraged by all that the organization is already doing to protect its vital assets.

There are various ways to go about examining a nonprofit's operations for risks that threaten its mission. And there are at least an equal number of ways to formulate strategies that will enable an organization to address major and minor risks. A multistep risk management process offers one approach to this important task. I explain one approach to this process on the pages that follow.

THE RISK MANAGEMENT PROCESS

Once the team that will tackle the assignment of integrating risk management into the operations of a nonprofit has been identified and formed and the broad goals of the effort have been articulated, a meeting should be held to discuss the process or steps the committee will follow to achieve its goals. The five-step process described here is a continuous loop. As soon as the committee reaches step 5, it's time to return to the beginning and reexamine the environment in which the organization operates. There is no set time frame in which the steps should be followed. Some organizations will try to come full circle in a year's time, while others will strive to begin at step 1 at least every two years. And in some cases, a shorter time frame will be required, due to the nature of the nonprofit's operations. Other organizations work to build risk management into the nonprofit's day-to-day planning and operational activities. For example, when the planning team for a fundraising event meets, it automatically includes a discussion of safety issues on its planning meeting agenda without a reminder to do so.

Step 1: Consider the Context

Before discussing the risks the nonprofit faces, the risk management committee should focus its attention on the environment in which the nonprofit operates. For example, the nonprofit's staff expertise, funding outlook, appetite for risk taking, past experience with losses and risk management, and economic and political circumstances are all aspects of the context in which any future risk management activities will take place. These contextual factors should be considered as the committee brainstorms risks and considers what strategies will work for the nonprofit.

The risk management committee should consider a wide range of factors as it discusses the environment in which future risk management activities will take place, including the following:

- *Personnel:* The attitudes and availability of staff members should be examined.
- *Financial resources:* Determine what funds, if any, are available to implement the committee's recommendations.
- *Past experience:* Past losses, crises, and risk management should be reviewed, as they will be instructive about the potential for future success.
- *Requirements:* Any changes that have been mandated by regulators, funders, and other bodies should be discussed.

The following questions may be helpful in unearthing the risk management context:

- What is the nonprofit's experience with accidental losses? If the organization has faced frequent or severe losses in the past, how well has it handled these events? What changes in operations were made as a result of these losses?
- What attitudes about risk prevail at the nonprofit? Do the organization's leaders support thoughtful risk taking in pursuit of its mission, or has an overly cautious approach led to the cancellation of mission-critical activities? (Some boards and executives may feel that they should be cautious, seeing themselves as stewards of the community's assets. This issue must be periodically discussed and agreed on.)
- What level of interest in risk management and loss prevention has been expressed by paid and volunteer staff? Is the organization likely to face resistance from key personnel when it tries to implement new risk management policies and procedures?
- Are there outside pressures to implement risk management from groups such as funders, regulators, and business partners?
- Have there been developments in the nonprofit's insurance program, such as the cancellation of coverage, new restrictions on coverage, or unprecedented premium increases, that have led to a greater interest in risk management?

Step 2: Identify Risks

During the second step of the risk management process, the committee works to identify the risks the organization faces. One approach is to encourage open brainstorming, during which every risk is written down without discussion about its merits or the nonprofit's level of exposure. A committee with diverse perspectives is in the best position to identify a wide range of risks, including those related to finance and administration as well as service delivery, collaborations, special events, governance, employment practices, and the nonprofit's reputation among stakeholders and in the community at large. This step works best when the committee members name specific rather than general risks. For example, during a brainstorming session, the members of a risk management committee for a nonprofit after-school tutoring program might come up with a long list that includes the following risks:

- The risk that a child will be picked up from the program by a non-custodial parent or another unauthorized person

- The risk that the reading levels of program graduates will not be markedly improved from their levels at the time of enrollment and that lack of change will be perceived as the organization's fault (Assessment of causes for change or no change in program participants— as Thomas thoroughly describes in Chapter Sixteen—is difficult, though participants and funders may expect improvement. Adequately responding to perceptions is important.)

- The possibility that two children enrolled in the program will have a physical confrontation

- The risk that a child or parent will accuse one of the program volunteers of inappropriate touching of a child

- The possibility that a volunteer tutor will establish inappropriate, out-of-program contact with a child or the child's family

The detail in such a list will be immeasurably helpful as the committee moves on to evaluating and addressing the risks it has identified. Risks stated in unspecific terms, such as "the risk that a client will be harmed," will be difficult, if not impossible, to quantify.

One of the concerns that is likely to be expressed by the members of the committee is the fear that it will not "cover the bases" in its risk identification efforts. A suggested approach for addressing this concern is to identify categories of exposure and then place identified risks within these categories. Some groups will do this by separating risks according to asset categories within the nonprofit: people, property, income, and goodwill or reputation. Others prefer to use the existing structure of the organization as a framework for identifying subcategories. For example, one national nonprofit social services organization used its organizational chart as the basis for the risk identification exercise. Risks that were articulated during the brainstorming exercise were listed under the nonprofit's six department headings: finance and administration, communications, development and special events, education programs, recreation programs, and facilities management.

This approach allows the committee to quickly see whether it has identified a least a minimum number of risks in each functional area. If the committee has difficulty naming risks in a particular area, this may signal the need to involve others who bring knowledge of day-to-day operations to the committee's deliberations.

Step 3: Evaluate Risks

The third step in the risk management process moves the committee from an exhaustive "laundry list" of risks to a more concise list of short-term and long-term risk management priorities for the nonprofit. There is no single or preferred way in which to analyze, review, or rank the list of risks identified in step 2. Nonprofits that operate informally may prefer to simply discuss the list and provide committee members with an opportunity to weigh in on the relative importance or urgency of the risks that have been identified. One guiding principle for an informal approach to risk evaluation is to single out recurring downside risks that can be avoided through simple or inexpensive means. For example, the committee at a shelter for homeless families may determine that several times each winter, a client slips on ice that has formed on the walkway in front of the shelter. This recurring event is a top candidate for risk management intervention because it is predictable and exposes the organization to financial loss. Another guiding principle for ranking risks is to give special notice to risks that rarely occur but would seriously threaten the mission and sustainability of the nonprofit if they did occur. The same shelter might identify the physical abuse of a family member by a paid or volunteer counselor as such an event. The organization expects that such an event may never happen, yet it recognizes that the aftermath of an incident—including media reports that a shelter intended to provide haven for homeless families is exposing clients to danger—could result in the loss of community support, public and private funding, and the ability to sustain the organization.

Another approach to evaluating or ranking the risks identified in step 2 is to assign scores or grades to each risk in terms of *frequency* (how likely it is to occur) and *severity* (how costly such an occurrence would be). Scoring systems of 1 to 10 (1 being extremely rare or inexpensive, 10 meaning likely to occur or costly) or A to F may provide the tools the committee needs to separate risks that deserve immediate attention from those for which no action is recommended.

Exhibit 21.1 illustrates how the committee for the hypothetical tutoring program might score the risks listed in the text. Given these results and assuming that the tutoring program must make choices about what risks it should address in the upcoming year, the organization is likely to focus on preventing pickup by noncustodial parents and preventing the abuse of children in the nonprofit's care.

Exhibit 21.1. Rating the Risks Identified by an After-School Tutorial Program.

Risk	Frequency	Severity	Score	Rank
The risk that a child will be picked up from the program by a noncustodial parent or another unauthorized person	2	9	11	1
The risk that the reading levels of program graduates will not be markedly improved from their levels at the time of enrollment and that lack of change will be perceived as the organization's fault	1	4	5	5
The possibility that two children enrolled in the program will have a physical confrontation	3	5	8	3
The risk that a child or parent will accuse one of the program volunteers of inappropriate touching of a child	1	9	10	2
The possibility that a volunteer tutor will establish inappropriate, out-of-program contact with a child or the child's family	3	4	7	4

Notes: Frequency and severity were rated on a scale of 1 (low) to 10 (high). Scores are the sum of the frequency and severity ratings.

Step 4: Decide What to Do and Take Action

The fourth step of the risk management process requires the greatest commitment of time. During this step, the committee makes decisions about the actions the nonprofit will take to address its priority risks. These actions can range from simple operational changes, such as requiring visitors to wear name tags while on the nonprofit's property or conducting a monthly fire drill, to potentially costly policy changes, such as requiring the rigorous screening of all volunteers seeking positions in a youth-serving organization. One way to approach this task is to create a table listing the organization's top risks— the risks that the committee has determined deserve immediate attention. Columns indicating the proposed action steps, due dates for implementation, and staff assignments are then added to the matrix. A sample is presented in Exhibit 21.2.

Exhibit 21.2. Sample Item on a Risk Management Action Plan.

Risk	Rank	Action Steps	Due Date	Staff
Child picked up from the program by a non-custodial parent or another unauthorized person	1	• Modify application to include verification of persons allowed to pick up client	Jan. 1	Mary
		• Draft new procedure and add to operations handbook	Jan. 5	Bob
		• Brief all staff on new procedure, including importance to safety of nonprofit and clients	Jan. 15	Bob

Step 5: Monitor and Adjust

Various outcomes are possible when a nonprofit adopts new risk management measures, including the following:

- The new policy, procedure, or practice is widely accepted as a practical way to reduce exposure to serious claims or other forms of harm to the nonprofit's assets.

- The new practice proves impractical and is followed inconsistently, thereby undermining its effectiveness.

- The new policy proves too difficult to follow or is communicated ineffectively, resulting in unintended policy violations,

- The new practice proves too costly in light of the risk to the organization or in the face of budget retrenchment at the nonprofit.

- The new risk management activity appears to have a neutral affect—it is unclear that it is making a difference with respect to preventing losses or increasing confidence among key stakeholders.

Most nonprofits are to some extent guardians of outdated, impractical, or ineffective policies and procedures. Like their counterparts in the business and government sectors, nonprofit managers find it difficult to spend time reviewing long-standing policies and practices and weed out those that no longer serve the organization well. Risk management activities that no longer serve the interests of the nonprofit should be modified to meet the nonprofit's needs or else abandoned. Ironically, the failure to do this could increase the nonprofit's exposure to liability claims. For example, a nonprofit that adopts a policy requiring the completion of fingerprint-based criminal history background checks for all staff is likely to discover that implementing the policy is very costly. An organization might be tempted to obtain such checks on only a small fraction of applicants in order to save time and money—perhaps those applicants whose appearance or demeanor generate suspicion among screening personnel. This practice could be potentially damaging evidence in a case against a nonprofit stemming from the hiring of an individual who wasn't subjected to the nonprofit's adopted screening procedure. Furthermore, an individual who was singled out for rigorous screening might pursue a claim alleging discrimination.

In addition to making changes to the existing risk management program based on the committee's analysis of the effectiveness of various strategies, the committee should also discuss changes in the nonprofit's environments, circumstances, and programs that warrant a new look at the exposures the organization faces. An important facet of step 5 is reexamining the nonprofit's exposure to risks and identifying new areas that deserve priority attention. For example, the hypothetical homeless shelter may, after an assault that resulted in the hospitalization of a young client, decide that addressing the risk of client-on-client violence deserves top attention.

APPLYING THE RISK MANAGEMENT FRAMEWORK

The risks nonprofits face vary with mission, clientele, geographical location, funding sources, and many other factors. For example, some of the risks identified by a nonprofit recreation program located on the coast of North Carolina will be quite different from those identified by a church located in rural Iowa. Yet many nonprofits will identify risk exposures that are common to nonprofits with polar-opposite missions. For example, a conservation nonprofit that takes children on wilderness hikes will face some of the same risks as a nonprofit organization that teaches adults and children how to hunt safely.

Here are some examples of these common exposures:

- Protecting vulnerable clients from harm
- Avoiding the theft of financial resources by insiders
- Minimizing disruptive and costly claims alleging wrongful employment practices
- Ensuring that the nonprofit is prepared to cope with a wide range of crisis situations, including those caused by natural hazards or events, as well as human-caused events such as workplace violence or equipment failure
- Minimizing the potential liability of volunteers for services delivered on the nonprofit's behalf and the apprehension of volunteers concerning their personal liability

All of these issues—in addition to the unique exposures a nonprofit faces— can be addressed by involving a group of people who understand and appreciate the organization's resources, operations, and constraints and following the steps in the risk management process.

Next we discuss the specific issue of volunteer liability and risk management. We single out this area because it is a common concern among a large number of nonprofits. It is also an area that continues to generate misunderstanding.

VOLUNTEER LIABILITY AND RISK MANAGEMENT

The topic of volunteer liability remains an important concern for nonprofit leaders. Some of the concerns that are raised under the volunteer liability umbrella include the following:

- Can we be sued and held liable for the mistakes or negligence of our volunteers?

- Can our volunteers sue us?

- What should I tell a volunteer who is concerned about his or her personal liability?

Volunteer Negligence

The simple answer to the first question is yes, an organization that deploys hundreds of thousands of volunteers who perform services, interact with clients and the general public, and represent the organization in other ways has a substantial exposure to the risk of being held liable for the actions of volunteers. Yet there is no need for the use of volunteers to cause alarm. As will be discussed later in this chapter, there are many things a nonprofit can do to enhance the safety of volunteer service and thereby reduce the risk of claims by volunteers. In addition, it is important to recognize that when a client or other participant is injured while participating in a nonprofit's program, a finding of liability is not automatic. Determining whether a nonprofit will be liable for harm resulting from the organization's acts or omissions depends on the confluence of various factors, including whether the nonprofit had a duty of care with respect to those who were harmed, the nonprofit breached its duty of care, harm actually occurred, the harm that occurred was foreseeable, the breach of the duty of care was a proximate cause of the harm that occurred, and there were reasonable measures available to the nonprofit that would have prevented the harm from occurring.

Each of these issues will be considered, along with the laws of a particular jurisdiction and the perspective and biases of the judge or jury who review the facts in a particular case. It is difficult, if not impossible, to predict whether liability will be imposed. Legal counsel representing the nonprofit, with full knowledge of all of the circumstances and facts at hand, will try to make this prediction and advise the nonprofit accordingly. Some commentators have observed that when children are hurt while participating in a nonprofit's programs, the imposition of liability on the nonprofit is increasingly likely and seemingly automatic. Under the legal concept of *respondeat superior* ("let the master answer"), a nonprofit is responsible for the acts and omissions of its agents. Volunteers—people who work on the nonprofit's behalf and whose labor benefits the nonprofits—are agents. There are some exceptions to this principle. For example, in some cases, a nonprofit may avoid responsibility for the negligent acts of a volunteer who is clearly acting outside the scope of his or her authority or whose actions are a direct violation of the nonprofit's rules and requirements.

Claims by Volunteers

Nonprofit leaders may also be concerned about the possibility of lawsuits filed by volunteers. The good news on this topic is that suits against nonprofits by volunteers continue to be rare events. The bad news, however, is that a claim by a volunteer—even one without legal merit—can be costly to a nonprofit. Two scenarios are most likely in regard to this exposure: (1) a volunteer suffers an injury and seeks compensation for it, or (2) a volunteer alleges nonphysical harm (such as defamation, discrimination, or wrongful termination). Injuries suffered by paid staff of the nonprofit are insured under mandatory workers' compensation coverage, which is triggered regardless of the fault of the employer and covers medical expenses and provides income replacement. The vast majority of nonprofits do not cover volunteers under their workers' compensation policies—it is generally cost-prohibitive to do so. Another option is to purchase an accident policy that ensures the availability of funds to cover medical expenses (up to a predetermined limit) following injury to a volunteer. At a minimum, an accident policy is a goodwill gesture by a nonprofit that conveys its concern for the safety of volunteers. At a minimum, a nonprofit should consider how it will react when a volunteer is injured and consider steps that will reduce the likelihood of a legal claim by the volunteer. Occasionally, a volunteer will seek redress for nonphysical harm, accusing the nonprofit of wrongful termination or discrimination. Although a number of such cases have reached the courts in recent years, most have ruled consistently that volunteers do not have standing to sue for wrongful employment actions. Although a nonprofit may prevail in the long run, the cost of defending such a claim can take a toll on the organization. Claims alleging defamation may be addressed on the merits. To guard against these claims, nonprofits must be cautious when screening, supervising, disciplining, and terminating volunteers: information that portrays the volunteer in a negative light should be shared only with persons who need to know it.

Fear of Liability Among Volunteers

During the years leading up to the adoption of the federal Volunteer Protection Act of 1997 (VPA), the legislation's supporters argued that large numbers of prospective volunteers had become increasingly fearful of being sued and that this widespread fear had a negative effect on the size of the pool of persons willing to volunteer for charitable organizations. Yet between 1980 and 1995—a long period in which volunteers' enthusiasm was allegedly dampened due to the fear of liability—the number of volunteers in the United States grew from 80 million to 93 million, an increase of 16 percent, and a record 90 percent of individuals volunteered when asked.

The recurring theme found in the federal and state volunteer protection laws is that certain volunteers serving nonprofit or government programs should, under certain circumstances, be protected from personal, civil liability for harm that results from their volunteer service. One of the recurring misconceptions about the protection afforded under the VPA (and the comparable state laws) is that the laws protect nonprofits as well as volunteers. The opposite is true. The proponents of the VPA argued forcefully that the new law would not leave victims of negligence by nonprofit personnel without recourse but instead ensure that the nonprofit, and not its volunteers, is responsible for negligent acts stemming from operations.

There have been positive benefits of the fear of personal liability among current or prospective volunteers as well as the fear that liability will be imposed on a nonprofit due to the actions of volunteers, including the following:

- Greater receptivity to policies adopted by the nonprofit pertaining to the screening of volunteers as well as operational policies and procedures related to safety

- Awareness and appreciation of the need to take care when providing service to a nonprofit

- Increased awareness by the paid staff and leaders of a nonprofit concerning the importance of carefully screening, selecting, and supervising volunteers

State Volunteer Protection Laws

Every state has a law that pertains specifically to the legal liability of some volunteers. These laws differ greatly. Some state volunteer protection laws protect only directors and officers serving nonprofits; others protect narrow categories of volunteers, such as firefighters or other emergency service personnel. The exceptions contained in the state statutes eliminate protection for volunteers in many circumstances. The most common exceptions in the various state statutes are the following:

- Willful or wanton conduct by the volunteer
- Gross negligence on the part of the volunteer
- Wrongful acts committed while operating a motor vehicle

These are some other exceptions featured in some of the state laws:

- Fraud or fiduciary misconduct
- Actions brought by an attorney general or other state official
- Delivery of certain professional services
- Knowing violation of the law

In addition to exceptions, there are various requirements that must be met in order for the limitation on liability to apply. Examples of conditions found in some of the various laws include these:

- The requirement that the nonprofit retaining the volunteer carry liability insurance at a specified level
- The requirement that the nonprofit amend its articles of incorporation or bylaws to specifically indemnify volunteers
- The requirement that certain volunteers receive training from the nonprofit
- The requirement that volunteers receive prior written authorization to act

The conditions are consistent with the federal law's intent: to ensure that the nonprofit, not the volunteer serving the nonprofit, is financially responsible for negligent acts or omissions committed by an uncompensated volunteer. However, there is great irony in these conditions. For example, the insurance requirement often means that volunteers serving the smallest nonprofits—those with only meager resources—may not receive protection under the state volunteer protection law, while those volunteering for larger organizations, which can arguably afford liability insurance, will enjoy protection.

The three other conditions lead to a similar outcome: volunteers who are serving smaller, more informal organizations are at greatest risk, because the lack of sophistication and resources of the nonprofits they serve removes the protection the volunteers would otherwise enjoy under the state volunteer protection law.

In short, state and federal volunteer protection statutes provide volunteers with a defense to claims that a volunteer should be legally responsible for harm stemming from his or her service for a nonprofit. They *do not* insulate volunteers from claims, provide protection or immunity for nonprofit organizations, or provide volunteers with a defense to many common claims, including those alleging negligence in the operation of a motor vehicle or wrongful employment practices.

When volunteers express concern about personal liability stemming from their service, a nonprofit should respond by providing information and resources that enable volunteers to better understand the exposure and protect themselves. For example, a nonprofit can direct its volunteers to an analysis of the state and federal volunteer protection statutes and caution volunteers about the importance of acting within the scope of their authority and not exceeding the instructions and guidelines provided by the nonprofit. Insurance coverage that the nonprofit has purchased for the benefit of its volunteers, including directors' and officers' liability or volunteer liability policies, should be explained to concerned volunteers.

Risk Management for Volunteer Programs

Every nonprofit that engages volunteers at the governance or service delivery level should examine the risks posed by the deployment of volunteers and identify practical measures available to address these risks.

It is neither necessary nor advisable to exhaust an organization's financial resources in an effort to foreclose the possibility of missteps or harm. Every proposed risk management activity should be evaluated in relation to its role in preventing foreseeable harm or increasing the organization's prospects of realizing success.

Several principles for managing volunteer-related risks can provide guidance.

1. *Apply common sense before dollars and cents.* While nonprofit leaders continue to view insurance as a primary risk management response, the truth is that many risk management measures cost little, if anything, to implement. For example, prohibiting volunteers from establishing out-of-program personal relationships with clients is a commonsense strategy for reducing the risk of out-of-program abuse of a client by an agent of the nonprofit. Yet this commonsense strategy is of little value unless the nonprofit carefully communicates the policy (and its rationale) to volunteers as well as clients and their parents or guardians.

2. *Involve volunteers in risk management planning.* On occasion, risk management programs are developed at the management level of a nonprofit and imposed on the people required to implement new procedures or adhere to new policy. In some cases, the top down approach is necessary and appropriate. But in other cases, this approach leads to a lack of commitment and support that jeopardizes the policy. It is prudent to involve volunteers in the design of strategies intended to protect them as well as activities that keep the nonprofit's clients and financial assets safe from harm.

3. *Provide explicit direction.* Some nonprofits shy away from providing explicit direction to volunteers out of fear of offending these unpaid but essential workers. Providing explicit instructions (including dos and don'ts) helps volunteers succeed. It also helps a nonprofit avoid potentially costly circumstances when a

volunteer claims, "I didn't know we weren't supposed to do that." For example, you may require an ongoing commitment of a certain number of service hours per week for volunteers working with vulnerable clients or that your volunteers attend a defensive driving course before driving your minibus. Don't forget to include prohibited activities when you provide instruction—including topics that may be difficult to discuss, such as your prohibition against volunteers dating or engaging in sexual acts with clients of any age or inviting clients into their homes.

4. *Maintain standards.* Directors of volunteers are generally well versed on the importance of recognizing and rewarding outstanding volunteer service. Yet it is sometimes difficult to acknowledge the need, from time to time, to discipline and even remove volunteers who fail to measure up. This is required when a volunteer performs at a level below your standards, does something prohibited by your program, or otherwise fails to meet your minimum requirements. It is critical that every nonprofit prepare for the day when it must remove a volunteer whose continued participation poses too great a risk to the health and safety of the organization, its clients, or other volunteers. Firing a volunteer, though never an easy task, may be absolutely necessary to protect the vital mission of an organization.

5. *Discuss responsibilities openly with partners.* Nonprofits often collaborate to achieve results that wouldn't be possible if the organizations operated alone. The greater an organization's reliance on volunteers, the more likely it is to partner with other organizations. Reduce the risk of these valuable collaborations by never assuming that the other organization has something covered. Every collaboration should begin with a frank discussion of who will do what, when, and where, including who will be responsible (and how) if harm to persons or property results from the collaboration.

6. *Establish and monitor policies.* Policies and procedures are crucial to the success of volunteer risk management. State-of-the-art eye protection is useless if volunteers aren't instructed that they must wear the protection before picking up a power tool. As a nonprofit develops policies that it requires its volunteers to follow, it must pay particularly close attention to the way in which these policies are communicated to all personnel. Using overlapping forms of communication and providing an opportunity for questions will reduce the risk that a key policy will go unnoticed or be misinterpreted.

7. *Guard client privacy.* Volunteers engaged in service delivery should be instructed about their responsibility for guarding client privacy. These instructions should include direction about the steps a volunteer should take to report accidental violations of privacy or concerns they may have about the organization's practices.

8. *Put expectations and duties in writing.* A growing number of nonprofits that rely on volunteers have adopted the use of written job descriptions or volunteer agreements. These resources serve several purposes, including making

it easier to determine and account for who is serving as a volunteer in your organization and what their responsibilities are; clearly establishing the terms of appointment and reappointment (for example, for one year, renewable by mutual agreement an unlimited number of times); reminding volunteers that they are serving at the discretion and will of the organization; and establishing a sense of accountability of the volunteer to the organization and its rules.

9. *Cast a wide net by making risk management a shared responsibility.* Strive to engage volunteers in all phases of your risk management program, and seek feedback from these valuable personnel as you work to integrate safe practices in the culture of your organization.

THE ROLE OF INSURANCE IN A RISK MANAGEMENT PROGRAM

A small percentage of nonprofit leaders continue to equate risk management with the purchase of insurance. When asked about their organization's risk management program, they reply, "We purchase several forms of liability insurance." Yet even though insurance is an important risk financing option—a way to pay for losses that result despite the nonprofit's attempt to avoid them—insurance plays no role in reducing the likelihood that harm will result from operations. In addition, there are many exposures faced by the vast majority of nonprofits for which no insurance is available. The best example is risk to reputation: no coverage is available to restore a nonprofit's sullied reputation following an attention-grabbing scandal reported on the front page of the local newspaper.

Insurance Market Cycles and Developments

Like other consumers of commercial insurance, nonprofits are subject to conditions in the insurance marketplace. One of the conditions that often has a dramatic effect on nonprofits is the cyclical nature of the industry. During the "soft market" phase of the cycle, insurers compete aggressively for new business. "Bells and whistles" may be added to commonly purchased policies, such as directors' and officers' liability, and insurers are willing to compete on price and coverage in order to retain customers and write new accounts. During the "hard market" phase of the cycle, nonprofits face a "seller's market." Typical hard market conditions include premium increases unrelated to an insured's loss history, restrictions in coverage, the requirement that buyers agree to higher deductibles, and the refusal of some carriers to offer the limits of liability that consumers wish to purchase. In the hard market cycle that began in 2000, many nonprofits have faced nonrenewal of core coverage by carriers that are walking away from segments of the nonprofit sector. Some organizations have found it difficult or impossible to purchase adequate coverage for such risks as improper sexual conduct, and many organizations have faced premium increases in the range of 10 to 50 percent or more with accompanying large increases in required self-insured retentions.

Insurance Dos and Don'ts

Although nonprofits have been purchasing commercial insurance for decades, the process has become only marginally simpler during this time. The insurance world remains a strange and daunting environment for most nonprofit managers. Before discussing various forms of coverage that nonprofits often purchase, I present the following list of dos and don'ts that should be considered as a nonprofit sets about procuring insurance.

Do

- Find a competent insurance professional (broker or agent) whom you trust to advocate for your nonprofit.
- Take the time to read your insurance policies.
- Investigate the financial stability of your insurers.
- Ask your broker or agent to respond to your questions in writing.
- Seek multiple bids for your insurance coverage once every three to five years.
- Give thoughtful consideration to how much risk your nonprofit can afford to retain.
- Provide your board of directors with a copy of your directors' and officers' liability policy.
- Discuss risk management and insurance issues at the board level.

Don't

- Delegate responsibility for your insurance program to a junior staff member.
- Simply renew your coverage each year without considering whether your needs have changed.
- Wait until the last minute to submit completed applications.
- Be evasive about your operations or risk exposures on your application.
- Be shy about asking questions concerning your coverage or the process.
- Regard your insurance coverage as your risk management program.

What's Appropriate Insurance Coverage?

Nonprofit managers and executives cope with many complex challenges on a regular basis. One of the perennial questions is whether the nonprofit's insurance program (the total of all coverage you purchase) is adequate. Unfortunately, there are no easy answers to what seems like a simple question. Every nonprofit must evaluate its exposures, risk-taking appetite, and budget constraints to determine how much insurance it can and should buy. Some experts urge nonprofits to purchase as much insurance as they can afford. Yet insurance is probably most economically efficient when it is an organization's risk financing method for unexpected or catastrophic exposures. Costs that can be readily predicted on the basis of past experience should be financed internally. During hard market conditions, the limits available to your nonprofit may be declining or the broadly worded coverage you purchased during the 1990s may be restricted through wording changes and new exclusions.

The following are some of the common property and casualty policies non-profits purchase.

Commercial general liability (CGL) coverage protects against third-party legal claims alleging bodily injury, property damage, and personal injury. There are numerous standard forms and a wide range of variations. For example, the CGL policy may include miscellaneous professional liability and improper sexual conduct, or it may explicitly exclude coverage of these claims.

Commercial auto liability and physical damage coverage protects against claims and damage stemming from use of the nonprofit's owned vehicles, including cars, vans, minibuses, buses, and trucks.

Directors' and officers' liability (D&O) coverage protects against claims alleging wrongful management acts. Most nonprofits that purchase D&O purchase nonprofit-tailored forms that provide broad protection for the nonprofit itself in addition to volunteer directors, other volunteers, and paid staff. Most nonprofit D&O policies also include coverage for claims alleging wrongful employment practices, although this coverage can also be purchased separately or as part of another policy.

Professional liability coverage protects against claims alleging negligence in the delivery of professional services. Nonprofits providing medical, legal, counseling, consulting, and many other services that require special training may be exposed to professional liability claims. This coverage can be purchased in a stand-alone policy or as part of a CGL or D&O policy.

Improper sexual conduct or sexual abuse coverage protects against claims alleging improper sexual contact. This policy may provide a defense for claims alleging improper contact between clients, or such conduct may be specifically excluded. Coverage may be purchased on a stand-alone basis or as part of another line of liability coverage.

Nonowned or hired auto policies provide excess coverage for damages and medical expenses that exceed the limit of the coverage on a car owned by a volunteer or employee acting on the nonprofit's behalf.

Property insurance covers property owned or leased by the nonprofit, including buildings and equipment.

Business interruption and extra expense coverage helps out in emergencies. The business interruption portion of the policy covers loss of income if premises are completely shut down for a period of time due to a covered property loss (such as a fire or a hurricane). Income from funding sources and participant fees are included, and the policy provides dollars for continuing expenses such as rent or salaries. The extra expense portion provides funds for additional costs a nonprofit might incur due to its inability to use its regular facilities, such as the cost of renting alternative space from which to deliver services.

Fidelity and crime insurance covers claims alleging theft of financial assets by an insider or a third party.

Umbrella insurance provides additional and even excess coverage over several primary policies, such as CGL, auto liability, and employers' liability. The policy increases the amount of liability coverage beyond that of the basic policies carried by the nonprofit and covers some areas that are missing from the basic insurance policy.

No-fault *workers' compensation* coverage is required by state law to cover medical expenses and lost income stemming from employee injuries. In some cases, volunteers can be insured under workers' compensation, although most nonprofits find this option to be cost-prohibitive.

Accident insurance is additional insurance that covers medical expenses (up to a preset limit) for volunteers or participants who are injured while serving the nonprofit or participating in the nonprofit's activities. Accident insurance covers any excess over the individual's health insurance and provides primary coverage for persons who are uninsured.

The Business Owner's Policy

Many nonprofit managers struggle with their insurance programs. Although purchasing adequate insurance is vitally important, doing so is complicated by the language contained in insurance policies as well as their confusing structure. Whether the nonprofit's policies, extent of coverage, limits, and deductibles are appropriate is a perennial question. When a nonprofit manager makes a mistake in selecting limits and coverage, the organization can wind up insurance-rich but coverage-poor. The ultimate goal, therefore, is to obtain appropriate coverage at an affordable premium. Most nonprofits require property coverage for the contents of their offices, and some require coverage for owned buildings. Liability insurance is a must for organizations concerned about lawsuits based on operations. The business owner's policy (BOP) is an important option. A

BOP is a terrific solution for some nonprofits under certain circumstances, but it is not a one-size-fits-all solution. A nonprofit that has unique risk exposures may be better served by purchasing separately the policies usually combined in a BOP. To begin the analysis of whether a BOP offers advantages for a nonprofit, it is therefore necessary to examine the types of coverage that are typically found in a BOP.

Keep in mind that insurance carriers develop distinctive BOPs as well as unique eligibility criteria. A BOP is generally available for nonprofits with retail, office, and general service operations. The key in determining eligibility is whether a nonprofit's operations are conducted principally on-premises or at others' premises. Insurers also have their own guidelines for determining eligibility for a BOP—for example, "a nonprofit occupying an area up to 25,000 square feet, an owned building up to 100,000 square feet and less than six stories, or revenues of $3 million or less." Once you have determined that your nonprofit meets the eligibility criteria established by a BOP provider, it's time to turn your attention to whether this type of policy addresses your coverage needs.

Sometimes a BOP includes property and business liability coverage in addition to a menu of additional, potentially valuable coverage. Generally covered in a standard BOP are the following:

- Property, including building, business personal property, and business income and extra expenses
- Business liability, including bodily injury and property damage, personal and advertising injury, fire legal liability, and medical expenses

The property coverage in the BOP is akin to the commercial property coverage often purchased separately. The coverage is written on either a basic form or a special cause-of-loss form. Some of the optional coverages that you might be able to purchase under the property section of the policy include crime, spoilage, mechanical breakdown, and computer. The crime portion covers money and securities (inside and outside the premises), employee dishonesty, and forgery or alteration. In most cases, rather low limits are available for these coverages, such as $250,000 for employee dishonesty or $10,000 for money and securities. Your nonprofit may require greater limits than those available through a BOP. Another potentially valuable coverage in the property section is computer coverage. However, the policy may be limited and not provide adequate coverage for your organization. One coverage area that has drawn increasing attention in recent years is loss of business income or extra expense incurred due to damage to the computers, data, or media. As nonprofits become increasingly dependent on technology for service delivery, the need to quickly restore systems following an interruption becomes paramount.

An attractive feature of the BOP is the fact that the policy's business income and extra expense coverage (for other than computers) is written without a limit. Coverage is based on the actual loss sustained by the insured over a twelve-month period.

The BOP's business liability coverage section is comparable to the commercial general liability or CGL form. Some insurers have chosen to provide additional exclusions on the BOPs that may make the policy inadequate in some instances. For example, some BOPs don't allow volunteers or members to be added as insureds or permit other endorsements that expand the provisions stipulating who is insured. And it is important to keep in mind that all BOPs exclude claims alleging abuse and molestation, and most exclude claims alleging negligence in the delivery of professional services. Another way that carriers reduce their exposure in the BOP is to include an endorsement that limits the coverage provided to designated premises or operations so that only *incidental* operations away from the nonprofit's designated premises are covered. For some nonprofits, this endorsement is acceptable, while for others, this endorsement leaves the nonprofit's principal activities unprotected. The BOP also includes coverage for hired and nonowned auto liability, but the option of adding employees as insureds is not available. A typical BOP also does not provide hired auto physical damage coverage.

While most nonprofits easily pass the eligibility test under the office classification, many organizations sponsor significant activities away from their principal office. The policy may cover these activities because they are not specifically excluded, but the rate charged for the policy doesn't fully contemplate these unique exposures. When the nonprofit files a claim stemming from one of these activities, the carrier may respond by canceling the policy, excluding off-site service delivery or activities, or increasing the premium substantially.

The most important benefit of a BOP is also its greatest weakness. The fact that the policy cannot be customized to meet a nonprofit consumer's preferences is appealing to many buyers, who simply want a package of policies at an affordable price. Yet for the more sophisticated buyer who understands his or her nonprofit's unique coverage needs, the BOP may prove inadequate. Another approach for larger organizations is to purchase a BOP and then purchase separate coverage to fill the gaps left by the BOP. As with all policies, it is essential to take time to read the full wording of the policy in order to understand the coverage it provides.

SUMMARY

Risk management is gradually being embraced by nonprofit leaders as an important management discipline. As managers learn more about risk management, the myths associated with the discipline are beginning to dissipate. A growing number of leaders are recognizing that a risk management program is vital to mission fulfillment and fully within their grasp. The risk management process can be coordinated by a task force consisting of paid and volunteer staff as well as outside advisers—only the largest nonprofits can afford to hire a full-time risk manager. The risk management process consists of the following steps:

Step 1: Consider the context

Step 2: Identify risks

Step 3: Evaluate risks

Step 4: Decide what to do and take action

Step 5: Monitor and adjust

The most important goal for risk management in a nonprofit organization is integrating the identification of risks and strategies to address them into the day-to-day operations of the organization so that the practice becomes intuitive and seamless.

PART FIVE

MANAGING PEOPLE

The final part of this book addresses any nonprofit organization's most important asset: the employees and volunteers who carry out the organization's mission through day-to-day work. Chapter Twenty-Two describes how to recruit and retain effective service volunteers; the chapter after that describes recruiting, hiring, and retaining the right employees. Both chapters give careful attention to legal issues involved in working with volunteers and in recruiting and selecting employees while also emphasizing the importance of keeping the mission in the forefront. Chapter Twenty-Four provides detailed information on designing and managing employee compensation and benefits in a total rewards framework. The final chapter in this part examines principles and practices for designing and carrying out appropriate training and development efforts for volunteers and for paid staff.

CHAPTER TWENTY-TWO

Keeping the Community Involved

*Recruiting and
Retaining Volunteers*

Stephen McCurley

Nonprofit agencies have long relied on the assistance of unpaid volunteers in delivering their services. In 2001, these volunteers provided the equivalent of over 9 million full-time employees to the nonprofit workforce in the United States (INDEPENDENT SECTOR, 2002). Similar volunteer activity has been recorded for the United Kingdom (Institute for Volunteering Research, 2003; Prime, Zimmeck, and Zurawan, 2002), Canada (Canadian Centre for Philanthropy, 2001), and Australia (Australian Bureau of Statistics, 2001). Similar growth has been observed in other countries (Anheier and Salamon, 1999). While there has been much debate in the literature as to whether volunteering is increasing or decreasing (see Baer, Curtis, and Grabb, 2001; Brown, 1999; Carlin, 2001; Goss, 1999; Tiehen, 2000; and Warburton and Crosier, 2001) and even as to how to measure volunteering (Carson, 1999), there is little doubt that the involvement of volunteers in the delivery of social services has become part of the institutional landscape.

As this unpaid workforce has become larger, as volunteer jobs have become more complex, and as competition among agencies for available volunteers has become more common, volunteer management practices have, of necessity, also become more sophisticated and more innovative (see McCurley and Lynch, 1996; Noble, Rogers, and Fryar, 2003; Wilson, 2001).

Effective involvement of volunteers demands a planned and organized process similar to that required by any organizational project or effort (McCurley and Lynch, 1996; Noble, Rogers, and Fryar, 2003; Volunteer Canada, 2001). The basic elements of this volunteer management process are shown in Figure 22.1.

The descending steps on the left side of the figure represent the major elements involved in determining the needs for volunteers within the agency, identifying suitable volunteers, and then creating a motivational structure that will support those volunteers. They are roughly analogous to personnel and supervisory procedures for paid staff. The elements on the right side of the figure represent the other universes that interact with and must support volunteer personnel (the community at large, upper management of the organization, and staff with whom volunteers will be in contact) and must therefore be involved in the process of volunteer utilization.

All of these elements are interactive and, as in most creative management processes, rarely proceed in a totally linear fashion. During the existence of the

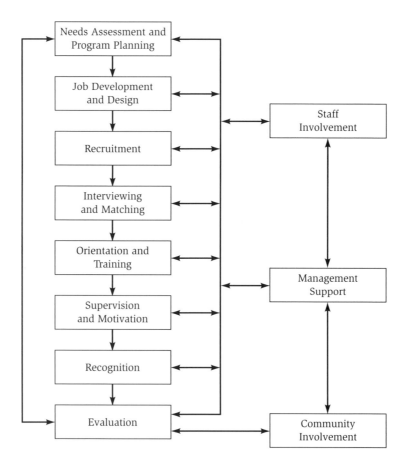

Figure 22.1. The Volunteer Management Process.

overall volunteer program, the elements within this process will tend to recur with the addition of each new area of volunteer utilization (as new projects or areas of usage are created) and with the addition of each new volunteer (as the process is customized to the requirements of the individual). The process will also be reenacted as new staff are added to the agency who must interact with volunteers.

This chapter will deal with the elements in this process for recruiting community volunteers to work with the agency and with means for maintaining motivational levels of those volunteers. It will concentrate on the volunteer recruited at the service provider level, not on the board or advisory committee volunteer who makes agency policy. The suggestions in this chapter will be aimed at the medium to large organizational structure in which there is significant paid staff presence, requiring a high degree of interaction and cooperation between these paid employees and the volunteers recruited from the community. Smaller agencies or those in which the primary service delivery is done by volunteers without interaction with paid staff can still follow the general principles offered but will need to adapt them to their less structured operational environment. The material discussed will generally apply both to nonprofit organizations and to the involvement of volunteers in public agencies (see Brudney, 1999, for specifics on the application of volunteer management practices to government agencies).

NEEDS ASSESSMENT AND PROGRAM PLANNING

Program planning and design begins with an assessment of why the agency wishes to use volunteers and what the benefits and problems are likely to be in volunteer use (Ellis, 1996).

Deciding on the Use of Volunteers

There are numerous possible benefits to using volunteers; you might find some or all of the following relevant to your situation:

- Delivery of services at reduced cost
- Access to additional expertise
- Better contact with the community
- Better assistance to clients
- Institutionalization of a community perspective

There are also possible disadvantages, including these:

- Lack of control and reliability of volunteers
- Time demands for volunteer supervision

- Potential negative impact on paid jobs
- Difficulties in recruiting enough qualified volunteers

It is essential that the agency and its staff have an overall appreciation that the use of volunteers will be worth the investment of organizational resources that are required to make the volunteer program operate. This appreciation is vital in explaining the need for volunteers both to staff within the agency (who must make changes in their own work styles to accommodate volunteers) and to the community (which must understand why the agency needs volunteers).

As the Grantmaker Forum on Community and National Service (2003) noted, "Nonprofit organizations that have a vision for incorporating volunteers in service delivery accrue advantages over time to their volunteer programs. The support, supervision and attention that volunteers require, not to mention the logistical aspects of scheduling volunteer labor, are significant burdens to an organization and cannot be established casually as an 'add on' service" (p. 11).

The philosophical determination by the agency to involve volunteers will often be written up as an official policy and approved by the agency's policy-setting group. The Juvenile Court of Spokane County, Washington, for example, makes use of the following statement in regard to volunteer involvement:

> The Spokane County Juvenile Court is committed to providing the best and most appropriate services possible. To realize this goal, our Department shall make every effort to enlist the cooperation of all available resources. The Department is committed to the development of a public-private partnership which includes volunteers as an important and necessary ingredient in the development and delivery of services.
>
> In addition to the above, our Department plans to actively implement and maintain a responsible program of citizen involvement because:
>
> 1. Our Department will never have sufficient resources to meet all service needs. Even if such resources were available (professional staff, finances, facilities, etc.), the Department would still believe it necessary for the community to become involved in juvenile issues.
>
> 2. It has been demonstrated repeatedly that volunteers can significantly enhance, expand, and upgrade services. With appropriate recruitment, screening, training, and supervision, volunteers can perform almost any task effectively and responsibly.
>
> 3. The Department feels it necessary to involve the community in the problems we are trying to alleviate or solve. Efforts to involve the community in agency affairs will help to educate the public about these problems and will create a more enlightened and active citizenry.

This official "endorsement" of the volunteer effort becomes the framework on which agency decisions regarding a consistent set of procedures for volunteer involvement can be based (Ellis, 1996).

Staff Involvement

Relationships between agency paid staff and volunteers have always played a crucial role in the eventual outcome of the volunteer program (Ellis, 1996; Lee and Catagnus, 1998). Developing a good working relationship between staff and volunteers has always been one of the major tasks of the director of the volunteer program. In the words of Ilsley (1990, p. 119): "One of the greatest fears among managers of volunteers is tension between volunteers and paid staff. So prevalent is this fear that when asked to name the most difficult aspect of their job, twenty-nine out of thirty managers of volunteers in organizations that have a paid staff responded that it is tension between that staff and volunteers." It is essential that the decision to use volunteers be agreed on by the staff of the agency. If these staff are uncomfortable with the decision to use volunteers, their resistance or even passive acceptance will serve as an effective barrier to volunteer involvement. Staff who do not support the concept of volunteer involvement will resist the development of creative or significant jobs for volunteers, thus reducing the agency's ability to offer desirable work opportunities to potential volunteers. Nonsupportive staff will also communicate their discomfort to agency volunteers, delivering a clear message that the volunteers are not really wanted by the agency despite its public pronouncements.

Nonsupportive staff will also function less effectively as volunteer supervisors. The relationship between the volunteer and his or her immediate staff supervisor will have direct bearing on the volunteer's job satisfaction (Gidron, 1983: Colomy, Chen, and Andrews, 1987).

In addition to obtaining staff agreement on the use of volunteers, it is also important to provide staff with training in how they can effectively work with volunteers (Skillingstad, 1989). This training should introduce staff to the operational procedures of the volunteer programs and should enable staff to learn the techniques of effective volunteer supervision. This training is particularly crucial when agency staff do not have much supervisory experience or training, as their work with volunteers may constitute their initial attempts at learning and implementing managerial skills. Expecting young and inexperienced staff members to acquire supervisory skills without assistance through a process of trial and error is optimistic and a bit foolhardy; expecting volunteers to enjoy the process of experimentation is delusionary.

POSITION DEVELOPMENT AND DESIGN

The next step in involving volunteers is to determine the uses to which those volunteers will be put. The development of these specific positions or volunteer assignments is the most important stage in volunteer recruitment and retention. Before any volunteers are sought, the agency should have a clear picture of what each volunteer will be doing and a clear written description of that work and the supervisory mechanisms and personnel that will surround the work situation.

The importance of a volunteer position description cannot be overstated. The position description is the agency's planning tool to help volunteers understand the results to be accomplished, what tasks are involved, what skills are required, and other important details about the job. A position description provides an organized means of creating continuity in a job from one volunteer to the next. It is also a living document that should be revised as the program changes or as the volunteer develops over time. Informative job descriptions are perhaps more vital in a volunteer environment than in the context of paid employees. Paid employees often function as generalists, partly as a result of their time commitment of forty-plus hours per week. As such, paid staff tend to learn their roles through on-the-job experience and have adequate time to do so. Volunteers, by contrast, commonly donate a lesser amount of time but view each donated hour as significant. "Wasting" time by waiting to learn what they are actually supposed to be doing is particularly demotivating to volunteers. Hence the volunteer position description must provide a clear guide as to what the volunteer is intended to do and what this work will contribute to the agency, its cause, and its clientele (McCurley and Lynch, 1996).

Position descriptions are the building blocks of the volunteer program, insofar as all recruiting, interviewing, placing, supervising, and evaluating is based on the information contained in the job description. The key to a good job description is to keep it short, succinct, and clear. The format for the job description is arbitrary, but its final content should be developed in concert with the volunteer who is accepting the position. The job description should provide the volunteer and the supervisor with a clear common conception of the purpose of the volunteer's job and of the expectation of results.

Developing ideas for potential jobs will require creative thought by current staff, who must be able to visualize tasks that might be suitable for volunteers. One way to approach this is to think of categories of potential tasks:

- Jobs that are of direct assistance to an individual client: counseling, visitation, mentoring, and so on

- Office administrative help: information services, filing, messengers, and the like

- Direct assistance to staff: research, training, computer assistance, and so forth

- Outreach to the community: speakers bureau, fundraising, client marketing, and similar activities

Each job design should meet certain requirements:

- The work must be meaningful and significant, both to the agency and to the agency's clientele. The work must be needed and should be interesting to someone. This means that the volunteer job must have a defined goal or purpose that the volunteer can work to accomplish and can feel good about having achieved.

• The volunteer ought to be able to feel some ownership in and responsibility for the job. Volunteers are not robots; they must feel that they have some input into and control over the work they are asked to do. This means including the volunteer in the flow of information and decision making within the office. It also means holding the volunteer responsible for the accomplishment of the job.

• The work must fit a part-time situation. Either the job must be small enough in scope to be productively approached in a few hours a week, or else it must be designed to be shared among a group of volunteers.

• The work must fit into the overall context of the agency, including strategic goals (relationship to agency mission and clientele), physical logistics (work site, equipment), and management procedures (assignment of a supervisor).

For the agency, this developmental planning will enable the creation of a structure that can effectively support the volunteer. For the volunteer, this planning will create a job situation that can be used in both recruitment (the volunteer can be attracted by the prospect of performing meaningful and contributory work) and retention (the volunteer will experience a more productive and enjoyable work environment) (see Gidron, 1983; Colomy, Chen, and Andrews, 1987; Wilson and Musick, 1999).

Since volunteer positions must both fit the configuration of time that the volunteer is able to contribute and also appeal to the volunteer's interests, it is desirable to be extremely flexible in developing volunteer positions in a wide variety of shapes and sizes. Thus the same type of work might be offered to a potential volunteer in different ways. Common ways to offer this variety include the following:

• Continuous, short-term, and one-shot projects

• Work done as individuals, families, or teams

• Periodic, on-call assignments

• Work done on-site, at home, or while at work

• Work done primarily with people, things, or ideas

The greater the options available to the prospective volunteer, the more likely that they will fit the prospective volunteer's requirements and interests.

RECRUITMENT

The next stage in incorporating volunteers into the nonprofit workforce is setting about attracting suitable volunteers.

Identifying Potential Recruitment Appeals

The agency must come up with appeals that might motivate potential volunteers to become involved. The possible range of volunteer motivations that may be appealed to in recruitment is very broad (Ellis, 2002), encompassing practically every psychological attribute. This tends to lead agencies to develop very broad motivational appeals, believing that at least a few of all those potential volunteers will respond. It is important, however, to realize that what is needed in the development of the recruitment appeal is a slightly narrower approach, motivating potential volunteers not just to decide to volunteer but to volunteer with this particular agency, doing this particular job (Dyer and Jost, 2002).

To create this more defined appeal, the agency should answer questions in four areas that can be used in communicating with the potential volunteer:

- Why should this job be done at all? What is the need in the community for this work? What bad things will happen if this volunteer job is not done?

- What will the benefit be to the community or to the clientele after the job is done? What will the work accomplish? What changes will it make in people's lives?

- What are some possible fears or objections concerning this job that must be overcome? The type of clients? The subject area? The skills needed to do the work? Geography?

- What will be the personal benefit to the volunteer in doing the job? Skills? Experience? Flexible work schedules? New friends?

The appeal can then focus on communicating to the potential volunteer why the agency and its work are important and why the potential volunteer should contribute to the accomplishment of that work. Different aspects of this message may be stressed more than others or may be communicated differently to various populations. An appeal to young persons, for example, may stress job experience possibilities, while an appeal to previous clients of the agency may talk about the effects of the problem and the ability to help others obtain the relief that they themselves have experienced.

Creation of this message is much more difficult than it seems, particularly for paid employees. Quite often their own innate knowledge interferes with writing an effective appeal; in a sense, they are too familiar with the subject to remember that others lack that knowledge. They will often forget to include the most basic of facts—numbers of persons in the community who face the problem; harmful effects of the condition—because they assume that others in the community are as familiar with the situation as they are. In truth, they are too close to the situation to see it objectively. This increases the importance of field-testing recruitment appeals, to make sure that the general population receives the appropriate information in a way that they can understand and relate to.

Designing a Recruitment Campaign

Effective volunteer recruitment consists of doing only as much work as needed to obtain the quantity and quality of volunteers required by the agency. Although this statement sounds simplistic, failure to heed it will subject the agency to one of the hidden dangers of volunteer involvement, the risk of ending up with too many of the "wrong" volunteers. Whereas an oversupply of workers to choose from is not considered problematic when dealing with candidates for paid jobs, it can be so when dealing with volunteer applicants. Either the agency must reject some applicants, who may then harbor negative feelings toward the agency, or the agency may accept applicants for whom it does not have available volunteer positions, following which the applicants will develop negative feelings toward the agency for wasting their time. In either case, an oversupply of applicants will consume valuable staff time in interviewing and screening.

Three different approaches to recruitment campaigns can help the agency focus more precisely on the number and types of volunteer applicants it seeks.

Warm-Body Recruitment. The warm-body recruitment campaign is used when the agency needs a relatively large supply of volunteers for tasks that can be easily taught to most people in a short period of time. A typical ideal warm-body recruitment situation involves recruiting volunteers for a weekend event, such as a Special Olympics contest in which volunteer huggers and judges are needed.

The operation of a warm-body recruitment campaign involves basic distribution of information about the agency and its need for volunteers to as wide a segment of the community as possible. Typical mechanisms include distribution of brochures and posters, announcements on TV and radio, articles in the newspapers, and talks to local groups.

Targeted Recruitment. The targeted recruitment campaign operates in exactly the opposite fashion as the warm-body campaign. Targeted recruitment is intentionally designed to limit the number of volunteer applicants by shaping the recruitment message and the information dissemination process. Design of the campaign involves working through a series of three questions about the volunteer position being filled:

- *What skills or aptitudes are needed to do this job?* If we draw a picture of the type of person who could do this job well and would *enjoy* doing it, what would that person look like? Cover age, sex, motivations, hobbies, possible occupations, related interests, and whatever else creates a clear and vivid picture.

- *Based on this picture, where can we find these types of people?* Think about work settings, educational backgrounds, leisure time organizations and activities, publications they might read, and parts of town in which they might live.
- *What motivations appeal to the type of person that we want to attract?* In particular, which psychological needs can be met through this job with our agency? Examples might include self-help, job enhancement, socialization, learning new skills, career exploration, leadership testing, giving back to the community, and keeping productively involved.

Using these planning questions should result in a more clearly targeted volunteer recruitment effort in terms of both dissemination sites and mechanisms and motivational appeal. This focus will tend to limit the applicants to those who more closely fit the profile of the ideal volunteer. Targeted recruitment works best for volunteer jobs that require a particular skill or interest or are appropriate for a specific age or cultural group.

Concentric Circles Recruitment. This type of recruitment campaign is designed to provide the agency with a small but steady flow of volunteer applicants. Concentric circles recruitment works through the application of word-of-mouth principles. In its day-to-day operations, the agency is in contact with a variety of populations: staff and their friends, volunteers and their friends, clients and their families, individuals in the surrounding neighborhood, and so on. These various population groups are already aware that the agency exists, and some of them have direct experience with its work or an indirect relationship through a friend who is familiar with the agency.

Concentric circles recruitment works efficiently because it relies on two favorable factors. The first is that it approaches a population whose familiarity with the agency makes it more receptive than those who do not know the agency or its work. And the second is that it makes use of the personal appeal factor by having individuals who already know the potential volunteer convey the recruitment message, thus piggybacking on their individual credibility. This method of recruitment is almost universal among agencies, with perhaps as many as 94 percent making some use of it (Watts and Edwards, 1983, p. 13).

Using Events to Recruit Volunteers

Recruiting volunteers for a short-term event is a relatively commonplace and relatively easy practice these days. On practically any given weekend, there are a variety of available volunteer activities that basically require the commitment of a few hours, often spent with friends, ranging from building houses to cleaning up parks to the various "-athons" that crop up throughout the year. There are even volunteer organizations that specialize in organizing these activities and targeting recruitment to people interested in short-term volunteering, such as CityCares, HandsOn Atlanta, and most local Volunteer Centers.

The only problem, of course, is that operating a sustained volunteer effort off one-shot events is a difficult, if not impossible, task. Most organizations need volunteers who are actively involved on more than a once-a-year basis and who are willing to come back once the fun event is over and do the hard work that really needs to be done. In particular, they need volunteers who are willing to accept responsibility and perform leadership functions.

Here are some tips for approaching this situation. Be forewarned that they require a planned and organized effort, and you'll have to do a lot of work before you earn your reward, but ultimately you'll find it well worth your time.

Step 1: Attractor Events. An attractor event is designed to engage the attention and short-term involvement of larger numbers of volunteers. It can be organized around a cleanup (park, home, nonprofit agency), community education (a mall show or a corporate fair), a fundraiser, or any other activity that meets the following requirements:

- It can involve large numbers of people in a variety of volunteer tasks and projects.
- The volunteer jobs don't require any substantial training or preparation.
- The work is fun and exciting and allows people to work with others.
- The activity is photogenic, thus attracting media attention.

The event itself should also accomplish something worthwhile, although this isn't the primary aim. In addition, the event should allow all who participate (volunteers and the general public) to get an introduction to the cause, clientele, and operation of your agency, with a particular highlighting of the contributions made by volunteers to the work of the organization. This introduction can be provided via print, demonstrations, or whatever medium seems to work in your setting. The key is that current volunteers should be a prominent part of the event.

Step 2: The Scouting Process. During the event, current volunteers should be assigned to work with groups of newcomers. Part of their assignment is to manage the work to be done during the event, but another part of their assignment involves scouting attendees, looking for those who show the most interest and potential.

These scouts should be encouraged to do the following:

- Establish personal contact with each of the volunteers with whom they are working
- Make the newcomers feel welcome and appreciated
- Get the names and addresses of attendees so that they can be thanked afterward

- Ensure that each new volunteer gets some basic information about the agency and the involvement of volunteers in it

There are a few specific things to look for in volunteers that indicate that they have potential for further development:

- They are having a lot of fun.
- They seem to like organizing others.
- They indicate interest in the cause.
- They seem to have some personal connection to the cause.

Particular attention should be paid to identifying individuals who are in charge of already established groups of volunteers, since they are likely to be people who enjoy being leaders and doing additional work.

Scouts should make notes about individuals they think have the potential for development, and a debriefing should be held following the event. The debriefing should discuss who might be receptive to further involvement, what types of volunteer work they have shown interest in, and how they will best be drawn further into the organization.

Step 3: The Nurturing Process. The process of cultivating individuals whose potential has been identified will vary with your circumstances, but here are some possible avenues to explore.

- If the event is a recurring one, you can increase involvement by offering additional work within the context of the event. This might include asking the volunteers to provide feedback about the event, offering them a promotion in the activity or group with whom they served in the past year, or asking them to participate in organizing and operating the event. This invitation should be offered by a scouting volunteer who has developed a personal relationship, and it should be based on being impressed with the quality of the work done by the potential volunteer.
- Volunteers should receive some sort of promotion after some time with the agency, such as an official title that indicates a new and higher status, access to materials or equipment, or a business card or some other item that creates an official link with the organization.
- While working on an event, volunteers should receive further indoctrination regarding the agency and its work. This should include information both about the work of the agency and about the variety of volunteer positions that are available within it. It greatly helps, by the way, to have a wide variety of volunteer jobs available, since the more options you offer, the greater your chance of resonating with potential volunteers.
- The types of volunteer work available should represent an ascending scale of complexity and requirements, from short and easy work to more difficult po-

sitions. New volunteers should be exposed to current volunteers in all these positions, who are given an opportunity to talk about their work and why they enjoy it. These discussions will reinforce the recruitment effort. From time to time, current volunteers can ask potential volunteers to "help them out" on a project. This work should expose the potential volunteers to what the volunteers are doing without requiring a big commitment.

• Potential volunteers should also be introduced to staff and volunteers at the agency and encouraged to get to know them. Becoming friends with others in the organization can serve as an anchor that tethers volunteers to the agency.

• During the exposure process, further scouting into the interests and reactions of potential volunteers should be undertaken. This scouting should fine-tune the effort to discover the types of motivations and possible volunteer positions that can be most appealing to the potential volunteers.

Potential Recruitment Dangers

As in any process, certain mistakes are easy to make. Here are some things to avoid.

• *Getting too greedy too fast.* Offering volunteers more than they want to do can be a fatal mistake. The trick, as in fishing, is to make volunteers want to take the bait, not to force it on them. Remember that volunteers, unlike fish, can always get off the hook.

• *Relying on make-work jobs.* The early steps of the recruitment process can succeed only if the initial jobs offered to volunteers are short-term and productive. If volunteers think at any stage that their time is being wasted, you've lost the battle. All of the jobs on the "career ladder" must be meaningful ones, and volunteers must be able to stop at any point in the process and feel good about the work they are doing.

• *Having too few opportunities for true advancement.* The implicit offer in this process is that a volunteer can become a real leader in your organization. This is true, of course, only if your organization has upward mobility for volunteers and if the current leaders are willing to step aside as new talent emerges. If your current volunteer structure is set in stone, it will be very difficult to get newcomers into the system.

Recruiting via the Internet

The Internet is rapidly becoming a handy method for recruiting volunteers. Most agencies with Web sites use them to describe the activities of the agency and to mention its need for volunteers. Some organizations go beyond this to formally incorporate mechanisms for volunteer involvement through the Web site, ranging from a simple transmission of contact information to a more formal Web-based application process. These will likely become almost universal.

In addition, Internet-based volunteer referral mechanisms are being developed in many countries. In the United States, the most active of these is VolunteerMatch (http://www.volunteermatch.org), which has established formal relationships with many nonprofit agencies to advertise their volunteer positions. Similar efforts are under way in the United Kingdom (http://www. thesite.org/do-it) and Australia (http://www.govolunteer.com.au). In 2001, according to INDEPENDENT SECTOR (2001, p. 2), "10% of [American adults] with Internet access used the Internet to search for volunteer opportunities." This figure will likely increase as the Internet becomes an even more primary means of communication and information gathering. The next generation of nonprofit Web sites is likely to introduce interactive methods for showing potential recruits what current volunteers are doing, using techniques such as those pioneered by the U.S. Army at its recruitment Web site (http://www.goarmy.com).

Recruiting for Volunteer Diversity

The volunteer recruitment process is one way in which the agency can attempt to broaden its base of community involvement. Various authors have examined the mechanisms by which the agency can attempt to increase the diversity of its volunteer component (see Vineyard and McCurley, 1992, for a look at a variety of populations). Chambre (1982) suggests that an agency wishing to recruit black and Hispanic volunteers should engage in efforts such as personalized approaches, establishing collaborative relationships with community groups, and arranging "trigger events" that crystallize individuals' decisions to volunteer. Latting (1990) suggests that black volunteers are more motivated by altruistic impulses than white volunteers and that recruiting attempts might best be targeted toward blacks who strongly identify with the black community and have strong feelings of social responsibility. Blakeman (1999) has examined the dynamics of recruiting male volunteers.

It is possible that agency concerns about the difficulty of minority recruitment are overstated. Carson (1987) offers data that suggests that contrary to perceptions, blacks, for example, actually volunteer more than is thought, noting, "the findings indicate that at every level of income, blacks are more likely than whites to volunteer their time" (p. 108). Data from a 1990 Gallup survey strongly suggest that if there is any problem with minority involvement, it lies with the agency rather than with the potential volunteer: "Among the 41% of respondents who reported they were asked to volunteer in the past year, 87% volunteered; among the 57% of respondents who reported that they were not asked, only 30% volunteered. Those respondents who were least likely to be asked were blacks (26%), Hispanics (27%), persons 18–24 years of age (31%), and those with household incomes below $20,000 (26%). Among the smaller proportion of these groups who were asked, the proportion who volunteered was more than three times higher than among those who were not asked"

(Hodgkinson and Weitzman, 1994, p. 5). Recent Gallup surveys on giving and volunteering have revealed similar patterns, but with an increase in the number of minorities engaged in volunteer work (INDEPENDENT SECTOR, 2002), which is perhaps one indication of the increased attention being given to outreach recruitment by traditional agencies.

All who have examined this issue have concluded that any attempt in this area can be effective only if it is matched with overall adjustments in the agency, including examination of staff recruitment practices, changes in the composition of the agency board, and reassessment of agency priorities to diverse community populations.

Providing a Responsive Recruitment Process

In some ways, volunteer involvement resembles any customer service relationship. Volunteers who feel that they receive good service are likely to continue with the agency, and those who do not feel as though a good relationship has been established are likely to leave. This relationship is most fragile in its early stages and is particularly vulnerable during the prospective volunteer's first contact with the organization, inquiring about the possibility of volunteering.

Most agencies pay far too little attention to making this process operate smoothly. In a study of 500 United Way–affiliated agencies in the Midwest, Hobson and Malec (1999, pp. 21–27) examined the experiences of prospective volunteers who phoned attempting to initiate volunteering:

- Only 49.3 percent received an offer of assistance ("May I help you?")
- 69.3 percent were not told the name of the staff person who answered the phone.
- 26.4 percent were not referred to the appropriate agency contact person.
- When the contact person was not available, only 48.7 percent were asked for their name and phone number.
- Only 30 percent received callbacks when a message was left.
- In 16.1 percent of the calls, prospective volunteers were not thanked for contacting the agency.

This pattern makes it easy to understand why many agencies have difficulty recruiting volunteers.

INTERVIEWING AND MATCHING

One of the most neglected areas of volunteer management training has been that of effective interviewing of volunteers. This is unfortunate, since good interviewing skills are essential to performing that most crucial of all volunteer management tasks, matching a potential volunteer with a task and a working environment the volunteer will enjoy. Saxon and Sawyer (1984, p.43) describe this interviewing and matching process as follows: "The selection and assignment of volunteers may be viewed as a process of matching skills and abilities to requirements, and work values to job activities. To maximize utilization and retention of volunteers, the director of volunteer services is attempting to assign volunteers to activities that meet each person's expectations and needs and that produce high levels of satisfaction. If skills and abilities also match the activity assignment, the value of the volunteer to the agency will be enhanced and the contribution to the agency will be maximized."

Even more unfortunate is the fact that much of the existing management training with respect to interviewing deals with employment interviewing, which is a totally inappropriate approach for interviewing volunteers. The main difference is quite easily stated: effective volunteer interviewing does not so much consist of examining an applicant's suitability for *one* job as it does of evaluating the ability and desire of that applicant to fit productively in *some* position within the agency. Employment interviewing focuses on the question "Who can do this job?" whereas volunteer interviewing should focus on the more creative question "How can this person help us?"

Purposes of Volunteer Interviews

Among other things, this difference in approach means that a volunteer interview has to accomplish more than the usual employment interview. There are two basic purposes: to identify fit and to recruit.

Identifying fit includes determining the interests and abilities of the potential volunteer, determining his or her suitability for particular jobs, and assessing how well suited the candidate is for the organization, its style of operation, and its mission.

The recruitment aspect involves answering any questions or concerns that the potential volunteer may have and convincing the volunteer of his or her ability to make a contribution to the agency and its clientele or to derive personal satisfaction from helping.

The Interviewing Site

Since a volunteer interview requires a greater exploration of personal characteristics, site selection can be important. Three attributes are critical: accessibility, a friendly atmosphere, and privacy.

Remember the old adage: "You never get a second chance to make a first impression." What the potential volunteer sees and feels during the first interview may shape his or her attitude toward the agency.

Advance Preparation

The following items should be ready before the interview:

- A list of possible jobs with descriptions of required work and qualifications
- A list of questions related to qualifications for each job
- An application form completed by the volunteer providing background information
- A set of open-ended questions to explore the motivations of the volunteer
- Information and materials on the agency and its programs

Opening the Interview

The beginning of the interview should focus on the following matters:

- *Making the applicant feel welcome.* Express appreciation to the person for coming to meet with you. Remember when interviewing potential volunteers that they are evaluating you while you are evaluating them, and this first introduction will have an enormous impact on their comfort level with the agency.
- *Building rapport.* Explain what you would like to accomplish and how the volunteer would fit into the process. Make it clear that the purpose of the interview is to permit the applicant to determine whether volunteering would be a suitable personal choice. Let the candidate feel "in charge."
- *Giving the applicant background about the agency.* Ask what questions he or she has about the agency and its purpose and programs. These questions will allow you to "sell" your agency to the potential volunteer and at the same time discover the person's interests and concerns.

Conducting the Interview

The major portion of the interview should be devoted to the following activities:

- *Exploration of the applicant's interests, abilities, and situation.* Determine why the applicant is considering volunteering and what types of work environment he or she prefers.
- *Discussion of various job possibilities.* Explain the purpose and setting of jobs, and let the applicant consider them. Use this as an opportunity to let the applicant discuss how he or she would approach various jobs, which will tell you more about the person's intentions and level of interest.

- *Discussion of agency requirements:* time commitments, training requirements, paperwork, confidentiality rules, and so on. Let the volunteer
  know what will be expected of him or her. Do not be afraid of telling the
  volunteer about requirements that are important to the agency, because
  the volunteer will learn about them sooner or later. You would much
  rather have a volunteer who honestly declines a potential job at the beginning rather than one who disappears from it later.

- *Further recruitment.* Remember that you are still recruiting the volunteer
  at this stage, so do not forget to explain why each job is important to the
  interests of the agency and the clientele.

- *Picking up on assignment cues.* Look for personality indicators that
  will help you in matching this person to a situation where he or she
  will be happy. This can include details such as whether the applicant
  is a smoker, likes working alone or in a group, and other preferences.

Don't be too quick to reach conclusions during interviews. You should not
assume that what volunteers tell you at first about their motivations presents a
complete picture of their interests. And do not assume that what they are currently doing, such as in their present job, automatically represents what they
should do as a volunteer. As Keyton, Wilson, and Geiger (1990, p. 13) explain it,
"Although a frequent way to uncover a person's abilities is to ask about work
experience, stereotyping a volunteer's ability by vocation can be harmful to the
volunteer's relationship with the organization." Remember that you are attempting to determine not just what a volunteer *can* do but also what he or she
will *want* to do. One way to approach matching volunteers to jobs is to attempt
to give them satisfactions that they do not have in their current paid work situation (McCurley and Lynch, 1996).

Once you have determined a possible job placement for a volunteer, the nature of the interview may change from open-ended exploration to determination
of the volunteer's qualifications and fitness for that position. This is commonly
done through the use of a structured interview, in which a consistent set of questions based on preidentified volunteer role performance indicators is used. This
more systematic format for interviewing has advantages in situations in which
candidates for a position are being compared and may also have some benefit
in screening out potential volunteers who may be inappropriate. It is very similar to interviewing individuals for paid employment positions.

One important skill to possess during the interview is the ability to detect an
unexpected talent in the volunteer and to begin to construct a possible volunteer
role making use of it. This requires a good understanding of the agency and its
programs. If you use volunteers to conduct interviews (a good technique for building rapport and for seeing things from the viewpoint of the potential volunteer),
make sure they have broad knowledge of the agency and its program needs.

Closing the Interview

The interview should be concluded by doing the following:

- Making an offer of a possible position to the volunteer or politely explaining that you have no suitable openings at this time.

- Explaining what will happen next: conducting background or reference checks, scheduling a second interview with staff, scheduling a training session, and so on. Explain the process, the time frame, and the role of all parties involved.

- Getting the permission of the volunteer to conduct any reference or background checks.

Matching Volunteers to Positions

Determining the correct job situation for a volunteer involves questions of both job qualifications and temperament. Volunteers must of course be capable of doing or learning to do the jobs for which they are selected. But it is equally important that the volunteers fit into the work situations for which they are being considered. This means that a volunteer must be satisfied with the job that is being offered and must view the job as desirable and fulfilling work. It means that the work setting (including the timing and site of the job) must also be amenable to the volunteer. And finally it means that the staff with whom the volunteer will be working must also be suitable. This last factor may ultimately be decided on the basis of issues as small as compatibility of personality type, style of work, or even whether one person smokes and the other doesn't.

Since it is difficult to make totally accurate decisions about such complicated matters based on a thirty-minute interview, it is desirable make all initial assignments on a trial-period basis. Let the volunteer know that the first thirty days of work will be done as a probationary period for both the volunteer and the agency. At the end of the thirty days, a second interview will be conducted in which both the agency and the volunteer will reevaluate the assignment. During this second interview, either party may request a change of assignment, based on firsthand knowledge of the situation.

This initial testing period will both make it easier to induce volunteers to try out jobs about which they are uncertain and make it more likely that any mismatches will be identified early and corrected quickly.

Risk Management and Volunteer Screening

The interviewing process is also the point at which the agency attempts to determine the suitability of the volunteer for the position, screening out candidates who are deemed inappropriate. This has become an issue with potential legal implications in recent years (Graff, 2003).

Volunteers, like paid staff, serve as representatives or agents of the organization, and the performance of their duties may lead the agency into potential litigation. The process of effectively screening volunteers is an integral part of risk management, focusing on ensuring the suitability of volunteers to successfully perform their assigned tasks. Screening also serves to ascertain the background of prospective volunteers, identifying those who might have interests that are counterproductive to that of the agency or its clients.

ORIENTATION AND TRAINING

Orientation involves giving volunteers an adequate background on the agency, its operation, and its procedures. Orientation is required because the volunteer needs to be made a part of the organizational environment, a process that requires the volunteer to understand what the organization is and how it operates.

A good orientation session will provide the volunteer with the following types of information:

- Description and history of the organization
- Description of the overall programs and clientele of the organization
- Sketch of the organizational chart of the organization
- Orientation to the facilities and layout of the organization
- Knowledge of general policies and procedures
- Description of the volunteer management system

The purpose is to provide the volunteer with a context within which to work and a feeling of comfort about the work setting. The better the volunteer understands what the organization is and how it operates, the better the volunteer will be able to fit his or her own actions into proper methods of behavior and to display initiative in developing further ways to be helpful to the organization. The orientation session also provides a formal opportunity to welcome volunteers into the agency and officially make them members of the team.

Training is the process of instructing volunteers in the specific job-related skills and behavior that they will need to perform their particular volunteer job. It is designed to tell volunteers

- How they are supposed to perform their particular job
- What they are *not* supposed to do in their job
- What to do if an emergency or unforeseen situation arises

An effective training program operates by identifying the skills, knowledge, and behaviors that are essential to good job performance and then designing a training format that instructs volunteers in those matters. It should be practical, experiential, and tailored to the individual needs of volunteers (Noble, Rogers, and Fryar, 2003).

This training should then be followed by a period of on-the-job coaching in which volunteers are given additional assistance and feedback (McCurley and Lynch, 1996). This coaching can be provided either by paid staff or by other volunteers.

It is helpful to involve other staff and volunteers in designing and delivering volunteer training. This both improves the content of the training and begins to cement the relationship between the volunteers and paid staff of the agency.

VOLUNTEER MOTIVATION

Numerous studies have examined the effect of volunteer motivation on overall service to the agency. Most have revealed the importance of job satisfaction to volunteers. In a study of fundraising volunteers, Dailey (1986) found that job satisfaction was crucial in determining level of organizational commitment. Gidron (1983), in a study of Israeli social services volunteers, found that organizational variables (such as adequate preparation for the task they were asked to do) and attitudinal variables (such as task achievement, relationships with other volunteers, and the nature of the work itself) were the best predictors of volunteer retention. Brown and Zahrly (1990), in a study of crisis intervention volunteers, examine an "investment motive" for volunteering, in which volunteers acquire skills while performing volunteer jobs that they may later use in their careers. Wilson and Musick (1997) have also noted connections between activity performed as a volunteer and work done in paid employment.

Colomy, Chen, and Andrews (1987), in a study of volunteers at various agencies, perhaps summarize all this work when they cite the importance that volunteers give to what they refer to as "situational facilities," a variety of job-related factors including suitable workload, clearly defined responsibilities, competence of their supervisor, and a reasonable work schedule. They conclude, "Perhaps the single most important finding reported in this study is the relatively high importance volunteers accord situational facilities. The high ranking and high mean score of situational facilities are evident both for the sample as a whole and for each of the three sub-groups of volunteers. In addition to the intrinsic and extrinsic incentives associated with volunteer work, then, it appears that individuals strongly desire conditions and organizational settings that facilitate effective and efficient volunteer work" (p. 23).

Much like paid workers, volunteers are motivated by their ability to perform their work well in compatible surroundings. Unlike paid workers, however, it is somewhat easier for volunteers to decide to leave their positions when limited in their ability to perform that work or when immersed in unpleasant working conditions. Failure to provide a satisfactory work environment may lead to reductions in volunteer retention levels (Morrow-Howell and Mui, 1987). This means that effective supervision of volunteers must concentrate on providing a management environment for the volunteers that enhances their overall job satisfaction.

SUPERVISION OF VOLUNTEERS

Supervising volunteers entails all of the aspects of supervisory practice exercised with paid employees.

General Aspects of Volunteer Supervision

The supervisory process involves three general elements:

- Establishing criteria of success, standards of performance, and program objectives, such as the job description and annual plan of work
- Measuring actual volunteer performance with respect to these stated criteria of success through observation, conferences, and evaluation
- Making corrections, as needed, through managerial action

Volunteers will need to be managed just as paid staff are managed and should in fact be treated just as paid staff are treated to avoid giving the impression that there are different classes of workers within the agency. Reporting, record keeping, and evaluation processes for volunteers should mirror those processes for paid staff. The agency should also have a process for dealing with problem supervisory situations (McCurley and Vineyard, 1998) and one for recognition of volunteer contributions.

Volunteers who are not satisfied with the organization are likely to leave, and poor management is one of the primary sources of this dissatisfaction.

In a survey of U.S. adults conducted by the United Parcel Service Foundation (1998), poor volunteer management was one of the two most frequent reasons cited to explain why people stop volunteering (see Table 22.1). The *1997 National Survey of Volunteering in the UK* uncovered similar responses (see Table 22.2).

Special Supervisory Issues

Although the supervision of volunteers is essentially no different in concept or execution from the supervision of any other type of staff for an agency, certain aspects of supervision need an extra emphasis in the volunteer relationship.

Table 22.1. Reasons Why People Stop Volunteering.

Reason Given	Percentage of Respondents
Poor volunteer management	65
Conflicts with more pressing demands	65
Charity was not well managed	26
Charity did not use volunteers' time well	23
Charity did not use volunteers' talents well	18
Volunteers' tasks were not clearly defined	16
Volunteers were not thanked	9

Source: United Parcel Service Foundation, 1998, p. 14.

Table 22.2. Negative Perceptions Among Volunteers in the United Kingdom.

Perception	Percentage of Respondents
"Things could be better organised."	71
"You sometimes get bored or lose interest."	34
"It takes up too much time."	31
"You can't always cope with the things you are asked to do."	30
"Your efforts aren't always appreciated."	29
"You find yourself out of pocket."	29
"You don't get asked to do the things you'd like to do."	20
"Too much is expected of you."	20
"The organisation isn't really going anywhere."	16
"Your help is not really wanted."	5

Source: Institute for Volunteering Research, 1997, p. 2.

Supervisory Responsibility. Is supervision to be provided by the volunteer co-ordinator or by the staff person with whom the volunteer will be working most closely? Both approaches work, but it is essential to make sure that all parties are in agreement regarding who is responsible for day-to-day supervision and management and who will deal with any problem situations that arise. In general, it is more desirable to give supervisory responsibility to whichever staff person will be working most directly and most often with the volunteer.

Flexible Management Approaches. Volunteers must be treated as individuals with different motivations and different styles. The supervisor must be able to accommodate individual variations. This may often require having to deal with situations that do not occur in paid-staff situations, such as those that arise because the volunteer position may have a lower priority than other things in the volunteer's life.

Allocating Time for Management. The pervasive myth that volunteers' work comes free of charge is the bane of good management. Staff who are responsible for volunteers must recognize that their own time must be allocated toward relating to, managing, and dealing with the volunteers on both a professional and a personal basis. Several methods can be instituted to encourage this availability. Open time can be scheduled in the week during which any volunteer can make an appointment. Specific lunch meetings for groups of volunteers can be regularly scheduled, during which open discussions are held. Supervisors can practice "management by walking around" so that they can be approached by volunteers. The intent is to develop an attitude of open and ready communication and access.

Integrating Volunteers into the Flow of the Organization. Above all, the supervisor is responsible for maintaining the communication flow between the volunteers and the organization and with ensuring that the volunteers feel informed of and included in decisions that may affect them and their ability to perform their work. Since volunteers most often work on a part-time or occasional basis, it is very easy for them to fall outside the general informational systems of the agency. If that situation is allowed to continue, their sense of separation deepens, and the volunteers may lost their sense of connection with the agency.

See Lee and Catagnus (1998) for a very practical overview of all aspects of volunteer supervision.

EVALUATION

Evaluation of the volunteer component should take place on the level of the individual and of the agency itself (McCurley and Lynch, 1996; Gouldourne and Embuldeniya, 2002). It may also need to take place on the project level, reviewing the accomplishments and operation of a special event operated by a team of volunteers.

At the level of the individual, volunteer evaluation is designed to give both the volunteer and the agency time to review progress and suggest improvements for the future. It is not designed to replace day-to-day supervision and management but rather to allow a more relaxed "big picture" examination of the volunteer's relationship with the agency. Much like an evaluation session for paid staff, a volunteer evaluation session should consist of a regularly scheduled meeting with supervisors to review past performance and expectations for the future. Unlike an evaluation session for paid staff, it should also provide an opportunity to review motivational aspects of the volunteer's involvement with the agency. This will allow identification of volunteers who have lost motivation due to burnout or who need a new challenge. In a sense, this session allows for rematching volunteers to the agency and rebuilding their commitment, as appropriate, by saluting their accomplishments, identifying new tasks and opportunities to provide service, or transferring them to an entirely new area of work within the agency.

At the agency level, the volunteer management component should engage in periodic evaluations. Input should be sought from current volunteers, paid staff, and agency clientele on the quality of services being provided by volunteers and on working relationships. Input should also be sought from volunteers who have left the agency, particularly if those individuals voluntarily resigned from volunteer service. These varying perspectives will allow the agency to identify ways to continually improve the volunteer utilization system. It will also allow the agency to determine whether the volunteer program is meeting the objectives identified in the program planning process.

INNOVATION IN VOLUNTEER MANAGEMENT

Although the content of this chapter encapsulates the essentials of creating an organizational system for volunteer involvement, it is important to operate this system *creatively*. In recent years, there have been a number of areas of innovation in volunteering, of which we'll examine four.

The Impact of the Workplace

The workplace has become a dominant factor in the lives of most people and thus has great significance for individuals attempting to connect with people. If people are usually at work, then work can serve as an effective mechanism for communication, a key to volunteer recruitment.

In the United States, the workplace has become a powerful force for volunteering (Conference Board, 1993; Points of Light Foundation, 1999a, 1999b). Its most immediate impact on volunteering is revealed in an INDEPENDENT SECTOR survey, which determined that 12 percent of those who volunteered were asked by someone at work and 24 percent learned about their volunteer activity through the workplace (1999, p. 12). Many corporations provide formal opportunities for community agencies to recruit their employees (Points of Light Foundation, 1999a, p. 2):

- 57 percent offer volunteer events on company premises.
- 32 percent provide a directory of community volunteer opportunities.
- 21 percent provide release time for volunteering.
- 21 percent operate a retiree volunteer program.

Accordingly, forming relationships with local businesses has become vital to the successful operation of a volunteer program. In many ways, workplaces are now serving as the modern counterparts to churches and social clubs, operating as feeder systems for volunteer programs.

Although the United States is currently significantly ahead of other countries in the level of involvement of the workplace, similar developments are occurring in other countries (see Imagine, 2001, 2002; Holroyd and Silver, 2001; Pancer, Baetz, and Rog, 2002).

The Shift Toward Shorter-Term Volunteering

Typical involvement patterns for volunteers were once built around a significant and ongoing contribution of time to a particular agency. This commitment might continue for years or decades. Recent years have witnessed considerable change in this ongoing commitment pattern.

An INDEPENDENT SECTOR survey (1999, p.17) reported that 41 percent of volunteers contributed time sporadically or at a onetime event, 39 percent preferred to work at a scheduled time, either weekly or monthly, and 9 percent volunteered only at special times, such as a holiday. Similar results were determined by Handy and Srinivasan (2002, p. 4), who found that among directors of volunteer programs in hospitals in Canada, 81 percent reported an increase in short-term volunteers and 63 percent reported an increase in volunteers requesting assignments of less than three months.

The immediate application of this shift in time donation militates the development of volunteer positions that are designed around projects or events as opposed to ongoing work (Macduff, 1991). This is obviously more suitable to some types of volunteer work than to others.

Volunteering via the Internet

The use of the Internet in volunteer recruitment was discussed earlier in this chapter, but it has also become a mechanism via which volunteering itself is performed. Online volunteering was originally conceived as a means by which computer professionals could assist nonprofit organizations and then expanded as a means to involve individuals in the workplace who might, for example, do mentoring during lunchtime without leaving their offices. Most volunteer positions that involve communication have some potential for being performed, at least in part, via computer. (See Ellis and Cravens, 2000, for a relatively complete overview of the history and development of virtual volunteer programs.)

Currently, about 3 percent of volunteers report performing volunteer work via computer (INDEPENDENT SECTOR, 2001, p. 2), but this percentage is expected to grow (Murray and Harrison, 2002). It has particular application to rural communities, where transportation is an issue, and to efforts to involve individuals with disabilities, particularly the homebound, for whom transportation may pose an absolute barrier.

Involving Families as Volunteers

Most volunteer positions are designed in a fashion similar to paid work—one person performing one job. Family volunteering works in a different fashion: recruiting the family unit as team to perform volunteer work. Extensive development of this concept was undertaken by the Points of Light Foundation (McCurley, 1999) in the United States and is now continuing in other countries (Bowen and McKechnie, 2002).

The most immediate implication of this approach is that it overcomes one of the biggest barriers to volunteering cited by working parents: volunteering requires them to give up time with their children and may impose the additional cost of babysitting. By involving the family as a volunteering unit, this barrier is removed. Interestingly, through proper design, many volunteer positions can be made suitable to family involvement (McCurley, 1999).

In addition to offering a source of assistance to agencies, family volunteering offers the potential for changing the attitudes of family members, both toward one another and toward their community, and of transmitting the values of volunteering to a new generation (Littlepage, Obergfell, and Zanin, 2003).

CONCLUSION

This chapter is intended to capture the basic structural components of a volunteer program and to stress the need for planning and attention to defining and developing that program. Successful volunteer involvement does not just happen; it requires the same meticulous thought and work as any complex task. Assuming that a volunteer program can operate without good management is to expect too much of good intentions.

At the same time, it is important to realize that behind this structure of operation exists the basic spirit of the volunteers, one that prompts them to do something simply because they feel it ought to be done, because there is someone in the community who needs help. It is important in the implementation of the processes described here to resist letting the management structure overwhelm this spirit. If the structure begins to interfere with the ability of the volunteers to accomplish good works and to enjoy their volunteer experience, it is the structure that will need to soften and adjust. The increasing need for sophistication in volunteer management, balancing the need for structure with the need for creative spirit, is illustrated in the listing of Internet resources in the Appendix to this chapter, outlining the growing network of voluntary organizations, technical assistance providers, research facilities, and other bodies who are identifying the means by which we can productively continue to involve volunteers.

Appendix:
Internet Resources for Volunteer Management

Web Sites

The following Internet sites contain material useful for volunteer programs.

Australia

Volunteering Australia: http://www.volunteeringaustralia.org

Volunteering SA: http://www.volunteeringsa.org.au

Volunteering Western Australia: http://www.volunteer.org.au/index.htm

Canada

National Survey on Giving, Volunteering and Participating: http://www.nsgvp.org

Volunteer Canada: http://www.volunteer.ca/volunteer/index.html

United Kingdom

Active Communities Unit, Home Office:
http://www.homeoffice.gov.uk/comrace/active/index.asp

Institute for Volunteering Research: http://www.ivr.org.uk

Millennium Volunteers: http://www.millenniumvolunteers.gov.uk

National Association of Volunteer Bureaux: http://www.vde.org.uk

National Centre for Volunteering: http://www.volunteering.org.uk

Volunteer Development Scotland: http://www.vds.org.uk

Wales Council for Voluntary Action: http://www.wcva.org.uk

United States

American Society of Directors of Volunteer Services: http://www.asdvs.org

Association for Research on Nonprofit Organizations and Voluntary Action (ARNOVA): http://www.arnova.org

Association for Volunteer Administration: http://www.avaintl.org

Corporation for National Service: http://www.cns.gov

Energize, Inc.: http://www.energizeinc.com

INDEPENDENT SECTOR: http://www.independentsector.org

National Mentoring Partnership: http://www.mentoring.org

Points of Light Foundation: http://www.pointsoflight.org

Virtual Volunteering Project: http://www.serviceleader.org

Internet Chat Groups

There are a number of major chat groups tailored to managers of volunteer programs. Each is free.

CyberVPM: http://www.avaintl.org/networks/cybervpm.html

GOV-VPM: http://www.pointsoflight.org/government/gov-join.html

OZVPMs: groups.yahoo.com/group/ozvpm

UKVPMs: groups.yahoo.com/group/UKVPMs

Volunteer Management Periodicals

Australian Journal on Volunteering (Volunteer Centre of South Australia Inc.): http://www.volunteer.org.au/vrn/journal.htm

Canadian Journal of Volunteer Resource Management (Johnstone Publishing, 1310 Upper Dwyer Hill Road, R.R. #2, Carp, Ontario K0A 1L0): (613) 256-5516

e-Volunteerism: An Electronic Journal for the Volunteerism Community (Susan Ellis and Steve McCurley): http://e-volunteerism.com

Grapevine (Sue Vineyard and Steve McCurley, Volunteer Marketplace, Points of Light Foundation): http://www.pointsoflight.org/volunteermarketplace.cfm

Journal of Volunteer Administration (Association for Volunteer Administration): http://www.avaintl.org

Leadership (Points of Light Foundation): http://www.pointsoflight.org

Nonprofit and Voluntary Sector Quarterly (ARNOVA): http://www.evans.washington.edu/nvsq

Nonprofit Management and Leadership (Mandel Center for Nonprofit Organizations, Jossey-Bass Publishers): http://www.josseybass.com

Voluntary Action (Institute for Volunteering Research): http://www.ivr.org.uk

Volunteering (National Centre for Volunteering): http://www.volunteering.org.uk

The Volunteer Management Report (Stevenson Consultants): http://www.stevensoninc.com

Volunteer Management Review (Charity Channel): http://charitychannel.com/resources/volunteer_management_review

Volunteer Today (Nancy Macduff): http://www.volunteertoday.com

Volunteer Recruitment Web Sites

Action Without Borders (global): http://www.idealist.org

Charity Village Volunteer Bulletin Board
(Canada): http://www.charityvillage.com/charityvillage/volbb.asp

Do-It (United Kingdom): http://www.thesite.org/do-it

Go Volunteer (Australia): http://www.govolunteer.com.au

The Interchange (Canada): http://www.web.net/ ~ interchg

International Volunteers (global): http://www.aitec.edu.au

Internet Volunteer Initiative (United States): http://www.4LaborsofLove/org

Nerd World (United States): http://www.nerdworld.com/nw721.htm

Network for Good (United States): http://www.networkforgood.org

ServeNet (United States): http://www.servenet.org

Volunteer Hub (United States): http://www.volunteerhub.com

Volunteer Match (United States): http://www.volunteermatch.org

Volunteer Opportunities Exchange (Canada): http://www.voe-reb.org/index.html

Volunteer Solutions (United States): http://www.volunteersolutions.org

Recommended Reading

This is a list of works, in addition to those in the References, that you may find useful.

AARP. *Volunteerism: A Survey of New York Members.* Washington, D.C.: AARP, 2002.

Active Community Unit, Home Office Communication Directorate. *Giving Time, Getting Involved.* London: Home Office, 1999.

Barbulak, W. *Connecting Volunteers with the Community.* Victoria, British Columbia: Volunteer Victoria, 2003.

Brudney, J. L. *Fostering Volunteer Programs in the Public Sector: Planning, Initiating, and Managing Voluntary Activities.* San Francisco: Jossey-Bass, 1990.

Brudney, J. L., and Warren R. "Multiple Forms of Volunteer Activity in the Public Sector: Functional, Structural, and Policy Dimensions." *Nonprofit and Voluntary Sector Quarterly,* 1990, *19,* 47–58.

Caro, F., and Bass, S. "Receptivity to Volunteering in the Immediate Post-Retirement Period." *Journal of Applied Gerontology,* 1997, *16,* 427–442.

Clary, E. G., Snyder, M., and Stukas, A. "Volunteers' Motivations: Findings from a National Survey," *Nonprofit and Voluntary Sector Quarterly,* 1996, *25,* 485–505.

Community Service Volunteers. *Giving Time: Volunteering in the 21st century.* London: Community Service Volunteers, 2000.

Community Service Volunteers. *Hidden Volunteers: Evaluating the Extent and Impact of Unrecognised Volunteering in the UK.* London: Community Service Volunteers, 2000.

Davis Smith, J. *The 1997 National Survey of Volunteering.* London: Institute for Volunteering Research, 1998.

Dorsch, K., Riemer, H., Sluth, V., Paskevich, D., and Chelladurai, P. *What Determines a Volunteer's Effort?* Toronto: Canadian Centre for Philanthropy, 2002.

Ellis, S. J., and Noyes, K. H. *By the People: A History of Americans as Volunteers,* (2nd ed.) San Francisco: Jossey-Bass, 1990.

Fischer, L. R. and Schaffer, K. *Older Volunteers: A Guide to Research and Practice.* Thousand Oaks, Calif.: Sage, 1993.

Fisher, R., and Ackerman, D. "The Effect of Recognition and Group Need on Volunteerism: A Social Norm Perspective." *Journal of Consumer Research,* 1998, *25,* 262–275.

Flick, M., Bittman, M., and Doyle, J. *The Community's Most Valuable [Hidden] Asset: Volunteering in Australia.* Sydney: Social Policy Research Centre, University of New South Wales, 2002.

Grossman, J. B., and Furano, K. "Making the Most of Volunteers." *Law and Contemporary Problems,* 1999, *62,* 199–218.

Handy, F., and Srinivasan, N. *Costs and Contributions of Professional Volunteer Management: Lessons from Ontario Hospitals.* Canadian Centre for Philanthropy, 2002.

Handy, F., and others. "Public Perception of 'Who is a Volunteer': An Examination of the Net-Cost Approach from a Cross-Cultural Perspective." *Voluntas,* 2000, *11,* 45–65.

INDEPENDENT SECTOR. *America's Teenage Volunteers.* Washington, D.C.: INDEPENDENT SECTOR, 2000.

Ironmonger, D. *Valuing Volunteering: The Economic Value of Volunteering in South Australia.* Adelaide: Office of Volunteers, Government of South Australia, 2002.

Kerr, L., Savelsberg, H., Sparrow, S., and Tedmanson, D. *Experiences and Perceptions of Volunteering in Indigenous and Non-English-Speaking Background Communities.* Adelaide: Social Policy Research Group, University of South Australia, 2001.

Lammers, J. "Attitudes, Motives, and Demographical Predictors of Volunteer Commitment and Service Duration." *Journal of Social Service Research,* 1991, *14,* 125–140.

Lukka, P. *Employee Volunteering: A Literature Review.* London: Institute for Volunteering Research, 2000.

Lynch, R., and McCurley, S. *Keeping Volunteers: A Guide to Volunteer Retention.* London: Directory for Social Change, 2004.

Miller, L. "Understanding the Motivation of Volunteers: An Examination of Personality Differences and Characteristics of Volunteers' Paid Employment." *Journal of Voluntary Action Research,* 1985, *14,* 112–122.

Miller, L., Powell, G., and Seltzer, J. "Determinants of Turnover Among Volunteers." *Human Relations,* 1990, *43,* 901–917.

National Centre for Volunteering. *Get It Right from the Start: Volunteer Policies—the Key to Diverse Volunteer Involvement.* London: National Centre for Volunteering, 2002.

Omoto, A., and Snyder, M. "Volunteers and Their Motivations: Theoretical Issues and Practical Concerns." *Nonprofit Management and Leadership*, 1993, *4*, 157–176.

Omoto, A., and Snyder, M. "Sustained Helping Without Obligation: Motivation, Longevity of Service, and Perceived Attitude Change Among AIDS Volunteers." *Journal of Personality and Social Psychology*, 1995, *68*, 671–686.

Pearce, J. *The Organizational Behavior of Unpaid Workers.* New York: Routledge, 1993.

Phillips, S., Little, B., and Goodine, L. *Recruiting, Retaining and Rewarding Volunteers: What Volunteers Have to Say.* Toronto: Canadian Centre for Philanthropy, 2002.

Quarter, J., Mook. L., and Richmond, B. J. *What Volunteers Contribute: Calculating and Communicating Value Added.* Toronto: Canadian Centre for Philanthropy, 2002.

Reed, P., and Selbee, K. *Formal and Informal Volunteering and Giving: Regional and Community Patterns in Canada.* Ottawa: Statistics Canada, 2000.

Reed, P., and Selbee, K. *Distinguishing Characteristics of Active Volunteers in Canada.* Ottawa: Statistics Canada, 2000.

Reeder, G., Davison, D., and Hesson-McInnis, M. "Identifying the Motivation of African American Volunteers Working to Prevent HIV/AIDS. *AIDS Education and Prevention*, 2001, *13*, 343–354.

Rehnborg, S., Fallon, C., and Hinerfeld, B. *Investing in Volunteerism: The Impact of Service Initiatives in Selected Texas State Agencies.* Austin: RGK Center for Philanthropy and Community Service, University of Texas, 2002.

Saunders, P. *Volunteering Vision, 2010.* Adelaide, Australia: Volunteering SA, 2000.

Statistics New Zealand. *Measuring Unpaid Work in New Zealand, 1999.* Wellington: Statistics New Zealand, 2001.

Sundeen, R. "Differences in Personal Goals and Attitudes Among Volunteers." *Nonprofit and Voluntary Sector Quarterly*, 1992, *21*, 271–291.

Uggen, C., and Janikula, J. "Volunteerism and Arrest in the Transition to Adulthood." *Social Forces*, 1999, *78*, 331–362.

Warburton, J., and Oppenheimer, M. (eds.). *Volunteers and Volunteering.* Sydney: Federation Press, 2000.

Wharton, C. "'Why Can't We Be Friends?' Expectations Versus Experience in the Volunteer Role." *Journal of Contemporary Ethnography*, 1991, *20*, 79–107.

Wilson, J., and Musick, M. "Who Cares? Toward an Integrated Theory of Volunteer Work." *American Sociological Review*, 1997, *62*, 694–713.

Wilson, J., and Musick, M. "The Contribution of Social Resources to Volunteering." *Social Science Quarterly*, 1998, *79*, 799–814.

References

Anheier, H. K., and Salamon, L. "Volunteering in Cross-National Perspective: Initial Comparisons." *Law and Contemporary Problems*, 1999, *62*(4), 43–65.

Australian Bureau of Statistics. *Voluntary Work, Australia, June 2001.* Canberra: Australian Government Printing Service, 2001.

Baer, D., Curtis, J., and Grabb, E. "Has Voluntary Association Activity Declined? Cross-National Analyses for Fifteen Countries." *Canadian Review of Sociology and Anthropology,* 2001, *38,* 249–274.

Blakeman, S. *Recruiting Male Volunteers: A Guide Based on Exploratory Research.* Washington, D.C.: Corporation for National Service, 1999.

Bowen, P., and McKechnie, A.-J. *Family Volunteering: A Discussion Paper.* Ottawa: Volunteer Canada, 2002.

Brown, E. "The Scope of Volunteer Activity and Public Service." *Journal of Law and Contemporary Problems,* 1999, *62,* 17–42.

Brown, E., and Zahrly, J. "Commitment and Tenure of Highly Skilled Volunteers: Management Issues in a Nonprofit Agency." Working Paper No. 12. San Francisco: Institute for Nonprofit Organization Management, University of San Francisco, 1990.

Brudney, J. L. "The Effective Use of Volunteers: Best Practices for the Public Sector." *Journal of Law and Contemporary Problems,* 1999, 62, 219–255.

Canadian Centre for Philanthropy, Volunteer Canada, and Statistics Canada. *Caring Canadians, Involved Canadians: Highlights from the 2000 National Survey of Giving, Volunteering and Participating.* Ottawa: Statistics Canada, 2001.

Carlin, P. "Evidence on the Volunteer Labor Supply of Married Women." *Southern Economic Journal,* 2001, *67,* 801–824.

Carson, E. D. "The Charitable Activities of Black Americans." *Review of Black Political Economy,* 1987, *12,* 100–111.

Carson, E. D. "On Defining and Measuring Volunteering in the United States and Abroad." *Journal of Law and Contemporary Problems,* 1999, *62,* 67–71.

Chambre, S. "Recruiting Black and Hispanic Volunteers: A Qualitative Study of Organizations' Experiences." *Journal of Volunteer Administration,* 1982, *1*(1), 3–10.

Colomy, P., Chen, H., and Andrews, G. "Situational Facilities and Volunteer Work." *Journal of Volunteer Administration,* 1987, *6*(2), 20–25.

Conference Board. *Corporate Volunteer Programs: Benefits to Business.* New York: Conference Board, 1993.

Dailey, R. "Understanding Organizational Commitment for Volunteers: Empirical and Managerial Implications." *Journal of Voluntary Action Research,* 1986, *15*(1), 19–31.

Dyer, F., and Jost, U. *Recruiting Volunteers: Attracting the People You Need.* London: Directory for Social Change, 2002.

Ellis, S. J. *From the Top Down: The Executive Role in Volunteer Program Success.* Philadelphia: Energize, 1996.

Ellis, S. J. *Volunteer Recruitment Book.* Philadelphia: Energize, 2002.

Ellis, S. J., and Cravens, J., *The Virtual Volunteering Guidebook.* San Francisco: Impact Online USA, 2000.

Gidron, B. "Sources of Job Satisfaction Among Service Volunteers." *Journal of Voluntary Action Research,* 1983, *12*(1), 7–19.

Goss, K. "Volunteering and the Long Civic Generation." *Nonprofit and Voluntary Sector Quarterly,* 1999, *28,* 378–415.

Gouldourne, M., and Embuldeniya, D. *Assigning Economic Value to Volunteer Activity: Eight Tools for Efficient Program Management.* Toronto: Canadian Centre for Philanthropy, 2002.

Graff, L. L. *Better Safe . . .: Risk Management in Volunteer Programs and Community Service.* Cayuga, Ontario, Canada: Graff Associates, 2003.

Grantmaker Forum on Community and National Service, *The Cost of a Volunteer: What It Takes to Provide a Quality Volunteer Experience.* Berkeley, Calif.: Grantmaker Forum on Community and National Service, 2003.

Handy, F., and Srinivasan, N. *Hospital Volunteers: An Important and Changing Resource.* Ottawa: Canadian Centre for Philanthropy, 2002.

Hobson, C., and Malec, K. "Initial Telephone Contact of Prospective Volunteers and Nonprofits: An Operational Definition of Quality and Norms for 500 Agencies." *Journal of Volunteer Administration,* 1999, *17*(4), 21–27.

Hodgkinson, V. A., and Weitzman, M. S. *Giving and Volunteering in the United States.* Washington, D.C.: INDEPENDENT SECTOR, 1994.

Holroyd, C., and Silver, A. *Corporate Volunteering: Helping to Build Business and Community Sustainability.* Joondalup, Western Australia: Centre for Regional Development and Research, Edith Cowan University, 2001.

Ilsley, P. J. *Enhancing the Volunteer Experience: New Insights on Strengthening Volunteer Participation, Learning, and Commitment.* San Francisco: Jossey-Bass, 1990.

Imagine and Volunteer Canada. *Volunteers at Work: How Canadian Businesses Encourage and Support Volunteerism.* Toronto: Canadian Centre for Philanthropy, 2001.

Imagine, Volunteer Canada, and the Calgary Workplace Volunteer Council. *Engaging Employees in the Community: How to Establish Employer-Supported Volunteerism in Your Community.* Toronto: Canadian Centre for Philanthropy, 2002.

INDEPENDENT SECTOR. *Giving and Volunteering in the United States, 1998.* Washington, D.C.: INDEPENDENT SECTOR, 1999.

INDEPENDENT SECTOR. *America's Family Volunteers.* Washington, D.C.: INDEPENDENT SECTOR, 2001.

INDEPENDENT SECTOR. *Giving and Volunteering in the United States, 2001.* Washington, D.C.: INDEPENDENT SECTOR, 2002.

Institute for Volunteering Research. *1997 National Survey of Volunteering in the UK* [http://www.ivr.org.uk/natinalsurvey.htm]. 2003.

Keyton, J., Wilson, G., and Geiger, C. "Improving Volunteer Commitment to Organizations." *Journal of Volunteer Administration,* 1990, *8*(4), 7–14.

Latting, J. "Motivational Differences Between Black and White Volunteers." *Nonprofit and Voluntary Sector Quarterly,* 1990, *19*(2), 121–136.

Lee, J., and Catagnus, J. *What We Learned (the Hard Way) About Supervising Volunteers.* Philadelphia: Energize, 1998.

Littlepage, L., Obergfell, E., and Zanin, G. *Family Volunteering: An Exploratory Study of the Impact on Families.* Indianapolis, Ind.: Center for Urban Policy and the Environment, School of Public and Environmental Affairs, Indiana University–Purdue University, 2003.

Macduff, N. *Episodic Volunteering: Building the Short-Term Volunteer Program.* Walla Walla, Wash.: MBA Associates, 1991.

McCurley, S. *Family-Friendly Volunteering: A Guide for Agencies.* Washington, D.C.: Points of Light Foundation, 1999.

McCurley, S., and Lynch, R. *Volunteer Management: Mobilizing All the Resources of the Community.* Downers Grove, Ill.: Heritage Arts, 1996.

McCurley, S., and Vineyard, S. *Handling Problem Volunteers.* Downers Grove, Ill.: Heritage Arts, 1998.

Morrow-Howell, N., and Mui, A. "Elderly Volunteers: Reasons for Initiating and Terminating Service." *Journal of Gerontological Social Work,* 1987, *13*(3–4), 21–34.

Murray, V., and Harrison, Y. *Virtual Volunteering: Current Status and Future Prospects.* Toronto: Canadian Centre for Philanthropy, 2002.

Noble, J., Rogers, L., and Fryar, A. *Volunteer Management: An Essential Guide.* Adelaide, Australia: Volunteering SA, 2003.

Pancer, S., Baetz, M., and Rog, E. *Developing an Effective Corporate Volunteer Program: Lessons from the Ford Motor Company of Canada Experience.* Toronto: Canadian Centre for Philanthropy, 2002.

Points of Light Foundation. *Corporate Volunteer Programs as a Strategic Resource.* Washington, D.C.: Points of Light Foundation, 1999a.

Points of Light Foundation. *Corporate Volunteer Programs: Benefits to Business.* Washington, D.C.: Points of Light Foundation, 1999b.

Prime, D., Zimmeck, M., and Zurawan, A. *Active Communities: Initial Findings from the 2001 Home Office Citizenship Survey.* London: Voluntary and Government Research Section, Immigration and Community Unit, Research Development and Statistics Department, Home Office, 2002.

Saxon, J., and Sawyer, H. "A Systematic Approach for Volunteer Assignment and Retention. *Journal of Volunteer Administration,* 1984, *2*(4), 39–45.

Skillingstad, C. "Training Supervisors of Volunteers." *Journal of Volunteer Administration,* 1989, *8*(2), 29–34.

Tiehen, L. "Has Working More Caused Married Women to Volunteer Less?" *Nonprofit and Voluntary Sector Quarterly,* 2000, *29,* 505–529.

United Parcel Service Foundation. *Volunteerism Today.* Nashville, Tenn.: United Parcel Service, 1998.

Vineyard, S., and McCurley, S. (eds.). *Managing Volunteer Diversity.* Downers Grove, Ill.: Heritage Arts, 1992.

Volunteer Canada. *A Guide to Volunteer Program Management Resources.* Ottawa: Volunteer Canada, 2001.

Warburton, J., and Crosier, T. "Are We Too Busy to Volunteer? The Relationship Between Time and Volunteering Using the 1997 ABS Time Use Data." *Australian Journal of Social Issues,* 2001, *36,* 295–314.

Watts, A., and Edwards, P. "Recruiting and Retaining Human Services Volunteers: An Empirical Analysis." *Journal of Voluntary Action Research,* 1983, *12*(3), 9–22.

Wilson, C. *"Lady Bountiful" and the "Virtual Volunteers": The Changing Face of Social Service Volunteering.* Wellington, New Zealand: Ministry of Social Development, 2001.

Wilson, J., and Musick, M. "Work and Volunteering: The Long Arm of the Job." *Social Forces,* 1997, *76,* 251–272.

Wilson, J., and Musick, M. "Attachment to Volunteering." *Sociological Forum,* 1999, *14,* 243–272.

CHAPTER TWENTY-THREE

Finding the Ones You Want, Keeping the Ones You Find

Recruitment and Retention in Nonprofit Organizations

Mary R. Watson
Rikki Abzug

T he attraction, selection, and retention of staff are perhaps the most important processes managers in organizations undertake. After all, the people of the organization are the architects and agents of everything that ultimately gets accomplished. Yet in many nonprofits, these processes garner woefully inadequate attention (Hecht and Ramsey, 2002). Overcrowded schedules, underfunded programs, endless client needs, irregular financial cycles, and demands for reports of accountability are among the never-ending pressures that crowd out the organization's ability to focus on the critical human dimensions of nonprofit management. With too little time, information, and money, not to mention staff needed yesterday rather than tomorrow, how can leaders learn how to plan a human resource system, much less implement one and then evaluate whether it is reaching the desired outcomes?

The purpose of this chapter is to help executive directors and staff at all levels reach their desired human resource goals within the realistic contexts of their own organizations. In the following pages, we strive to achieve two goals. The first goal is to demonstrate how thinking systemically about the role that people play in the organization leads to better long-term outcomes. Not only is it possible to save time and effort in recruitment, selection, and staff retention programs, but building an effective people-oriented culture is key to long-term success. The second goal of this chapter is to provide shorthand tips on managing critical human resource processes effectively. Although it is not possible to be comprehensive in every aspect of human resource management—volumes have been written on this subject—this chapter provides the essential knowledge regarding reaching out to find staff prospects, interviewing and evaluating applicants, keeping them motivated, and managing the circumstances under which staff will ultimately leave the organization (through retirement, voluntary turnover, termination, or layoffs). We also discuss important legislation related to various aspects of finding and keeping the right people that enable each nonprofit to reach its own unique objectives.

Staff and leaders might wonder what is different about the current approach to nonprofit human resources. In fact, one might simply pick up a current practitioner article on the "top ten tips for recruitment," for example, and conclude that the answers are stated there. The difference lies in the deliberate recognition of the variety of contexts in which organizations operate. We argue that there is no universal ("one size fits all") style of nonprofit human resource management. Further, contingency approaches that argue a simple set of "if . . . then" rules (for example, if an organization is in a rural area, then it must have a local recruitment strategy) are not sufficient. Measurements of returns on investment (ROI) (Bartel, 2000; Fitz-enz, 2000) on individual programs or practices are useful, but only when systems are considered holistically and in context. Rather, "configurational" (Delery and Doty, 1996) approaches are best because they recognize that there are unique synergies gained through human resource systems and that these synergies differ, depending on the context in which they exist. Executives who capitalize on the relationships among human resource approaches, the organization's environment, the mission and goals of the organization, and knowledge management principles are the ones who are successful in building momentum toward the organization's desired state.

The nonprofit sector has a vast array of organization types. People in organizations large and small work on very different missions, taking significantly different approaches, based on vastly different traditions, in different social and environmental contexts. Tax codes alone provide for twenty-six different categories of tax-exempt entities, the largest proportion of which fall in the 501(c)(3) category, which includes the subsectors of health care, education, and social services. Each subsector also has unique characteristics that drive human resource tradition and practice. Further, within nonprofit subsectors, definitions and dimensions of diversity differ in ways that have important implications for the crafting of a human resource strategy. Finally, nonprofits differ from for-profit organizations in many ways, yet research in nonprofit human resources is in its infancy and often draws too heavily on what has worked in the for-profit sector.

Successful nonprofit executives know the right questions to ask about their own contexts. They then use the answers to guide the way their organizations enact nonprofit recruitment and retention. They recognize the synergistic implications of effective management today on capacity building for the future. Throughout this chapter, we remind executives of the key questions that should be asked regarding elements of the human resource system in their organizations.

WHY PUT PEOPLE FIRST?

Given the humanistic missions of most nonprofit organizations, it is paradoxical that nonprofit leaders need to be reminded of the importance of the people in the organizations. Yet across organizations and time, multiple constituencies demand attention from nonprofit leaders (Kanter and Summers, 1987). Nonprofit mission statements typically do focus on people, but people who are external to the organizations—the clients—rather than internal staff.

Jeffrey Pfeffer's book *The Human Equation: Building Profits by Putting People First* (1998) outlines some of the people elements necessary for organization success in for-profits. It is exciting to note that most of Pfeffer's recommendations for success—passion, engagement, enthusiasm, lifelong learning—have always existed in most nonprofit organizations. The primary goal of nonprofits, for example, is to maximize the ability to deliver on mission. Nonprofits begin with staff attracted to and motivated by their organization's mission, an extremely powerful "human resource advantage." Indeed, even during the economic downturn of the past few years, the human resource consulting firm Towers Perrin (2003) reports that 42 percent of nonprofit employees remain "highly engaged" in their work, compared to 19 percent in the for-profit sector. Even in these cynical times, the motivations of nonprofit staff are precisely what will enable their organizations to thrive (Block, 2003; Light, 2002), if they avoid the pitfalls of adopting for-profit approaches without first considering their suitability for nonprofits.

So what is missing from the contemporary state of nonprofit human resources? We took an informal poll of a group of nonprofit managers interested in human resources at the Action Without Borders First Annual Nonprofit Human Resources Conference in June 2003. The respondents echoed the resounding cries of nonprofit managers everywhere: no time, no money, and no tools.

We put forward the concept of what we call the "People First" human resource approach for nonprofit organizations. We emphasize the unique elements of nonprofit sector organizations, arguing that the nature of nonprofits makes them ideally suited to maximize their outcomes through the people of the organizations. This focus on people results in additional organizational capacity, effective succession planning, engaged and motivated staff, and improved client service delivery. These are not just effectiveness outcomes; they are also the keys to the time, money, and information organizations need to survive and thrive. They also lead to reputation effects that attract staff and funders through positive profiles featured in outlets like *The 100 Best Nonprofits to Work For* (Hamilton and Tragert, 2000).

"People First" nonprofit organizations recognize that organizational success lies in the creative engagement of the human resources of the organization. They regard human resources not as a staff function outside the organization's operation but rather as the central conduit through which organizations succeed. They capitalize on the power of mission to attract and motivate staff. They recognize the critical nature of staff synergies in selecting new staff members. They leverage technology, where appropriate, to reduce recruitment costs and administer standardized human resource functions. They encourage diversity on many dimensions, and they enact cultures that are constituted by diverse groups working well together. They design motivation and retention systems that recognize both the intrinsic motivators that brought staff to the organization (such as mission focus or client focus) as well as the extrinsic motivators (such as pay, health care, or retirement) that are necessary for staff financial and physical health. They retain and develop talented staff whenever possible, and they manage terminations in humane and positive ways when layoffs are unavoidable.

Human Resources Is a System, Not a Set of Tasks

The "People First" approach is a systems approach to human resources. Thus the tasks of human resources cannot be thought about independent of one another, and effective leaders develop an overarching set of integrated human resource goals to guide their day-to-day decision making. Often staffing decisions come about as part of an immediate crisis: additional funding is received and staff must be hired quickly to scale up and deliver on the outcomes, a crucial staff person leaves the organization suddenly and needs to be replaced immediately, the organization is broadening its mission and needs additional kinds of talent, or executive succession planning uncovers a need to develop internal staff for future leadership. Falling prey to constantly solving immediate crises can lead to unintended long-term outcomes. Indeed, government contractors who consistently add and delete staff based on variable levels of program funding can inadvertently create a climate of insecurity and distrust. An individual decision, seemingly isolated, will cause reverberations inside and outside the organization, many of which may be unintended.

A large and well-established body of academic research has tested the relationship between systemic human resources and effective outcomes (for example, Becker and Huselid, 1998). Among the recommendations are strategic alignment of human resources with organization strategy (Becker, Huselid, and Ulrich, 2001), creating an executive position directly responsible for human resources in rapidly growing small organizations (Welbourne and Cyr, 1999), and incorporating IT systems design into human resources (Lengnick-Hall and Moritz, 2003). Although these findings have been tested primarily (but not exclusively) in the for-profit sector, caution in extrapolating them to nonprofits seems appropriate in these instances.

Not only are human resource functions interconnected, but in the aggregate they also represent the experienced culture of the organization. The organization's human resource goals are very important because they define the day-to-day quality of work life enjoyed by staff. Because of their centrality, informed executives engage all staff in imagining their ideal collective human resource culture. In this way, they begin at the desired end. First they figure out, collectively in their organization, where they want to go. Then they do a needs assessment of their current culture of human resources, assess their planning needs, engage staff at all levels in designing human resource processes, and later evaluate their progress toward the desired end. All along the way, effective nonprofits keep in mind where they are trying to go as they take the small steps that will get them there.

Most nonprofits (especially small ones) do not have time and resources for detailed and expensive planning. The good news is that for more than a decade, the management field has recognized that increasingly turbulent times call for flexibility in management along a guided course, not fixed planning cycles (Morgan, 1989). Rather than resulting in complex planning processes, engaging a "People First" human resource system is more a shift in way of thinking. Bolman and Deal (2003) write about how successful managers are able to reframe situations, focusing on the political, symbolic, structural, and human resource aspects at one time. Most managers have a predisposition to one approach over the others. For example, while many nonprofit leaders might be fixated on the political aspects of funding streams, others may be expert in the design of innovative structures for service delivery, others have special talents in using staff recognition ceremonies as powerful symbols of a mission-based culture, and still others specialize in the human resource talents of attracting and motivating staff with diverse and complementary skill sets. The "People First" approach takes this logic one step further and argues that effective executive directors know that all these elements of their organizations are important. Their focus on human resources as the vehicle to accomplish all organizational goals—political, structural, and cultural—is central to all their decision making.

Some examples will illustrate the point. Affirmative businesses, incorporated as or created by nonprofits, with goals of providing jobs and job training for mentally, physically, or economically disadvantaged individuals, often center human resources in their sustainability and growth plans. For organizations serving the mentally ill or the homeless, for example, the line between clients and staff can be amorphous, and best practices suggest an integrated approach that emphasizes job design, career pathing, motivational compensation, and respect for individual choice. Organizations from New York's Housing Works Bookstore to Seattle's Boomtown Café are "People First" organizations that try to do good by doing well (Kanter and Summers, 1987) by all of their people.

If You Build It, They Will Come (and Stay)

There are two key concepts to keep in mind while imagining the end state of a "People First" nonprofit: fit and embeddedness. These two concepts make clear that whereas successful executives design human resource systems, these systems are continually re-created by everyone associated with the organization. Therefore, in successful nonprofits, all staff are continually rebuilding a people-oriented culture. There is no true end result: human resource culture is a never-ending exercise in coevolution.

In a decade of studies on person-organization fit (see Chatman, 1989; O'Reilly, Chatman, and Caldwell, 1991; Werbel and Gilliland, 1999), a consistent finding is that staff are attracted to organizations with which they perceive an alignment between the goals of the organization and their own values and objectives. This is one explanation as to why recruiting by internal referral is so successful (Barber, 1998): individuals who know insiders are much more likely to understand what the organization is about and accurately assess whether or not they would like to work there. Thus self-selection on the part of prospective and current staff plays a huge role in shaping the ultimate human resource culture. This notion of perceived fit has also been shown to apply to the person and the job, as well as the person and the work group (Kristof-Brown, Jansen, and Colbert, 2002).

Nonprofit executives should keep in mind that these perceived fit processes are going on in all aspects of the human resource system (attracting, recruiting, selecting, retaining, and staff turnover). One productive task is to engage all staff in a dialogue around what constitutes fit in their organization. Work to make explicit what the fit dimensions are: examining the mission statement is a good way to start. A second task is to investigate perceptions of your organization held by those in similar and different organizations. Knowing how the culture of the organization is perceived by outsiders will provide key information about who might be attracted to the organization and who might be approaching staff to recruit them away. Once these dimensions are clearer, the human resource strategy of the organization can recognize the power and limitations of the notion of fit. Whether an organization makes it explicit or not, perceived fit (or lack thereof) is always an element of the human resource system.

One important clarification needs emphasis here. Fit is not a synonym for homogeneity. Successful organizations tend to seek and engage diverse viewpoints. In fact, one might have as an element of the mission an explicit goal of nourishing a culture of diversity. In this case, fit means attracting staff who share the value of honoring difference, not attracting similar staff. One good interpretation of diversity is articulated by scholar Taylor Cox (1994), who acknowledges and embraces the wide variety of social characteristics held by people who work together. Successful nonprofits shape their human resource systems around a broad and diverse set of views, using their historical, community, and mission contexts to define their diversity goals.

The second key element of a "People First" nonprofit human resource system is the notion of embeddedness. This refers to the extent to which the staff and their families are engaged in the organization and its community. Embeddedness is a broader concept than organization satisfaction and commitment, which have been argued to account for less than 5 percent of actual turnover (Hom and Griffeth, 1995). Drawing on Kurt Lewin's field theory (1951), research on embeddedness (Lee, Mitchell, Holtom, McDaniel, and Hill, 1999) suggests that staff who are more embedded in their organizations are less likely to leave voluntarily. There are three dimensions to embeddedness: the extent to which individuals have links to other people, the extent to which their job and community fit with other aspects of their lives, and the perception of what would be lost if the individual left his or her job (Mitchell, Holtom, Lee, Sablynski, and Erez, 2001).

For successful nonprofits, embeddedness is a powerful concept. Not only is it desirable that staff share a passion for the organization's mission, but they must also be motivated by the way in which their role facilitates reaching part of that mission. Further, the more extensive the networks of relationships they and their families have within the organization and the community, the more likely they are to stay with the organization. Finally, the understanding of what would be lost if they left the organization ("sacrifice," in embeddedness terms) helps leaders guide human resource systems closer to the ideal state that staff would imagine. Here a good exercise for executive directors would be to encourage open dialogue around human resource systems, eliciting from staff a shared understanding of the really unique elements of the nonprofit and the community it serves. Note that discussion of human resources includes all aspect of work, including the design of jobs themselves.

In addition to shared values, it is also important to recognize individual needs of staff, which will differ from person to person and family to family. The quality of the relationship that staff members have with leaders is a key factor in their intention to stay with the organization. Informal dialogue, or more formalized 360-degree performance appraisals systems, in which staff give constructive feedback to the executive staff (and vice versa), can help keep positive communication open across levels. Staff families matter too. Offering cafeteria-style benefits, allowing staff to choose from an array of human resource benefits what best fits their family needs, is one example of engaging with the "whole person." Flexible work schedules might also help in this area. At a minimum, open dialogue between staff and managers must be encouraged to keep shared lines of communication open.

FIRST THINGS FIRST: MAKE IT LEGAL

It is always wise to begin any discussion of the processes involved in human resource systems with a discussion of the existing law related to these human resource processes. Many nonprofit managers are unfamiliar with current legislative statutes, and the consequences of decisions that violate the law can be dire, particularly for smaller organizations without the resources to engage in lawsuits or absorb fines.

The United States has a centurylong tradition of creating policy to protect workers. Starting around the turn of the twentieth century with the birth of the union movement following the shirtwaist workers' strike, employment law emerged during the civil rights movement of the 1960s around race and equity, through advances in workplace safety in the 1970s, and today's work issues of HIV/AIDS, family-friendly policies, and procedures to reduce terrorism. We shall review the essential laws that all nonprofit professionals must know, whether "human resources" is part of their job title or not.

There are a variety of legislative frameworks around the world, made up of varying combinations of national, regional, and local legislation. Knowing how these levels of legislation interact in one's own country is important. For instance, in Canada, federal labor code covers less than 10 percent of the nation's employees, so most employment legal issues are determined by laws created by the various provinces (Bernier and Lajoie, 1986). In the United States, by contrast, federal regulations apply to all organizations with staff above a certain size (which varies, depending on the particular law). There are also state laws that provide more stringent standards than the federal legislation, and each nonprofit must familiarize itself with the laws of its own state and the states in which it operates. Due to space limitations, we review only U.S. federal law here. State laws vary considerably.

This section provides a general overview of the U.S. federal legislative framework, with particular emphasis on discrimination law. Using this chapter as a starting place, you may find that a user-friendly legal guide to U.S. federal employment law, like the one published by the American Bar Association (Fick, 1997), can help clarify key questions. However, general legal knowledge is not to be substituted for appropriate legal advice from qualified counsel. It is always necessary to consult an attorney for specific applications to your organization.

Title VII: The Civil Rights Act of 1964

Title VII of the Civil Rights Act, arguably the most influential piece of legislation regarding employee treatment, was passed into law in 1964. Building on energy from the civil rights movement that garnered more attention than previous civil rights bills, the Civil Rights Act was signed into law under Lyndon Johnson's administration. Title VII of that act focuses on employment, and it specifically prohibits employment discrimination based on race, skin color, religion, sex, and national origin. In addition, it establishes the Equal Employment Opportunity Commission (EEOC), a federal agency empowered with the enforcement of discrimination violations. Other sections of the Civil Rights Act relate to education and public facilities contexts. Here we focus only on the employment dimensions of the law specified in Title VII.

The prohibition of discrimination provided under Title VII applies to all aspects of the work relationship: recruiting, hiring, promoting, performance evaluation, access to training, discharging, and so on. A common misperception is that the coverage is narrowly applicable to hiring decisions. All organizations with fifteen or more employees are required to adhere to nondiscriminatory practices in all aspects of their treatment of employees. Furthermore, any organization of any size that receives substantial federal government funds or contracts (the dollar value varies by program) must comply. Also, any employment agency, labor organization, or joint labor-management committee controlling apprenticeship or other training or retraining must comply, regardless of size. Title VII was amended by the Civil Rights Act of 1991 to include the opportunity of compensatory and punitive damages for intentional discrimination, enable litigants to collect legal fees, and allow for jury trials.

There is one particularly notable exception to enforcement of antidiscrimination categories. In general, religious organizations have been considered exempt from the religion category and supported in their right to make employment decisions based on faith. However, some federal social programs (the Workforce Investment Act, for example) contain language explicitly prohibiting religious discrimination, others (such as community development block grants and Head Start) might be interpreted as prohibiting employment decisions based on religion, and other state and localities require religious organizations not to discriminate on the basis of religion in order to be eligible for funding. In 2004, the Bush administration's Office of Faith and Community Based Initiatives was considering legislation that would unify a position on a religious organization's ability to make employment decisions based on faith.

Disparate Treatment Versus Adverse Impact. Discrimination under Title VII falls into two categories. What is termed "disparate treatment" is sometimes also called deliberate or direct discrimination. Under a charge of disparate treatment, a litigant who is a member of a protected group (race, color, religion, sex, or national origin) would argue that he or she was treated differently because of his or her protected class. A litigant might argue that the interviewer indicated racial or national origin bias during the interview, for example. In addition to evidence of direct discrimination, disparate treatment charges require not only that the litigant has been denied access to the employment benefit but also that another person who is not a member of the protected class was chosen. Fortunately, most organizations have put human resource practices and staff training programs in place to alleviate many of the intentional discrimination charges.

Lesson: Make sure all staff are aware of the organization's intolerance of deliberately discriminatory practices, and ensure that training around these issues is delivered. Many issues are subtle.

Determining the much more common charge "adverse impact" is more complex. Sometimes called indirect or unintentional discrimination, adverse impact occurs when the aggregate outcomes for a protected group are less advantageous than for the majority group. The landmark case in this instance is *Griggs* v. *Duke Power* (401 U.S. 424, 1971). Griggs, an African American employee of the Duke Power Company in North Carolina, was denied promotion to a supervisory position because he did not hold a high school diploma. At that time in North Carolina, the high school graduation rates for blacks and whites were significantly different, with blacks earning diplomas at a lower rate (this disparity has since been corrected). The U.S. Supreme Court ruled that the high school diploma requirement discriminated against blacks because they had a lower graduation rate. Further, the organization failed to demonstrate why a high school diploma was necessary to do the job effectively. In fact, some supervisors promoted earlier did not have diplomas.

The *Griggs* case makes two things clear for nonprofit leaders. First, it is necessary to examine your own human resource practices to ensure that the outcomes for protected groups are not different from the outcomes for majority groups. Second, be certain that you can demonstrate the job-relatedness of any human resource criterion, regardless of whether you think it might be correlated with protected class. For example, imagine that you regularly select staff to attend a leadership development program. To encourage fairness, you make it a practice to choose individuals from across your organization's geographical locations to attend, and you make these decisions one by one over time. Imagine, however, that in compiling an analysis of your decisions in the past year, you discover that in the aggregate, women have been chosen less frequently than men, despite the fact that your workforce is balanced by gender. How would you know if you have enacted a discriminatory selection for training?

The first test is to see whether you have what is called a *prima facie* ("on its face") case of discrimination. The legal test is what is called the four-fifths rule: Was the rate of selection of the women at least four-fifths (80 percent) of the rate of selection for the men? Assume that there are ten women and ten men from whom you might have chosen. If you have chosen five men, you must also have chosen at least four women to diffuse a prima facie case. In the event that there appears to be discrimination after application of the four-fifths rule (in this example, if you chose fewer than four women), can you defend the decisions you made by arguing that the criteria on which you based the selection of trainees are related to job performance? Numerous court decisions based on gender, including well-publicized ones argued by airlines to defend female-only flight attendant positions, have established that gender is not a valid job criterion. You have a problem.

Consider another example. Imagine you are choosing among applicants for a counseling position where the clients speak English. Among your applicant pool are ten U.S.-born native English speakers and ten Chinese-born immigrants with Mandarin as their native tongue. If five of the Americans pass the initial English language test you use for prescreening but only one of the Chinese applicants does, is there discrimination based on national origin? On the face of it, there is a prima facie case of discrimination (50 percent of the U.S.-born make the cut, compared to only 10 percent of the Chinese-born, which fails the four-fifths test). In this situation, however, you may be able to successfully muster a job-relatedness defense that the skill on which you screened (language) is essential to performing the job (counseling clients). Although there are other defenses in the case of prima facie discrimination (seniority system, bona fide occupational qualification), job-relatedness is the best defense (Fick, 1997). Nonprofits need to be careful to use selection criteria that are quantifiable and empirically proven to be related to job performance. "Softer" general impressions of candidates and their attitudes do not hold up well in court.

Lesson: Use only human resource criteria that your organization can demonstrate are directly related to job performance. Do not rely on opinions or assumptions; collect hard data.

Interpretations of Title VII. An interpretation of Title VII surrounds the issue of sexual harassment. Although Title VII did not specifically identify sexual harassment as part of its domain, subsequent court cases have interpreted sexual harassment as discrimination based on gender. According to law, there are two kinds of sexual harassment. The first is called *quid pro quo,* Latin for "something in exchange for something." To meet the criteria under this category, a staffer (or in some legal findings, clients or board members) must have been the unwanted recipient of an advance that is sexual in nature, where the "submission to or rejection of this conduct explicitly or implicitly affects an individual's employment," including employment decisions (Equal Employment Opportunity Commission, 2002b). Most organizations have mechanisms in place to ensure that deliberate sexual harassment does not occur, as well as channels for safely reporting incidents.

The category of "hostile work environment" is more subtle. In general, a staffer must have been subjected to either sexual advances or other verbal or physical conduct of a sexual nature that either "unreasonably interfered with an individual's work performance" or created "an intimidating, hostile, or offensive working environment" (Equal Employment Opportunity Commission, 2002b). Courts typically consider whether the staffer made it known to the alleged harasser that the advances or behaviors were unwelcome, and the advances or behaviors must have been repeated. However, in some circumstances, courts have interpreted an act as so egregious as to not warrant meeting the conditions of notice and readvance.

Supreme Court cases clarify that both men and women are protected, and harassment can be perpetrated by individuals of the same sex regardless of the sexual orientation of either party (for example, *Oncale* v. *Sundowner Offshore Services, Inc.*, 523 U.S. 75, 1998). Further, the harasser can be connected to the organization in many capacities: as a supervisor, employee, agent of the organization, coworker, or nonemployee. Finally, the harassed does not need to be the direct recipient of the unwanted sexual behavior. A charge can be filed by anyone affected by the conduct.

Lesson: Make sure staff understand what constitutes sexual harassment, how to avoid harassing incidents, and the channels they should follow to report unwanted behaviors.

Legislation Protecting Other Groups

Other legislation has extended nondiscriminatory practices to other protected groups. For example, the Age Discrimination in Employment Act of 1967 (and amendments in the Older Workers Benefit Protection Act) applies to employers with twenty or more employees and protects workers over age forty (younger in some states) against discrimination based on age. The Pregnancy Discrimination Act (an amendment to Title VII) protects women who are pregnant against refusals to hire, requires treatment of pregnancy that interferes medically with the employee's ability to work to be treated as any other disability, requires that any health insurance offered by the employer include pregnancy coverage (but not abortion coverage), and requires that employees be given leave, vacation calculation, and pay under the same practices that are afforded to other employees on leave.

One final group deserves special explanation. The Americans with Disabilities Act of 1990 (ADA) protects those with physical and mental disabilities, whether perceived or real, from discrimination in employment (and public access). The act covers all employers with more than fifteen employees, as well as all state and government programs and activities. The ADA defines a person with a disability as "someone with a physical or mental impairment that substantially limits a major life activity, has a record of such an impairment, or is regarded as having such an impairment" (Equal Employment Opportunity Commission, 2002a).

The Council for Disability Rights emphasizes how widespread disabilities can be: An estimated 43 million Americans have physical or mental disabilities (Council for Disability Rights, 2003). Clarifications of the ADA by the EEOC indicate that the use of items like medications or prostheses does not disqualify a disabled person. Mental and emotional characteristics such as thinking and concentrating are covered, and short-term impairments are generally interpreted as less life-altering (Equal Employment Opportunity Commission, 2000). Active drug use is not a disability, although prior drug use can qualify if the person is discriminated against based on a record or perception of prior use. Although the ADA and its amendments do not specify the disabilities that qualify, case law has upheld such diverse conditions as mobility, vision, speech, and hearing impairments, asymptomatic HIV status, learning disabilities, and mental illness.

The passage of the ADA changed employment screening practices directly. Under the ADA, no employer may require a medical examination prior to extending a job offer. Further, where applicants or employees request "reasonable accommodation" of the physical workplace, the design of their jobs, or their benefits, employers are required to comply to the extent to which the accommodations do not cause the employer undue financial or logistical hardship. Examples of accommodations under ADA might include modifying work schedules, purchasing special equipment to facilitate reading or translation, physical alteration of the work site, or job reassignment.

Lesson: Be open to making accommodations to employees who might have disabilities. Encourage open dialogue so that staff with "invisible" disabilities feel free to come forward to request accommodation. Do not screen based on disability; ask only if the employee can do the essential functions of the work required.

Role of the EEOC in Discrimination Cases

Under federal law, discrimination charges must be filed with the EEOC within 180 days of the incident (or awareness that the incident might have caused discrimination). (Most state laws allow up to 300 days.) Charges can be brought forward by the individual affected or by any individual or any organization on behalf of the individual. No private lawsuit can be filed until the EEOC evaluates the case. Where EEOC investigation warrants, and where individuals request an EEOC "right to sue," private lawsuits can be started within a period of 90 days after the right to sue finding (Equal Employment Opportunity Commission, 2003).

Additional Legislation of Interest to Nonprofit Managers of Human Resources

In addition to the antidiscrimination legislation just described, there are many other major laws that affect your organization. Details about the key legal frameworks are listed here, and the U.S. government's official Web portal (http://www.firstgov.gov) is a great place for nonprofit managers to find resources to answer questions.

- Fair Labor Standards Act of 1938, which covers wages and hours standards, as well as overtime, for employees who work interstate. This act covers large employers (with $500,000 in annual revenue) and small employers whose employees operate across state borders. Of particular interest in this legislation is the determination of which staff are exempt from overtime pay for work in excess of forty hours per week. "Professionals," "executives," and "outside salespeople" are the official exempt categories, but interpretations are more complex.
- Equal Pay Act of 1963, which prohibits sex-based wage discrimination and applies to most organizations with one or more employees. Exceptions include seniority, merit pay, and job performance.
- Executive Order 11246, which requires nondiscrimination and affirmative action plans of federal government agencies and government contractors. At the time of this writing, the status of affirmative action in various states and at the Supreme Court level was in flux. Current legal findings should be investigated by the reader.
- Family and Medical Leave Act of 1993, which guarantees up to twelve weeks' unpaid leave to employees in organizations with more than fifty employees to welcome a natural or adoptive child into the family, to care for an immediate relative, or to recover from an illness.
- Homeland Security Act of 2002, which contains provisions regarding the hiring of foreign workers. The act created the Department of Homeland Security and transferred the processing of work authorizations from the Immigration and Naturalization Service to the Bureau of Citizenship and Immigration Services, a division of the Department of Homeland Security.
- Immigration Reform and Control Act of 1986, which requires employers to verify employee identity and legal eligibility to work in the United States.

- Occupational Safety and Health Act of 1970, which was designed to reduce workplace injuries and illnesses and resulted in the creation of the Department of Labor's Occupational Safety and Health Administration.
- USA PATRIOT Act of 2001, which broadens government ability to review employment records, conduct surveillance of employees and employers, and monitor financial flows.
- The Health Insurance Portability and Accountability Act of 1996 (HIPAA), which is designed to ensure that new staff can obtain health care benefits without being subjected to preexisting conditions clauses. This legislation is complex, and the reader can find details at the Health and Human Services Web site (http://www.hrsa.gov/website.htm).
- All state and local laws related to the workplace. Many of these follow the spirit of the federal laws but are likely to cover more organizations of smaller size. They may also cover groups (such as homosexuals) not protected by federal legislation.

Make It Legal, Make It Fair

There is a sometimes a paradox in legality and fairness: What is legal is not always perceived as fair, and what is perceived as fair is not always legal. It is, of course, necessary to meet legal standards in all human resource decisions, and the law is relatively clear on what those specifics might be. However, a higher and more complex standard is establishing human resource approaches that are perceived by everyone inside and outside the organization as fair. Promoting antidiscrimination, following legal hiring procedures, and creating legal wages and benefits are all important signals of the centrality of human resources to the nonprofit. Yet despite consensus on these concepts, implementation can often lead to staff feeling that they are not being treated fairly. Creating open communications channels to bring issues of fairness—and perceived unfairness—to everyone's attention is important. Finally, going beyond simply what is legal to embracing what staff feel is fair takes an organization a long way toward becoming "People First."

This is especially true for small or religious organizations that may be exempted from the requirements of many of these legislative initiatives. Small or religious organizations that do not respect the spirit of the law (even if not required to respect the letter of the law) do so at their own risk. They run the risk of disengaging the funding community, government opportunities, and local labor markets and talent pools, as well as segments of the giving public. With exemptions for religion-based discriminatory hiring for faith-based organizations seeking public support currently under contention, all organizations need to weigh the mission fulfillment and community needs argument in favor of exclusionary human resource practices against legal and public norms and expectations of fairness and diversity.

PUTTING IT ALL TOGETHER: THE PROCESSES OF HUMAN RESOURCES

This section of the chapter reviews effective approaches to recruiting and retaining motivated nonprofit staff. We begin by reinforcing the idea of beginning with the desired end state, and we recall the concepts of fit and embeddedness. We use the "People First" model, raising awareness about how recruitment and selection affect the culture of any nonprofit. Legal pitfalls related to each practice are raised. Throughout the discussion, we raise contextual considerations to be taken into account as a "People First" culture is crafted.

The Human Resource Audit

Earlier in the chapter, we introduced the idea of "starting at the desired end," that is, figuring out where the organization stands with respect to human resources and where it wants to go. Every nonprofit organization should regularly engage in systematically evaluating where it stands with respect to human resources. Exhibit 23.1 suggests the sorts of questions to be asked and answered. Each organization will of course develop its own set of questions based on its own situation.

Once the answers to the human resource audit questions are understood, the organization is ready to begin the process of adding additional staff in a way that will enhance the organization's movement toward its desired "People First" state. The goal is that every hiring and retention decision is made in the context of an overall plan for where the organization is headed. All staff should be involved in the human resource audit process as well as in developing plans for bridging any identified gaps.

The Staffing Plan

"People First" organizations are likely to address the issue of staff planning within the broader context of the organization's strategic plan, although all nonprofits would do well to strategically consider the staffing mix at start-up, at present, and for a future desired state. The motivating question for any staffing plan is, "What are the continuing activities that need to be performed to help the organization meets its goals (mission)?" The staffing plan involves a consideration of the complement of staffers (full-time or full-time equivalent, part-time, volunteer, consultant, and outsourced) that will most effectively contribute to achieving the organization's purpose. It is likely that planning such levels will involve careful review of state and federal laws around fair labor standards and the designation of employees as exempt versus nonexempt. The staffing plan will also likely designate staffing positions as belonging to central administration, general operations, or program staff.

Exhibit 23.1. Sample Human Resource Audit Checklist.

Organization and Job Structure

How accurate is the organization chart? Does it reflect both formal and informal reporting relationships? Is it current? Do staff at different levels agree that it is accurate?

How up-to-date are job descriptions and statements of knowledge, skills, and abilities (KSAs)? Do hiring, performance appraisal, and promotion standards support applicant matching and staff skill development for these jobs and KSAs?

Do the existing organization structure and distribution of work responsibilities match future operational plans? Which aspects of the structure seem appropriate for the next three to five years, and which will need modification?

Human Resource Planning

What skills are required for current projects? Do existing staff have the needed skills? What training might be needed?

What skills are anticipated to be needed for future projects? Does the organization have these skills on staff at this time? If not, how will they be acquired?

What turnover is anticipated within the next year? Will it likely be voluntary or involuntary? What gaps will this create in the organization's ability to meet its goals? What capacity may be lost due to turnover?

How strong is the internal promotion ladder? Are internal promotions a goal for this organization? If so, for what positions? How complete is the leadership succession plan?

What future hiring plans currently exist? Are there resources in place to fund these openings? What recruitment strategies have been developed in anticipation of upcoming recruitment?

How competitive is the organization in its labor market with organizations of similar size and purpose? Are salaries and benefits offered that will attract desired applicants? How does the organization's reputation affect potential recruitment success?

Organization Culture

What characteristics were identified in the organizational fit analysis as important? How well has fit been accomplished?

What were the outcomes of the internal embeddedness analysis? Which staff are embedded, and which staff are not committed? Are the most highly desired staff the most embedded? If not, how will the organization work to achieve this?

What is the state of staff motivation? What makes working in this organization desirable for staff? What are the negative aspects of the work environment? How and why do individuals vary in their motivation?

What characterizes the existing human resource culture? Is this culture consistent with the organization's mission? What values are central to the operation? What dimensions of diversity are desired?

Especially in the case of small grassroots organizations transitioning to professional staffed entities, the staffing plan must address the shift in day-to-day operations from a founding board or executive director to a supervised staff. Funding exigencies, growth projections, community and subsector expectations, and size and scope of expected service provision will all play a role in motivating or constraining the staffing levels set by organizational leaders. Staffing levels and complements for individual program areas may be set by constituent demands and supply for those services, while staffing levels and complements for central administration are likely to vary with the coordination and planning needs of the organization as a whole.

One of the most important yet most overlooked areas in staff planning in the nonprofit sector remains succession planning. In 2003, the United Way of New York City's study of CEOs, board members, and pipeline leaders confirmed sectoral fears that almost half of all New York executive directors were planning to leave their positions within five years at the same time that only one-third of all directors stated that they had a succession plan in place (Birdsell and Muzzio, 2003). Given demographic changes and likely competition for talent from other organizations and sectors, nonprofit leaders can both confirm commitments to "People First" cultures and give their organizations a leg up by engaging in reflective succession planning as well as thoughtful leadership development and training. "People First" staffing, succession, and training and development planning will also make staff retention (discussed later in the chapter) a less daunting challenge.

Recruitment

The first step in recruitment is figuring out what kind of staff the organization is seeking. Typically, a search is initiated by the creation of a new staff position or by the departure of staff in an existing role. In either case, it is important to begin any search with a clear idea of the characteristics the organization is seeking in a candidate.

Identifying Job Characteristics. In human resource terminology, these characteristics are called KSAs, for *knowledge, skills, and abilities. Knowledge* encompasses the content knowledge a staff person needs to know prior to being hired. Proficiency in many positions presumes a specific body of knowledge. Is an understanding of how arts management organizations are funded essential to the position? Is a knowledge of state laws related to nonprofit status required? When thinking about the term *knowledge,* it is useful to think about what facts an individual *should know.* The term *skills* refers to proficiency in doing things with objects or ideas. Is operating a computer necessary for this job? Does the applicant need to be able to calculate tax credits on a loan? When defining the term *skills,* think about what the applicant *needs to do*. Finally, *abilities* refers the capacity to undertake certain work responsibilities. Does the individual need to be able to communicate effectively? Are supervisory abilities paramount? When defining *abilities,* think about what the individual *has the capacity to accomplish.*

KSAs are similar to, but not the same as, *competencies.* KSAs have long been in use in government settings and made their way into the private sector nearly two decades ago. Although the term is somewhat less commonly used in the nonprofit sector, the KSA concept has an important legal distinction. In the event the nonprofit organization is required to demonstrate that a job requirement is related to the ability to perform the job, the organization will be asked to demonstrate what KSAs were used for hiring and how those KSAs are related to job performance. Thus they serve as the underpinnings for any legal and fair recruitment process.

Effective managers begin by determining what KSAs are desired for the available position through a process called job analysis. This process of discovery usually includes interviewing current and former staff incumbents (if any), dialogue among those who will work with the individual about what they feel is needed for success in the position, and strategic planning about what is needed for the organization in that role. Job analysis is a process of uncovering various perspectives on what the staff position is, might, and should encompass (see Chapter Twenty-Four for a discussion of the use of job analysis in compensation systems).

Writing Job Descriptions. After the job analysis phase, most organizations write job descriptions. The job description serves three purposes: to help those who will select among applicants consider what is needed for the position, to advertise to potential staff what the job will entail, and for use in legal defense against discrimination charges. It is important that the job description be both comprehensive and flexible. No candidate will meet all desired aspects, and the position's requirements will be fluid over time as needs arise. The effective non-profit manager strikes a balance, articulating clearly what the organization is seeking without writing an unrealistically rigid characterization.

There are commercially available products for job analysis and the writing of job descriptions, as well as technical assistance available from a variety of consulting firms who specialize in these tasks. Each organization must decide how it will undertake this responsibility. For larger organizations, crafting job descriptions in-house may be easier, as there may be numerous similar positions in-house. Conversely, it may be easier for outside consultants to compare positions with others in other organizations. For smaller organizations, the task is more difficult and is often best accomplished with outside advice from peer networks combined with sample job description materials found on the Internet.

Searching

Once the job description is in hand, the organization should consider how it will search for applicants. There are many sources of potential employees, grouped for the purpose of discussion here into external and internal types.

The primary consideration when drafting a recruitment strategy is determining the goal of the recruitment program. Is the organization trying to attract a large applicant pool? Is diversity of applications a major objective? Is promotion from within the desired outcome? What are implications of hiring from without versus hiring from within on a "People First" culture? Are the candidates likely to be available locally, or will a national search be required? Answers to these questions can help inform choices about recruitment strategies.

There is significant evidence that recruitment practices do matter to organizations. For example, there is a broad and extensive literature on the effect of different recruitment strategies on applicant perception (Barber, 1998). Less is known directly about recruitment strategies and organizational effectiveness, but anecdotal research suggests there is good fodder for investigation.

External Approaches. Under some circumstances, searching for potential staff from outside the organization is deemed desirable. Several types of sources can be used, depending on the applicant pool targeted.

• *Newspaper ads.* Running ads in newspapers or magazines is a broad recruitment approach: it will generate a large applicant pool with a wide range of general skills. Advertising in newspapers is a good idea when the organization is entering a new market, needs a large number of staff, wants to broaden its contacts, and has the capacity to review a large number of applications. The cost is related to the advertising rates of the newspaper or magazine itself and the staff to review applications that are generated. The typical urban newspaper ad can generate as many as one thousand applicants, so be prepared to manage the volume. Most newspapers have a local readership, so newspapers allow a geographically targeted search (national newspapers will attract a national pool). This is a good approach for attracting a diverse applicant pool, as a wide array of individuals will be exposed to the advertising.

• *Online (Web-based) recruitment.* Increasingly popular and very inexpensive, posting job listings through online databases enables nonprofits to reach out for applicants worldwide. Recent estimates suggest that recruitment costs can be reduced by as much as 95 percent through online recruiting (Cappelli, 2001). Services differ, but they generally allow the nonprofit to specify the characteristics they are seeking and to screen out applicants who lack requisite qualifications. One related issue is that Web recruiting acts as a stimulus for applicants to visit the hiring organization's Web site. There is evidence that Web site information is used by applicants to assess whether they fit with the organization or not (Dineen, Ash, and Noe, 2002), suggesting that nonprofits should make sure that their Web materials contain accurate information about the organization's mission and purpose.

- *Professional publications, associations, and conferences.* Releasing a job posting through a professional association or advertising in a professional journal is a good idea when the position the organization is seeking to fill is closely related to a specific profession. For example, if the organization is seeking a licensed social worker, advertising in professional social work outlets will attract a large proportion of qualified applicants. Conference listings are good when the organization can identify key conferences where applicants of interest would be in attendance.
- *College recruiting and internship programs.* Appropriate for positions requiring a college education, college recruiting is effective for reaching that market of applicants. For nonprofits, education about opportunities in the nonprofit sector needs to be part of on-campus recruitment efforts. Internships are particularly useful to test out staff before making a permanent hire and to allow students exposure to the organization.
- *Government job services offices and placement agencies.* These options are appropriate for locating entry and mid-level staff with little to some experience. Both types of agencies prescreen candidates, which can be a cost-saving measure for nonprofits with little time to cull through candidate files. Services are usually free to the organization; government-funded job services work for no fee, while placement agencies usually charge a fee to the applicant.
- *Professional search firms or executive recruiters.* Usually the most expensive of the options, professional search firms are a good source of high-level applicants with a specific skill set. Search firms usually offer expertise in identifying applicants with specific experience. They also offer the advantage of confidentiality, as they can make inquiries between the organization and potential applicants without identifying either party. Many search firms charge the hiring organization, not the applicant, and fees typically range from 10 to 25 percent of the first year's salary. Increasingly, search firms and recruiters are specializing in nonprofit placements, and in some cases, these services may be both less expensive and more targeted for the nonprofit sector.

Internal Approaches. In some cases, filling staff vacancies from inside the organization is the better strategy. The following are internal approaches that may be undertaken.

- *Employee referral.* As mentioned earlier, internal referral programs have advantages. Typically, employee referrals are relatively low in cost. Some nonprofits create staff incentive programs that give financial rewards to staff who recruit others who are hired and work successfully in the organization. Employee referrals lead to the identification of potential employees who know quite a bit about the organization and whose interest in the organization is therefore typically high. Employee referral programs tend to generate a geographically local applicant pool, and prospects are limited to candidates who are connected somehow to individuals already in the organization. One downside is that this can make diversifying the nonprofit more difficult.

• *Internal postings and promotion.* Making opportunities available to current staff is a critical dimension of a "People First" nonprofit. When hiring is consistently done from the outside for positions above the entry level, a signal is sent to staff that their opportunities are limited. Ensure that all staff are aware of upcoming openings, and give them access to ample information about the positions. Managing decisions to hire from the outside when there are qualified internal candidates can be difficult, but seriously considering insiders as applicants tends to lead to better perceptions of fairness, even if the internal candidates are not ultimately chosen.

• *Client and volunteer recruitment.* A rich source of candidates for nonprofits is the client and volunteer base of individuals who already have a relationship with the organization. These sources offer the benefits of familiarity with the organization and understanding of its basic operations. Many successful nonprofits make the boundaries between volunteers and paid staff permeable. Organizations with client bases can improve services by hiring clients as staff members. As already noted, many nonprofits and affirmative businesses, by mission and strategy, choose to hire mostly or exclusively from within client and volunteer ranks.

In general, what recruitment sources are most effective? Meta-analyses of studies of recruitment sources have found that individuals hired through internal sources are as much as 24 percent more likely to stay on the job for the first year (Zottoli and Wanous, 2000) and tend to be more satisfied than those recruited from the outside. Among the competing explanations for this effect are that the applicants have a realistic preview of the job, there is better person-job and person-organization fit for inside referrals, internal candidates are of higher quality, and employees are more credible as sources of job information.

Finally, what information should be included in the recruitment process? Effective and accurate communication is always a goal; candidates not hired by the organization will nevertheless learn a lot about it and should be left with a good impression. More information and accurate information both lead to positive outcomes. Friendliness and timeliness on behalf of everyone in the recruitment process leads to perceptions of a fair and friendly organization that is interested in the applicant (Breaugh and Starke, 2000). Inclusion of women and people of color in the recruitment process signals an organization open to diversity (Highhouse, Stierwalt, Bachiochi, Elder, and Fisher, 1999).

Choosing a Candidate

Perhaps the most challenging human resource task is determining which candidate or candidates from the pool of applicants should be chosen. As briefly described earlier, it is important that any applicant be evaluated on whether or not he or she has the ability to perform the required tasks. In nonprofits, the needs for flexibility of staff are often paramount; thus structured approaches are often not practical and are arguably less desirable.

Most nonprofit organizations are also particularly interested in the notion of fit—in many cases, this is interpreted as the extent to which the applicant shares a commitment to the mission. Mission drift is sometimes seen as one result of hiring key staff who do not share the organization's view on its future direction. In all selection decisions, the premiere challenge is finding a qualified, motivated, and adaptable candidate on whom various staff can agree.

Particularly applicable in large nonprofit contexts, staff selection can include highly technical procedures. For example, there is a plethora of well-established selection instruments, including personality, cognitive ability, and honesty testing; assessment centers that evaluate leadership and team performance; and work sample tests that replicate actual portions of the job to be performed. We will review each of these approaches briefly (more extensive details on these topics can be found in Gatewood and Feild, 2001).

Once the recruitment pool has been identified, the first selection step is to determine which of the applicants merit further consideration. Now is the time to apply what has been determined by the job analysis, examining which potential staff hold the best promise based on the KSAs previously identified for the position. It is best to review a variety of applicant materials, including résumés, letters of interest, and application forms (see Exhibit 23.2).

Step 1: Determine Which Applicants Have the Required Qualifications. Candidates who do not have the required qualifications should be immediately rejected from the pool. Most organizations write a polite letter to the candidate indicating that many other applicants who are more qualified for the position are being considered. It is important to thank candidates for their interest in the organization and to encourage them to apply for future openings as they become available. If possible, keep on file information about applicants who look promising but do not meet the organization's current needs.

For candidates who meet the required qualifications, the organization typically moves on to determine whether this is the best candidate for the position. Although the qualifications must eventually be verified (degrees actually awarded, employment checked, and so on), it is usually best to wait to verify these details after the candidate has shown interest through the interview.

Exhibit 23.2. The Candidate Selection Process.

Questions	Aspects to Consider	Details Needed	Action to Be Taken
Is the candidate qualified?	What required qualifications does the candidate clearly meet?	Degrees, certifications, credentials, past job titles, dates of employment	*If yes:* Verify facts from sources after candidate has reached the finalist pool. *If no:* Send rejection letter.
Is the candidate among the best available?	What evidence of past performance looks applicable to this position in this organization? What limitations does past experience suggest?	Statements of accomplishments, key positions held, experience in related organizations	*If yes:* Investigate or probe in the interview; administer selection tests, if used. *If no:* Send rejection letter.
Can this candidate's fit (with job and organization) be verified?	Who are key references for the applicant?	Extent to which listed references can evaluate various qualifications, experiences, motivation, and limitations; candidate consent to check other references not listed.	*If yes:* Conduct reference checks after the candidate has reached the finalist pool. *If no:* Send rejection letter.
Should this candidate be selected?	What do various staff sources say? How does all the evidence collected so far add up? (Consider using a team selection process.)	Candidate who best fits the job and the organization at this time	*If yes:* Tender an offer. *If no:* Wait until an offer has been accepted before rejecting other candidates, politely, in writing.

Step 2: Assess Which Candidates Are Among the Best for the Position. In this stage of the selection process, it is necessary to choose a pool of candidates whom the organization will consider further. The size of the reduced pool will be determined by the number of qualified candidates available, the organization's resources for further investigation, and the timetable under which the decision must be made. Most organizations will reduce the qualified candidate pool to between three and five candidates.

If the organization has the available resources and assessment instruments are considered appropriate for the position being considered, at this stage the organization may ask the candidates to submit to these tests. Many organizations (particularly in the private sector) use psychological tests, the most common of which is called the "Big Five" personality test. The five characteristics, identified through either the Five Factor Index instrument (Goldberg, 1990) or the NEO-PI instrument (Costa and McCrae, 1997) are based on decades of psychological research that suggests that the stable elements of personality include openness to experience, conscientiousness, emotional stability, agreeableness, and extroversion. Of the five, conscientiousness has been shown to be the best predictor of performance overall, and extroversion best for external relations positions like sales or fundraising (Gatewood and Feild, 2001). Tests of general cognitive ability, which research has shown to be among the best predictors of job performance for complex jobs across the United States, with even stronger relationships across Europe (Salgado, Anderson, Moscoso, Bertua, and De Fruyt, 2003), are also widely used. In recent years, honesty tests have become popular. Research findings about their general efficacy have reached even the popular business press (Fisher, 2003) but questions exist about the appropriateness of their use.

Psychological testing has been shown to be a good predictor of future performance and to have high "predictive validity," as there is empirical evidence that the traits they test are indeed related to some kinds of job performance. Thus such tests have generally been upheld in most court cases as legal, particularly where the organizations have tested the relationship between test scores and performance in their own organizations. However, personality tests often have low "face validity," that is, candidates may perceive the tests as inappropriate or invasive, and this sometimes gives rise to perceptions of inequity.

Other organizations use work sample tests to assess requisite skills such as financial management, software proficiency, or industry expertise. The challenge is to identify appropriate tests available for commercial sale or to develop one's own instruments in-house, an expensive undertaking that requires particular expertise. Assessment centers are very effective if the position requires leadership or team management skills, but their design and administration are expensive. In general, the advantage of work sample tests is that they assess work qualifications directly. Thus they tend to have high face validity and are usually perceived by applicants as fair since they are directly related to the work to be performed.

Perhaps the holy grail in selection is the personal interview. Historically conducted face to face, some organizations are finding that resource constraints and large applicant pools make preliminary telephone, video, or Web-based interviews an important first screening test. Empirical evidence about selection interviews is mixed. Research shows that interviews have low predictive validity for job performance but high face validity, as they are perceived as desirable by both interviewers and interviewees (Arvey and Faley, 1988).

Despite limitations, interviews are nearly universally conducted in selection. We offer the following guidelines to help interviewers do a better job at conducting effective interviews.

- *Use a structured interview format.* A consistent finding in the selection literature is that the same questions should be asked of all candidates for the position. Thus rather than using a free-flowing conversation to assess candidate appropriateness, determine ahead of the interview what questions will be asked of all candidates. This helps the organization keep the interview tied to the relevant KSAs being assessed, it encourages managers to consider carefully the characteristics they are seeking *before* the interview, and it ensures that each candidate is asked to address the same issues.
- *Stick with behaviors.* Successful interviewing relies on conversations that focus on the behaviors candidates have exhibited in past work settings. Interview questions should ask what the candidate *did* in past situations, as past behavior has been shown to be the best predictor of future performance.
- *Keep it legal.* As covered in detail earlier, there are many categories of protected employees. No interview questions should explore any protected category, either deliberately or inadvertently. For example, it is never appropriate to ask candidates if they have made child care arrangements or if they have spousal coverage on benefits (implying gender or parental status); instead, ask if the candidate is able to work the hours required. Never ask candidates when they graduated from high school or college or earned a professional certification (implying age); instead, ask if the degree has been obtained or if the certification is currently valid. Do not ask whether a candidate is a U.S. citizen; ask instead whether the candidate is authorized to work in the United States or can gain authorization if selected for the position.
- *Consider a team interview.* A relatively new development in selection involves team-based selection. Research suggests that conducting a team interview (with two to five members in diverse positions who are savvy about employment practices) and using a team selection process can enhance fit and improve commitment to selection decisions (Stewart, 2003). Team interviews

also enhance the likelihood of a realistic job preview (Wanous, 1980) that makes it more likely that the candidate will be informed about what the position will really entail, enhancing early commitment to the organization and encouraging self-selection out of the process for candidates who feel they would not be a good match.

Step 3: Verify Candidate Qualifications and Match. Once a candidate has passed the interview stage, it is time to check references. The candidate will have provided references in writing or listed names to be contacted. In either case, it is advisable to follow up with a telephone call with specific questions. These questions should be designed to probe information already obtained from other sources and to facilitate more detailed understanding of the candidate's qualifications.

The reference-checking process is fraught with difficulties. Many employers will provide only very basic information, including dates of employment and whether the employee is eligible for rehire. This reluctance is sometimes due to personal preferences and at other times is the result of legal counsel's advice to avoid possible slander or libel suits. Yet reference checking is a step that should never be skipped: It is imperative to show "due diligence" in the hiring process. A legal concept called "negligent hiring" can be invoked by staff members who feel that adequate precautions were not taken to ensure that the candidate does not prove dangerous to the other staff (Gatewood and Feild, 2001).

Step 4: Make the Selection Decision and Tender the Offer. Once all information has been collected, it is time to make an offer to the leading candidate. Ideally, there is agreement among those involved in the selection process as to who the best candidate is. Often there is more than one leading candidate. It is a good idea to keep all top candidates in the pool until a final offer is accepted.

The offer should be given by phone, followed up with details in writing. The offer letter should include the name of the position, annual (or hourly) salary, benefits to be included in the package, starting date, and terms of employment (full-time permanent, part-time temporary, and so on). The letter should include a deadline, usually within two weeks, by which the candidate must reply. Salary level should be discussed with the candidate before tendering the final offer (details about compensation and benefits are covered in Chapter Twenty-Four).

Summary of the Selection Process

To summarize, the selection process should be designed to attract and hire qualified candidates who fit both the job and the organization. Throughout the process, attention must be paid to the overall hiring strategy and staff and succession planning of the organization, in keeping with the "People First" approach. Performance standards must always be kept in mind during the selection process. A thorough job evaluation should help guide the criteria on which decisions are made. It is advisable to involve multiple staff members in the selection process to ensure an open dialogue among current and future staff. Legalities should be considered, and each step of the selection process should be valid in that it leads to the selection of a staff member who can succeed in the organization.

RETENTION THROUGH MOTIVATION

Once the organization has selected the right staff and the right complement of staff to achieve organizational goals, the next (ongoing) steps involve motivating and retaining (good) people. For-profit organizations and traditional business schools have spent the better part of a century trying to understand and enact the elusive motivation of staff that brings organizational effectiveness. The good news, as we noted at the beginning of this chapter, is that motivation of staff is one area where nonprofit organizations seem to have the inherent advantage. Study after study has demonstrated that nonprofit employees are more engaged, more motivated, and sometimes even more satisfied in and by their work than employees in other sectors. Yet turning that motivation into productivity and guarding against burnout remain confounding issues for nonprofit leaders. Furthermore, assuming that all nonprofits have the motivation advantage is misleading. Small nonprofits motivate employees toward goal achievement differently from larger nonprofits, and great variability in motivational techniques and organizational cultures exist across (and within) nonprofit subsectors. Indeed, motivating employees in large urban hospital systems may take a very different organizational culture and set of tools than motivating employees in a small rural community development corporation.

There are any number of theories that purport to explain how organizational actors are motivated. These include needs theories that emphasize how organizational life can help satisfy individual desires (Maslow, 1943) and process approaches like equity (Adams, 1963) and expectancy theories (Vroom, 1964), which emphasize the cognitive analyses and choices that individuals make in deciding how much exertion of effort is worth their while. These concepts have then been differentially applied by the generic management literature to construct techniques and programs aimed at increasing employee motivation and concomitant productivity. In the for-profit world, management flavors of the month have included the recognition of individual differences in designing motivation programs, managing by objectives (using goal setting to spur effort), basing rewards on performance, and enhancing opportunities for participation in decision making (for an overview, see Robbins, 2002). Many of these theories and applications start with the assumption that human resources need to be aligned with organizational goals, and motivation techniques exist to do just that.

Although these theories and applications are variably useful to nonprofit leaders, a critical review of them is beyond the purview of this chapter. They are, however, helpful to reconceptualize motivation in "People First" nonprofits as part of the larger human resource system embedded within the organization's culture, always with an eye toward the power of the mission. In nonprofit (and in particular service) organizations, human resources are not so much aligned with the organization as they *are* the organization. Further, it is often the case that nonprofits do not have to align employee goals with organizational goals because the selection process and the draw of the mission have already done that.

For "People First" nonprofits, then, activity around motivation might best be spent nourishing an organizational culture that values all constituencies, respecting each participant's contribution to fulfillment of mission. While such motivation may be complemented by compensation and benefit programs, it is also enacted by the management of organizational symbols, rites and rituals, and affirmative events and recognition (Bolman and Deal, 2003). "People First" cultures motivate employees through fair and humane compensation and benefits but also affirm people's value and commitment to the organization's mission in an ongoing fashion.

DISCHARGE, LAYOFFS, AND VOLUNTARY TURNOVER

Although we hope, and textbooks infer, that organizations can motivate people to stay goal-focused and loyal, we know that organizational turnover is a fact of life. Getting a handle on voluntary turnover seems especially important to nonprofit organizations that are, indeed, defined by their human resources. Costs of voluntary turnover, even in organizations not so dependent on labor, can be staggering, if not debilitating. Immediately, turnover means starting the recruiting, selecting, and even training processes all over and incurring their concomitant costs. There is also the disruption to the organization's processes, culture, and other constituents when old faces disappear.

Traditional advice to managers suggests a correlation between job satisfaction and voluntary turnover. However, many of the causes of turnover are varied and often not directly under the control of the organization. These include, most conspicuously, labor market conditions and alternative job (and life) opportunities. Recent literature has sought to explore how even these external factors might be addressed by organizational leaders eager to retain their most valued and valuable employees. A new wave of literature in the for-profit sector cited earlier posits that "job embeddedness" is an even better predictor of staying the organizational course than job satisfaction, organizational commitment, job alternatives, and job search (see Mitchell, Holtom, Lee, Sablynski, and Erez, 2001). As noted earlier, these researchers define job embeddedness as a multifaceted construct that includes three core components: links between individuals and coworkers, perceptions of fit with both organization and community, and the sense of sacrifice if the position were to be relinquished.

This line of thinking takes organizational leaders out of the realm of the at-work-only context and suggests that to promote a "People First" culture, leaders need to take a more holistic approach to employees' well-being. Encouraging employees' links to coworkers, boards, and clients might elevate employees' feelings of embeddedness, as would encouraging employees' connections to community activity. In many ways, these suggestions may be second nature to leaders of community-based organizations, but their value to organizational human resources has not been so acutely supported in the past. We suggest that in the nonprofit context, job embeddedness often morphs into organizational embeddedness, which is often overlaid with a sense of community embeddedness. If organizational leaders ignore the reality of embeddedness, within a job, an organization, or a community, they do so at their own peril. Conversely, finding organizationally sanctioned ways to encourage cross-linkages and social networks, as well as community involvement, will likely result in more embedded and then committed staffers and may go a long way toward supporting organization and community missions.

Particularly in the current dismal economic conditions at the time of this writing, some organizations inevitably need to lay off staff involuntarily. Inconsistent funding streams, failure to obtain grants or grant renewals, or a general downturn in demand can all lead to these difficult decisions that challenge the very fabric of the "People First" culture. Our general advice for downsizing (as it is bloodlessly called) is to avoid it where possible and where it is unavoidable to enact it mindfully. This includes careful performance-based identification of those to be eliminated, sufficient advance warning, adequate explanation of rationale, and assistance in outplacement (Cascio, 2002). Perhaps paradoxically, handling these issues with a personal touch is important. Although an executive's instincts may be to avoid face-to-face conversations with those being terminated or to delegate this responsibility to staff, handling these issues openly, honestly, and directly is the best approach. Legal considerations are also important. Many downsizings in the 1990s tended to target high-paid workers as a cost-cutting measure, resulting in class action lawsuits for discrimination based on age. Finally, managers also must not forget the remaining staff, termed "survivors" (Brockner, Grover, Reed, and De Witt, 1992). Research suggests that those who retain their jobs are often haunted by stress, fatigue, and guilt.

MAKE OR BUY: THE OPPORTUNITIES AND PERILS OF OUTSOURCING HUMAN RESOURCES

One contemporary trend is toward the outsourcing of human resource functions. For small nonprofits in particular, the attraction of delegating human resource functions to external experts may be strong: often there is little internal capacity to perform what are viewed as specialized tasks. Indeed, the outsourcing of recruitment, applicant screening, relocation services, payroll, and benefits is common in some subsectors.

Nonetheless, each organization must decide which human resource functions are core to its "People First" approach. For many organizations, this makes deciding to outsource payroll and benefits delivery (but not design) a clear choice: external vendors often have software and specialized expertise in delivering these services, and the cost can be advantageous. However, for human resource functions more central to the organization's mission, such as attracting and selecting staff, it often makes sense to keep these functions in-house. Although there can be economic benefits of scale when outsourcing recruitment and selection in small organizations (Klaas, McClendon, and Gainey, 1999), these reduced costs can sometimes also translate into loss of control of attraction of staff who fit the organization's culture. Outsourcing human resource functions that play critical roles in identifying and retaining staff who share the organization's mission are often best left inside.

One notable exception is the idea of collaborating across organizations to provide health care and retirement benefits. For small nonprofits in particular, purchasing power for health care packages and investment power for retirement are in short supply. Joining a benefits collaborative, or creating one, can dramatically decrease the cost of such services per individual employee.

When a decision to outsource is made, it is imperative to follow up with thorough management of the outsourced contracts as well as evaluation of the efficacy of those relationships after a short period. In addition to considering administrative costs, organizations are well advised to measure staff satisfaction with outsourced services.

SUMMARY: ALONG THE ROAD OF PEOPLE FIRST

If the more humanistic aspects of this chapter on "People First" organizations have been insufficient to jump-start a reluctant nonprofit human resource leader, consider this: research suggests that human costs (payroll, benefits, training, and so on) in labor-intensive nonprofit organizations can account for more than 75 percent of total costs, compared to under 15 percent in capital-intensive organizations (Macpherson, 2001). Obviously, inattention to the major resource of an organization is a recipe for trouble. But this chapter has recommended anything but inattention.

We began with the suggestion that human resources—which we define broadly as "the organization"—is usefully construed as a systems dynamic. "People First" organizational leaders work with staff to define organizational goals around human resources as well as mission fulfillment. The parts are interconnected—breakdowns in human resource leadership (a disintegration of organizational culture, a spate of voluntary departures, and so on) will likely lead to disrupted service delivery, which can tarnish reputation, diminish the ability to get funds, and cause harm in myriad other ways. A smooth-running organization will devote executive-level attention to planning around human resources.

We recognize that one size does not fit all; enabling dialogue around human resource goals is highly dependent on an organization's size and life cycle (not to mention cultural and industry or subsector norms). We argue that value-creating and value-diffusing nonprofits and their component parts are well advised to engage the whole of their labor force in the human resource process at all stages of the organization's growth. Executives in different contexts will necessarily face different human resource decisions and must ask context-relevant questions. To illustrate how some of these contextual elements might play out, a sampling of how size and life cycle of the organization influence what human resource questions should be asked is presented in Exhibit 23.3. These questions might be periodically reviewed to take stock of how well the organization is doing in developing and maintaining a "People First" approach.

Certainly, some subsectors (and within subsector, particular organizations) of the nonprofit universe are marred by less than stellar labor records, and so we underscore the importance of rethinking the organization from the standpoint of those who make it work. We call this putting "People First." All nonprofit leaders can be guided by the basic questions raised by this chapter, and the answers, of course, will vary: What motivates employees? What embeds them in their jobs, organizations, and communities? What laws model best practices even when size or subsector exempt an organization? What staffing plans best support an organization's human resource goals? What recruitment and selection processes are most likely to result in an augmentation of the most laudable components of the organization's unique culture? And finally, what are all of our goals for the people of the organization?

As the process of answering the questions is likely to be as important as the actual answers, it is through the continuous re-creation of human resource goals that a "People First" culture is developed and maintained.

Exhibit 23.3. Relevant Human Resource Questions as a
Reflection of Organization Size and Life Cycle.

Matter Under Consideration	Small or Start-Up	Large or Established
"People First" culture	Do our mission, vision, and strategy support a "People First" culture? Should our human resource systems be professionalized? If so, how? Should human resource responsibilities be part of existing staff roles, or are separate positions warranted?	Do our mission, vision, and strategy support a "People First" culture? Is our staff culture consistent with the values of our mission? Has human resources remained an integral part of our strategic thinking, or has becoming functionalized made it separate? Does our large organization feel small?
Legal	At what staff size do state labor and employment laws apply? At what staff size do federal labor and employment laws apply? Are we above those levels? Is our subsector subject to further labor regulation?	Are we compliant with state labor and employment laws? Are we compliant with federal labor and employment laws? Are we superseding legal standards in promoting an equitable workplace? Is our subsector subject to further labor regulation?
Human resource audits	When and how should we allocate funds to human resource audits? Where can we find sample materials and benchmarks?	What are the goals of our human resource audits? Do our audits meet those goals? Are our human resource audits comprehensive? Are we using a variety of metrics?
Staffing plan	Do we need to grow our staff to meet our mission? If so, how will we identify the resources to grow our staff?	Do we have the right complement of staff to meet our mission? Are we planning growth, transition, or downsizing?
Selection	Does our small size allow growth from inside, or is external recruitment more likely? Do religious orientation, regional culture, industry subsector, or other factors delimit our selection?	Does our culture promote growth from the inside? Have we identified appropriate channels through which to search for unique skills? Do religious orientation, regional culture, industry subsector, or other factors delimit our selection?

**Exhibit 23.3. Relevant Human Resource Questions as a
Reflection of Organization Size and Life Cycle (continued).**

Matter Under Consideration	*Small or Start-Up*	*Large or Established*
Retention and motivation	How much does our small size contribute to the "People First" culture we have developed? If we are growing, how is this affecting our culture?	What motivates our staff? How do we allocate resources to motivate and retain our proven staff? Which staff are leaving voluntarily, and why are they leaving?
Discharge, layoff, and turnover	Absent large size or long-term community track record, how do we embed our employees?	How do we leverage our size, standing, and reputation to help embed our proven employees?
Make or buy?	Do we "buy" to attempt to keep permanent staff size small?	Does our choice to "buy" alienate or support permanent internal staff?

References

Adams, J. S. "Toward an Understanding of Inequity." *Journal of Abnormal and Social Psychology,* 1963, *67,* 422–426.

Arvey, R. D., and Faley, R. H. *Fairness in Selecting Employees.* (2nd ed.) Boston: Addison-Wesley, 1988.

Barber, A. E. *Recruiting Employees: Individual and Organizational Perspectives.* Thousand Oaks, Calif.: Sage, 1998.

Bartel, A. P. "Measuring the Employer's Return on Investments in Training: Evidence from the Literature." *Industrial Relations,* 2000, *39,* 502–524.

Becker, B. E., and Huselid, M. A. "High-Performance Work Systems and Firm Performance: A Synthesis of Research and Managerial Implications." *Research in Personnel and Human Resource Management,* 1998, *16,* 53–101.

Becker, B. E., Huselid, M. A., and Ulrich, D. *The HR Scorecard: Linking People, Strategy, and Performance.* Boston: Harvard Business School Press, 2001.

Bernier, I., and Lajoie, A. *Labor Law and Urban Law in Canada.* Toronto: University of Toronto Press, 1986.

Birdsell, D. S., and Muzzio, D. "The Next Leaders: UWNYC Grantee Leadership Development and Succession Management Needs." [http://www.unitedwaynyc.org/pdf/the_next_leaders.pdf]. 2003.

Block, S. R. *Why Nonprofits Fail: Overcoming Founder's Syndrome, Fund-Phobia, and Other Obstacles to Success.* San Francisco: Jossey-Bass, 2003.

Bolman, L. G., and Deal, T. E. *Reframing Organizations: Artistry, Choice, and Leadership.* (3rd ed.) San Francisco: Jossey-Bass, 2003.

Breaugh, J. A., and Starke, M. "Research on Employee Recruitment: So Many Studies, So Many Remaining Questions." *Journal of Management,* 2000, *26,* 405–435.

Brockner, J., Grover, S., Reed, T. F., and De Witt, R. L. "Layoffs, Job Security, and Survivors' Work Effort: Evidence of an Inverted-U Relationship." *Academy of Management Journal,* 1992, *35,* 413–425.

Cappelli, P. "Making the Most of On-Line Recruiting." *Harvard Business Review,* Mar. 2001, pp. 139–146.

Cascio, W. F. "Strategies for Responsible Restructuring." *Academy of Management Executive,* 2002, *3,* 80–91.

Chatman, J. A. "Improving Interactional Organizational Research: A Model of Person-Organization Fit." *Academy of Management Review,* 1989, *14,* 333–349.

Costa, P. T., and McCrae, R. R. "Stability and Change in Personality Assessment: The Revised NEO Personality Inventory in the Year 2000." *Journal of Personality Assessment,* 1997, *68,* 86–95.

Council for Disability Rights. "Frequently Asked Questions." [http://www.disability rights.org/adafaq.htm#general]. 2003.

Cox, T. *Cultural Diversity in Organizations: Theory, Research, and Practice.* San Francisco: Berrett-Kohler, 1994.

Delery, J. E., and Doty, D. H. "Modes of Theorizing in Strategic Human Resource Management: Tests of Universalistic, Contingency, and Configurational Performance Predictions." *Academy of Management Journal,* 1996, *39,* 802–835.

Dineen, B. R., Ash, S. R., and Noe, R. A. "Web of Applicant Attraction: Person-Organization Fit in the Context of Web-Based Recruitment." *Journal of Applied Psychology,* 2002, *87,* 723–734.

Equal Employment Opportunity Commission. "Section 902: Definition of the Term *Disability.*" [http://www.eeoc.gov/policy/docs/902cm.html]. 2000.

Equal Employment Opportunity Commission. "The Americans with Disabilities Act." [http://www.eeoc.gov/ada/adahandbook.html]. 2002a.

Equal Employment Opportunity Commission. "Facts About Sexual Harassment." [http://www.eeoc.gov/facts/fs-sex.html]. 2002b.

Equal Employment Opportunity Commission. "Filing a Charge of Employment Discrimination." [http://www.eeoc.gov/charge/overview_charge_filing.html]. 2003.

Fick, B. J. *The American Bar Association Guide to Workplace Law: Everything You Need to Know About Your Rights as an Employee or Employer.* New York: Times Books/Random House, 1997.

Fisher, A. "How Can We Be Sure We Are Not Hiring a Bunch of Shady Liars?" *Fortune,* Oct. 2003, pp. 180–181.

Fitz-enz, J. *The ROI of Human Capital: Measuring the Economic Value of Employee Performance.* New York: AMACOM, 2000.

Gatewood, R. D., and Feild, H. S. *Human Resource Selection.* (5th ed.) Fort Worth, Tex.: Harcourt, 2001.

Goldberg, L. R. "An Alternative Description of Personality: The Big Five Factor Structure." *Journal of Personality and Social Psychology,* 1990, *59,* 1216–1230.

Hamilton, L., and Tragert, R. *100 Best Nonprofits to Work For.* (2nd ed.) Lawrenceville, N.J.: ARCO, 2000.

Hecht, B. L., and Ramsey, R. *ManagingNonprofits.org: Dynamic Management for the Digital Age.* New York: Wiley, 2002.

Highhouse, S., Stierwalt, S. L., Bachiochi, P., Elder, A. E., and Fisher, G. "Effects of Advertised Human Resource Management Practices on Attraction of African American Applicants." *Personnel Psychology,* 1999, *52,* 425–442.

Hom, P. W., and Griffeth, R. W. *Employee Turnover.* Cincinnati: South-Western, 1995.

Kanter, R. M., and Summers, D. V. "Doing Well While Doing Good: Dimensions of Performance Measurement in Nonprofit Organizations and the Need for a Multiple-Constituency Approach." In W. W. Powell Jr. (ed.), *The Nonprofit Sector: A Research Handbook.* New Haven, Conn.: Yale University Press, 1987.

Klaas, B., McClendon, J. A., and Gainey, T. "HR Outsourcing and Its Impact: The Role of Transaction Costs." *Personnel Psychology,* 1999, *52,* 113–136.

Kristof-Brown, A., Jansen, K. J., and Colbert, A. E. "A Policy-Capturing Study of the Simultaneous Effects of Fit with Jobs, Groups, and Organizations." *Journal of Applied Psychology,* 2002, *87,* 985–993.

Lee, T. W., Mitchell, T. R., Holtom, B. C., McDaniel, L., and Hill, J. W. "The Unfolding Model of Voluntary Turnover: A Replication and Extension." *Academy of Management Journal,* 1999, *42,* 450–462.

Lengnick-Hall, M. L., and Moritz, S. "The Impact of e-HR on the Human Resource Management Function." *Journal of Labor Research,* 2003, *24,* 365–370.

Lewin, K. *Field Theory in Social Science.* New York: HarperCollins, 1951.

Light, P.C. *Pathways to Nonprofit Excellence.* Washington, D.C.: Brookings Institution Press, 2002.

Macpherson, M. "Performance Measurement in Not-for-Profit and Public-Sector Organizations." *Measuring Business Excellence,* 2001, *5*(2), 13–17.

Maslow, A. H. "A Theory of Human Motivation." *Psychological Review,* 1943, *50,* 370–396.

Mitchell, T. R., Holtom, B. C., Lee, T. W., Sablynski, C. J., and Erez, M. "Why People Stay: Using Job Embeddedness to Predict Voluntary Turnover." *Academy of Management Journal,* 2001, *44,* 1102–1121.

Morgan, G. *Riding the Waves of Change: Developing Managerial Competencies for a Turbulent World.* San Francisco: Jossey-Bass, 1989.

O'Reilly, C. A., Chatman, J., and Caldwell, D. F. "People and Organizational Culture: A Profile Comparison Approach to Assessing Person-Organization Fit." *Academy of Management Journal,* 1991, *34,* 487–516.

Pfeffer, J. *The Human Equation: Building Profits by Putting People First.* Boston: Harvard Business School Press, 1998.

Robbins, S. P. *Organizational Behavior: Concepts, Controversies, and Applications.* (10th ed). Upper Saddle River, N.J.: Prentice Hall, 2002.

Salgado, J. F., Anderson, N., Moscoso, S. C., Bertua, C., and De Fruyt, F. "International Validity Generalization and Cognitive Abilities: A European Community Meta-Analysis." *Personnel Psychology,* 2003, *56,* 573–605.

Stewart, G. L. "Toward an Understanding of the Multilevel Role of Personality in Teams." In M. R. Barrick and A. M. Ryan (eds.), *Personality and Work.* San Francisco: Jossey-Bass, 2003.

Towers Perrin. *Working Today: Understanding What Drives Employee Engagement.* 2003 Towers Perrin Talent Report. [http://www.towersperrin.com/hrservices/webcache/towers/United_States/publications/Reports/Talent_Report_2003/Talent_2003.pdf]. 2003.

Vroom, V. *Work and Motivation.* New York: Wiley, 1964.

Wanous, J. P. *Organizational Entry: Recruitment, Selection, and Socialization of Newcomers.* Boston: Addison-Wesley, 1980.

Welbourne, T. M., and Cyr, L. A. "The Human Resource Executive Effect in Initial Public Offering Firms." *Academy of Management Journal,* 1999, *42,* 616–630.

Werbel, J. D., and Gilliland, S. W. "Person-Environment Fit in the Selection Process." In G. R. Ferris (ed.), *Research in Personnel and Human Resource Management.* Greenwich, Conn.: JAI Press, 1999.

Zottoli, M. A., and Wanous, J. P. "Recruitment Source Research: Current Status and Future Directions." *Human Resource Management Review,* 2000, *10,* 353–382.

CHAPTER TWENTY-FOUR

Total Rewards Programs in Nonprofit Organizations

Nancy E. Day

S ome profit and nonprofit organizations, particularly those that are smaller and less sophisticated, consider the compensation of their employees an onerous and expensive obligation on which as little time as possible should be spent. Salaries and benefits may be set haphazardly, based on "gut feelings" about how much certain jobs probably bring on the general market or on the difficulty of attracting qualified people to key positions. These organizations view compensation as extraneous to their organizations' overall mission or strategy. This is unfortunate and unwise, given that labor costs make up over 50 percent of total costs for many U.S. employers (Milkovich and Newman, 2002).

TOTAL REWARDS:
INTEGRAL TO ORGANIZATIONAL STRATEGY

It is essential that the compensation system attract and reward the best quality workforce it can afford, since the organization's human resources are indeed its most important resources. Without them, the organization's goals cannot be achieved and its values cannot be enacted. As Louis Mayer, of Metro-Goldwyn-Mayer, once said, "The inventory goes home at night." This is especially true for nonprofits.

On top of these considerations, the contemporary view of pay and benefits has become an integrative one that is more appropriately conceptualized as "total rewards" ("Welcome to WorldatWork," 2000). Although compensation includes anything of monetary value that the organization gives its employees in exchange for their services (pay and benefits, including perquisites), "total rewards" include all things that will motivate workers to be attracted to the firm, join it, perform well in it, and remain with the organization. This definition includes not only the basics, such as base salary, incentive pay, and benefits, but also the work environment characteristics that create a "workplace of choice": good supervision, safe and attractive facilities, access to training and development, and other elements that may attract potential employees and enhance their experiences once they are members of the organization. This definition is sweeping and inclusive and suggests that the job of compensation manager may be broader and more diverse than building sound pay programs and providing adequate benefits, including an entire constellation of programs and practices designed to support the organization's strategic goals.

However, for the purposes of this chapter, space necessitates that most of our discussion be confined to the more basic forms of compensation: salary, incentives, and benefits. Although incentives are still not pervasive in nonprofit organizations, particularly at nonexecutive levels, there is a trend to include them as part of the nonprofit pay package. Incentive pay is an avenue by which individual pay can be directly related to the "bottom line" results or mission of the organization, reducing fixed costs and encouraging top performance because it puts a percentage of an employee's pay "at risk." In times of tight budgets (as most are for nonprofits), pay programs that decrease fixed costs while increasing both individual and organizational performance are receiving more than passing attention from managers of nonprofit organizations.

Compensation Strategy and Organizational Mission

All organizations base their actions on goals that are either explicit or implicit. Long-term or strategic planning is done in well-managed organizations to ensure that current resources—financial, material, and human—are used in the manner most effective to the organization's raison d'être. Organizations with effective performance appraisal programs will require individual employees to set performance objectives that are based on department goals, which are in turn driven by division and organizational goals. This "cascading" effect allows effective organizations to link broad, often ambitious goals and values with the activities of their individual workers. Thus the individual employee is ultimately responsible for carrying out the fundamental mission of the organization. Because of this, it is imperative that the rewards system be part of the nonprofit's strategic mission or long-range plan and be consistent with the organization's goals, culture, and environmental pressures. Organizations need to decide where they want to go and how they will get there. Compensation is one of the many important cogs in the total organizational performance machine that must be carefully tended, frequently lubricated and repaired, and upgraded or replaced if it no longer functions adequately in contributing to the achievement of top performance.

For example, an organization that is changing its organizational structure must ensure that its pay strategy fits these changes. The most effective pay for self-directed work teams is probably not a traditional salary program; it will probably require careful analysis of the goals of the work teams and their structures, the reasons why teams are being implemented, and the pay strategy history of the organization.

It is imperative that workers be paid for what the organization wants to reward. This obvious yet crucial fact is illustrated by Steven Kerr's well-known article, "On the Folly of Rewarding A While Hoping for B" (1975), which cannot be quoted too often:

> Whether dealing with monkeys, rats, or human beings, it is hardly controversial to state that most organisms seek information concerning what activities are rewarded, and then seek to do (or at least pretend to do) those things, often to the virtual exclusion of activities not rewarded. The extent to which this occurs of course will depend on the perceived attractiveness of the rewards offered, but neither operant nor expectancy theorists would quarrel with the essence of this notion.
>
> Nevertheless, numerous examples exist of reward systems that are fouled up in that behaviors which are rewarded are those which the rewarder is trying to *discourage,* while the behavior he desires is not being rewarded at all. [p. 769]

A familiar example of this mistake occurred frequently several years ago when employees were given regular annual cost-of-living increases. Although high inflation demanded some salary escalation to keep workers even with living costs, organizations were in effect paying their employees merely to show up at work, whether or not they were performing in the best interests of the organization. A better way to use pay to accomplish organizational goals is to direct the largest increases at those workers who contribute the most and the best, not equally to all employees regardless of their performance. Another more disagreeable example was the situation at Green Giant, in which employees who were rewarded for finding pieces of insects in the vegetables began importing "home-grown" bug parts in order to increase their incentive rewards (reported in Milkovich and Newman, 2002).

The Need for a Rewards Policy

Environmental and market demands also have significant impacts on rewards systems. Organizations that have jobs requiring extremely high levels of technical skill and expertise, such as medical doctors or engineers, must design systems that reward these key positions adequately. Management needs to ensure that qualified people are attracted and retained while at the same time carefully balancing pay relationships across jobs within the company to avoid inequity.

Edward Lawler (1990, p. 11) recommends that managers should begin to develop an effective strategy "with an analysis of the outcomes or results they need from their pay system and then develop a core set of compensation principles and practices to support these directions." Aligning the reward system, including compensation, benefits, and work environment factors, to the organization's mission and strategic plan as well as its management style is critical. Thus before a reward program is seriously considered, the human resource (HR) professionals responsible for designing it need to evaluate carefully the organization's goals, values, culture, and strategy to ensure that rewards play a key role in accomplishing organizational goals. The key point here is that the nonprofit's top management should carefully and strategically assess *what knowledge, skills, and abilities the organization wants to reward.* This simple yet meaningful phrase should become the compensation manager's motto, continually guiding decision making on the content and process of the organization's total rewards strategy.

One way that many organizations define their total rewards strategy is through the development, communication, and maintenance of a *rewards policy.* This is generally a simple, relatively short statement that communicates how the organization plans to reward people, including pay, benefits, and work environment characteristics; how the system will be designed and maintained; and the philosophy of what rewards are supposed to accomplish. Also included should be a statement expressing the organization's intention to treat everyone fairly and equitably, regardless of race, sex, religion, age, disability, color, national origin, or any other relevant protected classes under laws and ordinances or organizational values and policies (for example, some jurisdictions and organizations now include sexual orientation as a protected class; some organizations do so simply because they believe it is the right thing to do). Although brief, much concern and deliberation needs to go into development of the rewards policy, as the organization's top management must make a commitment to adhere staunchly to its precepts so that employee trust is not shaken. The rewards policy should then be communicated to employees along with other key organizational policies.

Using Consultants

Before embarking on any major new salary or benefits program, the nonprofit organization should consider the value and cost-effectiveness of contracting with a compensation consultant. Organizations on tight budgets, particularly nonprofits, often fall into the trap of trying to save money by developing major programs in-house. If current HR staff have the needed expertise, this may be the appropriate avenue to take. However, even if current staff are equipped with necessary skills, the following points should be considered on the value of using consultants.

First, consultants generally have a wide range of experience across a number of organizations and therefore may know what will work best for your unique organization. Compensation programs, especially benefits, are sophisticated and complex systems, and even HR professionals with basic compensation knowledge may not have the breadth and depth of experience to develop and install programs that are truly a "good fit."

Second, consultants usually have access to a vast amount of salary and benefits survey data or have easily accessible sources and will thus be able to assess external competitiveness better than your organization alone can.

Third, consultants are outsiders, and this gives them an extremely valuable commodity: objectivity. Since the consultant's salary will not be part of the new compensation program, unlike the in-house HR professional's, he or she will be in a better position to tell top managers or the board of directors about unpopular or expensive compensation issues (for example, critical positions that are dramatically underpaid relative to the market and whose recommended salary increases may reach epic proportions). Objectivity is also a great asset in explaining to employees why some jobs have been downgraded and that their topped-out employees will not be receiving salary increases for the next year or so. Furthermore, if the consultant is to conduct a specially designed salary or benefits survey, other organizations may be more likely to participate and share their salary information since the consultant provides a greater guarantee of confidentiality than a rival organization.

The major disadvantage of using consultants is, of course, cost. But keep in mind the estimated wage costs cited earlier: 60 percent of GDP. Sometimes several thousand dollars in consulting fees is money extremely well spent if it is able to provide the organization with a compensation system that maximizes the value of the salary and benefit dollar.

To assist in-house compensation program development, HR professionals can gain useful technical knowledge through the certification program of WorldatWork (formerly the American Compensation Association). This program consists of nine two-day seminars and exams in core and elective compensation areas (WorldatWork also offers benefits certification). Those serious about establishing, installing, and maintaining a state-of-the-art rewards program should consider obtaining this certification.

Let us now turn to the components of developing a sound salary and benefits program. We will begin with base compensation, usually known simply as salary or wages. Executive pay and incentive programs in nonprofit organizations will be discussed before we move on to development of benefits packages.

TRADITIONAL
BASE COMPENSATION PRINCIPLES

Over the past decade or so, there has been a loosening of the concept of "job" from one that is tightly defined and controlled to one that is broader and more flexible. Given the competitive nature of labor markets as well as the need for organizations to maximize the value they receive from each individual, this makes a great deal of sense. Moving away from the attitude of "it's not in my job description" allows employers to use workers' knowledge, skills, and abilities (KSAs) to their utmost in accomplishing organizational and unit goals while at the same time providing employment that may be more rewarding, challenging and interesting than a traditional, narrowly defined job.

"To Job or Not to Job:" Job- or Person-Based Systems

Indeed, early predictions were that jobs as we know them would disappear into the mists of time (see Bridges, 1994). This possibility seems remote, since there are some impressive practical reasons to retain the job concept, especially in recruiting, conducting market analyses of competitors' pay levels, and training design. However, the way that management views how work will be accomplished, as either carefully prescribed "jobs" or as looser and more flexible "roles," will make a difference in the type of pay systems and procedures that should be developed. Thus nonprofits should carefully analyze their organizations' characteristics, the type of work that needs to get done, and the types of people most likely to have these skills and decide to what extent work should be conceived of as jobs or roles. One way to conceptualize this question is whether the organizations want to pay for a *job* to be done, in which the work requires a defined set of tasks and duties that are relatively stable and that a reasonable number of candidates in the labor market could be found to fill, or if the work requires a unique *person's* abilities and skills to be applied to a variety of changing organizational needs. Generally speaking, this strategy needs to be determined organizationwide, not job by job or person by person, so that the entire pay structure is coherent and consistent.

In my experience, few organizations, for-profit or nonprofit, have completely abandoned the convenience of the job; most have kept this useful concept and merely broadened its content and flexibility to one degree or another. Thus while "nonjob" approaches will not be ignored, this chapter will focus on more traditional job-centered compensation systems. For readers who believe a nonjob system would be more workable for their organizations, most compensation textbooks (Milkovich and Newman, 2002, is one) contain thorough descriptions of specific nonjob techniques.

Job or Work Analysis

As is true for many personnel practices (recruitment, staffing, performance management, training and development, and others), the foundation of salary systems is current, accurate, and thorough analysis of the work to be done. Traditionally called "job analysis," a variety of techniques can be used to observe, examine, record, and summarize the main components of jobs. However, given the interest in person-based ("nonjob") approaches, techniques are now being developed to analyze the work accomplished in organizations when it is done outside of a traditional job context. For example, work within an entire department, system, process, or skill set may be investigated as the unit of analysis, where multiple people may do many interchangeable tasks (Milkovich and Newman, 2002).

However, as noted earlier, since most organizations have retained the basic job concept for ease in recruitment, hiring, and compensation programs, job analysis is still a viable approach. Through job analysis, data on the content of jobs are gathered, evaluated, quality-controlled, compiled, and summarized (usually in the form of job descriptions) so that jobs are thoroughly and accurately understood. This somewhat time-consuming process is absolutely necessary for at least two reasons. First, accurate job knowledge is critical in establishing *external competitiveness* in that jobs must be compared across organizations by the *content* of the job (what the people actually do), not merely by a job title that may or may not truly describe the job. Second, only by understanding jobs can the level of *internal equity* in the organization be assessed and, if necessary, adjusted. Since establishing internal equity requires comparing jobs, it naturally requires that accurate and current job information be available in a usable format.

Job analysis employs a number of techniques, depending on its final use (job analysis is also used in designing programs for training, recruitment, and job design, among others, as well as compensation). These techniques include interviews of incumbents or supervisors (either individually or in groups), observations of workers, highly structured questionnaires or checklists ordinarily completed by the job incumbent (such as the well-known Position Analysis Questionnaire), or open-ended questionnaires completed by the incumbent or supervisor. The latter method is the one most frequently used by medium to small organizations, since it allows data to be gathered easily and relatively cheaply. Open-ended questionnaires are typically designed by the organization so that the data gathered fit the values and goals of the organization—in other words, they should collect data on *what the organization wants to pay for.* As will be discussed shortly, often *compensable factors* that will be used in the job evaluation process to establish internal equity are assessed through this questionnaire.

Organizations that do not have the resources to engage consultants or lack the in-house expertise to perform job analysis may find some relevant forms on several public domain Internet sites. However, it is critical to keep in mind two important points. First, job analysis, as mentioned, should measure jobs (or work) in relation to what the organization wants to reward. Therefore, off-the-shelf techniques or questionnaires may turn out to be a waste of time in that they don't really measure the work in ways that are useful or meaningful to effective pay system development. Second, job (or work) analysis can become a highly charged emotional and political activity in any organization, particularly if the results are to be used for pay determination. Employees who know that job analysis results may make a difference in how their job is valued have a vested interest in consciously or unconsciously making their work sound as important and complex as possible. If some believe that the process was unfair, incomplete, or contaminated, serious intraorganizational problems could arise. It is therefore strongly recommended that compensation experts be involved in this process as early as possible.

External Competitiveness

In the first edition of this book, external competitiveness, or the need for organizations to define their competition for labor and set pay levels in response to these competitors, was dealt with secondarily, after internal equity issues. However, several changes in the national (and global) economy have shifted the weight of pay system development from internal to external considerations. A primary change is that American organizations now recognize that they exist in a highly competitive labor environment and will for the next several decades. Indeed, even in times of economic downturn, the war for talent continues for many technical and highly educated workers. Given projections that KSAs in the American workforce will not meet American business needs over the next few decades (Heneman and Judge, 2003), external competitiveness has moved to the front of the line in pay system design. A second change is that this increase in competition for highly skilled labor has discouraged workers from limiting themselves to one sector or another. Indeed, public sector and nonprofit organizations may find themselves in competition with for-profits for the same people who previously saw themselves as nonprofit workers. Thus the ability to understand the entire labor market, both for-profit and nonprofit, enables the nonprofit compensation manager to make informed and intelligent decisions regarding total reward strategies. A third change that makes external competitiveness dominant over internal considerations is that technology requires hiring and retaining people with skills that are "market-driven." As nonprofit organizations rely more heavily on automation of information, Internet fundraising, and other technological functions, the need for the salary system to respond quickly and effectively to market forces that dictate salaries for these positions is critical. Without adaptive systems to gauge and react to market changes, retention of highly skilled workers will be extremely difficult.

With Whom Do We Compete for Employees? After ensuring that job information is complete and up-to-date, the first question that must be answered is "What are the salary markets for the jobs in this organization?" In nearly every organization, several salary markets, or *relevant labor markets,* will exist. The key to answering the question is to determine where the KSAs the organization needs exist in the labor market. For example, clerical jobs are nearly always recruited locally, probably from all types of organizations, not just other nonprofits, because that's where people with clerical KSAs can be found. Therefore, a wide local market is generally needed for clerical jobs. While it is true that many nonprofits will be unable to meet the pay levels for clerical workers paid by large private sector companies, it is still critical to have information about the pay level in the entire relevant market. Some professional jobs that are technically or specialty-oriented will most likely be recruited regionally, nationally, or even internationally, sometimes from other nonprofits with similar missions and goals and sometimes from other sources. Thus the relevant labor market for these specialty jobs may also include both for- and nonprofit firms. If key executive positions require skills specialized to particular nonprofit organizational needs, then their appropriate labor market will be national (or international) nonprofits in similar sectors. However, some executive roles may benefit from skills found outside the nonprofit arena. As in all positions, the appropriate relevant labor market for the nonprofit's executives must also be carefully considered and chosen, based on the organization's goals and strategies.

What Data? After identifying the relevant markets, benchmark jobs should be identified. These are jobs on which the salary system will be built, so they should be well defined and clearly understood within the organization. Every organization has its own unique jobs that do not exist in the rest of the world and for which no market data are available. However, benchmark jobs should be those that are easily found in other organizations in the relevant labor markets. Benchmarks should also be stable; as a group, they should represent nearly all levels within the organization; they should vary in levels of compensable factors (to be discussed shortly); and most should have multiple incumbents. Finally, jobs for which the organization is experiencing particular difficulty recruiting should be included as benchmarks (Wallace and Fay, 1988). Typically, it is desirable to choose a group of benchmarks representing a minimum of 25 to 30 percent of all jobs in the organization or many more if the organization wishes its rewards system to be market-driven.

A critical point in this process is that job *titles* are not determinants of bench-mark jobs; job *content* is. Therefore, to avoid confusion, an effort should be made to ensure that titles accurately reflect the content of the job and are not manip-ulated to reward employees or increase the prestige of the supervisor, as often happens in salary systems that are not adequately designed and maintained.

Salary data are generally collected from one of two broad sources: published salary surveys or surveys conducted by the organization or its consultants. Pub-lished surveys are undoubtedly the easiest to obtain but have drawbacks (a va-riety of published surveys are listed in Exhibit 24.1). First, some are extremely expensive. Some published by national consulting firms can cost more than $2,000. Such cost issues may be counteracted by payroll dollars saved in an ef-fective salary administration program, and several organizations may form a consortium to purchase them jointly. These surveys are generally of very high quality, with the data "cut" in many useful ways (for example, by region, by type of industry, and by budget size). However, because these surveys are geared to the private sector, they may have relevant data for a only few jobs in a nonprofit organization. But for some high-level technical or specialized jobs, the data found in them may be essential. Luckily, many cheaper published sources of salary data are available, such as those published by other nonprof-its, including professional associations and government entities.

Finding salary data for highly paid professional jobs that exist only in other nonprofits similar to yours may require a custom survey. An advantage of cus-tom surveys is that the organization has control over the data that are retrieved. The main disadvantage is that because surveying is a fairly sophisticated and technical activity, an organization must either have the internal staff with suf-ficient time and appropriate expertise or hire qualified consultants. Hence cus-tom surveys may be even more expensive than some purchased surveys.

Determining where salary data will be found will obviously be driven by what the relevant salary markets are. For local clerical markets, several sources are available. First, local human resource groups often publish salary surveys keyed to a general market. Check with the Society for Human Resource Man-agement (http://www.shrm.org) for the name of the local chapter. Second, the Bureau of Labor Statistics has a rich variety of data available on its Web site (http://www.bls.gov/home.htm) at no charge. Third, municipalities (often through the Chamber of Commerce) or states may conduct surveys of local mar-kets that may be available for a small fee. Nonprofit managers should be par-ticularly aware of organizations such as Abbott, Langer & Associates, Cordom Associates, and the American Society of Association Executives that publish data specifically for nonprofit markets, as listed in Exhibit 24.1. Consultants are often helpful in identifying more obscure sources for published surveys of un-usual jobs, and associations representing specific occupations may produce

Exhibit 24.1. Selected Sources of Salary Surveys.

U.S. Department of Labor, Bureau of Labor Statistics

National Compensation Survey: http://www.bls.gov/ncs/ocs/home.htm

Data for all fifty states and metropolitan areas are available at no charge; includes benefits data.

Professional Nonprofit Associations

American Society of Association Executives: http://www.asaenet.org/main

Association Executive Compensation and Benefits Study

Association Management Companies Compensation and Benefits Study

Association Staff Compensation and Benefits Study

Blue Chip Summary of Executive Compensation

Greater Washington Society of Association Executives:
http://www.gwsae.org/home.htm

GWSAE Compensation Survey Report

Nonprofit Industry Surveys

Abbott, Langer & Associates: http://www.abbott-langer.com

Compensation in Nonprofit Organizations

Fringe Benefits and Working Conditions in Nonprofit Organizations

Cordom Associates: http://www.cordom-salary-surveys.com

Salary Surveys of Nonprofit Organizations (Washington, D.C. area)

National Consulting Groups Publishing
Surveys for Various Industries and Professions

Abbott, Langer & Associates: http://www.abbott-langer.com

Executive Alliance: http://www.executivealliance.com

Hay Group (Hay PayNet): http://www.haypaynet.com/default.asp

Hewitt Associates (Hewitt Compensation Center: https://was4.hewitt.com/
compensationcenter/home/select_site.jsp

Mercer Human Resources Consulting: http://www.mercerhr.com/knowledgecenter

Towers Perrin: http://www.towersperrin.com/hrservices/global/default.htm

Watson-Wyatt Data Services: http://www.wwdssurveys.com

surveys that are available at reasonable cost. A word of caution must be said regarding these, however. Be sure that these surveys have been conducted using accepted and reputable survey methodologies. Since sometimes such associations desire that their occupations be viewed highly by the public and their constituents, these data should be compared with other, more objective sources to ensure their validity.

Simple Internet search engines may be able to locate hard-to-find salary sources, but as any wise Web surfer knows, data from the Internet, particularly salary data, must be accepted with a degree of skepticism. Many managers who have had conversations about competitive salaries with their employees in the past few years know that there is a seemingly infinite amount of salary data available for public access on the Internet, and employees frequently use this information to argue for pay increases. It is therefore critical that the nonprofit compensation manager be able to understand the basics of good salary survey methodology, which will be discussed shortly, and be able to communicate the importance of using only verifiably valid and reliable data in making pay decisions.

Using the Data. Good salary surveys report several statistics for each job, usually including the average salary, weighted average, minimum, maximum, median (50th percentile), and perhaps other percentiles. Generally, the most important statistic in the salary survey is the weighted average, since it represents the average salary across all the job incumbents (not just across organizations) in the market. Several points should be reviewed before using data from a salary source:

- How many organizations have participated? Make sure that the data are representative of a sufficiently large sample.
- Are the firms in the survey representative of the organization's relevant labor markets?
- How does the weighted average compare to the average salary? If the two are dramatically different, it may mean that one very large organization's data are skewing the results, since weighted averages are weighted by the number of employees in each organization.
- How do the average and weighted average salaries compare with the 50th percentile (median)? Again, a large discrepancy could indicate a skewed distribution that may mean it is a nonrepresentative sample.

At least three different sources of salary data should be collected for each benchmark job, more when possible. This ensures that final market data averages are valid. Because survey data are collected at different points in time (high-quality surveys will cite the effective date of the data), data must be aged by a reasonable inflation factor so that all data are comparable. This factor should be based on the general increase in salaries and salary structures currently occurring in the market (sources for these statistics will be discussed later). Next, the individual data points need to be checked to see that they are within a reasonable range of each other; outliers, either much higher or lower than others, should be removed. Then data for each job should be averaged, after which the jobs can be arrayed in order of market value.

A useful means of evaluating the organization's current standing in the market is through regression analyses. Using job evaluation points (to be discussed shortly) as the independent variable, one regression line should be calculated with market average salaries as the dependent. This regression line should be plotted and compared with the regression line for which current salaries is the dependent variable. By looking at the disparities between these two lines, the degree to which the organization conforms to the market can be ascertained. For example, such a comparison may show that the organization is paying competitively for lower-level jobs while upper-level jobs are being paid under their market rates (as in Figure 24.1). Using these graphs to illustrate discrepancies helps explain compensation needs to decision makers, such as boards of directors, who must consider economic impacts.

The convenience of adopting a job-based pay program is clearly seen when trying to gather market data for a non-job-based pay program. Simply speaking, it is difficult, if not impossible, to use market surveys to price "nonjobs" because they aren't jobs. Flexible, unique, and highly adaptable "roles" defy collecting competitive salary data. Efforts have been made that involve extrap-

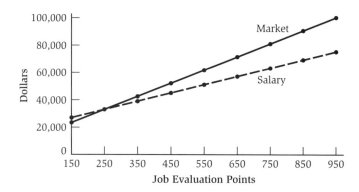

Figure 24.1. Regression Analysis Illustrating the Relationship of Current Salaries to Market Data.

olating key skills from job-based salary data, but this strategy, while theoretically workable, is time-consuming, difficult, and sometimes probably invalid. In a skill-based pay program, in which key skills are identified and individual workers are paid based on the number of skills in which they become adept, a "low-high" approach has been suggested (Milkovich and Newman, 2002) in which the lowest-paid and highest-paid benchmark jobs relevant to the skill in question are used as anchors. However, skill-based approaches to pay are workable only in limited circumstances and conditions and are thus beyond the scope of this chapter.

Internal Equity

Internal equity refers to the perception of fairness in pay for various jobs throughout the organization. In other words, in an internally equitable system, jobs that are of similar levels on key compensable factors, such as skill or knowledge required, supervisory responsibilities, accountability for budget and resources, complexity, or working conditions, will be paid at the same general level. For example, a job of accounting clerk may require some postsecondary education or experience, knowledge of basic accounting principles, no supervisory responsibilities, and little accountability for financial resources. If this job is compared to that of a beginning employee benefits claim clerk, a job also requiring some postsecondary education or experience, basic technical knowledge, no supervisory responsibilities, and little accountability for financial resources, we would conclude that the jobs are essentially worth about the same to the organization. However, the job of a custodian, compared to those jobs, would probably not be valued as highly, since custodial work usually requires less technical knowledge and experience. In an equitable system, these differences in internal job value would be appropriately reflected in the pay structure; in a system that is not equitable, the custodian may be paid the same as or more than the accounting clerk or benefits claims clerk, or the benefits claims clerk may make significantly more or less than the accounting clerk.

Internal equity is established using some form of *job evaluation*. This broad term describes a number of methods by which jobs are valued within the organization. Two of the most prevalent in small to medium-sized organizations will be discussed here: slotting and point-factor job evaluation.

Slotting. Slotting is appropriate for organizations that want to emphasize external competitiveness over internal equity, for those with a small number of jobs, for those for which a great deal of market data are available, or for those with flexible or quickly changing jobs. The slotting process begins with gathering as much market data as possible. After these data are tabulated and quality-controlled using the criteria presented earlier, the jobs are arrayed in order of their market value. Jobs for which no market data are available (usually jobs that are unique to the organization) are then *slotted* into this hierarchy. The slotting is done by comparing the job to those in the hierarchy and determining, based on the overall value of the job to the organization, where the job fits in the hierarchy. Slotting done in this manner is often referred to as a kind of "whole job" evaluation system, meaning that compensable factors (skill, education, working conditions, and so on) are not systematically determined and compared but that the job is instead looked at as a "whole." Of course, in practice, the actual cognitive decision processes that human beings naturally use tend to fall back on informally derived compensable factors. However, they are not formally defined or systematically applied.

In addition to allowing market responsiveness, the major advantage of the slotting method is the saving of time, effort, and costs. Since a more elaborate system is time-intensive, slotting saves much staff and management time and effort. Furthermore, the technical skill needed to develop and install other types of job evaluation systems is fairly high, and the cost of consultants in establishing internal equity can be avoided when slotting is used.

However, slotting has disadvantages. The most obvious is that some organizations have many jobs that are not found in the job market and hence market data may not be available for a large percentage of the organization's jobs. Second, because of the whole-job technique, the system is generally lower in reliability (when two people independently slot jobs, they are likely to come up with different solutions) than a point-factor system and thus may be more likely to face challenges from employees.

Point-Factor Job Evaluation. Of the more complex job evaluation systems, the most common is point-factor evaluation. The well-known Hay system is a sophisticated version of the point-factor method. There are three basic steps in establishing and implementing this system:

1. Identifying and weighting a set of factors that uniquely describe the job characteristics for which the organization wants to pay

2. Establishing levels within each factor and assigning points to each level

3. Carefully comparing each job to the factors and assigning points appropriate to each factor level that describes the job

The end result is a hierarchy that arrays the jobs from highest to lowest in their value to the organization.

Organizations have used a variety of compensable factors in their job evaluation systems, including the following:

Accountability	Interpersonal skills
Complexity of job	Physical exertion
Consequence of errors	Planning responsibility
Customer service responsibility	Problem solving
Decision making	Sales responsibility
Education and training	Scope of job
Experience	Supervision
Independent judgment	Technical knowledge
Interpersonal contacts	Working conditions

However, empirical research using factor analysis (a statistical procedure that defines basic underlying components) has found that these numerous factors generally reduce down to four basic concepts: skill, effort, responsibility and working conditions.

Compensable factors appropriate for the organization are determined by a number of methods, ranging from sophisticated computer programs to hand-picking the factors that "seem right." However, top management must be involved in the choice of these factors. There are several reasons for this. First, top management is closest to the mission, goals, and strategy of the organization and can define what the organization wants to pay for and translate that information into the compensable factors. Second, top management has a broad view of the organization's functions and thus understands the scope and content of the jobs. Third, as in any management program, it is imperative that top management "buy in" to the system. Nonprofit organizations should also consider the advisability of at least gaining the approval of the board of directors, if not including its members in the actual factor determination.

One of simplest and most straightforward methods used to guide top managers in factor choice is by using the following steps:

1. The HR professional in charge of developing this program identifies a universe of appropriate compensable factors. This can be done by reviewing a set of factors such as those just listed and eliminating the ones that are not relevant to the organization. For example, sales responsibility or physical exertion are often not relevant to nonprofits and may be removed.

2. After identifying an appropriate universe, the HR professional should carefully explain the overall point-factor evaluation concept and the meaning of each factor to the top managers.

3. Top managers then should *individually* rank the factors.

4. The HR professional compiles those rankings and selects a set of factors. While the number of factors needed to produce a workable job hierarchy can be as few as three or four, the key is to include enough to capture the major components for which the organization wants to pay. It is also advisable to consider factors that may improve the system's acceptability to employees and management (Milkovich and Newman, 2002). Several years ago, it was not uncommon for job evaluation systems to include up to ten compensable factors. Nowadays, given the increased emphasis on market data and consideration of the cost of complex systems, point-factor systems generally have between four and seven factors.

5. The HR professional presents this set of factors to the top management group, asking the managers to discuss the factors to ensure that they completely yet concisely describe the job characteristics for which the organization is willing to pay.

After the final compensable factors have been chosen, they should be weighted according to the relative importance of the factors to each other, in light of the organization's mission and strategy. For example, an association of physicians is probably driven by jobs that are highly dependent on education and technical training, so that factor would be heavily weighted. "Consequence of errors" may be less important, so it would be weighted accordingly. An easy method to accomplish this is to ask the top managers individually to divide 100 points among the set of factors. The HR professional can then compile their responses into one set of weightings, which top management as a group can again assess and approve.

After weighting the factors, they must be divided into *levels*. An easy example is education and training. Typical levels for this factor might be the following:

1. High school diploma (or equivalent); basic reading skills required

2. High school diploma (or equivalent) plus ability to operate simple equipment or use common computer applications such as word processing; basic office or technical skills

3. Some advanced training, typically found in a two-year college or certification program (or equivalent experience); ability to operate moderately complex equipment (such as for word processing); intermediate analytical skills

4. Theoretical understanding of a body of knowledge similar to that acquired in an academic field of study; may include a bachelor's degree, extensive technical training, or equivalent experience

5. Comprehensive understanding of one or several fields, normally gained through extensive study in an academic environment or business; may include a master's degree or equivalent experience

6. Knowledge of a subject such that the incumbent is an authority in the field; may include doctoral degree or equivalent experience

Note that "or equivalent" should be used for two important reasons. First, it allows flexibility in staffing. Practically every organization will have individuals who may be formally "overqualified" or "underqualified" for their jobs but are performing adequately or better. Second, it provides some protection from legal liability. Because protected classes may be adversely affected by educational requirements, it is important to show that these levels are not hard-and-fast requirements but are general levels of education that incumbents typically have.

If an outside consultant is not assisting in the project, it would be helpful for the HR professional to consult a compensation consultant or a comprehensive textbook listing typical compensable factors. Defining appropriately sensitive factor levels requires a degree of expertise that generally comes only from experience. Points must also be assigned to each factor level within each factor, guided by the factor weightings. Table 24.1 illustrates a typical example of the assignment of these values.

The product of these efforts at this point is essentially a device by which all of the organization's jobs can be measured. The next major phase of the point-factor job evaluation process involves using this point-factor "yardstick" to measure jobs. Benchmark jobs are evaluated first. Building the salary system is

Table 24.1. Assigning Points to Factor Levels.

Factor	Weight	Points	Level 1	2	3	4	5	6
Education and training	25%	250	50	75	100	150	200	250
Accountability	20%	200	35	75	100	135	175	200
Independent judgment	20%	150	25	50	75	100	125	150
Supervision	15%	100	15	30	45	60	80	100
Complexity of job	10%	100	15	30	45	60	80	100
Consequence of errors	10%	100	15	30	45	60	80	100
Total	100%	900						

easier if the benchmark jobs for which market data were collected are used as benchmarks in the job evaluation process.

Second, the individuals responsible for evaluating the jobs must be chosen. In the best of all possible worlds, a *job evaluation committee* made up of top managers is used. Under the guidance of the HR professional or compensation consultant, this group of five to eight executives spends several uninterrupted hours or even days carefully discussing each job, debating its rating on each factor, and finally reaching consensus on a final rating. Again, executives are ideal because they have a broad organizational perspective and understand overall organizational functions, are closest to the strategic goals and values of the organization, and are more likely to "buy in" to the system due to their participation. Also, this initial use of the new system on the benchmark jobs helps define the meaning of the factors in that particular organizational context more precisely. Top managers then better understand and appreciate its relevance. However, the disadvantage is clear: executives' time and energy are at a premium, particularly in these days of scaled-down management structures. Each nonprofit organization will need to carefully consider whether its executives' time should be used and if so, how much. A cheaper but less effective strategy is to use a middle-management committee to evaluate the benchmark jobs. (Committees made up of workers below middle management are generally not recommended because they become susceptible to political pressures from coworkers to overrate or underrate certain jobs.)

After the job evaluation committee has evaluated the benchmark jobs, a subcommittee, often the HR professional or consultant (or both) and one top manager, evaluates the rest of the jobs. Even using time-saving tactics, the committee process can be extremely expensive in terms of executive time and productivity. An alternative but less effective process is for the HR professional, in conjunction with a consultant or other HR staffer, to evaluate all jobs and then gain top management approval for the job hierarchy.

Regardless of the evaluation process, the same principles should be followed in evaluating the jobs:

- Evaluators must understand all the factors and levels. Time should be allocated for discussion of the system and how it relates to the organization.

- Evaluators must thoroughly understand each job. This is where current and accurate job descriptions are essential. If necessary, the job's supervisor should be consulted during the discussion to ensure that essential job functions are understood.

- A critical point that evaluators should remember is that they are evaluating *jobs* and not people. It is essential that discussion center on the requirements of the job and not the unusually high- or low-performing job incumbent.

- Each job should be discussed in terms of how it rates on each factor and what specific job tasks or responsibilities relate to the factor.
- If possible, a consensus on the job's rating on each factor should be reached. Majority rule should be used only as a last option.

After all jobs have been evaluated, the point values should be entered into a spreadsheet (an abbreviated example is presented in Table 24.2). This enables the evaluators to "quality-control" their results, ensuring that face-valid and sensible relationships between the jobs are maintained.

A final step in job evaluation is to review the hierarchy with each departmental manager. The array of jobs within the department, listed *without* point values, should be presented to the manager (point values of jobs should be known only by the job evaluation committee and relevant HR staff in order to avoid misunderstandings among those who do not understand the scope or application of the evaluation system). The manager should check to see that this hierarchy makes sense in the accepted understanding of the jobs' functions, values, and relationships. Some minimal fine-tuning may be needed. After all departments have reviewed these hierarchies, a spreadsheet illustrating all jobs in all departments can be produced, which may be reviewed by the top managers. This last step is to ensure that job relationships are equitable not only within departments but also throughout the organization.

Choosing and Maintaining the Right System. Regardless of the job evaluation method used, a system of regular review should be established so that jobs are analyzed and reevaluated about every three years, more often if they change frequently. Obviously, organizational needs, as well as jobs, change over time, and a regular system is necessary so that internal equity is maintained. Often HR departments will systematically review one-third of the jobs each year to eliminate having to undertake a major evaluation project every three years. Supervisors should also have a mechanism to appeal job evaluations to HR outside this regular cycle when they can substantiate a legitimate need to do so.

With innovative pay systems such as team-based pay, incentive systems, and skill-based pay increasing due to less traditional organizational structures, budget constraints, and market forces, the usefulness of extensive job evaluation programs has been questioned. All organizations, especially nonprofits, in which time and money are in extreme demand, need to decide the balance to strike between internal and external pressures and design an internal evaluation system that is the least administratively complex. In terms of administrative complexity, the point-factor system is definitely not for everyone.

Table 24.2. Job Evaluation Spreadsheet.

Job	Education and Training	Accountability	Independent Judgment	Supervision	Complexity of Job	Consequence of Errors	Total
Receptionist	50	35	25	15	15	10	150
Accounting clerk	75	100	75	30	45	30	355
Administrative assistant	150	135	125	45	60	40	555
Development director	200	175	125	60	80	80	720
Program director	200	175	150	80	80	50	735

Indeed, the hassles of creating an internally equitable salary structure are hard to exaggerate. They nearly always pay off in the long run, however. Although most managers believe that inequities with the external market will foster more pay dissatisfaction than inequitable internal relationships, experience in the private sector with two-tiered pay systems provides a valuable lesson on the impact of internal inequity. These systems were designed to help financially troubled employers reduce costs by paying new hires dramatically less for the same jobs that previously hired incumbents were doing, sometimes as little as one-half of the incumbents' pay. Research and experience found that not only did new employees show high levels of pay dissatisfaction, but longer-tenured, higher-paid employees were also extremely uncomfortable with the inherent inequities. Furthermore, internal inequities will be experienced by the employee on a daily or even hourly basis when interacting with other workers. External market inequities, on the other hand, may be directly experienced only occasionally as one reads the classified advertisements, surfs the Internet, or has a conversation comparing wages. Thus every organization should be cognizant of the consequences of internal inequity and install, implement, and maintain a sound job evaluation program, be it simple or complex.

External Competitiveness and Internal Equity: What Roles Should They Play?

The competitive pressures of the external labor market, plus the importance of creating organizations in which employees believe they are paid equitably relative to each other, require nonprofit managers to carefully weigh the relative importance of internal and external equity. It is possible that organizations that do not have to attract highly skilled technical workers may find their needs better served by ensuring first an equitable internal hierarchy of jobs and then making sure that it generally matches the relevant market. Alternatively, organizations that are dependent on the attraction and retention of highly skilled workers will probably need to first focus on developing a system in which jobs are paid competitively and then check to ensure that internal considerations are taken care of. As always, the mantra of "What is it that the organization wants to reward?" should inform and guide this strategic decision. It is on the basis of this important decision that the amount of market data needed and the complexity of the job evaluation procedure should be chosen.

Building the Externally and Internally Equitable Salary Structure

A salary structure creates an administrative means by which pay is determined. It serves to integrate the organization's policies relative to external competitiveness and internal equity in a manageable system that sets minimum and maximum pay levels for jobs, thereby serving to ensure that pay is within the range that supports the organization's rewards strategy.

Reconciling Contradictions Between the Data. Unless a totally market-based approach to pay is used, it is likely that the job hierarchies generated from market analysis and job evaluation will not match exactly; in other words, the market will probably value jobs higher or lower than the organization does. This requires that the organization have a strategy regarding the relative importance of each. Some jobs, such as those with valuable or rare skill sets, may need to be "market-driven," meaning that their values should be based primarily, if not solely, on current and accurate market data. An organization that has jobs that are particularly relevant to the organization's mission and strategy may choose to pay them above the market rates. An example from a for-profit organization may be helpful. In the banking industry, one of the most notorious low-paid jobs is that of teller. However, a bank that has formulated a strategy of preeminent customer service might choose to pay its tellers above the market because it wants to attract, motivate, and retain the very best candidates. Thus nonprofit HR managers must carefully consider what their strategy relative to internal and external equity should be and whether it should differ for any particular job or jobs.

Pay Level Policy. As part of the rewards policy formulation, top managers must decide where they wish to stand relative to their job markets. This decision then translates directly into how the organization "prices" its jobs, a fundamental part of building the salary structure.

Most organizations in the private sector attempt to maintain their pay levels at the median of their relevant markets. This does not mean that every employee will be paid the going market rate but that overall, the salary ranges and grades reflect the current market rates (more will be said about this later). Some organizations make policy decisions to pay at the 60th percentile or higher; they believe that paying premium salaries will ensure that they attract and retain the top performers in the job market. Some organizations may pay significantly under the market median; this strategy may be driven by the need for low-skilled, easily hired employees performing easily acquired duties. Obviously, the pay level decision is crucial to the organization's strategic planning, its long range goals, and its current environmental challenges.

Structuring the Structure. The HR professional or compensation consultant must make several decisions regarding the salary structure, which is merely the set of grades and their accompanying ranges. A salary grade involves several simple but key concepts: minimum, maximum, midpoint (or "control point"), and range spread. The minimum is the organization's estimation of the job's minimum value. Generally, newly hired workers with little or no specific job experience will be paid the minimum rate. The maximum reflects the most value the organization expects to receive from the job. Even if an incumbent performs the job superbly and has done so for the past fifty years, the job is simply worth no more than the maximum. In most cases, jobs of similar value will be grouped together in a single grade; systems that use only one job per grade are usually unwieldy and inefficient.

The midpoint or control point is a critical concept in base salary administration. It is the point in the salary range that is keyed to the organization's response to the market. For example, if the market rate for accountants is $3,000 per month and the organization's policy is to pay at 110 percent of the market, the midpoint for the grade in which accountants are found will be $3,300. New hires with little or no experience will be paid at the minimum of the range, and some longer-tenured accountants may be paid more, but generally the job of accountant, when performed by a full-performing incumbent, is worth $3,300 a month to the organization.

The term *control point* is preferable to *midpoint* for a couple of reasons, even though *midpoint* is more statistically descriptive. First, as we will see later, all employees should not expect to advance to the maximum of their job grade unless their performance over time is exemplary. In an effective salary structure, an employee who meets expectations for the job should receive the value the job is worth on the market (or our reaction to the market as determined by our pay level policy). Using the term *midpoint* is often interpreted by employees to mean that they have another 50 percent of the salary structure in which to move. Only top performers, however, should be paid in the top half of the grade. Second, *control point* is descriptive of the statistic's use in salary administration. It allows the organization to control costs around its policy toward the salary market.

Range Spread: Traditional or Broadbanding? The range spread is the difference between the maximum and the minimum, expressed as a percentage of the minimum. In older, more traditional salary systems, range spreads typically run from 35 to 50 percent, with the smaller ranges usually used for lower-level jobs. The idea here is that incumbents in lower-level jobs will stay in the range for less time than incumbents in higher-level jobs, since the lower jobs are less complex and easier to learn and incumbents will tend to be promoted quickly to higher levels. However, in the past decade or so, a useful concept called "broadbanding" has been adopted by organizations seeking to make their pay systems more flexible. Broadbanding collapses what would have been several grades into a broad "band," creating a more flexible system in which the pay for jobs can be adjusted without reclassifying a position from one grade to another. Figure 24.2 illustrates this concept. It also allows more managerial discretion, in that a manager has a wider range within which to pay people. Since there are fewer bands

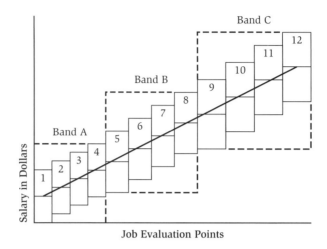

Figure 24.2. Broadbanding Superimposed on a Traditional Salary Structure.

than there are grades in a traditional salary structure, the broadbanded system is easier to administer and maintain. Although broadbanding may not formally assign a control point to the band, in practice there may be "shadow ranges" within the band that are keyed to market rates (Milkovich and Newman, 2002). In more traditional systems, salary grades group jobs that are of equal value to the organization. In broadbanding, a certain amount of precision is lost, and jobs in the same band will differ more in their organizational values than they would in a traditional system.

Broadbanding systems are useful when flexibility and nontraditional career paths are the preferred strategy of the organization. However, because there are fewer guidelines (since there are fewer ranges, there are fewer minimum and maximum pay rates in the system), broadbanding runs the risk of paying jobs over market rates, and the increased managerial discretion opens the door to wider potential for bias. As in all rewards system decisions, the mission, orga-nizational strategy, and HR strategies need to be carefully considered in deter-mining whether broad bands or more traditional ranges will be used.

Constructing Grades or Bands. Control point (or midpoint) progression, or the difference between the control points of two grades as expressed as a percentage of the lower grade's control point, should also be considered in constructing grades or bands. A key consideration here is the role of promotions to the or-ganization (if the organization wants to encourage employees to higher levels of achievement via promotion, making control points farther apart will provide substantial pay benefits to advancement). Also, if supervision is considered an important competency within the organization, larger progressions will more heavily reward those in supervisory positions. Sometimes organizations will split the structures into exempt (professional, supervisory, and managerial workers, including those exempt from the provisions of the Fair Labor Standards Act, who are not paid overtime) and nonexempt grades (those that are paid overtime) and use a larger control point progression for the exempt structure. The key issue is that job families have sufficient differentials between them to support the value of the jobs in the marketplace and within the organization.

Salary structures are built by beginning with the control points that are determined after the reconciliation of job evaluation points and market data for benchmark jobs. Minimums and maximums for each band or grade are then calculated. The widths should depend again on strategic considerations: how long incumbents are expected to remain in their positions (longer time calls for wider grades or bands) and the degree to which promotional opportunities should be rewarded (greater emphasis on promotions call for narrower grades or bands).

Maintaining the Structure. To maintain the salary structure, the market must be checked annually to ensure that the organization's grades or bands remain competitive. This is done through another kind of survey, the prototype of which is WorldatWork's annual *Salary Budget Survey* (available at a small fee to nonmembers). This survey presents data regionally, by industry and by job level, for present and anticipated structure increases. These data are presented as percentages and represent the amount the surveyed companies increased their midpoints (minimums and maximums change accordingly) in the year and the amount by which they expect to increase them in the next year. Organizations will typically use this information to adjust their own structures to remain competitive but usually do not correspondingly increase employees' wages unless an employee's salary is surpassed by the new minimum. Handling these "green circle employees" is discussed next.

Common Issues in Installing a New System. Upon installing a new salary system, it is likely that some employees' current salaries will be over the new maximums ("red circle" employees) or under the new minimums ("green circle" employees). Theoretically, red circle employees are being paid substantially over the market rate (or control point) for the job. Therefore, it does not make sense to continue to increase their base pay, and so it is typically "frozen" until the structure's maximum catches up and exceeds it in the course of normal salary structure maintenance, as described earlier. To maintain their level of motivation, however, many organizations will provide these individuals with annual lump-sum bonuses based on performance. This strategy gives the employees additional income but does not add to the fixed costs of their base salaries. Green circle employees' salaries are substantially below the market rates for their jobs and consequently should be moved at least to the new minimum as quickly as possible. For organizations with limited resources, that may mean giving small periodic increases to boost the salary gradually. Furthermore, some long-term employees may face severe inequity if their salaries are at the minimum and new workers are hired to work alongside them at the same pay level. In these cases, the HR professional must recommend the best approach to balance equity with financial resources. Often a simple formula combining years of services and performance is devised to move longer-term employees to a more equitable position in the grade or band.

Other Salary Administration Policies. Salary administration procedures must be written that coordinate with the goals and plans of the organization. There should be policies covering the salary impact of transfers, promotions, demotions, reclassifications (which happens when a job is reevaluated and placed in a different grade due to changes in its duties), and new hiring. It is essential that these be carefully thought out so that the intentions of the compensation plan are not subverted due to haphazard (and often nonmotivational) administrative procedures.

Pay satisfaction is often popularly regarded as the worker's satisfaction with the level of salary and benefits he or she may receive. However, since research shows that pay satisfaction depends on the structure and administration of the program as well as salary and benefits levels and raises (see, for example, Heneman and Schwab, 1985; Carraher, 1991), the wise HR professional will ensure that administrative processes are sound and equitable.

Increasing Individuals' Base Pay. In the past, nonprofit organizations, government entities, and school districts typically based salary increases on seniority rather than performance. In most cases, however, seniority-based pay has been regarded as strategically out of alignment with the leaner, more competitive business environment and has thus been discontinued in favor of a merit system (merit pay generally refers to an annual salary increase based on the employee's supervisory performance appraisal). A 1997 survey conducted by the American Society of Association Executives found that about two-thirds of participating associations reported using merit increases for nonexecutives and only 2 percent relied on seniority-based pay (Casteuble, 1997). Although association practices may differ from those in other nonprofits, there is in fact a trend across the nonprofit sector to move into what was once the domain of for-profit organizations: incentives and sometimes even pay-at-risk plans.

These more innovative pay systems do not eliminate the need for sound base compensation programs, however. Individuals must still receive a base wage, which will continue to represent a substantial expense to the organization and must be managed carefully. Therefore, the HR professional in charge of compensation in the nonprofit must decide the best method with which to move employees through their grades or bands. In addition to merit- and seniority-based systems, across-the-board or cost-of-living increases can be used. However, like seniority-based pay, these alternatives increase the fixed costs of salaries in a manner that has no relationship to the employee's level of performance.

Communicating Salary Plans

An effective compensation program should communicate several basic areas to all employees (Rubino, 1997):

- The employee's job description and how it was obtained (job analysis)
- The methods by which jobs are evaluated
- How market data are collected and analyzed
- How performance relates to pay
- How performance is measured and appraised
- Administrative policies and procedures
- Benefit plans

Beyond these sensible recommendations, organizations will have to make strategic decisions regarding how much information about the plan should be available to employees. Some public organizations, like federal, state, and local governments, make data regarding all salary grades and ranges available to employees as well as taxpayers; even individual salary levels can be easily discovered, often just by a search on the Internet or a trip to the library! Other organizations are less open, some making discussion of individual salaries among employees a disciplinary offense. Generally speaking, most organizations make the minimum, midpoint, and maximum of a salary range available to the individuals whose jobs fall within it. In this way, employees are aware of the earning power of their present jobs.

A case can be made for making the entire salary structure available to all employees because of the developmental (and thereby motivational) aspects. If individuals know the earning potentials of prospective jobs to which they may aspire, theoretically they may be motivated to acquire the necessary skills and experiences to get them there. Furthermore, the career-tracking characteristics of this scheme should encourage employees to remain with the organization in order to achieve their personal career goals. However, if such career options do not exist for most employees in the organization and if the culture does not permit such disclosure, it should not be done. While newer, innovative management strategies like "open-book management" would also argue in favor of increased openness about pay, like practically every human resource function, the method of communicating salary plans must be carefully determined on the basis of its impact on and coordination with the culture of the organization.

INCENTIVE PAY IN NONPROFITS

As has already been discussed, over the past decade or so, American business has had to become more competitive in many of its human resource practices. In many for-profit organizations, bonuses are now common at all levels of employees. Even equity or ownership incentives such as stock or stock options are now more frequently offered to nonexecutives (although concerns arising out of recent accounting scandals question the longevity of these plans, given that stock options may, in the future, be required to be expensed). Although some nonprofit organizations are so financially constrained that incentives may seem an impossible luxury, it is useful for the nonprofit HR professional to be aware of them, since some of these systems may have direct applicability to nonprofits that have productivity or motivational issues.

A recent survey found that over half of nonprofit organizations provide some type of cash incentive to employees, and although these are more common at the executive level, half also reported that all employees are eligible for these incentives (Klein, McMillan, and Keating, 2002; Towers Perrin, 1999). For the nonexecutive nonprofit employee, these are for the most part short-term incentives, designed to reward employees for a performance window of one year or less. Indeed, incentives can be effective in nonprofits if the following criteria are met (Wein, 1989):

- The top decision makers, usually the board of directors, must embrace a philosophy of pay-for-performance.

- Incentives can serve as effective motivators not only of CEOs but of lower-level managers as well. A particularly good candidate is the development officer, whose performance often has a direct and immediate impact on organizational revenue.

- Incentives should be used only if they can be based on improvements to the organization's financial condition, through either generation of revenue or enhanced cost savings.

- The performance on which the incentive is based must be measurable and achievable and should include nonfinancial measures that are critical to the organization's mission and strategy, such as quality of service delivery.

- Managers must find the financial rewards motivating. The amount of the incentive must therefore be large enough to "make a difference" in motivation.

- Incentives should be awarded only to employees whose performance is above average, perhaps substantially above average.

- The incentive plan will be successful only if it is communicated effectively and employees trust that their efforts will be appropriately rewarded.

These points underscore the case that has been made throughout this chapter that any rewards strategy must be carefully considered and closely aligned with the organization's mission, strategy, and other HR policies and practices.

Types of Incentives

Simple short-term bonuses are probably the most widely understood type of incentive. These bonuses are based on a measure of performance over which the employee has some level of control and can be awarded to individuals for individually based performance or to groups, departments, or units, depending on the appropriate level given the desired performance. "Spot awards," in which a supervisor allocates a pool of discretionary bonus money in relatively small amounts (usually around $50 to $100) to employees for excellent performance in isolated events, can be powerful if carefully used.

Gainsharing programs require significant up-front design time but may be more acceptable to board and public stakeholders because in the nonprofit context, they focus on cost savings generated by employee performance. This type of program may be particularly appropriate for nonprofits that are experiencing unnecessarily high operating costs. Although these plans vary widely, they nearly always include some employee participation mechanism whereby employee ideas and initiative not only encourage "buy-in" to the program but also at least partially determine methods to save costs. Usually, the organization will split the cost savings pool on an equal basis with the employees, and thus the plan benefits both the individual and the organization. The major downside to this type of program is that it involves deriving a fairly complicated formula by which productivity gains are measured, which may necessitate hiring sophisticated consultants to assist in the installation of the plan. Implementation of these complicated plans nearly always requires outside expertise.

Nonprofit organizations considering incentive plans should ensure that they remain in compliance with IRS regulations. While it is beyond the scope of this chapter, the IRS allows incentive plans as long as they do not violate rules that prohibit inappropriate private gain by executives, managers, employees, or other individuals (Klein, McMillan, and Keating, 2002).

Nonfinancial Incentives

Nonprofit organizations are generally not cash-rich. Board members or public constituents may also be resistant to providing cash incentives to employees who "are just doing their jobs" when those funds "should be" directed at the organization's core mission. When such attitudes exist, it is encouraging to note that other types of incentives may be powerful but less expensive motivators.

For example, a popular nonfinancial incentive used by nonprofits is flextime ("Innovative Compensation," 1996). "Employee of the month" or awards of clothing with organizational insignias can often reap motivational returns whose value far exceeds the cost of the reward itself. Wise managers will carefully consider these options in their rewards strategies. Nonprofit organizations may also want to consider the motivational implications of enhancing employee embeddedness (see Chapter Twenty-Three)

EXECUTIVE PAY IN NONPROFITS

Although for-profit organizations are nearly consistently under heavy fire by the media and labor groups for their top management compensation practices, such was not the case for top management of nonprofit organizations until the early 1990s, when nonprofit salaries reported in the media were repudiated out of hand, regardless of consideration of the market forces that probably made them necessary. It is imperative that top decision makers, including directors and major contributors, understand that superior performance in top management positions is critical and that the best performers are often in very high demand in the marketplace. However, even reasonable levels of pay for their services may seem unconscionably expensive to the uneducated, and individuals involved in determining executive pay should therefore be extremely thorough in their market analyses and decision making and meticulous in communicating market pressures for the top jobs to the directors and major contributors.

The pay of the nonprofit executive group should be determined in a similar manner to that for other employees described earlier, using market data analyses, job evaluation, sound policies and procedures, and carefully designed incentive pay. External competitiveness issues are usually weighted much more heavily for top managers, for a couple of reasons. First, the location of these positions in the organization means that internal equity considerations are limited to the jobs below them. Second, these are key jobs that are generally quite visible to organizations competing for talent. Thus external factors are more salient for these positions. In addition, since the overall performance of the nonprofit in accomplishing its mission is more clearly dependent on top management than on lower-level employees, an incentive program leveraged on achievement of mission and strategy should be seriously considered.

In response to the need for more market-based salaries, as well as external pressures for nonprofit executive pay to be correlated with organizational performance, nonprofits are increasingly turning to variable executive pay. In fact, in Buck Consultants' *2002 Nonprofit Survey,* nearly half the respondents, representing the entire nonprofit sector, reported having executive bonus programs (Gaeta, 2003). As is commonly known, for-profits are often criticized generally not for their base salaries, which tend to be relatively modest (*relatively* is a key word here), but for their incentive pay, often in the form of annual bonuses or stock options. However, nonprofit organizations have less to worry about in this regard, as nonprofit CEOs who are eligible for bonuses on average receive only about 15 percent of their base pay in incentives (Gaeta, 2003). In addition, non-profits are obviously often severely constrained by limited financial resources, making the magnitude of nonprofit executives' pay, in comparison to their for-profit counterparts, seem quite modest. However, wise nonprofit decision makers will monitor the level and composition of executive compensation packages to ensure that they are not only appropriate given market forces and IRS constraints but also acceptable to key stakeholders.

The most frequent strategy in nonprofit organizations for determining the basis for incentive pay is a relatively subjective board judgment. A better strategy is to establish executive performance measures that clearly delineate the criteria on which a bonus will be paid. An obvious strategy is to link executive bonuses with operational cost savings, which also serves to fund the incentives. Another financial criterion is "program ratio," the ratio of the amount spent on delivery of mission-related services to total expenses. However, in addition to financial components, measures should also be considered that reflect accomplishment of the organization's mission, such as number of clients served, as well as other practices found in "balanced scorecard" approaches, including investments in human capital, business processes, or innovation (Berman, 1998). (For a more thorough discussion of these measures and examples of how several nonprofits employ them, see Gaeta, 2003.)

It is often desirable, for obvious reasons, to contract with outside consultants to design the salary plan for top management. Not only do such professionals have access to more data, but they also have the objectivity needed to make recommendations to the board for paying these critical jobs.

BENEFITS

Careful design and implementation of benefits programs are essential in attracting and retaining a qualified workforce. It is now the rare job seeker who is willing to join an organization unless it offers a reasonable, if not generous, benefits package. The amount of money spent on benefits is staggering and continues to grow, costing the average U.S. employer 39 percent of its total payroll in 2001, about 4 percent higher than it was just one year earlier (U.S. Chamber of Commerce, 2003). Thus it is more than a good idea to make sure that benefits are effective in attracting and retaining good employees.

The breadth and depth of the topic of benefits could easily fill several volumes, so the scope of discussion here will be necessarily limited. The field has become highly technical and specialized, necessitating the HR professional who is inexperienced in this area to solicit help from outside in order to ensure that the organization's benefits programs are competitive and appropriate for its employee base. Many consultants are available to assist the nonprofit in this quest, some who are also brokers selling the products and some who merely analyze organizational needs and make recommendations. Either kind can be of great assistance to the nonprofit HR professional.

The same concepts of external competitiveness and internal equity applied to salary compensation are relevant in designing benefits programs. Organizations desiring to compete successfully for job candidates must design their benefits programs using current and reliable market data on the benefits offered by competitors. Short benefits surveys are often included as adjuncts to some salary surveys, and surveys specific to benefits are also available. Because of the divergence and variety of different packages, conducting a benefits survey from scratch can be an extremely difficult, frustrating, and cumbersome task. So if data are available from a published source, they are nearly always preferable to a survey conducted in-house.

Just as salary programs need to be developed with internal equity in mind, benefits programs should consider factors internal to the organization also. In other words, the program should meet key employee needs while satisfying the employer in terms of financial and other policy obligations.

In meeting employee needs, the HR professional should carefully consider what types and levels of benefits the employees want. Demographics of employee groups will undoubtedly have an impact on benefits attractiveness. For example, middle-aged or older employees may be more concerned with retirement and retiree health insurance than younger employees, whose interests may revolve around beginning families and whose desires may include health insurance, especially covering maternity expenses, family leave, and life insurance. However, it is a mistake to design benefits programs totally on demographics, since they are not always predictive of the benefits employees want. Employee surveys, focus groups, or other means of collecting data on the wants and needs of workers are essential.

One way that organizations can satisfy diverse employee groups is through flexible benefits, or "cafeteria plans." These plans, also called "125 plans" from the section in the IRS Codes that refers to the regulation, allow employees to choose to have pretax earnings deducted from their paychecks and set aside for particular benefits, such as child care or medical, vision, or dental costs. Not only does this option save the employee taxes, but it also offers flexibility by allowing employees to choose benefits that are particularly attractive to them.

Benefits in the Rewards Policy

As discussed earlier, a rewards policy needs to be formulated that explains precisely what the organization wants its rewards system to do. Just as pay and work environment considerations are included, the role of benefits in the rewards system needs to be clearly articulated. Information that should be considered for this policy include the following (McCaffery, 1983):

- The organization's desire to provide employees with meaningful welfare and security benefits
- The organization's intention to design benefits to fit employee needs
- The frequency and philosophy by which the program will be audited and evaluated in relation to benefits costs, salary increases, and external factors
- The organization's desire to use benefits as a means to motivate and achieve desired levels of productivity
- How the organization plans to fund the benefits (most often organizations require employees to pay at least part of the costs)
- The organization's intention to communicate thoroughly and explain changes to benefits programs to employees
- The content of individualized annual statements regarding the value of benefits, company contributions, and employee costs
- The market with which benefits will be compared
- The requirement that trustees and carriers will submit detailed reports annually to management
- The commitment that benefits plans will be assessed annually to ensure they meet the needs of changing demographics of the employee group

Health Care

The crisis in health care that has beset our country for the past several decades continues to escalate. The solutions to this complicated problem have been and will probably remain painful. The health care crisis involves two major issues: the dramatically rising cost of both health care and insurance and the large percentage of the population that is not insured or is underinsured.

Nonprofit organizations must confront both of these issues, one directly in our own rising health insurance costs and the other indirectly by making the difficult decision of whether health benefits can be offered to part-timers as well as full-timers. Unfortunately, many nonprofits, like many for-profits, simply cannot afford to offer expensive health benefits to part-time employees. However, some are offering prorated benefits to part-time employees, dependent on the number of hours worked.

To deal with the health insurance cost issues, nearly all organizations, for-profit and nonprofit, have turned to managed care programs. This is a catchall name for a variety of programs from health maintenance organizations (HMOs) to point-of-service plans (POSs) and preferred provider organizations (PPOs). These programs generally require significant monitoring and managing of individual health

care occurrences, including ensuring that individual care selections are prudently chosen and confirming that the costs associated with them are reasonable. Though variations are many, generally speaking, HMOs require employees
to choose physicians and other health care providers who belong to a network;
POSs and PPOs reward employees who choose within their networks but usually allow some coverage outside. In this way, employers can achieve reduced
rates for medical services by either paying en masse for services or receiving
discounts on certain procedures.

Although traditional cost containment strategies—such as raising copayments
and deductibles, encouraging preventive care, ensuring that medical billing is
accurate, and requiring second opinions—are still good ideas, new strategies to
manage health care costs include the following (Cascio, 2003):

- Forming purchasing coalitions to negotiate better rates with health
  care providers. Several jurisdictions have created community health purchasing alliances (CHPAs), organizations set up to create a group that
  qualifies for affordable health insurance for small businesses. Florida,
  California, North Carolina, Connecticut, and the city of Cleveland are
  among the jurisdictions that have such organizations (Volz, 1998).

- Treating hospitals, insurers, and providers like any other type of vendor
  by making information about them easily accessible to employees (for
  example, via the Internet) so that employees can make economical
  decisions.

- Offering flexible benefits plans that encourage employees to choose
  plans that meet their needs and also save costs.

- Establishing negotiation relationships directly with doctors to ensure
  the best prices.

- Ensuring that patients have "preadmission certification" given by
  physicians before they enter the hospital.

Most benefits professionals agree that managed health care hasn't turned out
to be the miracle cure that was hoped for. An innovative approach that has recently come under discussion is "defined contribution" health care, in which
employers shift the responsibility for provision of insurance to the employee,
as in defined contribution retirement plans. Though there are many variations
under discussion, the basic idea is that the employer would provide some sort
of cash stipend to employees, who would either choose their health insurance
on the open market or purchase it from providers sponsored by the employer.
Advantages to employers are that costs become more fixed and administrative
costs are reduced, but for employees the disadvantages probably outweigh the
advantages. Although technology may create a more open and affordable market for most employees, they will be required to understand complex medical

benefits plans and find affordable coverage in a confusing market. However, some employers are already implementing versions of this system (Sanicola and Johnson, 2001).

Retirement Plans

In the past, retirement plans aimed to provide retirees with 50 to 70 percent of their preretirement income. This was considered sufficient because in retirement, work-related expenses are no longer incurred, deductions are not withheld from pay, tax breaks give retirees a few advantages, and large sums of money need not be put away for retirement any longer. However, since most retirees nowadays have little desire to scale back their lifestyles and perhaps look forward to doing things for which they didn't have time before, most financial consultants now recommend that future retirees plan for a larger income, 80 to 100 percent of preretirement pay. Moreover, Americans are living longer, and more funds must be available for these longer retirements than previously.

Retirement income is usually achieved through the coordination of Social Security payments with income from retirement plans. Given the current state of Social Security and the recent lack of progress made by Congress in improving the situation, any substantial benefit for individuals retiring in the next fifteen to twenty years is not likely to come from Social Security. Americans will therefore need to do more careful planning than they have in the past in providing for retirement.

Two broad types of retirement plans exist: defined-benefit and defined-contribution. Defined-benefit plans have traditionally been the norm. These plans define the income that the employee will receive upon retirement, usually based on a percentage of the average compensation over all or a number of employment years. They require extensive actuarial support, making assumptions regarding future earning potential, number of years until retirement, and other pertinent factors. The contribution the employer makes is determined through actuarial assessments. Because of the expense of these programs and the requirement of a fairly large employee base, they are relatively rare in all but the largest nonprofit organizations, and their numbers are in decline in most sectors.

Defined-contribution plans, on the other hand, define the amount that is put into some kind of investment vehicle. Therefore, the actual retirement income the employee will receive depends on the success of the investment and is therefore unknown, but the amount contributed to the plan is defined. Often the investment is contributed by both employer and employee. These are commonly found in nonprofit organizations in the form of tax-sheltered annuity programs (TSAs) or 403(b) plans.

Similar to for-profit 401(k) plans, TSAs allow employees to reduce taxable income by contributing a percentage of their salaries on a pretax basis to one or more qualifying annuities or mutual funds. Plans can include an employer match along with the salary reduction or salary reduction alone. In 2003, individuals could contribute up to $12,000 a year.

Retirement plans for nonprofits, like for-profit plans, are subject to extensive IRS and other legislative regulations (especially the Employees' Retirement Income Security Act, or ERISA, and the IRS Codes), which are well beyond the scope of this chapter. Nonprofit HR professionals designing retirement programs should ensure that these complicated regulations have been complied with.

Given that generally defined contribution plans in the form of TSAs will be the preferred choice of most nonprofit employers, it is important that employees be aware of the financial risks of such plans. This is particularly critical given estimates that nearly 60 percent of Americans don't contribute even half of the maximum allowable to their TSAs (401khelpcenter.com, 2003). Many organizations offering defined contribution plans provide retirement or financial planning seminars for their employees many years before their normal retirement date. This type of training, which is generally free from TSA providers or fairly inexpensive, can assist employees in feeling comfortable about their retirement prospects and can aid employers by increasing the commitment level of the employee to the organization.

Paid Time Off

Often nonprofit organizations can more easily offer paid time off than cash to reward performance. In today's business environment, employees view vacations, holidays, and sick leave as an employment right, and thus paid time off has become a standard part of the total compensation package. Determining the best mix of paid time off requires application of the same principles used to determine other reward components: internal equity and external competition considerations. The demographics of the employee base may affect the particular kind of paid time off employees prefer. Younger workers may prefer sick leave, personal time off, or family leave to raise children. As employees age, they may prefer family leave programs that allow them time off to care for elderly parents. However, as in all benefits matters, be cautious about making unfounded assumptions based only on demographics. The best way to determine employees' preferences is to ask them, via a survey or other methods. Questions regarding employee preferences in paid-time-off issues should be included in any surveys or focus groups the organization uses.

Competitive market pressures must also be taken into consideration. For example, one nonprofit organization gives its employees all working days between Christmas and New Years as paid holidays because a major for-profit employer a few blocks away does the same. Although this may be an extreme example, it shows the necessity for nonprofits to be aware of the time-off policies of organizations with which they compete for labor. All organizations should carefully evaluate what their particular labor market competitors are offering before setting their own policies.

Most American employees in medium-sized and large organizations receive an average of 9.3 paid holidays per year, 9.6 days of vacation after one year of service, 13.8 days after five years of service, and 20.3 days after twenty years of service (U.S. Department of Labor, 2003). Some organizations also offer floating holidays, or days that change depending on the calendar and the needs of the organization. For example, if Independence Day falls on a Thursday, Friday may be given as a floating holiday to create a four-day weekend.

Note that many organizations now offer what is frequently referred to as personal days, often in lieu of sick leave. Although policies vary, personal days generally consist of a limited number of days that the employee may choose to take off for any personal reason, from sickness to birthdays to "mental health days." However, when personal days are used up, additional time off for illness must be taken without pay. The theory behind integrating personal time off with sick leave is that workers may then take time off to care for sick children, go to the doctor, or take care of other necessary personal business and not feel compelled to lie about being sick when they are not. Such programs can be effective in improving or maintaining trust in and commitment to the organization but must be carefully designed using historical sick leave data and employee preference information so that the program is as effective as possible. Some organizations incorporate all paid time off (except for holidays) in a personal-time-off program.

Other paid-time-off issues must be decided by the organization, including policies regarding jury duty, military leave, and death of a family member. Also, plans must be carefully formulated to ensure that policies deal appropriately with overtime pay, shift differentials, incentive pay, status of paid-time-off provisions during probationary periods, accrual of time off not used, and other relevant issues.

Tuition Reimbursement

According to a survey conducted by Abbott, Langer & Associates (2001), about half of surveyed nonprofit organizations reimburse tuition. However, this survey covered a broad range of nonprofit organizations, from "advocacy/consumer organizations through professional societies and trade associations . . . to youth organizations," and hence this statistic may not be representative of all types of nonprofit organizations.

Many nonprofits provide tuition reimbursement only for their employees who are pursuing degrees. Most require the student employee to receive satisfactory grades as well as to be working on a degree that is somehow related to his or her current job. Just as all compensation components need to be integrally linked to the organization's mission and strategic plan, however, tuition reimbursement programs should be carefully geared to some kind of career development philosophy that helps accomplish the organization's human resource strategy. In other words, nonprofits with limited resources need to understand what they are purchasing when they financially assist their student employees.

It could be simply employee goodwill or a more strategic goal of training workers to fill needed technologies or professions identified in the human resource planning process. Management should direct its tuition funds deliberately, as it would any other expenditure.

Communication of Benefits to Employees

Although effective communication is essential in nearly all aspects of human resources, perhaps no other area is so critically dependent on communication as the benefit program. Although ERISA requires that employees receive an annual summary plan description covering retirement benefits, this is not sufficient. Not only do employees need to know what their benefits are in order to use them effectively, but ensuring that they understand them is the only way for organizations to truly get the "bang for their benefit bucks." After all, both profit and nonprofit organizations spend an enormous amount of money on benefits. To obtain the optimum level of motivation and commitment from employees requires communicating the value of what they are receiving. McCaffery (1992) recommends several essential steps in effective communication:

- *Listen to employees.* Monitor the type of questions they ask, evaluate errors employees make in following procedures or filling out forms, listen to the employee "grapevine," and ensure upward communication channels are in place to monitor employee preferences.
- *Create and expand awareness.* Use "events-centered" communication that is structured around events such as time of hire, promotion, illness, or other relevant events that will make the information more salient, usable, and retainable for employees. Provide personalized reports that state clearly what each individual receives and the monetary value of his or her benefits package. Incorporate regular reminders of the value of benefits in newsletters, paycheck inserts, posters, and other communications devices.
- *Build understanding.* Ensure that literature is readable by evaluating the writing in benefits materials and use graphics and illustrations where appropriate. Communicate with employees face to face regularly to ensure that employees understand their benefits.
- *Gain employee trust.* Train company representatives to communicate effectively. Use nonsupervisory employees as benefits communicators so that knowledgeable and nonthreatening people are available to answer questions. Systematically audit benefits literature to ensure that it reflects current programs. Install internal complaint procedures that go beyond the requirements of ERISA. Balance themes of benefits messages to counter any bad news with the proactive communication of positive plan features.
- *Ensure that the benefits communication budget is adequate.* A standard is to budget 2 to 3 percent of the total cost of benefits.

JUSTIFYING REWARDS COSTS TO DIRECTORS

Some enhancements to total compensation programs may entail minimal cost increases but reap significant rewards in terms of increased employee satisfaction and retention or more successful recruitment. Often, however, improvements in salary and benefits programs result in potentially large financial outlays. In nonprofit organizations, as in many for-profit organizations, justifying such increases to boards of directors can be a formidable task. Faced with severe financial constraints and sometimes with constituent pressures, many directors are loath to approve policies that may have a long-lasting and sizable financial impact. Therefore, the HR professional in charge of formulating and proposing the program should follow some basic guidelines.

First, most of us realize that others will be more likely to accept a program if they are allowed some kind of input into it. Thus the HR professional should not begin developing any part of the total compensation program without the knowledge and blessing of the CEO and directors. He or she should carefully explain the need for the new program, the means by which it will be developed, and the method of implementation. Graphs of turnover statistics, current salaries compared to market data, and other preliminary information justifying the need for a new program should be presented concisely.

Second, directors should be informed throughout the process. Developing and implementing a salary program can take anywhere from six weeks to one year, depending on the size of the employee base, the number of jobs, and the culture of the organization. As the project progresses, the board should be given regular updates.

Third, directors should be involved in critical aspects of the project. It is essential, for example, that they approve the final relevant labor market determination before salary data are gathered. Unless the directors feel comfortable with the specific data sources to which jobs are being compared, any market data, no matter now painstakingly collected, will be virtually useless. Also, if an executive job evaluation committee is used, make sure that at least some members of the board, preferably those of longer tenure and greater respect, be included on the committee. Ensure that the board knows that it will approve all final job hierarchies and salary structures. Include directors, where possible, in focus groups that assess employee needs and desires.

When nonprofit operational needs are pressing, allocating money for salaries and benefits can be an imposing challenge. However, clear, concise, and thorough justification and explanation of the needs, development process, and final recommendations to directors will allow them to make reasonable and sensible decisions regarding this critical financial issue.

Also crucial is to ensure that corporate and foundation funders, as well as other major donors, understand the process by which the compensation decisions are made and the necessity for it. Although their communication and participation can be less involved, it is important that they believe that the systems and processes by which these crucial decisions are made have been conducted knowledgeably, professionally, and conscientiously.

SUMMARY

Organizations, both for-profit and nonprofit, are being challenged to compete effectively. To do this, they must have qualified employees who are motivated to accomplish the strategic goals of the organization. Attraction, motivation, and retention of high-caliber employees require that total compensation systems be carefully and thoughtfully designed. Pay strategies must fit the organization's culture and goals; thorough consideration must be given to identifying the behaviors the organization desires and designing reward strategies to ensure that they occur.

To do this, effective organizations must have up-to-date salary and benefits policies and communicate them to their employees. Second, organizations need to design and build effective base compensation programs, considering how external competitiveness and internal equity will be balanced. While job evaluation programs can be effective in communicating management's intentions to pay equitably, it is important that these time-consuming and expensive systems not be overused. Third, management must decide how it plans to encourage the key behaviors needed to accomplish strategic goals. This may be done through group or individual incentive programs, merit pay programs, or other plans. Each system has advantages and disadvantages that need to be weighed and evaluated in light of each organization's unique culture and characteristics.

Fourth, it is crucial that nonprofit organizations conscientiously evaluate necessary benefits levels. Especially in the area of health care, it is imperative that organizations understand both competitive pressures and employee desires. Finally, organizations need to design administrative policies and procedures that ensure that their salary and benefits programs are consistently, equitably, and effectively delivered to employees.

References

Abbott, Langer & Associates. "Nonprofit Fringe Benefits and Working Conditions Surveyed." [http://www.abbott-langer.com/snofsumm.html]. 2001.

Berman, S. J. "Using the Balanced Scorecard in Strategic Compensation." *ACA News,* 1998, *41*(6), 16–19.

Bridges, W. "The End of the Job." *Fortune,* 1994, Sept. 19, 1994, pp. 62–68.

Carraher, S. M. "A Validity Study of the Pay Satisfaction Questionnaire." *Educational and Psychological Measurement*, 1991, *51*, 491–495.

Cascio, W. F. *Managing Human Resources: Productivity, Quality of Work Life, Profits.* (6th ed.) New York: McGraw-Hill, 2003.

Casteuble, T. "What Today's Association Executives Earn." *Association Management*, 1997, *49*(4), 53–61.

401khelpcenter.com. "Retirement Savings Ranks High, But There Is a Clear Contradiction Between Intent and Action." [http://www.401khelpcenter.com/press/pr_putnam_060203.html]. 2003.

Gaeta, E. "Nonprofits at the Crossroads: A New Look at Executive Incentives." *WorldatWork Journal*, 2003, *12*(3), 64–71.

Heneman, H. G., and Judge, T. A. *Staffing Organizations.* (4th ed.) New York: McGraw-Hill, 2003.

Heneman, H. G., and Schwab, D. P. "Pay Satisfaction: Its Multidimensional Nature and Measurement." *International Journal of Psychology*, 1985, *20*, 129–141.

"Innovative Compensation: What Should You Try? What Should You Avoid?" *Nonprofit World*, Jan.-Feb. 1996, p. 54.

Kerr, S. "On the Folly of Rewarding A While Hoping for B." *Academy of Management Journal*, 1975, *18*, 769–783.

Klein, A., McMillan, A., and Keating, K. M. "Long-Term Incentives in Not-for-Profits: An Emerging Trend." *WorldatWork Journal*, 2002, *11*(3), 63–71.

Lawler, E. E., III. *Strategic Pay: Aligning Organizational Strategies and Pay Systems.* San Francisco: Jossey-Bass, 1990.

McCaffery, R. M. *Managing the Employee Benefits Program.* Boston: PWS-Kent, 1983.

McCaffery, R. M. *Employee Programs: A Total Compensation Perspective.* Boston: PWS-Kent, 1992.

Milkovich, G. T., and Newman, J. M. *Compensation.* (7th ed.) New York: McGraw-Hill, 2002.

Rubino, J. A. *Communicating Compensation Programs.* Scottsdale, Ariz.: American Compensation Association, 1997.

Sanicola, L., and Johnson, R. M. "D.C. Health Benefits: Big Questions, Few Answers." *Workspan*, August 2001, pp. 40–45.

Towers Perrin. *Management Compensation Report for Nonprofit Organizations.* New York: Towers Perrin, 1999.

U.S. Chamber of Commerce. "U.S. Chamber Survey Says Workers Receive More Job Benefits: Benefits Account for More of Payroll Costs." [www.uschamber.com/press/releases/2003/january/03-13.htm]. 2003.

U.S. Department of Labor, Bureau of Labor Statistics. "National Compensation Survey: Benefits." [http://www.bls.gov/ncs/ebs/home.htm]. 2003.

Volz, D. "If You Can't Beat 'Em." *Marketing Health Services,* 1998, *18*(3), 10–14.

Wallace, M. J., and Fay, C. H. *Compensation Theory and Practice.* Boston: PWS-Kent, 1988.

Wein, J. R. "Financial Incentives for Non-Profits." *Fund Raising Management,* 1989, *20*(7), 28–35.

"Welcome to WorldatWork: Integrated Solutions for Total Rewards." *Workspan,* June 2000, pp. 10–16.

CHAPTER TWENTY-FIVE

Principles of Training for Volunteers and Employees

Nancy Macduff

What is training? The dictionary says that training is to "gain knowledge of or skill in a subject through study, experience, or education." But what is it in the real world of nonprofit organizations and volunteer programs? It is any contact an organization or agency has with a volunteer or paid staff: a brochure, a Web site, a position description, an interview, an orientation session, an e-learning class, in-service education, or on-the-job training.

It usually begins with a brief news story on a local television show, a visit to the facility, surfing the Web, a brochure picked up at a library, a preassignment training session, orientation, in-service education, or a regional or national conference. Adult skill development and proficiency to carry out an assigned tasks begin with the first contact with the organization and last through the exit interview. This chapter focuses on formal training activities organized for volunteers and paid staff who work for nonprofit organizations and agencies or in volunteer programs.

Training can be divided into categories: micro and macro. Micro training exists for just one person or a small group of people; macro training exists for everyone within the organization, paid and unpaid. Training has two functions for the nonprofit organization. First, it establishes a minimum level of competency, and second, it is a benefit of being a part of the organization. (Laird, 1985)

Training is the way an organization publicly acknowledges that there is a necessary level of proficiency for the people working for the organizational mission.

It sends a clear message to people that the organization or agency has standards that those in its employ, paid or unpaid, are expected to meet. Expectations of growth and change through guided learning tells the potential volunteer or staff what the organization values.

Training is a benefit of volunteering or working. A benefit of working for Microsoft or the United Way is the continual and extensive training opportunities available to employees and volunteers. Volunteers also see a benefit in learning. Candace Widmer (1985), in a study of voluntary boards, found that 87 percent of board members surveyed listed learning as a benefit of membership in the group. Nonprofit organizations need to publicize how their training can help prospective volunteers on the job or in their personal relationships.

PRINCIPLES TO GUIDE ADULT LEARNING

There are two sources of information to help guide the individual who embarks on a journey to develop training and curriculum material. The first is the growing body of information about the brain and how information is stored in long-term memory, which is the goal of most training sessions. The second is the practical advice from modern adult educators who have been plying the waters of training for volunteers and paid staff for decades. We begin by examining knowledge about the brain.

The Brain

Early Egyptians, who preserved all the organs of the body after the death of an important personage, discarded the brain. They did not understand its function, so why keep it? As recently as the nineteenth century, phrenologists were palpating the skull to determine the location of the areas where wit was located in the head.

The advent of such sophisticated machinery as MRI, PET, and CAT scans (along with information from biology, physics, psychology, and neuroscience) have given us a picture of the brain as it has never been seen before—and with a profound impact on training. Lucia Jacobsen, psychologist and neuroscientist at the University of California in Berkeley, has described the brain as a rain forest, with symbiotic interconnected networks of associative relationships ("Why the Female Brain," 1999).

The following are but a few of the discoveries about the brain that affect how training should be organized to allow for the easiest mastery by learners (Reardon, 1999; Johnson, 1999; Colburn, 1999; Fishback, 1999; Begley, 2000a, 200b).

- Adults constantly make associations between incoming information and past experiences. Tie a training tidbit to something the learner already knows, and the person is halfway to remembering the key information.

- The adult brain operates simultaneously on many levels; multipath and multimodal experiences are best. For example, when a person crosses a street, the brain sorts out five functions simultaneously: visual pattern movement, shape, velocity, sound, and feelings. Training that operates in less than this engaging manner is often quickly forgotten.

- Memories are not stored intact in one spot in the brain. The information and experience are separated and distributed to different parts of the brain. To retrieve the information, the brain must reassemble it.

- The ability to pay attention during training is affected by fluctuations in brain chemistry during the day. About every ninety minutes, chemicals are released in the brain to allow for retention of incoming information. Giving breaks in training no less than every ninety minutes can improve the ability of the learner to pay attention.

- Optimal learning cycles correspond to our age plus or minus two minutes, up to a maximum of twenty to twenty-five minutes. A learner who is nineteen years old can focus for seventeen to twenty-one minutes. This means that training activities need to change about every twenty-five minutes. The topic or learning objectives might be the same, but the learner is doing something new.

- Learning can be increased by 35 percent with the use of "peripherals"— games, drawings, colors, and sounds to enhance learning.

- Different people use different strategies to accomplish the same thing. So learning needs to provide diversity in its delivery. It is also true that most adults are not consciously aware of their learning or cognitive style.

- Anatomical differences in the male and female brain are opening new windows into how to organize learning for the two genders.

As time goes on and the research grows ever more sophisticated, the way in which we train will be guided as much by brain structure and chemistry information as by the theories promoted by legions of educational professionals for the past hundred years.

Adult Learning Principles

In addition to information on the "hardware" of learning that comes from research on the brain, there is also "software" that provides information on the social and personal things that affect the ability of a volunteer or paid staff person to learn new information. The adult learning principles come from decades of work by authors as disparate as Paulo Freire, Stephen Brookfield, and Dugan Laird, who were operating independently and in different countries. Consequently, experts use an aggregate of principles that affect the ability of adults to absorb new information.

Training developers "need some learning theory upon which to base the activities they specify in the learning systems they create," writes Laird (1985, p. 113). These central principles guide informal learning activities (which is how much training for volunteers is conducted), and trainers who follow and apply the central principles have a greater chance of reaching their objectives and helping individuals grow and learn. The organizing principles mentioned are those for which the most research exists.

Russell Robinson (1994, p. 1) asserts that "the central organizing principles for adult education must be around problems adults face, not subject matter." Children and adults in educational institutions go to school and study subjects. Adults in informal training sessions are interested in solving problems or addressing issues important to their lives. In the case of staff in a nonprofit, paid or unpaid, they want to know how to do the job. A youth organization began its orientation training for new leaders of youth clubs with an hourlong overview of the national, regional, and local structure of the organization. Participant evaluations of the session said things like "I came here to find out what to do with eight twelve-year-old boys next Thursday. You didn't help at all." Most adults have immediate needs—and the hows usually take precedence over the whys. It is essential to determine those needs and set about organizing learning to meet them. (Needs assessment is discussed later in this chapter.)

Adult learners need a sense of ownership over both content and activities in training. They must see and feel a close connection between the topics under discussion and their own role within the organization. By engaging the learner, the trainer achieves two ends: the volunteer or staff member owns the final conclusions, or at least knows where the rules come from, and the learners' perceptions about the policies and how they affect their jobs are shared. "All modern learning theories stress that adults must have a degree of ownership of the learning process . . . and that they want to invest their previous experience in those processes" (Laird, 1985, p. 131). As mentioned earlier, the brain is constantly monitoring incoming information with referral to previous knowledge and experience.

Robinson (1994) assures us that adult learners are enthusiastic participants, desiring hands-on activities. This organizing principle is often incorrectly interpreted to mean that all adult learning must take place in small groups, but this is not so. A more useful descriptive word is *interactive*. To obtain ownership and address immediate needs, many adults want to participate through such activities as discussion; observation of clients, members, or patrons; role playing; demonstration; writing; and taking tests or using assessment tools. Robinson's point is that sitting and listening to someone else talk is not effective in adult education. Adults retain only about 20 percent of what they hear when there is no other participatory activity (Dale, 1969, p.129). Laird says that adult learners want to share their previous experience so that they can apply it. The adult learner is full of resources, ideas, experiences, and knowledge. The trainer's job is to bring the full force of that experience to bear on the job or task at hand. The trainer is not a "teller" of facts but an organizer of learning and a colearner with the trainees.

In reflecting on these organizing principles, one might see the person being trained as supremely confident and organized in the learning environment. The opposite is true. "Adults typically confront educational opportunity and partic- ipate in learning with mixed feelings and even fear" (Smith, 1982, p. 44). As you enter a room of learners, imagine them sitting in their chairs with their per- sonal baggage on the floor around them. The baggage contains such things as their previous educational experiences, their perceived success at learning, their knowledge of the topic or organization, their current life situation, and their adult life stage. Mixed feelings and fear can be reduced by a trainer who un- derstands that the majority of volunteers and staff have some level of anxiety about the impending experience. The sooner the trainer moves ownership of activities into the hands of the learner and addresses their needs, the more the anxiety level is reduced.

Another principle of learning is that of *praxis*. Praxis provides an "opportu- nity for interplay between action and reflection for the student" (Brookfield, 1986, p. 50). Brookfield diagrams it as a circular process (see Figure 25.1). Praxis is always present in an adult learning situation. The trainer's responsi- bility is to help adults bring their previous experience together with new infor- mation. It is the struggle between knowing general principles; exploring new concepts, behaviors, or skills; and applying all of these to a situation. For ex- ample, most adults think they understand the principles of confidentiality. A volunteer working in a hospice-sponsored AIDS residential center called a radio talk show that was focusing on the AIDS epidemic. He didn't mention names but provided enough personal information about one client that anyone casu- ally affiliated with the organization could easily identify the person. The direc- tor of volunteers contacted the volunteer and found that his understanding of

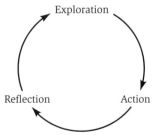

Figure 25.1. Praxis.

Source: Courtesy of Stephen Brookfield. Used by permission.

confidentiality did not go far enough. He thought that by omitting the name, he was following organizational policies (Murrant and Strathdee, 1992).

Robert Smith (1982) summarizes six conditions that must exist for adult learning to take place. First, the adult must feel a need to learn and have some input into the identification of that need. This provides the impetus for the instructional process. Adults resent others orchestrating their lives. They know they have knowledge and experience and want to affect the direction of the instructional activities.

Second, the content of the training must have a perceived relationship to past experience so that what is already known is used as a resource for new learning. Adult learners bring a wealth of experience to the training session. By validating that experience, the trainer validates the person and gives encouragement to use existing knowledge to reach greater levels of knowledge and skill. For example, imagine teaching a group of volunteers how to use a computerized cash register. Some may have high levels of anxiety and no knowledge. An effective way to begin is to ask if anyone in the group has used a pocket calculator or a microwave oven. Many people will say yes. These common appliances are computers, and it is easy to begin the transfer of what the adult already knows to the skill to be learned.

Third, learning is related to the individual adult's developmental stage. Just as children go through stages or cycles, so do adults. McCoy (1977) outlined the developmental stages in the life of an adult: from ages eighteen to twenty-two is "leaving home," twenty-three to twenty-eight is "becoming adult," twenty-nine to thirty-four is "catch thirty," thirty-five to forty-three is "midlife reexamination," forty-four to fifty-five is "restabilization," fifty-six to sixty-four is "preparation for retirement," and sixty-five and older is "retirement." McCoy's work has helped identify the need for trainers of adults to consider developmental stage when planning training. Helping a volunteer or staff member see how learning certain skills can help them in their paid employment works for someone at age thirty-five but has little impact on someone who is seventy-five. A person who is organizing learning activities must take into account the differences in adult developmental stages. As adults evolve, their sense of self and approach to decision making change This development occurs with the interrelationship of cognitive style and intellectual tasks (such as perceiving, thinking, and problem solving) with ego development (feelings about self, impulses, aspirations, and relationships with other people) (Knox, 1986).

Knox is emphatic about the trainer's responsibility to accommodate developmental stages. He points out, for example, that "performance in learning tasks such as rote memory, discovering figurative and mathematical relations, and inductive reasoning steadily declines from young adulthood into old age. Consequently, as adults grow older, they tend to substitute wisdom for brilliance when dealing with intellectual tasks" (1986, p. 22).

Smith's fourth condition for learning to take place is that autonomy in training needs to relate to the autonomy the learner will experience on the job. If volunteers or paid staff are expected to wait on customers and handle monetary transactions with few or no supervisors to oversee the process, training should move them to autonomous performance relatively quickly. Conversely, if a person's work is going to be closely supervised, the most appropriate training methods might be to work with the person and supervisory personnel together and begin the process of building working teams. If the actual supervisory staff are not available, surrogates who can replicate the work situation are needed.

Fifth, attention to the learning climate can reduce anxiety and encourage risk taking. The climate includes the physical amenities, the formality or informality of the trainer, and the environment in which the learning takes place. It is the feeling, atmosphere, and attitude present in the learning situation.

Sixth, diversity of individuals and learning styles needs to be addressed directly by the training activities. Adult needs are often dictated by life circumstance. Volunteers have very practical needs. They want to be comfortable carrying out the assigned task. This common characteristic crosses ethnic, racial, economic, and educational barriers. It presents a common goal for the trainer. The commonality, however, stops at that point. Learning styles vary from person to person.

"The characteristic and preferred way in which an adult engages in learning activities is termed learning style" (Knox, 1986, p. 20). Learning style inventories developed for adults include the Myers-Briggs Type Inventory, Neurolinguistic Communication Profile, Gregorc Style Delineator, and the Group Embedded Figures Test. These instruments measure such things as cognitive style, the processes adults use to interpret new experiences, and the habitual ways in which we conduct learning activities, like goal setting or generating evaluative information (Brookfield, 1990). It is not clear how learning style is related to developmental stages. What is known is that adult learning styles change over time. "Learning ability and style change gradually throughout life. The result is a stable plateau of general earning ability through most of adulthood, but with shifts in what seems important to learn and in how easy it is to master various types of learning tasks" (Knox, 1986, p. 21).

Previous experiences, bad and good, influence the learner. Physical matters such as eyesight, hearing, and disabilities do, too. Lack of attention to the specific concerns of an adult audience is risky business. Knox sums up the application of necessary conditions for the trainer of adults, saying, "Effective teaching depends on being responsive to the learners in the program, not to adults in general" (1986, p. 38).

Creating a hospitable environment for learning is not the only responsibility of the trainer. An understanding of the motivation of adults to learn is also important. Just as their physical and cognitive development changes, adults experience stages in what motivates them to learn. In a model to measure multiple components of motivation, K. Patricia Cross (1981) identifies five steps: (1) engaging in training, (2) retaining skill or knowledge, (3) applying the skill or knowledge, (4) gaining material reward, and (5) gaining symbolic reward. When adults are paid for training, as when staff attend training during working hours, the motivation to learn is enhanced. Trainers recognize, however, that pay alone is not sufficient as a motivator.

Monetary rewards are not always possible for volunteers, but other tangible rewards are. Some trainers of volunteers use donated coupons from retail merchants or restaurant gift certificates as rewards for attending training. In other cases, promotion is contingent on attendance at certain types of training sessions, and the promotion is a motivating reward.

Symbolic rewards such as diplomas and certificates can also be effective in recognizing that a person has completed training. The volunteer coordinator at a large performing arts center decided to offer advanced training for people working at the center's gift shops. Upon completion of training, volunteers received a symbolic reward—a gold star to attach to the nameplates they are required to wear when working. The coordinator launched a publicity campaign with the theme "Ask a Gold Star Volunteer." This had the effect of a material reward: volunteers were stopped by staff and patrons who needed help solving problems. It also had the effect of allowing the volunteers to apply what they had learned in a real situation. The trainer designed a program in which all of the motivational steps were addressed. She followed Laird's admonition: "The ultimate behavior of adult learners is to apply knowledge over a long range of time, not just to acquire and retain it for a few days" (1985, p. 115).

An exception to this principle is the increasing number of episodic or short-term service volunteers. The temporary volunteer comes and goes in a matter of hours. Training for them is quick and brief, rarely rigorous or challenging. Frequently, the training is done by another volunteer with more experience.

The central principles constitute the foundation of all training for adults. They guide the tasks of conducting needs assessments, writing training plans, and evaluating the training. Imagine the central principles as the foundation of a house; without it, a good windstorm and the house might blow over.

CONDUCTING A NEEDS ASSESSMENT

The first step in planning training is to understand the needs of the potential participants. The adult learning principles tell us that learning is more apt to take place if the learner sees the information as relating directly to his or her life. By understanding the discrepancies between what the attendees currently know and what they need to know in order to perform a new job or task, the trainer can make the instruction responsive to learner needs (Knox, 1986). The needs assessment is a process of uncovering information that guides the trainer's planning efforts.

Robinson (1994) identifies three elements that make up a needs assessment. The first is *relevancy*. The content to be discussed and the activities to be undertaken must make sense to the learners attending the training session. For example, a training session for dog walkers at an animal shelter should include contact with the animals. Lectures and pictures are fine, but the learners will be worried about their ability to handle unknown animals of indeterminate size and disposition. The relevant information for the attendees is very practical. It is ideal to ask experienced dog walkers what they needed to know first. It is also useful to check with those who have never done this job about the information they feel they need.

Relationship is the second area to be considered in doing a needs assessment. By this Robinson means that the trainer must learn something about the learners' previous experience with this topic. An experienced trainer was presenting a workshop on leadership skills at a large national conference for volunteer leaders. She was using the Myers-Briggs Type Inventory, a standard psychological instrument that is used to understand the differences in how people take in information and process it. During the introductions, she asked the participants, one by one, what they hoped to learn from the workshop. One member of the group said she was an experienced administrator of the Myers-Briggs Type Inventory and was there to get new ideas about using that tool. Throughout the workshop, the trainer called on this individual to assist in explaining certain concepts and had her lead one of the exercises. The needs assessment at the beginning of class helped the trainer know the experience level of her learners and strive to relate the concepts and theories to real life.

It is important to remember that starting where the learner is and moving forward will enhance learning. It is hooking relevancy to relationship. That can happen only if the trainer determines the learners' needs in advance.

Most learning from early childhood through the teen years places responsibility for organizing and conveying information on the teacher. Children are largely passive participants. Adult learners are aided by the trainer or teacher who helps them take control of their own learning and understand how they learn. The needs assessment process is a means to move control of content and teaching activities into a joint responsibility between the trainer and the learner. Robinson refers to *responsibility* as the third element in needs assessment.

By encouraging learners to take responsibility for participating in the identification of needs, the trainer conveys an interest in moving the responsibility for the actual learning during the training session into the hands of the learners. This is, of course, in addition to giving learners a say in the training course's content and activities.

There are other important processes involved in carrying out a training event. In addition to assessing learners' needs, the trainer will have to prepare a training plan, arrange for the physical facilities and equipment, and present the event. All of this takes time, and time is the first issue in the planning process. How much time is being asked of the volunteer or staff member? The value of a training session can be calculated by taking the hourly wage of staff and multiplying that by the length of the session. The same can be done for volunteers, using wages paid to staff for a comparable job. This tells the cost in time, translated into money. There may be other costs as well, for both the trainer and the trainee; these might include such things as parking or transportation fees, child care, lost work time, clothing costs, and supplies. Even volunteering is never free—for the staff or for the volunteers. A needs assessment must determine the actual costs of being trained.

Needs assessments should also consider such things as the energy demanded of the learners and their physical comfort. Training sessions planned for evening hours are best with a slower pace, but they must be interactive and end at a definite time. Why? The needs assessment might tell you that the evening hours are the most convenient for people with busy daytime schedules, but evening is also the time of the day when most adults' mental energy is sapped. By keeping this in mind, the trainer can organize learning activities that will be active and fun, thus keeping energy levels high just when they might be sinking.

An important consideration for the trainer is physical surroundings. Wheelchair or handicapped access is important. Microphones or headsets are in order for those who might be hearing-impaired. Even the comfort of the chairs can affect the number of breaks the group takes during the training session. The trainer must consider these things in advance of the actual event.

Another key consideration in needs assessment is the type of learning activity planned. How much room is needed? Will people be writing during the session? What special equipment will be needed? (A flashy multimedia presentation at a primitive campsite might flop for want of electricity.) The level of audience expectation about training is also an important factor. Is the audience one that expects some amount of formal presentation or one that expects only interactive groups? Those pieces of information gathered through the needs assessment lead directly to an effective training event.

Sometimes it is possible to contact each person who will be attending a training session to learn of his or her personal needs ahead of time, but more likely the trainer must employ a variety of needs assessment methods at the first meeting to gather information to guide the next training session. Any of the following needs assessment techniques can serve this purpose:

- *Evaluation reports* of previous training sessions should be read and the data compiled for future reference. Today's participants in a training session are excellent representatives of those who will attend the next one.

- *Observation* of actual volunteer and staff jobs is another excellent way of determining needs for training.

- *Incumbents* in the role being trained for are a good source of information about training needs. People who are currently doing the tasks can identify the gaps between what they learned in training and what they needed to know to do the job. This is especially true for the short-term or episodic volunteer. An exit evaluation for this group of volunteers should ask about the training provided.

- *Past participants* (employees or volunteers) are also useful sources of information. They are not so closely connected to the program. Time and distance may have given them perspective on their learning experience.

- *Performance evaluations* are done by many nonprofit organizations for both staff and volunteers. These reports may be useful in the planning of training sessions.

- *Experts* are good sources of ideas. They generally have the most recent information on a topic and can help the trainer bring learners up to date on the latest developments. For example, changes in laws and regulations regarding children happen fast. Contact the individuals most in know.

- *Standard measures* or pretests are a good way to determine learners' knowledge of a topic. These can include tests on the use of machines such as copiers, cash registers, and computers, as well as conceptual knowledge.

An effective way to explore needs is to assemble a surrogate committee to represent the group who will be in the training session. The committee should include people with experience in the organization and people who know nothing about either the organization or the job in question. This meeting can be a short onetime event to get at the issues of relevancy, relationship, and responsibility.

When conducting a needs assessment, it is important to distinguish between training needs and supervisory responsibilities. Sometimes a problem develops with volunteers or staff that is an issue best addressed by the supervisor. The trainer who is doing a needs assessment may be asked to conduct a training session to help eliminate the problem. Laird (1985) contends that performance problems can occur that are not related to training needs. The way to distinguish between the two is to ask whether training is needed to solve the problem. For example, if volunteers report late to a work unit on a regular basis, the problem is not a training problem; it is an issue to be addressed by the supervisor. Having a training session on time management is not going to fix the problem.

Individuals who organize and conduct training must learn to educate others about what is a training need and what is a performance problem. If paid staff are fearful of addressing performance issues with volunteers, for instance, skill training in effective supervision of volunteers can help them overcome the fear. At the same time, they must be encouraged to solve performance problems immediately, as ignoring such problems is frustrating for staff and other volunteers and can even affect clients, members, or patrons.

STAFF AND VOLUNTEER TRAINING

The principles delineated in this chapter apply equally to volunteers and paid staff. The principles of adult learning do not change when a person is paid to attend a training session. However, a common question with regard to the training of paid staff and volunteers is, Should they be trained together? What are the advantages and disadvantages? The decision should be made consciously, rather than haphazardly. Thoughtlessly putting volunteers and paid staff together in the same session has the potential for missing the mark on instruction and offending both groups. If staff and volunteers are trained together, teaching and training activities need to be adjusted to accommodate the presence of both groups. By choosing to train volunteers and staff together, you can send a message about teamwork, planning, cooperative relationships, and the values of the organization or agency. Some training lends itself to being done jointly, such as orientation. Many municipal governments train all new hires at the same time. This puts attorneys, secretaries, garbage collectors, and social workers together in the same session.

One of the issues to address when training volunteers and paid staff together is timing. Quite often training for volunteers must be scheduled for evenings, early mornings, weekends, or lunchtime. Such time slots are designed to accommodate the volunteers, more than 50 percent of whom are employed outside the home. These are often not convenient times for the paid staff. They might also be costly to the organization if overtime must be paid. So time of training is a factor in who will attend.

Content is another issue that determines who might attend. If the topic is medical benefits, insurance, and retirement options, it is likely that the training session would be held for paid staff. If the content deals with job roles, a joint training session is ideal. Murrant and Strathdee (1992) report on a nurse working full-time in a hospital setting who agreed to volunteer at an AIDS residential treatment center. As a volunteer, her role was defined by the nurse or medical professional on duty; she was not a decision maker. In her paid job as a nurse, she was in a leadership position. After a while, she became uncomfortable with this role reversal. Her role at the residential center could have been effectively clarified in a joint volunteer–paid staff training session.

If the decision is made to train staff and volunteers separately, the quality and content of the sessions need to be consistent. Trainers for both groups need to work together to ensure consistency. An excellent way to provide new job challenges to experienced volunteers is to have them lead training sessions. This also gives the person coordinating volunteers some relief from the time needed to plan, organize, and implement training. But volunteers, like anyone providing training, need to be involved in discussions about quality and content.

Many nonprofit organizations provide little or no training for people who supervise volunteers. Supervisory training is usually available only to those who oversee paid workers. This policy sends a message to staff that supervising volunteers "doesn't really count." Anyone who works with volunteers has management and supervisory responsibilities and should be trained accordingly. This is an ideal situation for training volunteers and paid staff together. Often volunteers are in the position of supervising other volunteers, and many paid staff supervise only volunteers. This training includes such topics as the motivation of volunteers, roles and responsibility of the supervisor in relationship to an unpaid workforce, formal and informal recognition strategies, and techniques of evaluating volunteer performance.

FORMAL AND INFORMAL TRAINING

"Volunteer managers train on a daily basis. Whenever a volunteer is asked to do something new, or change past behavior, teaching and learning are at work. The volunteer is the learner and the volunteer program manager is the teacher" (Macduff, 1988, p. 38). Most people think of training as what happens in a classroom setting or in an on-the-job "here's how you do it" session. In fact, a nonprofit organization is conveying messages to potential staff and volunteers long before they are hired to work. The first informal contacts come during recruitment and screening. "A key feature of the recruitment process is the imparting of information about a volunteer-based program to rouse people's interest and ultimately persuade them to volunteer" (Ilsley and Niemi, 1981, p. 45).

The first contact with your organization may be through a printed brochure, a Web site, a volunteer center ad about positions at the organization, a radio announcement, or a want-ad listing. The principles of adult learning apply to those early contacts just as they do to the planning of learning activities. Robinson's tests of relevancy, relationship, and responsibility are good tools to use when evaluating whether the message you think you are sending is the one likely being received.

Volunteers and paid staff are the biggest recruiters of other volunteers. Do you train those people in the appropriate things to say to prospective applicants? Have you developed a brochure for staff and volunteers to use when they are talking to their friends about the positions available in your organization? By doing these things, you can exert more control over the first formal training effort your organization offers to the people it recruits. This is especially important when a volunteer brings to an event or activity a friend who might volunteer episodically. The current volunteer needs to know how the organization deals with short-term or episodic volunteers, and that's something the volunteer can know only if informed about it by the manager of volunteer programs.

Minimal information needed by staff and volunteers are the mission statement; information about clients, members, or patrons served; hours required to give full-time service; application process for volunteer or staff jobs; telephone and fax numbers; and address. If the information is written so as to appeal to adults, there is a greater chance that the training you want to happen will take place.

Screening of prospective volunteers and paid staff usually includes the completion of an application, an interview, and the signing of some type of work agreement. The interview and work agreement allow the manager to establish the role of formal training in the organization. Training and job expectations are communicated and clarified.

This step is especially important to volunteers. If the organizational message is "You don't need to worry about attending training sessions," training will have a low priority for the volunteer. Applications should ask questions about availability for training, interviews should include reviews of the different types of training (on-the-job, orientation, and in-service), and the contract should be clear as to expectations related to training. People cannot be expected to attend educational sessions without being informed as to why doing so is important to them and to the organization.

Training for temporary service volunteers, such as those working at an event or a fundraising activity, is usually done right at the time of service. One way in which this is done is to train experienced volunteers to train those giving temporary service. The experienced volunteer is trained in advance and carries out his or her duties during the event by preparing the inexperienced. This frees paid staff to do more demanding tasks.

Virtual volunteers, whose service is given online, are presenting new challenges in training. Virtual volunteers rarely meet face to face with the managers of volunteer programs, yet they need training. As with the long-term service volunteer, the intake process is the time to begin training.

There needs to be a clear position description with qualifications spelled out, duties listed, and time for training indicated. There should also be an explanation of how training is to be conducted. It seems obvious that to run a virtual volunteer program means an organization has to develop, design, and launch online learning modules.

E-learning modules need to follow the same principles as have been outlined in this chapter to this point. Relevancy, relationship, and responsibility apply in cyberspace, too. The content needs to be relevant to what learners already know and what they need to learn to carry out the task. Intake for a volunteer should include skill and knowledge identification. The relationship between what prospective volunteers already know and what they need to know is a means to determine where training begins. The responsibility for training is joint, with the volunteers and the manager of volunteers discussing how training is to be designed and carried out. Some organizations go so far as not placing virtual volunteers until they have successfully completed training, which can include testing.

Formal training is a learning event, with objectives, a training plan, and methods of evaluation. A trainer may be part of the presentation, but not necessarily. Volunteers and staff can learn from interactive videos, workbooks, audiocassettes, or other media. These are, however, planned and prepared in exactly the same fashion as a face-to-face training session. "Portable" training sessions that use technology are an important growth area for nonprofit organizations. It is especially crucial for organizations whose staff and volunteers are spread over large geographical distances or whose volunteer pool is large. The development of e-learning capacity with the volunteer program is an essential part of planning for the future. It is not just the virtual volunteer that can be trained online. Shortening the time to train, through the use of electronic methods, means that volunteers can go to work fast. Large volunteer programs that offer training only twice a year could move people into service sooner with the availability of e-learning. E-learning is a specialized form of education, requiring a skilled and knowledgeable person to develop it for maximum effectiveness. Putting current books online and expecting people to sit and read on their computer is not e-learning; it is just bad educational planning. The wise organization either develops internal education specialists or contracts with reputable individuals or companies to create e-learning modules.

Some nonprofit organizations use formal training as part of the screening process. A large performing arts center has learned that by requiring pre-assignment training participation, they weed out people who are not truly interested in the commitment required to be a volunteer. They offer weekday and weekend all-day training sessions for individuals who have completed an application and have expressed an interest in becoming a volunteer. They lose between 25 and 35 percent of the applicants before actual assignments are made. This preassignment formal training session saves both time and money for the staff and for the volunteers.

Most nonprofit organizations provide an orientation for staff and volunteers after they have been hired but before they begin actual work assignments. This is an opportunity to have volunteers and staff in one training session. The material covered in an orientation is usually similar for staff and volunteers. It includes such things as tours of the facility, introductions to key personnel (including supervisory staff), an organizational overview, policies on confidentiality, appropriate attire, parking, security of personal belongings, the relationship between volunteers and paid staff, and methods of recording work hours.

The issue of benefits is different for volunteers and paid staff, but most programs offer some "perks" for volunteers.

Part of the orientation is job-related. Volunteers and paid staff are anxious to learn about their specific job assignment. This training can be done during the orientation or at a second session. The challenge in the orientation is to provide enough information to give people the confidence to go to their work assignment ready to work and to help them feel confident enough to ask questions and listen to the experts who are their supervisors and colleagues.

Formal training does not stop with orientation, nor does informal training end with an on-the-job explanation of duties by the supervisor. Continuing in-service education is a part of all successful nonprofit organizations. Nothing in any organization or agency is static. Social trends, client needs, membership services, and staffing patterns require constant change and updating. The foundation for active participation in in-service training begins with the first contact with staff, paid and unpaid, and continues as long as the person is affiliated with the organization. In-service education programs are designed to enhance current job skills, build new skills, and train the person for expanded duties. In-service training might also include opportunities for personal development, such as stress management, time management, conflict management, and reduction of burnout.

Another area often missed by nonprofits is training in organizational change. Volunteers are sometimes the last to hear about important structural changes. This sends a powerful message about the importance of volunteers to the mission of the organization or agency. It is much better to arrange for in-service education programs to keep volunteers and staff fully informed about such changes as downsizing, staff restructuring, or major changes in client, member, or patron services.

Some nonprofit organizations provide clinic-type in-service programs for volunteers and paid staff. Hospice is a notable example. Hospice volunteers are expected to attend monthly meetings where specific problems are discussed and policy and procedural changes are reviewed. The primary focus is to bring staff and volunteers with the most direct client contact together. The sessions usually have an organized formal training component, but the bulk of the time is devoted to talking about the personal impact of the clients on the volunteers or staff members. In doing this, hospice has reduced its loss of volunteers due to burnout. This type of in-service training is especially useful when the emotional toll of the work on the volunteers or staff is high.

ORGANIZING TRAINING ACTIVITIES FOR EFFECTIVENESS

Planning training activities begins with concern for the learning climate. Carl Rogers says, "Trainers should be as concerned with their relationship with students as they are about the content of the course" (quoted in Laird, 1985, p. 178). This is not to suggest that teaching or training is in any way a popularity contest. It means that the teacher cares enough about the relationship with the learners to make certain that each person achieves all of the desired learning objectives. In some cases, this requires nudging people away from their comfort zones into uncharted territory.

Climate Setting

Once the needs assessment is complete, the trainer must focus on organizing a training plan. The training plan begins with attention to the climate. Climate is made up of five things: responsiveness, respect, reasons, options, and proficiencies (Knox, 1986).

Responsive teachers are those who consider the needs of diverse learners when organizing their training plan. The needs assessment helps them organize the content so that visual, auditory, or kinesthetic learners can absorb it. Responsive teachers factor in physical differences, disabilities, age, previous experience, culture, ethnicity, and developmental life stage into their plan.

Respect means that the trainer views his or her role as that of colearner. Trainers of adult learners know that learners have information and experience to offer in the learning situation. They support, encourage, and honor learners, never ignoring or ridiculing them.

A guiding principle in all adult learning is the importance of making the content relevant to the learners' lives. Adults have a variety of *reasons* for attending training sessions. The trainer's job is to organize the training plan so that learners' needs are met and participants know early on how and when the topics they are concerned about will be covered. It is almost as if the trainer plans around the question "When will you get to the issue I came to talk about?"

Lectures, small groups, or demonstrations are different types of teaching techniques. Some learners prefer one over the others. An effective trainer provides *options* for learners so that there are different activities during the session (Knox, 1986).

Proficiencies refers not only to ensuring each learner's competency in the skills or concepts being taught but relates as well to the proficiency of the trainer in terms of both content and process. Learner and teacher must know the skills needed to function on the job. There must be time to practice those skills during the training and the opportunity to evaluate each person's abilities.

Trainers must be well versed in the content they present. Staying current is a must. It is also essential that trainers learn as much as possible about adult education and continually enhance and improve their skills in creating a learning environment.

The Lesson Plan

Bringing the needs assessment, principles of adult education, and content together in a cohesive whole is the training design, and its written format is the training plan. Laird and other authors on adult education call the training plan a "lesson plan." The lesson plan consists of six elements: the purpose, the learning objectives, the time allotted for specific activities, a detailed explanation of the activities designed to accomplish the learning objective, the techniques used to evaluate learner performance (summative and formative), and the resources needed to carry out the training activities. Exhibit 25.1 is an example of a form that can be used to record the lesson plan.

Purpose. The *purpose* is an overview of the things that are to be accomplished by the training session. For example, "The purpose of the orientation training is to acquaint volunteers and paid staff with an overview of this organization and their places in it." The statement of purpose is usually global in scope and does not need to be measurable.

Learning Objectives. Robert Mager (1984) says that instruction is of little use if it doesn't change anyone; it has no effect and no power. The only way to ensure that change has occurred is to begin by identifying behaviors or knowledge that the learner must possess before leaving the training session. The written objective describes that behavior. An *objective* is a description of a performance you want learners to be able to exhibit before you consider them competent. "An objective describes an intended result of instruction, rather than the process of instruction itself" (p. 3). For example, if the CEO and board president were creating a lesson plan for board orientation, one learning objective might be

Exhibit 25.1. Training or Lesson Plan.

Purpose of this session: _____

Learning Objective	Time	Teaching Activity	Evaluation	Resources (handouts, overheads, supplies)

"The learner will be able to identify the six areas of responsibility of members of the board of directors: legal, financial, personnel, public relations, asset management, and risk management." This learning objective says that the two trainers will have tested the knowledge of the learners before they leave the training session to determine their understanding of the six areas of responsibility. (Mager's book, *Preparing Instructional Objectives,* is an excellent self-study guide to writing objectives.)

Few people who train volunteers and staff have education courses in their background and thus rarely write learning objectives to guide their training plan. This can lead to a lack of focus and an inability to determine the effects of the training session. It can also lead to an incredible waste of time. Writing the learning objectives is the equivalent of zeroing in on the content to be covered, the most effective means of conveying the material, and the best way of evaluating the learners' grasp of the material. It is the single most important step in designing a lesson plan.

Learning objectives are always written from the point of view of the learner; they never describe what the trainer will do. There are no rules for how many learning objectives are needed for a given length of time, but it is reasonable to assume that a four-hour training session would have no more than four learning objectives.

Time. In the process of organizing and sequencing the teaching activities (discussed in the next section), the trainer should figure out the time required and record it on the written lesson plan. Whether to record the running time for the session or the actual time for each activity is a matter of personal preference.

Training Activities. "Training is the subsystem that acquaints people with material and technology. It helps them learn how to use the material in an approved fashion that allows the organization to reach its desired output" (Laird, 1985, p. 6). The basic function of training is to help the volunteer or staff person get control of his or her job. This control comes through activities that are designed to achieve the learning objectives. They define and demonstrate the right way to do the job by means of standards, models, and examples of the job done properly. They should acquaint the learners with the written and unwritten "laws" that govern the jobs they will be doing. Volunteers delivering midday meals to shut-ins, for example, need to know whether they should stop and visit for twenty minutes at each location or move quickly to deliver hot food.

Training activities must also help learners identify the differences in their current level of knowledge and the skills they need to acquire. Training boards and advisory groups is challenging. The learners in these sessions are often community leaders, who feel they have a good understanding of the roles and responsibilities of boards and advisory committees. How can a training plan be organized to help them identify the gap between what they know and what they need to learn?

One trainer divides the members of a board into three small groups. She makes one of the subgroups a nonprofit board, another is a board for a for-profit hospital, and the third is an advisory group to a government agency in the community. Each board is given two problems. In the first problem, an individual has fallen in a facility owned or leased by the organization. The person is in the hospital and may die. In the second problem, the organization's money is drying up, and significant program cutbacks and layoffs of paid staff may be required if something isn't done soon. The groups are told to imagine that they have been called together in an emergency meeting to address these issues. Participants are to identify the roles and responsibilities of the group to which they were assigned at the beginning of the exercise. Each "board" discusses its problems separately, and then the trainer stops everyone to ask some of the following questions: Who had legal responsibilities? Who had personal responsibilities? What and why? Who is responsible for coming up with needed funds?

This exercise has several consequences. Board or advisory members who are being trained suddenly realize that they do not share the same roles and responsibilities and that each person has brought different "baggage" to the training session. Individuals' previous experiences are validated by giving all participants the opportunity to discuss their solutions to the problems, but these views are tempered by peers who add their current knowledge. The trainer serves as devil's advocate and resource person. The exercise ends with the distribution and discussion of information on appropriate roles and responsibilities for the nonprofit organization in question and an organizational chart.

In this example, the teaching activity has helped the learners identify the gaps in their knowledge and begin to see what they can do to close the gap between what they thought they knew and what they need to know in order to function effectively as board members. This type of activity helps create a receptiveness toward the remaining material.

Adults learn "in layers," and the lesson plan must accommodate that fact. Once adults see the gap in their skill or knowledge, they must be given the material and time to close the gap. Trainers quite often resort to the lecture format because they can cover a great deal of material with it. And that is true: they are covering the material! However, the learner is not working with the material or processing the information. If there is one irrefutable rule in teaching adults, it is to get them involved in an interactive teaching activity as quickly as possible.

Trainers must be reasonable in what they expect adults to retain. They must establish realistic learning objectives given the time, resources, skills, and previous experiences of the learners. Effectively pacing a training plan depends on having clear data from the needs assessment and a realistic approach to what can be accomplished in a two-hour training session.

"One crucial aspect of the teaching/learning transaction is the way you sequence learning activities for progression," writes Knox (1986, p. 9). In the example of board members who were being trained to understand their organizational role, suppose the session began with a lecture by a risk management expert. It is unlikely that the board members would grasp the connection between their roles and risk management issues. The most effective way to arrange the sequence of activities is to plan them with the learning objectives. Write them out on small cards and arrange them in a logical progression, from basic information to more complex concepts.

Nonprofit organizations have three basic modes in which they train: individual, small group (less than fifty), and large groups (more than fifty). Different training activities are needed, depending on the size of the group. For individual learners, effective techniques and devices include such things as coaching, computer-assisted instruction (CAI), correspondence, e-learning, reading, television, and tutoring. For large groups, some of the most effective techniques and devices are lectures, panels, debates, subgroup discussion, and forums. Small groups are especially responsive to discussions, seminars, case study analyses, simulations, role playing, and demonstrations (Knox, 1986). There are certainly a wealth of other techniques and devices available, including skits, field trips, programmed instruction, brainstorming, nominal groups, "buzz groups," games, clinics, overhead projections, flipcharts, whiteboards, videotaped programs, audiocassettes, slide shows, puzzles, handouts, and photographs.

Adults generally prefer learning that is interactive. Interactive learning is not necessarily limited to groups, although there seems to be a rush to put all volunteer and staff training into the format of small discussion groups. "Interactive" means that the learner interacts with the information or skill to be learned. Knowledge about the history and organizational structure of a nonprofit could be interactively taught to adults through the use of a crossword puzzle and a video. For example, learners would receive a crossword puzzle at the beginning of a training session. The puzzle would be based on a history of the organization and its current structure. In working through the puzzle, the learners laugh, struggle, and are encouraged to share answers with their neighbors. *Fun* is the operative word. Then a video describing the history of the organization and its structure is shown to the group. Afterward, the learners are allowed more time to complete their puzzles. Closure comes with a discussion of the correct answers to the key points (the learning objectives) and any unanswered questions. This is an example of interactive learning but not a small group activity.

Less experienced trainers need to be wary of using small groups. The interpersonal dynamics unleashed in small groups are fraught with peril, and even the most experienced teachers can have a bad time with them. Small group work is an effective means to learning for the vast majority of adults, but the trainer must be comfortable with all aspects of this teaching technique. "The fundamental criterion in selecting a learning method should be the appropriateness of the method to the learning objective," Laird writes (1985, p. 130). The learning objective should tell the trainer whether a small group is an appropriate technique to use. The trainer must then figure out how to physically move the learners into groups and how to provide instructions for the assigned task. Then the trainer must consider what to do while the groups are working: Stand still and observe? Walk around and consult? And perhaps the most important issue for the trainer is how to bring the participants out of the small groups and launch into providing validation, new information, closure, and review. "The undoubted value of small group work is lost almost entirely if you rush into this too early in the belief that students will feel insulted by your obvious authoritarianism if you don't," counsels Brookfield (1990, p. 61).

Evaluating Learner Performance. "Just as needs assessment is viewed as the overture to the program development process, so evaluation becomes its final movement," writes Brookfield (1986, p. 261). Preparing the training lesson plan involves designing formative and summative evaluation techniques. Formative evaluations are done during the training to allow for midcourse corrections. Summative evaluations are done after the training is completed to ensure that the objectives were achieved.

"Evaluative models applied to adult learning tend to be drawn from secondary school or higher education settings and then adapted to the circumstances of adult learners. Rarely are they grounded in or reflective of the concepts, philosophies, and processes of adult learning" (Brookfield, 1986, p. 262). Many adult educators argue for the inclusion of learners in the evaluation process. They argue that the participatory nature of teaching techniques that are most effective in adult learning situations must be used in evaluating the learning. Adults in training sessions must also learn how to evaluate their success. Brookfield (1986) is "compelled by the argument for participatory evaluations," but says, "The educator who abrogates responsibility for setting evaluative criteria to participants is guilty of professional misconduct" (p. 277).

Practicality suggests that teacher and learner need to be engaged in evaluative processes together. Time and activities need to be provided as part of the training plan to allow learners time for reflection, for comparing skill or knowledge acquisition with preestablished standards, to apply the relevant skill or knowledge, and to engage in mutual feedback with the trainer with regard to skills and knowledge covered in the training session. This ongoing process needs to be planned simultaneously with the activities.

Formative Evaluation Techniques. Dick and Carey (1985) define formative evaluation as "the process instructors use to obtain data in order to revise their instruction to make it more efficient and effective" (p. 198). They assert that the formative evaluation process is essentially positive, constructive, and non-judgmental. They suggest several types of formative evaluation, many of which are included in a needs assessment. They include such things as field tests, small group evaluation, and one-to-one evaluation. It is also essential that formative evaluation be done during the actual training sessions. The following are a small sample of formative evaluation techniques:

- When planning a discussion group, write out the expected responses in advance. As reports are presented from groups, review the list to ensure that all appropriate topics have been covered.
- Create learning activities in which learners are evaluating their own and a partner's performance on information or skill to be learned.
- Solicit and record comments or notes made by learners with regard to instructional material, explaining where they encountered difficulties.
- Appoint learner review teams. These groups do periodic reviews to provide midtraining assessments of the material to be learned up to the point of the review.

Summative Evaluation Techniques. "The process of evaluation is essentially the process of determining to what extent the educational objectives are actually being realized . . . since educational objectives are essentially changes in human beings," wrote Tyler in 1949. He went on, "Evaluation is the process for determining the degree to which these changes in behavior are actually taking place" (p. 110). It is the summative evaluation that in fact measures quantitatively and qualitatively the learners' progress in meeting the learning objectives. It is the device for determining if the training has been successful and effective. The following are some types of summative evaluation tools:

- Pretest and posttest comparative scores
- Tabulations of such things as units of work per hour, units of work per volunteer or employee, tasks completed, personnel turnover, or dollar value per task completed
- Self-reported proficiencies by participants in the training session
- Observations of trainees on the job

Resources. The last part of the training lesson plan is the list of resources and supplies essential to the delivery of the training program. This should include such things as equipment, handouts, overheads, flipchart displays, pencils, and markers. By including these details in the lesson plan, the trainer reduces the chances of arriving at the scene of training only to discover that some essential item has been forgotten.

THE COST OF TRAINING

A lesson plan must consider the cost of training. A budget for training events must include the cost of equipment rental, resources for learners, trainer fees, room rental, staff time, food and beverages, and supplies. Training is often just another one of the duties delegated to the organization's staff. Some larger nonprofits have training departments, but they are few. It is rare to see "training" as a line item for in-house costs. Usually that item refers to the expenses of sending paid staff and volunteers to training away from the main office.

Budgets can help in determining whether the current training events and training plans are the wisest use of resources. A large volunteer program offered an orientation to prospective volunteers each month on a Saturday. The cost included room and equipment rental, supplies, beverages, and compensatory time for paid staff. Attendance ranged from twenty-five to thirty-five individuals most Saturdays. A budget analysis revealed that the actual and indirect costs were higher than they had at first appeared. The CEO, the paid staff responsible for training, and volunteers decided to experiment with four sessions per year. A needs assessment was completed, and the training plan was redesigned to accommodate more learners. Projected group size was between sixty-five and eighty.

In this case, the organization saved considerable staff time and equipment and supply expenses. Careful monitoring has shown little change in the volunteer program. Even though a person volunteering today may not be placed for two months, the dropout rate is close to what it was with the one-per-month training schedule. The size of the group presented challenges to paid staff and volunteers, who were used to training smaller groups. As they tested and refined the presentation, however, the group of volunteers responsible for training wanted to offer new large group in-service training sessions. Their experience in the orientation training gave them both the knowledge and the courage to try out activities with a larger group. "Decisions about teaching activity are multidimensional. They involve the learning objective, the inventory of the learners, and the norms of the organization, to say nothing of the available budget" (Laird, 1985, p. 130).

An issue for nonprofit organizations is the need for alternatives to face-to-face training. Statistics show a growing need to accommodate volunteers interested in short-term assignments or virtual volunteer assignments (J. C. Penney and National Volunteer Center, 1989). Many volunteer groups are serving population segments in geographically and culturally diverse communities. English may not be the language of choice for some volunteers. These issues are prompting many organizations to consider the use of technology in training, especially interactive video, e-learning, and television downlinks. The principles of adult education and the techniques needed to create a training plan are no different when a technological delivery system is used. If anything, the individuals responsible for expending training dollars must determine that the training is in fact planned in a careful way. An interactive video can cost $20,000 and up. E-learning courses are especially susceptible to the "just put it up on the Web" philosophy. Violating the principles of learning described in this chapter and producing a videotape or an e-leaning course based on wishful thinking could be a costly mistake.

COMPETENCIES OF THE TRAINER

"The teacher is not so much a purveyor of knowledge . . . [as] a facilitator, an encourager of another's finding the knowledge for himself" (Robinson, 1994, p. 56). A trainer cannot make adults learn. Each individual learner controls his or her own learning. The ability of the trainer lies in creating an environment that encourages discovery. It is forming a setting where it is impossible *not* to learn. Adult views of training are often rooted in childhood formal educational experiences. As trainers and learners, it is challenging to change that image.

The person who is responsible for training needs to see that role as one of enabler, facilitator, guide, encourager—rarely as teller of facts. Sometimes the most challenging part of training is waiting while learners grope toward answers when it would be so easy to just give the answers out. It is in discovery that learning takes place—for adults and for trainers. Trainers must know the answers unequivocally and in depth. Then they can help guide the learning struggle in productive ways. This requires competencies beyond "I know this and will tell it to you." "The competencies vary from understanding of adult learning to computer competency, from questioning skills to presentation skills, from futuring skills to library skills, and from cost-benefit analysis skills to group process skills," writes Laird (1985, p. 14).

In *The Skillful Teacher* (1990, pp. 192–211), Brookfield offers "truths" about skillful teaching. The following list is adapted to apply to the training prepared and delivered in nonprofit organizations.

- *Be clear about the purpose of your training.* From on-the job training to an orientation for new volunteers, the individual responsible for the training should have a written purpose for the training session.
- *Reflect on your own learning.* You are a biased trainer. Understand how you like to learn and then work against it. Most trainers teach the way they like to learn. As they plan a training activity, they mentally evaluate it based on their own preferences. The audience is diverse, and each person has his or her learning style. By understanding your own learning preferences, you can broaden the choices you offer learners.

- *Welcome ambiguity.* Despite the best efforts to apply a systematic and rational process in addressing training issues, the actual training is a journey into uncertainty. Trainers often cross the borders of chaos into zones of ambiguity. Even when there is a well-designed training plan based on a needs assessment, the teacher can experiences outcomes that confound explanation. The effective trainer needs to welcome those experiences and realize that ambiguity is part of learning.

- *Perfection is impossible.* Striving to be better from training session to training session is an admirable trait. Thinking perfection is possible can only frustrate. Adult participants will be different, and that makes each training event new and challenging. Some events will be better than others. The ambiguity of learning makes perfection in training sessions an impossible and unrealistic goal.

- *Know your learners.* Research the learners' backgrounds, including how they experience learning. This is more important than ever in our diverse society. The more the trainer knows about volunteers, staff, board members, clients, members, or patrons, the better the chance of organizing learning to meet their needs and attain organizational goals.

- *Talk to your colleagues.* Training is carried out in all nonprofit organizations and agencies. Find out what others are doing. It is especially important to talk to people who provide a different type of service. There is much to be learned from those who do not see the world from your perspective.

- *Trust your instincts.* Use all your faculties to assess your progress as a trainer. Listen and observe the learners in the training session and at work. Touch the things they will touch. Immerse yourself in the learning, and then trust your sense of what works and what doesn't.

- *Create diversity.* Seek a variety of methods and techniques and devices to address the same learning objective. Experiment with different models, and encourage your learners to do the same.

- *Take risks.* Model for others in your organization that risk taking is acceptable. Modeling is one of the most powerful training tools.

- *Accept the emotionality of learning.* Learning the simplest task is not a sterile experience. Brain research shows us that the emotional centers in the brain are incredibly active when someone is learning (Fishback, 1999). Learners report their experiences using highly emotional terms. Exploration of new territory, being a board president, chairing a committee, serving as a direct service volunteer, staffing a work team, accessing services of a nonprofit organization—all present threats to self-esteem as the individual explores new and difficult knowledge and skills. When training people to take on new challenges, acknowledge the emotionality of the experience.

- *Learning satisfaction is not the only evaluation.* Be wary of the evaluations at the end of a training session. Learning is often defined as a change in behavior. Change is painful and is resisted by most adults. Happy learners who have never had their knowledge, skills, values, or beliefs challenged are not necessarily "trained." Likewise, hostile evaluations should not be given any greater weight than positive ones. Remember that learning is emotional, and if the training experience was challenging, the learner may be experiencing pain and anxiety. Sometimes volunteers work for a year or two before recognizing the value of the early training they received. This is why needs assessments are such an important evaluation tool.

• *Balance supporting and challenging the learner.* This is the most difficult training skill to develop. By trusting your instincts, you get better at creating a balance between the support of sometimes fragile egos and the challenge of exploring alternative perspectives. Challenge for challenge's sake rarely teaches anything but hostility. Volunteers are not a captive audience; they can choose to avoid future training sessions.

• *Recognize the significance of your actions in all aspects of your job.* View yourself as a helper of learning.

SUMMARY

Training is a regular activity for nonprofit organizations. Staff and volunteers are a team delivering both formal and informal training to one another, the community, clients, members, and patrons. The best training creates a team of staff and volunteers who use adult education principles as a guide. The team of trainers conducts needs assessments, which produce information about potential learners and their individual needs. The assessments draw on issues of diversity, costs, competencies, relevancy, responsibility, and relationship for each learner. Once training needs have been determined, decisions are made to present informal training opportunities or organize formal training events. Organizing the training activities includes determining the purpose, assessing and planning for a nourishing learning climate, writing learning objectives, designing training activities, planning to evaluate learner performance, and arranging for appropriate resources. Individuals with training responsibilities must be attentive to their style of training and how it fosters a climate of healthy adult learning.

References

Begley, S. "Getting Inside a Teen Brain." *Newsweek,* Feb. 29, 2000a, pp 58–59.

Begley, S. "Mind Expansion: Inside the Teenage Brain," *Newsweek,* May 8, 2000b, p. 68.

Brookfield, S. D. *Understanding and Facilitating Adult Learning: A Comprehensive Analysis of Principles and Effective Practices.* San Francisco: Jossey-Bass, 1986.

Brookfield, S. D. *The Skillful Teacher: On Technique, Trust, and Responsiveness in the Classroom.* San Francisco: Jossey-Bass, 1990.

Colburn, Don. "The Infinite Brain." *Washington Post-Health Magazine,* Sept. 28, 1999, pp. 12–17.

Cross, K. P. *Adults as Learners: Increasing Participation and Facilitating Learning.* San Francisco: Jossey-Bass, 1981.

Dale, E. *Audio-Visual Methods in Teaching.* (3rd ed.) Austin, Tex.: Holt, Rinehart and Winston, 1969.

Dick, W., and Carey, L. *The Systematic Design of Instruction.* (2nd ed.) Glenview, Ill.: Scott, Foresman, 1985.

Fishback, S. J. "Learning and the Brain." *Adult Learning,* Apr. 1999, pp. 18–22.

Ilsley, P. J., and Niemi, J. A. *Recruiting and Training Volunteers.* New York: McGraw-Hill, 1981.

J. C. Penney and National Volunteer Center. *Report on Volunteering in America.* Arlington, Va.: National Volunteer Center, 1989.

Johnson, G. "How Much Give Can the Brain Take?" *New York Times,* Oct. 24, 1999, pp. 1–6

Knox, A. B. *Helping Adults Learn: A Guide to Planning, Implementing, and Conducting Programs.* San Francisco: Jossey-Bass, 1986.

Laird, D. *Approaches to Training and Development.* Boston: Addison-Wesley, 1985.

Macduff, N. "Training Adult Volunteers." *Journal of Volunteer Administration,* 1988, *6*(3), 38–39.

Mager, R. F. *Preparing Instructional Objectives.* Belmont, Calif.: David Lake, 1984.

McCoy, V. R. "Adult Life Cycle Tasks." In *Lifelong Learning: The Adult Years.* Washington, D.C.: American Association of Adult and Continuing Educators, 1977.

Murrant, G., and Strathdee, S. "AIDS, Hospice, and Volunteers: Casey House Volunteer Program." *Journal of Volunteer Administration,* 1992, *10*(4), 11–17.

Reardon, M. "The Brain: Navigating the New Reality: An Exploration of Brain-Compatible Learning." *Adult Learning,* Apr. 1999, pp. 10–17.

Robinson, R. D. *An Introduction to Helping Adults Learn and Change.* (rev. ed.) West Bend, Wis.: Omnibooks, 1994.

Smith, R. M. *Learning How to Learn.* New York: Cambridge University Press, 1982.

Tyler, R. W. *Basic Principles of Curriculum and Instruction.* Chicago: University of Chicago Press, 1949.

"Why the Female Brain Is Like a Swiss Army Knife." *USA Weekend,* Jan. 1, 1999.

Widmer, C. "Why Board Members Participate." *Journal of Voluntary Action Research,* 1985, *14*(4), 8–23.

CONCLUSION: THE FUTURE OF NONPROFIT MANAGEMENT

Robert D. Herman

As I reflect on the variety, depth, and scope of information presented in the preceding chapters, I am again reminded of how great a challenge effective nonprofit leadership and management are. Changes since the publication of the first edition of this book suggest that the challenge is in some ways greater, though many nonprofit organizations and the people who lead and manage them are achieving much.

It is impossible to summarize the detailed information contained in the foregoing chapters, and rather than try to do so in this concluding chapter, I will again, as in the first edition, use it to reflect on a couple of key themes, particularly in relation to the future of nonprofit management. The future of nonprofit management would seem to be very rosy. As Lester Salamon describes in Chapter Four, the number and revenues of U.S. nonprofit organizations continue to grow. Also, the number of universities offering degree programs in nonprofit management continues to increase, as do specialist professional and academic journals devoted to nonprofit management. All this indicates a professional field in progressive development. Nonetheless, the idea and practice of nonprofit management may be short-lived. Undoubtedly, nonprofit organizations will continue to exist and even continue to increase, as there are definite advantages to the "ownerless" nonprofit form, but will management in nonprofit organizations continue to be distinct? Will nonprofit management continue to exist?

As Lester Salamon and Cynthia Massarsky observe in Chapters Four and Eighteen, respectively, many public service nonprofit organizations have adapted to the challenges of recent decades by increasing their efforts to earn income. Some of this is perhaps just increasing the amount earned from fees and other standard charges, but clearly efforts to create new ventures (even if they are mission-related and thus not subject to unrelated business income tax and also hard to find on the Forms 990 filed by U.S. nonprofit organizations with the IRS) have also increased dramatically. Many foundations and other funders and donors are actively encouraging public service nonprofit organizations to become more commercial and more businesslike. "Venture philanthropists" are promoting a "business model" for nonprofit organizations. No doubt the increasingly popular view that business and market values are appropriate for nonprofit organizations in part represents the triumphalism of U.S.-style capitalism at the turn of the twenty-first century (notwithstanding the spectacular instances of business malfeasance).

As a result of the spreading use of commercial activities and of thinking and acting in market terms, will nonprofit leaders and managers come to identify themselves as fundamentally like leaders and managers in business? The answer is, of course, unknowable, and much will depend on social, political, and economic trends and events that are not yet obvious. Here I want to raise some questions about the possible consequences of the disappearance of nonprofit management and suggest some actions that might possibly promote a distinct nonprofit management model (and explain why I think that is desirable).

One very good reason to suspect that nonprofit management will not disappear is that nonprofit organizations will not disappear. Scholars in several disciplines have, over the years, developed explanations for the existence of various types of nonprofit organizations (beyond the obvious one that it is legally possible). As Frumkin (2002) has recently observed, many of these explanations have emphasized the demand side; that is, nonprofit organizations, particularly public service (as opposed to member benefit) organizations, are theorized to arise because of both "market failure" and "government failure." The nature of some goods or services prevents the formation of a market, in that the goods or services are nondivisible and "free riders" are difficult or impossible to prevent. For example, providing for clean (or cleaner) air and water must be done over very large areas, and it is impossible to prevent those who did not help pay for cleaner air or water in that area from consuming either. Government is typically the provider of such public goods, but democratic governments often produce less of a public good than some people desire (leading to government failure). Hence to produce services with public goods characteristics, nonprofit public benefit organizations are created in response to demand for the undersupplied public services.

Such explanations are plausible, though they also conjure up an "invisible hand," one that responds to the demand for public services by somehow inducing an organization to supply the services. Frumkin (2002) further observes that more recently, supply-side explanations for the creation of nonprofit organizations have been receiving greater attention. Rather than nonprofit organizations rather automatically, if somewhat mysteriously, arising because of need, the supply-side explanation draws attention to the motives and desires of those who actually take the time and effort to create and sustain an organization. Certainly, many motives underlie the creation of nonprofit organizations, including the desire to meet public needs, but also including a passion for a particular idea, solution, or way of living.

The demand-side explanations of the origin of public-benefit nonprofit organizations citing market and government failure imply first that organizations providing such benefits cannot cover their costs solely by sales to customers. Thus at a minimum, such organizations must convince some individuals to voluntarily support the organization by giving both time and money. Many early nonprofit organizations, founded in the nineteenth century, relied on philanthropy for substantial proportions of their revenue. Following the Second World War and particularly with the expansion of the American welfare state, governments began to contract more frequently with nonprofit public-benefit organizations to offer an increasing array of services. Frumkin (2002) argues that the core problem for public-benefit nonprofit organizations that provide services that donors or government contractors want—and hence a threat to the legitimacy of such nonprofit organizations—is that they become strictly vendors. Businesses can and increasingly do offer to provide such services as government contractors. If nonprofit organizations are merely service providers, why should government (and ultimately donors) choose them rather than commercial businesses?

Correspondingly, the supply-side explanation for nonprofit public-benefit organizations implies that some donors, who conceive of themselves as social venture investors (though the return they seek is presumably not financial but emotional, a feeling of accomplishing a social value of importance to them), will donate (or invest) funds to create an organization that promotes their cause or their solution. Furthermore, these businesslike ("social entrepreneurial") public-benefit nonprofit organizations will also seek to respond to market demand and create ventures to enhance their earned income.

The core problem Frumkin (2002) identifies for such business-oriented nonprofit organizations is commercialism. While such organizations may become increasingly successful financially (perhaps programmatically, but that is a more difficult achievement to assess), many observers will wonder why they should be treated as nonprofits, why they aren't just treated as ordinary businesses, even if they also have a social purpose.

Of course, many public-benefit nonprofits have been pursuing both strategies—trying to identify and provide services that government (and major donors) will pay for and identifying and pursuing earned income ventures that provide additional funds to advance the mission. As Salamon observes in Chapter Four (citing Gray and Schlesinger, 2002), more and more nonprofit organizations are facing a conflict between the "distinctiveness imperative" and the "survival imperative."

Does the strategy of seeking to provide services for which someone is willing to pay (either governments or direct customers) risk erasing the distinctiveness of nonprofit management and hence the legitimacy of the nonprofit organizational form? What is the distinctiveness of nonprofit management, anyway? To simplify, what is distinctive about public service nonprofit management is, I would like to think, that it is founded on a moral imperative—that of responding to the unmet (or undermet) needs of some portion of the living and future community (see Ostrander and Schervish, 1990, for the full development of this claim and for how they distinguish the moral basis of philanthropic exchange from the commercial and political bases of exchange). Public-benefit nonprofit organizations require mission statements not solely or most importantly as a means of strategic management but fundamentally as a way of explaining and affirming their moral basis. If the values and moral basis of the mission are not affecting the decisions and actions of the organization's leaders, then indeed such organizations risk becoming something other than a true public-benefit nonprofit, managed as a nonprofit.

I believe that much will be lost if nonprofit organizations come to exist only as a legal form and are managed as if they were businesses (though that will continue to be very difficult, as the lack of a monetized bottom line will prevent assessing how much various activities and units contribute to the bottom line). Surely, public trust will erode and volunteers and donations will disappear from those nonprofit organizations that seem to serve no purpose beyond their continued existence. Important unmet needs will expand. Our moral claims on one another will be ignored, even though the number and size of nonprofit organizations may be growing.

Admittedly, I have overdramatized the consequences of the disappearance of a distinctive nonprofit management, but the direction in which it is headed is clear. How can the moral distinctiveness of nonprofit management be retained and even strengthened? Some experts might argue that really there is nothing that be can done. If social forces and trends are moving nonprofit organizations away from a distinctive management approach, then that is what will happen. Exhortation will not work. Some basis for the distinctiveness must be structured into the operation of nonprofit organizations; that basis has until now been that the moral values of an organization are crucial to attracting and retaining donors, volunteers, and often employees.

An argument invoking the power of social forces and trends, of course, assumes (1) that one has identified the forces and trends correctly and that other countervailing forces are not operating or in the offing and (2) that forces and trends are inevitable. The exhilarating example of many nonprofit organizations (and their managers) is that they have rejected the second assumption. Only forces unresisted are inevitable. All those who accept that maintaining the distinctiveness of nonprofit management is important can certainly act in ways that may help make that possible.

Thus in a period when nonprofit organizations have often undergone considerable stress and adapted to substantial changes in ways that may increasingly put their distinctiveness and legitimacy in jeopardy, it is important to reflect on how we want nonprofit organizations to be managed in the future. I hope others will join me in concluding that the distinctive character of nonprofit management (which might be called "managing toward the morality of the mission") deserves to be preserved.

References

Frumkin, P. *On Being Nonprofit.* Cambridge, Mass.: Harvard University Press, 2002.

Gray, B., and Schlesinger, M. "Health." In L. M. Salamon (ed.), *The State of Nonprofit America.* Washington, D.C.: Brookings Institution Press, 2002.

Ostrander, S. A., and Schervish, P. G. "Giving and Getting: Philanthropy as a Social Relation." In J. Van Til and Associates, *Critical Issues in American Philanthropy: Strengthening Theory and Practice.* San Francisco: Jossey-Bass, 1990.

NAME INDEX

SUBJECT INDEX

647–649; organizational, 451–455, 462–463. *See also* Evaluation; Outcome assessment/measurement

Assessment centers, 647

Asset management analysis, 487, 488, 499–500; ratios in, 503, 506–507

Asset replacement: differential cost accounting and, 537–539; surplus and, 494, 495–496

Asset turnover ratio, 506–507

Assets: accounting problems with, 485; accounting standards for, 470–471, 476–477, 478–479; assessment of, for business venture, 453–454, 462–463; distribution of, 80; ownership of, 72; ratio of equity to, 492; return on, 495–496, 504–505, 545, 547; surplus and financing, 494, 495–496

Association for Healthcare Philanthropy, 95

Association of Fundraising Professionals (AFP), 56, 95; Code of Ethical Principles and Standards of Professional Practice, 432, 433–435

Association of Small Foundations, 95

Associations, 7–9; in colonial America, 4–6; 1860–1890, 9–13; 1890–1930, 13–16; for enterprise strategies, 438–439; for government contracting organizations, 385–386; as legal entities, 65; for lobbying support, 236, 238; 1930–1980, 16–22; 1980–2000, 22–24; number of, 28*n.*2; salary information from, 669–671; 1780–1860, 7–9; statewide, 385–386; trade, 12, 15–16. *See also* Sector-serving organizations

Associations of retarded citizens (ARCs), 376

Assumptions: in differential cost accounting, 534; erroneous, in strategic alliances, 268; underlying, in evaluation, 351

"-athons," 596

Atlantic Constitution, 44–45

Attac, 117

Attorney counsel: on earned income, 449; on employment law, 630; on lobbying, 237; on risk management, 563, 564

Audits: compliance, 78–79; external performance, 356; human resource, 638, 639, 655; organizational, 451–454

Australia: Internet resources for volunteer management in, 600, 614, 616; volunteer recruitment Web site in, 600, 616; volunteers in, 587

Australian Bureau of Statistics, 587, 619

Auto insurance, 580, 581

Autonomy: in strategic alliances, 260; in training, 709

Average-days-inventory ratio, 506

Average-days-receivable ratio, 506

B

Baby boomers, intergenerational transfer of wealth to, 90

Background checks, 570–571

Balance sheet: accounting standards for, 467, 470, 482–483; problem areas of, 485–486; ratio analysis and, 501; sample, 474

Balanced evaluation, 403–404. *See also* Program evaluation

Balanced scorecard (BSC), 181, 182, 358–359, 691

Balancedscorecard.org, 358

Banding, salary, 683–684

Bank account, 67

Baptist Church, 6

Base compensation: data sources for setting, 669–671; executive, 690–691; external competitiveness of, 666, 667–674, 681–682; increasing, 686–687; installing a new system of, 685–686; internal equity in, 666, 673–681; job- versus person-based systems of, 665, 672–673; job/work analysis for, 666–667; principles of, 665–687; structuring, 681–687

Benchmarks and benchmarking: for board effectiveness, 132–134; job, for compensation setting, 668–673, 677–678; for organizational effectiveness evaluation, 355, 360–361

Beneficiaries, 59

Benefits, employee, 691–698; cafeteria-style, 629–630, 692; collaboratives for, 653; communication about, 698; costs of, 691; external competitiveness of, 692, 696; health care, 693–695; internal equity of, 692, 696; paid-time-off, 696–697; retirement plan, 695–696, 698; in rewards policy, 692–693; tuition reimbursement, 697–698

Benhaven's Learning Network, 444

Berkeley Art Center Association, 20, 29

Bertelsmann Stiftung, 113

Best-practice benchmarking: for board of directors, 132–134; for organizational effectiveness evaluation, 360–361

Better Business Bureau (BBB), Wise Giving Alliance, 57, 219, 347, 361

Bewilderment, 172

Big Brothers Big Sisters, 305, 323

Big Five personality test, 647

Big government: conservative revolution against, 22–23; history of nonprofit sector and, 16–22, 81–82

Bill and Melinda Gates Foundation, 25

Bill of Rights, 64

Blendedvalue.org, 441

Block grant programs, 373

Entertainers, as politicians, 46

Entitlement programs: conservative revolution and cuts to, 24; expansion of, 90–91, 373; financial accounting for, 484

Environmental context: assessment of, in Strategy Change Cycle, 179–182; board understanding of, 139; for boards, 131–132; changes in, 81–99; chief executive in, 159–167; for enterprise strategies, 436–437; for fundraising, 426, 427, 429; for government contracting, 371–374; for internationalizations, 115–120; nesting of organizational life in, 40–42; overview of, 42–53; for risk management, 565–566; scanning and, 40–42; staff turnover and, 651–652; for strategic alliances, 254–256, 264–265. *See also* Change, environmental

Environmental organizations: case study of legal framework for, 63–80; international, 113

Envisioning, 157

Episcopal Church, 42

Episodic volunteering, 324, 326–327, 612; training for, 710, 716, 726–727

Equal Employment Opportunity Commission (EEOC), 657; role of, in discrimination cases, 635–636; Title VII and, 631–634, 635

Equal Pay Act of 1963, 636

Equipment: assessment of, for enterprise strategies, 453; insurance coverage of, 582, 583

Equity: financial accounting for, 470, 477, 478; as financing source, 494; interperiod, 478; long-term solvency and, 507; ratio of assets to, 492; return on, 495, 505; surplus and, 494, 495. *See also* Internal equity in compensation

Equity capital, 460, 461

Equity theory, 650

Espoused theories versus theories-in-use, 166–167

Ethics, 204–227; board oversight and, 149–150; core values and, 206–207, 211–226; culture of, 222–227; definitions of, 207, 208–209; education for, 226; erroneous assumptions about, 205–206; of experimental designs, 410; in fundraising, 214–216, 224–225, 430–432, 433–435; at individual level, 222; in international nongovernmental organizations, 121; leadership modeling of, 224, 226–227; moral accountability and, 347; organizational culture and, 206–227; at organizational level, 222–223; overview of, 206–208; professional, 209–211, 216, 220; program evaluation and, 406–407; responsibility for, 205; scandals and surge of interest

in, 204–206; structural aspects of, 224–226, 227; translation of, to behavior, 207–208, 222–223; utilitarian perspective on, 210–211

"Ethics and the Nation's Voluntary and Philanthropic Community," 211

Europe: international nongovernmental organizations in, 109, 110, 111; international philanthropy in, 114

European Commission, Humanitarian Office, 107

European immigrants, in early nineteenth century, 8

European Union, 109

Evaluation: of advertising program, 304–305; of fundraising program, 425; of learner performance, 724–725; of organizational effectiveness, 275–276, 345–368; process, 413–414; of program effectiveness, 275–276, 391–416; in responsibility accounting, 553–554; of staff, 334–336; of strategic alliance, 264, 271; tools for, 357–362; of trainers, 728–729; of volunteer program, 336–338, 611; of volunteers, 333–336, 610–611. *See also* Organizational effectiveness evaluation; Outcome assessment; Performance measurement; Program evaluation

Evaluators: boards of directors as, 366; external, 404–405, 412, 413, 414, 415; external funders or contractors as, 366–367; internal, 404, 405; for organizational effectiveness evaluation, 366–368; political/relationship problems with, 366–368; for process evaluation, 413; professional/outside consultant, 357, 404–405; for program evaluation, 404–405, 412, 414, 415–416

Evangelical Council for Financial Accountability, 219

Events: attractor, 597; scouting during, 597–598, 599; volunteer recruitment at, 595, 596–599

Excessive compensation, 75

Exchange, marketing and, 278–281, 285, 306–307

Executive Alliance, 670

Executive Order 11246, 636

Executive Order 132224, 79

Executive recruiters, 643

Executives, nonprofit: compensation of, 690–691; ethical modeling by, 224, 226–227; leadership role of, 129, 142–143, 153–169; role of, in cost accounting, 515–516; role of, in responsibility accounting, 545–549. *See also* Chief executive officers; Nonprofit managers

(PLC) of, 292–293; responsibility accounting for, 544–556, 554; strategic alliances and, 257
Promotions: posting opportunities for, 644; salary grades and, 684
Prompt Contracting Law, 386
Property income, 436–437, 444–448; hard, 444; soft, 444–448
Property insurance, 581, 582
Property tax revenue, 480
Proprietary funds, 481
Protestant church, 21, 45
Psychic reward, 55
Psychographic market segmentation, 284
Psychological contract, with volunteers, 316–317
Psychological tests, 647
PTL Ministries, 214
Public benefit: accountability and, 218; ethics and, 211, 218, 220–221, 227; fundraising and, 430–431; service and, 220–221; through strategic alliances, 257
Public choice economics, 120–121
Public Law 94-455 (1976 law), 239–253. See also Lobbying regulations
Public trust: board responsibility and, 151; commercialism and, 734; ethical behavior and, 207; rhetoric and, 314; scandals and erosion of, 98, 151, 204–205, 214–216; threats to, 97–98
Publication sales, legalities of, 69, 70, 76, 77
Publications, nonprofit management: on enterprise strategies, 441; growth in, 95, 731; job posting in, 643; on volunteer management, 615–618
Purposive-rational model, 154–155

Q

Qualitative measures, 401
Quasi-experimental designs, 410–412
Questionnaires, 399–400
Quick ratio, 505
Quid pro quo sexual harassment, 633–634

R

Racism, 47–48
Radicals, nonprofit internationalization and, 115
Randomization, 409–410, 411, 412
Range spread, salary, 681, 683–684
Rating services, 361–362
Ratio analysis, 487–491; categories for, 487–489, 502, 503–504; primer on, 501–510; standards for comparison in, 489–491; summary of ratio computations in, 503–504; using, 499, 510

Readiness: for enterprise strategies, 450, 462, 465; for fundraising, 428–429; market, 303–304
Reagan administration, 22–23, 50, 83–84, 90, 91, 373
Real Clout (Meredith and Dunham), 232
Real Collaboration (La Piana), 264
Real estate. See Property income
Realization principle, 469
Rebekahs, 12–13
Recessions, economic, 47, 52, 84, 256
Reciprocal allocation method, 527
Reciprocity, 221
Recognition: of staff, 335–336; of volunteers, 335
Reconstruction era, 10
Record keeping, on lobbying activities, 235–236
Recruitment. See Employee recruitment; Volunteer recruitment
Red circle employees, 685
Red Cross, 102, 113, 122, 300–301. See also American Red Cross; International Federation of Red Cross and Red Crescent Societies
Redistributive globalizers, 118
Reengineering, 177
Reference checking, 646, 649
Referendum lobbying, 245
Reflective practitioner, 206
Reformer-globalizers, 118
Refreezing, 188
Refugees, increase in, 89
Regime, contracting, 374–379
Regime building, in Strategy Change Cycle, 191
Regional foundations, defined, 56
Registry of Charitable Trusts, 78
Regression, 409, 411
Regression analysis, of salary competitiveness, 672
Regressive globalizers, 118
Regulations: community values and, 51–52; compliance mechanisms and, 78–79; employment, 75; government impact and, 51–52; international, 120, 121; lobbying, 51, 68, 70, 79, 231–232, 239–253. See also Legal issues
Regulators: categories of, 57–58; of legal entity formation, 65
Regulatory change, lobbying for, 241–242
Reimbursement rates, for federal entitlement programs, 91
Reimbursement system reform, 386–387
Reinvention, 177
Reliability, 397–398

of, 561; monitoring and adjusting, 570–571; phases of, 563–564, 584; responsibility for, 562–564; risk management process of, 565–571; risks identification for, 566–568, 569; starting a, 562–565; tangible benefits of, 562; volunteer liability and, 571, 572–578; for volunteer programs, 576–578; volunteer screening and, 605–606

Risk managers, 562

Rituals, 222–223

Robert Bosch Stiftung, 113

Roberts Enterprise Development Fund (REDF), 442

Robin Hood pattern, reverse, 52

Rochester Rehabilitation Center, 443

Rockefeller Foundation, 25; international philanthropy of, 113

Rockefeller General Education Board, 14

Roles and players: beneficiaries and customers, 59; in enterprise strategies, 438–439; givers, 54–55; intermediaries, 55–57; perspectives of, on nonprofit work, 40, 59; regulators, 57–58; in responsibility accounting, 545–549; in risk management, 562–564; in volunteer programs, 320–322. See also Board of directors; Chief executive officers; Executives; Staff

Rolfe Larson Associates, 439

Roman Catholic Church, 59; faith-based services and, 45; family values debate and, 43; history of nonprofits and, 3, 8, 21; sexual misconduct in, 48, 53, 204; transnational operations of, 102

Rotary, 15

Rowan College of New Jersey, 54

Rowntree Foundation, 113

Royalty income, 76, 77

Rural volunteers, 612

Russell Sage Foundation, 14

S

Saatchi & Saatchi Public Relations, 446

Salaries. See Base compensation; Compensation; Rewards

Salary administration policies, 685

Salary Budget Survey (WorldatWork), 685

Salary grades and bands, 682–685

Salary structure, 681–687

Salary surveys: for salary structure maintenance, 685; sources of, 669–671; using data from, 671–673

Salvation Army, 59

San Francisco, nonprofit regulation in, 78

Sarbanes-Oxley corporate reform legislation, 141, 150

Save the Children Federation, 102, 103, 448

Scandals: board oversight and, 143, 149–150, 151; board scrutiny and, 132, 149–150, 151; erosion of public trust and, 98, 151, 204–205, 214–216; examples of, 214–216, 225–226; impact of, 204–205; integrity and, 214–216; in international nongovernmental organizations, 121, 122; mass media and, 53; nonprofit executive, 53; responses to, 205–206; in Roman Catholic Church, 48, 53, 204; structural causes of, 225–226. See also Abuse; Ethics

Scandinavian welfare state, 49

Scanning, environmental, 40–42; for marketing opportunities, 290–291

Scenarios, 180

Scojo Foundation, 443

Scouting, for volunteers, 597–598, 599

Scrip, 447

Search, job candidate, 642–644

Search firms, 643

Second sector. See Government

Sector-monitoring organizations, 57, 219; for organizational effectiveness evaluation, 347–348, 361–362

Sectors, categories of, 41

Sector-serving organizations, 56, 58; for government contracting organizations, 385–386. See also Associations

Seedco, 440

Selection process, candidate, 645–650, 655

Selective perception, 302–303

Selective retention, 303

Self-defense activity, 242

Self-directed work teams, 662

Self-regulation, board, 150, 151

Self-serving hypothesis, 156

Semifixed costs. See Semivariable costs

Semivariable costs, in differential cost accounting, 529–530, 531, 532, 542

Senate report 94-938, 250

Senior managers. See Chief executive officers; Executives; Nonprofit managers

Seniority-based pay, 686

Sensitivity analysis, 535

September 11, 2001: American cynicism and, 48, 98, 314; American Red Cross and, 122, 215; antiterrorist laws and, 78; impact of, on nonprofit sector, 52, 98; Internet fundraising and, 88; transnational organizations and, 25

Servant leadership, 221

Service: as core value, 207, 220–221; ethical management for, 220–221; as volunteer motivation, 328, 329, 330, 331, 594